www.ingramcontent.com/pod-product-compliance
Lightning Source LLC
LaVergne TN
LVHW080614300926
849162LV00005B/1160

Architecting the Digital Future:

Platforms, Design, and Application

Jean-Éric Pelet
Institut d'Administration aux Entreprises d'Amiens, LEFMI, Université de Picardie Jules Verne, Amiens, France

IGI Global
Scientific Publishing
Publishing Tomorrow's Research Today

Vice President of Editorial Melissa Wagner
Managing Editor of Acquisitions Mikaela Felty
Managing Editor of Book Development Jocelynn Hessler
Production Manager Mike Brehm
Cover Design Phillip Shickler

Published in the United States of America by
IGI Global Scientific Publishing
701 East Chocolate Avenue
Hershey, PA, 17033, USA
Tel: 717-533-8845
Fax: 717-533-7115
Website: https://www.igi-global.com E-mail: cust@igi-global.com

Library of Congress Cataloging-in-Publication Data

Names: Pelet, Jean-Éric, 1976- editor.
Title: Architecting the digital future: Platforms, design, and application / edited by: Jean-Eric Pelet.
Description: Hershey PA : Engineering Science Reference , [2025] | Includes bibliographical references. | Summary: "This book will aim to provide relevant theoretical frameworks and the latest empirical research findings in the area. It will be written for professionals and academics who want to improve their understanding of the strategic role of User Experience at different levels of the information and knowledge society, that is, e-commerce and e-learning at the level of the global economy, of networks and organizations, of teams and work groups, of information systems and, finally, e-learning and e-commerce at the level of individuals as actors in the networked environments"-- Provided by publisher.
Identifiers: LCCN 2024042531 (print) | LCCN 2024042532 (ebook) | ISBN 9798369329733 (hardcover) | ISBN 9798369344439 (paperback) | ISBN 9798369329740 (ebook)
Subjects: LCSH: User interfaces (Computer systems) | User-centered system design. | World Wide Web.
Classification: LCC QA76.9.U83 A23 2025 (print) | LCC QA76.9.U83 (ebook) | DDC 303.48/33--dc23/eng/20241212
LC record available at https://lccn.loc.gov/2024042531
LC ebook record available at https://lccn.loc.gov/2024042532
British Cataloguing in Publication Data
A Cataloguing in Publication record for this book is available from the British Library.

The talk commences with analyzing the influence of user experience in e-learning and the transition from Web 2.0 technologies to the current Web 3.0 paradigm. The chapter delves into the theory and application of designing contemporary ubiquitous interfaces, with a focus on the significance of developing immersive and captivating learning environments. This study delves at the role of serious games and entertainment technologies in improving educational experiences, with a focus on their capacity for facilitating successful learning. The investigation encompasses the utilization of online communities and social media platforms for both business and education, emphasizing the interdependent nature of digital engagements. The chapter explores the importance of human-computer interaction in meeting the varied demands of learners and customers. It highlights the function of interfaces in structuring educational experiences.

In order to improve functionality, security, and user experience, this chapter examines the design and implementation of a Web3 mobile platform that combines blockchain technology with artificial intelligence (AI). The methodology addresses major issues in usability, security, and scalability by employing an exploratory and developmental approach that prioritizes user-centered design principles and iterative feedback loops. The results show that greater trust and uptake of decentralized technologies are fostered by Web3 applications that are easy to use, safe, and scalable. The chapter emphasizes that in order to remove obstacles and build a strong Web3 ecosystem, stakeholders—including developers, investors, regulatory agencies, and users—must work together. The work's ramifications highlight how crucial it is to resolve present issues in order to fully utilize Web3 technologies' promise to transform digital interactions.

The purpose of this chapter is to examine the ethical concerns and benefits associated with the integration of Artificial Intelligence (AI), particularly chatbots, in education. A comprehensive literature review was conducted to identify and analyze ethical considerations related to AI in education. The applicability of the web3 application in the identification and analysis of ethical concerns of AI chatbots is also explored. The findings revealed a spectrum of ethical concerns spanning fairness, transparency, privacy, autonomy, and educational inequality. Ethical concerns also include the misuse of private data, algorithmic biases, surveillance, and threats to job security. Conversely, the benefits of AI in education encompass improved learner experiences, enhanced teaching efficiency, and personalized learning opportunities. Chatbots, in particular, demonstrate potential in fostering engagement, increasing interest in subjects, and offering immediate support to students.

First introduced in the early 2010s, the term "gamification" is now widely used. It has been implemented in fields as varied as marketing and healthcare or crowdsourcing. Here, the authors focus on its use in education. Today, many students lack motivation and show little interest for learning in class. Given the choice, many would rather play video games than read a book or complete an assignment. This study was conducted to identify the potential effects of gamification on learner motivation and engagement. The study was carried out involving students enrolled at a Moroccan university. The major findings of the study showed that gamification had a positive effect on students' lives. This was shown by their greater motivation to learn and their commitment to taking part in the games.

In today's internet economy and Web 3.0, firms are using virtual Internet portals for co-design. Product design by firms have focused predominantly on the significance of product aesthetics. Virtual co-design by firms are moving towards new product design using creative themes to focus on the aesthetics of design in association with a product function. Firms are integrating the internet for co-design, customization and the personalization of products and web portals are facilitating the personalization and customization of ideas, concepts and designs and are co-creating value for firms. Firms today have become agents of change and are adding value to professions and vocations. Today, firms acknowledge the fact that products can be designed virtually.

This chapter explores the advancements in human-machine interfaces (HMIs) and their potential to enhance user experience and interaction in information applications, particularly within Web3 environments. As decentralized technologies like blockchain and dApps grow, interface design becomes crucial for improving user engagement and usability. The paper examines the latest developments in HMIs, such as natural language processing, gesture recognition, augmented reality (AR), and virtual reality (VR), and their impact on Web3 applications. These technologies offer innovative ways to enhance user experience by providing more intuitive and immersive interactions in decentralized systems. Additionally, the paper discusses the challenges of implementing advanced HMIs in Web3, including issues of compatibility with blockchain protocols and the need for seamless user experiences.

preservation empower us to explore and safeguard heritage across time and space. By catering to diverse heritage types (tangible and intangible), these platforms offer valuable tools for education and global exchange. With the integration of Web3 technologies, these initiatives can further enhance their impact. Decentralized networks enable more equitable access to digital heritage, preventing gatekeeping and censorship. Blockchain can ensure transparent and immutable records of heritage artifacts, addressing ethical concerns related to digital representation. Additionally, the tokenization of cultural assets offers allowing communities to retain control over their heritage. However, the adoption of Web3 also necessitates careful consideration of data sovereignty and digital rights to ensure inclusive and responsible cultural preservation.

C. V. Suresh Babu, Hindustan Institute of Technology and Science, India
P. M. Akshara, Hindustan Institute of Technology and Science, India
Dhanush Harsha, Hindustan Institute of Technology and Science, India
Iniyavan M. Afeef, Hindustan Institute of Technology and Science, India
J. Jowin, Hindustan Institute of Technology and Science, India

The study aims to display the application of multiclass algorithms in machine learning for educational settings, particularly for skill assessment, learning style prediction, and peer recommendation. The method of skills assessment uses the RandomForestClassifier model to forecast learners' skill proficiency by using a mock dataset that represents the learners having different skill levels. The module of learning style prediction employs the model to categorize all students into their cognitive preference spectrum according to the dataset which contains their neurocognitive attributes and learning preferences. Through Peer recommendation, the system suggests to the study partners that students typically will be matched together with similar standards, interests, and learning styles. The study stresses the utility of personalized learning freed by multi-class algorithms for students to be assessed on basic skills, their learning patterns to be predicted as well as promotion of cooperative learning which eventually results in improvement of the learning experience and academic success.

This study aims to propose a website for the preservation and accessibility of street art in Türkiye with crowdsourcing methods. The proposed website is based on the literature about the usability of street art websites. The related literature showed that the websites are weak regarding institutional information and policies, including copying and copyrights, and that descriptive data regarding the works is insufficient. Additionally, it has been observed that the most common crowdsourcing method is collection completion. Street artworks created by street artists and then converted into digital form are also prone to change and metamorphosis, requiring specific digital solutions for long-term preservation. The rise of Web3 technologies offers new opportunities to overcome the challenges of documenting, preserving, and sharing these digital street arts. It is thought that this study, conducted in the case of Türkiye, will contribute to the literature on preserving and accessing street art as a cultural heritage.

The purpose of the module reported on in this chapter is that it will be used by students as an introduction to object-oriented programming in the context of developing the knowledge, skills, and values needed to develop a working computer-based program and to add interactive functionality to the program through structured object-oriented programming. Against the background of Mobile Platforms, Designs, and Applications for Web3, the novelty of the chapter is emphasized by this module being presented at a Comprehensive Open and Distance e-Learning (CODeL) university.

The digital landscape is transforming cultural heritage preservation. Online mapping initiatives, like UNESCO's GIS and Historypin's community-driven maps, are fostering engagement and accessibility. Europeana's digital library and CyArk's 3D

The use of information technology and related processes has permeated into organizations of all sizes. Higher learning institutions are described as open, multi-modal platforms whose organizational complexity can increase vulnerability to information security breaches. Several high-profile cyberattacks have occurred on universities and colleges, including ransomware attacks resulting in data breaches and system shutdowns. In some cases, universities have had to pay large sums to regain system access. The following research objective guided the study: (1) Establish cyber security posture in Higher Learning institutions. The literature highlighted that the critical cybersecurity challenges in most Higher learning institutions, in general, are a lack of cybersecurity governance and risk assessment frameworks, a lack of incident management plans, and a lack of national and regional legal frameworks related to cybersecurity, a lack of security awareness and education programs; and a lack of national and international legal frameworks related to cybersecurity.

The internet has evolved from Web 1.0 to emerging Web 3.0. E-learning platforms have revolutionized education but face security threats. As Web 3.0 technologies integrate into e-learning, new cybersecurity concerns arise. This chapter reviews Web 3.0 and cybersecurity challenges in e-learning including data privacy, smart contract vulnerabilities, and malware. An experimental approach evaluates real-world issues in Web 3.0 e-learning. Results show decentralized technologies enhance privacy and security but vulnerabilities must be mitigated through controls and audits. User awareness is critical. A multifaceted strategy encompassing strong safeguards, training, and collaboration is required to address the cybersecurity landscape of Web 3.0-enabled e-learning. As technologies advance, cybersecurity must remain a priority to develop resilient platforms. This bridges the academic-practical gap.

in the development of dynamic and captivating learning environments. We shall illustrate the effectiveness of these technologies in improving understanding and memory of intricate ideas by including case studies from different educational settings. This discussion will focus on the utilization of VR and AR in virtual laboratories, simulations, field trips, and cultural immersion. The emphasis will be on the potential of these tools to facilitate experiential learning and bridge the divide between theoretical understanding and practical implementation. Although VR and AR have the ability to bring about significant changes in education, there are various obstacles that prevent their widespread use.

Karnika Srivastava, Shri Ramswaroop Memorial University, India
Manoj Kumar, Shri Ramswaroop Memorial University, India
Rinki Verma, Babu Banarasi Das University, India
Shreyanshu Singh, Babu Banarasi Das University, India
Pratibha Maurya, Amity University, Lucknow, India

Learners face problems while using traditional e-learning systems but AI introduces an innovative stage of advancement in technology that gives revolution in e-learning process. Study investigates factors that influence learner behavioral intention to use AI and actual usage in higher education. The study proposed UTAUT and IS model with additional external variables like perceive risk, work engagement and self-efficacy of learner. Cross-sectional study was used to measure research models based on several theories related to AI that brings cutting-edge technologies that enhance e-learning. Data was analysed using SEM technique. Research model and hypothesis testing was done by AMOS. Study investigate performance expectancy, effort expectancy, facilitating condition, system quality, service quality information quality, perceived risk, work engagement; self-efficacy had significantly influenced behavioral intention and actual use of AI. Finding gives practical references to stakeholders for adoption and acceptance of AI within e-learning process in higher education in NCR.

Detailed Table of Contents

This study analyzes web services' functionalities and performance, focusing on mobile platforms and Web3 applications. Web services enable communication between applications but pose challenges due to different types (RESTful, SOAP), data formats, and protocols. Choosing the right service requires considering scalability, security, and interoperability. The study provides a comparative analysis of web service types, evaluating their strengths, limitations, and suitability for mobile platforms. It highlights challenges in selecting services and offers insights to guide decision-making. By assessing performance metrics, this research aids in optimizing web-based applications, enhancing decision-making for Web3 and mobile development.

The incorporation of Virtual Reality (VR) and Augmented Reality (AR) in educational environments has fundamentally transformed the manner in which learners interact with educational material, offering immersive encounters that surpass conventional teaching approaches. This chapter examines the pragmatic uses of VR and AR

Table of Contents

Preface

User experience (UX) is an essential factor that shapes perceptions, interactions, and behaviors in the digital age. As the Internet evolves into its next iteration—Web3—understanding the implications of user experience in this new paradigm becomes crucial for academia and business alike. Web3 introduces decentralized platforms, blockchain technologies, and enhanced user control over data and digital assets, making it imperative to rethink traditional UX design principles.

The mobile user experience (MUE) is particularly critical in this evolution. Studies have shown that a frustrating experience on a website or mobile application negatively affects brand perception and consumer trust. Mobile UX is not just about functionality but also about engagement, accessibility, and security. The demand for intuitive and responsive interfaces extends beyond e-commerce into e-learning, where digital interfaces shape the educational landscape. The rise of augmented reality (AR), virtual reality (VR), artificial intelligence (AI)-powered chatbots, and blockchain-based learning management systems further complicates the UX landscape, necessitating a multidimensional approach to designing effective digital experiences.

E-commerce, particularly in the post-COVID-19 era, has witnessed an increasing demand for seamless last-mile delivery solutions, driven by consumer expectations for efficiency and sustainability. Innovations in urban logistics, sensor-driven marketing, and AI-powered recommendation systems are revolutionizing how businesses interact with consumers. Similarly, e-learning is undergoing a transformation through immersive technologies like the Metaverse, blockchain-based certification, and non-fungible tokens (NFTs) for credential verification. These developments necessitate a reassessment of the UX principles guiding digital education and commerce.

One of the key variables in UX design is visual perception. Research indicates that up to 80% of information processed by users comes from visual stimuli, making elements like color schemes, contrast, and typography crucial in digital environments. Studies on mobile commerce (m-commerce) websites have demonstrated how design choices affect users' emotions and behavioral intentions. Accessibility, data privacy, and cybersecurity also play pivotal roles in shaping digital interactions, ensuring that applications cater to diverse user needs while maintaining robust security protocols.

With Web3 technologies integrating AI, decentralized finance (DeFi), and voice user interfaces (VUIs), the design considerations extend beyond aesthetics and usability. Ethical concerns regarding data ownership, transparency, and inclusivity need to be addressed to build trust in Web3 applications. As smart contracts and decentralized autonomous organizations (DAOs) gain traction, the UX of blockchain-based applications must evolve to accommodate users with varying levels of technical expertise.

This edited volume brings together theoretical frameworks and empirical research to provide a comprehensive understanding of UX and mobile applications in Web3. It aims to equip professionals, academics, and industry practitioners with insights into how UX shapes digital interactions in e-commerce and e-learning. By exploring interdisciplinary perspectives, this book offers a holistic view of the strategic role of UX in networked environments, from multinational corporations and higher education institutions to healthcare providers and digital marketplaces.

The target audience for this book includes researchers and professionals in marketing, information systems, human-computer interaction, cognitive psychology, change management, and education. It also serves as a valuable resource for executives managing digital transformation initiatives, knowledge management systems, and organizational development projects. As digital technologies continue to reshape societies, this book provides a timely exploration of UX principles in the context of Web3, ensuring that digital experiences remain user-centric, secure, and inclusive.

ORGANIZATION OF THE BOOK

Chapter 1: A Comprehensive Review on Comparative Analysis of Web Services

This chapter presents a critical comparative analysis of web services, examining their functionalities, performance metrics, and diverse applications. Web services serve as essential tools for seamless data exchange and communication across platforms, yet choosing the most suitable option remains a challenge for developers and researchers. By evaluating RESTful and SOAP services, the chapter highlights their advantages, limitations, and key differences in scalability, security, and interoperability. This study provides invaluable insights for decision-makers seeking to optimize their digital infrastructure and enhance the efficiency of web-based applications.

Chapter 2: Virtual and Augmented Reality for Immersive Learning Experiences: Practical Applications and Challenges

Virtual Reality (VR) and Augmented Reality (AR) are revolutionizing educational environments by offering immersive, interactive experiences that transcend traditional learning methodologies. This chapter explores practical applications of VR and AR in virtual laboratories, simulations, cultural immersion, and field trips. By incorporating case studies, the discussion underscores the effectiveness of these technologies in fostering experiential learning. While highlighting their potential to bridge the gap between theoretical concepts and practical applications, the chapter also addresses key challenges hindering their widespread adoption, such as cost, accessibility, and technological constraints.

Chapter 3: Analyzing the Drivers of Adoption in Higher Education E-Learning: Exploring Factors Affecting Behavioral Intentions and Actual Usage

E-learning continues to evolve with advancements in Artificial Intelligence (AI), offering innovative solutions to traditional learning challenges. This chapter investigates factors influencing learners' behavioral intentions and actual AI adoption in higher education using the UTAUT and IS models. External variables such as perceived risk, work engagement, and self-efficacy are examined, with a cross-sectional study employing structural equation modeling (SEM) for data analysis. The findings provide practical implications for stakeholders, offering a roadmap for integrating AI technologies effectively within higher education institutions.

Chapter 4: Taxonomy of Challenges of Cybersecurity Risk Assessment in Higher Learning Institutions

Higher learning institutions face increasing cybersecurity threats due to their open, multi-modal structures, which heighten their vulnerability to cyberattacks. This chapter examines the key cybersecurity challenges in these institutions, including the lack of governance frameworks, incident management strategies, and legal policies at national and international levels. By analyzing case studies of high-profile cyberattacks, the discussion underscores the urgent need for robust cybersecurity postures, risk assessment strategies, and comprehensive awareness programs to safeguard institutional data and infrastructure.

Chapter 5: Securing the Future of E-Learning with Web3 Technologies and Cybersecurity

As Web3 technologies gain traction in e-learning, new cybersecurity concerns emerge. This chapter explores how decentralized technologies can enhance privacy and security while also introducing vulnerabilities such as smart contract risks and data breaches. An experimental approach evaluates these challenges in real-world Web3 e-learning environments. The findings highlight the importance of security audits, user awareness programs, and a multifaceted strategy to ensure a resilient cybersecurity framework for next-generation educational platforms.

Chapter 6: Access to Street Art via Crowdsourcing Methods: A Web Page Proposal for Türkiye

Street art preservation in Türkiye faces challenges related to documentation, accessibility, and copyright concerns. This chapter proposes a crowdsourced web platform to digitally archive and enhance the accessibility of street art. By analyzing existing platforms, the study identifies gaps in institutional policies and metadata management. Web3 technologies present new opportunities for long-term digital preservation, ensuring the sustainability of street art as cultural heritage while addressing the ethical and technological aspects of digitization.

Chapter 7: Mobile Platforms, Designs, and Applications for Web3 Towards Reducing Students' Cognitive Load: Online Meetings and Recordings for Support

This chapter explores the role of Web3 technologies in mobile learning platforms, particularly in reducing students' cognitive load. By integrating object-oriented programming modules, the discussion focuses on enhancing interactivity and knowledge retention in digital education. With an emphasis on open and distance learning models, the chapter demonstrates how Web3-powered applications can support students by providing interactive content, streamlined user interfaces, and real-time collaborative tools.

Chapter 8: Mapping Cultures Together Online Heritage Initiatives

Digital initiatives are transforming cultural heritage preservation through interactive mapping and archival projects. This chapter discusses platforms such as UNESCO's GIS, Historypin, and Europeana, showcasing how these tools facilitate global access to heritage. With the integration of Web3 technologies, decentralized networks can enhance equitable access, while blockchain ensures transparent record-keeping. The chapter also examines ethical concerns surrounding data sovereignty, digital rights, and community ownership of cultural assets in the online space.

Chapter 9: Neurocognitive Learning Design and Multiclass Algorithms: Academic and Business User Experience in Web3

Machine learning and neurocognitive models are reshaping user experiences in education and business. This chapter examines how multiclass algorithms can personalize learning through skill assessment, cognitive preference prediction, and peer recommendation systems. By employing RandomForestClassifier models on diverse learner datasets, the study demonstrates how adaptive learning platforms can enhance engagement, collaboration, and academic success in Web3 environments.

Chapter 10: Value Co-Creation of Design in the Internet Economy

The evolution of product design in the internet economy is shifting toward virtual co-creation and personalization. This chapter explores how firms are leveraging Web3-powered internet portals for product customization, aesthetic enhancements, and consumer-driven design processes. By facilitating interactive co-design experiences, businesses can enhance customer engagement, foster innovation, and create value through collaborative product development.

Chapter 11: Advanced Human-Machine Interfaces for User Experience and Interaction in Information Applications

The advancement of human-machine interfaces (HMIs) is revolutionizing user interaction in information applications. This chapter examines emerging technologies such as natural language processing, gesture recognition, augmented reality, and virtual reality. By analyzing their impact across industries, the chapter identifies challenges and opportunities for optimizing user experiences through seamless, intuitive interface design.

Chapter 12: Chatbots as Learning Companions: Exploring Ethical Dimensions of AI in Education

AI-powered chatbots are increasingly used as learning companions, raising ethical concerns regarding autonomy, data privacy, and educational integrity. This chapter presents a comprehensive literature review on the ethical implications of AI in education. By exploring the intersection of Web3 applications, chatbot-driven learning, and responsible AI development, the discussion provides insights into balancing technological innovation with ethical accountability in digital education.

Chapter 13: Gamification of Learning to Boost Students' Motivation and Study Engagement

Gamification has emerged as a transformative approach to education, leveraging game-like elements to enhance student motivation and engagement. While initially adopted in fields such as marketing and healthcare, its application in education has gained traction as educators seek innovative solutions to counter declining student interest. This chapter explores the impact of gamification on learning by examining a study conducted with university students in Morocco. The findings reveal that incorporating game mechanics into the educational experience significantly boosts motivation and fosters active participation. By examining the intersection of gaming and pedagogy, this chapter provides valuable insights into how gamification can be harnessed to create more dynamic and engaging learning environments.

Chapter 14: Advancements in Educational Technology: Navigating the Landscape of User Experience in Web3

As digital education evolves, the transition from Web 2.0 to Web3 is reshaping how learners interact with technology. This chapter investigates the role of user experience in e-learning and the design of modern, ubiquitous interfaces that foster immersive learning. It examines how serious games and entertainment technologies contribute to effective education, while also exploring the symbiotic relationship between online communities, social media platforms, and digital learning. Additionally, the chapter highlights the importance of human-computer interaction in meeting diverse learner needs and optimizing educational interfaces. By bridging theoretical foundations with real-world applications, this work provides a comprehensive exploration of how Web3 is transforming digital education.

Chapter 15: Designing and Developing a Web3 Mobile Platform: Integrating Blockchain and AI for Enhanced Functionality, Security, and User Experience

The integration of blockchain and artificial intelligence (AI) within Web3 mobile platforms represents a significant leap in digital innovation. This chapter presents a comprehensive analysis of designing and implementing a Web3 mobile platform that prioritizes security, functionality, and user experience. Employing an exploratory and developmental approach, the study addresses key challenges such as usability, scalability, and trust in decentralized technologies. The findings underscore the necessity of collaboration among developers, investors, regulatory bodies, and users to establish a robust Web3 ecosystem. By tackling present limitations, this chapter highlights the transformative potential of Web3 technologies in shaping secure, user-friendly digital interactions for the future.

CONCLUSION

As education continues to evolve in the digital age, the chapters in this volume highlight the transformative potential of emerging technologies in shaping the future of learning. From the gamification of educational experiences to the integration of Web3 technologies, each contribution underscores the need for innovative approaches that enhance student engagement, optimize user experience, and improve security in digital learning environments. The research presented not only explores theoretical frameworks but also provides practical insights into how these advancements can be implemented effectively.

As we navigate the intersection of technology and education, it is evident that a multidisciplinary and collaborative approach is essential. Educators, technologists, policymakers, and industry leaders must work together to ensure that these innovations are accessible, scalable, and inclusive. By addressing current challenges and embracing the opportunities presented by gamification, Web3, and blockchain-driven platforms, we can create more dynamic and effective learning environments that empower students and educators alike. This volume serves as a foundation for future discussions and developments in digital education, paving the way for a more interactive, engaging, and secure learning landscape.

Introduction

WEB3: THE THIRD GENERATION OF THE WEB

Web3 represents the third generation of the Internet, characterized by decentralization and user autonomy. Built on blockchain technology, Web3 offers users transparency and ownership of their data. Non-fungible tokens (NFTs) and metaverses are widely regarded as emblematic of Web3's current evolution. Web3 has significant implications for various sectors, including education, commerce, and marketing:

- **In education:** Web3 introduces innovative learning approaches through metaverses and NFTs. Metaverses provide immersive and interactive learning environments, while NFTs can serve as rewards for student achievements or as certificates of accomplishment.
- **In commerce:** Web3 enables businesses to engage directly with consumers, as seen in the wine industry. Consumer cooperatives can leverage social media to establish new distribution channels, while blockchain technology ensures traceability and transparency in supply chains.
- **In marketing:** Web3 facilitates novel communication strategies, such as metaverse marketing. Businesses can utilize social media to foster deeper connections with customers and build long-term relationships.

Despite its transformative potential, Web3 faces challenges, particularly related to energy consumption and environmental impact. The extensive use of blockchain technology and data centers for streaming and storage contributes to greenhouse gas emissions. It is essential to mitigate these environmental effects by adopting sustainable practices, such as eco-design.

While challenges remain, Web3 represents a critical evolution of the Internet, offering potential for groundbreaking innovations and new business models. The rapid evolution of the digital landscape has heralded the advent of Web3, a decentralized and user-centric iteration of the Internet. Unlike its predecessor, Web 2.0, which centralized control in the hands of a few dominant platforms, Web3 is underpinned by transformative technologies such as blockchain, non-fungible tokens (NFTs), and the metaverse. Together, these innovations are reshaping industries and redefining user experiences across academia and business.

Blockchain ensures transparency, security, and trust in digital interactions, providing the foundation for decentralized applications and smart contracts. NFTs have emerged as a revolutionary means of representing ownership and value in digital ecosystems, with implications spanning the arts, education, and consumer goods. The metaverse, a networked digital universe of interconnected spaces, offers unparalleled opportunities for immersive learning and collaboration. These developments are not only reshaping commerce but are also transforming the way knowledge is shared and consumed.

The transformative potential of Web3 technologies continues to shape various industries. The following sections explores how blockchain, NFTs, and other Web3 advancements are revolutionizing the wine supply chain, enhancing consumer engagement, and redefining education and marketing strategies in the industry. By delving into the challenges, opportunities, and future prospects of integrating Web3 into business, this section offers insights into how traditional practices can merge with cutting-edge innovations for a more sustainable, efficient, and interactive industry.

This is what is explained in this book, which description of the details of each chapter is presented in a table in the Appendix. A detailed description of title, abstract, keywords and authors from each chapter waits for the reader. A glossary summarizing the 100 main technical terms of the book is also presented right after the appendix of this introductive chapter.

The Role of Blockchain in Sustainable Logistics for the 2024 Paris Olympics

The Paris 2024 Olympic Games present a significant opportunity to showcase sustainable urban logistics innovations, with blockchain (BC) technology playing a pivotal role. Shippr, a logistics provider specializing in last-mile delivery via cargo bikes, is exploring the integration of BC to enhance transparency, traceability, and operational efficiency. This initiative aligns with the event's sustainability goals while addressing the complexities of urban logistics (Pelet, Taieb and Alkhudary, 2025).

Blockchain technology offers unique benefits, including immutable data recording, decentralized information sharing, and enhanced security. For Shippr, integrating BC could improve real-time tracking, minimize delivery errors, and bolster consumer trust. By leveraging BC, stakeholders—including municipal authorities, businesses, and end-users—can ensure efficient coordination while promoting eco-friendly delivery methods.

The adoption of BC in Shippr's logistics operations must align with the needs of various stakeholders. Internal stakeholders, such as operational teams, need reliable tools for managing data transparency. Externally, consumers seek traceable deliveries that reinforce the company's green credentials. Collaborating with municipalities is crucial to meet regulatory requirements and support sustainable urban mobility policies during the Olympics.

Despite its potential, integrating BC faces barriers, including high implementation costs and scalability concerns. For a successful rollout, Shippr must choose the appropriate BC model—public, private, or hybrid—tailored to the delivery network's needs (Bitcoin, Ethereum, and Litecoin). Additionally, stakeholders need to address technological literacy and infrastructure readiness to ensure seamless integration.

This case written by Pelet, Taieb and Alkhudary (2025) serves as an invaluable resource for students, educators, and professionals. It enables students to bridge theoretical concepts with practical applications, fostering critical skills in strategic decision-making, technological leadership, and sustainability. Educators can use this case to introduce interdisciplinary discussions, while logistics and technology managers gain insights into deploying BC in complex operational settings.

As urban logistics evolve, BC adoption could set new benchmarks in efficiency and transparency. Shippr's approach during the Olympics may pave the way for broader adoption in urban mobility, inspiring innovations in other industries. The lessons learned here could influence global strategies, demonstrating the viability of green logistics powered by advanced technology.

In summary, blockchain technology represents a transformative tool for addressing the challenges of sustainable urban logistics at the 2024 Paris Olympics. By integrating BC with cargo bike delivery solutions, Shippr can enhance operational efficiency, align with sustainability goals, and set a precedent for future innovation in the logistics sector.

Redefining Trust and Sustainability in the Wine Supply Chain

The article from Pelet, Alkhudary and Taieb (2025) explores the transformative role of Blockchain-Connected Cargo Bikes (BCCB) in enhancing sustainable last-mile logistics, examining how this innovative system improves efficiency, transparency, and sustainability in urban delivery processes. Using the Information System Success Model (ISSM), the study investigates the system's impact from the perspectives of logistics professionals and end consumers. The integration of blockchain with cargo bikes is shown to address key urban logistics challenges such as traffic congestion, pollution, and inefficiencies in delivery operations. Through real-time tracking, data transparency, and agile delivery methods, the BCCB system optimizes logistics processes while meeting growing consumer demand for eco-friendly and reliable delivery services.

The study highlights the significant improvements in system quality, information quality, and service quality resulting from the adoption of the BCCB system. Blockchain provides a secure, transparent ledger that enables accurate and real-time tracking of parcels, enhancing decision-making and consumer trust. This technological integration ensures the confidentiality and accuracy of data shared between logistics professionals and consumers. Cargo bikes, with their ability to navigate urban traffic and reduce carbon emissions, complement blockchain's strengths, offering a sustainable and efficient alternative to traditional delivery methods. The system's focus on transparency, security, and environmental impact aligns with the demands of both the logistics sector and end consumers for sustainable urban solutions.

End consumers report high satisfaction with the BCCB system, appreciating the real-time tracking, personalized delivery options, and reduced delivery times. The system also addresses consumer concerns regarding transparency, ensuring that they are informed about the status of their deliveries and can easily track the location of delivery personnel. The ability to communicate directly with delivery personnel further enhances the consumer experience, fostering a sense of control and satisfaction. The adoption of blockchain and cargo bikes in last-mile logistics not only meets consumer expectations for fast, secure, and eco-friendly delivery options but also promotes loyalty and repeat purchases.

The study also finds that the BCCB system delivers substantial economic and managerial benefits. By optimizing operations, reducing fuel consumption, and minimizing delivery delays, logistics professionals achieve cost savings while enhancing delivery reliability. Blockchain technology streamlines inventory management and route planning, leading to more efficient use of resources and better decision-making. The environmental benefits of cargo bikes are significant, with reductions in carbon emissions and energy consumption contributing to the sustainability goals of both companies and consumers. This combination of efficiency and sustainability positions the BCCB system as a forward-thinking solution to urban logistics challenges.

Moreover, the study's findings suggest that the BCCB system's integration of blockchain and cargo bikes creates a competitive advantage for e-commerce and logistics companies. By improving operational efficiency, transparency, and service quality, the system strengthens consumer trust and satisfaction. The eco-friendly nature of cargo bikes aligns with growing consumer demand for sustainable practices, making the BCCB system a valuable asset in the context of environmentally-conscious consumer behavior. The managerial implications of the study emphasize the importance of integrating innovative technologies to optimize urban delivery systems and enhance customer loyalty.

While the study provides valuable insights into the benefits of BCCB systems in urban logistics, it also presents several limitations and opportunities for future research. The technical aspects of blockchain models, particularly in relation to consensus mechanisms and their environmental impact, require further exploration. Additionally, the study's focus on the French market limits the generalizability of its findings, and future research should expand to different geographical contexts. A quantitative validation of the ISSM constructs in the context of sustainable urban logistics is also needed to reinforce the study's conclusions. Future studies should also explore the role of moderating variables such as company size and develop comprehensive sustainability metrics to assess the alignment of BCCB systems with global sustainability goals.

The integration of blockchain with cargo bikes offers a promising solution for addressing the challenges of urban last-mile logistics. This study contributes to the growing body of knowledge on sustainable logistics systems by highlighting the role of advanced technologies in improving operational efficiency, enhancing customer satisfaction, and reducing environmental impacts. The BCCB system represents a significant step forward in the development of eco-friendly and efficient urban logistics, providing valuable insights for both academic researchers and industry practitioners interested in the future of sustainable logistics solutions.

The Role of the Edu-Metaverse in Promoting Diversity, Equity, and Inclusion in Education

The integration of Web3 technologies, such as the metaverse, into education offers promising solutions to enhance diversity, equity, and inclusion (DEI) in learning environments. As educational institutions increasingly adopt immersive virtual platforms, the metaverse provides opportunities to address long-standing challenges related to accessibility, representation, and student engagement. By creating virtual spaces where individuals can interact without the constraints of traditional physical classrooms, Web3 technologies can foster a more inclusive environment for all learners, especially those from marginalized or underrepresented backgrounds.

One of the key advantages of the metaverse is its ability to promote diverse forms of expression. Avatars, which represent students in these virtual environments, allow learners to control how they present themselves, enabling those who may feel marginalized in traditional settings to express their identities freely. This enhanced self-expression can reduce social anxiety and improve students' sense of belonging, especially for individuals who face challenges in face-to-face interactions due to factors such as appearance, physical disabilities, or social anxiety. By providing a safe space for interaction, the metaverse encourages more active participation, thus supporting greater social integration.

Moreover, the immersive nature of metaverse platforms facilitates personalized learning experiences, catering to a range of learning styles and needs. These virtual environments allow for adaptive teaching strategies that can accommodate different cognitive abilities and preferences. For instance, visual simulations and interactive experiences enable students to grasp complex concepts more effectively, contributing to improved learning outcomes. In addition, asynchronous communication within these platforms offers students the flexibility to engage at their own pace, further supporting equitable access to education.

Incorporating DEI principles within the design of the edu-metaverse requires careful attention to both technological accessibility and content development. To ensure inclusivity, it is essential to integrate multilingual support and assistive technologies, which allow students with diverse needs to navigate and engage with the platform effectively. This approach promotes equity by providing equal access to educational resources, regardless of students' backgrounds or physical limitations. Furthermore, fostering an inclusive environment requires that institutions implement ongoing evaluation processes, such as collecting user feedback and tracking engagement metrics, to assess the impact of the platform on learning experiences and outcomes.

Despite these advantages, challenges remain in implementing the metaverse as an educational tool that fully realizes DEI objectives. Issues such as the digital divide and privacy concerns could act as moderating factors that influence the effectiveness of these platforms. Future research should examine how these barriers interact with perceived benefits to shape students' intention to use the metaverse, as well as how these factors evolve over time. Longitudinal studies are essential for understanding the sustained use and impact of the metaverse on learning, as user perceptions and technological advancements are likely to change.

Additionally, faculty training and development are critical to ensuring the effective use of the metaverse in educational settings. Training programs that equip educators with the skills to leverage the metaverse's features for inclusive teaching will be pivotal in ensuring that all students benefit from these platforms. By focusing on the potential of Web3 technologies to create inclusive, diverse, and engaging learning environments, educational institutions can contribute to advancing the goals of DEI in a rapidly evolving digital landscape.

The edu-metaverse holds significant potential to transform education by promoting DEI principles through its immersive, adaptable, and accessible features. As Web3 technologies continue to develop, it is crucial for institutions to address existing challenges and continuously refine their platforms to ensure equitable and inclusive learning opportunities for all students. By doing so, the metaverse can play a key role in creating a more diverse, inclusive, and accessible educational experience for the future.

Reducing Carbon Footprints Through Edu-Metaverse: Sustainability and Challenges in Higher Education

As educational institutions face growing concerns about their environmental impact, the integration of Web3 technologies such as the metaverse offers a promising approach to reducing carbon footprints. This study explores the role of the edu-metaverse in higher education institutions (HEIs), focusing on its potential to offer sustainable, eco-friendly learning environments. By providing students with virtual learning experiences that eliminate the need for physical commuting, the edu-metaverse contributes to lowering the carbon footprint associated with traditional educational models. However, despite its benefits, there are challenges in balancing innovation with environmental sustainability.

The research highlights several key benefits of using the edu-metaverse in higher education. Primarily, the use of Web3 technologies facilitates deeper engagement, motivation, and retention among students. Through immersive, gamified, and interactive learning environments, students are better equipped to acquire essential 21st-century skills. Furthermore, edu-metaverse courses emphasize eco-design principles, enhancing students' understanding of sustainability. This combination of pedagogical innovation and environmental consciousness positions the edu-metaverse as a valuable tool in advancing sustainability education.

The study underscores the growing importance of online learning platforms, including the metaverse, in the effort to reduce carbon emissions associated with traditional educational models. Commuting to physical campuses contributes significantly to the carbon footprint of higher education. By adopting online, metaverse-based learning environments, HEIs can reduce the need for travel, offering a more sustainable alternative. However, while the edu-metaverse presents potential energy savings, its own environmental impact remains a subject of debate. The metaverse's energy consumption, particularly its computational power requirements, must be carefully considered in the context of sustainability.

While students generally recognize the environmental benefits of metaverse-based learning, there are challenges regarding the technological demands and the learning curve associated with Web3 tools. Many students face difficulties in understanding and navigating platforms like Figma and the metaverse itself. Despite these hurdles, students appreciate the added value of these technologies in enhancing their learning experiences. However, the perceived environmental benefits are often seen as more symbolic than demonstrable, indicating the need for HEIs to provide clear evidence of the sustainability advantages of edu-metaverse adoption.

For HEIs, the adoption of the edu-metaverse presents an opportunity to strengthen their commitment to sustainability. By incorporating eco-conscious practices into their pedagogical frameworks, institutions can enhance their reputation as environmentally responsible educational providers. However, it is crucial for HEIs to position the edu-metaverse not as a replacement for traditional education but as a hybrid approach that complements existing methods. The metaverse offers a modern alternative to in-person classes, replicating key aspects of classroom interactions while promoting eco-friendly learning practices.

The success of edu-metaverse adoption hinges on strategic communication and effective positioning. HEIs must highlight the environmental advantages of the edu-metaverse to attract students who are increasingly concerned with sustainability. However, the adoption of edu-metaverse should be framed as part of a broader, hybrid learning strategy rather than a standalone solution. Additionally, the communication should address students' varying levels of familiarity with Web3 technologies, ensuring that the benefits of eco-design and sustainability are emphasized for all students, particularly those who are already experienced with metaverse-based learning.

While this study provides valuable insights into the potential of edu-metaverse in promoting sustainability, it also identifies areas for future research. There is a need to assess the true environmental impact of the metaverse compared to other online and traditional learning models. Additionally, exploring the perceptions of students from diverse educational contexts and cultural backgrounds could shed light on the global applicability of edu-metaverse strategies. HEIs must continue to monitor the carbon footprint of their educational technologies and adopt strategies that balance pedagogical innovation with genuine environmental benefits. By doing so, they can contribute to a more sustainable future while providing students with high-quality, eco-conscious education.

Exploring the Role of the Metaverse in Supporting Students With Selective Mutism and Social Anxiety in Education

This study from Pelet and Taieb (2025) explores the potential of the metaverse in supporting students with selective mutism and social anxiety, particularly within educational contexts. Selective mutism, a condition marked by the inability or unwillingness to speak in certain social situations, poses significant challenges for learners, especially in classroom settings. Traditional educational models often exacerbate these issues by requiring verbal participation in front of peers, leading to heightened anxiety. The metaverse, however, with its immersive and flexible nature, offers an alternative environment where learners can engage without the same pressure. The study investigates how the metaverse's features, such as avatars, asynchronous communication, and gamification, create opportunities for students to interact and learn at their own pace, reducing the barriers posed by anxiety.

The findings suggest that avatars play a central role in reducing anxiety and facilitating engagement. By allowing learners to express themselves through digital representations rather than their physical bodies, avatars mitigate the fear of judgment associated with face-to-face interactions. Participants indicated that the ability to control their avatar's appearance and behavior, coupled with the anonymity it provides, leads to increased comfort in expressing themselves. In particular, the use of avatars can lessen the social pressures typically found in traditional classroom settings, enabling learners to engage more freely with course content and peers. This feature is particularly helpful for students who might otherwise withdraw from participation due to fear of being judged based on their real-world identity.

The study also highlights the importance of passive engagement in the metaverse, especially for those who may be hesitant to actively participate. Passive observation, such as watching others' interactions or exploring virtual environments, provides valuable opportunities for learners to process information and build confidence before engaging directly. This reflective approach allows students to familiarize themselves with social dynamics and course material in a less intimidating space. While active participation is still essential for deep learning, passive engagement serves as a crucial first step for learners who need time to acclimate to the virtual environment.

Moreover, the metaverse's immersive nature supports various learning styles, including visual and kinesthetic learners. By providing interactive and exploratory experiences, such as virtual field trips or simulations, students can engage with content in a more hands-on manner than traditional educational tools allow. For instance, students can explore complex concepts, such as the structure of the solar system or human anatomy, in ways that are not feasible in the physical world. This approach not only increases engagement but also aids retention, as learners are able to interact with and visualize concepts in a dynamic, memorable way.

Despite the promising benefits, the study acknowledges several limitations. The sample size was small, and participants were already familiar with immersive technologies, which may not fully represent the broader student population. Additionally, the reliance on qualitative data, while offering rich insights, limits the ability to generalize findings or measure the long-term effectiveness of metaverse-based learning. The study also points out that while the metaverse offers a novel approach to overcoming communication barriers, over-reliance on virtual environments could potentially hinder the development of face-to-face communication skills, which remain essential in many contexts.

Looking ahead, the study suggests several avenues for future research. Longitudinal studies could explore how sustained use of the metaverse impacts student outcomes, particularly in terms of social anxiety and academic performance. It would also be valuable to investigate the types of activities and interactions that most effectively promote engagement and self-efficacy among learners with selective mutism. Furthermore, examining how metaverse environments foster social dynamics, such as the roles learners adopt in virtual communities, could provide valuable insights into how these platforms contribute to peer learning and socialization.

The metaverse therefore represents a promising educational tool for students with selective mutism and social anxiety. Its immersive, flexible, and inclusive nature can help reduce traditional barriers to participation and create more accessible learning experiences. While more research is needed to understand its long-term effectiveness, the metaverse has the potential to transform how learners with communication challenges engage with educational content and collaborate with their peers, offering a more supportive environment for those who struggle with face-to-face interactions.

Blockchain's Potential for Cost Reduction and Operational Optimization

Web3, as a transformative technological framework, presents unique opportunities for the wine industry (Pelet et al., 2023; Pelet and Haller, 2025; Pelet and Terblanche, 2025). This decentralized ecosystem, built on blockchain technology, is characterized by its ability to offer transparency, enhanced security, and traceability of assets. In the context of the wine industry, integrating Web3 technologies, particularly blockchain and non-fungible tokens (NFTs), could address long-standing challenges related to authenticity, traceability, and supply chain efficiency. Given the global nature of wine distribution, where provenance and quality are paramount, the adoption of Web3 technologies could lead to significant benefits such as cost reduction, improved customer trust, and greater transparency.

The wine industry has faced increasing concerns about fraud and counterfeiting, particularly in regions where counterfeit wines are a major issue (Lecat, Brouard & Chapuis, 2017). Blockchain technology could provide an effective solution to these challenges, as its immutable ledger ensures that information related to a wine's origin, production, and distribution cannot be altered or manipulated. Additionally, the rise of NFTs, which are uniquely linked to digital assets, offers a new layer of authentication, allowing consumers to verify the legitimacy of wine products, from vineyard to bottle.

The concept of Web3 extends beyond traceability and authentication, fostering a more decentralized and consumer-centric market (Pelet and Terblanche, 2025). By leveraging blockchain's transparency and security, wine producers and distributors can create new ways to engage with customers and build brand loyalty. In addition to improving operational efficiency, these technologies also introduce opportunities for direct customer interaction through NFTs, offering exclusive experiences or digital collectibles that can further enhance customer loyalty.

One of the most significant advantages of adopting blockchain and NFTs within the wine industry is the potential for cost reduction and process optimization. Blockchain's distributed ledger system eliminates the need for intermediaries, such as brokers and centralized data storage systems, reducing the costs associated with traditional methods of managing inventory and sales. Moreover, blockchain enables efficient tracking of wine products, automating processes such as shipment tracking, reducing human error, and improving overall supply chain management.

Interviewees in the wine industry have identified opportunities for substantial savings through blockchain integration. For example, blockchain-based systems can streamline invoicing and payment processing, ensuring transparency and reducing the risk of fraud. As these technologies enhance efficiency, companies could benefit from lower operational costs while maintaining product quality and customer satisfaction. The ability to automate and streamline key aspects of the supply chain also minimizes the need for labor-intensive tasks and ensures quicker transaction times.

Another area where blockchain could lead to cost savings is in inventory management. By utilizing smart contracts and decentralized networks, wine producers can more effectively track stock levels in real time. This would reduce the likelihood of overstocking or stockouts, leading to more accurate forecasting and reduced waste. Furthermore, the transparency offered by blockchain could simplify auditing processes, providing regulators with a clear, verifiable record of compliance that reduces the need for expensive oversight and inspections.

Enhancing Customer Trust Through Traceability and Authenticity

Trust is a cornerstone of the wine industry, particularly when it comes to ensuring product authenticity. Consumers are increasingly concerned about the authenticity of the wine they purchase, with counterfeit wines presenting a major risk to both brands and customers (Pelet and Terblanche, 2025). Blockchain offers a secure, transparent method of tracking a wine's journey from vineyard to consumer, ensuring that every stage of the production process is recorded and verifiable. This transparency provides customers with confidence that the wine they are purchasing is genuine and of high quality.

NFTs play a crucial role in this process by certifying ownership and authenticity. Each NFT associated with a wine bottle or collection can be tied to specific attributes, such as the vineyard's location, harvest date, and production methods. By offering NFTs as proof of authenticity, producers and distributors can provide an extra layer of security against counterfeit products. This digital certification can be easily verified by consumers, offering an added layer of trust and distinguishing high-quality wines in a competitive market.

The implementation of Web3 technologies also offers wine producers a way to engage with customers on a deeper level. For instance, by incorporating blockchain-based provenance information, consumers can trace the journey of their wine, gaining insight into the vineyard's sustainability practices, the region's terroir, and other unique features that contribute to the wine's characteristics. This level of transparency not only builds customer trust but also supports sustainable practices within the wine industry by rewarding producers who emphasize quality and ethical production methods.

Despite the many advantages of Web3 technologies, there are challenges to overcome in their adoption within the wine industry (Pelet and Terblanche, 2025). One major barrier is the complexity and perceived technical barriers of blockchain and NFTs. Many industry professionals, particularly those in traditional wine production or distribution roles, may not fully understand the technology or its potential applications. Training and awareness campaigns will be necessary to ensure that wine industry professionals are equipped with the knowledge to implement and manage Web3 technologies effectively.

Another concern is the initial investment required to adopt blockchain-based systems. Implementing a blockchain infrastructure, particularly one that integrates NFTs, can require significant resources, both in terms of time and money. Smaller producers or distributors may find these costs prohibitive, particularly if the perceived return on investment is unclear. As the technology matures and becomes more accessible, however, it is likely that these costs will decrease, making adoption more feasible for businesses of all sizes.

Moreover, the regulatory landscape surrounding blockchain and NFTs remains uncertain. While many countries are beginning to adopt frameworks for digital assets, there is still a lack of uniformity in how these technologies are regulated, particularly in the wine industry. In some regions, the use of NFTs for authenticity may be subject to legal scrutiny, and businesses may need to navigate complex regulatory environments as they adopt these technologies.

The integration of Web3 technologies into the wine industry offers the potential for significant sustainability benefits. Blockchain's transparency and traceability capabilities can ensure that every step of the wine supply chain is documented, providing consumers with insight into the environmental impact of their purchases. This level of visibility can be particularly appealing to consumers who are increasingly concerned with sustainability and ethical sourcing.

Wine producers who prioritize sustainability could use blockchain and NFTs as a way to communicate their efforts to consumers. For example, by integrating sustainability metrics into the blockchain, producers can showcase their commitment to reducing carbon footprints, conserving water, or supporting local communities. These verifiable claims can enhance a producer's reputation and differentiate their brand in an increasingly eco-conscious market.

Additionally, by reducing the number of intermediaries in the supply chain, blockchain technology could lower the environmental impact of wine logistics. For example, fewer intermediaries would lead to more direct shipping routes, potentially reducing carbon emissions associated with transport. Furthermore, digitalizing the wine production and distribution process would reduce the need for paper-based record-keeping, further minimizing the industry's ecological footprint.

Web3 technologies, including blockchain and NFTs, offer the wine industry an opportunity to address some of its most pressing challenges, such as counterfeiting, inefficiency, and environmental sustainability. By leveraging these technologies, wine producers can improve traceability, reduce costs, and enhance customer trust, all while fostering deeper engagement with consumers. However, challenges related to technical knowledge, costs, and regulation must be addressed to ensure the successful integration of Web3 technologies into the industry.

As blockchain and NFTs continue to evolve, it is likely that their applications will expand, offering even more ways to optimize the wine supply chain. Whether through enhanced product authenticity, streamlined logistics, or better sustainability practices, the future of the wine industry appears poised for transformation. The growing interest in these technologies from both producers and consumers alike signals that Web3 could become an integral part of the wine industry's next generation of operations.

Consumer Engagement and Social Media Marketing in the Wine Industry

Exploring the intersection of consumer engagement and social media marketing within the wine industry, with a focus on how these elements drive business performance, can reveal interesting as Pelet et al. (2023) show. Social media platforms, such as TikTok, Meta, Instagram, and X, have become integral tools for engaging with consumers, facilitating interaction, and creating brand loyalty. The work conducted by Pelet et al. (2023) highlights how wine producers use these platforms to communicate with their target audiences, cultivate brand awareness, and ultimately influence consumer purchasing behavior. It also addresses the growing importance of digital engagement for the wine market, particularly as younger generations increasingly turn to online platforms to make purchase decisions, and reveal the necessity to connect Web 2.0 (social media) to Web3 (blockchain, NFT, metaverses).

Social media plays a pivotal role in shaping consumer behavior in the wine industry (Pelet et al., 2023). Through these platforms, wine producers and distributors are able to connect directly with consumers, fostering a sense of community and engagement around their products. The research suggests that consumers' online engagement with wine brands is motivated by a desire for information, entertainment, and connection. By leveraging social media, wine brands can provide consumers with content that is both informative and emotionally resonant, which enhances their decision-making processes. Furthermore, this digital engagement has significant implications for brand loyalty, as it can help build long-term relationships between wine brands and their customers.

The influence of online reviews and user-generated content (UGC) is another critical aspect of the paper. User reviews on social media platforms and dedicated wine review sites offer consumers the opportunity to share their experiences and opinions about specific products. These reviews not only impact the reputation of wine brands but also shape the perceptions of potential buyers. The paper examines the increasing reliance on UGC in influencing consumer choices, noting that consumers often trust peer reviews over traditional advertising. The authenticity of UGC and its ability to provide a more personalized perspective on wine products are key factors that drive its influence.

The wine industry's adaptation to digital marketing trends is explored in the contribution from Pelet et al. (2022), highlighting how brands are using social media to promote their products and engage with customers. Traditional methods of wine marketing, such as print advertising and in-store tastings, are being supplemented or replaced by digital strategies. These include influencer partnerships, targeted ads, and content marketing tailored to specific consumer segments. By aligning their marketing efforts with the preferences of digital-savvy consumers, wine brands are able to reach a broader audience and remain competitive in an increasingly crowded market. This adaptation is especially crucial given the growing significance of younger consumers, such as millennials and Generation Z, who are more likely to engage with brands through social media.

Despite its potential, there are several challenges associated with consumer engagement on social media in the wine industry. One key challenge is the management of brand identity across multiple platforms (Ettis, Pelet & Zaichkowsky, 2023). Wine producers must ensure that their messaging is consistent and aligns with the values and expectations of their target audience. Additionally, the sheer volume of content on social media can make it difficult for wine brands to stand out and capture the attention of consumers. The paper also discusses issues related to privacy, data protection, and the ethical implications of targeted marketing on social media platforms. These challenges require wine brands to adopt strategic approaches to digital engagement that balance consumer expectations with brand objectives.

The work by Pelet et al. (2023) also investigates the direct impact of social media engagement on consumer purchase intentions in the wine industry. It highlights how interactions with wine brands on social media can influence consumers' attitudes and behaviors, ultimately leading to increased purchase likelihood. Research suggests that consumers who engage with wine brands online are more likely to make a purchase, especially when they feel a personal connection to the brand. The paper discusses various factors that influence this connection, such as the quality of content, the responsiveness of the brand, and the level of emotional engagement. These elements contribute to creating a positive online brand experience, which translates into real-world sales.

As technology continues to evolve, new platforms and tools will likely emerge that further reshape consumer engagement strategies. The rise of virtual reality (VR), augmented reality (AR), and artificial intelligence (AI) could offer new opportunities for wine brands to engage consumers in innovative ways. Additionally, the ongoing shift towards sustainability and environmental consciousness among consumers may prompt wine brands to adopt more transparent and socially responsible marketing practices. The paper emphasizes the need for ongoing research to understand the long-term effects of social media engagement on consumer behavior and to develop strategies that effectively leverage these digital tools for sustainable business growth.

Integration of NFTs and the Metaverse in Wine Education

The rapid evolution of virtual technologies has given rise to a novel paradigm in education, where the metaverse emerges as a transformative tool for immersive learning (Pelet and Haller, 2025). In this context, wine education benefits from both its rich cultural heritage and the potential of emerging digital platforms. The integration of NFTs (Non-Fungible Tokens) into the educational process offers a unique approach to rewarding students, making their learning experience not only interactive but also financially meaningful. NFTs, which serve as digital certificates or representations of ownership, can be linked to specific wine bottles or educational milestones, effectively gamifying the journey of knowledge acquisition.

Viticulturists and wine producers are increasingly leveraging the metaverse to enhance their visibility, utilizing NFTs to establish a connection between the digital and physical worlds of wine. In this ecosystem, each bottle of wine is represented by a unique NFT, providing both a form of certification and a potential revenue stream. The educational journey within this "oenophilic metaverse" transcends traditional learning by allowing students to collect NFTs as proof of their progression, blending the acquisition of knowledge with the excitement of accumulating digital assets.

The fusion of NFTs with the European Credit Transfer System (ECTS) credits introduces an innovative approach to student assessment. In this model, wine becomes the currency of achievement, where learners accumulate wine-related rewards as they progress through their studies. This system not only serves as a motivational tool but also reflects the tangible value that the metaverse can provide, where virtual rewards correspond to real-world products, fostering a deeper connection with the subject matter.

One key aspect of this project is the development of a Learning Management System (LMS) within the metaverse, built by students themselves. Using tools such as Unity, Sketchfab, and Spatial, students are tasked with creating virtual scenes that simulate real-world wine-related environments, such as vineyards, wine merchant shops, and educational laboratories. These scenes are designed not only as immersive experiences but also as platforms for selling both physical wine and its digital counterparts in the form of NFTs. The goal is to aid young winemakers in gaining visibility within the metaverse while simultaneously enriching the educational process through interactive, hands-on projects.

In tandem with the creation of metaverse scenes, students are asked to design and execute a TikTok campaign aimed at boosting brand engagement. The campaign serves as a practical exercise in digital marketing, drawing inspiration from successful real-world campaigns. By using tools like CapCut, students create video content that is designed to capture the attention of a broad audience, showcasing both creativity and strategic thinking. The TikTok project encourages the students to apply their understanding of branding and engagement tactics in a fast-paced, popular medium.

The evaluation of these projects is based on both creativity and technical execution. For the metaverse scenes, students are assessed on the clarity of their pedagogical objectives, the realism of their proposed environments, and the use of diverse techniques to enhance the educational experience. The TikTok campaign is similarly evaluated on creativity, humor, and provocation, with an emphasis on the quality of the final product. Both components serve as a reflection of the students' ability to integrate modern technological tools into a cohesive educational strategy that balances both theory and practical application.

The integration of NFTs and the metaverse into wine education represents a forward-thinking approach that blends traditional knowledge with cutting-edge technology. This model not only offers a novel method of learning and assessment but also provides a platform for the wine industry to engage with a digitally savvy, future-oriented audience. As virtual and augmented reality technologies continue to evolve, such innovations may become standard in educational environments, offering students and industry professionals new ways to engage, learn, and thrive.

In those recent research and publications, I have explored the strategic integration of Web3 into various sectors. For instance, the potential of NFTs as educational rewards is discussed in the work. These contributions, alongside our analysis of consumer cooperatives and retail logistics, underscore the breadth of Web3's transformative potential.

As we transition into examining the broader impacts of Web3 technologies, particularly in relation to mobile applications, the upcoming book, *Architecting the Digital Future: Platforms, Design, and Application*, offers a comprehensive exploration of these advancements. Spanning 16 chapters, this book delves deeply into the intersection of Web3 and user experience, providing critical insights into how mobile platforms are being shaped by decentralized technologies and blockchain innovations (Please see the appendix for a detailed description of title, abstract, keywords and authors).

Each chapter within this volume covers a specific aspect of Web3's influence on mobile application design and user experience. The first few chapters set the stage by introducing the core concepts of Web3, emphasizing the transformative potential of decentralized systems and how they promise to redefine the way users interact with mobile platforms. These foundational discussions explore the concept of decentralized identities, the rise of tokenization, and the impact of blockchain on the privacy and security of mobile app users.

As the book progresses, the focus shifts to practical applications, with several chapters examining the design strategies that enhance UX within mobile Web3 environments. These include designing for cross-platform accessibility, understanding the unique challenges of integrating blockchain into user-friendly interfaces, and the role of mobile wallets and NFTs in the evolving mobile ecosystem. Insights from leading experts in design and technology offer actionable guidance on how businesses can ensure that their Web3 mobile applications are intuitive, engaging, and secure for end users.

In subsequent chapters, the book explores the real-world applications of these design principles across various sectors, such as e-commerce, entertainment, education, and healthcare. For example, in the context of academia, the book discusses the growing adoption of Web3 in educational platforms, particularly the use of NFTs for credentialing and gamifying learning. The education sector stands to benefit from Web3 by providing students and educators with new ways to interact with digital content, certify achievements, and enhance global collaboration through decentralized platforms.

Furthermore, the book delves into the intersection of Web3 with business practices, highlighting how companies across industries are utilizing decentralized mobile platforms to improve customer experience and streamline operations. Through detailed case studies, readers gain insights into how businesses can leverage Web3 to foster innovation, create more personalized customer experiences, and even reduce operational costs.

Of particular interest is the exploration of user behavior and expectations in the Web3 space. The book discusses the unique challenges that come with the transition from centralized to decentralized applications, addressing issues such as user onboarding, educating consumers about new technologies, and building trust in Web3 environments. These insights provide a blueprint for businesses aiming to integrate Web3 technologies in a way that enhances rather than alienates their user base.

Finally, the book concludes by examining the long-term implications of Web3 on mobile applications and business models. It speculates on future trends, such as the role of AI in shaping Web3 experiences, the potential of virtual and augmented reality within mobile apps, and the continued evolution of blockchain technologies. With its forward-thinking approach, the book offers a roadmap for companies and academic institutions looking to stay ahead of the curve in a rapidly changing technological landscape.

This book, *Architecting the Digital Future: Platforms, Design, and Application*, offers a comprehensive examination of Web3 technologies and their implications for user experience (UX) in mobile applications, spanning theoretical insights, design strategies, and real-world applications. The 16 chapters in this volume delve into the interplay between technological advancements and practical outcomes, as highlighted below:

CONCLUSION

This book bridges theoretical explorations and practical applications of Web3 technologies, offering insights into their transformative potential across academia and business. By highlighting blockchain, NFTs, and the metaverse, the chapters collectively chart a path forward, equipping readers with the knowledge to navigate and leverage Web3's unprecedented opportunities. The integration of Web3 technologies into mobile applications represents a seismic shift in how users interact with digital platforms, businesses operate, and even how industries, such as the wine sector, harness the potential of decentralization, blockchain, and NFTs. This introductory chapter has set the stage for a deeper dive into the myriad ways in which Web3 is transforming both the academic and business landscapes, particularly within the domain of user experience (UX) and mobile platforms.

By embracing Web3, organizations across various sectors, from retail to education, are beginning to uncover the vast potential for more secure, transparent, and decentralized digital ecosystems. Whether through the use of NFTs to verify product authenticity in the wine industry, or through the creation of immersive, gamified educational environments within the metaverse, Web3 offers an entirely new paradigm for digital engagement. Through these innovations, Web3 is not just altering how industries operate but also how consumers perceive and interact with these industries.

As we move forward, the role of user experience design becomes ever more critical. The way Web3 technologies are integrated into mobile applications can determine the success or failure of these innovations. This book aims to unpack the complexities of these transitions, offering valuable insights for both industry professionals and academics who are looking to navigate the emerging Web3 ecosystem.

Managerial Implications

For business leaders, the adoption of Web3 technologies can open new doors to efficiency, enhanced security, and deeper customer engagement. From a managerial perspective, the integration of blockchain into mobile applications can help reduce operational costs, improve traceability, and foster customer loyalty through transparent, verifiable product journeys. However, the complex nature of Web3 also requires a strategic approach. Managers must invest in educating their teams and developing an understanding of these technologies' long-term potential, as well as their immediate practical applications. The successful integration of decentralized systems requires significant planning, collaboration, and investment, particularly in areas like training and resource allocation.

In the wine industry, for example, blockchain's potential to automate invoicing and reduce fraud offers a significant opportunity for operational efficiency (Pelet and Terblanche, 2025). However, managers must balance these technological advances with an understanding of the industry's traditional processes and the hesitancy toward adopting new technologies. The integration of NFTs into the supply chain, as discussed in the wine sector, can be seen as a pathway to authenticate products and offer customers a more transparent and trustworthy purchasing experience, but this requires strong managerial leadership to guide the transition smoothly.

Methodological Implications

The methodologies employed in researching Web3 technologies and their application within mobile platforms require a multidisciplinary approach, combining fields such as design, technology, and consumer behavior studies. The methodological implications of this book suggest that future research must not only investigate the technical aspects of Web3 but also consider its practical implementation from both a user-experience and business-strategy perspective. Moreover, qualitative research methods, such as interviews, case studies, and ethnographic research, can help capture the nuanced experiences of users and organizations as they transition to these new systems. Surveys and user testing, including usability studies, will be essential in understanding how consumers engage with decentralized applications, particularly as Web3 technologies evolve rapidly.

Furthermore, research methodologies in this space should incorporate the feedback of stakeholders in industries adopting Web3 to better understand adoption barriers and identify effective strategies for overcoming challenges related to education, training, and regulatory compliance.

Theoretical Implications

From a theoretical perspective, this work contributes to the ongoing discourse around the intersection of decentralized technologies, user experience, and mobile application design. As Web3 continues to gain traction, the theoretical frameworks that have traditionally governed UX design must adapt to account for the complexities of decentralization. Theoretical frameworks must evolve to accommodate the decentralization and tokenization paradigms introduced by Web3. Existing theories on trust, value co-creation, and user engagement can be reexamined in light of blockchain's ability to reduce information asymmetry and enhance transparency. Similarly, consumer behavior theories may require expansion to account for the interplay between digital and physical assets, as well as the influence of NFTs and social media platforms on decision-making. Future research should also consider how Web3 technologies reshape organizational structures and governance, challenging traditional hierarchies and fostering more participatory models.

Limitations and Future Research Directions

Despite its potential, the integration of Web3 technologies faces several challenges. The high costs of adoption, technical complexity, and lack of standardized regulations remain significant barriers for many businesses and academic institutions. Additionally, concerns around data privacy, energy consumption, and digital inequality could hinder widespread acceptance.

Future research should focus on addressing these limitations by exploring scalable solutions for small and medium-sized enterprises, developing energy-efficient blockchain technologies, and ensuring equitable access to Web3 tools. Longitudinal studies could examine the long-term impacts of Web3 on business performance, while cross-cultural research could uncover variations in adoption and perception across different markets. As the metaverse and virtual environments continue to evolve, further investigation into their role in education and consumer engagement is warranted.

Looking Ahead

The adoption of Web3 technologies represents more than a technological evolution—it is a paradigm shift that redefines how value is created, shared, and experienced. As we look to the future, the convergence of blockchain, NFTs, and immersive technologies such as the metaverse holds immense potential for reshaping academia, business, and society. However, realizing this potential will require collaborative efforts among researchers, practitioners, and policymakers to address the challenges and ensure that Web3 technologies are harnessed for inclusive and sustainable development.

This book serves as a starting point for understanding these transformative trends, offering both theoretical insights and practical applications. As the subsequent chapters unfold, readers will gain a deeper appreciation for how Web3 can empower businesses and educators to navigate the digital frontier, setting the stage for a new era of innovation and engagement.

REFERENCES

Ettis, S., Pelet, J.-É., & Zaichkowsky, J. (2023). Comparing Online User Experience across Different Digital Business Ecosystems and Platforms When Booking Vacations. *Review of Managerial Science*, •••, 1–30. DOI: 10.1007/s11846-023-00712-2

Lecat, B., Brouard, J., & Chapuis, C. (2017). Fraud and counterfeit wines in France: An overview and perspectives. *British Food Journal*, *119*(1), 84–104. DOI: 10.1108/BFJ-09-2016-0398

Pelet, J.-É., & Haller, C. (2025 forthcoming). *Immersive wine pedagogy in the metaverse: NFTs as potential rewards for graduation*. Springer.

Pelet, J.-É., & Taieb, B. (2025a). *«Silent No More: Harnessing the metaverse to support students with selective mutism»*, WorldCist'25 - 13rd World Conference on Information Systems and Technologies, to be held in Florianópolis, at Federal University of Santa Catarina, Brazil, 15 - 17 April 2025.

Pelet, J.-É., & Taieb, B. (2025b). (forthcoming). Leveraging the metaverse for inclusive education: Exploring the perceived benefits of edu-metaverse. *The Journal of Strategic Information Systems*.

Pelet, J.-É., Taieb, B., & Alkhudary, R. (2023). Measuring consumer perceptions of home-delivery convenience – the case of cargo bikes. *International Journal of Retail & Distribution Management*, *51*(9/10), 1371–1387. Advance online publication. DOI: 10.1108/IJRDM-11-2022-0483

Pelet, J.-É., Taieb, B., Lecat, B., Terblanche, N.-S., & Alkhudary, R. (2023). Exploring how consumer cooperatives might strategically incorporate social media to distribute wine. *Journal of Consumer Behaviour*. Advance online publication. DOI: 10.1002/cb.2255

Pelet, J.-É., & Terblanche, N.-S. (2025). Trying to Solve South Africa's Port Logistics Challenges with Blockchain-Enabled Traceability, AMS World Marketing Congress held at Dijon, July 02-04, 2025 • Dijon, Burgundy, France.

KEY TERMS AND DEFINITIONS

Administrative Paperwork: The documentation necessary to manage and execute logistics operations, often involving records, forms, and permits.

Augmented Reality (AR): Technology that overlays digital content on the real world, enhancing physical environments with interactive features.

Blockchain: A decentralized and secure digital ledger technology that records transactions across multiple systems to ensure transparency and immutability.

Blockchain: A decentralized and secure digital ledger technology that records transactions across multiple systems to ensure transparency and immutability.

Brand Engagement in the Metaverse: Strategies for interacting with consumers in virtual environments, often incorporating NFTs, immersive storytelling, and gamification.

Carbon Footprint of Blockchain: The total greenhouse gas emissions generated by the energy-intensive processes involved in blockchain operations, particularly consensus mechanisms.

Carbon Footprint: The total amount of greenhouse gases emitted, directly or indirectly, by an individual, organization, or activity.

Cargo Bikes: Bicycles specifically designed for carrying goods, often equipped with storage compartments or trailers.

Consensus Mechanism Environmental Impact: The energy consumption and ecological effects associated with the processes used to validate blockchain transactions.

Consensus Mechanism: A process used in blockchain systems to agree on a single source of truth among distributed participants.

Consensus Mechanism: A process used in blockchain systems to agree on a single source of truth among distributed participants, ensuring data integrity and authenticity.

Consumer Personalization: Customizing products, services, or experiences to meet individual preferences, often enabled by data analytics and Web3 technologies.

Consumer Trust: Confidence in the reliability, integrity, and performance of blockchain systems or services, particularly in transactions or data handling.

Consumer Trust: The confidence that users have in the reliability, integrity, and performance of a service or system.

Crypto Wallet: A digital application used to store, send, and receive cryptocurrencies or digital assets securely.

Data Confidentiality: Ensuring that sensitive information is accessible only to authorized users.

Data Traceability: The capability to track the origin, history, and movement of data throughout a system.

Data Traceability: The capacity to track the origin, history, and movement of data or assets within a blockchain or supply chain system.

Decentralized Education Models: Learning frameworks that use blockchain to provide transparent, secure, and equitable access to educational resources.

Decentralized Systems: Systems where control and decision-making are distributed across multiple participants rather than centralized.

Decentralized Systems: Systems where control and decision-making are distributed across multiple participants, eliminating central authority.

Delivery Automation: The use of automated systems or vehicles to streamline logistics operations, improving efficiency and reducing costs.

Delivery Automation: The use of technology to streamline and perform delivery processes without human intervention.

Delivery Flexibility: The ability to adjust delivery schedules or methods to suit consumer preferences or changing conditions.

Delivery Notifications: Alerts or updates provided to consumers about the status and progress of their deliveries.

Delivery Reliability: The consistency and dependability of delivery operations in meeting expected times and conditions.

Dematerialized Orders: Paperless order processing, using digital systems to manage and fulfill orders.

Digital Asset Security: Measures to ensure the protection and safe storage of digital assets, including NFTs and cryptocurrencies, from breaches or theft.

Digital Citizenship in the Metaverse: The responsible and ethical use of virtual environments, emphasizing security, respect, and collaboration.

Digital Collaboration Spaces: Virtual environments in the metaverse that enable teams to work together on projects, blending physical and digital interactions.

Digital Collectibles: Unique digital items such as NFTs, often valued for their rarity, artistic appeal, or association with specific communities or brands.

Digital Ecosystem: A network of interconnected technologies, platforms, and communities operating within the blockchain or metaverse space.

Digital Identity: A representation of an individual's or entity's online persona, often secured and managed using blockchain technology.

Digital Marketing in Web3: Strategies leveraging blockchain, NFTs, and the metaverse to engage audiences, enhance branding, and promote products or services.

Digital Ownership: The ability to own and trade digital assets securely and transparently using blockchain technology.

Digital Provenance: The ability to verify the origin and history of digital or physical assets through blockchain technology.

Digital Rewards: Incentives issued in digital form, such as NFTs or tokens, to recognize achievements or encourage participation.

Digital Twins: Virtual representations of physical objects, systems, or environments, enabling simulation and analysis in the metaverse.

Eco-Friendly Blockchain Innovations: Developments aimed at reducing the environmental impact of blockchain technology, such as energy-efficient consensus mechanisms.

Eco-Friendly Delivery Options: Logistics practices that minimize environmental impact, often through reduced emissions or sustainable transportation methods.

E-Commerce Markets: Online platforms and industries where goods and services are bought and sold digitally.

Educational Metaverse: A virtual space designed for immersive learning experiences, combining real-world content with interactive digital simulations.

Edu-Metaverse: A subset of the metaverse tailored for education, offering immersive and gamified learning experiences.

End Consumers: The individuals who are the final recipients of goods or services in a supply chain.

Energy Consumption: The amount of energy used in performing logistics operations, including transportation and warehousing.

Environmental Sustainability in Web3: Efforts to minimize the ecological impact of blockchain technologies, particularly in energy-intensive systems.

Environmental Sustainability: Practices and processes that minimize environmental impact and preserve natural resources for future generations.

Gamification in Education: The use of game-like elements to enhance engagement and learning outcomes, frequently integrated with AR and VR technologies.

Geolocation: The identification or estimation of the geographic location of an object, such as a delivery vehicle, using GPS or similar technologies.

Immersive Educational Experiences: Learning activities designed to fully engage users in simulated environments, combining realism with interactivity.

Immutable Ledger: A record-keeping system where data entries cannot be altered once they are added, ensuring authenticity and reliability.

Immutable Ledger: A record-keeping system where data entries cannot be altered or deleted once they are added, ensuring transparency and reliability.

Immutable Record: A data entry in a blockchain that cannot be altered or deleted, ensuring permanent accuracy.

Information Quality: The accuracy, relevance, and timeliness of data provided by a system.

Interactive Delivery Interfaces: User-friendly platforms or applications that enable real-time interaction with delivery systems.

Interactive Delivery Interfaces: User-friendly platforms that allow real-time interaction with logistics or delivery systems, enhancing transparency and engagement.

Interoperability: The ability of different blockchain systems, platforms, or technologies to communicate and exchange data seamlessly.

Inventory Management: The process of monitoring and controlling stock levels to meet demand while minimizing excess inventory.

Last-Mile Logistics: The final phase of the delivery process where goods are transported from a distribution hub to the end consumer.

Metaverse Tokenomics: The economic systems governing digital transactions and rewards within virtual spaces.

Metaverse: A virtual shared space that combines augmented reality (AR), virtual reality (VR), and the Internet, enabling immersive experiences and interactions.

Net Benefits: The overall advantages or value derived from implementing a system, balancing its costs and benefits.

NFT (Non-Fungible Token): A unique digital asset stored on a blockchain, representing ownership of a specific item or piece of content such as art, music, or virtual goods.

NFT Educational Certificates: Blockchain-based digital credentials that verify skills, qualifications, or achievements, ensuring authenticity and permanence.

Operational Delays: Disruptions or slowdowns in the logistics process that affect timely delivery.

Operational Efficiency: The ability to deliver goods or services in the most cost-effective manner without compromising quality.

Operational Efficiency: The ability to perform business processes effectively while minimizing waste, cost, and time.

Operational Uncertainties: Unpredictable factors that can affect the efficiency or effectiveness of logistics operations.

Personalization: Tailoring services or experiences to individual consumer preferences and needs.

Proactive Issue Resolution in Blockchain Systems: Identifying and addressing potential challenges in blockchain operations before they escalate into significant problems.

Proactive Issue Resolution: Addressing potential problems before they occur by anticipating challenges and taking preventive actions.

Real-Time Tracking: Monitoring and reporting the location or status of an object or process instantly and continuously.

Real-Time Visibility in Logistics: The capability to access live updates on the location, status, or condition of goods within the supply chain.

Real-Time Visibility: The capability to access live updates and insights about the current status and location of assets or processes.

Route Optimization: The process of determining the most efficient path for deliveries, minimizing time, cost, and energy consumption.

Secure Data Protocols: Established methods for protecting data integrity and privacy during transmission and storage.

Secure Information Sharing: The exchange of data in a manner that protects it from unauthorized access or breaches.

Service Quality: The ability of a system or service to meet or exceed user expectations through responsiveness, reliability, and empathy.

Smart Contracts: Self-executing contracts on a blockchain where the terms are directly written into code, automatically enforcing agreements without intermediaries.

Spatial Computing: The blending of digital and physical environments through AR, VR, and advanced computing, facilitating metaverse interactions.

Sustainability Metrics: Quantitative measures evaluating the environmental, social, and economic impact of blockchain technologies or logistics practices.

Sustainability Metrics: Quantitative measures used to evaluate the environmental, social, and economic performance of a system or practice.

Sustainable Delivery Practices: Delivery methods designed to reduce environmental harm, such as using renewable energy or low-emission vehicles.

Sustainable Delivery Practices: Environmentally conscious methods for transporting goods, often involving low-emission vehicles or renewable energy sources.

Sustainable Urban Logistics Systems: Logistics practices designed to reduce the environmental impact of operations in urban areas, emphasizing efficiency and sustainability.

System Quality: The overall performance and technical soundness of a system, including its reliability, usability, and scalability.

System Use: The degree and manner in which users engage with a technological system in their workflows or routines.

Tokenization: The process of converting rights to an asset into a digital token stored on a blockchain.

Tokenomics: The study of economic systems and incentives within blockchain-based ecosystems, focusing on the use and value of tokens.

Traceability in Wine Logistics: Blockchain-enabled tracking of wine production, from vineyards to consumers, ensuring authenticity and quality.

Traceability: The ability to track and verify the history and movement of goods or data throughout a supply chain.

Transparency: The characteristic of processes being open and easily observable, fostering trust and accountability.

Urban Congestion: Overcrowding in urban areas, often caused by high volumes of traffic, which affects transportation and logistics.

Urban Logistics: The management of logistics operations within urban areas, often focusing on efficiency and sustainability.

Urbanization Challenges: Problems arising from increasing population density in cities, such as pollution, congestion, and resource depletion.

User Satisfaction: The degree to which users' needs and expectations are met by a product or service.

Virtual Goods: Items that exist only in digital environments, such as in games or the metaverse, which can be purchased, traded, or sold.

Virtual Marketplaces: Online platforms where goods, services, or digital assets are bought and sold, often using blockchain for transactions.

Virtual Reality (VR): Fully immersive experiences created using computer-generated simulations, allowing users to explore and interact within a digital environment.

Web3: A decentralized Internet powered by blockchain technology, focusing on user control, privacy, and peer-to-peer interactions.

APPENDIX

Table 1.

Title	Abstract	Keywords	Authors/Institution
A Comprehensive Review on Comparative Analysis of Web Services	This research paper offers a comparative analysis of web services, focusing on functionalities and performances. It examines types like RESTful and SOAP, addressing scalability, security, and interoperability challenges. The findings guide decision-makers in optimizing web-based applications and services.	Web Services, RESTful, SOAP, Scalability, Interoperability	Kuldeep Vayadande, Vishwakarma Institute of Technology, India; Varsha Jujare, Sharad Institute of Technology, India; Maya Patil, St. John College of Engineering, India; Ajit Patil, Bharati Vidyapeeth College of Engineering, India; Gitanjali Yadav, Vishwakarma Institute of IT, India; Sachin Takmare, A. P. Shah Institute of Technology, India; Rahul Mirajkar, Bharati Vidyapeeth College of Engineering, India
Optimizing Web Services for Mobile Platforms: Comparative Insights on Design and Applications	This research paper examines web services tailored to mobile platforms and Web3 applications. It explores RESTful and SOAP services, focusing on scalability, security, and performance. Insights aim to enhance understanding and decision-making in optimizing mobile web-based applications.	Mobile Platforms, RESTful, SOAP, Scalability, Web3	Kuldeep Vayadande, Vishwakarma Institute of Technology, India; Priya Ghate, Sharad Institute of Technology, India; Maya Patil, St. John College of Engineering, India; Yogesh Bodhe, Government Polytechnic Awasari, India; Ajit Patil, Bharati Vidyapeeth College of Engineering, India; Gitanjali Yadav, Vishwakarma Institute of IT, India; Rahul Mirajkar, Bharati Vidyapeeth College of Engineering, India
Virtual and Augmented Reality for Immersive Learning Experiences: Practical Applications and Challenges	This chapter explores VR and AR applications in education, highlighting their potential to enhance comprehension through virtual labs, simulations, and cultural immersion. Challenges to widespread adoption are also discussed.	VR, AR, Immersive Learning, Education, Cultural Immersion	Pankaj Bhambri, Guru Nanak Dev Engineering College, India

continued on following page

Table 1. Continued

Title	Abstract	Keywords	Authors/Institution
Analyzing the Drivers of Adoption in Higher Education E-Learning	This study investigates AI's role in e-learning, examining behavioral intentions and actual usage. Using models like UTAUT, factors such as perceived risk, work engagement, and self-efficacy are analyzed. Findings provide practical insights for AI adoption in higher education.	AI, E-Learning, Behavioral Intentions, UTAUT, Self-Efficacy	Karnika Srivastava, Shri Ramswaroop Memorial University, India; Manoj Kumar, Shri Ramswaroop Memorial University, India; Rinki Verma, Babu Banarasi Das University, India; Shreyanshu Singh, Babu Banarasi Das University, India; Pratibha Maurya, Amity University, India
Taxonomy of Challenges of Cybersecurity Risk Assessment in Higher Learning Institutions	This chapter identifies critical cybersecurity challenges in higher education, including governance gaps, incident management, and security awareness. Recommendations focus on improving institutional cybersecurity postures.	Cybersecurity, Risk Assessment, Governance, Higher Education, IT Security	Beatrice Owino, USIU, Kenya; Collins Oduor, University of Nairobi, Kenya; Gerald Chege, USIU, Kenya; Mahona Paschal, TELTA, Tanzania
Securing the Future of E-Learning with Web 3.0 Technologies and Cybersecurity	This chapter reviews cybersecurity concerns in Web 3.0 e-learning, such as data privacy and malware. Recommendations include robust safeguards, training, and collaboration to create resilient e-learning platforms.	Web 3.0, Cybersecurity, E-Learning, Data Privacy, Decentralization	Er. KRITIKA, Independent Researcher, India
Access to Street Art via Crowdsourcing Methods: A Web Page Proposal for Türkiye	This study proposes a website for preserving street art in Türkiye using Web3 and crowdsourcing. It addresses challenges like digital preservation, copyright issues, and equitable access to cultural heritage.	Street Art, Crowdsourcing, Web3, Preservation, Türkiye	Orhun Ugur, University of Exeter, UK; Semanur Öztemiz, Hacettepe University, Turkey
Mobile Platforms, Designs, and Applications for Web3 Towards Reducing Students' Cognitive Load	This chapter focuses on Web3 mobile platforms' potential to enhance learning by reducing cognitive load. It highlights online meetings and recordings as support tools in programming education.	Web3, Mobile Platforms, Cognitive Load, Education, Online Tools	Dalize van Heerden, University of South Africa; Leila Goosen, University of South Africa

continued on following page

Table 1. Continued

Title	Abstract	Keywords	Authors/Institution
Mapping Cultures Together: Online Heritage Initiatives	This chapter explores online mapping tools like GIS and blockchain for preserving cultural heritage. Web3 offers decentralized solutions for equitable and transparent heritage access.	Cultural Heritage, Mapping, Web3, Blockchain, Digital Preservation	Munir Ahmad, Survey of Pakistan; Maida Maqsood, Government College Women University, Pakistan
Neurocognitive Learning Design and Multiclass Algorithms	This study applies machine learning algorithms to assess skills, predict learning styles, and recommend peers in educational settings. Personalized learning fosters cooperative and effective education.	Machine Learning, Neurocognition, Education, Peer Recommendation, Personalization	C.V. Suresh Babu, Hindustan Institute of Technology and Science, India; Akshara P M, Hindustan Institute of Technology and Science, India; Dhanush Harsha, Hindustan Institute of Technology and Science, India; Afeef Iniyavan M, Hindustan Institute of Technology and Science, India; Jowin J, Hindustan Institute of Technology and Science, India
Value Co-Creation of Design in the Internet Economy	This chapter examines virtual co-design and customization in Web3, emphasizing the role of aesthetic and functional design in value creation.	Co-Design, Web3, Customization, Design Aesthetics, Value Creation	Balaji Gopalan, CMS Business School, India; Ravishankar Ulle, CMS Business School, India; Yogananthan S, CMS Business School, India
Advanced Human-Machine Interfaces for User Experience and Interaction in Information Applications	This research highlights advancements in HMIs, such as gesture recognition and natural language processing, to improve user experience and productivity in information systems.	HMI, User Experience, Gesture Recognition, Natural Language Processing, Productivity	SANJAY TANEJA, Graphic Era University, India; Reepu Reepu, Chandigarh University, India; Mandeep Singh, Chandigarh University, India
Chatbots as Learning Companions: Exploring Ethical Dimensions of AI in Education	This chapter examines ethical concerns in AI chatbot usage in education, including privacy, bias, and transparency. It also highlights the benefits of personalized and engaging learning experiences.	AI Ethics, Chatbots, Education, Privacy, Transparency	Maida Maqsood, Government College Women University, Pakistan; Hafsa Hamid Butt, Minhaj University, Pakistan; Muhammad Awais Ali, Bahria University, Pakistan; Caleb Chinedu, Universiti Tun Hussein Onn Malaysia, Malaysia; Munir Ahmad, Survey of Pakistan
Gamification of Learning to Boost Students' Motivation and Study Engagement	This study explores the positive effects of gamification in education, highlighting increased motivation and engagement among students.	Gamification, Education, Motivation, Engagement, Learning	Laila Zeroual, National School of Commerce and Management – Tangier, Morocco

continued on following page

Table 1. Continued

Title	Abstract	Keywords	Authors/Institution
Advancements in Educational Technology: Navigating the Landscape of User Experience in Web 3.0	This chapter explores user experience advancements in Web3 education, focusing on immersive learning environments, serious games, and the role of interfaces in enhancing educational outcomes.	Web3, UX, Education, Serious Games, Immersive Learning	Pankaj Bhambri, Guru Nanak Dev Engineering College, India; Sita Rani, Guru Nanak Dev Engineering College, India
Designing and Developing a Web3 Mobile Platform: Integrating Blockchain and AI for Enhanced Functionality, Security, and User Experience	This chapter discusses the design and implementation of a Web3 mobile platform using blockchain and AI to improve usability, security, and scalability. Collaborative efforts are emphasized for a robust Web3 ecosystem.	Web3, Blockchain, AI, Mobile Platforms, Security	C.V. Suresh Babu, Hindustan Institute of Technology and Science, India; Malini William, Mirage Software, Inc., USA

Chapter 1
A Comprehensive Review on Comparative Analysis of Web Services

Kuldeep Vayadande
https://orcid.org/0000-0002-0848-5407
Vishwakarma Institute of Technology, India

Ajit R. Patil
https://orcid.org/0009-0002-4278-2277
Bharati Vidyapeeth's College of Engineering, India

Varsha Jujare
https://orcid.org/0009-0009-4596-0711
College of Engineering, Sharad Institute of Technology, Yadrav, India

Gitanjali Bhimrao Yadav
https://orcid.org/0000-0002-6724-8612
Vishwakarma Institute of Information Technology, India

Maya Yogesh Patil
https://orcid.org/0009-0001-7853-7196
St. John College of Engineering and Management, India

Sachin Balawant Takmare
https://orcid.org/0009-0008-4868-0670
A.P. Shah Institute of Technology, India

Rahul Prakash Mirajkar
https://orcid.org/0009-0004-8021-7601
Bharati Vidyapeeths College of Engineering, India

ABSTRACT

This study analyzes web services' functionalities and performance, focusing on mobile platforms and Web3 applications. Web services enable communication between applications but pose challenges due to different types (RESTful, SOAP), data formats, and protocols. Choosing the right service requires considering scalability, security, and interoperability. The study provides a comparative analysis of web service types, evaluating their strengths, limitations, and suitability for

DOI: 10.4018/979-8-3693-2973-3.ch001

mobile platforms. It highlights challenges in selecting services and offers insights to guide decision-making. By assessing performance metrics, this research aids in optimizing web-based applications, enhancing decision-making for Web3 and mobile development.

I. INTRODUCTION

Testing plays an important role in the software development life cycle (SDLC) to ensure the correctness and functionality of the software. It shows the importance of Web services and the problems associated with testing Web applications, especially in terms of loading and response time. This study aims to compare the response times of three performance measurement tools: Apache JMeter, Grinder and Http Rider, (Dhiman & Sharma, 2009). The purpose of this qualitative literature review is to gain a deeper understanding of MWS detection systems and identify new research, (Wagh & Thool, 2008). The challenge of building quality Web services in Quality of Service (QoS) reflects the complexity of many NPhard services. Most existing systems simplify this process by using scaling aggregated into global scores, (Cremene et al., 2019). The importance of decentralized cloud computing innovation in providing various services to customers through network connections. Setiawan and Setiyadi (2015) emphasizes the on-demand nature of cloud computing, offering infrastructure-based services through models like IaaS, PaaS, and SaaS. Mohammed and Zeebaree (2004) focuses on the importance of cloud computing by comparing and discussing three main services: Software as a Service, Platform as a Service, and Infrastructure as a Service. Previous research on these services is reviewed in terms of methods, products, and key results, providing an overview of their origins and key features in the cloud business. This article provides an overview of the historical development and recent achievements of serverless research. Sharma and Sharma (2010) surveys serverless applications across eight domains, discussing objectives and viability in each. The challenges faced by serverless applications are categorized into nine topics, with proposed solutions outlined. The study concludes by highlighting areas requiring additional attention from the research community and identifying open problems within the serverless computing landscape.

The contemporary emergence of blockchain technologies and cloud computing. As both technologies extend beyond their initial applications, there is a growing fusion, particularly seen in Blockchain-as-a-Service (BaaS).

Onik and Miraz (2016) presents results, compares various BaaS platforms, and discusses applications, challenges, and risks. The study concludes by recommending that BaaS platforms be designed to maximize their benefits.

The use of web services continues to increase and there is an urgent need for format selection, especially during the development of SOAP (Simple Object Communication) and REST (Representational State Exchange Process) standards. Managing REST and SOAP websites is considered a major challenge in their growing environment. This study aims to compare SOAP and REST based web services using benchmarking software, (Mohammed & Zeebaree, 2021).

This will be done through a qualitative literature review focusing on evaluating and comparing these Web services against various software evaluation methods.

This research addresses the challenge of selecting and optimizing web services for mobile platforms and Web3 applications by examining the complexities of scalability, security, interoperability, and performance. It evaluates various web services, including SOAP, REST, GraphQL, and WebSocket, to determine their suitability for different use cases, focusing on response times, security features, and incident response capabilities. The study also compares hosting environments, such as shared and virtual private servers, highlighting their impact on application performance. By providing performance benchmarks, insights into fault tolerance, and guidelines for matching web service characteristics (e.g., SOAP for reliability, REST for simplicity) to project requirements, the research equips developers with the knowledge to make informed decisions. This contributes to building robust, scalable, and secure applications optimized for mobile and Web3 environments.

II. LITERATURE SURVEY

Shikha Dhiman and Pratibha Sharma's research paper titled "Performance Evaluation: A Comparative Study and Analysis of Web Services and Evaluation" (2009) takes a look at important works on software testing in a general context and with a specific focus performance evaluation. History of the Software Development Life Cycle (SDLC) shows the importance of ensuring software reliability and performance through effective testing, especially in the world of web applications that are full of problems such as unpredictable loading and response times. The author introduces and analyzes three well known performance measurement tools (e.g., Apache JMeter, Grinder, and HttpRider), providing an overview of their functions, requirements, and what is required for testing Web services through comparative research. In conclusion, the authors evaluate the findings by emphasizing that HttpRider is a risky choice due to its highly functional features.

The challenges of quality of service (QoS) were examined in the research paper titled "Comparison of multi objective evolution algorithms for QoS-compliant Web services" by Marcel Cremene, Mihai Suciuc, D. Dumitrescu and Denis Pallezc (2015). Be aware of web services and solve the NP problem through design Value or Pareto based optimization problem. To close this gap, this work performs a comparison of state-of-the-art multi-objective evolutionary algorithms (EMOA) and evaluates their performance in solving QoS and gaining insight into the composition of the program. This analysis uses datasets from real web services to measure performance and uses statistical analysis to identify algorithms with the best performance and lowest time, thus helping to understand and improve the web service process.

The article titled "Comparison Study of SOAP and REST Web Services Provisioning Techniques for Mobile Host" was written by Dr. Kishor Wagh and Ravindra Thool (2012) discuss the importance of Web services in the mobile wireless world and present a comparison of SOAP and REST frameworks for providing Web services on mobile devices. It highlights the need for lightweight, persistent web services on resource efficient mobile devices in wireless environments. The guide provides an overview of the role of mobile devices in Web usage, delivery, and integration, illustrating the transition to mobile devices as a web service provider. The results showed that foreign shared hosting servers performed best overall and used the lowest time of 8,267 milliseconds; This makes them the first choice for customers looking to host their applications online.

A study by E. B. Setiawan and A. Setiyadi (2023) compared the performance of different web hosting servers, including Indonesian shared hosting servers, foreign shared hosting servers, Indonesian virtual private servers, and foreign virtual private server devices. They use tools like Dotcom-Tools, Pingdom.com, Web Page Testing, and site speed to measure parameters like load time, Domain Name System (DNS), connection, and Secure Sockets Layer (SSL). The results showed that foreign shared hosting servers performed best with the lowest time of 8,267 ms; This makes them the first choice for users who can monitor their applications online. A literature review by Tihomirovs and Grabis (2016) provides a good comparison between SOAP and REST-based web services, focusing on software testing. Their work begins with a general introduction to the importance of Web services and should choose the appropriate type (for example, SOAP or REST). The author examines in depth the theoretical foundations of Web services and He explains that SOAP is an older protocol with comprehensive standards and XML-based data transfer structures, compared to REST, which leverages the simplicity and familiarity of HTTP and JSON. They used systematic literature searches, obtained data from reputable digital libraries, and used strict and exclusionary criteria to select relevant studies.

The article "Performance Evaluation and Comparison of Blockchain as a Service (BaaS) Platforms" (2021) by Md Mehedi Hassan Onik and Mahdi H. Miraz provides an in-depth discussion on the current position of the BaaS patch. Evaluating technology development, implementation, market potential, and decisions comparing various BaaS platforms. Start by discussing the evolution of blockchain technology beyond cryptocurrencies and changes in cloud computing to meet the needs of Industry 4.0. The authors highlight the fusion of blockchain and cloud computing in BaaS as a means to provide value to enterprises, offering a survey of BaaS platforms provided by major companies like Microsoft, Amazon, IBM, Oracle, SAP, and Hewlett Packard (HP).

The article titled "A Comparison of Cloud Computing Services: IaaS, PaaS and SaaS: An Analysis" published by Chnar Mustafa Mohammed and Subhi R. M. Zeebaree in the International Journal of Science and Business (2021). It provides an examination and comparison of Infrastructure as a Service (IaaS), Platform as a Service (PaaS) and Software as a Service (SaaS) in cloud computing. It provides an in depth look at the main concepts, features and service models of cloud computing, highlighting their main features and benefits. The author discusses all service models in detail, elucidating their roles, functionalities, and examples of prominent providers. Through a thorough literature review, the paper examines previous studies and findings related to each service model, encompassing aspects such as performance analysis, optimization algorithms, security measures, and integration techniques.

There are many studies and studies related to Chnar Mustafa Mohammed and Subhi R. M. Zeebaree's talk in the article "Cloud Service Comparison: IaaS, PaaS and SaaS: Analysis" (2021). Number of clouds; They include services as a service (IaaS), platform as a service (PaaS), and software as a service (SaaS). Additionally, the review explores research on the development of security measures, capacity building, and usability of PaaS systems, with examples such as access control strategies that control traffic for smart elastic scaling algorithms for volume groups. Moreover, the literature review encompasses investigations into the quality of service (QoS) aspects of SaaS, including studies on service selection frameworks, multi-tenant management systems, and continuous delivery (CD) flows for personalized solutions. The review highlights the diverse range of topics addressed in the existing literature, showcasing the depth and breadth of research conducted to advance the understanding and utilization of cloud computing services.

Tihomirovs and Grabis' literature review. A comprehensive review of SOAP and REST protocols focusing on software testing, titled "Comparison of SOAP and REST based web services using software testing". Through comprehensive analysis of SCOPUS, Web of Science and IEEE Xplore, this article compares SOAP and REST in terms of various parameters such as cost, performance, line of code, speed, memory, force experience, complexity, efficiency, reliability and control. It provides comprehensive understanding by recommending REST for analysis, activation, and performance-oriented tasks and SOAP for security- and reliability-oriented applications, thus improving your understanding of the Web's software design options.

This paper conducts qualitative data analysis (SLR) to understand trends in web services (MWS) discovery in a dynamic mobile environment (DME). It examines 76 articles on competition in the DME and offers solutions. It introduces the detection of anomalies by classifying methods according to parameters such as network service descriptions and matching methods. This article highlights the importance of SLR and lays the foundation for future research on MWS detection in DME.

III. COMPARISON TABLE

Table 1. Comparison table of research papers

Methods used	Results	Applications / limitations	References
This model consist Apache JMeter, Grinder, HttpRider tools for automate testing processes, making it easier to simulate test environments and improve software quality.	Among open-source web tools such as Apache Jmeter, Grinder, HttpRider, it is clear that each tool has its own architecture and internal processes; these form the basis of response time benchmarking tools such as Apache. Jmeter (1309.5), Grinder (1079.725), HttpRider (1015.84)	The paper compares three testing tools for performance and stress testing but is limited in scope, focusing on a single web service and a narrow selection of tools.	Wagh & Thool (2008)
The research paper uses four network performance testing tools (dotcom-tools, pingdom.com, web page test, website speed)	Foreign shared hosting servers are the best hosting servers because such servers outperform other servers in many parameters and have the least (best) value, Total 8,267 milliseconds.	The limitations of the research paper include conducting tests on hosting servers from only two geographical locations and using a single website for evaluation, potentially limiting the generalizability of the findings.	Tihomiroves (2016)
The paper analyzes the role of permanent establishments in a digital economy and their attribution of assets, risks, and liabilities. It also examines how the Authorized OECD Approach, including the "Unified Approach" under Pillar One, interacts with digitalization.	The research emphasizes the need to update tax systems for digital business models, proposing changes to profit allocation and nexus rules under Pillar One, with implementation details still pending.	The limitations of the research include a focus on digital business models and proposed changes to tax rules, with implementation details yet to be determined.	Wagh and Thool (2008)

continued on following page

Table 1. Continued

Methods used	Results	Applications / limitations	References
The researchers uses web service crawel engine which passes the tools as VerifyWS, ValidateWS, MetaCollector	The study underscores the need for specialized web service crawlers and centralized repositories with the growing number of web services. It highlights the increasing reliance on search engines for service discovery and advocates for advanced techniques to enhance relevancy.	In this paper simplistic search, voluntary registration, lack of data validity guarantees, and absence of QoS measurements and lifecycle management. WSDL documents, while abundant, often lack descriptive information, hindering proper indexing by search engines.	
The paper employs a comparative analysis methodology to evaluate and compare various BaaS platforms based on performance metrics such as scalability, transaction throughput, latency, security features, cost-effectiveness, ease of deployment, and integration capabilities.	Comparative performance metrics such as scalability, transaction throughput, latency, and security features of different BaaS platforms. Evaluation of the advantages and disadvantages of each platform in terms of ease of deployment, integration capabilities, cost-effectiveness, and regulatory compliance. Identification of potential challenges, risks, and opportunities associated with adopting BaaS solutions. Recommendations for standardization or best practices to promote interoperability and usability across different BaaS offerings.	Decision Making Healthcare: HR Management Supply Chain Management Securities Settlement	Garba & Mohmad (2021)

continued on following page

Table 1. Continued

Methods used	Results	Applications / limitations	References
Comparative Analysis of Results Decisions on Evaluation Tools Decisions on Evaluation Evaluations Decisions on Websites Decisions on Hosting Server	The article compares the performance of four types of web hosting servers: Indonesian shared hosting (SH I), foreign shared hosting (SH LN), Indonesian virtual private server (VPS I) and foreign virtual private server (VPS LN). Use various tools to measure parameters such as loading time, DNS resolution, connection speed, and SSL handshake duration. The results showed that foreign shared hosting had the best overall performance with a total time of 8,267 milliseconds, which was better than other hosting options tested.	Dotcom-Tools: Dotcom-Tools is a free web browser and activity tracker. Pingdom. com: Pingdom.com is a website performance and monitoring tool. Site speed web test	Setiawan & Setiyadi (2015)
Systematic Literature Review Selection of Source Repositories Identification of Search Keywords Classification Scheme and Data Extraction Method	Contemporary Web Service Discovery Techniques Effectiveness of Proposed Solutions: Techniques for Addressing Challenges: Contributions and Drawbacks: Assessment Procedures	Mobile Application Development Enhanced Mobile Service Provisioning: Improved User Experience Optimized Resource Utilization Context-Aware Mobile Applications	Garba & Mohmad (2021)

IV. RESULTS

Table 2. Security levels of different types of web services

	Web Service Type	Security (Arbitrary Units)
1	API (RESTful, GraphQL)	3
2	Software as a Service (SaaS)	2
3	Platform as a Service (PaaS)	1.5
4	Infrastructure as a Service (IaaS)	1
5	Serverless Computing	2.5
6	Microservices	2.75

Figure 1. On security

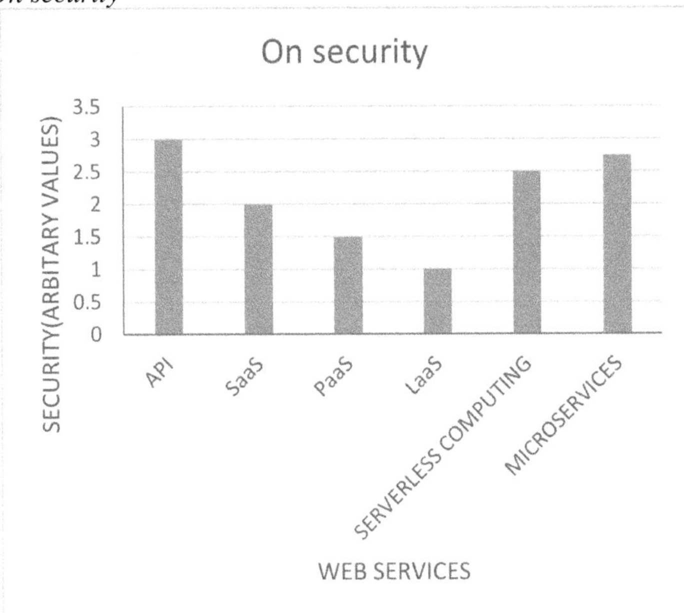

Table 3. Performance of different types of web service

	Web Service Type	**Performance (ms)**
1	SOAP	50
2	REST	60
3	JSON-RPC	55
4	XML-RPC	65
5	GraphQL	70
6	Microservices	45
7	WebSocket	75

Figure 2. Types of web services

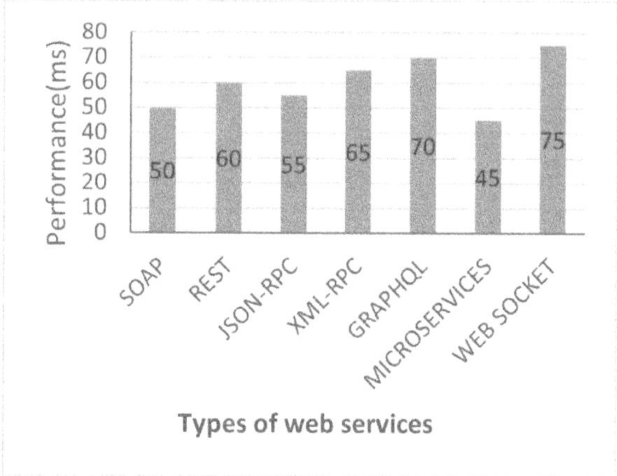

Table 4. Incident response capability of different types of web services

	Web Service Type	Incident Response Capability (Points)
1	Content Delivery Network (CDN)	7
2	E-commerce Platform	5
3	Social Media Platform	4
4	Cloud Storage Service	6
5	SaaS Application	3
6	API Gateway	2

Figure 3. Incident response capability

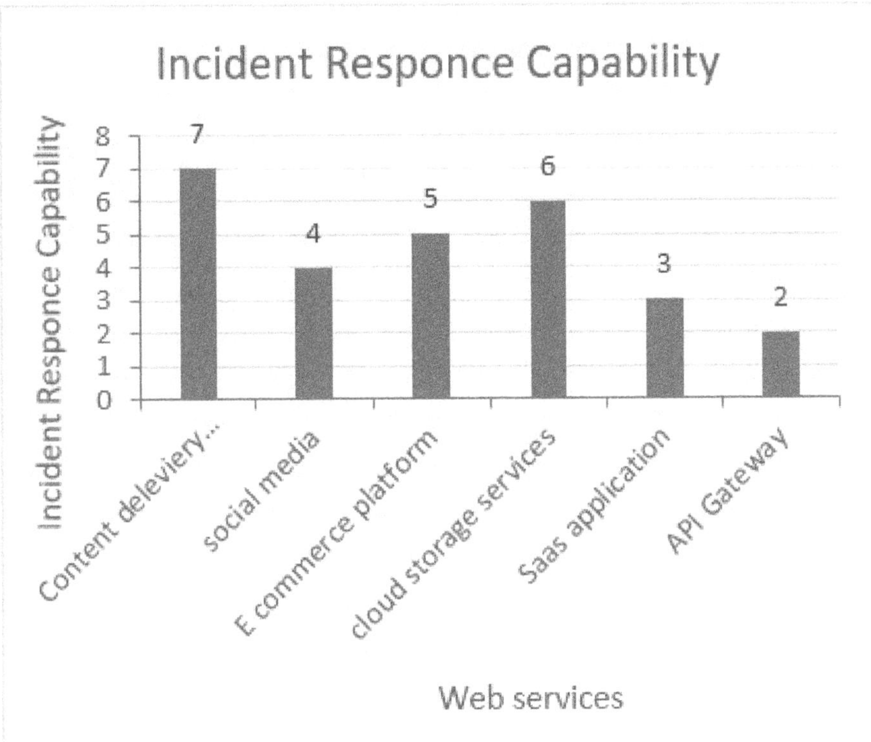

Table 5. Freidman graphs

	GraphQL-Mongo	REST-Mongo	SOAP-Mongo	GraphQL-MySQL	REST-MySQL	SOAP-MySQL
GraphQL-Mongo	1	509	365	56	698	568
REST-Mongo	510	0	144	153	189	59
SOAP-Mongo	366	144	0	309	333	203
GraphQL-MySQL	57	153	309	0	642	512
REST-MySQL	699	189	333	642	0	130
SOAP-MySQL	599	59	203	512	130	0

Figure 4. Friedman's performance

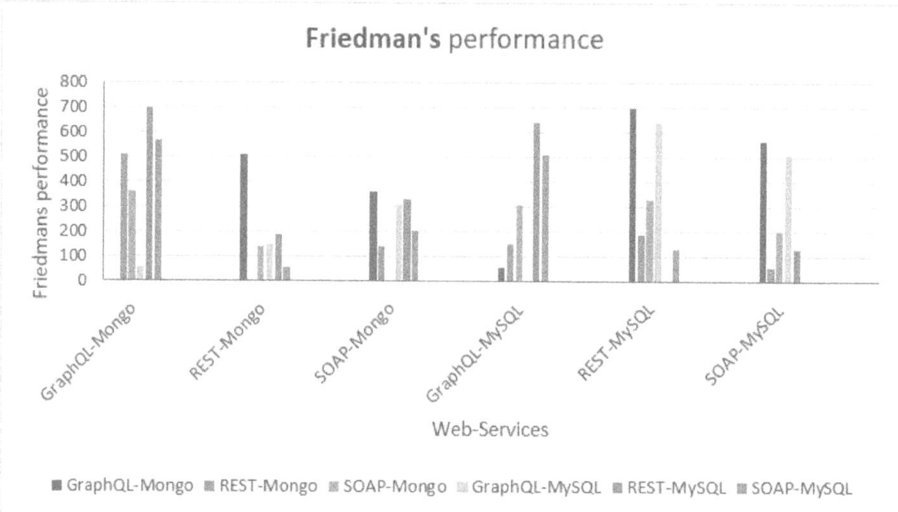

V. DISCUSSION

In the graph of Web Service Types vs. Incident Response Capability. Incident response capabilities can vary greatly depending on factors such as resources, expertise, and specific implementation. CDNs typically have robust incident response protocols due to the critical nature of their services. They often have dedicated security teams and automated incident detection and response systems. E-commerce platforms handle sensitive data and financial transactions, so they have a strong focus on security. However, their authorization mechanisms, but vulnerabilities can exist in their implementation or integration with other systems. SaaS offerings often have robust security practices due to economies of scale, but user configuration and data management practices can impact overall security. PaaS platforms offer varying levels of security depending on the provider and chosen configuration. Security is often shared responsibility between provider and user. IaaS provides the underlying infrastructure, and security is entirely the responsibility of the user. Configuration and patching are crucial for maintaining security. Serverless providers manage vulnerabilities in the underlying infrastructure, but user code and configurations can introduce security risks. Security in microservices architectures depends on securing each individual service and their communication channels. This difficulty increases the attack surface.

In the performance graph of different web services, the performance of SOAP as a web service is 50 milliseconds. SOAP is a protocol that uses XML as the message format and usually operates over HTTP or SMTP. Although SOAP services are a mature and widely used technology, the performance of SOAP services may be slightly slower than other new methods due to the overhead of parsing XML and adding contract work. The processing time of a RESTful website is 60 milliseconds. REST (Representational State) is a framework for creating simple, non-embedded web-based communication over HTTP. RESTful services are known for their lightness and simplicity, resulting in excellent performance in many applications. The performance of the JSONRPC web service is 55 milliseconds. JSONRPC is a remoting protocol that uses JSON to exchange data. Because of the lightweight of JSON and the simplicity of the protocol, JSONRPC generally provides fast processing. The processing time of XMLRPC web services is 65 milliseconds. XMLRPC is a remote protocol that uses XML for data encoding and HTTP as transport. Due to the XML parsing overhead, performance of XMLRPC services may be slightly slower than JSON-based alternative. The performance of the GraphQL based web service is 70 milliseconds. GraphQL is a query and runtime framework used to execute queries against APIs. While GraphQL provides clients with a powerful and flexible data retrieval capability, performance may vary depending on the complexity of the query and the performance of the data retrieval layer. The performance of microservices based web services is 45 milliseconds. Microservices architecture involves breaking applications into small, independent services. Microservices can provide operational speed by optimizing service boundaries and increasing the value of details in a part.

The differences between web services in this study are addressed in terms of several key factors that impact their suitability for different use cases, particularly in mobile platforms and Web3 applications. These differences include:

SOAP-based web services are shown to have the lowest response time (50ms), making them ideal for high-performance applications. RESTful services, though slightly slower (60ms), are still widely used for their simplicity and ease of integration. GraphQL services offer flexibility but have a higher processing time (70ms) due to the complexity of data retrieval. Microservices, on the other hand, provide superior performance (45ms) by breaking applications into smaller, independent services, optimizing operations for distributed systems.

VI. RESEARCH GAP IDENTIFIED

There is a lack of a comprehensive comparison of how different web service types handle and recover from faults, errors, and unexpected events, which influences the robustness of the overall system, especially within mobile platforms and Web3 applications. Hybrid Web Service Architectures: Limited research explores the benefits and challenges of hybrid architectures that combine different web service protocols (e.g., REST, SOAP, GraphQL) within a single application or system on mobile platforms. Context-aware Decision Support Systems: There's a gap in developing context-aware decision support systems that can assist developers and stakeholders in choosing the most suitable web service based on project-specific requirements, including design considerations for mobile and Web3 applications.

The challenges faced in achieving interoperability are often overlooked when integrating traditional web services with newer technologies like serverless computing or blockchain within mobile platforms and Web3 environments. Real-world Performance Metrics and Benchmarks: Many studies focus on theoretical aspects, but there's a need for more research providing real-world performance metrics and benchmarks for different web service types under various conditions, particularly in the context of mobile platform design and Web3 applications.

VII. CONCLUSION

This survey paper conducted a comparative analysis of web services, exploring dimensions such as performance, security, scalability, and interoperability. The findings emphasize the dynamic nature of the field, with each platform exhibiting unique strengths and considerations. Decision-makers should align their choice of web service with project-specific requirements. This survey serves as a valuable guide for practitioners, offering insights into the diverse landscape of web services and paving the way for informed decision-making in the ever-evolving technological landscape.

REFERENCES

Dhiman, S. andSharma, P. (2009). "Performance Testing: Comparative and Statistical Analysis of Web Services and Tests", International Journal of Computer Science and Network Security (IJCSNS), Vol. 9. No. 4, p. 84-90.

Cremene, M., Suciuc, M., Dumitrescu, D., and Pallezc D. (2019). "Comparison of multi-objective evolutionary algorithms for QoS:aware web service composition", published July 14, 2019 in the Springer Nature LNICST Series.

Garba, S. andMohmad, R. (2021). "Web Services for Dynamic Mobile Environments": A Case Study - International Journal of Electronic Services and Mobile Applications Volume 13 - Issue 4 - October-December.

Md, M. H. O., & Miraz, M. H. (2016). Comparative Performance Analysis of Blockchain as a Service (BaaS) Platforms. *Applied Soft Computing*, *39*, 124–139.

Mohammed, CM. and Subhi R. M. (2021). Zeebaree Cloud Comparison: IaaS, PaaS and SaaS: A Review. Journal of Web Semantics Volume 1, Issue 3, April 2004, No. Page 309 - 320 page

Setiawan, E. B., & Setiyadi, A. (2015). A compares the performance of different web hosting servers. *International Journal of Database Theory and Application*, *8*(3), 297–312.

Sharma, D., Sharma, A.K. (2010). "Comparative Analysis of Web Page Ranking Algorithms". International Journal of Computer Science thiab. *Engineering (London)*, *2*(08), 2670–2676.

Tihomiroves, J., & Grab, J. (2016). "Comparison of SOAP and REST-based web services using software benchmarks." ISSN 2255-9086 (Print) December, Vol. 19 Ib., p. 92-97 DOI: 10.1515/itms-2016-0017

Tihomirovs and Grabis. (2004). Comparison of SOAP and REST-based web roles. *Management*, *17*(2), 275–297.

Wagh, K. and Thool, R. (2008). "A Comparative Study of SOAP and REST Web Services Configuration Techniques for Mobile Hosting," Proceedings of the 17th International World Wide Web Conference, p. 287-296.

Chapter 2

Virtual and Augmented Reality for Immersive Learning Experiences: Practical Applications and Challenges

Pankaj Bhambri
https://orcid.org/0000-0003-4437-4103
Guru Nanak Dev Engineering College, India

ABSTRACT

The incorporation of Virtual Reality (VR) and Augmented Reality (AR) in educational environments has fundamentally transformed the manner in which learners interact with educational material, offering immersive encounters that surpass conventional teaching approaches. This chapter examines the pragmatic uses of VR and AR in the development of dynamic and captivating learning environments. We shall illustrate the effectiveness of these technologies in improving understanding and memory of intricate ideas by including case studies from different educational settings. This discussion will focus on the utilization of VR and AR in virtual laboratories, simulations, field trips, and cultural immersion. The emphasis will be on the potential of these tools to facilitate experiential learning and bridge the divide between theoretical understanding and practical implementation. Although VR and AR have the ability to bring about significant changes in education, there are various obstacles that prevent their widespread use.

DOI: 10.4018/979-8-3693-2973-3.ch002

1. INTRODUCTION

Virtual Reality (VR) and Augmented Reality (AR) have transformed educational approaches by providing immersive learning experiences that surpass conventional teaching methods. These technologies facilitate learners' engagement with instructional content in dynamic and fascinating manners, promoting a more profound comprehension and recall of intricate topics (Reinoso & Monzonis, 2023). VR allows users to fully engage with simulated environments such as virtual laboratories and realistic simulations. On the other hand, AR enhances real-world experiences by overlaying digital information onto the user's surroundings, making field trips and cultural immersion more enriching. This chapter investigates the profound influence of VR and AR in educational environments (Vaquero-Gonzalez & Alcover, 2022). It examines how these technologies effectively connect theoretical knowledge with practical implementation. Additionally, it explores the challenges and opportunities that arise from using VR and AR to enhance learning within the framework of Web3 technologies.

1.1 Overview of VR and AR

VR and AR are sophisticated technologies that manipulate or enhance the user's view of reality to create immersive experiences. VR immerses people in completely virtual surroundings using head-mounted displays and sensory feedback methods, enabling interactive encounters in simulated worlds. In contrast, AR superimposes digital content onto the physical environment, thereby increasing the way we see and interact with our surroundings (Liu & Kang, 2022). This is achieved through the use of devices such as smartphones or AR glasses. Both VR and AR have been utilized in a wide range of industries, such as gaming, entertainment, healthcare, and education. In the realm of education, these technologies are revolutionizing the way people learn by facilitating interactive simulations, virtual field excursions, and practical training situations. These technologies have the capacity to profoundly transform education by enhancing the level of engagement, retention, and accessibility for learners across various age groups and backgrounds.

1.2 Importance of Immersive Learning Experiences in Education

Immersive learning experiences are essential in education since they create dynamic environments that improve engagement, comprehension, and retention of educational content. Immersive technologies like VR and AR allow students to actively engage with knowledge, promoting a better understanding through hands-on exploration and experiential learning, as opposed to traditional techniques that frequently rely on passive learning (Heidemann & Elgert, 2023). VR and AR enable the practical implementation of theoretical concepts by replicating real-world scenarios. This helps bridge the divide between classroom education and real-life conditions. Furthermore, these technologies accommodate a wide range of learning styles and preferences, hence enhancing the inclusivity and accessibility of education. Additionally, they equip students with the necessary skills to navigate the intricacies of a swiftly changing digital landscape.

1.3 Significance of VR and AR in Transforming Educational Practices

VR and AR have the potential to greatly impact education by fundamentally changing how students learn and interact with instructional material. VR provides learners with the opportunity to engage in realistic simulations and virtual settings, allowing them to experience and learn in ways that are challenging or impossible to recreate in traditional classrooms (Moura & Borges, 2022). This immersive program allows students to investigate intricate concepts through practical application, thereby deepening their comprehension through interactive encounters. AR enhances teachings by superimposing digital information onto the physical world, incorporating interactive components like 3D models, animations, and real-time data overlays. VR and AR enhance education by creating a more dynamic, personalized, and effective learning experience. They cater to different learning styles and prepare students for future occupations that require digital literacy and problem-solving skills.

1.4 Relationship Between Mobile Platforms, VR/AR, and Web3

Mobile platforms are essential for the advancement and acceptance of VR and AR technologies, particularly in the context of Web3. The emergence of high-performance mobile devices has made immersive experiences more accessible, allowing a wider range of people to interact with VR and AR applications. Web3 seeks to establish a decentralized internet that empowers users with greater authority over their data and interactions. Mobile platforms play a crucial role as the main entry point for accessing these experiences. Mobile devices enable consumers to effortlessly engage with decentralized applications (dApps), virtual worlds, and digital assets like NFTs, by integrating VR and AR capabilities. This interaction takes place within the Web3 ecosystem. This convergence improves user experiences by providing more interactive and personalized information, which in turn promotes the adoption of both Web3 and immersive technologies (Bhambri, 2024a).

The combination of mobile platforms, virtual reality/augmented reality, and Web3 technology promotes the development of creative applications in several industries, such as education, entertainment, and commerce. Mobile devices with VR/AR capabilities facilitate immersive learning experiences, enabling students to engage in virtual classrooms and interactive simulations. These experiences coincide with the decentralized and user-centric principles of Web3. Mobile platforms in the entertainment industry enable users to easily access metaverse environments, where they can engage in social interactions, play games, and participate in virtual events. Importantly, users retain full ownership and control over their digital identities and assets. Mobile-based VR and AR applications in commerce offer improved shopping experiences, including virtual try-ons and augmented product views. These applications are coupled with blockchain technology to guarantee transparency and security. The convergence of these technologies not only enhances user involvement but also lays the foundation for a more interconnected and decentralized digital future.

1.5 Introduce of Web3 and its Relevance to Mobile VR and AR Applications in Education

Web3 embodies the subsequent iteration of the internet, distinguished by decentralization, user ownership, and improved privacy, constructed on blockchain technology. The objective is to establish a digital ecosystem that is more open and focused on the needs of users, allowing individuals to have more authority over their data and interactions. Web3's significance in the realm of mobile VR and AR applications in education is substantial. Due to their widespread presence and ease of use, mobile devices are well-suited for implementing VR and AR instructional applications. The utilization of immersive technologies, facilitated by the decentralized infrastructure of Web3, allows for customized and interactive learning experiences. Students have the opportunity to utilize virtual classrooms, carry out simulated experiments, and participate in collaborative projects within a secure and transparent setting. By integrating Web3, educational content and user data can be managed in a decentralized manner, which improves security, privacy, and trust. This integration also promotes an innovative and engaging learning ecosystem (Javornik & Verhagen, 2022).

2. BACKGROUND

Web3, often known as the decentralized online, signifies a significant departure from the conventional, centralized internet (Web2). The system is constructed using blockchain technology, allowing a network of decentralized nodes to collectively oversee data, guaranteeing transparency, security, and user autonomy. Web3 enables decentralized peer-to-peer connections, eliminating the reliance on middlemen that typically store and govern data in Web2. The decentralized structure of this system empowers users by granting them full control over their data and digital identities, hence improving privacy and minimizing the likelihood of censorship or data breaches. Web3 relies on key technologies such as smart contracts, and decentralized finance (DeFi). These technologies are designed to foster a more inclusive and fair internet.

The incorporation of VR and AR with Web3 on mobile platforms has great potential, especially in improving accessibility and user involvement. Mobile devices, because to their extensive accessibility and powerful functionalities, are perfect tools for delivering immersive experiences to a large range of people (Khoshelham & Elberink, 2022). Through the utilization of Web3 technologies, VR and AR applications on mobile platforms may provide decentralized and user-focused experiences. For instance, educational VR and AR applications can employ blockchain technology to guarantee the reliability and genuineness of learning materials. Blockchain can provide secure and direct sharing of educational resources among peers. This integration not only provides equal access to high-quality, engaging learning experiences but also guarantees that users have full control over their educational data and digital footprints.

The combination of VR, AR, and Web3 on mobile platforms has the potential to bring about a significant transformation in multiple industries through the development of groundbreaking applications and services. Within the field of education, students have the opportunity to engage in interactive and gamified learning experiences that are further improved by the security and transparency provided by blockchain technology. AR applications in healthcare can offer immediate, tailored medical advice while safeguarding patient data confidentiality using decentralized storage options (Wang & Yang, 2023). Within the realm of entertainment, individuals have the opportunity to delve into virtual realms and engage in captivating activities, all the while possessing and overseeing their digital possessions in a secure manner. The decentralized structure of Web3 guarantees that these interactions are not only highly safe but also very resistant to manipulation and censorship, thus establishing a more robust and user-focused digital economy.

3. PRACTICAL USES OF VR AND AR IN EDUCATION

VR and AR have a wide range of practical uses in education, improving learning by providing immersive experiences in many areas. VR enables the creation of simulated laboratories, providing students with the opportunity to perform experiments in a secure and regulated setting. This promotes experiential learning in subjects such as chemistry, biology, and physics (Rana & Bhambri, 2024). AR enhances field excursions by superimposing historical material, geographical data, or interactive components onto real-world locations, offering contextual learning experiences beyond the confines of the classroom. Furthermore, both technologies facilitate the use of simulations that replicate intricate scenarios, such as medical operations or engineering simulations, enabling students to engage in realistic settings to enhance their skills and problem-solving abilities. These applications enhance learning by making it more captivating and interactive. Additionally, they help students connect theoretical knowledge with practical application, equipping them to tackle real-world difficulties in their academic and professional pursuits.

3.1 Virtual Laboratories: Enhancing Scientific and Technical Education

Virtual laboratories utilizing VR and AR technology are a notable progression in scientific and technical education, providing engaging and interactive learning experiences. These virtual environments replicate authentic laboratory settings, enabling students to do experiments, manipulate apparatus, and witness phenomena in a secure and regulated manner (Ijaz & Ahmad, 2022). VR facilitates intricate three-dimensional depictions of scientific topics, empowering students to engage with intricate simulations that could be expensive, dangerous, or otherwise unattainable in conventional laboratories. AR improves these experiences by superimposing supplementary information, such as live data, annotations, or instructions, directly onto the student's field of vision. Virtual laboratories offer a safe and practical space for experimentation and exploration. They improve learning outcomes by reinforcing theoretical knowledge with hands-on application. Additionally, they promote curiosity, critical thinking, and problem-solving skills, which are crucial for scientific inquiry and technical expertise.

3.2 Simulations: Practical Applications in Complex Scenarios

Simulations are a crucial use of VR and AR in education, especially in situations when real-life experiences are neither feasible nor dangerous. Virtual reality simulations fully immerse learners in authentic surroundings that accurately reproduce intricate scenarios, such as medical operations, engineering simulations, or historical reconstructions (Bhambri, 2024b). These simulations enable students to engage and make choices in a secure yet immersive environment, promoting experiential learning and the enhancement of skills. AR improves simulations by adding contextual information to physical objects, which is helpful in training settings that require real-time data display or instructional prompts. Both VR and AR simulations enhance comprehension through hands-on experience and equip learners with essential problem-solving skills and situational awareness required for their future careers.

3.3 Field Trips and Cultural Immersion: Experiential Learning Beyond the Classroom

VR and AR enhance field excursions and cultural immersion, providing educational institutions with advanced capabilities to extend learning beyond traditional classrooms. VR allows students to engage in virtual field trips to historical landmarks, natural environments, or scientific laboratories, offering immersive experiences that vividly recreate distant settings (Gadelha & Silva, 2023). AR promotes cultural immersion by superimposing digital information onto actual items or settings, enabling students to engage with historical artifacts or cultural monuments in significant and meaningful ways. These technologies enhance the learning process by increasing engagement and facilitating better retention. Additionally, they remove limitations related to distance and practicality, guaranteeing that all students may access valuable learning opportunities that promote a greater understanding of different cultures and situations.

3.4 Case Studies from Different Educational Settings

Below are case studies from various educational contexts that demonstrate practical applications of VR and AR in improving learning experiences:

- **Virtual Laboratories and Simulations:** Stanford University and other medical education institutes have included VR simulations into surgical training. By utilizing a realistic virtual environment, students have the opportunity to enhance their surgical abilities and confidence through practicing procedures (Lai, 2024). This allows them to gain valuable experience before doing actual operations on real patients. Universities like MIT employ VR technology to replicate intricate technical procedures and experiments in their engineering curricula. Students have the opportunity to engage with three-dimensional models of machines and structures, which allows them to acquire practical knowledge about design concepts and problem-solving.

- **Field Trips and Cultural Immersion:** The British Museum in London provides AR tours that enhance the experience of viewing ancient artifacts by bringing them to life. By utilizing AR equipment, students have the opportunity to investigate historical items inside their authentic settings, so enriching their comprehension of cultural history and archaeology (Nardo & Carminati, 2023). VR is utilized in geography and environmental science classrooms at schools around the globe to facilitate virtual field trips. Students have the opportunity to explore ecosystems, geological formations, and remote areas, allowing them to witness real-world events without having to physically leave the classroom.
- **Interactive Learning Modules:** Language learning systems such as Rosetta Stone have incorporated AR technology to enhance vocabulary acquisition and provide an immersive language learning experience. AR applications superimpose foreign words onto real-world objects, resulting in interactive language learning experiences that improve memory retention and comprehension (Sayedi & Santhanam, 2022). VR simulations are used in physics and chemistry lectures to help students visualize abstract topics, such as atomic structures and molecular interactions. Students have the ability to control particles and witness scientific phenomena in ways that improve their conceptual knowledge and experimentation.
- **Accessibility and Inclusive Education:** AR apps are employed in special education programs to offer customized learning experiences for children with disabilities. AR adaptations of educational resources can accommodate the specific requirements and preferred learning methods of individuals, promoting inclusiveness and active participation in a wide range of educational settings. Museums and cultural organizations utilize VR technology to develop displays that are easily accessible to visitors who have physical disability or are limited by geographical constraints (Bhambri & Khang, 2024). VR experiences allow users to investigate museum collections and historical sites using improved accessibility features, guaranteeing fair access to educational resources.
- **Decentraland University:** Decentraland, a virtual world that operates without a central authority and is constructed on the Ethereum blockchain, has broadened its educational services by introducing Decentraland University. By utilizing VR technology on mobile devices, students have the ability to engage in virtual lectures, partake in interactive simulations, and communicate with others in virtual study groups. In this Web3 ecosystem, educational credentials and learning achievements are securely stored on the blockchain,

ensuring that academic records can be verified and are resistant to tampering. Implementing decentralized identification systems guarantees that students maintain authority over their educational data, hence enhancing privacy and security.

- **EdChain's Augmented Reality Learning Modules:** EdChain is a decentralized education platform that utilizes blockchain technology to offer secure and easily accessible learning resources. The company has created mobile AR instructional courses that can be accessed using smartphones and tablets. These modules provide engaging and realistic teaching material, including virtual laboratory experiments and three-dimensional historical reconstructions. EdChain's blockchain infrastructure guarantees the verification and authenticity of material, while smart contracts enable secure and transparent transactions for accessing high-quality educational resources.
- **Integration of Lifeliqe's Augmented Reality and Blockchain:** Lifeliqe, a mobile company that offers educational information using AR, has incorporated blockchain technology to improve its services. Students get the opportunity to examine intricate 3D models in areas such as biology and chemistry. They can utilize their mobile devices to actively engage with the content in real-time (Bose et al., 2021). Lifeliqe utilizes blockchain technology to guarantee that educational content is both engaging and protected, while also being able to be verified. This connection enables educators to monitor student progress and accomplishments in a clear and open manner, while students may safely communicate their learning outcomes to prospective educational institutions or companies.

3.5 Highlighted Mobile Apps and Platforms

- **Mobile App- Unimersiv:** Unimersiv is a mobile app that offers VR educational experiences in various subjects, from history to science. In the context of Web3, Unimersiv could leverage blockchain to provide secure access to VR learning modules and to ensure the authenticity of the educational content. This would also allow students to earn and store digital credentials on the blockchain, which can be shared and verified by educational institutions or employers (Chen et al., 2022).
- **Platform-Blockchainedu:** Blockchainedu is a decentralized platform that integrates VR and AR to create immersive learning environments. Using mobile devices, students can access a wide range of educational experiences, from virtual field trips to interactive science lessons. The platform utilizes blockchain to manage digital identities, secure educational data, and facilitate transparent transactions for premium content. This ensures that learners have

full control over their educational journey within a decentralized and secure environment.

4. EFFECTIVENESS OF VR AND AR IN ENHANCING LEARNING

VR and AR have become influential technologies in education, providing distinctive capacities to enhance learning experiences beyond conventional techniques. These technologies provide learners with immersive and dynamic settings, allowing them to interact with instructional information in new and exceptional ways (Javornik & Verhagen, 2022). VR enables immersive learning by replicating real-world situations and intricate settings, providing students with a secure and regulated virtual environment to practice and apply skills and concepts. AR superimposes digital information onto the real world, enhancing educational materials with interactive aspects that improve understanding and memory. This chapter investigates the efficacy of VR and AR in boosting learning outcomes. It examines how these technologies enhance comprehension, motivation, and engagement in different educational fields (Kuzhaloli et al., 2020). VR and AR have the ability to greatly enhance students' preparation for the difficulties of a digitally-driven future by offering practical, hands-on experiences that bridge the gap between theoretical knowledge and real-world application.

4.1 Understanding and Memory Improvement

Understanding and memory improvement are critical outcomes of using VR and AR in educational settings. These immersive technologies offer unique advantages by providing sensory-rich experiences that engage multiple senses simultaneously, thereby enhancing cognitive processes involved in learning. VR allows learners to interact with 3D environments and simulations, fostering active exploration and spatial understanding. AR overlays contextual information onto real-world objects, reinforcing connections between theoretical knowledge and practical applications (Milgram & Kishino, 2023). Studies indicate that the spatial presence and interactive nature of VR and AR experiences can lead to deeper engagement and better retention of information compared to traditional learning methods. This chapter explores how VR and AR contribute to enhancing understanding and memory retention in educational contexts, supported by evidence from research and case studies across various disciplines.

5. CHALLENGES IN IMPLEMENTING VR AND AR IN EDUCATION

Implementing VR and AR in education presents several challenges that must be addressed for these technologies to realize their full potential. One significant challenge is the cost associated with acquiring and maintaining VR/AR hardware and software, which can be prohibitive for many educational institutions (Rana et al., 2024). Moreover, there are technological constraints such as the need for robust network infrastructure to support high-quality VR/AR experiences and compatibility issues with existing educational technology ecosystems. Another critical hurdle is the requirement for educators to undergo specialized training to effectively integrate VR/AR into curriculum and instructional practices. Additionally, ensuring accessibility and inclusivity remains a challenge, as not all students may have equal access to VR/AR devices or environments. Addressing these challenges requires strategic planning, investment in infrastructure, ongoing professional development for educators, and proactive measures to promote equitable access to immersive learning experiences in education.

5.1 Challenges of Developing and Deploying Mobile VR and AR Applications Within the Web3 Framework

Distinct Difficulties in Creating and Implementing Mobile Virtual Reality and Augmented Reality Applications inside the Web3 Framework are listed below (Uzunboylu & Ozdamli, 2023):

- **The Presence of Technical Complexity and the Need for Integration:** The technical complexity involved is a major issue in developing mobile VR and AR applications within the Web3 platform. Combining blockchain technology with VR and AR necessitates a profound understanding of both domains, along with proficiency in mobile app development. Developers must maintain a smooth and uninterrupted connection between decentralized systems and immersive technologies, which might be technically challenging. This encompasses the integration of intelligent agreements, the management of decentralized storage, and the guarantee of real-time synchronization between the blockchain and the virtual reality/augmented reality settings. The requirement for expertise across multiple disciplines might increase the difficulty and resource requirements of the development process.
- **Problems With Performance and Latency:** Performance is a crucial aspect for VR and AR apps, as they necessitate high frame rates and minimal delay to deliver a seamless and captivating user experience. Nevertheless, the de-

centralized structure of Web3 can give rise to latency problems caused by the duration needed for blockchain transactions and data synchronization across a distributed network. Optimizing the performance of VR and AR apps on mobile devices, which often have constrained processing capabilities and low battery endurance, introduces an additional level of intricacy. Developers must enhance the efficiency of their apps while upholding the integrity and security offered by the blockchain.

- **User Experience and Accessibility:** Ensuring a user-friendly experience is crucial for the widespread acceptance and usage of any technology, especially in the case of VR and AR applications. Ensuring a smooth and user-friendly experience can be difficult inside the Web3 architecture, as it is inherently tricky to deal with blockchain. Unfamiliar users may find it challenging to handle digital wallets, comprehend decentralized identities, and navigate blockchain transactions. In order to ensure that VR and AR applications can be used by a large number of people, it is important to consider the different capabilities of hardware and the variable levels of internet connectivity. This is particularly important in countries where mobile infrastructure is not as advanced.
- **Issues Regarding Security and Privacy:** Web3 seeks to bolster security and privacy by means of decentralization, but VR and AR apps present distinct issues in this domain. To guarantee the security of immersive environments and safeguard user data in these apps, it is essential to provide strong encryption and reliable authentication systems. VR and AR applications frequently gather substantial user data, including movement patterns and biometric information, necessitating secure management and storage on the blockchain. Developers face a tremendous difficulty in finding a balance between creating immersive, data-rich experiences and meeting strict security and privacy regulations.
- **Regulatory and Compliance Matters:** Engaging with the Web3 framework requires adeptly maneuvering through an intricate and constantly changing regulatory environment. The development and implementation of mobile VR and AR applications might be affected by varied legislation in various jurisdictions, as they pertain to blockchain technology and decentralized applications. Ensuring adherence to data protection laws, financial rules, and other legal obligations is crucial, but it can be challenging due to the decentralized and frequently global nature of Web3 technology. Developers must remain updated on regulatory modifications and be ready to adjust their applications accordingly.
- **Scalability and Interoperability:** Web3 applications must address scalability as a crucial issue, as blockchain networks can experience congestion

and reduced speed due to increased usage. Ensuring scalability is crucial for maintaining a high-quality user experience in mobile VR and AR applications that require real-time interactions and handle enormous amounts of data. Furthermore, it is imperative to provide compatibility among diverse blockchain platforms and VR/AR technologies in order to facilitate smooth and uninterrupted user experiences, as well as to promote extensive acceptance and usage. Creating applications that can function on many blockchains and virtual reality/augmented reality devices introduces additional intricacy and necessitates the use of standardized protocols and frameworks.

5.2 Financial Constraints: Cost of hardware, software, and maintenance

The implementation of VR and AR in education is hindered by many financial limitations associated with the expenses of hardware, software, and maintenance. Below is a comprehensive breakdown of the challenges:

- **Hardware Expenses:** Acquiring top-notch virtual reality headsets that can provide captivating experiences can incur significant costs. Schools and educational institutions may be required to purchase many units in order to accommodate a class or group of students, hence further escalating expenses. Similarly, AR gadgets like smart glasses or tablets with AR capabilities can be expensive, particularly when there is a desire to disseminate them extensively among students.
- **Software Expenses:** Creating or acquiring educational content and applications tailored for VR and AR platforms might incur significant costs. VR/AR educational software must possess interactivity, captivation, and alignment with learning goals, necessitating customization and development endeavors (Trujillo-Torres & Trujillo-Pisanty, 2024). The overall cost of using certain software may be increased by continuous licensing fees or subscriptions, depending on the specific product being used.
- **Maintenance and Support:** VR and AR technologies necessitate technical proficiency for installation, upkeep, and problem-solving. Educational institutions may need to invest money for the purpose of providing training to their IT staff or recruiting specialized experts to oversee the management of these technologies. Maintaining the newest improvements and security fixes for VR/AR hardware and software can result in increased expenses over time. Maintenance and Substitution: Regular usage or mechanical malfunctions may require repairs or replacements of VR/AR gear, which can put a financial burden on budgets.

- **Infrastructure Requirements:** To ensure optimal performance of VR/AR experiences, a strong and reliable internet connection and network infrastructure are essential. Implementing these technologies may require substantial upfront investments to upgrade the infrastructure. Virtual reality/augmented reality setups may necessitate specific areas with sufficient power infrastructure and ample space for mobility, perhaps resulting in supplementary expenses for remodeling or building.
- **Cost-Benefit Analysis:** Educational institutions must evaluate the advantages of adopting virtual reality/augmented reality technology in comparison to the associated expenses (Papagiannis, 2022). It is essential to provide evidence of the educational worth and the learning results linked to these technologies in order to justify the financial expenditure.

To tackle these financial limitations, it is necessary to engage in meticulous strategizing, allocate funds wisely, and take into account the long-term viability of the strategy. Grants, collaborations with technology companies, and agreements to share resources amongst educational institutions might provide opportunities to reduce expenses and enable wider availability of virtual reality and augmented reality in education.

5.3 Technological Challenges: Hardware requirements and compatibility issues

The integration of VR and AR in education has great promise, but it also poses various technological obstacles. Principal among these are the necessary specifications for the hardware and the potential problems related to compatibility.

- Minimum System Specifications: Enhanced Computing Capability
- **VR:** VR experiences necessitate robust CPUs and top-of-the-line graphics cards to efficiently generate realistic environments. Consequently, schools and educational institutions must allocate resources towards acquiring costly, top-of-the-line computers.
- **AR:** Although AR can be supported by widely used devices such as smartphones and tablets, the development of intricate AR experiences still requires substantial computational capabilities.
- Specialized Devices:
- **VR Headsets:** VR experiences require the use of certain devices such as the Oculus Rift, HTC Vive, and PlayStation VR. These headsets are expensive and may necessitate supplementary devices such as motion controllers and sensors (Bhambri & Gupta, 2018).

- **Augmented Reality Glasses:** Augmented reality glasses such as Microsoft HoloLens or Magic Leap are costly and not as widely used as mobile devices, which poses difficulties for their general adoption.
- Maintenance and Upgrades:
- **Lifecycle Management:** Both VR and AR hardware necessitate periodic maintenance and updates. Staying abreast with technological progress in order to maintain compatibility with new software can put a financial burden on school budgets.
- **Degradation:** Regular usage by students might result in accelerated degradation, requiring frequent maintenance or replacements.
- Physical Space:
- **VR:** Adequate physical space is necessary for the safe and immersive setup of VR settings. This can pose a difficulty in schools that have a restricted amount of space.
- Incompatibility Problems: Software Compatibility
- **Multiple Systems:** VR and AR applications are designed to work on many systems, including Windows, macOS, Android, and iOS (Raghav & Joshi, 2023). Ensuring that the hardware of an educational institution can adequately support the required software on various platforms poses a substantial difficulty.
- **Regular Changes:** VR and AR applications undergo regular changes that may not always be compatible with current technology, requiring additional investment in new equipment or updates.
- Standards and Interoperability:
- **Absence of Standardization:** The VR and AR market suffers from a lack of consistent standards, resulting in compatibility problems among various devices and apps. The fragmentation can impede the smooth integration of VR and AR technologies in educational environments.
- **Content Portability:** Ensuring that instructional content developed for one VR or AR platform can be easily transferred to another platform might present challenges, which can restrict the capacity to reuse and share resources across various systems.
- Connectivity Requirements:
- **High-Speed Internet:** VR and AR apps typically need fast internet connections to efficiently download huge files and stream content without interruptions. Several educational institutions, particularly those located in rural or underfunded areas, may face difficulties in providing the required bandwidth.
- **Network Infrastructure:** The process of improving the network infrastructure to accommodate the simultaneous operation of many virtual reality (VR)

and augmented reality (AR) devices can be expensive and technically challenging (Kaur & Bhambri, 2019).

- Compatibility with Existing Infrastructure:
- **Legacy Systems:** The integration of VR and AR gear with educational technology infrastructure may pose difficulties, especially if the current systems are obsolete.
- **Peripheral Integration:** The process of ensuring seamless compatibility between VR and AR devices and other classroom technologies, including as projectors, smartboards, and audio systems, necessitates meticulous preparation and sometimes additional financial resources.

5.4 Training and Support for Educators: Skills and Knowledge Needed for Effective Integration

The integration of VR and AR in education presents various difficulties, namely with the training and assistance provided to educators. The requisite competencies and expertise for successful integration encompass:

- Skills and Knowledge Required for Successful Integration
- **Technical Proficiency: - Device Operation:** Acquiring knowledge on the configuration, utilization, and resolution of issues related to VR and AR equipment.
- **Software Navigation:** Mastery in utilizing specialized VR/AR software and applications that are pertinent to the program.
- **Content Creation:** Proficiency in generating or modifying VR/AR content to cater to educational requirements (Bose et al., 2021).
- **Pedagogical Strategies: - Instructional Design:** Creating instructional plans that seamlessly incorporate VR/AR technology, in accordance with educational goals and desired results.
- **Classroom Management:** The act of effectively overseeing a classroom where students are utilizing virtual reality/augmented reality technology, with the goal of promoting active participation and reducing any factors that may hinder focus and attention.
- **Evaluation Methods:** Creating strategies to evaluate the learning results attained through virtual reality/augmented reality encounters.
- **Adaptability and Continuous Learning: - Remaining Current:** Ensuring knowledge of the most recent advancements in VR/AR technologies, trends, and educational applications.

- **Professional Development:** Participating in continuous training and professional development activities specifically focused on virtual reality and augmented reality.
- Obstacles in the Implementation of Virtual Reality and Augmented Reality in Education
- **Resource Limitations: - Technology Accessibility:** Ensuring equitable access to essential VR/AR hardware and software for all students.
- **Infrastructure:** Possessing the necessary infrastructure, including fast internet and ample room for virtual reality/augmented reality activities.
- **Training and Professional Development: - Introductory Training:** Offering extensive introductory training for educators to develop fundamental skills in VR/AR technologies.
- **Continual Support:** Guaranteeing uninterrupted assistance and improved educational possibilities for teachers to remain up-to-date and enhance their abilities (Tobar-Munoz & Ruiz-Blanco, 2023).
- **Time Constraints:** Ensuring educators have enough time to participate in training while also handling their usual teaching responsibilities.
- **Curriculum Integration: - Conformity with Standards:** Ensuring that VR/AR content adheres to educational standards and curriculum prerequisites.
- **Content Availability:** Ensuring the presence of a diverse selection of high-quality educational virtual reality/augmented reality content that is pertinent to various subjects and grade levels (Lee & Wong, 2022).
- **Lesson Planning:** Supporting educators in seamlessly incorporating VR/AR into their lesson planning without causing them to feel overwhelmed.
- **Technical Challenges: - Device Maintenance:** Consistent upkeep and upgrades of VR/AR equipment and software.
- **Technical Support:** Offering prompt technical assistance to resolve any issues that may emerge during VR/AR lessons.
- **Cost: - Initial Investment:** The acquisition of VR/AR equipment and software entails a significant expense.
- **Sustainability:** Continual expenses associated with updates, maintenance, and content subscriptions.

6. ADDRESSING CHALLENGES: SOLUTIONS AND STRATEGIES

In order to overcome the difficulties associated with deploying VR and AR for immersive learning, it is crucial to adopt a comprehensive and diverse strategy. Schools must to allocate resources towards comprehensive professional development programs, which offer both initial and continuous training for educators to cultivate and sustain technical expertise and pedagogical skills. Partnering with technology businesses can provide access to cutting-edge gadgets and software, while also offering technical assistance and maintenance services. Establishing collaborations with content developers can facilitate the integration of VR/AR resources into curricular standards and learning objectives (Singh et al., 2021). Moreover, obtaining financial support via grants, collaborations, and government programs can help alleviate the substantial upfront and recurring expenses. Establishing a collaborative network of educators to exchange experiences and resources would promote ongoing enhancement and flexibility, guaranteeing the successful integration of VR and AR technologies in educational settings to boost student engagement and learning results.

6.1 Cost-Effective Approaches to Implementation

To implement VR and AR for immersive learning experiences cost-effectively, schools and institutions can leverage a combination of strategies. Utilizing affordable VR headsets like Google Cardboard or smartphone-based AR applications can significantly reduce hardware costs. Collaborating with universities or tech companies for shared resources or pilot programs can provide access to cutting-edge technologies at a lower cost (Uzunboylu & Ozdamli, 2023). Additionally, educators can tap into free or low-cost VR/AR content and open-source platforms, while investing in professional development through online courses and workshops to enhance their skills without incurring high expenses. By gradually integrating VR/AR, starting with smaller, scalable projects, and seeking grants or funding opportunities, institutions can make immersive learning technologies more accessible and sustainable.

6.2 Technological Advancements and Future Prospects

The progress in VR and AR technologies is transforming the way we study by providing exceptional chances for interactive and captivating educational experiences (Bakshi et al., 2021). VR has made substantial progress in the advancement of more cost-effective and easily obtainable headsets, such the Oculus Quest. This allows students to engage with lifelike simulations and virtual settings, which in turn improves their comprehension and memory recall. AR, utilizing technologies such as Microsoft HoloLens, superimposes digital information onto the physical environment, offering interactive educational tools and real-time viewing of data. Promising future developments encompass the incorporation of AI to tailor learning experiences, the implementation of 5G networks to enable smooth streaming and instantaneous interactions, and the broadening of VR/AR content repositories to encompass a wide range of educational disciplines (Faiella & Ricciardi, 2023).

These developments have the potential to revolutionize traditional education by promoting hands-on learning, improving cooperation, and catering to different learning preferences, ultimately equipping students for a technology-driven society.

6.3 Training Programs for Educators and Support Staff

Training programs for educators and support staff in VR/AR are essential for properly incorporating new technologies into education. These programs often cover a wide-ranging curriculum that includes an overview of VR/AR technology, practical experience with VR/AR hardware and software, and instructional design techniques specifically designed for immersive learning (Kline & Best, 2023). Teachers receive training to develop and execute virtual reality/augmented reality lesson plans that are in line with educational standards, while support personnel are educated to resolve technical problems and upkeep virtual reality/augmented reality equipment. Moreover, these training programs frequently integrate optimal strategies for promoting student involvement and evaluating educational achievements in virtual settings (Sutherland & Goodchild, 2022). These programs seek to improve the educational experience by providing educators and support workers with the essential skills and knowledge, resulting in more engaged and meaningful learning.

6.4 Strategies for Ensuring Accessibility and Inclusion

To guarantee accessibility and inclusiveness in VR and AR for immersive learning experiences, it is necessary to cater to the diverse physical, sensory, and cognitive requirements of all users. Here are multiple tactics to accomplish this:

- **Universal Access Design - Versatile Content Presentation:** Offer many methods of presenting information, including text, audio, and visual prompts. This guarantees that individuals with diverse requirements can have the content in a manner that is most suitable for their needs.
- **Customizable Environments:** Enable users to personalize the VR/AR environment by modifying settings like brightness, contrast, and audio levels, to suit their particular preferences and requirements.
- **Physical Accessibility - Sitting and Standing Modes:** Create experiences that can be experienced in both sitting and standing positions, enabling people with limited mobility.
- **Alternative Controllers:** Suggest alternative input modalities for individuals who are unable to utilize conventional virtual reality controllers, such as voice recognition, eye-tracking technology, or personalized peripheral devices.

- **Sensory Accessibility - Subtitles and Captions:** Ensure that all audio content includes subtitles and captions for non-verbal noises to accommodate users who are deaf or have hearing impairments.
- **Haptic Feedback:** Utilize haptic feedback to offer sensory input to individuals with visual impairments, aiding them in navigating and engaging with the virtual environment (Wang & Yang, 2023).
- **Cognitive Accessibility - Streamlined Interfaces:** Develop user interfaces that are straightforward and effortless to navigate, featuring explicit directions and minimum cognitive burden.
- **Guided Experiences:** Offer structured experiences or lessons to assist users in comprehending how to engage with the VR/AR world, hence minimizing the difficulty in learning.
- **Content Inclusivity - Diverse Avatars:** Provide a comprehensive selection of configurable avatars that accurately depict various ethnicities, genders, and body shapes. This ensures that users can identify with and feel represented in the virtual environment.
- **Inclusive Situations:** Generate situations and storylines that encompass a wide range of perspectives, ensuring that the information is relatable to a diverse audience.
- **Technical Considerations - Cross-Platform Compatibility:** It is important to ensure that VR/AR experiences can work on different hardware and software platforms, so that there are no obstacles preventing people from accessing them.
- **Optimal Solutions for Limited Bandwidth:** Enhance user experiences for individuals with limited internet bandwidth or less advanced gear, hence expanding the accessibility to a wider audience.
- **User Testing and Feedback - Inclusive Testing Groups:** Engage users with a range of disabilities and diverse backgrounds during the testing phase to obtain feedback on accessibility and inclusiveness.
- **Iterative Enhancement:** Consistently enhance and refine VR/AR experiences by incorporating user feedback and advancements in accessibility technologies.
- **Training and Education - Developer Accessibility Training:** Offer comprehensive training sessions to VR/AR developers, focusing on the implementation of accessibility best practices and emphasizing the significance of inclusive design (Li & Hsiao, 2023).
- **User Guides and Support:** Provide extensive user guides and support materials to assist all users, including individuals with impairments, in maximizing their VR/AR experiences.

- **Policy and Standards Compliance - Comply with Accessibility Standards:** To maintain compliance and adhere to best practices, it is important to follow recognized accessibility criteria, such as the Web Content Accessibility criteria (WCAG) and those developed by the World Wide Web Consortium (W3C).
- **Ethical Considerations:** Integrate ethical issues into the design process to uphold user privacy, autonomy, and diversity.

7. FUTURE TRENDS AND INNOVATIONS IN IMMERSIVE LEARNING

The future of immersive learning is poised to transform education through enhanced interactivity, personalization, and engagement. The progress in artificial intelligence and machine learning will facilitate the development of adaptive learning environments that customize educational content according to the specific needs and learning preferences of each learner (Bhambri et al., 2019). The integration of haptic technology with advancements in virtual reality/augmented reality hardware will provide more authentic and tangible experiences, hence augmenting the acquisition of practical skills in domains such as medicine and engineering. The incorporation of the metaverse would establish extensive virtual campuses where students from all parts of the globe can engage in real-time collaboration, thereby eliminating geographical limitations. Furthermore, the utilization of blockchain technology for credentialing and secure data management would guarantee transparency and confidence in digital school records. These advancements hold the potential to enhance accessibility, inclusivity, and effectiveness in learning, hence revolutionizing the educational environment.

7.1 Integration of VR and AR with Web3 Technologies

The incorporation of VR and AR with Web3 technology signifies a noteworthy forthcoming trend and advancement in immersive learning. The integration of Web3, which is defined by the principles of decentralization, blockchain technology, and increased user autonomy over data, has the potential to significantly revolutionize educational experiences. VR and AR can utilize blockchain technology to guarantee safe and transparent credentialing, allowing learners to possess verifiable and unchangeable records of their accomplishments (Khoshelham & Elberink, 2022). Decentralized platforms have the ability to enable peer-to-peer learning environments and content development, which promotes a more collaborative and democratized education system. In addition, the utilization of non-fungible tokens (NFTs) might facilitate the creation of distinct and interactive educational resources that students can possess and exchange, thereby augmenting their level of involvement and motivation. The integration of these technologies holds the potential to establish a learning environment that is tailored to individual needs, highly protected, and fosters active engagement, in line with the principles of the next-generation internet.

7.2 Potential of Blockchain for Secure and Scalable Educational Platforms

Blockchain technology holds significant potential for secure and scalable educational platforms, especially as immersive learning continues to evolve. By leveraging blockchain, educational institutions can enhance the security and transparency of academic records, ensuring that credentials and achievements are tamper-proof and easily verifiable (Lin & Hsu, 2023). This decentralized approach can streamline the management of student data, reducing the risk of fraud and enhancing trust among stakeholders. Additionally, blockchain can facilitate the creation of decentralized learning environments where educators and learners interact directly, bypassing traditional intermediaries (Anand & Bhambri, 2018). This can lead to more personalized and flexible learning experiences, supporting innovations such as smart contracts for automated credentialing and micro-credentialing. As immersive learning technologies like VR and AR become more prevalent, integrating blockchain can ensure these platforms are not only secure but also capable of scaling efficiently to meet the demands of a global, digital-first education landscape.

7.3 Advances in Interactive Simulations and Pedagogical Innovations

The future of immersive learning is being shaped by advancements in interactive simulations and pedagogical innovations. These advancements utilize technologies such as VR, AR, and Mixed Reality (MR) to enhance educational experiences. Below are few significant forthcoming developments and advancements in this particular domain:

- **Tailored Learning Experiences - Intelligent Learning Algorithms:** Artificial intelligence-powered systems assess how learners behave and adjust the information in real-time to match their unique learning methods and speed.
- **Tailorable Scenarios:** Virtual and augmented reality environments enable learners to delve into scenarios that align with their individual interests or

professional trajectories, fostering heightened engagement and pertinence (Siemons & Markopoulos, 2023).

- **Collaborative and Social Learning - Virtual Classrooms:** Virtual reality environments enable learners and instructors to collaborate in real-time, regardless of their physical location.
- **Collaborative Experiences:** AR allows several people to work together to solve problems by interacting with virtual items in a shared physical environment.
- **Experiential Learning via Simulations - Realistic Scenarios:** Virtual reality simulations recreate genuine situations (such as medical surgeries or engineering projects) to provide practical learning experiences without any real-life repercussions.
- **Real-Time Feedback:** Simulations provide learners with instant feedback, allowing them to comprehend the outcomes of their choices and enhance their abilities.
- **Improved Accessibility and Inclusivity - Adaptive Interfaces:** Virtual reality and augmented reality systems accommodate a wide range of learning requirements, including the ability to adapt text sizes, provide audio descriptions, and offer alternate input methods (Dede, 2022).
- **Inclusive Design Principles:** Technologies are intentionally created to prioritize accessibility, guaranteeing that all individuals, regardless of their physical or cognitive limitations, may fully engage and contribute.
- **Data-Driven Insights and Analytics - Learning Analytics:** VR and AR systems gather data on how learners engage and perform, offering valuable information for customized interventions and enhancements to the curriculum.
- **Predictive Analytics:** Artificial intelligence systems utilize past data and performance metrics to forecast student progress and provide customized learning routes.
- **Immersive Storytelling and Narrative-Driven Learning - Emotional Engagement:** Virtual reality and augmented reality settings foster emotional connections by employing captivating narratives and immersive storytelling approaches.
- **Interactive Narratives:** Learners engage as active players in evolving narratives, making choices that impact the result and enhancing their comprehension of intricate subjects.
- **Integration with Emerging Technologies - IoT and Wearable Devices:** VR and AR can be combined with IoT devices and wearables to generate interactive learning experiences. For example, virtual scientific laboratories can be created using linked sensors (Chen et al., 2022).

- **Artificial Intelligence:** AI-driven virtual tutors and assistants offer immediate assistance and guidance tailored to the specific needs of each learner.
- **Gamification and Interactive Elements - Game-Based Learning:** Virtual reality and augmented reality gamification strategies inspire learners through the use of challenges, prizes, and engaging gameplay experiences.
- **Interactive Items:** AR superimposes digital information onto tangible items, so converting static educational resources into dynamic and interactive learning aids.
- **Cross-disciplinary Applications - Industry Training:** VR and AR simulations provide secure and economical training environments for sectors such as healthcare, manufacturing, and aviation.
- **Cross-Cultural Education:** Utilizing virtual field trips and cultural exchanges, students from diverse places can develop a heightened sense of global awareness and comprehension.
- **Ethical and Social Implications - Digital Citizenship:** Educating individuals on the proper utilization of immersive technology and promoting ethical deliberations within virtual worlds.
- **Data Security and Safety:** Guaranteeing the protection of personal information and creating secure virtual and augmented reality experiences, particularly for younger students and others who are more susceptible to harm.

8. CONCLUSION

The exploration of VR/AR for immersive learning reveals transformative potential across educational landscapes. Key findings underscore the pivotal role of VR/AR in fostering experiential learning, personalized engagement, and inclusive education. Advances in interactive simulations and pedagogical innovations are reshaping learning paradigms, offering adaptive learning environments tailored to individual needs (Parsons & Cobb, 2023). Moreover, VR/AR's capacity to simulate real-world scenarios enhances practical skill development and deepens conceptual understanding, transcending traditional classroom constraints. These technologies not only amplify educational content but also nurture collaborative learning and cross-disciplinary exploration, preparing learners for dynamic future challenges.

Looking ahead, the integration of immersive learning into Web3 contexts holds significant promise. As decentralized technologies and virtual economies evolve, VR/AR will facilitate novel educational experiences rooted in blockchain-based platforms (Bhambri et al., 2023). Smart contracts could enable credentialing and certification within virtual environments, ensuring transparency and authenticity in learning achievements. Furthermore, the interoperability of digital assets in Web3 could foster cross-institutional collaboration and global knowledge sharing. Embracing these innovations may empower educators to cultivate digital literacy and ethical awareness in learners navigating a digitally interconnected world.

Educators and institutions are urged to embrace a proactive approach in integrating VR/AR into educational frameworks. First, fostering digital fluency among educators is crucial, enabling effective integration and utilization of immersive technologies in curriculum design. Second, prioritizing accessibility and inclusivity ensures equitable access to immersive learning experiences for diverse learner populations (Peters & Edler, 2024). Third, continuous research and development efforts should focus on refining VR/AR applications to meet evolving educational needs and technological advancements. Lastly, collaboration with industry partners can facilitate the creation of immersive simulations that align with workforce demands, preparing learners for future career pathways in a digitally driven economy.

In conclusion, the future of immersive learning in VR/AR is poised to redefine educational standards, offering dynamic, interactive, and personalized learning environments. Educators and institutions must navigate this transformative landscape with foresight and innovation, leveraging VR/AR's potential to cultivate engaged learners and shape tomorrow's educational ecosystems in Web3 contexts.

REFERENCES

Anand, A., & Bhambri, P. (2018). *Rotation, Scale and Translation Invariant Character Recognition System using Neural Network. I.K.Gujral Punjab Technical University*. Jalandhar.

Bakshi, P., Bhambri, P., & Thapar, V. (2021). A review paper on wireless sensor network techniques in Internet of Things (IoT). Wesleyan Journal of Research, 14(7), 147-160. Retrieved from https://www.wesleyanjournal.in/

Bhambri, P. (2024a). NFTs: Transforming Digital Ownership in the Web 3 Era. In Darwish, D. (Ed.), *Decentralizing the Online Experience With Web3 Technologies* (pp. 151–167). IGI Global., DOI: 10.4018/979-8-3693-1532-3.ch007

Bhambri, P. (2024b). Wallets and Transactions. In Darwish, D. (Ed.), *Decentralizing the Online Experience With Web3 Technologies* (pp. 90–106). IGI Global., DOI: 10.4018/979-8-3693-1532-3.ch004

Bhambri, P., & Gupta, O. P. (2018). Implementing Machine Learning Algorithms for Distance based Phylogenetic Trees. I.K.Gujral Punjab Technical University, Jalandhar (Ph.D. thesis).

Bhambri, P., & Khang, A. (2024). Basics of greener living. In Khang, A., Abdullayev, H. V., Litvinova, E., Musrat, G. E., & Avramovic, Z. Ž. (Eds.), *Revolutionizing automated waste treatment systems: IoT and bioelectronics* (pp. 396–412). IGI Global., DOI: 10.4018/979-8-3693-6016-3.ch024

Bhambri, P., Singh, S., Jain, S., & Dhanoa, S. I. (2023). Plants recognition using leaf image pattern analysis with focus on advanced smart computing technologies. In AIP Conference Proceedings 2916, 020003 (2023). https://doi.org/DOI: 10.1063/5.0179534

Bhambri, P., Sinha, V. K., & Jaiswal, M. (2019). Change in iris dimensions as a potential human consciousness level indicator. *International Journal of Innovative Technology and Exploring Engineering*, *8*(9S), 517–525. DOI: 10.35940/ijitee.I1082.0789S19

Bose, M. M., Yadav, D., Bhambri, P., & Shankar, R. (2021). Electronic customer relationship management: Benefits and pre-implementation considerations. *Journal of Maharaja Sayajirao University of Baroda*, *55*(01(VI)), 1343–1350.

Chen, J., Liu, L., & Zhu, L. (2022). An intelligent training system based on virtual reality technology. *Computers in Human Behavior*, *130*, 107086. DOI: 10.1016/j.chb.2022.107086

Dede, C. (2022). The future of immersive technologies in education. In Khine, M. S. (Ed.), *Immersive Learning and Virtual Reality in Education* (pp. 1–17). Springer., DOI: 10.1007/978-981-16-9164-6_1

Faiella, F., & Ricciardi, M. (2023). Virtual reality in education: A tool for learning in the experience age. Journal of e-Learning and Knowledge Society, 19(1), 167-178. https://doi.org/DOI: 10.20368/1971-8829/1866

Gadelha, M. R., & Silva, A. P. D. (2023). Design and evaluation of an augmented reality-based educational game for teaching mathematics to children. *Computers & Education, 178*, 104343. DOI: 10.1016/j.compedu.2022.104343

Heidemann, W., & Elgert, L. (2023). Virtual and augmented reality in education: Recent developments and future trends. *Educational Technology Research and Development, 71*(1), 1–14. DOI: 10.1007/s11423-022-10040-w PMID: 37016716

Ijaz, K., & Ahmad, S. (2022). Augmented reality: An innovative approach in education and learning. *Journal of Educational Computing Research, 60*(5), 1081–1106. DOI: 10.1177/07356331211058791

Javornik, A., & Verhagen, H. (Eds.). (2022). *Augmented Reality and Virtual Reality in Education: Innovative Instructional Approaches* (1st ed.). Routledge., DOI: 10.4324/9781003189983

Kaur, J., & Bhambri, P. (2019). Design of Paddy Crop Prediction Technique based on K-Mean, Naïve Bayes, KNN and SVM Classifiers. I.K. Gujral Punjab Technical University, Jalandhar (M.Tech. thesis).

Khoshelham, K., & Elberink, S. O. (2022). Augmented reality in education: A review. *Journal of Computer Assisted Learning, 38*(1), 3–13. DOI: 10.1111/jcal.12663

Kline, B., & Best, S. (2023). Virtual reality in higher education: A comparative case study. *Interactive Learning Environments, 31*(1), 80–95. DOI: 10.1080/10494820.2021.1977123

Kuzhaloli, S., Devaneyan, P., Sitaraman, N., Periyathanbi, P., Gurusamy, M., & Bhambri, P. (2020). Invention titled "IoT based Smart Kitchen Application for Gas Leakage Monitoring" (Application No. 202041049866A). Published on 27th November 2020 (Issue No. 48/2020, Page No. 59674). Retrieved from http://ipindia .nic.in/writereaddata/Portal/IPOJournal/1_4929_1/Part-1.pdf

Lai, K. W. (2024). Augmented reality in education: A meta-analysis. *Educational Technology Research and Development, 72*(2), 331–349. DOI: 10.1007/s11423-023-10051-1

Lee, E. A. L., & Wong, K. W. (2022). Enhancing student engagement through augmented reality in education. *Interactive Learning Environments, 30*(8), 1121–1134. DOI: 10.1080/10494820.2021.1923496

Li, L., & Hsiao, K. F. (2023). Exploring the affordances of virtual reality in education: A systematic review. *British Journal of Educational Technology, 54*(2), 308–327. DOI: 10.1111/bjet.13183

Lin, H. Y., & Hsu, Y. C. (2023). The effects of virtual reality and augmented reality on learning outcomes in K-12 education: A meta-analysis. *Computers & Education, 181*, 104450. DOI: 10.1016/j.compedu.2022.104450

Liu, Z., & Kang, J. (2022). Virtual reality in education: A comprehensive review. *Education and Information Technologies, 27*(5), 5189–5211. DOI: 10.1007/s10639-022-11063-4 PMID: 35013667

Milgram, P., & Kishino, F. (2023). Taxonomy of mixed reality visual displays. *IEICE Transactions on Information and Systems, E77-D*(12), 1321–1329. DOI: 10.1587/transinf.77.d.1321

Moura, A. M. C., & Borges, M. R. S. (2022). Virtual reality in the education of health professionals: A systematic review. *Revista Brasileira de Enfermagem, 75*(1), e20200401. DOI: 10.1590/0034-7167-2020-0401

Nardo, D., & Carminati, L. (2023). Using virtual reality to enhance soft skills: A systematic review. *Interactive Learning Environments, 31*(2), 228–244. DOI: 10.1080/10494820.2021.1978540

Papagiannis, H. (2022). *Augmented Human: How Technology Is Shaping the New Reality*. O'Reilly Media.

Parsons, S., & Cobb, S. (2023). Augmented reality and education: A review of the literature. *Journal of Interactive Learning Research, 34*(3), 293–316.

Peters, M., & Edler, J. (2024). The potential of augmented reality in education: A systematic review. *Educational Research Review, 43*, 100518. DOI: 10.1016/j.edurev.2021.100518

Raghav, S., & Joshi, S. (2023). Virtual reality in education: A systematic review of empirical studies. *Education and Information Technologies, 28*(2), 1597–1626. DOI: 10.1007/s10639-022-11097-8

Rana, R., & Bhambri, P. (2024). Digital Twin for Sustainable Industrial Development. In Rani, S., Bhambri, P., Kumar, S., Pareek, P. K., & Elngar, A. A. (Eds.), *AI-Driven Digital Twin and Industry 4.0: A Conceptual Framework with Applications* (1st ed., pp. 241–253). CRC Press., DOI: 10.1201/9781003395416-15

Rana, R., Bhambri, P., & Chhabra, Y. (2024). Evolution and the Future of Industrial Engineering with the IoT and AI. In *Integration of AI-Based Manufacturing and Industrial Engineering Systems with the Internet of Things* (pp. 19–37). CRC Press.

Reinoso, M. S., & Monzonis, J. L. (2023). Augmented reality and mathematics education: A systematic review. *Journal of Educational Computing Research, 60*(4), 871–896. DOI: 10.1177/07356331211019019

Sayedi, M., & Santhanam, R. (2022). The impact of virtual reality on learning and student engagement: A meta-analysis. *Computers & Education, 174*, 104332. DOI: 10.1016/j.compedu.2021.104332

Siemons, J., & Markopoulos, P. (2023). Augmented reality in primary schools: Designing and evaluating a learning tool. *Journal of Educational Computing Research, 59*(5), 829–856. DOI: 10.1177/0735633119863108

Singh, S., Lal, Y., Bhambri, P., Kumar, A., & Dhanoa, I. S. (2021). Advancements in social data security and encryption: A review. *Natural Volatiles and Essential Oils, 8*(4), 15353–15362.

Sutherland, A., & Goodchild, A. (2022). Virtual reality for learning: A critical review of the use of VR in primary and secondary education. *Education and Information Technologies, 27*(3), 2139–2172. DOI: 10.1007/s10639-022-10859-2

Tobar-Munoz, H., & Ruiz-Blanco, J. A. (2023). Impact of augmented reality on creativity in primary education. *Computers & Education, 182*, 104505. DOI: 10.1016/j.compedu.2022.104505

Trujillo-Torres, J. M., & Trujillo-Pisanty, D. (2024). Virtual reality and augmented reality in education: A review and systematic meta-analysis. *Computers & Education, 174*, 104385. DOI: 10.1016/j.compedu.2022.104385

Uzunboylu, H., & Ozdamli, F. (2023). A meta-analysis on the effects of augmented reality applications in education. *Computers in Human Behavior, 126*, 107018. DOI: 10.1016/j.chb.2021.107018

Vaquero-Gonzalez, L. M., & Alcover, C. M. (2022). Virtual reality and mathematics learning: A systematic review of empirical studies. *Journal of Educational Computing Research, 60*(4), 897–924. DOI: 10.1177/07356331211019020

Wang, T., & Yang, M. (2023). Using augmented reality to support learning: A systematic review and meta-analysis. *Journal of Educational Computing Research, 60*(3), 587–613. DOI: 10.1177/07356331211019023

Chapter 3
Analyzing the Drivers of Adoption in Higher Education E-Learning:
Exploring Factors Affecting Behavioral Intentions and Actual Usage

Karnika Srivastava
Shri Ramswaroop Memorial University, India

Manoj Kumar
https://orcid.org/0000-0002-8325-6612
Shri Ramswaroop Memorial University, India

Rinki Verma
Babu Banarasi Das University, India

Shreyanshu Singh
https://orcid.org/0000-0001-8745-6227
Babu Banarasi Das University, India

Pratibha Maurya
https://orcid.org/0000-0003-1988-1146
Amity University, Lucknow, India

ABSTRACT

Learners face problems while using traditional e-learning systems but AI introduces an innovative stage of advancement in technology that gives revolution in e-learning

DOI: 10.4018/979-8-3693-2973-3.ch003

process. Study investigates factors that influence learner behavioral intention to use AI and actual usage in higher education. The study proposed UTAUT and IS model with additional external variables like perceive risk, work engagement and self-efficacy of learner. Cross-sectional study was used to measure research models based on several theories related to AI that brings cutting-edge technologies that enhance e-learning. Data was analysed using SEM technique. Research model and hypothesis testing was done by AMOS. Study investigate performance expectancy, effort expectancy, facilitating condition, system quality, service quality information quality, perceived risk, work engagement; self-efficacy had significantly influenced behavioral intention and actual use of AI. Finding gives practical references to stakeholders for adoption and acceptance of AI within e-learning process in higher education in NCR.

1. INTRODUCTION

In India, the rapid advancement in technology has enhanced the present education system. There is a use for new tools in order to enhance the teaching and learning process. Platforms like online learning, e-learning, mobile e-learning applications etc. provide widespread availability of online courses and degree programs authorised by universities that makes e-learning easy and feasible (Dieguez et al., 2021). This practise may offer greater opportunities for their e-learning process and evolve large number of students to access higher education (Neumann et al., 2021). Technological changes leads to cover a wide range students enrolling from cross-cultural upbringing, innovation and research that carry global citizenship (Amornkitpinyo et al., 2021).

Academia needs to collaborate between the industries that focus more on entrepreneurship and commercialization. The educational industry tries to meet the expectations day by day, which upgrade the technology by introducing AI (Khan et al., 2022). Artificial Intelligence (AI) enforcement enhances the higher education system (Chedrawi & Howayeck, 2019). In the current situation, the use of AI in edification system is truly convincing, as technology has upgraded the e-learning pattern (Mishra, 2019). The adverse situation during the COVID-19 pandemic, forced us to move to e-learning process from traditional e-learning. The higher education system needs to be upgraded with the development of upgraded intelligent machines and technologies.

AI-based e-learning proves how important innovation in technology has now become an intrinsic part of our life (Rodríguez et. al., 2021). The use of learning applications for AI has increased rapidly from 2020 till date. With the advancement in technology *i.e.* AI, the government should assess and upgrade the higher learning system from time to time (Holmes et al., 2021a; Pardamean et al., 2022).

AI plays a dominant role in enhancing learning in the higher education system (Choi, 2020). User personal data and performance record according to their strengths and weaknesses provided by AI-powered e-learning in the education system is customized according to one's requirements. The AI approach provides better outcomes more effectively by gaining raw knowledge from the users (Aldosari, 2020). Advanced based technology like AI-powered Chatbots, Adaptive E-learning system and Virtual Assistance tools provide a wide range of e-learning experiences that offers students easy solutions in the best possible manner with interactive and meaningful ways from complex theories (Pradana, et al., 2023, Chaudhry, et al., 2023). AI- powered tools improvise the assessment that refers to grading students' assignments and appraisals like detecting similarities by Turnitin, monitoring students' participation in library resources and so on. AI will provide fast and precise feedback with quick instructions to students to concentrate on work (Essien et al., 2020).

AI-powered chatbots provide many facilities, like providing information regarding course materials, student's registration and student's grievances. It can assist students immediately and give personalized assistance for academic and organizational needs. This system will help in the analysis and predict the data of those students who are going to struggle in academics and have a chance of dropping out. AI filtration applications and tools like Turnitin, Coursera, Mendeley and Bit. AI analyse the large set of data, formulates the insights, predict at an early stage which helps academic instructors to convey the academic risk (Wenge, 2021). Improvisation and evolution in technology increase the expectation for more effective and innovative application of AI- powered education. It leads to work engagement of academicians in higher education and e-learning experiences for learners (Li et al., 2021).

In higher learning, teaching staff adopted AI that makes assignment grading easy, maintaining attendance records and provide feedback to students' etc. AI plays a vital role in administrative and academic engagement and activity (Bisen et al., 2021). AI providing opportunity in personalised professional development and teaching skill which improvise teacher's performance and the area of expertise (Minkevics & Kampars, 2021). But, higher education still faces many challenges, such as limited access and diversifying style of e-learning, etc. (Odhiambo, 2016). Traditional teaching tools lack in engaging students in different e-learning activities, actively participation in tough thinking and logical skill that describe the understanding of students' skill, competency, practical knowledge (Rudolph et al., 2023; Kistyanto et al., 2022). Traditional teaching methods, same for all teaching methods fail to prove due to lack of insufficient addressing opportunity, diversified cultural exchanges with international collaboration in higher education. Integration of AI actually fills the gap to find the solution for these challenges.

The AI-algorithm offers filtered coursework by analysing the capacity of individual e-learning patterns and identifies the diverse patterns and preferences. The adoption of AI analytics predicts and analyse at early stage, the academic journey of students who are at risk and facilitating them timely. AI-powered tools deliver the educational content, which provides easy adaptability according to students' pace, knowledge gaps and e-learning styles. AI gives liberty to teachers, staff and faculties from daily work engagement, so that they can focus on other knowledgeable and impactful activities. Many research papers explore the adoption of AI that's makes immense contribution in the higher learning system. The findings of this research paper endeavour to assist policymakers of different institutions in knowing how AI as a new technology will enhance higher education by providing them necessary infrastructure and training to solve the challenges.

AI plays an inevitable role in the future e-learning process of education. So the present study aims to find out the satisfaction level of student's e-learning processes, that are empowered by artificial intelligence in higher education system. The paper also explores how students' e-learning experience may be enhanced by AI, which impacted the creativity, efficiency, productivity and work engagement of teachers in higher education. The above mentioned issues are the main research problems of this study. The IS success model and UTAUT model has the theoretical groundings to fill this gap in the literature regarding the variables, perceived risk, perceived security, work engagement and self-efficacy. To fulfill the above research gap, the present study will fulfill the following objectives:

- To examine IS success model and UTAUT model framework by integrating the perceived risk, work engagement and self-efficacy of learners using AI in e-learning in higher education.
- To study the variables i.e. Performance Expectancy (PE), Facilitating Conditions (FC), Effort Expectancy (EE), System Quality (SYQ), Service Quality (SQ), Perceived Risk (PR), Information Quality (SQ), Self-Efficacy (SE) and Work Engagement (WE) which influenced the learner behavioural intention to use AI in e-learning in higher education and the actual usage of AI in e-learning process in higher education.

In this present study, the first section highlights the role of e-learning powered by AI in higher education system, that creates the opportunity for students, administrative staff, policy makers and teachers etc. The second section discusses on e-learning powered by AI related existing literature. The third section focuses on methodology, which is used to justify the current research. Further, the fourth section presents the result and discussion that came from the previous section and correlates the result with supporting literature. Lastly, study concluded with theoretical and practical implications.

2. THEORETICAL BACKGROUND

Rapid advancement in technology makes e-learning in higher education easier and convenient for teachers, staff and students. This section of the paper discusses the existing literature and a conceptual base for implementing AI in e-learning (Hooda, et. al, 2022) and measures the user' satisfaction. E-learning education is getting drastic transformation by AI and an undeniable impact on work engagement and performance. This will increase students confidence, active participation in coursework and proper engagement in work without alteration (Chen et. al., 2020). E-learning applications with the support of AI facilitate personalised study material recommendations that help students to access the relevant resources to make learning goals easier for learners (Zhou & Feng, 2017).

2.1 E-Learning Technology

The e-learning technology upgraded the level of education. It raises the standard for student learning outcomes. E-learning is described as a medium that is easily available and scatters the unlimited learning skills, knowledge in innovative and interactive ways to the users. Traditional learning basically related with face-to-face communication between students and teachers, integrated with online learning like e-learning models and applications from real-time classroom meetings. Universities and educational institutions can upgrade teaching methodologies and improvise the learning outcome with the help of e-learning (Mishra et. al., 2019)

The e-learning model helps to maintain and retain the academic performance of users in many new orientation courses (Boudreau, & Kromrey, 1994), this would lead to the growth and development of universities and educational institutions towards teaching and learning. The overall usage of e-learning platform will be useful in enhancing and continuous intention to use various activities related to collaboration, communication, and creativity (Nuaimi et. al., 2022). Traditional teaching combined with technology can raise the standard of academic performance and increase the interest of students' motivation.

2.2 Artificial Intelligence

Artificial Intelligence is the most upgraded, advanced and best technology used today. IBM defines Artificial Intelligence (AI) as an advanced technology that leverages computers and machines that mimic the problem and capability of solving, with decision-making like human mind (Mitic, 2019; Jarrahi, 2018). Computer technology changes itself have the capacity to do many things that were left for humans to do so (Signorelli, 2018). Computers combined with AI algorithms can perform any task or work with more accuracy and efficiency (Mitic, 2019, Sutton & Barto, 2018). The algorithms of AI can learn by themselves and guide according to what they have been programmed to do, which is termed as Reinforcement Learning.

Usage of new technology *i.e.* AI has tremendously increased in numerous fields that targets in increasing human intelligence or working as human (Ahmed et. al., 2022; Kolotylo-Kulkarni et. al., 202; Ahmed et. al., 2021). AI assesses the routine process related to mind (Ahmed et. al., 2022). The growth of AI is significantly related with social and economic progress (Bazoukis, 2022).

Table 1. Education and AI

SCENARIOS	TECHNIQUES
Evaluation and Grading	Computer Vision, Image Recognition, Prediction System
Smart School	Virtual Labs, Face Reorganization, Speech Recognition
Thoughtful Instruction and Individualised	Intelligent Teaching System, Data Mining, Learning Analytics
Online and Remote Education Analysis	Virtual Personalized Assistant, Edge Computing, Real Time Analysis
Assessment	Learning Analytics, Adaptive Learning Method

Source: Journal of Higher Education Theory and Practice Vol. 22(13) 2022

2.3 Conceptual Frame Work: Extended UTAUT with IS Success Model

2.3.1 The Unified Theory of Acceptance and Use of Technology (UTAUT) Model

The "Unified Theory of Acceptance and Use of Technology" (UTAUT) Model was originally proposed by Venkatesh et al. (2003), where the UTAUT Model found four initial key variables like (performance expectancy, social influence, effort expectancy and facilitating conditions). The UTAUT model is used in many studies related to technology acceptance and is considered most effectively convenient to measure the behaviour intention to use technology and actual usage of IT (Kalavani et al., 2018; Sumak & Sorgo, 2016).

The UTAUT Model is considered useful as it has been used in the advancement and technological innovation of digitalised learning in higher education (Halili & Sulaiman, 2018). The Educational environment has been immensely changed, which brings "virtual learning" like clouds, web conferences, meetings and whiteboards (Suki & Suki, 2017). The UTAUT model proposes four variables that significantly impact user behaviour, intention to use and actual usage of technology (Williams et al., 2009). "Performance Expectancy refers to an individual belief that their job performance is enhanced by using technology". "The Effort Expectancy concerned to the degree of ease while using technology effortlessly" (Sanusi, 2022). Similarly, "facilitating conditions refers to an individual belief that technical support and resources are available and will be totally supported by the use of technology" (Zabri et al., 2023).

2.3.2 The DeLone and McLean Information System (Information System (IS) Success Model)

Various models are used in the existing studies for technology adoption, like TAM, TAM2, etc. In this study, the IS success model is used in perspective of technology acceptance. Previous studies using IS success model shows positive results. The model is used to find out the causal relationship and its impact between the variables. IS success model has three exogenous quality variables shown in the model given below i.e. SYQ (System Quality), IQ (Information Quality) and SQ (Service Quality) that influenced the users behaviour intention and AI actual usage in e-learning in higher education. "System quality refers to the performance, functions and quality of an information system" (DeLone & McLean 1992). "Information quality refers to the accuracy and format provided by an information system, including some dimensions like relevance, scope, accuracy, timeliness, completeness, and efficiency of information" (Cheng 2012; Almarashdeh et. al., 2010; DeLone & McLean, 1992). "Service quality refers to the quality which users receive from the information system" (Wang & Wang 2009; Kim et. al., 2008; Delone & McLean, 2003). This model successfully finds the impact on users and benefits of accepting the new technology, which can explore two different sides of an individual's i.e. belief and their satisfaction. In this study, the IS success model has been used for measuring the constructs of information system with behaviour intention and actual usage of technology (Cheng, 2012).

Table 2. Existing studies of AI in higher education

Study	Main focus	Findings
AI application and Learning Environment	Faculty members	Faculty motivated to apply AI in their teaching method. Use of AI in Higher education brings numerous opportunities.
Curriculum design and future direction using AI.	Higher Education Institutions	Students learning through AI teaching methods influenced students' by using learning Management systems and curriculum design.
Reforming education using AI.	Higher Education Institutions	Explore the adoption of AI by institutional will transforms, emphasis, enhanced accessibility, and better learning outcomes.
Challenge of integrating AI in Higher Education	Universities and Colleges	Integration AI in learning education brings many challenges including barriers that hinder and ethical concern in higher education.
Role of faculty Transition	Teaching Professionals	Identifies the role of faculty to shift towards facilitation by being AI-driven learning environments.

3. RESEARCH MODEL AND HYPOTHESIS FORMULATION

The "Unified Theory of Acceptance and Use of Technology (UTAUT)" models were developed by Venkatesh et al. (2003), while Information System (IS) Success Model was originated by DeLone & McLean, (2003). These models were used in the proposed research model, which has a theoretical framework that shows the impact of facilitating conditions, performance expectancy, effort expectancy and behaviour intention to use (UTAUT Model) whereas, course system quality, content quality, service quality and actual usage (IS Success Model) of AI in e-learning in higher education. In addition to above eight variables, three more variables are introduced to enhance the study by individual beliefs like perceived risk, perceived satisfaction, work engagement and self-efficacy of e-learning empowered by AI in the higher education system (Sohn & Kwon, 2020a).

Both the IS Success Model and UTAUT Theoretical Models analyse and forecast the factors which influenced the users' perception, acceptance and use of information technology (Dulle & Minishi-Majanja, 2011). Information technology has been accepted and used due to the quality aspects that make working easier (Popenici & Kerr, 2017). The present study identifies the primary factors that influence user behaviour intention. The UTAUT model helps to form an authentic design that can allow the implementation of AI technologies, which is more effectively used by learner. Similarly, IS success model contains additional factors that influence the usage of AI in e-learning in higher education. The construct descriptions are displayed in Table 3.

Table 3. Description of variables

Name used in model	Narration	Narration/Description
PE	Performance Expectancy	"Performance Expectancy refers to the benefits that are usefulness for new system to perform like AI in the education system".
EE	Effort Expectancy	"Effort Expectancy refers to ease of use of a new system effortlessly".
BI	Behaviour intention to use	"Behavioural Intention refers to a specific behaviour or sense of assessing the strength of an individual to perform".
FC	Facilitating conditions	"Facilitating conditions refers to an individual ready accessible the technical infrastructure of AI in the system".
CCQ	Course content quality	"Course content quality refers to how much the learning materials are accurate, complete, relevant, easy and up-to-date with the help of AI".
SYQ	System quality	"System quality refers to the extent to which e-learning Platforms with help of AI are perceived to be technically and functionally sound".
SQ	Service quality	"Service quality refers to the reliability, accuracy, and quality of delivered content".
PS	Perceived satisfaction	"Satisfaction is defined as the fulfilment of subjects' emotional expectations regarding digital learning".
SE	Self- efficacy	"Self-efficacy refers to an individuals' competency and self-belief to use the AI-empowered technology which he/she possesses".
PR	Perceived Risk	"Perceived Risk refers to the belief related to an unfavourable outcome or loss that can incur while using or operating AI- empowered technology".
WE	Work Engagement	"Work engagement here refers to the participation and performance of students' through AI-empowered pedagogy that engaged students in other activities".
AAI	Actual usage of AI in Higher Education	"Artificial intelligence in Higher Education refers to the use of AI in learning by the teachers to improve the content, coursework and enhance the teaching experience".

Factors that Influenced Behaviour Intention to Use E-Learning Empowered AI in Higher Education

In the present study, three factors of UTAUT have been taken into consideration ie performance expectancy, effort expectancy and facilitation condition, which influenced users' behavioural intention to use e-learning with the help of AI and its usage in higher education. Performance expectancy is the degree that believes that users' can achieve job performance. Here, job performance refers to users performance related to study, maintenance of records, interactive work engagement, etc. (Venkatesh et. al., 2003). It is the most important variable used in TAM, which measures the behaviour intention of users (Chang, 2013; Dijk et. al., 2008).

Effort expectancy refers to how easily and effortlessly any technology can be accepted. It shows perceived ease to use any challenge (Venkatesh et al., 2003). EE variable denotes the users' ease in using e-learning empowered by AI in e-learning (Alrawashdeh, 2012). It reflects that EE has significantly influenced BI related to online learning (Venkatesh & Davis, 2000; Venkatesh, 2000).

Facilitating conditions signifies how an individual deals with the organizational and technical infrastructure that is mandatory and available. Venkatesh et al. (2003), investigated the users acceptance of information technology, which explained how the FC affects users' BI to use the technology. Raza et al. (2021) studied that FC directly and positively influenced users' BI to use smartphones for health services (Boontarig et. al., 2012).

Hence, we propose the following hypothesis:

H1. Performance expectancy influenced the users' behavioral intention to use e-learning empowered by AI in higher education.

H2. Effort expectancy influenced the users' behavioral intention to use e-learning empowered by AI in higher education.

H3. Facilitating Conditions influenced the users' behavioral intention to use e-learning empowered by AI in higher education.

According to the IS success model, System Quality denotes the degree to which e-learning empowered by AI technically and functionally used. In other words, it may defined as features that shows technical level of system from where information has been generated (DeLone & McLean, 1992). Lin and Lu (2000) state that the usage of internet emphasize the users' for e-learning, only the problems that make them resist are lack of accessibility, heavy traffic, poor design, etc. System quality and behavioural intention to use have a positive relationship due to service quality of technology which may encourage user to use it (Srivastava et. al., 2024; Tajuddin et. al., 2013; Roca et. al., 2006).

Information quality is an important construct that influences the usage of e-learning platforms through AI. Course content and information quality have an influence on usage of e-learning empowered by AI (Srivastava et. al., 2024). It refers to how easy, understandable, accurate, update and relevant e-learning material is provided through AI. Ramayah et al. (2010), explore that course content quality influenced the e-learning through AI. Course content quality significantly depicted behaviour intention to use e-learning platforms by AI. Hence, the course content quality related to information systems influence the user's beliefs of e-learning (Lin & Lu, 2000).

Service quality influenced the behaviour intention to use e-learning platforms through AI (Li et. al., 2021; Ramayah et. al., 2010). Ramayah et. al., (2010) found that SQ significantly and positively influenced the usage of e-learning system amongst universities in Malaysia. In China, SQ effects positively on the BI to reuse e-learning systems (Srivastava et. al., 2024; Li et. al., 2012). In COVID-19 pandemic, it was found that SQ had significantly influenced the BI to use e-learning (Mailizar et. al., 2021).

Hence, we propose the following hypothesis:

> H4. System quality influenced the users' behavioral intention to use e-learning empowered by AI in higher education.
> H5. Course content quality influenced the users' behavioral intention to use e-learning empowered by AI in higher education.
> H6. Service quality influenced the users' behavioral intention to use e-learning empowered by AI in higher education.

Applications of AI in e-learning and Perceived Risk

Perceived risk is the "potential loss that is incurred from the desired outcome of using an e-learning platform" (Featherman & Pavlou, 2003). This study explores the risk factor that is investigated in online learning and e-learning had to be measured. Users might feel risks like problems related to system errors, privacy, lost passwords, inability to operate systems, software security, and poor system quality (Srivastava & Kumar, 2017; Hanafizadeh et. al., 2014). It was found that PR has negatively influenced BI, and barrier for users.

Hence, the developed hypothesis is:

> H7: Perceived Risk (PR) has influenced the behaviour intention to use AI in higher education.

Applications of AI in e-learning and Perceived Self-Efficacy (SE)

Self-efficacy with reference to an individual's own competency and belief means that he/she has the level of competence that he/she can hold (Bandura, 1986). In other words, an individual can judge the capabilities that he/ she can unify and accomplish a course of action needed to perform (Christensen & Knezek, 2015). It is a kind of self-confidence, judgement and potential that an individual can use to deal in different situations (Hong et. al., 2019; Nardi & Ranieri, 2019; Durak, 2018; Joo et. al., 2000; Bandura, 1986). Self-efficacy is the central point of this study, explains "an individual belief that, ability to successfully use technology to increase learning outcomes" (Durak, 2018; Mikusa, 2015; Venkatesh & Davis, 1996).

Hence, it is proposed that:

> H8: Perceived Self-efficacy (SE) has influenced the behaviour intention to use AI in higher education.

Applications of AI in E-learning and Users' Work Engagement

AI is a tool that is useful for educational institutions in bringing more productivity in e-learning and teachers' engagement with students in numerous ways. It has the capability to transform the present education system (Cui et. al., 2019). Rahimi & Tafazoli, (2022) and Franzoni et. al., (2020) has explored the users' behaviour intention to use AI and work management of faculties in personalized course design, grading, assessment, professional development and student support. Existing studies explored teachers' engagement in AI-integrated CRM system including digital competencies, which will improve work engagement (Chatterjee et al., 2021).

Hence, we proposed the following hypothesis:

> H9: Work engagement influenced the behaviour intention to use AI in higher education

Behaviour Intention to Use and Actual Usage of AI in Higher Education.

The introduction of AI has changed the dimensions of higher education system in the learning process (Khoza & Mpungose, 2022). AI actually improvises the learning experienced by teachers, staff and students. It is a collaborative approach where teachers improve teaching skills with interactive and creative activity involvements, students with their work engagement and a digital platform for various courses available to them in association with AI (Carvalho et. al., 2022; Ge & Hu, 2020).

Behavioral intention measures an individual's strength and behaviour to willingly perform and respond to use the system (Fishbein & Ajzen, 1977). BI is an extent to which users' students plan out to perform specific behaviour (Davis, 1989; Warshaw & Davis, 1985). Behavioral intention to use and actual usage are strongly associated with each other (Bhattacherjee & Hikmet, 2008). Furthermore (Kelly et al., 2023; Chang et al., 2022) the perception of society towards education has transformed by acceptance of AI, identified how it raised the concern as it fulfils all the issues of users regarding cultural, demographic and behavioral profile (Chang et. al., 2022).

This study highlighted the relationship between users, behaviour intention to use AI and its actual usage in higher education.

Therefore, the following hypothesis developed:

H10: Behaviour intention of users' to use AI in e-learning influenced usage of AI in higher education.

4. METHODOLOGY USED

4.1 Sample and Survey Method

A questionnaire designed from the above proposed model has been tested by the quantitative method. The questionnaire consists of two sections and questions taken from existing literature are displayed in Table 4. A survey was done to obtain responses on a questionnaire from the users' of AI in the higher education system i.e. faculties, staff and administrative members of different designations from different parts of NCR (National Capital Region) i.e. Faridabad, Ghaziabad, Gurugram and Noida. The data was collected from 72 academic staff members for the purpose of pilot study. "For conducting a survey, pilot study of 30 respondents' as sample size is required (Hunt et al. 1982)". The responses, comments and feedback helped us in improving the questionnaire.

4.2 Data Collection

The probability proportional stratified sampling technique has been used to cover a wide number of administrative, academic and staff members from different universities and educational institutions working in higher education institutions in the NCR. The structured questionnaire was distributed through social media applications like (WhatsApp, LinkedIn and Gmail on personal basis). Research purpose and confidentiality about the personal details were briefed in the survey. 1776 self-administered questionnaires were attempted to be filled, from which 1565 were completely filled, indicating 88.1% response rate. Only, 7 responses were not considered in the study, because of incomplete answers. 1558 responses are used for further testing and analysing by using SPSS-21. AMOS was used to study the relationship between latent and observed variables for Structural Equation Modeling (SEM). The proposed model was tested through the outcome of SEM by AMOS for model fit from observed data.

4.3 Instrument Measurement Items

The extended UTAUT model with IS success model was developed (Venkatesh et al., 2003; DeLone & McLean, 2003). This proposed research model provides a base structure for knowing the users' acceptance for AI and usage of AI in higher education. Each independent and dependent variable was designed to be represented by a set of questionnaire shown in Table 4. AI-empowered technology in e-learning in higher education has been measured by the researcher through a set of 45 questions. The set of questions covered each construct related to AI tools like e-content customisation, AI-empowered chatbot technology, etc. in higher education and the rise in usage of AI technology in managing procedures of admission, impact of AI on behaviour, self-efficacy to use AI, system quality provided by AI, course content provided by the faculties, work engagement and regular academic practices through AI tools.

4.3.1. Factor Loading

Factor loadings "+ 1 to – 1" represent the principal component correlated with each item, ranging between "higher factor loadings, closer to + 1", represents a stronger correlation with the construct (De Roover et. al., 2022). The result shows that all items "more than 0.5, below 0.5" (Li et. al., 2002) were excluded.

4.3.2. Multicollinearity Indicator

To administer the consistency in the research, a multicollinearity test was used. The "Variance Inflation Factor (VIF) statistics should be below 5", that is according to the inception (Miles, 2014). The result depicts the value in Table 6, which is within the range of correlation between independent and dependent variables.

4.3.3. Test for Reliability and Validity

The test for reliability can be administered by Cronbach's alpha by considering 30 samples. The alpha value should be more than 0.7 (Taber, 2018). The result shows all the values are above the threshold limit, if some statements or items (questions) are irrelevant or less than 0.7 were deleted. The composite reliability of all variables is displayed in Table 4.

Convergent validity and discriminant validity tests were administered by using AMOS 21, where "Average Variance Extracted (AVE) is "> 5" (Olapade et. al., 2023) and discriminant validity was analysed (Roemer et. al., 2021; Fornell &

Larcker, 1981) by (square root value) “AVE >” in correlation with other variables, all the values are in acceptable limit and are shown in Table 6.

Table 4. Questions and reliability

Constructs	No. of items	Questions	Reliability (α)	Sources
Performance Expectancy (PE)	4	“AI-powered learning activities will enhance the efficiency of the higher education system.” “Educational content prepared by AI technology is useful.” “Using AI-powered chatbot technology I can get an accurate answer.” “Smart educational content can be prepared using AI technology”	0.841	“Venkatesh et al., 2003”
Effort Expectancy (EE)	4	“AI technology is not easy to learn.” “If I know basic AI technology, I can easily learn AI-based applications.” “I can have my query answered quickly using AI chatbot technology.” “Individualized content can be prepared using AI technology.”	0.759	“Sohn & Kwon, 2020a”
Facilitating Condition (FC)	4	“My institute has all the necessary resources to use AI technology for smart.” “My institute sponsors any AI-related learning opportunity.” “All the classrooms of my institute are equipped with the necessary devices for using AI technology for teaching purposes.” “My institute encourages its staff to use modern technology.”	0.812	“Venkatesh et al., 2003”
Content Quality (CCQ)	4	“AI- powered learning provides information that is relevant to my needs.” “AI- powered learning provides comprehensive information.” “AI- powered learning provides me with organized content and information.” “AI- powered learning provides up to date content and information.”	0.747	“Lee et al.2009 Cheng (2012)”
System Quality (SYQ)	4	“AI- powered learning makes easy for me to interact with my teachers.” “AI- powered learning is a compatible with different platforms.” “AI- powered learning to be useful, it is important to be the size and resolution of the interface is a good.” “AI- powered learning has well- designed menus and icons.”	0.736	“Delone and Mclean (2003), Pituch and Lee (2006), Cheng (2012)”

continued on following page

Table 4. Continued

Constructs	No. of items	Questions	Reliability (α)	Sources
Service Quality (SQ)	4	"AI- powered learning provides learning services anywhere." "AI- powered learning provides learning services any time." "AI- powered learning provides me a prompt service." "AI- powered learning service responds in a cooperative manner."	0.882	"Al-Mushasha and Nassuora (2012) Mohammadi (2015)"
Behaviour Intention to use (BI)	5	"I believe AI technology is very easy to learn for beginners." "I am willing to use AI technology for developing smart content." "I believe AI technology could be used for answering student's queries." "I shall recommend all the stakeholders in higher education explore AI." "I intend to use AI technology for teaching-learning purposes in the next couple of years."	0.857	"Sohn & Kwon, 2020a"
Work Engagement (WE)	4	"AI technology made my learning and teaching experience more interactive and interesting." "The adoption of AI technology and tools fostered my classroom engagement." "AI technology developed my performance and engagement in research activities." "AI technology and resources are enhanced by participation and performance in professional and personal development activities."	0.864	"Braganza et al., 2021"
Self- Efficacy (SE)	3	"I am confident that I can perform effectively on many different tasks." "When facing difficult tasks, I am certain that I will accomplish them." "I believe I can succeed at most any endeavour to which I set my mind."	0.840	"Luo & Du 2022"
AI in higher education (AAI)	5	"I apply AI technology to create teaching material and content development." "I apply AI tools to review homework, tests, and other written assignments, monitor student achievement, and provide feedback." "I apply AI tools to detect plagiarism in student papers and courses works." "The application of AI in my higher education academic journey is cost-effective." "I am using AI technologies and tools in my teaching and learning activities."	0.831	"Chatterjee & Bhattacharjee, 2020"

4.3.5. Data Analysis and Interpretation

The collected data was analysed using SPSS 21 and AMOS. Descriptive statistics was used to interpret features of the sample. The tests were applied to identify the significance of the variables in the proposed model by using SPSS 21. Structural Equation Modeling (SEM) was applied using SPSS and AMOS, to study the correlation between the factors.

5. RESULTS

5.1. Characteristics of Sample

The sample collected for the present study was limited to academic staff working in various universities and educational institutions in the NCR. The sample consists of 79% of male and 21% of female's respondents from different designations. The survey respondents were from different regions of NCR. All participants in the demographical survey were mainly from higher educational institutions of NCR as shown below in Table 5.

Table 5. Demographical details

Characteristics	Demography	Frequency	Percent
Age	23-35	796	51.1
	35-50	595	38.2
	50-65	167	10.7
Gender	Male	1230	79
	Female	328	21
Courses	Commerce and management	498	32
	Science and engineering	872	56
	Law and humanities	188	12
Education	Masters	809	51.9
	PhD	460	29.5
	Post Doc	289	18.6
Designation	Assistant professor	732	47
	Associate professor	483	31
	professor	125	8
	others	218	14

continued on following page

Table 5. Continued

Characteristics	Demography	Frequency	Percent
NCR	Noida	654	42
	Ghaziabad	546	35
	Gurugram	265	17
	Faridabad	95	6

5.2. Correlation and Validity

Regression analysis has a conjoint issue of multicollinearity, when the factors are highly correlated with each other. This method will help to maintain the stability of the model and moderate the correlation between predictor variables. Acceptable "VIF values up to 5 is considered as higher threshold and set a lower threshold of 3.3 or even lower" (Table 6).

The Average Variance (AV) of individual variable is the (square root) AVE, for establishing the discriminant validity, AV of each construct were compared with correlation coefficients of the construct in the model with the other constructs shown in the Table 6.

Table 6. Correlation and validity

	PE	EE	FC	CCQ	SYQ	SQ	PR	SE	WE	BI	AAI	CR	AVE	VIF
PE	**0.83**											**0.87**	**0.69**	**3.9**
EE	0.66	**0.92**										**0.94**	**0.85**	**3.7**
FC	0.65	0.69	**0.88**									**0.91**	**0.77**	**4.1**
CCQ	0.67	0.7	0.61	**0.85**								**0.88**	**0.72**	**3.8**
SYQ	0.60	0.72	0.74	0.70	**0.87**							**0.81**	**0.75**	**4.2**
SQ	0.58	0.68	0.69	0.70	0.61	**0.90**						**0.90**	**0.81**	**3.6**
PR	0.62	0.63	0.74	0.68	0.64	0.70	**0.88**					**0.87**	**0.77**	**3.3**
SE	0.66	0.69	0.69	0.70	0.63	0.70	0.64	**0.87**				**0.90**	**0.76**	**4.0**
WE	0.66	0.70	0.68	0.60	0.64	0.70	0.65	0.69	**0.86**			**0.89**	**0.74**	**4.3**
BI	0.64	0.69	0.69	0.65	0.66	0.73	0.62	0.68	0.69	**0.89**		**0.92**	**0.79**	**3.7**
AAI	0.60	0.72	0.64	0.63	0.67	0.72	0.63	0.64	0.65	0.68	**0.85**	**0.94**	**0.73**	**3.9**

Source: AMOS analysis, CR: Composite Reliability, AVE: Average Variance Extracted

In this study, after data analysis, the next step was model testing that confirms that model is fit for the study. The result shows model was supported by "Goodness of Fit" (Tabachnick & Fidell, 2013). In this research model, the model- fit indices has been checked by using "Confirmatory Factor Analysis" (CFA) shown in Table 7.

Table 7. Model-fit analysis

Fit index	Proposed model	Threshold value
"x^2 /d.f"	3.897	'<5.00'
"GFI"	0.904	'>0.90'
"AGFI"	0.821	'>0.80'
"RMSEA"	0.023	'<0.06'
"SRMR"	0.051	'<0.08'
"NFI"	0.952	'>0.90'
"NNFI"	0.921	'>0.90'
"CFI"	0.935	'>0.90'
"IFI"	0.910	'>0.90'

5.3. Structural Equation Model (SEM)

Researchers have used SEM to test the relationship between latent variables and observed variables. Estimation in the study was done by using AMOS. The study shows the theoretical framework which consists of total ten hypotheses are listed for analysis. Result shown all the hypotheses are supported, except H7. The relationship between perceived risk (PR) and behaviour intention (BI) of AI user, being insignificant "($p > 0.005, \beta = 0.046$)", that shows perceived risk insignificantly influenced the behaviour intention of AI users in higher education. Where, performance expectancy (PE) and behaviour intention of users' towards AI (BI) as shown is significant. Hence, H1 supported "($p < 0.001$ and $\beta = 0.743$)". Effort expectancy has significantly influenced the behaviour intention of users' (H2) "($p < 0.001$ and $\beta = 0.816$)" shown in the Table 8. Facilitating condition (FC) and behaviour intention of users' (H3) was significant "($p < 0.001$ and $\beta = 0.653$)". Course content quality and users' behaviours towards AI in higher education data represent (H4) CCQ has significantly influenced the BI "($p < 0.001$ and $\beta = 0.794$)". Data depicts (H5) the significant relationship between system quality (SYQ) and behaviour intention to use AI "($p < 0.001$ and $\beta = 0.599$)". Hence, H5 is supported. In this case, a relationship between service quality and behaviour intention "($p < 0.001$ and $\beta = 0.811$)" has significantly influenced each other. Hence, H6 is accepted. Similarly, self-efficacy (SE) has significantly influence the BI "($p < 0.001$ and $\beta = 0.745$)", So H8 is also supported. Work engagement (WE) and BI of users towards AI "($p < 0.001$ and $\beta = 0.611$)". Therefore, H9 supported. Similarly, behaviour intention of users' of e-learning empowered by AI has significantly influenced the actual usage of AI in higher education "($p < 0.001$ and $\beta = 0.734$)", therefore, H10 supported. The results indicate that PE, EE, FC, and BI support the AAI to 78.3%. Similarly, CCQ, SYQ, and SQ support BI to 65.1%. The variable BI supports perceived risk, self-efficacy and work engagement shows the accuracy of model 64.2%, BI support the actual usage of AI in higher education for 61.6%.

Table 8. Hypothesis testing

Constructs	Hypothesis	Result (β-value)	Significance	Supported
PE->BI	H1	0.743	0.001	Yes
EE->BI	H2	0.816	0.000	Yes
FC->BI	H3	0.653	0.002	Yes
CCQ->BI	H4	0.794	0.001	Yes
SYQ-> BI	H5	0.599	0.000	Yes
SQ->BI	H6	0.811	0.000	Yes
PR->BI	H7	0.046	0.284	Not
SE->BI	H8	0.745	0.000	Yes
WE->BI	H9	0.611	0.000	Yes
BI->AAI	H10	0.734	0.000	Yes

Source: Data Analysis

6. DISCUSSION

AI has brought the technology to the apex level and has the huge potential to enhance the quality of higher education. So, it becomes essential to use AI-based algorithms for teaching purposes. The finding of the study explores effectively, the integration of AI empowered learning in higher education with lots of diligence and thorough planning, taking ethical consideration as a precaution (Bates et al., 2020). The UTAUT model and IS Success Theory has been used to explore the acceptance of AI in higher education, (Sohn & Kwon, 2020a; DeLone & McLean, 2003; Venkatesh et al., 2003). The proposed model consists of ten variables. The research has considered faculty, staff, administration and others in higher education institutions for acceptance and usage of AI (Chatterjee & Bhattacharjee, 2020).

The study has been conducted with different variables i.e., effort expectancy, perceived expectancy, facilitating conditions, course content quality, service quality, system quality, perceived risk, self-efficacy, work engagement, behaviour intention to use and actual usage of AI in learning in higher education. The results indicate that the user's PE, EE, FC have a noteworthy influence on BI of users' towards AI and increase the actual usage of AI in higher education. This research finding was supported by Audet et. al., (2021), which states that learners' are adopting online learning and e-learning due to the adverse effect of COVID-19 pandemic, this study is supported by Marks & Thomas, (2022); Silic & Back, (2017). Hence, the advancement in technology keeps on updating, which brings innovation in learning system in higher education. Using AI in e-learning system shows the globalisation and flexibility in education system that brought much support to learning system (Chang, 2013; Abu-Al-Aish & Love, 2013). Faculties and academic staff maintained the record of students' can customise the study material according to requirement and teachers can guide the students without any hindrances. The result indicates that faculties and academic staff have positive behaviour towards AI, its make their life more comfortable and ease.

The results suggest that faculties teach and maintain all students' data without any difficulties in higher education institutions. This is possible due to better and upgraded technological system introduced in teaching and learning process. The results identified that CCQ, SYQ and SQ have positively influenced the users BI towards AI in their routine academic practices. Upgraded technology might create the best productivity that attracted the new generation toward AI (Srivastava, et al., 2024; Sun et al., 2022, Kour & Karim, 2020).

This research finding also indicates that the perceived risk has not influenced the behaviour intention to use AI in higher education. AI embraces users' learning process whether it's a faculty, staff or students. PR doesn't make any difference to the users' behaviour because AI makes every user more comfortable than before. AI may improve, enhance and create more productive outcome to users'. This study was supported by Teng et. al., (2022) and Mnhrawi & Alreshidi, (2022). The research identified that self-efficacy and work engagement have significantly influenced the behaviour intention to use AI, that significantly influenced the actual usage of AI in higher education, also supported by Marcinkowski et. al., (2020). The benefits by implementing proper training and learning programs in higher educational institutions would accept the new and upgraded technology (Beerkens, 2022).

The result shows that faculty members, who use and incorporate AI into their work, will involve the skill of work engagement. Faculty members need to be encouraged for their efforts and self-confidence to accept the AI tools in their work

(Hooda et al., 2022). For this genuine effort and innovative practices, faculty members receive positive responses. This step will help to motivate the academicians to generate new idea of integrated AI empowered learning, which will reinforce the learners' engagement.

7. CONCLUSION

The existing study predicts the association between factors and usage of AI-empowered learning in the higher education system. The study identifies factors like effort expectancy, performance expectancy and facilitating conditions that significantly influenced behaviour intention to use AI in e-learning and usage of AI in higher education. The outcome of this study shows that technology with better upgraded AI has made it easier to implement it in various fields, including higher education. This study indicates the quality factors related to AI like content quality, system and service quality that influence behaviour intention to use AI and its usage in higher education. The outcome of study notices that the role of AI in learning will improve personalized learning, engagement in work, knowing the students at risk, and administrative tasks. Finally, the result shows that actual usage of AI in higher education will be useful in the routine teaching process. The research hypothesis also shows the external factors like perceived risk, work engagement and self-efficacy, which make teaching and learning more interesting by transforming and swift in the advancement of AI. The research study highlights that risk did not affect the usage of AI rather, it made easy and comfortable teaching that made teacher and staff self-sufficient to use AI, which can change the face of teaching and uplift it to a higher level.

7.1. Implications

The acceptance and adoption of upgraded technology in learning processes empowered by AI in higher education is implemented in various educational institutions across India. AI empowered tools used in the learning process such as intelligent systems tutoring, chatbots, maintaining the data and automated grading systems. This paper will be helpful for policy makers, software developers and educational institutions.

The policymakers should generate funds that promote and create the financial aid that supports the infrastructure in universities and educational institutions. This will embrace the collaboration between educators, staff, students, and service providers, so that they can work together for innovation in the implementation of AI enabled tools. Safety and privacy are the main challenges for any technology that create risk. It provides E-learning platforms and shares personal data, with full secrecy and confidentiality. This issue is related to privacy and security of data, along with ethical concerns.

For educational institutions, it is essential to keep some reserve to provide free training programs and support to develop educator's skill, self- confidence and knowledge to operate AI empowered tools in the process of learning. AI- based software solutions, systematic resource development programs, partnerships with leading industry in AI research and development. Upgraded curriculum and skill program will increase the knowledge and skills of students' to survive and succeed.

8. LIMITATIONS AND SUGGESTIONS

The present study has certain limitations that must be addressed. Firstly, this study only covers some urban area universities and educational institutions related to higher education in NCR. The study has not covered large size of population that studies in higher education. Secondly, Due to time constrain many other factors need to be explored. Thirdly, in this study sample size is limited to only universities and educational institutions situated in NCR's, other areas need to be explored with different ideology, psychological and demographical factors can be considered. Lastly, there is still insufficiency faced by many universities and educational institutions in effective implementation of AI. The main concerns of implementing AI based learning process solution are its cost and complexity. There is a need of more institutions that implement the AI-empowered learning so that population size can be extended and real picture will display.

REFERENCES

Abu-Al-Aish, A., and Love, S. (2013). Factors influencing students' acceptance of m-learning: an investigation in higher education. Int. Rev. Res. Open Distributed Learn. 14, 83–107. acceptance model: four longitudinal field studies. Manage. Sci. 46, 186–204.doi: .DOI: 10.19173/irrodl.v14i5.1631

Ahmad, S. F., Alam, M. M., Rahmat, M. K., Mubarik, M. S., & Hyder, S. I. (2022, January). Academic and administrative role of artificial intelligence in education. *Sustainability (Basel)*, *14*(3), 1101. DOI: 10.3390/su14031101

Ahmad, S. F., Rahmat, M. K., Mubarik, M. S., Alam, M. M., & Hyder, S. I. (2021, November). Artificial intelligence and its role in education. *Sustainability (Basel)*, *13*(22), 12902. DOI: 10.3390/su132212902

Al-Mushasha, N. F., & Nassuora, A. B. (2012). Factors determining e-learning service quality in Jordanian higher education environment. *Journal of Applied Sciences (Faisalabad)*, *12*(14), 1474–1480. DOI: 10.3923/jas.2012.1474.1480

Al-Nuaimi, M. N., Al Sawafi, O. S., Malik, S. I., Al-Emran, M., & Selim, Y. F. (2022, April). Evaluating the actual use of learning management systems during the covid-19 pandemic: An integrated theoretical model. *Interactive Learning Environments*, •••, 1–26. DOI: 10.1080/10494820.2022.2127777

Alalwan, A. A., Rana, N. P., Dwivedi, Y. K., & Algharabat, R. (2017). Social media in marketing: A review and analysis of the existing literature. *Telematics and Informatics*, *34*(7), 1177–1190. DOI: 10.1016/j.tele.2017.05.008

Aldosari, S. A. M. (2020). The future of higher education in the light of artificial intelligence transformations. *International Journal of Higher Education*, *9*(3), 145–151. DOI: 10.5430/ijhe.v9n3p145

Almarashdeh, I. A., Sahari, N., Zin, N. A. M., & Alsmadi, M. (2010). The success of learning management system among distance learners in Malasian universities. *Journal of Theoretical and Applied Information Technology*, *21*(2).

Alrawashdeh, T. A. (2012). Factors affecting acceptance of web-based training system: Using extended Utaut and structural equation modeling. *Int. J. Comput.Sci. Eng. Inf. Technol.*, *2*(2), 45–54. DOI: 10.5121/ijcseit.2012.2205

Amornkitpinyo, T., Yoosomboon, S., Sopapradit, S., & Amornkitpinyo, P. (2021). The structural equation model of actual use of cloud learning for higher education students in the 21st century. *Journal of E-Learning and Knowledge Society*, *17*(1), 72–80. DOI: 10.20368/1971-8829/1135300

Audet, É. C., Levine, S. L., Metin, E., Koestner, S., & Barcan, S. (2021). Zooming their way through university: Which Big 5 traits facilitated students' adjustment to online courses during the COVID-19 pandemic. *Personality and Individual Differences*, *180*, 110969. DOI: 10.1016/j.paid.2021.110969 PMID: 36540325

Bandura, A. (1986). *Social foundations of thought and action*. Prentice-Hall.

Bates, T., Cobo, C., Mariño, O., & Wheeler, S. (2020). Can artificial intelligence transform higher education? *International Journal of Educational Technology in Higher Education*, *17*(1), 42. Advance online publication. DOI: 10.1186/s41239-020-00218-x

Bazoukis, G., Hall, J., Loscalzo, J., Antman, E. M., Fuster, V., & Armoundas, A. A. (2022). The inclusion of augmented intelligence in medicine: A framework for successful implementation. *Cell Reports Medicine*, *3*(1), 1–8. DOI: 10.1016/j.xcrm.2021.100485 PMID: 35106506

Beerkens, M. (2022). An evolution of performance data in higher education governance: A path towards a "big data" era? *Quality in Higher Education*, *28*(1), 29–49. DOI: 10.1080/13538322.2021.1951451

Bhattacherjee, A., and Hikmet. (2008). Reconceptualizing organizational support and its effect on information technology usage: Evidence from the health care sector. *Journal of Computer Information Systems*, *48*, 69–76. DOI: 10.1080/08874417.2008.11646036

Bisen, I. E., Arslan, E. A., Yildirim, K., & Yildirim, Y. (2021). *Artificial intelligence and machine learning in higher education. In machine learning approaches for improvising modern learning systems*. IGI Global., DOI: 10.4018/978-1-7998-5009-0.ch001

Boontarig, W., Chutimaskul, W., Chongsuphajaisiddhi, V., & Papasratorn, B. (2012). "Factors influencing the Thai elderly intention to use smartphone for e-Health services," in *2012 IEEE Symposium on Humanities, Science and Engineering Research*, 479–483. DOI: 10.1109/SHUSER.2012.6268881

Boudreau, C. A., & Kromrey, J. D. (1994). A longitudinal study of the retention and academic performance of participants in freshmen orientation course. *Journal of College Student Development*, *35*, 444–449.

Braganza, A., Chen, W., Canhoto, A., & Sap, S. (2021). Productive employment and decent work: The impact of AI adoption on psychological contracts, job engagement and employee trust. *Journal of Business Research*, *131*, 485–494. DOI: 10.1016/j.jbusres.2020.08.018 PMID: 32836565

Carvalho, L., Martinez-Maldonado, R., Tsai, Y.-S., Markauskaite, L., & De Laat, M. (2022). How can we design for learning in an AI world? *Computers and Education: Artificial Intelligence*, *3*, 100053. DOI: 10.1016/j.caeai.2022.100053

Chang, C.-C. (2013). Library mobile applications in university libraries. *Library Hi Tech*, *31*(3), 478–492. DOI: 10.1108/LHT-03-2013-0024

Chang, C. C., Yan, C. F., & Tseng, J. S. (2012). Perceived convenience in an extended technology acceptance model: Mobile technology and English learning for college students. *Australasian Journal of Educational Technology*, *28*(5), 809–826. DOI: 10.14742/ajet.818

Chang, Y.-H., Yan, Y.-C., & Lu, Y.-T. (2022). Effects of Combining Different Collaborative Learning Strategies with Problem-Based Learning in a Flipped Classroom on Program Language Learning. *Sustainability (Basel)*, *14*(9), 9. Advance online publication. DOI: 10.3390/su14095282

Chatterjee, S., & Bhattacharjee, K. K. (2020). (2020)Adoption of artificial intelligence in higher education: A quantitative analysis using structural equation modelling. *Education and Information Technologies*, *25*(5), 3443–3463. Advance online publication. DOI: 10.1007/s10639-020-10159-7

Chatterjee, S., Rana, N. P., Khorana, S., Mikalef, P., & Sharma, A. (2021). Assessing organizational users' intentions and behavior to AI integrated CRM systems: A meta-UTAUT approach. *Information Systems Frontiers*, *25*(4), 1299–1313. DOI: 10.1007/s10796-021-10181-1

Chaudhry, I. S., Sarwary, S. A. M., El Refae, G. A., & Chabchoub, H. (2023). Time to revisit existing student's performance evaluation approach in higher education sector in a new era of ChatGPT — A case study. *Cogent Education*, *10*(1), 2210461. DOI: 10.1080/2331186X.2023.2210461

Chedrawi, C., & Howayeck, P. (2019). Artificial intelligence a disruptive innovation in higher education accreditation programs: Expert systems and AACSB. *Lecture Notes in Information Systems and Organisation*, *30*, 115–129. DOI: 10.1007/978-3-030-10737-6_8

Chen, C., Landa, S., Padilla, A., & Yur-Austin, J. (2021). Learners' experience and needs in online environments: Adopting agility in teaching. *J. Res. Innov. Teach. Learn.*, *14*(1), 18–31. DOI: 10.1108/JRIT-11-2020-0073

Cheng, X., Bao, Y., Zarifis, A., Gong, W., & Mou, J. (2022, March). Exploring consumers' response to text-based chatbots in e-commerce: The moderating role of task complexity and chatbot disclosure. *Internet Research, 32*(2), 496–517. DOI: 10.1108/INTR-08-2020-0460

Cheng, Y. M. (2012). Effects of quality antecedents on e-learning acceptance. *Internet Research, 22*(3), 361–390. DOI: 10.1108/10662241211235699

Cheng, Y. M. (2012). Effects of quality antecedents on e-learning acceptance. *Internet Research, 22*(3), 361–390. DOI: 10.1108/10662241211235699

Choi, K.-S. (2020). Opportunities for higher education of artificial intelligence in korea. *International Journal of Engineering Research & Technology (Ahmedabad), 13*(11), 3428–3430. https://www.scopus.com/inward/record.uri?eid=2-s2. DOI: 10.37624/IJERT/13.11.2020.3428-3430

Christensen, R., & Knezek, G. (2015, October). The technology proficiency self-assessment questionnaire (TPSA): Evolution of a self-efficacy measure for technology integration. In Proceedings of the KEYCIT2014: Key Competencies in Informatics and ICT Conference, KEYCIT, Potsdam (pp. 311–318).

Chuan-Chuan Lin, J., & Lu, H. (2000). Towards an understanding of the behavioural intention to use a web site. *International Journal of Information Management, 20*(3), 197–208. DOI: 10.1016/S0268-4012(00)00005-0

Cui, W., & Xue, Z., & Thai, K.-P. (2019). Performance comparison of an AI-Based adaptive learning system in China. In 2018 Chinese Automation Congress, CAC 2018, pp. 3170–3175. Institute of Electrical and Electronics Engineers Inc. https://doi.org/DOI: 10.1109/CAC.2018.8623327

De Roover, K., Vermunt, J. K., & Ceulemans, E. (2022). Mixture multigroup factor analysis for unraveling factor loading noninvariance across many groups. *Psychological Methods, 27*(3), 281–306. DOI: 10.1037/met0000355 PMID: 33271027

DeLone, W. H., & McLean, E. R. (1992). Information systems success: The quest for the dependent variable. *Information Systems Research, 3*(1), 60–95. DOI: 10.1287/isre.3.1.60

Delone, W. H., & McLean, E. R. (2003). The DeLone and McLean model of information systems success: A ten-year update. *Journal of Management Information Systems, 19*(4), 9–30. DOI: 10.1080/07421222.2003.11045748

Dieguez, T., Loureiro, P., & Ferreira, I. (2021). *Entrepreneurship and leadership in higher education to develop the needed 21st Century skills. In 17th European Conference on Management, Leadership and Governance, ECMLG 2021*. Academic Conferences International Limited., https://www.scopus.com/inward/record.uri?eid=2-s2

Dulle, F. W., & Minishi-Majanja, M. K. (2011). The suitability of the unified theory of acceptance and use of technology (utaut) model in open access adoption studies. *Information Development*, *27*(1), 32–45. DOI: 10.1177/0266666910385375

Durak, H. Y. (2018). Flipped learning readiness in teaching programming in middle schools: Modelling its relation to various variables. *Journal of Computer Assisted Learning*, *34*(6), 939–959. DOI: 10.1111/jcal.12302

Essien, A., Chukwukelu, G., & Essien, V. (2020).

Featherman, M. S., & Pavlou, P. A. (2003). Predicting E-Services Adoption: A Perceived Risk Facets Perspective. *International Journal of Human-Computer Studies*, *59*(4), 451–474. DOI: 10.1016/S1071-5819(03)00111-3

Fishbein, M., & Ajzen, I. (1977). Belief, attitude, intention, and behavior: An introduction to theory and research. *Philosophy & Rhetoric*, •••, 10.

Fornell, C., & Larcker, D. F. (1981). Evaluating structural equation models with unobservable variables and measurement error. *JMR, Journal of Marketing Research*, *18*(1), 39–50. DOI: 10.1177/002224378101800104

Franzoni, V., Milani, A., Mengoni, P., & Piccinato, F. (2020). Artificial intelligence visual metaphors in e-learning interfaces for learning analytics. *Applied Sciences (Basel, Switzerland)*, *10*(20), 1–25. DOI: 10.3390/app10207195

Ge, Z., & Hu, Y. (2020) Innovative application of artificial intelligence (AI) in the Management of higher education and teaching. In *2020 International Conference on Artificial Intelligence and Information Technology, ICAIIT 2020*. Institute of Physics Publishing. https://doi.org/DOI: 10.1088/1742-6596/1533/3/032089

Halili, S. H., & Sulaiman, H. (2018). Factors influencing the rural students' acceptance of using ICT for educational purposes. *Kasetsart Journal of Social Sciences*, *40*, 574–579. DOI: 10.1016/j.kjss.2017.12.022

Hanafizadeh, P., Behboudi, M., Koshksaray, A. A., & Tabar, M. J. S. (2014). Mobile-Banking Adoption by Iranian Bank Clients. *Telematics and Informatics*, *31*(1), 62–78. DOI: 10.1016/j.tele.2012.11.001

Holmes, E., Nicholson, J. K., Lodge, S., Nitschke, P., Kimhofer, T., & Wist, J.. (2021a). Diffusion and relaxation edited proton NMR spectroscopy of plasma reveals a high-fidelity supramolecular biomarker signature of SARS-CoV-2 infection. *Analytical Chemistry, 93*(8), 3976–3986. DOI: 10.1021/acs.analchem.0c04952 PMID: 33577736

Hong, J. C., Hwang, M. Y., Tai, K. H., & Lin, P. H. (2019). Improving cognitive certitude with calibration mediated by cognitive anxiety, online learning self-efficacy and interest in learning chinese pronunciation. *Educational Technology Research and Development, 67*(3), 597–615. DOI: 10.1007/s11423-018-9628-4

Hooda, M., Rana, C., Dahiya, O., Rizwan, A., & Hossain, M. S. (2022). Artificial intelligence for assessment and feedback to enhance student success in higher education. *Mathematical Problems in Engineering, 2022*, 1–19. DOI: 10.1155/2022/5215722

Hunt, S. D., Sparkman, R. D.Jr, & Wilcox, J. B. (1982). The pre-test in survey research: Issues and preliminary findings. [intrinsic motivation, and emotion into the technology acceptance model. Inf.]. *JMR, Journal of Marketing Research, 19*(2), 269–273. DOI: 10.1177/002224378201900211

Jarrahi, M. H. (2018). Artificial Intelligence and the Future of Work: Human-AI Symbiosis in Organizational Decision Making. *Business Horizons, 61*(4), 577–586. DOI: 10.1016/j.bushor.2018.03.007

Joo, Y. J., Bong, M., & Choi, H. J. (2000). Self-efficacy for self-regulated learning, academic self-efficacy, and internet self-efficacy in web-based instruction. *Educational Technology Research and Development, 48*(2), 5–17. DOI: 10.1007/BF02313398

Kalavani, A., Kazerani, M., & Shekofteh, M. (2018). Acceptance of evidence based medicine (EBM) databases by Iranian medical residents using unified theory of acceptance and use of technology (UTAUT). *Health Policy and Technology, 7*(3), 287–292. DOI: 10.1016/j.hlpt.2018.06.005

Kelly, A., Sullivan, M., & Strampel, K. (2023). Generative artifiicial intelligence: University student awareness, experience, and confiidence in use across disciplines. *Journal of University Teaching & Learning Practice, 20*(6). Advance online publication. DOI: 10.53761/1.20.6.12

Khan, N., Sarwar, A., Chen, T. B., & Khan, S. (2022). Connecting digital literacy in higher education to the 21st century workforce. *Knowledge Management and E-Learning, 14*(1), 46–61. DOI: 10.34105/j.kmel.2022.14.004

Khoza, S. B., & Mpungose, C. B. (2022). Digitalised curriculum to the rescue of a higher education institution. *African Identities, 20*(4), 310–330. DOI: 10.1080/14725843.2020.1815517

Kim, B., Lim, H., Chung, J., Kim, J., Lim, K., Sohn, D., Cho, J.-Y., Yu, K.-S., Shin, S.-G., Paick, J.-S., & Jang, I.-J. (2008). Safety, tolerability and pharmacokinetics of udenafil, a novel PDE-5 inhibitor, in healthy young Korean subjects. *British Journal of Clinical Pharmacology, 65*(6), 848–854. DOI: 10.1111/j.1365-2125.2008.03107.x PMID: 18318773

Kistyanto, A., Rahman, M. F. W., Adhar Wisandiko, F., & Setyawati, E. E. P. (2022). Cultural intelligence increase student's innovative behavior in higher education: The mediating role of interpersonal trust. *International Journal of Educational Management, 36*(4), 419–440. DOI: 10.1108/IJEM-11-2020-0510

Kolotylo-Kulkarni, M., Xia, W., & Dhillon, G. (2021). Information disclosure in e-commerce: A systematic review and agenda for future research, March 2020. *Journal of Business Research, 126*, 221–238. DOI: 10.1016/j.jbusres.2020.12.006

Kour, R., & Karim, R. (2020). Cybersecurity workforce in railway: Its maturity and awareness. *Journal of Quality in Maintenance Engineering, 27*(3), 453–464. DOI: 10.1108/JQME-07-2020-0059

Lee, B. C., Yoon, J. O., & Lee, I. (2009). Learners' acceptance of e-learning in South Korea: Theories and results. *Computers & Education, 53*(4), 1320–1329. DOI: 10.1016/j.compedu.2009.06.014

Li, H., Edwards, S. M., & Lee, J.-H. (2002). Measuring the intrusiveness of advertisements: Scale development and validation. *Journal of Advertising, 31*(2), 37–47. DOI: 10.1080/00913367.2002.10673665

Li, J., Li, J., Yang, Y., & Ren, Z. (2021). Design of higher education system based on artificial intelligence technology. *Discrete Dynamics in Nature and Society, 2021*, 1–11. DOI: 10.1155/2021/3303160

Li, J., Li, J., Yang, Y., & Ren, Z. (2021). Design of higher education system based on artificial intelligence technology. *Discrete Dynamics in Nature and Society, 2021*, 1–11. DOI: 10.1155/2021/3303160

Li, J., Li, J., Yang, Y., & Ren, Z. (2021). Design of higher education system based on artificial intelligence technology. *Discrete Dynamics in Nature and Society, 2021*, 1–11. DOI: 10.1155/2021/3303160

Li, Y., Duan, Y., Fu, Z., & Alford, P. (2012). An empirical study on behavioural intention to reuse e-learning systems in rural China. *British Journal of Educational Technology, 43*(6), 933–948. DOI: 10.1111/j.1467-8535.2011.01261.x

Luo, Y., & Du, H. (2022). Learning with desktop virtual reality: Changes and interrelationship of self-efficacy, goal orientation, technology acceptance and learning behavior. *Smart Learning Environments, 9*(1), 1–22. DOI: 10.1186/s40561-022-00203-z

Mailizar, M., Burg, D., & Maulina, S. (2021). Examining university students' behavioural intention to use e-learning during the COVID-19 pandemic: An extended TAM model. *Education and Information Technologies, 26*(6), 7057–7077. DOI: 10.1007/s10639-021-10557-5 PMID: 33935579

Marcinkowski, F. (2020). Implications of AI (un-)fairness in higher education admissions: The effects of perceived AI (un-)fairness on exit, voice and organizational reputation. In 3rd ACM Conference on Fairness, Accountability, and Transparency, FAT* 2020. Association for Computing Machinery, Inc, pp. 122–130. https://doi.org/DOI: 10.1145/3351095.3372867

Marks, B., & Thomas, J. (2022). Adoption of virtual reality technology in higher education: An evaluation of five teaching semesters in a purpose-designed laboratory. *Education and Information Technologies, 27*(1), 1287–1305. DOI: 10.1007/s10639-021-10653-6 PMID: 34257511

Mikusa, M. E. (2015). The effect of technology self-efficacy and personal engagement on students' and teachers' attitudes toward technology use in education(Doctoral dissertation). Appalachian State University

Miles, J. (2014). Tolerance and Variance inflation factor. Wiley StatsRef: Statistics Reference Online, https://doi.org/.DOI: 10.1002/9781118445112.stat06593

Minkevics, V., & Kampars, J. (2021). Artificial intelligence and big data driven is security management solution with applications in higher education organizations. In Chemouil, P.. (Ed.) *17th International Conference on Network and Service Management, CNSM 2021*. Institute of Electrical and Electronics Engineers Inc. pp. 340–344. https://doi.org/DOI: 10.23919/CNSM52442.2021.9615575

Mishra, N., & Mukherjee, S. (2019). Effect of artificial intelligence on customer relationship management of Amazon in Bangalore. *International Journal of Management (Kolkata), 10*(4), 168–172. DOI: 10.34218/IJM.10.4.2019.016

Mishra, R. (2019). Usage of data analytics and artificial intelligence in ensuring quality assurance at higher education institutions. In *2019 Amity International Conference on Artificial Intelligence, AICAI 2019*. Institute of Electrical and Electronics Engineers Inc. pp. 1022–1025. https://doi.org/DOI: 10.1109/AICAI.2019.8701392

Mitic, V. (2019) Benefits of Artificial Intelligence and Machine Learning in Marketing. In Sinteza 2019-International Scientific Conference on Information Technology and Data Related Research (pp. 472-477). Singidunum University.

Mohamed Zabri, S., Mohammad Abakar, Y., & Ahmad, K. (2023). Exploring the acceptance of online learning among students in technical and non-technical programmes at a higher education institution. *Cogent Education*, *10*(2), 2284552. DOI: 10.1080/2331186X.2023.2284552

Mohammadi, H. (2015). A Study of Mobile Banking Usage in Iran. *International Journal of Bank Marketing*, *33*(6), 733–759. DOI: 10.1108/IJBM-08-2014-0114

Nardi, A., & Ranieri, M. (2019). Comparing paper-based and electronic multiple-choice examinations with personal devices: Impact on students' performance, self-efficacy and satisfaction. *British Journal of Educational Technology*, *50*(3), 1495–1506. DOI: 10.1111/bjet.12644

Neumann, C., Stroud, K. M., Bailey, S., Allison, K., & Everts, S. S. (2021). 21st-century competencies in higher education: A practitioner's guide. In *Handbook of research on barriers for teaching 21st-Century competencies and the impact of digitalization* (pp. 293–315). IGI Globalpp., DOI: 10.4018/978-1-7998-6967-2.ch016

Odhiambo, G. (2016). Higher education in Kenya: An assessment of current responses to the imperative of widening access. *Journal of Higher Education Policy and Management*, *38*(2), 196–211. DOI: 10.1080/1360080X.2016.1150551

Olapade, D. T., Aluko, T. B., Adisa, A. L., & Abobarin, A. A. (2023). A framework for assessment of customary land delivery institutions: Instrument development, content validity and reliability testing. *Property Management*, *41*(5), 729–752. DOI: 10.1108/PM-06-2022-0041

Opportunities and challenges of adopting artificial intelligence for learning and teaching in higher education. In Fostering communication and learning with underutilized technologies in higher education, pp.67–78. IGI Global. https://doi.org/ .DOI: 10.4018/978-1-7998-4846-2.ch00

Pardamean, E., Roan, W., Iskandar, K. T. A., Prayangga, R., & Hariyanto, T. I. (2022). Mortality from coronavirus disease 2019 (Covid-19) in patients with schizophrenia: A systematic review, meta-analysis and meta-regression. *General Hospital Psychiatry*, *75*, 61–67. DOI: 10.1016/j.genhosppsych.2022.01.010 PMID: 35182908

Pituch, K. A., & Lee, Y. (2006). The influence of system characteristics on e-learning use. *Computers & Education*, *47*(2), 222–244. DOI: 10.1016/j.compedu.2004.10.007

Popenici, S. A. D., & Kerr, S. (2017). Exploring the impact of artificial intelligence on teaching and learning in higher education. *Research and Practice in Technology Enhanced Learning*, *12*(1), 22. Advance online publication. DOI: 10.1186/s41039-017-0062-8 PMID: 30595727

Pradana, M., Elisa, H. P., & Syarifuddin, S. (2023). Discussing ChatGPT in education: A literature review and bibliometric analysis. *Cogent Education*, *10*(2), 2243134. DOI: 10.1080/2331186X.2023.2243134

Rahimi, A. R., & Tafazoli, D. (2022). The role of university teachers' 21st-century digital competence in their attitudes toward ICT integration in higher education: Extending the theory of planned behavior. *The JALT CALL Journal*, *18*(2), 238–263. DOI: 10.29140/jaltcall.v18n2.632

Ramayah, T., Ahmad, N. H., & Lo, M. C. (2010). The role of quality factors in intention to continue using an e-learning system in Malaysia. *Procedia: Social and Behavioral Sciences*, *2*(2), 5422–5426. DOI: 10.1016/j.sbspro.2010.03.885

Raza, S. A., Qazi, W., Khan, K. A., & Salam, J. (2021). Social isolation and acceptance of the Learning Management System (LMS) in the time of COVID-19 pandemic: An expansion of the UTAUT Model. *Journal of Educational Computing Research*, *59*(2), 183–208. DOI: 10.1177/0735633120960421

Roca, J. C., Chiu, C.-M., & Martínez, F. J. (2006). Understanding elearning continuance intention: An extension of the Technology Acceptance Model. *International Journal of Human-Computer Studies*, *64*(8), 683–696. DOI: 10.1016/j.ijhcs.2006.01.003

Roemer, E., Schuberth, F., & Henseler, J. (2021). HTMT2–an improved criterion for assessing discriminant validity in structural equation modeling. *Industrial Management & Data Systems*, *121*(12), 2637–2650. DOI: 10.1108/IMDS-02-2021-0082

Roemer, E., Schuberth, F., & Henseler, J. (2021). HTMT2–an improved criterion for assessing discriminant validity in structural equation modeling. *Industrial Management & Data Systems*, *121*(12), 2637–2650. DOI: 10.1108/IMDS-02-2021-0082

Rudolph, J., Tan, S., & Tan, S. (2023). ChatGPT: Bullshit spewer or the end of traditional assessments in higher education? *Journal of Applied Learning & Teaching*, *6*(1). Advance online publication. DOI: 10.37074/jalt.2023.6.1.9

Sanusi, M. S. (2022). Action research to reassess the acceptance and use of technology in a blended learning approach amongst postgraduate business students. *Cogent Education*, *9*(1), 2145813. DOI: 10.1080/2331186X.2022.2145813

Sayed Al Mnhrawi, D. N. T. A., & Alreshidi, H. A. (2022). A systemic approach for implementing AI methods in education during COVID-19 pandemic: Higher education in Saudi Arabia. *World Journal of Engineering*, *20*(5), 808–814. DOI: 10.1108/WJE-11-2021-0623

Signorelli, C. M. (2018). "Can computers overcome humans? consciousness interaction and its implications," in *2018 IEEE 17th International Conference on Cognitive Informatics & Cognitive Computing* (Berkeley, CA). DOI: 10.1109/ICCI-CC.2018.8482038

Silic, M., & Back, A. (2017). Impact of gamification on user's knowledge-sharing practices: Relationships between work motivation, performance expectancy and work engagement. In T. X. Bui. and R. Sprague (Eds.), 50th annual Hawaii international conference on System Sciences, HICSS 2017 (pp. 1308–1317). IEEE Computer Society. https://www.scopus.com/inward/record.uri?eid=2-s2.0-85086568517&partnerID=40&md5=

Sohn, K., & Kwon, O. (2020a). Technology acceptance theories and factors influencing artificial intelligence-based intelligent products. *Telematics and Informatics*, *47*, 101324. DOI: 10.1016/j.tele.2019.101324

Sohn, K., & Kwon, O. (2020b). Technology acceptance theories and factors influencing artificial intelligence-based intelligent products. *Telematics and Informatics*, *47*, 101324. DOI: 10.1016/j.tele.2019.101324

Srivastava K., Kumar M, Verma R, Maurya P., (2024). Assessment of Quality Attributes of Mobile Learning Applications on Students' Satisfaction Source Title: Architecture and Technological Advancements of Education 4.0. DOI:.DOI: 10.4018/978-1-6684-9285-7.ch007

Srivastava. K, Kumar. Manoj (2017). An Empirical Examination of Perceived Risk in Mobile-Banking Business, Economics, Computer Science Adhyayan: A Journal of Management Sciences DOI: Corpus ID: 169118936DOI: 10.21567/adhyayan.v7i02.10762

Suki, N. M., & Suki, N. M. (2017). Determining students' behavioural intention to use animation and storytelling applying the UTAUT model: The moderating roles of gender and experience level. *International Journal of Management Education, 15*(3), 528–538. DOI: 10.1016/j.ijme.2017.10.002

Šumak, B., & Šorgo, A. (2016). The acceptance and use of interactive whiteboards among teachers: Differences in UTAUT determinants between pre- and post-adopters. *Computers in Human Behavior, 64*, 602–620. DOI: 10.1016/j.chb.2016.07.037

Sun, H., Ni, W., & Farouk, A. (2022). Design and application of an AI-Based text content moderation system. *Scientific Programming, 2022*, 1–9. DOI: 10.1155/2022/2062791

Sutton, R. S., & Barto, A. G. (2018). *Reinforcement learning: An introduction* (2nd ed.). The MIT Press. Syst. Res. 11, 342–365. DOI: 10.1287/isre.11.4.342.11872

Tabachnick, B. G., & Fidell, L. S. (2013). Using multivariate statistics: International edition. Pearson 2012.

Taber, K. S. (2018). The use of Cronbach's alpha when developing and reporting research instruments in science education. *Research in Science Education, 48*(6), 1273–1296. DOI: 10.1007/s11165-016-9602-2

Tajuddin, R. A., Baharudin, M., & Hoon, T. S. (2013). System quality and its influence on students' learning satisfaction in UiTM Shah Alam. *Procedia: Social and Behavioral Sciences, 90*, 677–685. DOI: 10.1016/j.sbspro.2013.07.140

Teng, Y., Zhang, J., & Sun, T. (2022). Data-driven decision-making model based on artificial intelligence in higher education system of colleges and universities. *Expert Systems: International Journal of Knowledge Engineering and Neural Networks, 40*(4), e12820. Advance online publication. DOI: 10.1111/exsy.12820

van Dijk, J. A. G. M., Peters, O., & Ebbers, W. (2008). Explaining the acceptance and use of government Internet services: A multivariate analysis of 2006 survey data in the Netherlands. *Government Information Quarterly, 25*(3), 379–399. DOI: 10.1016/j.giq.2007.09.006

Venkatesh, V. (2000). Determinants of perceived ease of use: Integrating control intrinsic motivation, and emotion into the technology acceptance model. *Information Systems Research, 11*(4), 342–365. DOI: 10.1287/isre.11.4.342.11872

Venkatesh, V., & Davis, F. D. (1996). A model of the antecedents of perceived ease of use: Development and test. *Decision Sciences, 27*(3), 451–481. DOI: 10.1111/j.1540-5915.1996.tb01822.x

Venkatesh, V., & Davis, F. D. (2000). A theoretical extension of the technology acceptance model: Four longitudinal field studies. *Management Science*, *46*(2), 186–204. DOI: 10.1287/mnsc.46.2.186.11926

Venkatesh, V., Morris, , Davis, , & Davis, . (2003). User acceptance of Information technology: Toward a unified view. *Management Information Systems Quarterly*, *27*(3), 425–478. DOI: 10.2307/30036540

Wang, W. T., & Wang, C. C. (2009). An empirical study of instructor adoption of web-based learning systems. *Computers & Education*, *53*(3), 761–774. DOI: 10.1016/j.compedu.2009.02.021

Warshaw, P. R., & Davis, F. D. (1985). Disentangling behavioral intention and behavioral expectation. *Journal of Experimental Social Psychology*, *21*(3), 213–228. DOI: 10.1016/0022-1031(85)90017-4

Wenge, M. (2021). Artificial intelligence-based real-time

Williams, M. D., Dwivedi, Y. K., Lal, B., & Schwarz, A. (2009). Contemporary trends and issues in IT adoption and diffusion research. *Journal of Information Technology*, *24*(1), 1–10. DOI: 10.1057/jit.2008.30

Zhou, Z. H., & Feng, J. (2017) Deep Forest: Towards an Alternative to Deep Neural Networks. arXiv *preprintarXiv*:1702.08835. https://arxiv.org/pdf/1702.08835.pdf DOI: 10.24963/ijcai.2017/497

Chapter 4
Taxonomy of Challenges of Cybersecurity Risk Assessment in Higher Learning Institutions

Beatrice Akoth Owino
https://orcid.org/0000-0003-4185-3846
United States International University Africa, Kenya

Collins Oduor
University of Nairobi, Kenya

Gerald W. Chege
United States International University Africa, Kenya

Mahona Joseph Paschal
https://orcid.org/0000-0001-9842-9849
St. Augustine University of Tanzania, Tanzania

ABSTRACT

The use of information technology and related processes has permeated into organizations of all sizes. Higher learning institutions are described as open, multi-modal platforms whose organizational complexity can increase vulnerability to information security breaches. Several high-profile cyberattacks have occurred on universities and colleges, including ransomware attacks resulting in data breaches and system shutdowns. In some cases, universities have had to pay large sums to regain system access. The following research objective guided the study: (1) Establish cyber security posture in Higher Learning institutions. The literature highlighted that the

DOI: 10.4018/979-8-3693-2973-3.ch004

critical cybersecurity challenges in most Higher learning institutions, in general, are a lack of cybersecurity governance and risk assessment frameworks, a lack of incident management plans, and a lack of national and regional legal frameworks related to cybersecurity, a lack of security awareness and education programs; and a lack of national and international legal frameworks related to cybersecurity.

INTRODUCTION

The rate of technological progress in computing has accelerated in the recent century. A complex integration of information systems (IS) and information and communication technology (ICT) is now an inevitable result of this progress, coupled with the pervasive globalization of businesses and organizations (Sadaf Hina et al., 2019). Modern companies and institutions prioritize cyber security risk assessment in response to the daily volume of data and an increase in successful cyberattacks. Information is a significant business asset in all organizations. The ICT systems are prone to failures caused by malicious actors attacking the systems, accidents, or even natural disasters that could interrupt their normal functions. These failures and interruptions are called cyber incidents, costing companies millions of euros every year (Sharma, 2022). The interconnectivity in universities continues to increase, and the attack surface grows proportionately. One of the most challenging issues with technological advancements is securing systems from cyber-attacks (Farheen Ansari, 2022).

According to Microsoft Security Intelligence, the education industry accounted for 61% of the 7.7 Million malware encountered by businesses (Alexei & Alexei, 2021). Fouad (2021) cites three main implications of cyber attacks on higher education that warrant attention to the sector's cybersecurity. The first is substantial financial losses caused by ransomware attacks or data breaches. The second critical impact of cyber threats on education is the disruption of learning processes. Third, the involvement of many universities in strategically or economically significant research makes them attractive targets for intellectual property theft.

Melaku (2023) discovered that the critical cybersecurity challenges in the East African region, in general, are a lack of cybersecurity governance and risk management frameworks, a lack of incident management plans, and a lack of national and regional legal frameworks related to cybersecurity, a shortage of sufficient cybersecurity professionals, capability, and skills; a lack of security awareness and education programs; and a lack of national and international legal frameworks related to cybersecurity (Njoroge, 2021).

HLIs' most significant challenge is determining which maturity model to use because different models are used for various purposes. Alshar'e's (2023) study points out that security needs are different for every organization. This means no one-size-fits-all solution for securing an organization's information assets exists. Every business has unique security needs and requirements that change over time (Alshar'e, 2023).

Cyber risk assessment standards and methodologies are necessary for the secure governance of any enterprise since cyber-attacks dramatically grow in parallel to technological innovations. HLI's are now integrating information and communication technology (ICT) into its core operations and functionalities, learning and teaching, communication and collaboration, research, innovations and developments, and information-sharing to fulfill their mandate (P. M. Njoroge, 2021).

KPMG's report of August 2023 (KPMG, 2023) shows that Higher Learning Institutions have recently been determined as the most likely educational body to become a target for cyberattacks. Universities promote the free flow of ideas and information, telecommuting, and BYOD, and have an ever-changing student and faculty population. Because there are inadequate cyber security controls in place, there is an increase in general business risks and cyber security threats in most Higher Learning Institutions. Universities sit at one of the most crowded intersections of the digital economy: these open-by-design, decentralized, multi-stakeholder, transient platforms are traditionally associated with technology, research, and innovation. Students, academics, staff, and visitors regularly access universities' IT infrastructures to consume and produce data in a multi-modal fashion: from personal mobile phones and smart-watches (bring your-own-device, BYOD) through corporate laptops and tablets to laboratory sensors and swipe access card systems, the data exchange among universities as organizations and their different categories of end-users are continuous (Bongiovanni, 2019).

According to Ulven and Wangen (2021), higher learning institutions collect data from donors, trustees, board members, alumni, students, parents, applicants, faculty, staff, medical patients, consumers, and vendors. The type of data they collect and maintain is widespread, including sensitive research, financial, medical, employment, personal, and tax data. The universities are not only institutions of higher learning institutions but also financial institutions, medical institutions, and retail establishments, and they are subject to state and international regulations related to those industries (Ulven & Wangen, 2021). Bongiovanni (2019) describes universities as open, multi-modal platforms whose organizational complexity can potentially increase vulnerability to information security breaches. This culture of openness is a crucial contributor to the sector's peculiar security challenges as it contradicts conventional security frameworks characterized by centralized governance and rigid architectures (Fouad, 2021). As an open-by-design sector, higher education appears to be uniquely positioned to balance access and security, whereas most other sectors would prioritize security and restrict access. On the one hand, the online resources of universities can be accessed by a huge number of partners and collaborators beyond institutional and geographical boundaries (Fouad, 2021).

Due to this open culture of HLIs, sensitive information on employees and students, financial and personal details, confidential medical records, and profitable research, colleges and universities have become high-value targets for cyber hackers (Yaokumah & Dawson, 2019). Ulven and Wangen (2021) noted that higher learning institutions store thousands of pieces of information from each student, faculty, and staff member, including bank accounts, addresses, school transcripts, and other valuable data. The PII (Personal Identifiable Information) processed in Higher Learning Institutions can include information about applicants, students, employees, guests, alumni, and participants in research projects. Students' PII includes email ID, contact number, financial information, and records; admission, examination, administration details, and employee PII are assets Ulven and Wangen, (2021) cited as critical for cybersecurity, making bulk PII on staff and students are typical targets of a cyberattack. Figure 1 shows the personally identifiable information about students and employees processed for multiple purposes at a university.

Figure 1. Overview of breached data record types (y-axis) and percentages (x-axis) approximate n = 1150

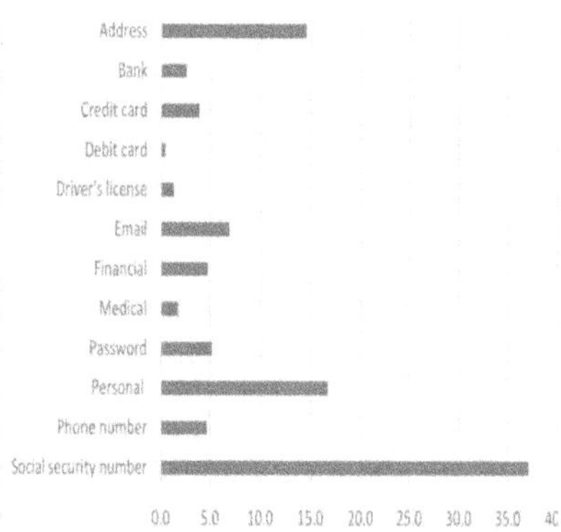

(Ulven & Wangen, 2021)

Ahmed et al. (2023) noted that many universities had reported high rates of cyber-attacks, with the information systems of these institutions being particularly vulnerable. Cybercriminals have increasingly targeted higher learning institutions since the COVID-19 Pandemic, where almost all life activities were forced to become digital (Alzighaibi, 2021). Moreover, universities have increased their reliance on digital technology to execute their core operations and functionalities, increasing their exposure to cyber threats and unprecedented security risks. Higher Learning Institutions are becoming increasingly technologically advanced and data-driven (Prinsloo & Kaliisa, 2022). However, technology adoption and use bring notable benefits, new opportunities, and inherent risks. Further, the study by Njoroge (2021) indicated that over 36 percent of the Universities in the United Kingdom were affected by cyber-attacks on an hourly basis and that many of the hacking attacks were targeting the student exam results, intellectual property theft and exfiltration of the research data.

Cyber threats can also exacerbate financial pressure on higher education even when no ransoms are paid. A security report conducted by IBM in 2020 shows that the cost of data breaches in education accounts for $3.90 million, higher than sectors like transportation, communication, and retail and higher than the global average of $3.58 million (Fouad, 2021). These financial losses can result in reputational damages and affect universities' ability to secure funding from private entities. Yaokumah and Dawson (2019) state that data breaches may result in potential direct financial costs, including legal representation, fines, and the expense of notifying affected individuals.

STATE OF CYBERSECURITY ATTACKS ON ACADEMIC INSTITUTIONS

Higher Learning Institutions have become a prime target for cyber-attacks due to invaluable user information, computing resources, instrument designs, proprietary compounds, and personal communications. According to a study by Kaur (2023), the rapid pace of technological change and innovation and the rapidly evolving nature of cyber threats further complicate the situation. Carnegie Mellon University's Computer Emergency Response Team (CERT, 2019), the availability of automated tools capable of launching sophisticated attacks is increasing. As a result, the technical knowledge the attacker needs to launch the attacks does not need to be as high. According to research, the defender's capabilities have also increased due to the availability of better tools. Lallie and Titis (2023) noted that university networks are extraordinarily complex, with tens of thousands of users logging on daily using various personal devices, hosting a range of cyber security protections. In addition, users log on from a wide range of locations and have a wide range of motivations for accessing the data that they do. This technical landscape creates more accessible opportunities for perpetrators to launch cyber attacks, mainly targeting people in jobs that have access to strategic or confidential data.

A 2019 university phishing attack resulted in a cost of £65,000 related to staff response time and high legal expenses; a 2020 phishing campaign against a UK college led to recovery costs of £30,000; a 2020 password compromise led to a response cost of £40,000; another 2020 password compromise led to around 1,000 accounts compromised and about 80 days of response effort. These figures do not include the opportunity cost created by the redeployment of staff and resources, which might not otherwise have been expected to have been applied, nor the time lost for end users (Lallie & Titis, 2023).

According to Alzighaibi (2021), in June 2019, the Australian National University was a victim of a cyber-attack, targeted for its payroll and personal information dating back to nineteen years. As such, cybersecurity is a risk management function in all sectors. In 2020, Northumbria University canceled exams, and Newcastle University's IT system in the UK was offline for weeks due to cyberattacks (Fouad, 2021) Likewise, in April 2021, attacks on two of Ireland's top colleges, the National College of Ireland and Technological University Dublin, hindered students and staff from accessing library services, the learning management system, and the entire on-site IT system for days, resulting in postponing classes and assessments (Fouad, 2021).

Badamasi & Utulu (2021) Cited the Denial of Service (DoS) attack in which an unknown person abused the Network Time Protocol (NTP) server at the Federal University of Technology Akure, Nigeria. Madonna University in Eastern Nigeria also reported that hackers accessed and tempered over 25,000 data in their database (Egbunike, 2019). In 2016, 2017, and 2018, Ahmadu Bello University, Zaria, Nigeria, disclosed incidents that potentially exposed a severe breach of the university website that compromised student and staff data (Badamasi & Utulu, 2021). A cyber security report for Kenya uncovered the hacking of the Twitter handle for the University of Nairobi and web defacements. The rise of cyber-attacks directed at Kenyan universities to tamper with students' grades, fee balances, and records of students and employees was recorded (Macharia Njoroge, 2021). The hack against the University of Yale in the US was discovered in 2018, in which personal information, social security numbers, and addresses of 119,000 students and staff were at risk (Fouad, 2021).

These examples demonstrate how cyber security is a critical defensive maneuver and a strategic decision that may increase an organization's competitive advantage. Furthermore, they emphasize the growing need to develop economic models to assess cyber risk and derive insights on investing in measures to mitigate it (Tsiodra et al., 2023).

Although these increasing cyber incidents create an apparent intellectual demand for investigating cybersecurity in the Higher Learning Institutions sector as an area of research and policy analysis, it is not currently getting as much attention as other sectors like banking and finance, manufacturing, and healthcare (Fouad, 2021). As a result, higher learning institutions and universities should learn from prior hacking scenarios in Higher Learning Institutions services and be prepared to fight against any potential cyberattacks that may target their digital, computer-based systems and begin strengthening security at all levels: technical, physical, and administrative (Aborujilah et al., 2024).

CYBER ATTACK TYPES IN HIGHER LEARNING INSTITUTIONS

Cyber Security threats are any digital activity that could threaten content integrity or endanger access to data and users' privacy (Yousif Yaseen, 2022). Cyber threats to Higher Learning Institutions IS and data come from various common attack vectors, including deliberate threats (e.g., ransomware attacks) and accidental acts (e.g., unintentional disclosure by an employee).

Higher learning institutions are rich in population and private data that attract substantial amounts of various forms of attack. (Yusif & Hafeez-baig, 2023) describe universities as "loosely coupled systems", thus open, making them susceptible to all sorts of physical attacks, necessitating a balance between openness and safety. Like other organizations, Higher Learning Institutions are vulnerable to various types of cyberattacks. These attacks can target sensitive data, intellectual property, financial information, and the overall integrity of academic and research activities. Higher Learning Institutions house large and critical biographical and financial data and data on cutting-edge research and development of emerging and new technologies (Yusif & Hafeez-Baig, 2023). The Higher Learning Institutions are highly concerned about cybersecurity, particularly in this post-pandemic period. Higher education institutions had accumulated enormous amounts of data from professors, staff, and students even before the pandemic (Pillay & Sharma, 2022). The types of attacks and threats on the security of information systems also vary, both from within the institution and from outside (Mantra et al., 2020). Cyberattacks on higher learning institutions can take various forms, each with unique characteristics and impacts. The category of the attacks includes Technical Challenges, Human Factors Challenges, Governance and Compliance Challenges, Emerging Threat Landscape Challenges, and Cultural and Organizational Challenges:

TECHNICAL CHALLENGES

Technical challenges in cybersecurity within Higher Learning institutions are multifaceted due to the complex nature of their IT environments and the evolving threat landscape. Addressing these technical challenges requires a holistic approach, including implementing robust security architectures, leveraging advanced security technologies, adopting best practices frameworks (e.g., NIST Cybersecurity Framework), and fostering a culture of security awareness and collaboration within the Higher Learning Institutions communities.

i. Internal Threats

Internal threat is a critical security problem. Intimidation of intrinsic persons may be presented inadvertently or intentionally by injured persons. Internal threats are defined as threats posed by a person who has authorized access privileges and knowledge of an organization's computer systems and is inspired to affect the organization adversely.

Ndeda et al. (2019) noted that insider threats are characterized by employees deliberately attacking organizational cyberspace assets. High-level access users, for example, system, such as administrators, look for system loopholes to gain unauthorized access, ride on other users' access privileges without their authority to attack the organizational systems for several reasons ranging from disgruntlement, revenge, and blackmail (Ndeda et al., 2019).

ii. Identity and Access Management (IAM)

Effective identity and access management (IAM) enables open interaction between an institution's students (Uddin & Preston, 2015). The identity access management concept is evolving. Managing user identities and controlling access to systems and data is challenging in large, dynamic higher learning institutions. Proper authentication, authorization, and identity lifecycle management are critical for preventing unauthorized access and data breaches. IAM is an essential component of cybersecurity in universities, ensuring secure access to resources, protecting sensitive data, and maintaining compliance with regulations. By implementing robust IAM strategies and technologies, universities can strengthen their cybersecurity posture and safeguard their academic and administrative environments (Uddin & Preston, 2015).

Addressing IAM challenges requires a comprehensive approach that includes implementing robust IAM policies and technologies, conducting regular access reviews and audits, providing user training and awareness programs, and fostering collaboration among the university's IT, security, and academic departments.

iii. Cloud Security

Many HLI leverages cloud services for storage, collaboration, and computing resources. Securing cloud environments involves challenges such as data encryption, access control, configuration management, and ensuring the security of cloud provider services.

HUMAN FACTORS CHALLENGES

i. Phishing Attacks

Al and Stefano (2022) define phishing as a typology of cyber-attacks heavily grounded in social engineering, where an attacker sends a malicious message to trick the victim into performing a specific action. Phishing is a problem that affects colleges and institutions frequently. Phishing attacks are performed by sending forged emails from an authentic entity looking legitimate to a victim or a group of victims (Salahdine et al., 2021). In a phishing attack, the hacker will assume the identity of a reliable source and take advantage of that relationship to coerce the user into disclosing personal data like passwords or even social security numbers (Pillay & Sharma, 2022). Social engineering attacks can cost organizations more than 100,000 USD per instance (Alsulami et al., 2021). Phishing exploits the victim's lack of knowledge about technology or inattention to presented information.

Figure 2. Complexity and dimensions of phishing attacks

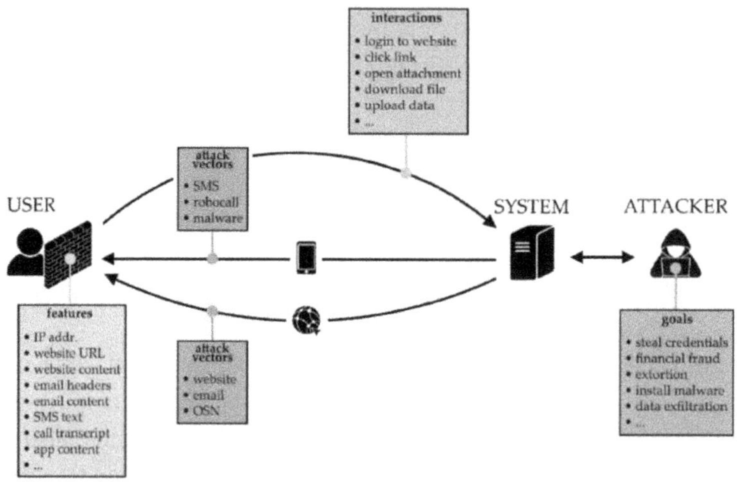

(Al & Stefano, 2022)

ii. Insider Attacks

An insider attack occurs when an individual who has authorized access to the university's systems and data intentionally or unintentionally causes harm. Lallie and Titis (2023) pointed out that having a unique level of institutional access, students may present a particular type of threat either as targets of phishing attacks or for deliberate malicious reasons such as viewing and altering grades, playing pranks, testing their hacking abilities, or carrying revenge. The literature discusses incidents of student grade manipulation, such as attacks at Austin's Business School and incidents in Kenyan colleges where some students' outstanding fees were changed (Maranga, 2019). Moreover, a student compromised over 3,300 accounts at the University of Alberta, whereas an insider at Rutgers University took down the institution's central authentication server that maintained the gateway portal to deliver assignments and assessments (Lallie & Titis, 2023).

EMERGING THREAT LANDSCAPE CHALLENGES

The growth and sophistication of cybersecurity threats, encompassing techniques such as ransomware, malware, DoS, and DDoS assaults, persistently provide significant challenges (Jony & Hamim, 2024).

i. Ransomware

Yusif and Hafeez-baig (2023) define Ransomware as "malicious software that, once loaded on a victim system, encrypts the hard drive and issues a warning that unless a ransom is paid within 24–48 hours, all the data will become unrecoverable." Hackers use Ransomware to target colleges and universities because they retain valuable student data and conduct important high-level research (Pillay & Sharma, 2022). Ransomware has three main core stages: infection and distribution vectors, data encryption, and ransom demand. All ransomware variants follow these three fundamental phases, but different Ransomware may use a different implementation or incorporate more processes.

Cyber attacks against universities have been increasing in recent years, with the average cost of addressing a cyber attack amounting to £620,000 in 2021 (Lallie & Titis, 2023). The most significant rise in cyber attacks has come from ransomware attacks. Ransomware attacks first occurred in 1989 in the healthcare domain, and it was estimated that WannaCry infected an estimated 10,000 organizations with 200,000 computers in more than 150 countries via phishing emails and a user visiting a malware-infected website (Yusif & Hafeez-Baig, 2023).

Although law enforcement does not encourage, endorse, nor condone the payment of ransom demands, several universities have reported paying cybercriminals to unlock their systems, such as Maastricht University in the Netherlands, paid nearly €200,000 of bitcoin to regain access to research and recover its commercial operations and the University of California, San Francisco that paid attackers $1.14 million to recover hacked data from its School of Medicine (Haque et al., 2023; Lallie & Titis, 2023; Fouad, 2021), University of Utah paying $457,000, and the University of California paying $1.14 million in 2020 (Fouad, 2021). As in Regis University's case, ransom payment does not guarantee a return to complete system restoration, which had day-to-day operational disruption for months after paying a ransom (Lallie & Titis, 2023).

It is estimated that ransomware attacks against education increased from 6 percent in 2019 to 15 percent in 2020, whereas in healthcare, they increased from 21 percent to 23 percent during the same period (Fouad, 2021). Figure 5 shows a summary of how Ransomware works. Ransomware is typically delivered through phishing emails, malicious attachments, or compromised websites. It can also be spread through malicious emails or social media links.

Figure 3. How ransomware works

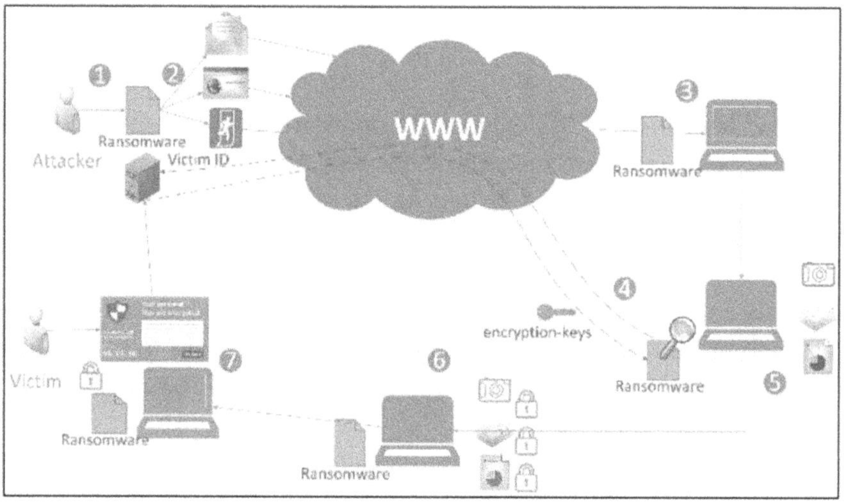

(Pillay & Sharma, 2022)

ii. Distributed Denial of Service (DDoS)

In a DDoS attack, the attacker floods a server or network with traffic or requests, overwhelming its capacity to respond to legitimate requests and causing it to crash or become unavailable to users (Haque et al., 2023). Yusif & Hafeez-Baig (2023) state that cybersecurity threats and incidents negatively impact cybersecurity infrastructure and digital assets associated with organizations and individuals and their reputations. When an institution suffers a complete network outage from a Denial of Service (DoS) attack disrupting teaching and learning, it endures a dent in its status.

DDoS attacks can disrupt a university's online systems and services, including email, websites, and learning management systems, causing significant disruption to students, staff, and faculty. In a DDoS attack, the attackers take control of a vast network of compromised computers or other devices and launch a concerted assault on the targeted system (Pillay & Sharma, 2022). According to Lallie & Titis (2023), In 2016, 63 UK universities suffered from DDoS attacks, while in 2019, DDoS attacks continued to be on the rise, with a successful attack on the University of Edinburgh making headline news. In 2021, there was a 102% increase in such attacks targeting universities, colleges, and schools, with a DDoS attack occurring every three seconds (Lallie & Titis, 2023). Figure 4 shows DDoS attack patterns between 2018 and 2023.

Figure 4. Distributed denial of service attack

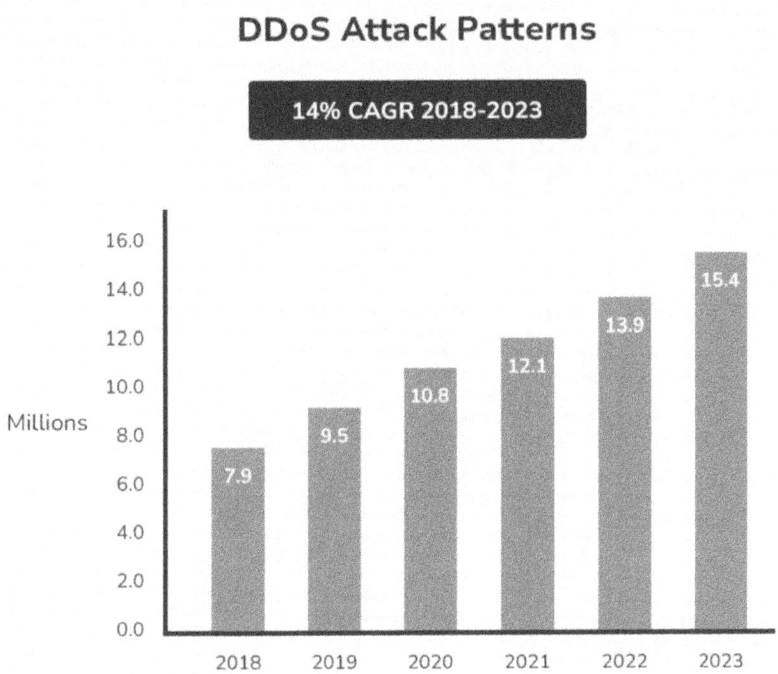

(https://www.stationx.net/ddos-statistics/)

CULTURAL AND ORGANIZATIONAL CHALLENGES:

As the leadership, organizational structures, and processes involved in the protection of informational assets, a governance approach to organizational cybersecurity has been recommended (Cheng & Wang, 2022). This approach calls for bringing cybersecurity to the attention of senior management. Besides senior management involvement, the leadership's will and attitudinal commitment are equally crucial. Additionally, leadership needs to recognize that, while cybersecurity is an integral component of IT governance, it should no longer be solely the responsibility of IT departments but the focus of institution-wide efforts. As digital technologies are strategically aligned with business strategy, the same should be done with cybersecurity (Cheng & Wang, 2022).

According to Cheng & Wang (2022), a fundamental transformation underlying and responsible for many of the changing practices has been the movement toward the "corporatization" of higher education, a rationale that, by adopting the structure and practices of the corporate world, higher education will be better able to meet its current challenges.

The cultural and organizational challenges include:

i. Institutional resilience
ii. Leadership and governance
iii. Organizational culture

Figure 5. Cyber-attacks taxonomy in higher learning institutions

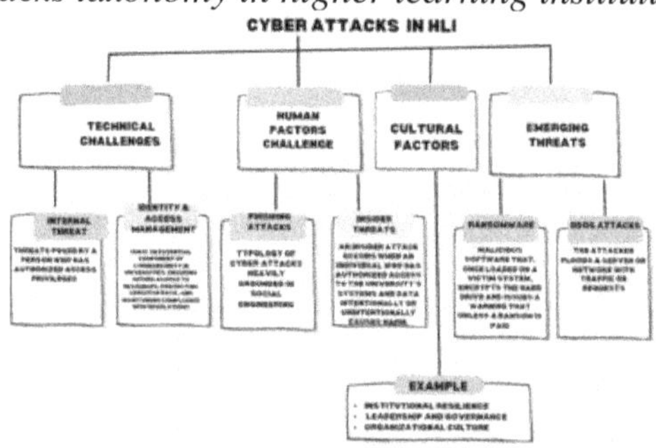

(Author)

CYBERSECURITY RISK ASSESSMENT CHALLENGES WITHIN HIGHER LEARNING INSTITUTIONS

i. Diverse IT Infrastructure

Higher learning institutions often maintain complex and heterogeneous IT environments comprising legacy systems, on-premises infrastructure, cloud services, and decentralized networks across various departments and campuses. This diversity in infrastructure introduces several challenges for cybersecurity risk assessment, making it challenging to assess and manage cybersecurity risks comprehensively.

ii. BYOD (Bring Your Own Device) Policies

Many higher education institutions allow students and faculty to use personal devices for work and study, introducing additional cybersecurity risks due to varying security standards and potential vulnerabilities in these devices.

iii. Data Protection and Privacy Compliance

Compliance with data protection regulations (such as GDPR or HIPAA) can be complex in educational settings, particularly concerning sensitive student and research data, posing risk assessment and mitigation challenges.

iv. Limited Resources

Budget constraints and limited staffing in higher education institutions may result in inadequate cybersecurity resources, hindering effective risk assessment efforts and leaving systems vulnerable to cyber threats.

v. High Volume of Users and Devices

The large number of users (students, faculty, staff) and devices (laptops, smartphones, IoT devices) connected to university networks increases the attack surface. It makes it difficult to monitor and assess risks effectively.

vi. Cybersecurity Awareness and Training

Lack of cybersecurity awareness among students, faculty, and staff can lead to inadvertent security breaches, emphasizing the need for ongoing training and education initiatives to promote a security-conscious culture.

vii. Emerging Threat Landscape

The rapidly evolving nature of cyber threats, including malware, Ransomware, phishing attacks, and zero-day vulnerabilities, presents ongoing challenges for risk assessment and mitigation strategies within higher learning institutions.

viii. Complex Regulatory Environment

Higher education institutions must navigate a complex regulatory landscape, including sector-specific regulations (e.g., FERPA for student data) and general data protection laws, requiring careful assessment of compliance requirements and associated risks.

ix. Integration of Third-Party Services

Many higher education institutions rely on third-party vendors and service providers for various IT functions, necessitating thorough risk assessments to evaluate the security posture of these external partners and ensure they meet cybersecurity standards.

To effectively mitigate risks and protect the integrity and confidentiality of university information systems, addressing these issues and implementing appropriate mitigation strategies call for a comprehensive approach to cybersecurity risk assessment. This strategy should incorporate technical solutions, policy development, staff training, and continuous monitoring.

CYBER ATTACKS MITIGATION STRATEGIES IN HIGHER LEARNING INSTITUTIONS

Organizations have introduced various security technologies, i.e., database security protection, networking security protocols, and intrusion detection methods (among others), to protect their cyber and information technology from cyber threats(Sulaiman et al., 2022). Sulaiman et al. (2022) state that poor and dangerous security practices among individuals in an organization should be identified. Mitigation efforts such as continual education and awareness are needed to prevent cyber crimes such as phishing and malware attacks on security systems resulting from human intervention.

At the personal level, various measures are available to strengthen one's cybersecurity; these include adopting antivirus software, antispyware software, cloud-based backup systems, and identity theft avoidance services. Undeniably, external factors pose the biggest threat to cyber security in HLIs. Hence, studies highlighting risk assessment practices to provide the best understanding for cyber security practitioners in the HLI that contribute to the most significant risk identification and mitigation.

i. User Awareness

By raising people's consciousness about cybersecurity issues, security awareness programs aim to make campuses safer (Pillay & Sharma, 2022). Users are taught the basics of cyber security, made more aware of potential dangers, and given guidance on protecting themselves from online attacks. The goal is to instill a culture of security compliance among students, faculty, and staff at the institution so that they think about cybersecurity whenever they use a computer or check their email. The importance of cyber awareness is highlighted in many national strategies, but promoting awareness amongst students varies. Extending the level of cyber security training to students and across more traditional courses would enhance community awareness (Lang et al., 2022).

Higher Learning Institutions experience a constant influx of students and staff each year, and they all need to be aware of the importance of maintaining safe online behaviour to avoid a cyber security breach. It is also necessary to update existing students and staff on the expected security behaviour to prevent complacency among them (Arogbodo, 2022).

Vogl (2023) argues that compromised user accounts are the origin of almost all attacks (vulnerabilities of systems that allow privileged access from outside without first having a local, unprivileged account are very rare). So, preventing users from being tricked by phishing emails or websites is critical. Additionally, Russia's war on Ukraine has led to an increase in spear-phishing activity targeting educational institutions in NATO countries (Godejord & Godejord, 2023). This situation calls attention to the need to raise awareness about personal cybersecurity. Regular drills with simulated phishing attacks can help to gauge the awareness level.

According to Godejord & Godejord (2023), Nord University in Norway is one of a few universities focusing on security and preparedness, including cyber security awareness. The university has two information security courses: one belonging to furthering education and one within the MBA-study program in Security and Preparedness Management. Both courses use computer games and online quizzes to enhance the students' understanding of cybersecurity threats.

Educating staff and students in the information security field will reduce the IT team's effort and increase cyber security through distributed efforts (Alexei & Alexei, 2021). Awareness, training, and certification are three of five solutions posited in the first version of the JISC report as mechanisms to reduce the likelihood of a cyber attack against a university, the other two being strong leadership and adherence to technical basics (Lallie & Titis, 2023).

ii. Securing the Windows Active Directory

Since the Windows Active Directory is the predominant target for attacks, it must be closely monitored for suspicious activities and potential configuration errors (Vogl, 2023). Commercial and freeware tools are available for continuous auditing of the Active Directory. An additional recommendation of Vogl (2023) is that essential infrastructures like VMware ESX/vSphere, backup systems, network management, etc, should be kept completely separated from Windows AD with their administration accounts (even if this is inconvenient) to prevent attacks from spreading to these assets.

iii. Security Patching

Timely security patching is, upon discovery or notification of a security flaw in a system or product, the release of a security update within a reasonable time that patches and updates the security of a system; sometimes this is automatic, sometimes the security patch is merely a notification that you can and should patch your system (Maurushat & Nguyen, 2022). The lack of a legal requirement to offer security support, let alone prompt security support, is one element that contributes to this. This indicates that the law does not require patching known security flaws and vulnerabilities or releasing automated updates.

The study by Alexei & Alexei (2021) also recommends updating information systems and applications, patch management, and automating these processes to ensure consistent security. Users cannot easily navigate security patching and automatic updates (Maurushat & Nguyen, 2022). Researchers at CACE (Centre for Cybersecurity Aid and Community Engagement) at Western Sydney University conducted research that analyzed automatic update functionality in operating systems, browsers, emails, and smartphones. The results demonstrate these systems' complexity and built-in assumptions (Maurushat & Nguyen, 2022).

iv. Multi-Factor Authentication

Multi-factor authentication, which combines several authentication factors such as something the user has, knows, or is, is a new state-of-the-art technology being adopted to strengthen systems' authentication security (Kimani et al., 2023). Authentication is verifying a user's process or device's identity to allow access to the system's resources.

According to (Vogl, 2023), there is a need for Mandatory multi-factor authentication for all users when accessing from outside the campus network: the common attack vector is compromised user accounts, giving attackers from the internet access to systems in the campus network from where they can scout for exploits. It is necessary to invalidate stolen credentials by mandatory multi-factor authentication for all access from outside the campus network - via VPN, accessing VDI virtual machines, and accessing Remote desktop servers. All web applications requiring login should be accessible only from the campus's internal network (Vogl, 2023).

Kimani et al. (2023) call for improving ERP authentication mechanisms to ensure tougher systems securities. OTP (one-time password) provides a solution that can quickly be established for all users, even in large communities like a university with 60,000 users. It integrates nicely with VPN Clients, VDIs, and several web-based software systems. A portal allowing users to self-service their MFA settings is mandatory here, which requires MFA protection. Ultimately, MFA only makes sense when it is not optional but compulsory for all users; otherwise, criminals can activate MFA for stolen user accounts with the users themselves potentially not noticing (Vogl, 2023).

According to Liluashvili (2021), any privileged account must be constantly monitored because cyber-criminals target administrative credentials to access high-value assets and gain more control in exposed networks.

v. Antivirus Software

Antivirus software are known as Computer programs designed to identify, stop, and eliminate harmful software, including worms and viruses. To detect new viruses as soon as they are identified, the majority of antivirus applications come with an auto-update capability that allows the program to download profiles of newly discovered infections. Every system needs antivirus software as a basic requirement.

Standalone antivirus software is no longer sufficient for cloud-based solutions gathering and consolidating threat intelligence from all institutional systems, allowing early warning of rising threat levels as the standard to adopt (Vogl, 2023).

vi. Cloud-Based Backup Systems

A study by Pillay & Sharma (2022) recommends that regular data backups are crucial to any data storage security system. Data backups can help establish which systems, applications, etc., were compromised and assist IT administrative employees in communicating relevant information to individuals impacted, even if a cyber attacker successfully retrieves data. For enhanced data protection, backups should be encrypted and stored offsite and offline when possible. Also, it supports complete system recovery and reconstitution of all devices. IT staff should perform systematic testing and evaluate the backup plan.

vii. Firewall

A firewall serves as the first line of protection for any system or network. The classification of a firewall is determined by its function (Nassoura, 2022). Create access control lists and firewalls - IT and cybersecurity personnel can provide user and investigative support more easily before, during, and after a data breach if they have easy access to control lists and firewalls (Pillay & Sharma, 2022). This technology was created to keep the internal infrastructure safe from illegal transactions and to ensure that nothing harmful could get through (Nassoura, 2022).

viii. Intrusion Detection System (IDS) and Intrusion Prevention System (IPS)

Nassoura (2022) defines IDS as an application that analyzes all network traffic entering an organization to guarantee it is not harmful. It can also be used to manage traffic and notifications to see if they are malicious or the consequence of a potentially untrustworthy cause. This method is primarily concerned with inspecting traffic to assess whether it should be approved in the first place.

IPS is a system or tool that detects and responds to unauthorized traffic detected by IDS. When a packet is flagged as unreliable by the IPS, it is meant to leave the system (Nassoura, 2022). It acts as a first line of defense, preventing hostile traffic from entering the organization's network. The IPS should ensure that all traffic seeking to access the structure complies with the organization's policies, ensuring the system's operation is not jeopardized. According to Nassoura (2022), the Network IPS resides on the edge of the higher learning institutions' networks and the internet, protecting them against harmful traffic outside the higher learning institutions. The IPS allows higher learning institutions to defend their wireless networks by providing sophisticated threat detection.

ix. Cybersecurity Risk Assessment Framework

Cybersecurity risk assessment frameworks help institutions prioritize and implement appropriate controls and measures to mitigate cyber risks and comply with relevant regulations and standards. Proactive risk management strategies anticipate and mitigate potential risks before they manifest. The background and significance of cybersecurity risk assessment in higher learning institutions highlight the transformative impact of digitalization, the evolving nature of cyber threats, and the critical role of robust risk assessment methodologies in safeguarding institutions and preserving public trust. Cybersecurity risk assessment methodologies are systematic approaches to identify, analyze, and manage potential risks to an organization's information systems and data. These methodologies provide a structured framework for evaluating the likelihood and impact of various threats, vulnerabilities, and risks. The Cybersecurity Risk Assessment Framework provides a flexible and widely adopted framework for managing and improving an organization's cybersecurity posture. It helps organizations align with industry best practices and improve cybersecurity risk management.

CONCLUSION

This research explored the cybersecurity security literature to identify ideal components of a cybersecurity posture in higher learning institutions. This information was used to develop subcomponents of the ideal taxonomy of cybersecurity risk for Higher Learning Institutions. While the amount of cybersecurity research is growing extensively, our findings show that empirical research on security practices within Higher Learning Institutions is severely lacking. The threats in higher learning institutions can exploit vulnerabilities in the administrative, technical, and physical domains, such as the lack of information security knowledge and awareness or the missing best-practice security controls.

Though the strategies listed above are not comprehensive and may not prevent every attack, they do, from a system-wide perspective, represent a relatively straightforward means that can yield significant benefits in higher learning institutions' fight against cyber threats.

Recommendations

Combining the literature review findings, we recommended the adoption of the Cybersecurity risk assessment framework within Higher learning institutions, training, workshops, seminars, media adverts on cybercrime, and multilateral cooperation and needs. Future research may empirically examine the effectiveness of the proposed strategies' applicability in higher learning institutions.

REFERENCES

Aborujilah, A., Al-othmani, A. Z., Hussien, N. S., Mokhtar, S. A., Long, Z. A., & Nizam, M. (2024). Cybersecurity Risk Assessment Approach for Malaysian Organizations : Malaysian Universities as Case Study. *2022 9th International Conference on Electrical and Electronics Engineering (ICEEE)*, 440–450. DOI: 10.1109/ICEEE55327.2022.9772546

Ahmed, A. A., Elmi, A. H., Abdullahi, A., & Ahmed, A. Y. (2023). *Cybersecurity awareness among university students in Mogadishu : a comparative study. 32*(3), 1580–1588. DOI: 10.11591/ijeecs.v32.i3.pp1580-1588

Alexei, A., & Alexei, A. (2021). Cyber security threat analysis in higher education institutions as a result of distance learning. *International Journal of Scientific & Technology Research, 10*(3), 128–133. www.ijstr.org

Alshar'e, M. (2023). *Cyber Security Framework Selection: Comparison of Nist and ISO27001. 3*(1), 245–255.

Alsulami, M. H., Alharbi, F. D., Almutairi, H. M., & Almutairi, B. S. (2021). *Measuring Awareness of Social Engineering in the Educational Sector in the Kingdom of Saudi Arabia*. 1–13.

Alzighaibi, A. R. (2021). Cybersecurity Attacks on Academic Data and Personal Information and the Mediating Role of Education and Employment. *Journal of Computer and Communications, 09*(11), 77–90. DOI: 10.4236/jcc.2021.911006

Badamasi, B., & Utulu, S. C. A. (2021). Framework for Managing Cybercrime Risks in Nigerian. *Proceedings of the 1st Virtual Conference on Implications of Information and Digital Technologies for Development,* 2021, 853–866.

Bongiovanni, I. (2019). *The least secure places in the universe? A systematic literature review on information security management in higher education*.

Cheng, E. C. K., & Wang, T. (2022). Institutional Strategies for Cybersecurity in Higher Education Institutions. *Information (Basel), 13*(4), 192. Advance online publication. DOI: 10.3390/info13040192

Farheen Ansari, M. (2022). An Effective Cybersecurity Awareness Training Model: First Defense of an Organizational Security Strategy. *International Research Journal of Engineering and Technology (IRJET), 9*(4), 1–6. www.irjet.net

Fouad, N. S. (2021). *Securing higher education against cyberthreats : from an institutional risk to a national policy challenge*. DOI: 10.1080/23738871.2021.1973526

<jrn>Hina, S., Selvam, D. D. D. P., & Lowry, P. B. (2019). Institutional governance and protection motivation: Theoretical insights into shaping employees' security compliance behavior in higher education institutions in the developing world. Computers & Security, 87, 101594. </jrn>

Jony, A. I., & Hamim, S. A. (2024). Navigating the Cyber Threat Landscape: A Comprehensive Analysis of Attacks and Security in the Digital Age. *Journal of Information Technology and Cyber Security*, *1*(2), 53–67. DOI: 10.30996/jitcs.9715

Kaur, R. (2023). *Artificial intelligence for cybersecurity : Literature review and future research directions. 97*(January). DOI: 10.1016/j.inffus.2023.101804

Lallie, H. S., & Titis, E. (2023). *Understanding Cyber Threats Against the Universities, Colleges, and Schools*. Elsevier.

Macharia Njoroge, M. P. (2021). An Examination of Threats facing Assets in Use in Kenyan Public Universities. [IJSRP]. *International Journal of Scientific and Research Publications*, *11*(5), 687–695. DOI: 10.29322/IJSRP.11.05.2021.p11372

Mantra, I. Abd. Rahman, A., & Saragih, H. (2020). Maturity Framework Analysis ISO 27001: 2013 on Indonesian Higher Education. In *International Journal of Engineering & Technology* (Vol. 9, Issue 2, p. 429). DOI: 10.14419/ijet.v9i2.30581

Maranga, J. (2019). *Emerging Issues in Cyber Security for Institutions of Higher Education. August.*

Melaku, H. M. (2023). Context-Based and Adaptive Cybersecurity Risk Management Framework. *Risks*, *11*(6), 101. Advance online publication. DOI: 10.3390/risks11060101

Ndeda, L. A., Odoyo, C. O., Systems, I., Town, B., & Town, K. (2019). Cyber Threats and Cyber Security in the Kenyan Business Context. *Global Scientific Journal*, *7*(9), 576–582.

Njoroge, P. M. (2021). An Examination of Threats facing Assets in Use in Kenyan Public Universities. *International Journal of Scientific and Research Publications*, *11*(May), 687–695. Advance online publication. DOI: 10.29322/IJSRP.11.05.2021.p11372

Pillay, A. K., & Sharma, N. A. (2022). Applicable Cyber Security Recommendations to Prevent Cyber Attacks in Universities. *2022 IEEE Asia-Pacific Conference on Computer Science and Data Engineering (CSDE)*, 1–5. DOI: 10.1109/CSDE56538.2022.10089360

Prinsloo, P., & Kaliisa, R. (2022). Data privacy on the African continent : Opportunities, challenges and implications for learning analytics. *British Journal of Educational Technology Published by John Wiley & Sons Ltd on Behalf of British Educational Research Association. 894, December 2021*, 894–913. DOI: 10.1111/bjet.13226

Salahdine, F., Mrabet, Z. El, & Kaabouch, N. (2021). Phishing Attacks Detection A Machine Learning-Based Approach. *2021 IEEE 12th Annual Ubiquitous Computing, Electronics & Mobile Communication Conference (UEMCON)*, 250–255. DOI: 10.1109/UEMCON53757.2021.9666627

Sharma, A. (2022). Review on Major Cyber security Issues in Educational Sector International Journal of Computer Sciences and Engineering Open Access Review on Major Cyber security Issues in Educational Sector. *International Journal on Computer Science and Engineering*, (January). Advance online publication. DOI: 10.26438/ijcse/v9i12.2629

Tsiodra, M., Panda, S., Chronopoulos, M., & Panaousis, E. (2023). Cyber Risk Assessment and Optimization: A Small Business Case Study. *IEEE Access : Practical Innovations, Open Solutions*, *11*(May), 44467–44481. DOI: 10.1109/ACCESS.2023.3272670

Uddin, M., & Preston, D. (2015). Systematic Review of Identity Access Management in Information Security. *Journal of Advances in Computer Networks*, *3*(2), 150–156. DOI: 10.7763/JACN.2015.V3.158

Ulven, J. B., & Wangen, G. (2021). A systematic review of cybersecurity risks in higher education. *Future Internet*, *13*(2), 1–40. DOI: 10.3390/fi13020039

Yaokumah, W., & Dawson, A. A. (2019). Network and Data Transfer Security Management in Higher Educational Institutions. *Advances in Information Security, Privacy, and Ethics*, (February), 1–19. DOI: 10.4018/978-1-5225-8455-1.ch001

Yousif Yaseen, K. A. (2022). Importance of Cybersecurity in The Higher Education Sector 2022. *Asian Journal of Computer Science and Technology*, *11*(2), 20–24. DOI: 10.51983/ajcst-2022.11.2.3448

Yusif, S., & Hafeez-baig, A. (2023). Cybersecurity Policy Compliance in Higher Education : A Theoretical Framework Cybersecurity Policy Compliance in Higher Education : A. *Journal of Applied Security Research*, *0*(0), 1–22. DOI: 10.1080/19361610.2021.1989271

Chapter 5
Securing the Future of E-Learning With Web 3.0 Technologies and Cybersecurity

Er. Kritika
https://orcid.org/0000-0002-1186-6032
Independent Researcher, India

ABSTRACT

The internet has evolved from Web 1.0 to emerging Web 3.0. E-learning platforms have revolutionized education but face security threats. As Web 3.0 technologies integrate into e-learning, new cybersecurity concerns arise. This chapter reviews Web 3.0 and cybersecurity challenges in e-learning including data privacy, smart contract vulnerabilities, and malware. An experimental approach evaluates real-world issues in Web 3.0 e-learning. Results show decentralized technologies enhance privacy and security but vulnerabilities must be mitigated through controls and audits. User awareness is critical. A multifaceted strategy encompassing strong safeguards, training, and collaboration is required to address the cybersecurity landscape of Web 3.0-enabled e-learning. As technologies advance, cybersecurity must remain a priority to develop resilient platforms. This bridges the academic-practical gap.

INTRODUCTION

The way we approach learning and the distribution of knowledge has changed dramatically as a result of technology's incorporation into the educational system. Because they give students flexible and accessible learning possibilities, e-learning

DOI: 10.4018/979-8-3693-2973-3.ch005

platforms have become an essential component of modern education. To maintain the integrity and security of these virtual learning environments, new cybersecurity issues have been brought about by the growth of e-learning, as is the case with any technical development. A variety of issues are covered by cybersecurity in e-learning, such as the preservation of intellectual property, system vulnerability, and data privacy. A major concern associated with e-learning systems is the possibility of unapproved access to private student and school information. malicious actors might try to take advantage of system flaws to get personal data, academic records, or even financial data (Alotaibi, 2020). As a result, e-learning platforms must implement robust security measures, such as encryption, access control mechanisms, and regular security audits, to safeguard the confidentiality and integrity of data. Intellectual property protection is a crucial component of cybersecurity in e-learning. A multitude of educational resources, such as course materials, lectures, and tests, are frequently available on e-learning platforms. Copyright violation and possible legal repercussions may result from unauthorized access to or dissemination of these content (Mohammadi et al., 2020). Strong security measures, such watermarking and digital rights management (DRM) programs, can help reduce these risks and guarantee that intellectual property is properly attributed and protected.

Moreover, the increasing use of online tests and assessments in virtual learning environments raises significant security issues. Maintaining the legitimacy and credibility of the educational process depends on ensuring the authenticity and integrity of these evaluations (Apampa et al., 2020). To stop cheating, impersonation, and other types of academic dishonesty, strategies like biometric authentication, remote proctoring, and secure browser environments can be used. The systems and infrastructure that underpin these platforms are likewise covered by cybersecurity in the e-learning space. Malware infections, distributed denial of service (DDoS) attacks, and other cyberthreats might interfere with the availability and operation of e-learning platforms, possibly seriously impairing the educational process (Alotaibi, 2020). Strong network security protocols, frequent software upgrades, and incident response procedures can all assist reduce these risks and ensure the continuity of e-learning operations. In recent times, there has been a significant disruption in the e-learning landscape due to the swift advancements in technology and the increasing demand for digital learning solutions. However, this modification has resulted in new cybersecurity challenges. For a considerable amount of time, traditional e-learning systems have been under attack from various cyberthreats, including malware outbreaks, phishing efforts, and data breaches. Phishing attempts(Kritika, 2024), for example, sometimes target teachers and students by seeming to be reliable emails or websites in order to steal personal data or login credentials. However, systemic flaws can lead to data breaches, which can result in unauthorized access to vast amounts of private data.

Comprehensive cybersecurity measures are required for e-learning platforms in order to overcome these obstacles. According to Mohammedi et al. (2020), this method should include technical controls, organizational rules, user awareness, and education in a multi-layered manner. Security coding techniques, intrusion detection and prevention systems, and firewalls are examples of technical measures that can be used to stop and identify cyberattacks. To provide a uniform and well-coordinated approach to cybersecurity, organizational rules and procedures should clearly outline expectations for data handling, access control, and incident response. Additionally, preserving a secure e-learning environment depends greatly on user knowledge and education. Apampa et al. (2020) state that education and training are necessary for administrators, teachers, and students to identify possible cyberthreats, handle data and passwords according to best practices, and report questionable activity right once. Via fostering a culture of cybersecurity awareness, e-learning institutions can empower their communities to become active participants in maintaining a secure and trusted learning environment. Web 3.0 technologies offer transformative potential for e-learning by providing more secure, transparent, and efficient systems. However, they also introduce new challenges and vulnerabilities, such as smart contract bugs, the complexity of managing decentralized identities, and the difficulty of regulating data flows in decentralized networks.

Web 3.0 technology integration in e-learning signifies a paradigm shift in the management and delivery of digital education, not just a technical advancement.

1. WEB 3.0: A COMPREHENSIVE EXPLORATION OF THE NEXT GENERATION WEB

The evolution of the World Wide Web has been nothing short of transformative, transitioning from the static Web 1.0 to the interactive Web 2.0, and now ushering in the era of Web 3.0, also known as the decentralized web (Frivold et al., 2023; Xu et al., 2024). This new iteration of the internet promises a more open, transparent, and user-centric ecosystem built on blockchain technology, decentralized applications (dApps), and advanced security protocols. The World Wide Web has undergone a transformational growth from web 1.0 to web 3.0 in the way people communicate, interact with information, and do business. Timothy John Berners-Lee suggested a distributed textual system known as the Web, which kicked off the first phase (Goel et al., 2022). This system had static pages that allowed users to carry out basic tasks based on the graph and link organisation method that became easier to use and much more adaptable. Proposed in a brain-stream forum, the second-generation Web, or Web 2.0, offered new technologies including the document object model, asynchronous JavaScript and XML, Cascading Style Sheets, and JavaScript object notation.

Using this, people could now produce and publish different kinds of content to the internet, which is why interactivity is essential to Web 2.0 design. The maturation of social media platforms, music and video websites, and online business platforms has impacted the creative passion of young people. However, Web 2.0 platforms collect users' data as much as possible and maximize their revenue, leading to confusion about how and for what their information will be used. The Web 3.0 era, also known as the era of the semantic web or the Decentralised Web, is already emerging (Gan et al., 2023). Drafting the concept of an increasingly intelligent, decentralised, and user-centric internet, this thorough investigation explores the fundamental ideas, potential technological advances, current trends, and possible ramifications of Web 3.0. Web 3.0 is built on user-generated content and user-generated authority, giving individuals the ability to manage the information that is visible to other users and platforms. Blockchain (Lacity & Lupien, 2022) technology is renowned for introducing a new model of organisation governance, known as decentralisation, providing for a more transparent architecture, decentralized, and aims to create a more intelligent web that emphasizes machine understanding of human semantic expression. Ethereum co-founder Gavin Wood believes that centralized services cause corporate monopolies, and the next Web flood will change the status of Web 2.0 (Gan et al., 2023). Table 1 highlights the comparison between web 1.0, web 2.0 and web 3.0. Web 3.0, also known as the "Decentralised Web" or the "Semantic Web," is the next wave of internet technology, distinguished by increased intelligence, decentralisation, and interactivity. By integrating cutting-edge technologies like blockchain, smart contracts, and decentralised applications (dApps), Web 3.0 seeks to create a more intelligent and autonomous internet experience than its predecessor, Web 2.0, which concentrated on user-generated content and social media.

Blockchain: A decentralised ledger system that uses cryptographic techniques to guarantee data integrity and security, blockchain technology is the foundation of Web 3.0. Blockchain technology can be utilised in e-learning to securely verify credentials, making academic achievements and certificates tamper-proof and verifiable.

Smart contracts are self-executing agreements that have the provisions of the contract explicitly encoded into the code. Smart contracts automate and enforce the execution of agreements without the need for intermediaries. In the context of e-learning, they can streamline processes such as course registration, payments, and content licensing.

Decentralized Applications (dApps): Unlike traditional applications, dApps operate on a decentralized network, reducing the risk of single points of failure and enhancing data security. They can offer personalized learning experiences by securely managing user data and preferences.

Web 3.0 technologies offer transformative potential for e-learning by providing more secure, transparent, and efficient systems. However, they also introduce new challenges and vulnerabilities, such as smart contract bugs, the complexity of managing decentralized identities, and the difficulty of regulating data flows in decentralized networks.

Table 1. Comparison between Web 1.0, Web 2.0 and Web 3.0

Parameters	Web 1.0	Web 2.0	Web 3.0
Foundation	Read only	Read-write	Portable and personal
Central focus	Organisation focus	Company focus	Individual focus
Type of Content	Home Pages	Blogs/Wikis	Live Stream/ Waves
Content focus	Owning	Sharing	Consolidating
Interaction examples	Web Forms	Web applications	Smart applications
Interactions predicted on	Directories	Tagging	User Behaviour
Advertising depends on	Banner	Interactive	Behavioural
Data	Not focussed	Controlled by mediatory	Personalised
Goal	Information sharing	Interaction	Immersion
Technologies Involved	Web and file servers, HTML	AJAX, Javascript, CSS, HTML5	Blockchain, AI, Decentralised Protocols

1.1 Components of Web 3.0

Figure 1 represents the components of web 3.0.

Figure 1. Components of web 3.0

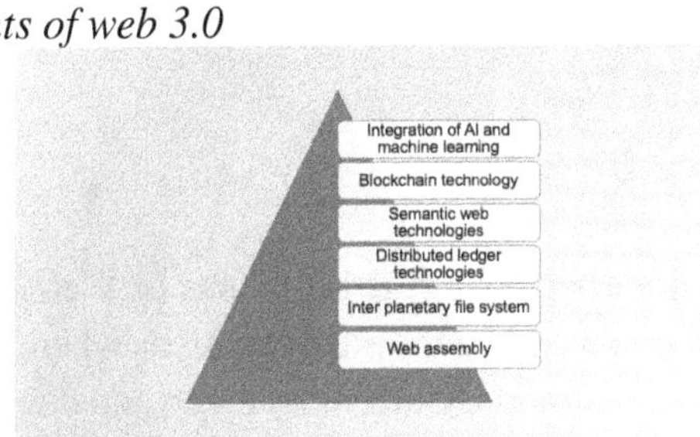

Integration of AI and Machine Learning: Web 3.0 improves user experiences by using advances in AI and machine learning woven throughout web 3.0 from engineered recommendations to automated virtual assistants and allowing systems to develop and adapt, these technologies for the provision of context-awareness and intuitive personalised services.

Blockchain Technology: It forms the foundation of Web 3.0 by introducing trust, transparency, and security in originally designing it as the backbone of cryptocurrency, a key component of decentralised apps, making it possible for agreements to be automatically executed in a transparent, tamper-proof manner using features like smart contracts.

Semantic Web Technologies: The Semantic Web is based on the ideas of machine-readable data linkage, structure, and understanding to create significant connections between data points to improve information all round. A semantic layer is created in large part by technologies like OWL (Web Ontology Language), SPARQL (Query Language for RDF), and RDF (Resource Description Framework).

Distributed Ledger Technologies: The decentralisation of Web 3.0 is facilitated by distributed ledger technologies that go beyond conventional blockchain topologies altering for building safe, distributed systems without one point of control include hash graphs, directed acyclic graphs (DAGs), and other consensus techniques providing boosts in efficiency and scalability.

Inter Planetary File System (IPFS): This system aims to overcome the drawbacks of conventional, centralised online file storage. IPFS is a content-addressable system-based decentralised file storage technology. It makes data distribution possible throughout a network of nodes, improving data retrieval efficiency, robustness, and dependability.

Web Assembly (Wasm): Web Assembly (Wasm) is a binary instruction format designed to allow web browsers to run programmes at fast speeds and overcome the constraints of conventional web programming languages by enabling developers to create apps in languages like C++ and Rust to create more potent and effective online apps.

Challenges in Web 3.0

Scalability: One major obstacle to the broad use of Web 3.0 technology is still scalability. Transaction speed and latency are two areas where blockchain networks in particular suffer from constraints. Current research and development endeavours try to tackle these obstacles by investigating layer 2 remedies, shading, and further scalability-improving methodologies.

Sustainability: The applications of web 3.0 pose a significant issue in terms of sustainability which includes energy consumption, e-waste and hardware upgrades. Transitioning to more energy-efficient consensus mechanisms and exploring layer-two scaling solutions can mitigate the environmental impact of Web 3.0. Corporate miners can mitigate the carbon footprint associated with Bitcoin mining by increasing their utilization of stable and renewable energy sources.

E-waste and hardware upgrades: Electronic waste and hardware upgrades pose another challenge to Web 3.0 applications which lead to shorter hardware life cycles and increased e-waste. Encouraging sustainable manufacturing practices, promoting recycling initiatives, and exploring alternative approaches like cloud-based computing can address these challenges.

Regulatory compliance: Legal and regulatory compliance challenges related to Web 3.0 technologies, including Blockchain and AI, are crucial that requires careful consideration of potential challenges affecting their development and adoption. These challenges include decentralized finance, distributed energy networks, and energy consumption. For example, Japan is considering legal modifications aimed at classifying bitcoin and other cryptocurrencies as currencies(Rathor et al., 2023).

User acceptance: The achievement of Web 3.0 depends on obtaining broad user acceptance. Initiatives to raise user understanding of the advantages of decentralisation, enhanced privacy, and increased control over their digital lives are required. Reducing barriers to access requires solving usability issues and designing intuitive interfaces.

Prospects of Web 3.0

Integration of the Metaverse: Web 3.0 is becoming more and more integrated with the metaverse, a communal virtual shared environment to create an easily navigable and user-controlled environment where digital assets and identities move across virtual worlds with ease. The way we interact with digital and virtual surroundings might be completely changed by this integration.

The Internet of Things (IoT): More intelligent and secure ecosystems might be produced by combining Web 3.0 and the Internet of Things (IoT) and guaranteeing data integrity and lowering vulnerabilities, decentralised networks can improve the security and interoperability of devices. This confluence gives up new opportunities for novel applications in smart cities, healthcare, and industrial processes.

Decentralised Finance: It is a rapidly evolving industry with decentralised exchanges, lending platforms, and trust-less financial instruments created with the aid of smart contracts and blockchain technology to provide financial services that are more inclusive and accessible.

Environmental Sustainability: A major topic of conversation these days is how blockchain networks' energy usage affects the environment. Future advances in Web 3.0 could concentrate on developing consensus processes that are more environmentally friendly and lowering the carbon footprint that comes with decentralised technology. This is in line with the larger worldwide objectives of reducing climate change and encouraging environmentally friendly alternatives.

With a focus on semantic understanding, decentralisation, and interoperability, represents a dramatic change in the development of the World Wide Web ushering in a new era of increased security, inventive apps, and user empowerment vitalising necessity for ethical concerns, developing regulatory frameworks, and resolving problems. A promises to redefine information exchange, commerce, and virtual places by creating a more intelligent, decentralised, and user-centric internet by envisioning a day where openness, inclusiveness, and personal empowerment are reflected in a dynamic networked ecosystem.

1.2 Cyber Security: Safeguarding the Digital Realm

The critical field of cybersecurity protects digital networks, systems, and data from data breach, unauthorised access, and malicious intention(Kritika, 2023). Threat actors may take advantage of the weaknesses in digital platforms as our dependence on them increases urging the need of cybersecurity to act as a barrier to keep people, businesses, and countries safe from the constantly changing world of online dangers. In order to guarantee the availability, confidentiality, and integrity of digital information, a comprehension of wide range of procedures, tools, and regulations is vital. Computer science, information technology, risk management, and legislation are all combined in the interdisciplinary discipline of cybersecurity to provide a strong defence against online attacks. It is crucial to comprehend and use efficient cybersecurity techniques to secure from breach from financial as well as reputational damage as well as securing national security infrastructure. Cybersecurity refers to the automation and delineation of measures to prevent theft, vandalism, and unauthorised access to systems, websites, programmes, and information on a personal, confidential, or public basis(Sarkar et al., 2020). Protecting the CIA triad—confidentiality, integrity, and availability of the data which is the core tenet of the resolve(Lodh & Dalave). Figure 2 represents the key components of cybersecurity.

Figure 2. Key components of cybersecurity

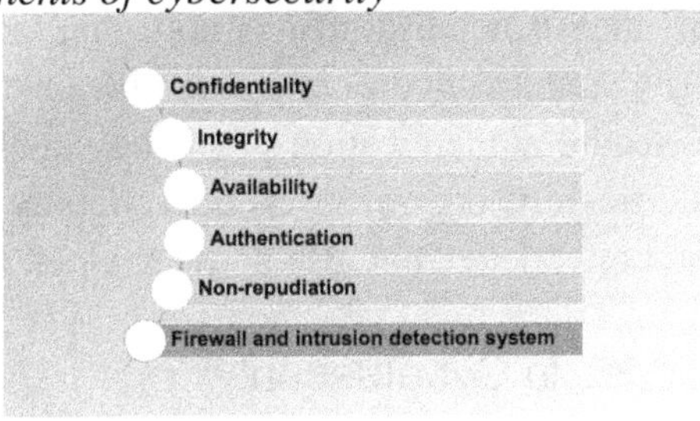

Key Components of Cybersecurity

Confidentiality describes the ability of authorised persons to disclose and alter information. It is possible for confidentiality to be violated inadvertently or maliciously. A direct breach of duty might take the shape of securing prohibited entry into software systems, prosecution, or confidential credentials of an organization's assets with the intention of stealing or tampering with the data. Inadequate safeguards, carelessness, or inadvertent intents are all considered causes.

Integrity frequently implies that the data or information is unadulterated and unaltered, necessitating its reliability. It can be resolved by direct attack employing different threat trajectories, disregard, or pathetic security procedures.

Availability often refers to the capacity for authorised workers to access the information upon request. However, this accessibility can frequently be impeded by denial-of-service attacks, power outages, unanticipated disasters, or malicious web application breaches.

Authentication is preventing unwanted access requires people and systems to have their identities verified. To guarantee that only authorised users are granted access, multi-factor authentication, passwords, and biometrics are employed.

Non-repudiation is the concept makes sure that the sender cannot dispute the message's origin or its integrity. Audit trails and digital signatures are often employed methods for proving non-repudiation.

Firewall and Intrusion Detection Systems (IDS) is an essential component of modern day cybersecurity strategies, aims to protect networks from unwarranted access, malicious activities, and potential security threats, acting as a barrier between trusted internal networks and outlawed external networks by monitoring and controlling incoming and outgoing network traffic based on agreed security rules which can be implemented at various levels such as network level for filtering traffic based on IP addresses whether to allow or disallow and application level which inspect and filter traffic at the application layer.

When an IDS detects suspicious activity, it generates alerts or takes predefined actions, such as blocking the suspicious traffic or notifying security administrators. A comprehensive security strategy incorporates multiple layers of defense, including antivirus software, secure authentication practices, regular software updates, and user education. Additionally, organizations often deploy Intrusion Prevention Systems (IPS), which not only detect but also actively block malicious activities.

Multifaceted Challenges in Cybersecurity

Advanced Persistent Threat (Alshamrani et al., 2019) is defined by three words: advanced, persistent, and threat is a type of cyber attack that involves a group of advanced attackers, often well-funded by an organization or government, who use advanced tools and methods to gain confidential information about their target. Advanced attackers are well-funded and have access to advanced tools and methods, including multiple attack vectors. Persistent attackers are highly determined and persistent, planning evasive techniques to evade detection by their target's intrusion detection systems. They follow a "low and slow" approach to increase their success rate. The attackers pursue their objectives repeatedly over an extended period, adapt to defenders' efforts to resist them, and maintain the level of interaction needed to execute their objectives which includes establishing footholds, internal network scanning, and moving laterally.

Zero-day attacks (Guo, 2023) exploit vulnerabilities not disclosed publicly or employ novel tactics to avoid detection by existing detection tools often targeting while remaining unrecognized. A typical zero-day attack lasts 312 days before being detected, and the volume of attacks increases by up to five orders of magnitude after vulnerabilities are disclosed publicly. An "in the wild" zero-day attack is discovered every 17 days, and it takes 15 days on average to develop a patch for the vulnerability exploited by active attacks. A recent study by the Ponemon Institute concluded that 80% of security breaches are derived from zero-day attacks, with an average incurred cost of 1.2 million dollars per attack. Cyberattack detection systems are traditionally classified into signature-based detection systems, deployed in operational environments to detect known attacks with high precision and recall whereas anomaly-based detection systems identify abnormal or unexpected behavior within a system or network by establishing a baseline of normal behaviour and raise alerts when deviations occur.

Cloud service providers (CSPs) (Akbar et al., 2023) have data centers in different geographical locations, presenting security issues and dangers to consumers. Conventional security measures like host-based antivirus, firewalls, and intrusion detection technologies do not provide sufficient security in server virtualization. Crypto-cloud architecture which involves three primary components, namely, the data's owner (Data Authority), the data's end user (consumer), and the Cloud Storage Service Provider (CSSP) has several advantages but also security hazards, such as potential damage to data privacy and authenticity.

Supply Chain threats (Sharma et al., 2023), the globalized nature of modern supply chains has brought about unprecedented efficiency and interconnectedness, but has also introduced significant vulnerabilities that can be exploited by malicious actors manifested at various stages, posing threats to the security, integrity, and resilience of the entire ecosystem that lead to product failures, security vulnerabilities, and safety risks. The dependency on third-party entities, supply chain attacks, software and firmware risks, counterfeit components, regulatory compliance challenges, physical security risks, lack of transparency, globalization and complexity, communication weaknesses, and insufficient due diligence are some of the challenges faced by organisations (Gupta et al., 2023). The implementation of strict vendor and supplier management procedures, conducting thorough risk assessments, utilising blockchain technology to improve transparency, adhering to industry-specific security standards and regulatory compliance, creating and routinely testing disaster recovery plans, continuous monitoring, diversifying suppliers, and educating and training supply chain stakeholders are some of the mitigation strategies to be applied by professionals.

Awareness and training are crucial for building a resilient defense against cyber threats such as changing threat landscape, employee engagement, limited time and resources, lack of personalisation and much more. However, organizations often face challenges in implementing comprehensive and impactful programs.

To address these challenges, organizations should regularly update training content, engage employees, prioritize key cybersecurity topics, leverage cost-effective online platforms, and integrate training into existing onboarding processes. Customize training programs based on employees' roles, responsibilities, and specific cybersecurity risks, and consider cultural nuances when offering diverse learning formats. Technological advancements can outpace organizations' ability to keep training content up-to-date, so organizations should implement a continuous learning culture, encourage employees to stay informed about technological changes, and provide resources for ongoing education. Resistance to change is another challenge, as employees may resist changes in security policies and practices. Organizations should communicate the importance of cybersecurity, address concerns proactively, and involve employees in decision-making processes to foster a sense of ownership.

Remote work challenges can also be addressed by utilizing virtual training platforms, conducting regular awareness sessions, and tailoring content to address specific remote work-related security concerns. Measuring behavioral change in response to training can be challenging, but simulations, periodic assessments, and real-world incidents can help gauge the effectiveness of training in influencing behavior.

1.3 E-Learning

The advent of electronic learning (e-learning) has revolutionized the way knowledge is accessed and disseminated in the 21st century. E-learning platforms offer numerous advantages, including flexibility, accessibility, cost-effectiveness, interactive learning, and global collaboration (Khamparia & Pandey, 2020). However, these platforms also face challenges such as technological barriers, lack of face-to-face interaction, quality assurance, and motivational difficulties (Fayomi & Sani, 2023).

The inception of electronic learning or e-learning has significantly mutated the way individuals access information and acquire knowledge in the 21st century. It has a rich history dating back to the 1960s, with its seeds deep rooted in computer-based learning flourished in 1990s with the spread of availability of the internet evolved with the emergence of interactive platforms, multimedia tools and high speed internet. The transition from traditional classroom-based education to online learning platforms marked a paradigmatic change in educational delivery methods which has evolved from simple text-based courses and basic multimedia elements to a diversity of formats, including audio-video lectures, virtual classrooms, simulations, and gamified content. With the increasing accessibility of computers in the late 20th century, the term "e-learning" gained popularity with the initialisation of digitised instructional materials on virtual platforms(Martinez et al., 2023). There are various advantages offered by e-learning platforms, namely:

Flexibility and Accessibility: Geographical and demographical obstacles are eliminated since learners may access instructional materials from nearly any location with an internet connection providing schedule flexibility, enabling students to acquire knowledge at their own convenience and pace.

Cost-Effectiveness: Since e-learning does not require physical infrastructure, typical classroom expenses like building upkeep and utilities are reduced providing affordability to large number of individuals regardless of their financial income.

Interactive Learning: To actively include students, contemporary e-learning systems make use of multimedia components, simulations, and interactive information. By improving understanding and retention, this participatory method makes learning more efficient and pleasurable.

Global cooperation: Students from all around the world may communicate and work together on projects thanks to e-learning, which promotes global cooperation. This promotes inclusive and varied learning environments and gets people ready for a workforce that is more globalised.

Challenges to E-Learning

Technological Barriers: The digital divide that has been brought about by technology, made e-learning a possibility. The stark reality is not every student has equal access to gadgets, high-speed internet, or the required technological know-how.

Absence of Face-to-Face Interaction: A need to invest in innovative ways to inculcate e-learning as part of daily life to aid students develop their social skills, collaborate, and can freely ask questions and get quick responses.

Assurance of Quality: With digital learning expanding so rapidly, questions have been raised concerning the quality of online education. One of the constant issues faced by educational institutions and certifying agencies is ensuring that online courses maintain stringent academic requirements while offering accreditation for e-learning programmes.

Motivational Difficulties: Students must possess a high degree of self-control and drive to stay away from procrastination and show dedication towards the learning.

Impact of E-Learning

Educational Inclusion: The promotion of educational inclusion consistent with the overarching goals of democratising education has been greatly aided by e-learning, giving people options who otherwise may not have been able to pursue education because of geographical limitations or other obstacles.

Lifetime Learning: By offering a platform for ongoing skill improvement and knowledge growth, and in order to keep up to date in fields that are in demand, professionals may participate in online courses and receive certifications, encouraging a culture of lifelong learning.

Professional Development and Corporate Training: A lot of companies have adopted e-learning for their corporate training initiatives that is effective and economical which guarantees the skills and information required to fulfil the responsibilities of their positions from anywhere and at anytime.

Teaching Methods' Evolution: The advent of e-learning has forced a change in teaching strategies. In order to improve the learning process, educators are currently investigating cutting-edge strategies including gamification, flipped classrooms, and group projects conducted online. Traditional classrooms may benefit from this growth of teaching techniques as well.

With its affordability, customisation, and accessibility, e-learning has completely changed the educational scenario. However, for sustained expansion, concerns with quality assurance, absence of face-to-face connection, and technical impediments must be resolved. The navigating frontiers of e-learning is full of exciting possibilities as technology develops, and integrates augmented reality, virtual reality, and artificial intelligence, well-positioned to have a significant impact on how education will be delivered on global front. The chapter further navigates to challenges in e-learning via web 3.0, mitigation strategies, experimental analysis and future scope of the e-learning platforms.

2. NAVIGATING CYBERSECURITY CHALLENGES IN E-LEARNING VIA WEB 3.0

The Semantic Web, decentralised technology, and increased interconnection define Web 3.0, a paradigm change that has emerged in recent years as a result of the internet's expansion is a revolutionary phase emerging in a number of fields, including schooling, where it takes the shape of e-learning systems driven by Web 3.0. The incorporation of cutting-edge technologies presents a new range of cyber-security issues in addition to previously unheard-of possibilities for personalised and collaborative learning experiences. The security environment is becoming intricate and dynamic as more and more of schools and online platforms use distributed technologies, smart contracts, and decentralised frameworks. In this quickly changing digital world, protecting the integrity, confidentiality, and availability of educational materials requires an understanding of the possible dangers and taking appropriate action.

Web 3.0 is coming ashore, and its waves are washing over the educational beaches and calling e-learning to a brave new world. However, concealed reefs of cyberthreats exist amid the glittering promises of decentralisation and interaction. In order to continue the learning journey, this chapter delves further into this unexplored security environment, examining the perilous seas of smart contract shortcomings, data privacy storms, and Sybil assaults.

The need to successfully traverse these treacherous seas armed with strong security standards, privacy-preserving technology, and attentive user education. Our compass will be cooperation and constant innovation, leading us to a Web 3.0 e-learning paradise where information is openly and securely shared, enabling everyone to start their educational journey. Figure 3 represents the cybersecurity challenges to e-learning in web 3.0.

Figure 3. Cybersecurity challenges to e-learning

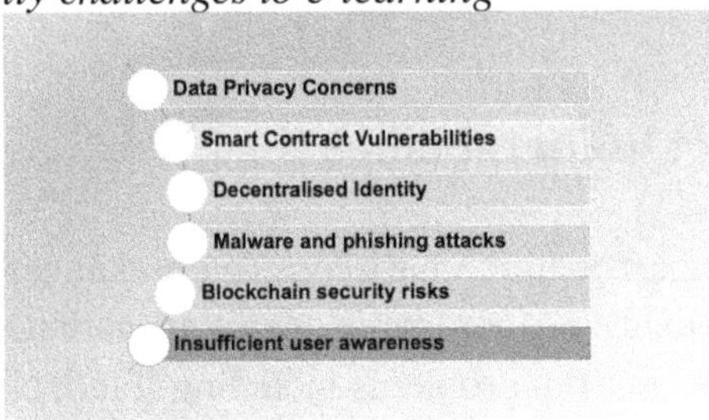

2.1 Data Privacy Concerns

With the increased collection, processing, and storage of personal data in the digital era, data privacy is a crucial problem. With its decentralisation and interactivity, the Web 3.0 is set to revolutionise education. But there are concerns about how data privacy must be balanced. With the use of tailored data analysis and artificial intelligence, it provides a personalised learning experience which offer insights into pupil participation, learning styles, and progress. Digital privacy, the right to control one's personal data, faces a myriad of challenges in this interconnected world. The proliferation of digital platforms has revolutionized communication, toiling, and socializing, but it has led to an unprecedented amount of personal data being shared and stored on various platforms, presenting a challenge in ensuring individuals retain control over their data while utilising. The pervasive collection of user data by tech giants, governments, and third-party entities raises significant concerns about digital surveillance. Striking a balance between legitimate data use for service improvement and protecting user privacy is a delicate challenge.

The erosion of anonymity poses a substantial challenge to digital privacy, as advanced tracking technologies, pervasive surveillance, and the aggregation of data across platforms make it increasingly difficult for individuals to navigate the digital realm without leaving a trace. Legal and regulatory intricacy in digital privacy is a significant challenge for businesses and individuals while navigating through a patchwork of regulations and compliance requirements. The rapid pace of technological innovation often outpaces the development of comprehensive legal frameworks, leaving gaps that may be exploited by entities with less regard for user privacy.

Due to the complexity of the issue, digital privacy requires an all-encompassing and cooperative solution. Informed consent, cybersecurity risks, data gathering, monitoring, evolving technologies, legal difficulties, and corporate accountability are all addressed. These problems are essential to establishing a safe online space where people may browse around safely and yet be in charge of their personal data. In the digital era, protecting privacy and individual liberty requires finding workable solutions.

2.2 Smart Contract Vulnerabilities

Blockchain-based smart contracts have completely changed the e-learning industry by making transactions safe, automated, and transparent. while having certain weaknesses which may result in problems including fraud, abuse, and unapproved access. It is vital to comprehend the nature of smart contracts and their possible repercussions in order to reduce these dangers. E-learning systems can guarantee user safety and security as well as the quality of the educational process by putting strong governance and security mechanisms in place. Smart contracts are frequently used by e-learning systems to validate and store academic credentials on the blockchain, which makes them susceptible to unwanted access. The integrity of educational records may be jeopardised by manipulation or forgery of these contracts. Attacks known as denial of service (DoS) have the potential to interfere with the contract's regular operation and limit the accessibility of learning materials. If instructional materials are not sufficiently protected, unauthorised access may result. Payment fraud may result in monetary losses or incorrect money distribution. Furthermore, there are privacy problems associated with smart contracts that handle student data, especially in decentralised identification systems. These contracts may violate privacy laws if personal information is unintentionally disclosed or handled improperly, jeopardising the privacy of student records.

It also results in reputational harm, monetary losses, disruptions to educational services, and compromises to academic integrity. The educational ecosystem's credibility can be damaged by fraud, unauthorised access, and credential manipulation. Unauthorised transactions, poor money management, and payment vulnerabilities can all lead to financial losses. Attacks known as denial of service (DoS) have the potential to interfere with the platform's regular operation, leading to service outages, postponed course delivery, and worse educational outcomes.

The incorporation of smart contracts into e-learning systems results in increased efficiency and transparency, but also presents special risks that need to be carefully considered. Addressing these weaknesses becomes critical as the blockchain age of education continues to change taking proactive steps like regular security audits, following best practices, and implementing strong access restrictions. Realising the revolutionary potential of smart contracts in influencing the future of online education requires striking a balance between innovation and security.

2.3 Decentralised Identity

One important aspect of blockchain technology is decentralised identification, which gives people authority over their personal data which may be used in e-learning to deliver safe and user-focused learning environments along with offering obstacles. Blockchain-based decentralised identity systems allow users to maintain their educational credentials, govern access to their personal data, and identify themselves. Although these systems might be difficult to work around, they offer a safe and dependable method of managing their data. The adoption of decentralized identity solutions in e-learning platforms presents several challenges, including interoperability issues, user adoption and education, privacy concerns, security risks, and credential standardization. The lack of standardized protocols and interoperability lead to difficulties in seamless integration and collaboration between platforms.

Users, including educators and learners, may find it challenging to adapt to new identity management processes, and educating them about the benefits and functionalities of decentralized identity is crucial for successful adoption. Balancing the transparency and immutability of blockchain with selective disclosure and confidentiality is a delicate challenge, especially in an educational context where varying levels of data disclosure may be necessary. Standardized formats and protocols for educational credentials on the blockchain are essential for consistency and compatibility across different e-learning platforms.

Frustration and disengagement resulting from the splintered user experience of e-learning systems caused by uneven standards and interoperability problems. Security flaws in decentralised identification systems can lead to data breaches that compromise personal or academic credentials that may impede resistance to adoption. Digital learning systems may find it difficult to persuade consumers to adopt the new paradigm if they are unable to clearly convey the advantages and security of decentralised identification in handling unauthorised data, privacy violations, and regulatory standards. Though its implementation necessitates cooperation from parties including e-learning platforms, universities, developers, and regulatory authorities, decentralised identity has the ability to completely transform online learning identity management with strong security measures, standardisation efforts, and a focus on user education, addressing some of its drawbacks.

2.4 Malware and Phishing Attacks

With the advent of e-learning platforms, education has undergone a transformation and has become more accessible and flexible to students all over the world making it susceptible to malware and phishing attempts, among other cybersecurity risks. Malware can damage a platform or device's security and functioning by taking different forms by means of spyware, ransomware, or viruses, and phishing attempts use trickery to deceive people into disclosing personal information.

Phishing attempts may jeopardise user credentials and let unapproved users access to e-learning environments leading to data breaches and privacy violations, revealing personal information, academic records, and communication logs, which can result in identity theft. . Malware attacks, particularly those that involve ransomware, have the potential to impede educational operations by encrypting important data or making computers unusable, resulting in the loss of priceless educational materials and interrupt the flow of instruction by unwittingly corrupting materials. Phishing attacks that target financial information instead of only e-learning platforms can potentially result in financial crime by exposing sensitive data to unapproved transactions or financial fraud.

An attentive and proactive approach is necessary given the dynamic and linked nature of e-learning platforms. The e-learning community may establish a safe and reliable online environment by being aware of the possible dangers posed by malware and phishing attempts, taking precautions, and encouraging a culture of cyber resilience. Administrators, teachers, and students all have a critical responsibility to play in protecting the virtual classroom from the constant hazards that exist online.

2.5 Blockchain Security Risks

As a ground-breaking invention with broad applications in numerous industries, blockchain technology has come to light. According to Yaga et al. (2018), a blockchain is fundamentally a distributed, decentralized digital ledger that securely and openly documents transactions. An unchangeable and impenetrable record of data can be created thanks to this cutting-edge technology, which is based on the concepts of consensus processes, peer-to-peer networking, and encryption. Blockchain technology is a series of interconnected blocks that prevents edits or deletions without discovery by creating an auditable trail of transactions connected to earlier blocks(Crosby et al., 2016). Because it is decentralized, there is no need for a central authority, which fosters confidence among users of the network. In order to avoid double-spending and preserve data integrity, consensus mechanisms like as proof-of-work or proof-of-stake algorithms make sure that all participants concur on the legitimacy of each new block. This consensus-driven method encourages accountability and transparency since it eliminates the need for substantial processing capacity or resources needed for data modification (Kshetri, N., 2018).

Blockchain technology enhances security and promotes transparency and has potential uses in government services, healthcare, finance, and supply chain management. Its tamper-proof and unchangeable characteristics make it a desirable option for high-level trust applications such as intellectual property protection, identity management, and land registry(Zheng et al., 2018). Blockchain technology has advantages, but it also has drawbacks, including scalability, energy consumption, and legal frameworks. Notwithstanding these obstacles, the potential of blockchain technology to transform sectors and foster confidence in digital transactions continues to be a motivating factor for continued study and advancement in this area.

Improvements in security, transparency, and trust within educational ecosystems are anticipated with the use of blockchain technology into e-learning platforms. It does, however, potentially bring possible security risks. These dangers are examined in this article along with their effects and mitigation techniques. Because of its decentralised structure, blockchain technology has applications in e-learning, such as transparent record-keeping and safe credential verification. It seeks to completely transform the administration, vetting, and accessibility of educational data.

Blockchain technology offers transparency but also raises privacy concerns when dealing with sensitive educational data which may expose certain information to all participants, potentially violating privacy regulations and compromising confidentiality. A 51% attack, which occurs when an entity or coalition controls the majority of the network's computing power, could compromise data integrity and disrupt the platform's normal functioning in absence of standardized protocols to securely interact and share data. Integration challenges arise when integrating blockchain technology with existing e-learning systems and infrastructure along with regulatory compliance crucial for educational institutions, as the decentralized and transparent nature of blockchain may conflict with certain privacy requirements. Scalability issues may arise as the number of transactions and users on an e-learning platform increases, leading to slower transaction times and increased vulnerability to attacks. Immutable data challenges arise when dealing with erroneous or outdated educational records, as it becomes difficult to alter or correct once recorded on the blockchain, raising concerns about the accuracy of information over time.

E-learning might be revolutionised by using blockchain technology, but it needs aggressive security precautions in order to safeguard the integrity, privacy, and continuity of virtual classrooms, educational institutions need to be aware of the dangers, put strong safeguards in place, and take part in standardisation and compliance activities.

2.6 Insufficient User Awareness

There are possibilities and problems associated with the digital revolution of education. One enduring difficulty is the lack of user education about the proper use of e-learning systems which includes tutorials and instructions necessary to inculcate the rapid advancements in technology and resistance of users to adapt. A lack of user education can be caused by a numerous factors, including scarce training resources, quick technical advancements, reluctance to change on the part of the user base, and the presumption of digital literacy.

The issue of inadequate user education must be addressed if e-learning systems are to reach their full potential. Through the identification of knowledge gaps, comprehension of their underlying causes, and use of focused tactics to overcome these gaps, educational establishments may enable teachers and students to confidently traverse the digital terrain. All stakeholders will benefit from a more efficient and interesting e-learning experience if a culture that values ongoing learning is fostered and easily accessible resources are made available.

3. MITIGATING CYBER THREATS IN E LEARNING WITH WEB 3.0 SAFEGUARDS

Web 3.0 technologies also referred to as decentralised web is transforming e-learning systems by offering cutting-edge methods for user identification, content distribution, and credential verification that call for specific mitigating techniques. Regular security audits are crucial for smart contracts, decentralized identity systems, and blockchain infrastructure engaging third-party auditors to provide an unbiased evaluation of the platform's security posture incorporated into decentralized identity systems, implementing encryption, data minimization, and user-controlled consent mechanisms. A robust scalability plan should be developed, including anticipatory measures for increased user loads. Standardization advocacy is essential within the Web 3.0 and e-learning communities, enhancing interoperability. User education and awareness programs should be implemented to empower users to identify and respond to potential threats effectively. Decentralized governance models should be implemented for e-learning platforms, enhancing transparency and fostering a more resilient ecosystem. Incident response plans should be developed and regularly updated to address Web 3.0 threats. Federated learning approaches, where machine learning models are trained across decentralized devices, can reduce the need for centralized data storage, mitigating data breaches and enhancing overall platform security. Figure 1 represents the mitigation strategies to be adopted for preventing cyber threats in e-learning platforms.

- *Code Reviews:*

Before being deployed, smart contracts may be made more secure by identifying and fixing vulnerabilities through regular, comprehensive code audits conducted by qualified experts. This preventive action is essential to safeguarding the contract's integrity and averting further exploitation.

- *Best Practices and Standardisation:*

Vulnerabilities can be minimised by adhering to best practices and recognised standards for developing smart contracts, such as Ethereum's ERC standards. Standardisation promotes uniformity and aids in developers' adherence to tested procedures.

- *Frameworks for Secure Development:*

Using safe development frameworks created especially for smart contracts might improve the code's resilience. These frameworks offer an organised approach to development and frequently have built-in security measures.

- *Gas Limit Control:*

Vulnerabilities connected to gas consumption can be avoided by careful control of gas limitations and comprehensive testing under varied scenarios. Developers ought to think about the possible effects of transaction fees and resource constraints on smart contract execution.

- *Constant Observation and Reaction:*

It is imperative to deploy real-time monitoring tools in order to identify anomalous activity or possible assaults. Furthermore, having a clear response strategy in place makes it possible to act quickly in the case of a security problem.

- *Mechanisms of Access Control:*

To guarantee that only authorised people or entities have access to private information or premium educational content, implement strong access control measures within smart contracts. Appropriate permission and authentication procedures are part of this.

- *Designing for Privacy:*

Develop smart contracts that manage student data by including privacy by design principles. To safeguard people's privacy, use data reduction, encryption, and pseudonymization techniques.

- *Plans for handling incidents:*

To effectively handle security breaches, create and update incident response strategies on a regular basis. A clear plan in place makes it possible to respond to security incidents quickly and efficiently.

- *User-Centric Instruction and Design:*

Give user-centric design concepts first priority while developing user interfaces and experiences. Additionally, spend money on educational initiatives that educate users about the advantages, safety precautions, and procedures related to decentralised identity in e-learning.

- *Cooperation & Joint Ventures:*

Encourage cooperation between educational institutions, blockchain developers, and e-learning platforms. Forming alliances may speed up the integration of decentralised identities throughout the education sector, exchange best practices, and aid in the creation of standardised solutions(Le et al., 2024).

- *Gradual Integration and Transition:*

Use a phased-in method to incorporate decentralised identification into e-learning systems. Permit users and organisations to move gradually to provide a seamless transition while preserving identity compatibility.

- *Multi-factor authentication:*

To provide an extra degree of security, e-learning systems should use multi-factor authentication methods as it requires secondary verification, it helps prevent unauthorised access even in the event that login credentials are compromised.

- *Anti-malware programmes and email filtering:*

To identify and stop phishing efforts before they get in users' inboxes, deploy email filtering technologies. Use anti-malware software to scan e-learning platform files and URLs in order to stop harmful code from running.

- *Safe File Sharing Procedures:*

Encourage people to share data securely and to only download files from reliable sources. Put limitations on the kinds of files that can be posted to the platform in order to reduce the possibility of files containing malware.

- *Planning for Scalability:*

Making sure e-learning platform is scalable from the start by using scalable blockchain technologies or putting in place safeguards against future scalability issues. Scalability plans should be periodically reviewed and updated in light of changing requirements.

- *Unchangeable Data Management:*

Establish governance protocols to manage blockchain-based immutable data. Provide procedures for confirming and updating inaccurate or out-of-date records while preserving the general security and integrity of the educational information.

- *Mechanisms of Feedback:*

Put feedback tools in place to find out what users thought about their training experiences and what needs to be improved. The creation of focused treatments and the improvement of educational programmes can both be influenced by user input.

Securing these decentralised ecosystems becomes crucial as Web 3.0 technologies embrace the revolutionary potential in e-learning. A multifaceted strategy that includes strong technological controls, user education, and cooperative efforts within the larger Web 3.0 community is needed to mitigate cyber dangers. Through proactive vulnerability management and ongoing threat detection, e-learning platforms may use the advantages of decentralisation while guaranteeing a safe and robust learning environment for all parties involved.

Blockchain's decentralized and immutable ledger system provides a secure method for storing and verifying information, making it nearly impossible for malicious actors to alter data. This is particularly beneficial for maintaining the integrity of academic records, certificates, and other critical information. Transparency and trust are also significant benefits of blockchain technology. All transactions and changes are recorded on a public ledger, providing a clear and verifiable history of events.

However, the complexity of smart contracts can introduce significant risks, as they can be exploited for unintended outcomes or financial losses. Regulation and compliance challenges arise from the decentralized nature of Web 3.0 technologies, as traditional regulatory frameworks are often not well-suited to decentralized systems, creating legal ambiguities. Additionally, decentralized platforms can be vulnerable to 51% attacks, where malicious actors gain control of the network's computing power, posing environmental concerns.

4. EXPERIMENTAL EVALUATION AND ANALYSIS

With the advent of Web 3.0 technologies, a newer age of decentralisation and user-centric experiences has begun, which holds the potentiality to completely mould into a number of industries, including distance education. In order to protect the integrity, privacy, and security of e-learning platforms and their users, the integration of these cutting-edge technology also brings with it a host of cybersecurity issues that need to be resolved. The application of Web 3.0 technologies in e-learning systems is connected with certain hazards and weaknesses, which this project aims to explore through an experimental approach. Our goal is to identify workable answers and industry best practices that can be implemented to improve the cybersecurity posture of Web 3.0 e-learning platforms by means of a thorough examination of real-world situations, simulations, and controlled environments. By leveraging a combination of theoretical and empirical methods, this study seeks to bridge the gap between academic research and practical implementation. The experimental approach encompasses various techniques, including penetration testing, vulnerability assessments, user studies, and simulated attack scenarios, to provide a holistic understanding of the cybersecurity challenges and their potential impact on e-learning environments. Table 2 illustrates the research questions along with possible approach to be followed in order to bridge the gap.

Table 2. Research questions and possible approach to be followed

Research Question	Possible Approach
RQ1: How can Web 3.0 technologies address data privacy concerns in e-learning platforms?	Web 3.0 technologies like decentralized data storage, encryption, and differential privacy can help address data privacy concerns by enhancing user control and data security.
RQ2: What are the potential vulnerabilities of smart contracts in e-learning systems, and how can they be mitigated?	Smart contracts can be vulnerable to fraud, DoS attacks, and unauthorized access. Mitigation strategies include security audits, access controls, best practices, and incident response plans.
RQ3: How can decentralized identity solutions improve security and user control in e-learning environments?	Decentralized identity gives users control over credentials and data sharing. Adoption requires addressing standardization, privacy, and interoperability challenges.

continued on following page

Table 2. Continued

Research Question	Possible Approach
RQ4: What measures can be taken to protect e-learning platforms from malware and phishing attacks in the Web 3.0 era?	Multi-factor authentication, anti-malware software, secure protocols and ongoing user education help protect against evolving malware and phishing threats.
RQ5: What are the security risks associated with integrating blockchain technology into e-learning systems, and how can they be addressed?	Risks include privacy issues, integration challenges, and scalability. Solutions involve governance protocols, regulatory compliance, and planning for scalability.
RQ6: How can user awareness and education be improved to enhance cybersecurity in Web 3.0-based e-learning platforms?	Improving awareness involves updated training content, online resources, role-based customization, and addressing resistance to change.
RQ7: How effective are advanced biometric authentication methods in securing e-learning platforms against unauthorized access?	Biometrics like fingerprint and facial recognition provide robust security against unauthorized access, but require strong safeguards and user education to address privacy risks.
RQ8: What are the potential benefits and challenges of implementing quantum-safe cryptography in Web 3.0 e-learning systems?	Quantum-safe cryptography future-proofs confidentiality and integrity of data. Challenges include performance, interoperability, and standardization.
RQ9: Can AI-assisted threat detection systems effectively identify and mitigate cyber threats in e-learning environments?	AI can boost security by analyzing patterns and responding to threats in real-time. Effectiveness depends on algorithm resilience and training data quality.
RQ10: How can decentralized storage solutions enhance data resilience and mitigate the risk of single-point failures in e-learning platforms?	Decentralized storage improves availability and redundancy. Challenges include scalability, performance, and storage overhead.
RQ11: What role can collaborative threat intelligence sharing play in protecting e-learning systems from emerging cybersecurity threats?	Sharing real-time threat intelligence improves detection and response. Addressing privacy, trust and standardization issues enables effective collaboration.
RQ12: How can e-learning platforms leverage privacy-enhancing technologies, such as zero-knowledge proofs and differential privacy, to protect user data while maintaining functionality?	These technologies preserve privacy while enabling essential platform interactions. Challenges include performance, scalability and user adoption.
RQ13: What are the challenges and best practices for implementing secure cryptographic protocols in Web 3.0 e-learning applications?	Best practices include following industry standards, proper algorithm selection and key management, and frequent security upgrades.
RQ14: How can e-learning platforms effectively manage and update immutable data stored on the blockchain to ensure accuracy and compliance?	Governance protocols and consensus mechanisms enable updating while preserving integrity and transparency of blockchain data.
RQ15: What impact do cultural and regional factors have on user adoption and awareness of Web 3.0 cybersecurity measures in e-learning environments?	Factors like technological literacy and cultural norms affect adoption. Localization of content and addressing barriers improve engagement.
RQ16: How can cybersecurity be incorporated into the application design phase for Web 3.0 based e-learning platforms?	Following security-by-design principles from the start, conducting risk assessments, architecting zero-trust models, and static/dynamic testing of apps.

In terms of cybersecurity, the incorporation of Web 3.0 technologies into e-learning systems offers a special combination of potential and risks. We have learned a great deal about reducing worries about data privacy, safeguarding smart contracts, putting decentralised identity solutions in place, preventing malware and phishing scams, controlling blockchain security risks, and improving user awareness and education thanks to this experimental research.

The findings underscore the significance of utilising a comprehensive strategy that blends technology advancements, strong security measures, user awareness, and cooperative endeavours across the Web 3.0 community. E-learning platforms may successfully address data privacy concerns and enable learners to manage their personal information by incorporating decentralised data storage, encryption techniques, and user-controlled permission processes.

To further mitigate vulnerabilities in smart contracts and guarantee the integrity of transactions and educational records, regular security audits, adherence to best practices, and the deployment of safe development frameworks are essential. Decentralised identity solutions can improve user control and encourage the safe management of educational credentials when combined with standardised protocols and strong privacy safeguards.

E-learning platforms need to be on the lookout for malware and phishing attempts, and they should use multi-factor authentication, anti-virus software, email filtering, and secure file-sharing protocols to help combat this constantly changing threat landscape. Furthermore, for blockchain technology to be successfully integrated into e-learning systems, scaling plans, governance procedures, and regulatory compliance are necessary to handle blockchain security issues.

The study's experimental methodology has yielded useful conclusions and doable suggestions for improving e-learning platforms' cybersecurity in the Web 3.0 age. We have discovered efficient methods for reducing the risks associated with data privacy, safeguarding smart contracts, putting decentralised identity solutions in place, thwarting malware and phishing attacks, controlling blockchain security risks, and encouraging user awareness and education through extensive testing, simulations, and user studies.

As Web 3.0 technologies find increasing traction in e-learning, stakeholders must make cybersecurity a top priority and a cornerstone of their digital transformation plans. Through adoption of the research findings and a cooperative methodology, the e-learning sector may effectively manage the intricacies of Web 3.0, guaranteeing a safe, reliable, and robust learning milieu for generations to come.

5. EXPLORING THE FUTURE SCOPE

The dynamic nature of e-learning platforms, in conjunction with the revolutionary potential of Web 3.0 technologies, offers a unique blend of novel prospects and complex cybersecurity difficulties. Through the lens of Web 3.0 cybersecurity, this section investigates the potential future applications of knowledge defence in e-learning. Understanding new trends and preventative actions is essential for maintaining the safety and authenticity of the online learning environment as we expect the ongoing growth of digital education. Figure 4 represents the future aspects of the e-learning platform.

Figure 4. Future application of security in e-learning

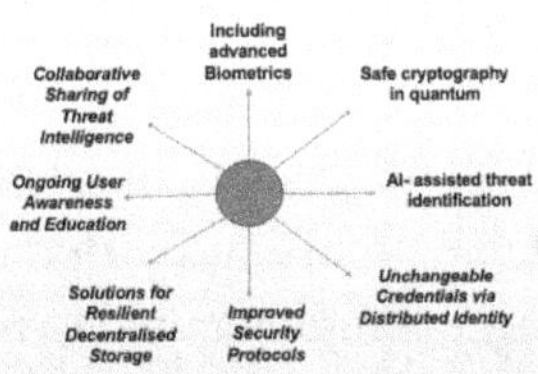

- *Including Advanced Biometrics:*

In Web 3.0 frameworks, enhanced biometric authentication will be included for knowledge defence in e-learning systems. Utilising biometric information, such as fingerprint and face recognition, provides an additional degree of security by guaranteeing that only those with the proper authorization may access learning materials.

- *Safe Cryptography in Quantum:*

The possible threat posed by quantum(Xu et al., 2023) computing to establish cryptography systems is becoming more and more obvious, requiring the use of quantum-safe encryption in order to future-proof e-learning systems, guarantying the security of educational data even in the midst of quantum developments.

- *AI-Assisted Threat Identification:*

The integration of artificial intelligence (AI) into cybersecurity protocols is an essentiality for safeguarding knowledge in online learning environments. The entire security posture of educational platforms is strengthened by AI-powered threat detection systems that function inside Web 3.0 ecosystems. These systems can analyse trends, spot abnormalities, and respond to possible cyber attacks in real-time.

- *Unchangeable Credentials via Distributed Identity:*

Immutable credentialing in e-learning is made possible by Web 3.0's decentralised identification capabilities along with tamper-proof educational credentials will be created using blockchain technology, which will increase confidence and lower the possibility of credential-related fraud in the context of digital education.

- *Improved Security Protocols:*

Future knowledge defence will necessitate more privacy controls in Web 3.0 e-learning systems. Zero-knowledge proofs and differential privacy are examples of privacy-centric features that may be implemented to maintain user data confidentiality while still enabling essential interactions within the educational environment.

- *Solutions for Resilient Decentralised Storage:*

Decentralised storage options are introduced, which disperse data over a network to improve data resilience and lower the chance of single-point failures is necessary for knowledge defence in the future in order to protect instructional materials from manipulation or unwanted access.

- *Ongoing User Awareness and Education:*

The future of knowledge defence against evolving cyber dangers depends on ongoing user education and awareness campaigns. In order to keep teachers, administrators, and students up to date on the newest cybersecurity best practices, emerging threats, and platform-specific security features, Web 3.0 e-learning platforms will incorporate continuous training programmes.

- *Collaborative Sharing of Threat Intelligence:*

Collaborative threat information sharing will be essential to protecting knowledge in e-learning in the Web 3.0 used by educational institutions and platforms to share information about new cyberthreats in real time and to coordinate defence efforts.

The future necessitates a comprehensive and progressive approach to cybersecurity in order to safeguard knowledge incorporating cutting-edge technology, robust cryptographic safeguards, and a cooperative security network will influence the direction of reliable and safe digital education in the future. E-learning platforms can strengthen the digital classroom against new cybersecurity threats by being proactive, adaptable, and embracing the innovative potential of Web 3.0. This will guarantee a robust and safe learning environment for future generations.

REFERENCES

Akbar, H., Zubair, M., & Malik, M. S. (2023). The Security Issues and challenges in Cloud Computing. *International Journal for Electronic Crime Investigation*, *7*(1), 13–32. DOI: 10.54692/ijeci.2023.0701125

Alotaibi, M. B. (2020). A comprehensive cybersecurity framework for e-learning systems. *Computers & Security*, *97*, 101963. DOI: 10.1016/j.cose.2020.101963

Alshamrani, A., Myneni, S., Chowdhary, A., & Huang, D. (2019). A survey on advanced persistent threats: Techniques, solutions, challenges, and research opportunities. *IEEE Communications Surveys and Tutorials*, *21*(2), 1851–1877. DOI: 10.1109/COMST.2019.2891891

Alshamrani, A., Myneni, S., Chowdhary, A., & Huang, D. (2019). A survey on advanced persistent threats: Techniques, solutions, challenges, and research opportunities. *IEEE Communications Surveys and Tutorials*, *21*(2), 1851–1877. DOI: 10.1109/COMST.2019.2891891

Apampa, K. M., Wills, G., & Argles, D. (2020). Cybersecurity and in-course assessment practices in distance learning: Perspectives from international institutions. *Computers & Security*, *96*, 101924. DOI: 10.1016/j.cose.2020.101924

Crosby, M., Pattanayak, P., Verma, S., & Kalyanaraman, V. (2016). Blockchain technology: Beyond bitcoin. Applied Innovation, 2, 6-10. https://j2-reed.com/papers/npb16.pdf

Fayomi, J. O., & Sani, Z. A. (2023). Application and challenges of web 3.0 in smart cities. *JO. Fayomi and ZA. Sani. Application and Challenges of Web*, *3*, 31–42.

Frivold, G., Krokstie, R., & Hassini, E. (2023). Exploring the Role of Web 3.0 in Higher Education: A Systematic Literature Review. *Education Sciences*, *13*(2), 112.

Gan, W., Ye, Z., Wan, S., & Yu, P. S. (2023). Web 3.0: The Future of Internet. *arXiv preprint arXiv:2304.06032*. DOI: 10.1145/3543873.3587583

Goel, A. K., Bakshi, R., & Agrawal, K. K. (2022). Web 3.0 and decentralized applications. *Materials Proceedings*, *10*(1), 8.

Guo, Y. (2023). A review of Machine Learning-based zero-day attack detection: Challenges and future directions. *Computer Communications*, *198*, 175–185. DOI: 10.1016/j.comcom.2022.11.001 PMID: 36741076

Gupta, S., Modgil, S., Choi, T. M., Kumar, A., & Antony, J. (2023). Influences of artificial intelligence and blockchain technology on financial resilience of supply chains. *International Journal of Production Economics*, *261*, 108868. DOI: 10.1016/j.ijpe.2023.108868

Khamparia, A., & Pandey, B. (2020). Association of learning styles with different e-learning problems: A systematic review and classification. *Education and Information Technologies*, *25*(2), 1303–1331. DOI: 10.1007/s10639-019-10028-y

Kritika (2024). A comprehensive literature review on phishing URL detection using deep learning techniques. Journal of Cyber Security Technology, 1–29. DOI: 10.1080/23742917.2024.2378552

Kshetri, N. (2018). Blockchain's roles in strengthening cybersecurity and protecting privacy. *Telecommunications Policy*, *41*(10), 1027–1038. DOI: 10.1016/j.telpol.2017.09.003

Lacity, M. C., & Lupien, S. C. (2022). *Blockchain Fundamentals for Web 3.0*. University of Arkansas Press.

Le, T. D., Le-Dinh, T., & Uwizeyemungu, S. (2024). Search engine optimization poisoning: A cybersecurity threat analysis and mitigation strategies for small and medium-sized enterprises. *Technology in Society*, *76*, 102470. DOI: 10.1016/j.techsoc.2024.102470

Martinez-Garcia, A., Horrach-Rosselló, P., & Mulet-Forteza, C. (2023). Evolution and current state of research into E-learning. *Heliyon*, *9*(10), e21016. DOI: 10.1016/j.heliyon.2023.e21016 PMID: 37867823

Mohammadi, M., Zahedi, M., & Baraani, A. (2020). Cybersecurity in e-learning systems: A systematic review. *Journal of Computer Assisted Learning*, *36*(5), 648–662. DOI: 10.1111/jcal.12440

Rathor, S., Zhang, M., & Im, T. (2023). Web 3.0 and Sustainability: Challenges and Research Opportunities. *Sustainability (Basel)*, *15*(20), 15126. DOI: 10.3390/su152015126

Sarkar, I.H., Kayes, A.S.M., Badsha S., Alqahtani, H., Watters, P. and Ng, A., (2020). Cybersecurity data science: an overview.

Sharma, S. K., Srivastava, P. R., Kumar, A., Jindal, A., & Gupta, S. (2023). Supply chain vulnerability assessment for manufacturing industry. *Annals of Operations Research*, *326*(2), 653–683. DOI: 10.1007/s10479-021-04155-4 PMID: 34149141

Xu, M., Ren, X., Niyato, D., Kang, J., Qiu, C., Xiong, Z., & Leung, V. C. (2023). When quantum information technologies meet blockchain in web 3.0. *IEEE Network*.

Yaga, D., Mell, P., Roby, N., & Scarfone, K. (2018). *Blockchain technology overview*. National Institute of Standards and Technology., DOI: 10.6028/NIST.IR.8202

Zheng, Z., Xie, S., Dai, H., Chen, X., & Wang, H. (2018). Blockchain challenges and opportunities: A survey. *International Journal of Web and Grid Services, 14*(4), 352–375. DOI: 10.1504/IJWGS.2018.095647

Chapter 6
Access to Street Art via Crowdsourcing Methods:
A Web Page Proposal for Türkiye

Orhun Uğur
https://orcid.org/0000-0002-9274-0414
University of Exeter, UK

Semanur Öztemiz
https://orcid.org/0000-0003-1560-8062
Hacettepe University, Turkey

ABSTRACT

This study aims to propose a website for the preservation and accessibility of street art in Türkiye with crowdsourcing methods. The proposed website is based on the literature about the usability of street art websites. The related literature showed that the websites are weak regarding institutional information and policies, including copying and copyrights, and that descriptive data regarding the works is insufficient. Additionally, it has been observed that the most common crowdsourcing method is collection completion. Street artworks created by street artists and then converted into digital form are also prone to change and metamorphosis, requiring specific digital solutions for long-term preservation. The rise of Web3 technologies offers new opportunities to overcome the challenges of documenting, preserving, and sharing these digital street arts. It is thought that this study, conducted in the case of Türkiye, will contribute to the literature on preserving and accessing street art as a cultural heritage.

DOI: 10.4018/979-8-3693-2973-3.ch006

INTRODUCTION

Street art generally encompasses the artworks produced by the artist, along with the artist using urban spaces to create and exhibit his works (Ayhan, 2021, p. 96). Street art's temporal and vulnerable nature is key in determining the necessary steps for sustainable preservation. Digitalization is the most important preservation stage since physical artifacts can easily be damaged and lost. In the literature, the relationship between cultural heritage and street art (Bates, 2014; Nomeikaite, 2017), the aesthetic characteristics of street art (Nogel, 2015), the effect of promotions with street art on the number of spectators in art organizations (Poole, 2020), the relationship of street art with political movements (Taş and Taş, 2015; Cowick, 2016; Tulke, 2020), copyrights of street artworks (Davies, 2012; Bonadio, 2017; Bonadio, 2018a; Bonadio, 2018b), public view of street art (Conklin, 2012; Vanderveen and van Eijk, 2016). Studies are addressing this issue. Various studies have also been conducted in the literature regarding the documentation of street art. Novak (2014), one of the prominent names in this context, emphasized in his study that size information is not a consideration in documenting street art. The author also touched upon the characteristics of 4 street art forms classified as "piece", "character", "tag" and "throw up" and determined their average dimensions (width and height) by measuring 268 works. Gottlieb (2008) and Novak (2015) focused on the classification of street art in their studies. In another study, Novak (2015) touched upon the importance of photography in documenting street art and offered a guide for photography and identifying photographed works. In a survey documenting street art on online platforms (Graf, 2018), the open coding method was used to determine the architectural features of organizational labels and websites used on 241 sites. In the study, facets related to the website were determined under two code categories named "general features" and "other media", facets about the works and sub-facets depending on them were determined under the categories "general", "supporting", "genre" and "location". In the last part of the study, interviews were held with the website administrators to determine the importance of the information facets obtained in line with the findings. In line with the data collected, it was revealed that the facets were used differently, and the most frequently repeated facets were supporting facets such as canvas, wall, and train. It was concluded that location information is used most frequently at the city level, followed by the country level. As a result of the interviews, it was seen that there were different ideas about which terminology or categories to organize the photo collections. However, everyone described the name of the artist/gang, the year of production, and the location of the work as the most important facets. Curators have touched on the impact of the size of the collection, its geographical focus, and the diversity of works in terms of site organization (Graf, 2018).

There are many websites in the world where street art is a product of cultural heritage, is preserved and made accessible. Although street art is produced in Türkiye, there is no platform where these works can be preserved and made accessible. In this study a website proposed for the preservation and accessibility of street art in Türkiye with crowdsourcing methods.

WEB 3.0, MOBILE COMMERCE, AND STREET ART

In recent decades, there has been a significant increase in the use of digital technology for the documentation of both tangible and intangible digital cultural heritage (DCH) materials. These developments have affected street art, which can be seen as an important part of tangible cultural heritage products. The rise of Web3 technologies provides new opportunities for addressing the challenges associated with documenting, preserving, and sharing street art. Digital artifacts, such as those created by street artists, are inherently prone to change and transfiguration, which can complicate their long-term preservation (Marchese & Shergill, 2012). However, Web3 technologies, including blockchain, decentralized storage, and non-fungible tokens (NFT), offer solutions to these challenges, allowing for the creation of immutable and verifiable digital art records.

One of the key benefits of using Web3 technologies for street art is the ability to create "smart collectibles" or non-fungible tokens that can serve as digital representations of physical artworks. These NFTs can document street art's provenance, ownership, and authenticity, creating a tamper-proof record that the public can access and verify (Chevet, 2018). Furthermore, the decentralized nature of blockchain technology ensures that this information is not subject to the whims of centralized authorities, providing a more reliable and secure means of preserving the historical record of street art.

In addition to documentation, Web3 technologies can enable new methods of preserving and sharing street art. Decentralized storage solutions, such as those provided by platforms like IPFS, allow for the secure and distributed preservation of digital art files, ensuring they are not susceptible to the same risks of loss or corruption as traditional centralized storage (Persistence, 2023).

In the digital age, the evolution of technology has transformed how we engage with the world, particularly in Web3 and mobile commerce. These platforms have been shaped by design principles that aim to enhance user experience, foster innovation, and drive business growth (Ablyazov & Rapgof, 2019; Dumanska et al., 2021; Schallmo et al., 2017).

One of the fundamental design principles for Web3 and mobile commerce platforms is "designing with the user" (AlSheikh Theeb et al., 2022). This approach emphasizes understanding the user's needs, preferences, and behaviors through comprehensive research and co-creation. By gathering information about the user through conversations, observations, and collaborative efforts, developers can ensure that the selected technologies are relevant, sustainable, and tailored to the specific needs of the intended audience. Another key design principle emphasizes modular structure and simple mobile platforms. This principle encourages the development of easily configurable, scalable, and adaptable systems to the evolving needs of users. By adopting a modular approach, developers can ensure that their platforms remain relevant and responsive to the changing technological landscape (Bakri et al., 2019).

Moreover, the design of Web3 and mobile commerce platforms should strive to enhance the behavioral interaction and emotional guidance of users. Strengthening the interaction modes, improving efficiency, and establishing a good dialogue between users and products can lead to a more satisfying and immersive experience (Jun & Shaokang, 2018).

The use of blockchain technologies in the field of art has been increasing for seven years. Blockchain is a technology that creates meaningful contributions in terms of processes such as increasing the visibility of works of art, discovering who/which country produced them, and ensuring that works reach their interested parties. One of the most prominent examples and pioneering initiatives of Blockchain's contributions to art is the sale of some of Andy Warhol's works with cryptocurrencies on Maecenas, a blockchain platform (Maecenas, 2018).

ETHICAL AND LEGAL DIMENSIONS FOR STREET ART

In recent years, the importance of street art has increased significantly. While in previous years the rise in graffiti in an area was often considered a precursor to crime based on the "broken window theory" (Kelling and Wilson, 1982), today, with the evolution of street art into new forms, an opposing perspective has emerged. Although still technically illegal, street artworks have become assets that add value to the locations where they are created.

A notable example is the wall where Banksy's artwork Aachoo!! was painted, which increased the market value of a house from £300,000 to £5 million (Sputniknews, 2020). Banksy even included a complaint from a resident in his book. The resident expressed concern in an email that students and young city dwellers were moving into the area, driving up prices significantly (Banksy, 2005, p. 20).

With this shifting positive perception, street art has turned into a profitable avenue for artists. Municipalities, private businesses, and events have begun hiring artists to paint murals to attract attention. However, it has also drawn the attention of "advertisers and marketing gurus", particularly in industries like fashion, fast food, and entertainment (Bonadio, 2018b, p. 84).

During this transformation, attempts were made to commercialize artworks without granting copyright to the artists. One example involves Revok and H&M. In 2018, the brand recorded an ad video featuring a model backflipping off a wall containing artwork created by Revok. The artist sent a cease-and-desist letter to the company, which responded with a countersuit, claiming the artwork was painted illegally. However, after facing public backlash on social media, the company withdrew the lawsuit, and an agreement was reached (Neuendorf, 2018).

Another important legal victory for street artists involves the famous 5Pointz building in New York City. Known as the "Mecca of Graffiti," the building was a graffiti center showcasing works from 21 artists. In 2014, the owner demolished the building to construct luxury condominiums, increasing the value of the property from $40 million to $200 million, thanks to the artwork. Following the demolition, the artists sued the owner for damages under the Visual Artists Rights Act (VARA). The judge awarded $6.7 million to the artists, marking the first case where graffiti artists were protected under moral rights, including the right to prevent the destruction of their work (Bonadio, 2018a).

These examples come from the United States, but each country has its own approach to street artists and copyright. In general, to claim rights over their work, artists must prove ownership, which can compromise anonymity, a crucial aspect for some street artists.

To address this issue and credit artists while maintaining their anonymity, Mendelson-Schwartz, Schwartz, and Mualam (2023) proposed an NFT-based model for protecting street art rights. They suggest that artists use an app installed on their mobile devices to create a profile and upload their work. That app would register, authenticate, and timestamp the artwork, with the evidence stored on a public blockchain ledger. The image would also be stored in an external database with bidirectional links. While the ledger and database would be publicly accessible, the artist's identity could remain anonymous, reachable only through a blockchain-secured contact mechanism connecting their public profile to an anonymous messaging system.

PARTICIPATORY HERITAGE AND DIGITAL ACCESS TO STREET ART

There are mainly two approaches to preserving street art collections. The first is institutional preservation, exemplified by organizations such as the Street Art Museum Amsterdam1 or the Urban Spree Galerie Berlin2, which incorporate works created by invited artists, either on the streets or in enclosed spaces, into their collections. Since these works are produced with the institution's knowledge, their digitization can follow similar processes to those used for other heritage objects of artistic or historical value.

However, an action beyond this institutional approach is necessary to protect street art that exists in public spaces without permission. Street art, which can appear overnight in any corner of a city and vanish just as quickly, is extremely difficult for cultural memory institutions to identify and document on their own. This challenge gave rise to the second approach, which can be referred as participatory preservation. Thanks to advancements in digital technologies and the ubiquity of smartphones capable of capturing photographs and connecting to the internet, the digitization of cultural heritage has become much more accessible. Today, anyone, from amateurs to professionals, can contribute to this process (Zahidi, Lim, & Woods, 2013, p. 13). These innovations have enabled users to transition from being 'passive observers' to 'active participants' (Carletti, 2016, p. 196).

The European Commission, in its report 'Towards an Integrated Approach to Cultural Heritage for Europe' (2014), emphasized the need of:

- "Reaching out to new audiences and engaging young people in particular."
- "Continuing to develop more participatory interpretation and governance models better suited to contemporary Europe, through greater involvement of the private sector and civil society."

In another report published the following year (European Commission, 2015), it was noted that in conservation practices conducted solely by cultural heritage professionals, local communities have little responsibility for protecting their own cultural heritage. The report also highlighted that the innovative use of cultural heritage has the potential to actively involve people in the process. Such engagement could support integration, inclusivity, social cohesion, sound investment, and the necessary components for smart, sustainable, and inclusive growth. The report emphasized that digital technologies have already facilitated interaction in terms of accessing collections and sharing knowledge. It also pointed out the positive aspects of participation for both young and older generations:

- For young people and the unemployed, involvement in heritage management processes could help them build self-confidence and acquire skills that enhance their employability.
- For older individuals with free time, engaging in an activity can provide motivation and positively impact their health (European Commission, 2015, p. 9).

Various definitions have been made for participatory heritage, which generally aims to increase the interaction of the user with cultural heritage and to keep them closer to the heritage management process. In their book "Participatory Heritage", Roued-Cunliffe and Copeland defined participatory heritage as "a space in which individuals engage in cultural activities outside of formal institutions for the purpose of knowledge sharing and co-creating with others" (Roued-Cunliffe and Copeland, 2017, p. xv). They stated that in participatory heritage practices, the focus is on content rather than medium, process or expertise, and that action is taken under the leadership of a common authority formed by the combination of various expertise. They evaluated heritage institutions as "institutions, which are governed by policies and procedures and are hindered by legal and budgetary constraints" (Roued-Cunliffe and Copeland, 2017, p. xv) and stated that heritage management is already being carried out outside institutional frameworks through a do-it-yourself (DIY) approach, involving family historians and amateur collectors.

In his study examining the views of users on participatory heritage websites, van der Hoeven (2020) has adopted a broader definition of participatory heritage than Roued-Cunliffe and Copeland (2017). As in their definition, he has included not only "those outside official institutions" but also projects in which heritage institutions seek the participation of citizens (van der Hoeven, 2020, p. 134). Intriligator (2015, p. 63) has classified the participatory approach in the heritage sector into three separate groups: 'participatory digital heritage', 'crowdsourced cultural heritage', 'independent public digital heritage and community archives'. He has included open-ended heritage projects developed by academics working in the field of heritage using digital tools and carried out with the participation of local communities under the category of participatory digital heritage applications. He has placed digital projects in which cultural memory institutions want to benefit from public labor in line with their goals under the category of crowdsourced cultural heritage. He also classified projects carried out by local communities and small software developers on a smaller scale, outside of traditional heritage institutions, as independent public digital heritage and community archives (Intriligator, 2015, p. 63). Although participatory approaches in the field of heritage can be categorized based on the institutions or objectives driving the project, crowdsourcing remains one of the most popular methods for fostering a participatory understanding of heritage (Carletti, 2016, p. 197).

Crowdsourcing is the voluntary involvement of crowds in helping to solve a problem. Oomen ve Aroyo (2011) classified crowdsourcing methods used in cultural heritage management by aligning them with the stages of the "digital content life cycle" model of the National Library of New Zealand, chosen among many similar models. The digital content life cycle consists of a chain of stages, including creation, description, management, discovery, use, reuse, and returning to the beginning to create again (DigitalNZ, n.d.). According to the digital content life cycle, Oomen and Aroyo matched the stages with complementing collection, correction, contextualization, co-curation and crowdsourcing methods (Oomen and Aroyo, 2011, p. 141).

These methods can be used in the management of any cultural heritage, as well as for street art, which, due to its ephemeral nature, requires participation and the digitization for its survival. New artworks can be collaboratively created with communities under the guidance of artists. People with more knowledge about a particular artwork can correct or enhance its information online or help classify it. Communities can add new dimensions to the artwork by sharing their personal stories or memories related to a piece or the space it occupies, thus contextualizing the artwork. They can also curate or contribute to the curation of new collections by adding new perspectives to digital street art information. Furthermore, they can support artists or art events through funding, embodying the spirit of crowdsourcing.

There is a mutual relationship between street art and the community. Street art thrives through participation, and in return, it contributes to the community by enhancing the aesthetic appeal of urban spaces, fostering a sense of cultural identity, encouraging tourism, and supporting local economies through increased foot traffic and public interest.

CULTURAL AND HISTORICAL SIGNIFICANCE OF STREET ART IN TÜRKİYE

The historical development of street art in Türkiye has not been much different from the rest of the world. Leaving aside the graffiti encountered in ancient cities, the first graffiti in the modern sense appeared in the 1960s, aiming to mark political territory and express ideas (Erdoğan, 2009, p. 76). Modern graffiti, which went beyond political writings and diversified, began to appear in the mid-1980s and became widespread with Hip Hop culture in the 1990s. Street art other than graffiti became visible in various forms in the 2000s and became more intense in 2010 (Çakır, 2015, p. 21).

An example of striking importance in the history of Türkiye was seen at the 13th International Antalya Film and Art Festival held on June 13, 1976 (Salt Araştırma, 2023). Artists were invited to the exhibition by the municipality to make murals and street sculptures, but the works were destroyed by opposing groups by pouring black paint on them or breaking them (see Figure 1).

Figure 1. Zehra Aral, İsimsiz

(https://archives.saltresearch.org/handle/123456789/206819)

Street art represents the expression of the impact of social events, political and political transformations on the public. After street art became effective as a political tool and the 1980 coup, people associated painting walls in the middle of the night with politics and terrorism for a long time. Tunç "Turbo" Dindaş, a member of the group "S2K", and one of Türkiye's first graffiti artists, is one of the people who suffered the pain of this period. However, unlike the artists who started in the same period and later abandoned graffiti, Turbo still produces works today (Kaçmaz, 2019, p. 121). Since there was no spray paint at that time, the works were drawn on sketchbooks, and the first graffiti made with spray was produced by Turbo in 1985. Street art has continued to live and evolve in Türkiye, thanks to hip hop culture, which Turbo was also interested in, punk, DIY culture, magazines and fanzines, and young people who showed civil disobedience as a result of pressure (Kaçmaz, 2019, p. 121-127).

In addition to what is practiced illegally, graffiti and street art have also been produced legally. GNG Klan, founded in 1998 and consisting of 7 people, is the first group to legally engage in graffiti in Turkey (Erdoğan, 2009, p. 78). Political graffiti made in the 1970s are among the examples of graffiti in Turkey. The Gezi Park events in 2013, which caused concepts such as public, politics and resistance to be mentioned together, deeply affected society (Pehlivan, 2021). Street art, which emerges more effectively in events that deeply affect society, showed itself on the walls of the city, on the ground, on billboards, and sometimes in the soil as a guerrilla gardening action during the Gezi Park protests in 2013 (see Figure 2 and Figure 3). Many murals made during the protests have led to potential crimes due to both the adaptation of art reflecting social events to the street and the unauthorized use of public space, even with an art theme.

Figure 2. "Revolution will not be televised it will be tweeted"

(http://1.bp.blogspot.com/-JeK_vfQO6iw/Ua9PKK9AvBI/AAAAAAAAovE/op5Bd7iFlh4/s1600/68.jpg)

Figure 3. Gasmask

(https://www.farklibirbakis.com/turkiye-ve-dunyadan-en-iyi-45-sokak-sanati-ornegi/)

Another incident in which 301 people lost their lives and deeply affected society was the Soma massacre (Soma Disaster, 2014). A critical mural was painted for the mine, which was criticized for not taking adequate safety measures (see Figure 4).

Figure 4. It's not a disgrace, it's coal black, that's how you earn your living

(https://listelist.com/somayi-unutma/)

After two major earthquakes occurred on February 6, 2023, with a magnitude of 7.8 Mw (± 0.1) centered in Kahramanmaraş Pazarcık at 04:30 and a magnitude of 7.5 Mw centered in Kahramanmaraş Ekinözü at 13:24, 10 provinces suffered major damage. According to official figures, at least 50 thousand 96 people died in Türkiye and at least 8 thousand 476 people in Syria, and more than 122 thousand people were injured in total (2023 Kahramanmaraş earthquakes, 2023). The graffiti in Figure 5 was found in Hatay and Antakya, one of the most damaged regions due to the late arrival of aid, right after the earthquake.

Figure 5. "Don't lose hope, we will come back Hatay", 12 February 2023. Graffiti: Özgür Bilgin, Photographer: Diego Cupolo

(https://twitter.com/DiegoCupolo/status/1624794140553760771)

In recent years, the importance of street art has been increased in Türkiye. Undoubtedly, this development is greatly influenced by international developments. While in previous years, the increase in the number of graffiti in an area was considered a precursor to all kinds of crimes based on the broken window theory (Kelling and Wilson, 1982), today, with the evolution of street art into new forms, an opposing perspective has begun to emerge. Although still illegal, street artworks have become products that add value to the place where they are made. The wall on which Banksy created his work Hapşu! (Aachoo!!) increased the market value of a house from 300 thousand pounds to 5 million pounds (Sputniknews., 2020). Banksy included a complaint made by a resident of a neighborhood for this reason in his book. The resident complained in an e-mail that students and young city dwellers were moving to that area because of the work and that prices had increased a lot (Banksy, 2005, p. 20).

In Türkiye, street art appears as cultural products that shed light on history, both as the creative expressions of artists and as a direct reflection of social events, and continue to exist legally or illegally in our country, as in the world. Local governments also noticed the positive attitude of society towards street art and carried out projects to have the walls of the cities painted. With the "Mural Art" event organized in 2019, Ankara Municipality invited street artists to color the walls of Ankara, known as the "Grey City" (Ankara Metropolitan Municipality, 2019). Although these works are considered public art rather than street art because they are made legally, it is possible to say that municipalities in Türkiye have a positive approach to seeing works of art on the street.

METHODOLOGY

This study, which proposes a website that will provide access to street art, was conducted based on the limited literature on the subject. In literature, apart from some studies (Graf, 2018; Uğur, 2023; Uğur and Öztemiz, 2024), no study has been found that evaluates websites that provide access to street art. Based on these works (Graf, 2018; Uğur, 2023; Uğur and Öztemiz, 2024), general conclusions regarding street art sites around the world are as follows:

- Each site uses different metadata fields to describe street art. No common areas have been developed to identify websites or works within the street art community. In line with Graf's (2019, p. 189) results, it was observed that the most frequently used field when defining street art was an artist. However, unlike his work, it turns out that the areas that follow the artist identifier are location and genre. It can be said that such a small number of identifiers is insufficient because street art requires special fields in addition to the metadata fields used to describe other cultural heritage works.
- Most sites do not contain informative texts regarding acquiring works, copying, and copyrights. It has been observed that legal regulations regarding access to works hosted by street art sites are ignored.
- Crowdsourcing methods are not used sufficiently on street art sites that require user participation for digitization and archiving.
- According to the usability evaluations of street art websites, it can be said that street art websites are weak in terms of institutional information and policies regarding the reproduction of artworks and copyrights and that descriptive data on artworks is insufficient. As a result of the related research (Graf, 2018; Uğur, 2023; Uğur and Öztemiz, 2024), it was understood that the platforms were strong in terms of aesthetic and minimalist design, consistency, and standards, but weak in terms of features such as user control and freedom, flexibility, and efficiency. These findings regarding existing street art websites and the best among them guided the website proposed within the scope of the study. The recommended website includes street artworks in Ankara that were digitized by researchers.

A WEB PAGE PROPOSAL FOR ACCESSING STREET ART

The purpose of the web page is to access street artworks in Türkiye and ensure their preservation in the digital environment. This page provides:

-Using crowdsourcing methods and introducing them to the user
-To inform the user about street art, cultural heritage, digitalization
-Informing the society about the relationship between street art and cultural heritage
-Relating the usability features of existing websites with the design principles of Web3 and mobile commerce platforms

The long-term goals of the site are to support street artists, soften society's view of them, and perhaps become a platform that can offer different job opportunities. In line with these purposes, the name of the site, which aims to archive “art” works on the street, has been determined as “street art archive”.

Technical Specifications of the Web Page

The sample web application can be created by using four technologies that can be written in Javascript language. React library was used to code the front end, NodeJS was used to set up a web server, Express was used to run the back end, and PostgreSQL was used as a relational database (see Figure 6). All technologies are open source and are also known as P.E.R.N, which is a combination of their initials. The costly part encountered while preparing the application is the storage fee to be spent on obtaining a web address/domain and storing visual data. Instead of storing the data locally, it might be preferable to save it in a cloud service like Amazon S3, which offers free usage for the first year. However, since the service can become expensive after the initial free period, decentralized data storage solutions like IPFS can be utilized as a more cost-effective alternative.

Additionally, implementing XML (Extensible Markup Language) and RDF (Resource Description Framework) in the system architecture could provide robust benefits for managing metadata and enabling interoperability. XML would offer a flexible way to structure and store the data, while RDF (Resource Description Framework) would enhance the ability to represent complex relationships between data entities, making the platform more scalable and semantically rich.

Figure 6. Technologies used when developing the prototype

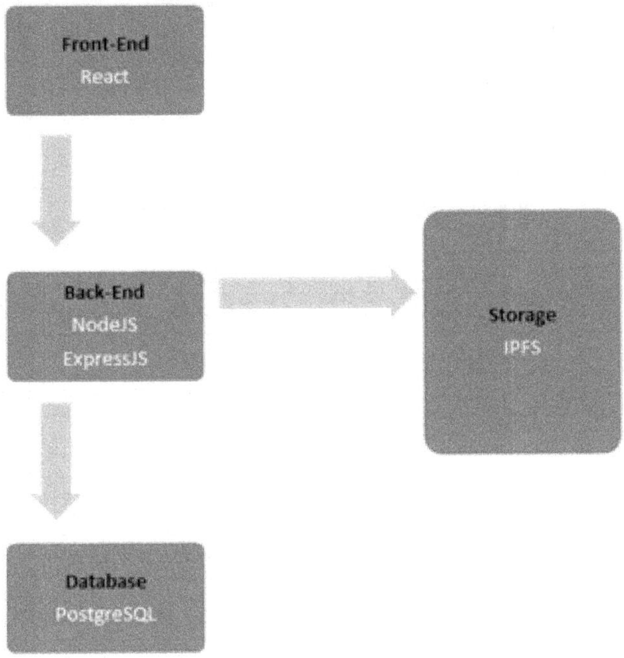

The site must be kept as simple and useful as possible, taking into account the aesthetic and minimalist design principle. The colors that will appear throughout the site can be created by applying the 60-30-10 rule. This rule means using the main color in approximately 60% of the site, the secondary color in 30%, and the supporting color in 10% (Gordon, 2021). The main color that forms the area where the content is presented is cream, beige tone (HEX code: #e6e5b6), and the accompanying green fog (HEX code: #d6d5a8). The second color is black (HEX code: #000000) and the supporting color is green (HEX code: #28a745), which is mostly used on buttons, and dark green (HEX code: #218838), which is formed when the button is hovered over).

Metadata

Street artworks, like other cultural heritage objects, at least need to be defined at a basic level. It is thought that the basic level Dublin Core (DC) standards such as title, subject, description, creator, publisher, date, genre, format, identifier, source, language, relationship, and location can often be used when defining street art. In Table 1, the basic DC fields are given on the left, and next to them, their equivalents, explanations, and mandatory statuses to be used in the proposed web page are given. As seen in the table, most fields were able to directly match DC fields. The source, language, and relationship metadata fields available in DC were not initially considered a priority for this website.

Table 1. Metadata mapping

Dublin Core Title	**Proposed Title**	**Title Description**	**Obligation Situation**
Work Name	Work name	Work name	Yes
Subject	Subject	Subject (Satirical, political etc.)	No
Definition	Explanation	Description of the work	Yes
Creator	Artist	Artist name/nickname	Yes
Posted by	Photographer	Photographer name/nickname	Yes
Contributor	Uploaded by	Uploader name/nick	Yes
History	Construction date	Production date of the work	No
	Date photographed	Date of photography of the work	No
	Release date	Date of publication of the work on the site	Yes
	Date of disappearance	Date of disappearance of the work	
	Lost work reporting date	Date when the work was first seen missing	No
Type	Type	Type (Graffiti, Mural, Stencil etc.)	Yes
Format	Artifact size	Artifact size	No
Descriptive Scope	WorkID	WorkID	Yes
	Province	Province	Yes
	District	District	No
	Village/Neighborhood	Village/Neighborhood	No
	Specification	Specification	No
	Location(latitude)	Location(latitude)	Yes
	Location(longitude)	Location(longitude)	Yes
Rights	CC license	CC license	Yes
Source	Not a priority for this site		No
Language	Not a priority for this site		No
Relationship	Not a priority for this site		No

Location and date information has been made more detailed by creating different subheadings according to DC basic standards. For historical metadata, this is because the existence and extinction of street art can change very quickly compared to other cultural heritage works. Just like the date of construction, the date of destruction is also important information for the works. If the works are not digitized by the artist himself, it is difficult to know the date of production. But at least the date of the photograph's shooting provides "terminus ante quem" information, which is used to date the work in archaeology. Since the uploading date of the work and the shooting date of the photo may be different, they require separate metadata fields. The upload date of the work is automatically created by the system by taking the timestamp of the moment the work was uploaded. If the date of extinction of the work is known by the artist or the uploader of the work, the "date of disappearance" field can be used. If the date of disappearance is not known clearly, a "lost work reporting date" field should be provided to record this date if any user can no longer see the work while passing through the same street. This information will indicate that the work could not have been seen after this date and that it was destroyed before this date, that is, "terminus ante quem". Loss of information will be possible if the person who uploaded the work can edit the uploaded work. If a different user notices this, the site administrator and the person who uploaded the work will be informed via the "report disappearance" button on the work page. The photo added by the user who noticed and documented the disappearance and the date of disappearance will be presented to the user as evidence on the page containing the relevant work.

Location information can also be defined by dividing it into different subfields, such as date. The smaller the information is divided into smaller pieces, the easier and more meaningful it is to manage and subsequently analyze it. The user is given the opportunity to select a location by clicking on the map. The system automatically records the latitude and longitude information of the selected location. This information allows the works to be presented on the map again. At the same time, information was also requested at the provincial, district, village/neighborhood level. The provincial part is required because it may be useful especially in statistical studies or filtering processes later. However, other fields are left to the user's choice. The description metadata field offers user the opportunity to make additional explanations about the location. The field can be used to provide detailed information about the location. An expression such as "behind the transformer next to the rose garden" can also help user to detect the artwork that are difficult to see in the first place.

Corporate Information and Policies

Mission statement, work acquisition, work copying policy, information about the physical location of the institution (if any), and contact information that can be accessed to get information about the collection or a different subject are the types of information that the user must easily access to resolve the question marks in their minds.

In Street Art Cities, the website examined by experts, the mission statement was created on a page called "community", not "about" (Uğur, 2023; Uğur and Öztemiz, 2024). This page can be accessed with the title "Community" in the navigation bar at the top of the site (see Figure 7) and with the title "About us" under the title "Company" in the footer. This situation is ranked in Nielsen's (2001) usability criteria. Two buttons with different names opening to the same page are not correct in terms of meeting the standard. At the same time, related studies (Uğur, 2023; Uğur and Öztemiz, 2024) states that it is not very easy to access information, the information on the "About" page should be presented with the same title, like all information.

Figure 7. Street art website navigation bar and about page

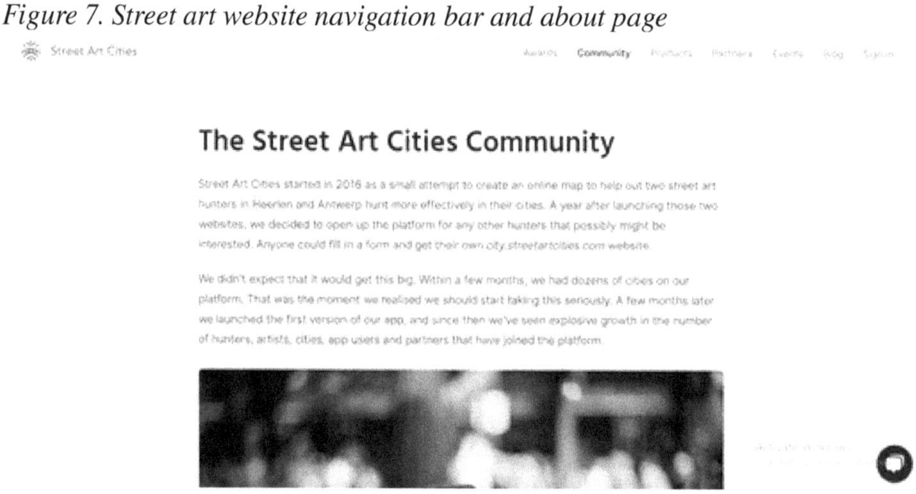

(https://streetartcities.com/about)

The "About" page is not only used to explain the mission statement/purpose of the site. According to Nielsen (2001), the about page should provide general information about the institution/company and links to details about the product, service, team, and values. When considering a street art website, this page should not only serve its purpose, but also provide simple information and guiding links about what the user can find on this site, how to use it, legal terms of use and project details, especially for a sample site to be produced as a result of a scientific thesis.

All works added to the site are licensed with "CC BY-SA 4.0". For more detailed information about adding works, using them and licenses, you can check out the "Legal" page. If you are an artist or someone who advocates street art, you can join the movement by going to the "Join" page. You can access the pages from the top or bottom navigation bar or use the buttons below."

An example interface can be created as in Figure 8.

Figure 8. Street art web page for Türkiye, "About" page

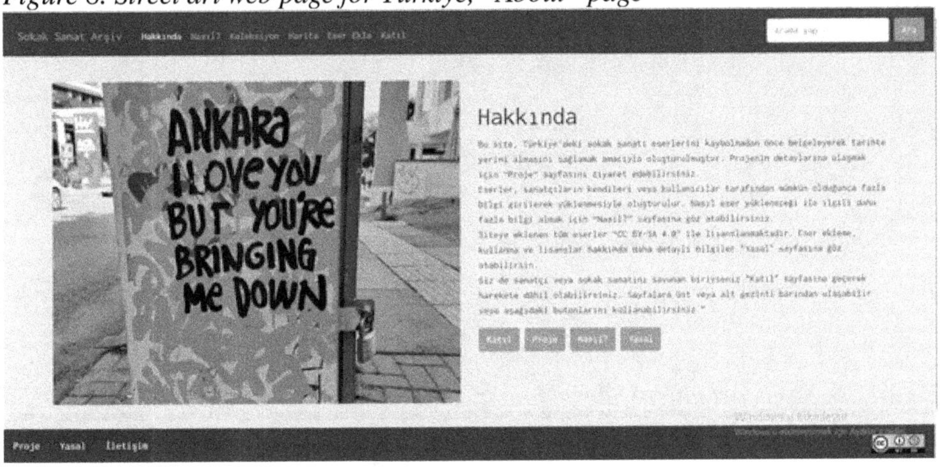

It is necessary to provide the user with access to information through different means. The Street Art Cities website has chosen to provide information regarding acquisition, copying, and copyright in general under the "Legal" page (see Figure 9). Access to the "Legal" page is given under the "Company" heading in the footer area (see Figure 10).

Figure 9. Street art cities website "legal" page

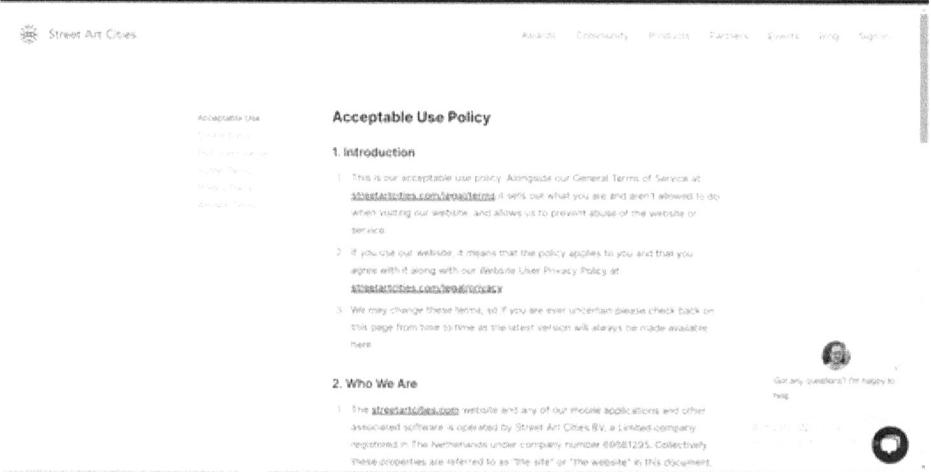

(https://streetartcities.com/legal/acceptable-use)

Figure 10. Street art cities website footer

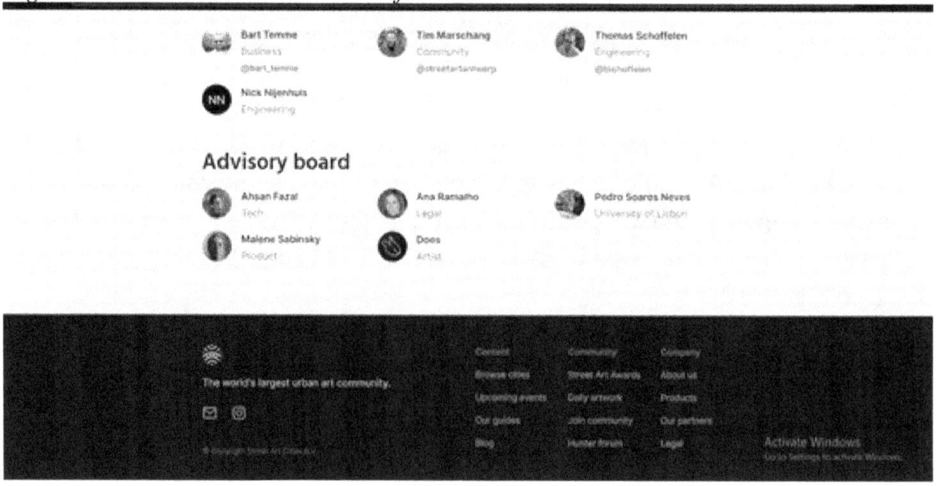

(https://streetartcities.com/legal/acceptable-use)

The information is presented in six subheadings. When each title is clicked, the relevant text is presented on the right. This layout can be used similarly on the site prepared for Türkiye. However, research (Uğur, 2023; Uğur and Öztemiz, 2024) has pointed out that the selected button may be more distinguishable than the unselected ones. The black and tone text color used in the headings on the left side of this page may be distinguishable. The web page to be created should be prepared more simply and understandably, considering this article.

Street Art Cities website explains its policies for acquiring and copying works in the "Acceptable Use" section, under the heading "Use of Content", with the description of the content, the owner of the metadata, and the license clauses used. The following statements can be made in a similar vein on the website to be created for Türkiye:

> *"Users add photos of street art works and different information and metadata about the work such as location, artist name, title, etc. to this website. Metadata is owned by users and they have the right to publish it on this site. Redistribution of metadata is prohibited without permission from the site administration or content owner. Photos and metadata are licensed under Creative Commons Attribution-ShareAlike 4.0 (CC BY-SA 4.0). CC BY-SA 4.0 license means that the content can be used and published freely, provided that the creator is credited. However, it is recommended to talk to the creator of the content and get permission."*

Apart from the person taking the photo, the street artist who creates the work may also have concerns about his or her work being displayed on this website. To protect the artist's rights, an explanation as follows should be added:

> *"If the creator of street art is in any way disturbed by the publication of his work and wants it to be removed, he can directly contact the site management and remove the records containing his work. You can find the contact addresses on the Contact page. Just as the copyright of the artist performing street art is protected, the user who digitizes the digital work, that is, street art, and uploads it to the system must also be informed of this."*

Finally, the user can be adequately informed by adding the following information to the legal page:

> *"The creator of the digital copy of the street art, the user who takes the photo and uploads the metadata must accept this situation and accept the upload. Informing all kinds of users is a basic requirement of the Help and Documentation criterion. In addition, the CC BY-SA 4.0 icon to be added to the footer area will ensure that the user who does not read the "legal" page will be informed about copyright."*

When all the information is added, the "Legal" page may look like Figure 11.

Figure 11. Sample legal page view

Contact information should be included on the contact page as an e-mail address and should encourage the user to write for any reason such as feedback or questions.

Document Access Tools

This title is related to the general search features of the site, not to the level of collections and works. There must be a search bar on the home page of the site to be designed. The words written in the search bar should query all kinds of text on the site and sort the results page by page, from the most related to the unrelated, on a new page. The user should be given the chance to choose by providing some text from the title and content of the results. There is no general search feature on the Street Art Cities website. The expression "I Support Street Art" allows searching the entire site by word (see Figure 12). The site lists the search results as a simple list. A similar results page should also be created on the site to be designed for Türkiye.

Figure 12. I support street art site "rights" search result

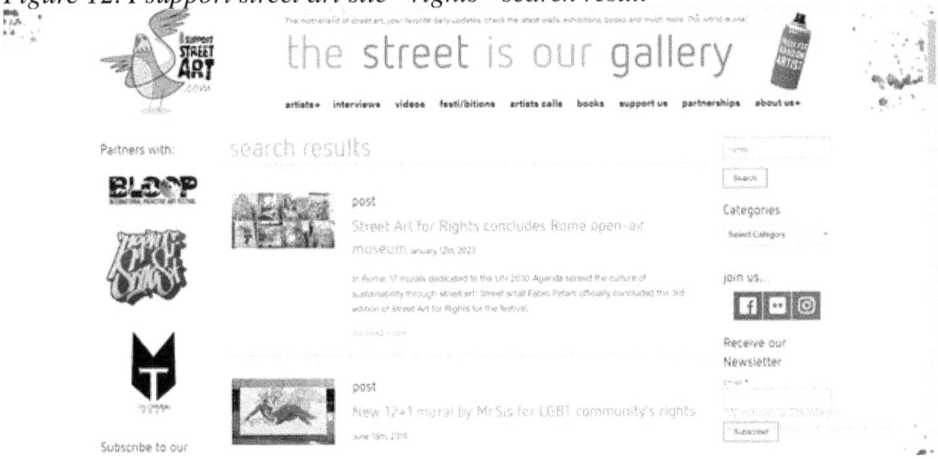

(https://www.isupportstreetart.com/)

Menu options are document access tools that are directly in front of the user and direct them to the information they are looking for. Whitenton (2015) gave the example that even the most important content will not matter if it cannot be found and stated that navigation on the website is the feature that should be given the highest priority. He pointed out that although the site has a search feature, importance should not be given only to the search bar.

Menu items should contain the descriptive titles of all the pages that the user may need. By the Flexibility and Efficiency criteria propositions, menu items should be limited to seven. Brief explanations of these headings and their contents are given in Table 2.

Table 2. Pages and contents in the menu

Location	Page Name	Content
Navigation Bar	Main Page	Brief introduction of the site and contact call
(1)	About	Brief information and links about the purpose of the site, communication method, ethical rights and how to use the site
(1)	How?	Information on how to use the site, how to digitize
(1)	Collection	All works in the collection can be accessed on the work page, with word search and filtering options
(1)	Map	All works in the collection presented on the map
(1)	Add Work	Adding work page

continued on following page

Table 2. Continued

Location	Page Name	Content
(1)	Join	Membership transactions page
SubInformation Bar	Project	Information about the project links to external street art collections, relevant literature
(1)	Legal	Legal information stating the rights of acquiring works, copying them, the license used, and the rights of works and users in general.
(1)	Contact	Communication ways

The position of the navigation bar on which the menu items are located should be designed to follow the user as he scrolls down the page (see Figure 13).

Figure 13. Navigation bar that follows the user

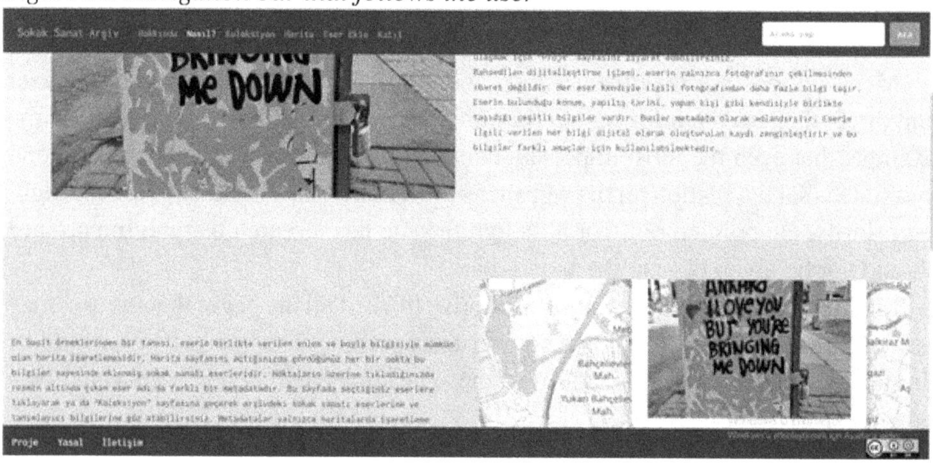

User Information

On the "about" page of the Global Street Art website, which has the second highest usability level as a result of formal evaluation (Uğur, 2023; Uğur and Öztemiz, 2024), while making a call for contribution, they also addressed a direct audience by saying "If you are an artist or photographer and want to contribute, please register and upload photos to our website. If you just want to say hello or give us some suggestions, you can email us at dudes@globalstreetart.com". The target audience referred to on this page is "artist", "photographer" or "anyone who might contribute". On the Street Art Cities website, the target audience is expressed with the term "hunter", which is used frequently on the site.

Although the target user base of the website to be created includes the entire society, artists, collectors and people interested in street art are in the priority group. In this regard, this group should be addressed first, as the Global Street Art site does, but beyond that, since the site will have an archive feature, researchers from various fields such as archaeology, history, art history and architecture should also be included in the target audience. The last group can be addressed under the title "researcher". While these groups are mentioned directly, it should also be emphasized that the site is a platform open to users from all walks of life.

The home page, the name of the website is "Street Art Archive", the purpose of the short site is "The website that archives street art works made in Türkiye together with its users." (see Figure 14).

Figure 14. Main page

Getting feedback is the easiest way to learn about the shortcomings of the site directly from the person using it. The contact page should be located in the footer bar where the user can always see it. As on the home page, there is "about" and "how?" Expressions such as "Feel free to contact us to express your questions and opinions" should be used on pages where users can ask questions. Problems (if any) should be grouped and a "frequently asked questions" page should be prepared and presented as questions/answers responded to by the site, without the user having to wait for an e-mail. Thus, the usability level of the site will increase in terms of both user feedback and accessibility to information. While explaining the "Compatibility Between the System and the Real World" criterion, Nielsen (2020) pointed out that the terms that are familiar to the creators of the site may be unfamiliar to the users. Accordingly, the words to be used on the page should be chosen very simple and understandable. Even if the user is not directly interested in street art, they should be informed to avoid this confusion. Therefore, the page should be prepared to provide explanations for all types of users.

Collection

According to Dyson and Moran (2000, p. 404), the user should be able to access the information he wants by clicking on the options before typing a word in the search bar. On the proposed website, the works should be visible shortly and concisely (Aesthetic and Minimalist Design) by clicking on the menu item in the top bar with the title “Collection”.

Works should be presented to the user in filterable lists based on both map and metadata fields. However, both document access tools do not need to be presented on the same page. The Street Art Cities website only allows you to open a map of a single city and search for artworks and search options in a small area on the right. However, this page is among the sections that are considered problematic by experts (Uğur, 2023; Uğur and Öztemiz, 2024).

Instead, a “collection” page with filtering and search features, where the works are directly visible, and a separate “map” page, where the locations of the works on the map can be created, can be created on the site to be designed. The coordinate information of the works is one of the fields created by selecting the location on the map and is required for the user to fill in. With the “Map” page, it is possible to effectively present all works visually on the map. In the site to be suggested, all works can be presented on an interactive map on the left side of the page, offering drifting and zooming in/out options (see Figure 15). When you click on the icons, it is possible to see basic work data such as work name, artist name, and work image on a card. When you click on this card, you can go to the work page with all the details of the work. One of the metrics measured in the Dyson and Moran (2000) survey is the number of works in the collection. This information should be presented n the page in a way that the user can easily see.

Figure 15. Map page view

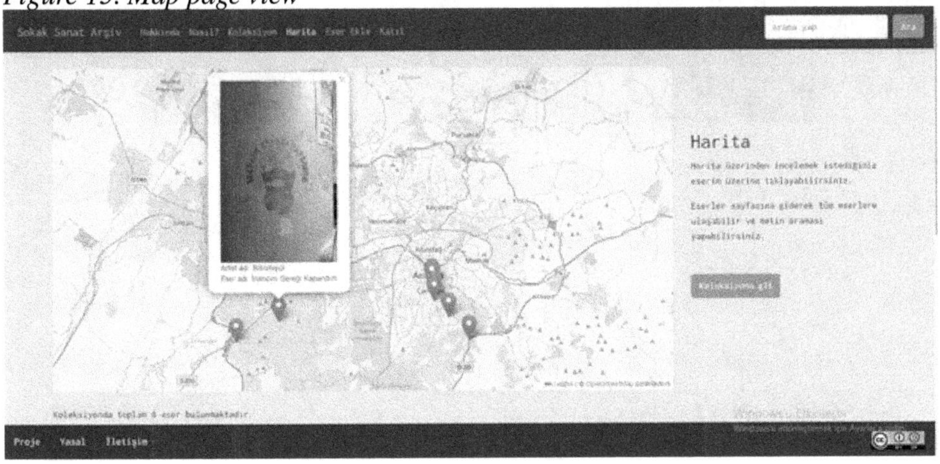

On the left side of the prepared sample page, there are all the works in the collection, and on the right side there is a section that offers filtering and search features. The search and filtering area should be created on a card that follows the user even if he or she scrolls the page. By scrolling down through the collection, the user should be able to start a new search at any time.

While the Collection and Map pages display the collection, a page should also be designed for each work. All information about the work should be given on this page. The big picture of the work can be presented in the middle, with the meta below and the location information on the map shown side by side (see Figure 16). Thus, the user will be able to access all visual, spatial, and textual information on the same page. At the bottom, there will be "edit", "delete" and "report lost" buttons designed to inform you that the work is no longer in the same location.

Figure 16. Sample work page

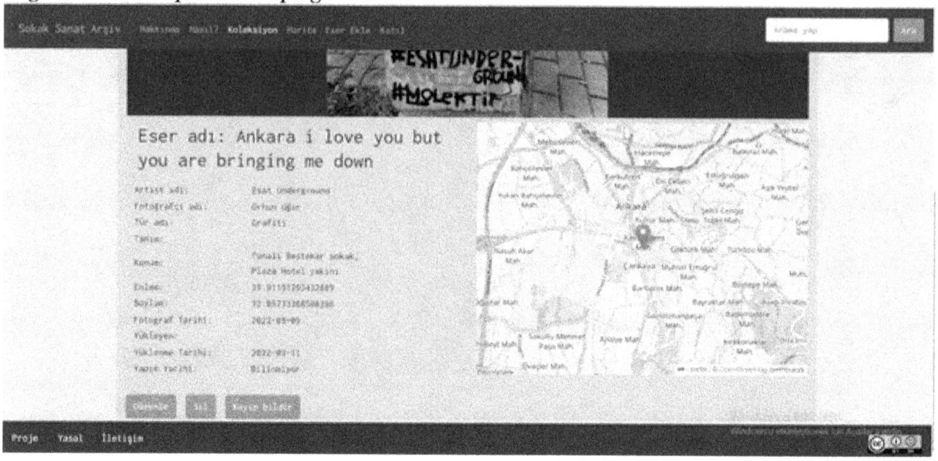

Pages throughout the website have been created using works from the collection. The user may also want to access the works on these pages. When you move the cursor over the image without the need for any search, you can access the work and artist name information at the bottom of the image (see Figure 17). When you click on the area where the information is provided, you can go back to the work page.

Figure 17. Interacting with the work displayed on the pages

Structural Context

Access to the collection, both as a map and as listed works, is possible with just a single click on the collection page. Additionally, when you click on the works in the collection exhibited on other pages, you can go directly to the work page. The website may provide external links to different collection pages, as does the Art-Crimes site. The "project" page, which will contain detailed information about the project, should provide links to different collections as well as links to literature on street art, digitalization, and participatory heritage. In this way, the user will be able to see street art digitalization projects with examples from around the world and realize the importance of this site for our country, in which he is or is considering becoming a participant.

Another item examined under this heading is the up-to-dateness of the website. The fact that this information is not directly available to the user during the formal evaluation makes data collection difficult. Information that the site is up-to-date can be presented to the user along with the date in the footer bar.

Search Mechanism

Collection-based searches can be done in three ways: Filtering, searching on the map, and searching by word. Most of the websites examined (Uğur, 2023; Uğur and Öztemiz, 2024) provide menu options, allowing the user to search by filtering on areas such as artist, genre, and date. Similarly, on the created "collection" page, filtering can be done using artist, genre and city information. For example, someone who wants to see the works in Ankara will be able to see the listed cities when they hover over the "city" button (see Figure 18). When you select Ankara, the page will automatically be updated to display all the works in Ankara. Since the website initially does not have enough data to create its controlled dictionary, using these basic fields will be sufficient. As time progresses and data entry increases, features such as uploader, date, and disappearance status can also be included in the filter options.

Figure 18. Work search options

Search should also be made with the search bar on the same page. The searched text should search through all the information in the work and present the relevant results on the left (by updating the page). Later, with the advanced search option, you may be given the option to search only in specified areas. An advanced search feature can also be added to the right-hand column. The web page should also allow searching via the map. The "Map" page was established for this purpose. The page, which currently lists all works on the map, may become more useful in the future by adding filtering options here. Additionally, if the user cannot select the locations on the map, they should have the option to search not only for the work but also for the locations on the map. Considering different user types, search options should be offered as much as possible without straining the eyes. However, since the information to be used during searching or filtering will be created as data is entered, basic search tools will be sufficient in the beginning.

Call Return and Records

On the web page to be designed for Türkiye, search results are displayed directly with cards on the collection page, while they are presented as points on the map on the map page. The filtering or word search results are presented on the same page by updating the entire collection. In this way, all data containing similar texts or classified in the same type will be available to the user. If the search can directly find a single example, the single result should be displayed alone. If the search result is not possible, the user must be informed. According to usability analysis in literature (Uğur, 2023; Uğur and Öztemiz, 2024), one of the usability criteria that experts considered most problematic was the recognition, diagnosis, and treatment of errors. Users need to take precautions against errors that may be encountered, especially when searching for work. For a work that cannot be found as a result of the search, the user should be informed that the work can't be found, and alternative ways to find it should be shown.

There is no need to give the user a lower or upper limit in terms of image quality. The image quality of today's cameras or mobile phone cameras will be sufficient. However, a standard can be offered regarding the format of the image file by recommending .jpg or .png. It should be stated to the user that the photo should be brought without any action on it.

Decentralizing Street Art

When street art is reconsidered from a Web 3 perspective, it reveals innovations in the art itself, the role of the artist, and the long-term preservation of cultural heritage. To ensure the sustainability of street art, there must be a mechanism for monetization. Street art, which is often not directly funded by a single entity due to its unique and anonymous nature, can benefit from support through decentralized financial structures.

Related literature (Uğur, 2023; Uğur and Öztemiz, 2024) highlights that only three crowdfunding platforms were utilized, but these platforms are crucial for enabling street art to be created freely and without censorship. The proposed website for Türkiye should offer users various payment options, including cryptocurrency, to support this model.

In Uğur's (2023) study, street artworks were successfully converted into NFTs on the platform '99 Rooms' (https://opensea.io/collection/99-rooms). For the proposed website in Türkiye, if the artist's identity is known, an account can be created in their name. If the artist remains anonymous, revenue from sold products could be held in a communal pool until the rightful owner claims their earnings.

Another way to monetize street art is by transforming it into a source of tourism revenue, as demonstrated by the Street Art Cities website. As the site attracts more visitors, the potential for advertising revenue increases. The proposed website could allocate space for campaigns that support street art and artists, thereby contributing to the tourism industry in areas where street art is prominent. Additionally, cities could enhance their visibility on social media through influencer campaigns, similar to those implemented by Street Art Cities. This model of social interaction could evolve into a system where not only the art and artist benefit financially, but users can also earn income by promoting street art.

CONCLUSION

In this research, in line with the literature, a web page proposal was made to digitalize and make accessible street art in Türkiye. In line with the findings obtained under the title "A Web Page Suggestion for Türkiye", some street arts in Ankara were digitized and a sample web page was designed as a practical application. In line with the results obtained from the study, it is possible to make the following suggestions:

- The web page should be designed via crowdsourcing methods and involve the users in the project. Since street artworks can disappear quickly, the digitalization process must be done directly with the user. In particular, the user should be allowed to create works, to interact with them to provide information about lost or changed works, and to provide different information about the work. Crowdfunding, one of the crowdsourcing methods, enables users to financially support the project. A system that can survive only with the user budget will be able to be maintained without the need for requests and censorship from cultural memory institutions or different special funds. Liking and sharing the works, and creating new works or collections by using them in different ways will increase the visibility of the website. This will cause more users to examine the site, gain awareness about street art as a cultural heritage product, and perhaps become involved in the site development process through crowdsourcing methods, allowing street art to be preserved sustainably.
- The target user audience should be determined and users at all levels should be informed about street art as a cultural heritage product, crowdsourcing methods, and digitalization. In a "project" page that can be created, it should first be explained to the user why street art is a product of cultural heritage and has the nature of a historical document. Afterward, crowdsourcing methods should be mentioned so that the user can participate in the system in any way. Digitization and its stages should be explained so that new works can be added to the collection, identified, and organized. In addition, there is a "how?" section containing content that informs the general user, such as how to use the site, how to upload a work, how to provide support. A page should also be added to the site. The proposed site and the work data it contains should be able to be used by researchers in various ways. For researchers who may need works or metadata, the works should be presented as tabular data in addition to their appearance on the page, and how to use them should be explained.
- The website should be as clear as possible. Street art can be preserved by digitalization due to its ephemeral nature. Since street artworks can be seen

anywhere at any time and disappear quickly, digitalization should be done with the participation of society, not by cultural heritage professionals. The user's inability to access, share, or use the works will negatively affect the interaction of the web page with the user. This will harm the sustainable management of street art, whose preservation depends directly on user participation. In the Horizon 2020 program, the European Commission has determined the principle of "as open as possible, as closed as necessary" for access to research data (European Commission, 2016, p. 4). Since heritage data can also be used as research data by various scientists, the same principle should be used for street art data. Roued-Cunliffe (2019, p. 2) pointed out that openness to heritage data can be brought at 3 levels with physical, online, and data-level access. The site to be designed for Türkiye should provide online access to the works as well as access at the data level. Heritage data should include metadata of the work rather than just the photograph of the work. As suggested by Berners-Lee (2006), presenting all data of the artworks to researchers in an open format such as CSV and by integrating semantic languages and frameworks like XML and RDF will help adapt to the open data universe.

- The user should be informed about copyrights and should be able to access the content regarding permissions and conditions such as uploading, using, and copying the work. Although openness is one of the main features of the site, the legal regulations necessary to protect the rights of artists and the expression "closed as necessary" mentioned in Horizon 2020 (European Commission, 2016, p. 4) should be taken into consideration. On a "legal" page that can be created, the work and metadata must be defined and its owner must be shown. The examined website Street Art Cities defines the owner of the works and metadata added to the site as the person who uploaded the work. The preferred license for reuse and distribution on the site is Creative Commons BY SA 4.0 (Creative Commons., 2023). Likewise, on the site to be proposed for Türkiye, the owner of the digitized work should be determined as the uploader and CC BY-SA should be used as an open license. Apart from the person who uploads the work, the street artist who produces the physical work also has the right to have a say on the work. Since the street artist creates his work in a public area where everyone can see it, it is thought that he will not have any problems with his work being seen. However, even if he does not want the work to be seen or not to be published on this site, his choice should be respected to protect his rights. If contacted, the work should be removed. This information must be given on the same page, as it shows both the user uploading the work that the street artist will have the priority right to speak in such a case and that the street artist can contact in such a case.

- Metadata should be created taking into account information that is particularly important for street art. When describing the works on the site, the simple descriptive fields provided by DC (DCMI Usage Board, 2020) should be used. However, street art differs from other cultural heritage products in that it can disappear very quickly. Extinction information should be included alongside other metadata describing the work, and an encouraging "report edit" option should be provided for users who notice the disappearance to report it. Since the works will be uploaded with a participatory approach, there is a possibility that not every user will know all the metadata about the works. For works whose description remains incomplete, except for the mandatory fields (see Table 1), metadata containing defined or undefined information must be submitted. Users who want to add information to missing works or direct artists will be able to easily access the works as a result of a search based on the information in this field. As works and information about works are entered into the site, commonly used terms should be grouped and in-site authority files should be created. In this way, the term with the same meaning will be prevented from being written in two different ways.
- Navigation and error prevention features should be given importance. As a result of related studies (Uğur, 2023; Uğur and Öztemiz, 2024) heuristic evaluation, the weakest aspects of the site were navigation and error prevention features. Menu titles on the website to be proposed for Türkiye should be kept short and should be designed to provide information about the content. The website should be designed in a way that allows the user to always return to the previous page. External pages that open to different web addresses, such as the "blog" on the website under review, should be avoided as they may confuse the user and do not provide an opportunity to return. Any error encountered on the website should inform the user of the reason for the error. In case of an error occurring while searching for a work or a work not being found, suggestions should be made to the user as to why the work could not be found or how to perform alternative searches. In both the work and general search results, similar or close possibilities should be presented to the user even if the work cannot be accessed directly.

DISCUSSION

The Street art platform created should support street artists. The sustainability of street art is directly related to the fact that artists continue to produce works and the addition of new artists. Interviews with artists, projects that can be carried out together, community pages where experienced artists and novices can meet, job opportunities that can be offered to indexed artists, paint and various equipment that can be purchased from the artist support budget that can be created from the site fund, should be among the features that the site to be developed can offer.

Possibilities offered by Web 3 technologies should be considered. Besides crowdfunding methods, securing ads for the website, running influencer campaigns, and especially utilizing NFTs can help monetize the projects. Using decentralized and more cost-effective options such as IPFS for long-term storage can also help reduce the financial pressure on the project's budget.

The website to be prepared must be redevelopable in the light of new research and user feedback. Due to reasons such as the scope of the study and time limit, only one web page has been suggested for access to Türkiye's street art. The following suggestions can be offered for new research at the website development level:

- A usability evaluation is also required for the website created for Türkiye. For this evaluation, not only the heuristic evaluation method should be used, but also different types of tests should be performed. According to the evaluation results, the website can be updated and become more useful.
- Generating new ideas on how the works on social media can be combined and presented with metadata or how the works can be integrated into the site that can be recommended for Türkiye may lead to a more efficient portal.
- Opinions of street artists will provide information about their copyright, necessary metadata, and their views on street art. Communicating and learning about their needs and ideas will allow the platform to become a more collaborative project.
- Accessing street art via digital platforms not only provides an understanding of social events, social resistance efforts, and social thoughts. Street art also provides an understanding of society's perspective on art and the reflections of art on the street. Accordingly, street art platforms can be useful in contributing to educational initiatives such as school curricula or public art workshops.
- Street art is among the material and spiritual cultural products of society. Street art has the potential to provide ideas and encourage innovation in art not only for the society it belongs to but also for all humanity at a universal level. Platforms that provide digital access to street art can develop project-based collaborations with institutions responsible for the survival of cultural memory, such as libraries, archives, museums, and art galleries. This will contribute to the sustainability of access to street art as a cultural heritage, and may also provide project-based income opportunities for institutions.
- Platforms that provide access to street art can cause street artworks, which are a part of cultural identity, to be visible on a mass level. The desire of those

interested in these works to see these works physically can contribute to the development of cultural tourism in cities where street artworks are located.

- Street art, which is accessed through digital platforms and whose content is enriched with mass participation, can contribute to the appropriate use of the digital environment, the presentation of the right content by integrating it with the right information, and thus the development of digital literacy skills as an educational tool.

NOTE

This study is based on Uğur's (2023) master thesis written under the supervision of Semanur Öztemiz.

REFERENCES

Ablyazov, T., & Rapgof, V. (2019). Digital platforms as the basis of a new ecological system of socio-economic development. *IOP Conference Series. Materials Science and Engineering*, *497*, 012002. DOI: 10.1088/1757-899X/497/1/012002

Advan, A. (2015). Taksim Gezi Park protest in the framework of social movements and the use of social media (Doctoral thesis). Retrieved from: https://tez.yok.gov.tr/UlusalTezMerkezi/tezDetay.jsp?id=ebVax1OsckbMgNOJfdQ3Mg&no=kBZOEKmrfhGGibOKiM4rig

AlSheikh Theeb, T., Chuang, R., & Pandit, S. (2022). *Key considerations when developing an ICT in Education strategy (Helpdesk Response No. 43)*. EdTech Hub., DOI: 10.53832/edtechhub.0100

Ankara Metropolitan Municipality. (2019). The capital walls are colorful… Retrieved from: https://www.ankara.bel.tr/haberler/baskent-duvarlari-rengarenk

Ayhan, A. (2021). Kent mekânında bir çeviri biçimi olarak sokak sanatı. *Çeviribilim ve Uygulamaları Dergisi*, [Street art as a form of translation in urban space. Journal of Translation Studies and Applications] 31, 91-107. Retrieved from: chrome-extension://efaidnbmnnnibpcajpcglclefindmkaj/https://dergipark.org.tr/en/download/article-file/2059888

Bakri, M. Q., ... (2019). A review on service robots: mechanical design and localization system. IOP Conf. Ser.: Mater. Sci. Eng. 705 012003. Retrieved from: chrome-extension://efaidnbmnnnibpcajpcglclefindmkaj/https://iopscience.iop.org/article/10.1088/1757-899X/705/1/012003/pdf

Banksy (2005). *Banksy wall and piece.* Wemding: Apply Druck.

Bates, L. (2014). *Bombing, Tagging, Writing: An Analysis of the Significance of Graffiti and Street Art.* (Master thesis). University of Pennsylvania, Philadelphia, PA. Retrieved from: https://repository.upenn.edu/hp_theses/570/

Berners-Lee, T. (2006). Linked data. Retrieved from: https://www.w3.org/DesignIssues/LinkedData.html

Bianet (2017). More than 20 thousand gas cartridges were used in ıstanbul during the gezi resistance. Retrieved from: https://bianet.org/bianet/insan-haklari/187962-gezi-direnisinde-istanbul-da-20-binden-fazla-gaz-fisegi-kullanildi?utm_content=buffer620bd&utm_medium=social&utm_source=twitter.com&utm_campaign=buffer

Bonadio, E. (2017). Copyright protection of street art and graffiti under UK law. *Intellectual Property Quarterly,* 2, 1-39. Retrieved from: https://papers.ssrn.com/sol3/papers.cfm?abstract_id=2946360

Bonadio, E. (2018a). Graffiti gets vara protection: The 5Pointz case (March 6, 2018). *European Intellectual Property Review, 2018,* Forthcoming, Retrieved from: *SSRN*: https://ssrn.com/abstract=3135118

Bonadio, E. (2018b). Street art, graffiti and copyright. In Bonadio, E., & Lucchi, N. (Eds.), *Non-conventional copyright – do new and atypical works deserve protection?* (pp. 83–110). Edward Elgar. DOI: 10.4337/9781786434074.00012

Çakır, M. S. (2015). Graffiti and street art in Türkiye (Master thesis). Retrieved from: https://tez.yok.gov.tr/UlusalTezMerkezi/tezDetay.jsp?id=z1h8wuUu352yX48C4QpBMw&no=dTdcSQotHaQ44PhQzSb5xg

Carletti, L. (2016). Participatory heritage: Scaffolding citizen scholarship. *The International Information & Library Review, 48*(3), 196–203. DOI: 10.1080/10572317.2016.1205367

Chevet, S. (2018). Blockchain technology and non-fungible tokens: reshaping value chains in creative industries. Retrieved from https://papers.ssrn.com/sol3/papers.cfm?abstract_id=3212662

Conklin, T. R. (2012). *Street Art, Ideology, and Public Space* (Master thesis). Doi: DOI: 10.15760/etd.761

Cowick, C. (2015). Preserving street art: uncovering the challenges and obstacles. *Art Documentation: Journal of the Art Libraries Society of North America, 34,* 29-44. Retrieved from: https://www.jstor.org/stable/10.1086/680563

Creative Commons. (2023) Attribution-sharealike 4.0 international (CC BY-SA 4.0). Retrieved from: https://creativecommons.org/licenses/by-sa/4.0/

Davies, J. (2012). Art crimes?: Theoretical perspectives on copyright protection for illegally-created graffiti art. *Maine Law Review*, *65*, 27–35. https://digitalcommons.mainelaw.maine.edu/mlr/vol65/iss1/3/

Digital, N. Z. (n.d.). *Getting started with digitisation*. Retrieved from: https://digitalnz.org/make-it-digital/getting-started-with-digitisation

Dumaska, I.. (2021). E-commerce and M-commerce as global trends of international trade caused by the Covid-19 pandemic. *WSEAS Transactions on Environment and Development*, *17*, 386–397. DOI: 10.37394/232015.2021.17.38

Dyson, M. C., & Moran, K. (2000). Informing the design of web ınterfaces to museum collections. *Museum Management and Curatorship*, *18*(4), 391–406. DOI: 10.1080/09647770000501804

Erdoğan, G. (2009). Street Art in Public Space: Graffiti Istanbul, Beyoğlu, Yüksek Kaldırım Street Analysis (Master thesis). Retrieved from: https://tez.yok.gov.tr/UlusalTezMerkezi/tezDetay.jsp?id=eSyrdfAApPq4gJghJX9Txw&no=Ljcw59xkWxqAsNt4-QQreg

European Commission. (2014). Communication from the commission to the European Parliament, the council, the European Economic and Social Committee and the Committee of the Regions, towards an integrated approach to cultural heritage for Europe. Retrieved from: https://eur-lex.europa.eu/legal-content/en/ALL/?uri=CELEX:52014DC0477

European Commission. (2015). Getting cultural heritage to work for Europe, report of the Horizon 2020 expert group on cultural heritage. Retrieved from: https://op.europa.eu/en/publication-detail/-/publication/b01a0d0a-2a4f-4de0-88f7-85bf2dc6e004

Gordon, K. (2021). Using color to enhance your design. Retrieved from: https://www.nngroup.com/articles/color-enhance-design/

Gottlieb, L. (2008). *Graffiti art styles a classification system and theoretical analysis*. McFarland & Company, Inc., Publishers.

Graf, A. M. (2018). *Facets of graffiti art and street art documentation online: A domain and content analysis* (Doctoral thesis). Retrieved from ProQuest Dissertations and Theses. (UMI No. 10810618).

Intriligator, S. S. (2015). *Local heritage as a participatory digital culture: the rise and fall of "Anglesey: a bridge through time" website* [PhD Dissertation]. ProQuest Dissertations and Theses (UMI No. 27609710)

IPFS. (2024). Persistence, permanence, and pinning. Retrieved from https://docs.ipfs.tech/concepts/persistence/#long-term-storage

Jun, Z., & Shaokang, G. (2018). Exploration of product design based on behavioral interaction and emotional guidance. *2018 1st International Conference on Education, Art, Management and Social Sciences (EAMSS)*. Retrieved from chrome-extension://efaidnbmnnnibpcajpcglclefindmkaj/https://www.clausiuspress.com/conferences/LNEMSS/EAMSS%202018/E0431.pdf

Kaçmaz, O. (2019). *Contemporary street art in Kadıköy special* (Master thesis). Retrieved from: https://www.proquest.com/openview/d4528d067e0e4c24ec0b59d773ff2aa3/1?pq-origsite=gscholar&cbl=2026366&diss=y

Kelling, G. L., & Wilson, J. Q. (1982). Broken windows: The police and neighborhood safety. Retrieved from: https://www.theatlantic.com/magazine/archive/1982/03/broken-windows/304465/

KONDA. (2014). Trip report. Society's perception of the 'Gezi Park Events'. Who were the people in Gezi Park? Retrieved from: https://konda.com.tr/uploads/konda-geziraporu2014-be80cf101d80fe3a74322f7690203132abd2f22b1c69b31a6bbad80d1a227cf1.pdf

Maecenas (2018). Andy Warhol's 14 small electric chairs to be sold in blockchain art auction. Retrieved from: https://blog.maecenas.co/andy-warhols-14-small-electric-chairs-to-be-sold-in-blockchain-art-auction/

Marchese, F. T., & Shergill, M. P. K. (2012). 500 year documentation. In *Proceedings of the 2012 ACM symposium on Document engineering (DocEng '12)*. Association for Computing Machinery, New York, NY, USA, 157–160. https://doi.org/DOI: 10.1145/2361354.2361391

Mendelson-Shwartz, E., Shwartz, O., & Mualam, N. (2023). Protecting street art rights using an NFT-based system. *Journal of Urban Technology*, *30*(3), 81–100. DOI: 10.1080/10630732.2023.2180983

Neuendorf, H. (2018). Street artist revok and H&M settle dispute over an ad that featured his work without permission. Retrieved from: https://news.artnet.com/art-world/revok-hm-ad-campaign-1345127

Nielsen, J. (2001). 13 design guidelines for homepage usability. Retrieved from: https://www.nngroup.com/articles/113-design-guidelines-homepage-usability/

Nielsen, J. (2020). 10 usability heuristics for user interface design. Retrieved from: https://www.nngroup.com/articles/ten-usability-heuristics/

Nogel, C. N. (2015). Decolonial arts pedagogy and the visual metaphor: the great wall of los angeles mural project. (Master thesis). Retrieved from: https://escholarship.org/uc/item/99m0v13q

Nomeikaite, L. (2017). Street art, heritage, embodiment. *Street Art and Creativity, 3*, 43-53. Doi: https://doi.org/DOI: 10.25765/sauc.v3i1.62

Novak, D. (2014). Methodology for the measurement of graffiti art works: Focus on the piece. *World Applied Sciences Journal*, *32*, 40–46. DOI: 10.5829/idosi.wasj.2014.32.01.301

Novak, D. (2015). Photography and classification of information. *SAUC - Street Art & Urban Creativity Scientific Journal,* 1, 13-25. Doi: DOI: 10.25765/sauc.v1i1.22

Oomen, J., & Aroyo, L. (2011). Crowdsourcing in the cultural heritage domain: opportunities and challenges. Proceedings of the 5th International Conference on Communities and Technologies (C&T '11) In Association for Computing Machinery (p. 138–149). New York, USA. Doi: https://doi.org/DOI: 10.1145/2103354.2103373

Pehlivan, S. (2021). Sanatın ve hareketin mekânı sokaklar. Retrieved from: https://narmanlisanat.com/sokak-sanati/

Poole, K. (2020). Arts organizations engaging audiences through street art. Unpublished master thesis. ProQuest Dissertations and Theses veri tabanından erişildi. (UMI No. 27999258)

Roued-Cunliffe, H. (2019). *Open heritage data: an ıntroduction to research, publishing and programming with open data in the heritage sector*. Facet., DOI: 10.29085/9781783303618

Roued-Cunliffe, H., & Copeland, A. (Eds.). (2017). *Participatory heritage*. Facet., DOI: 10.29085/9781783301256

Salt Araştırma. (2023). 13th news about Antalya international film and art festival painting and sculpture symposium. (1976). Pure research archive. Inventory Number: DRKDOC010. URI: https://archives.saltresearch.org/handle/123456789/11637

Salt Beyoğlu. (2013). They are afraid of the mural. Retrieved from: https://saltonline.org/tr/471/duvar-resminden-korkuyorlar

Schallmo, D., Williams, C. A., & Boardman, L. (2017). Digital transformation of business models best practice, enablers, and roadmap. International Journal of Innovation Management, 21, 08, 1740014. Retrieved from https://www.worldscientific.com/doi/abs/10.1142/S136391961740014X?srsltid=AfmBOooPZRAZ8Kwl83b9pqgDCfgNQTZsGO5ZqDCpxse21h_mkd2fHINl

Soma Disaster. (2014, May 14). In Wikipedia. Retrieved from (26 March 2023): https://tr.wikipedia.org/wiki/Soma_Facias%C4%B1

Taş, O., & Taş, T. (2015). Street art in Ankara: right to the city, protest and resistance. Mulkiye Journal, 39, 85-114. Retrieved from: https://dergipark.org.tr/en/download/article-file/1093

Tulke, J. (2020). Archiving dissent: (ım)material trajectories of political street art in Istanbul and Athens. A. McGarry, I. Erhart, H. Eslen-Ziya. In Jenzen, O., & Korkut, U. (Eds.), *The Aesthetics of Global Protest* (pp. 121–140). Visual Culture and Communication., DOI: 10.2307/j.ctvswx8bm.11

Tuncel, R. (2021, May 29). We commemorate those who died in Gezi with a demand for justice. Bianet. Retrieved from: https://m.bianet.org/bianet/insan-haklari/244857-gezi-de-olenleri-adalet-talebiyle-aniyoruz

Uğur, O. (2023). *Sokak sanatına erişim: Türkiye için bir web sayfası önerisi* [Access to street art: A webpage proposal for Türkiye]. Unpublished master thesis. Hacettepe University, Ankara.

Uğur, O., & Öztemiz, S. (2024). Usability evaluation of street art websites. *Bilgi Yönetimi*, 7(2), 305-324. https://dergipark.org.tr/tr/pub/by/issue/89621/1578190

van der Hoeven, A. (2020). Valuing urban heritage through participatory heritage websites: Citizen perceptions of historic urban landscapes. *Space and Culture*, *23*(2), 129–148. DOI: 10.1177/1206331218797038

Vanderveen, G., & van Eijk, G. (2016). Criminal but beautiful: A study on graffiti and the role of value judgments and context in perceiving disorder. *European Journal on Criminal Policy and Research*, *22*(1), 107–125. DOI: 10.1007/s10610-015-9288-4

Whitenton, K. (2015). Menu Design: Checklist of 15 UX Guidelines to Help Users. Retrieved from: https://www.nngroup.com/articles/menu-design/

Zahidi, Z., Lim, Y. P., & Woods, P. C. (2013). User experience for digitization and preservation of cultural heritage. In *2013 International Conference on Informatics and Creative Multimedia,* 2013, (p. 13-16). Kuala Lumpur, Malaysia Doi: DOI: 10.1109/ICICM.2013.11

ENDNOTES

1 https://www.streetartmuseumamsterdam.com/

2 https://www.urbanspree.com/

Chapter 7

Mobile Platforms, Designs, and Applications for Web3 Towards Reducing Students' Cognitive Load:

Online Meetings and Recordings for Support

Dalize van Heerden
https://orcid.org/0000-0002-7539-8995
University of South Africa, South Africa

Leila Goosen
https://orcid.org/0000-0003-4948-2699
University of South Africa, South Africa

ABSTRACT

The purpose of the module reported on in this chapter is that it will be used by students as an introduction to object-oriented programming in the context of developing the knowledge, skills, and values needed to develop a working computer-based program and to add interactive functionality to the program through structured object-oriented programming. Against the background of Mobile Platforms, Designs, and Applications for Web3, the novelty of the chapter is emphasized by this module being presented at a Comprehensive Open and Distance e-Learning (CODeL) university.

DOI: 10.4018/979-8-3693-2973-3.ch007

BACKGROUND

This section of the chapter will provide broad definitions and discussions of the topic of Reducing Students' Cognitive Load by using Online Meetings and Recordings for Support and incorporate the views of others (in the form of a literature review) into the discussion to support, refute, or demonstrate the authors' position on the topic.

Theme 1: Digital Learning and Pedagogy

1.1 Online and Blended Learning

"The growing shift toward online learning" had "brought new expectations for teachers, including" the "skills needed to combine content knowledge with engaging pedagogical strategies that leverage the affordances of" technologies. Against the background of educational psychologists, Archambault, Leary and Rice (2022, p. 178) presented a framework for teaching in online learning environments in terms of the so-called 'pillars' of online pedagogy.

The effects of various modes of online learning on learning results was the focus of an international journal article on advanced computer science and applications by Rusli (2020, p. 100). "The demand for online learning particularly" at the college level means that this mode of delivery needs "to be developed and implemented as an alternative method of" delivering "learning materials in this millennial era."

Best Practices in Online Course Design

At the Frontiers in Education (FIE) conference, the paper by Velaj, Dolezal, Ambros, Plant and Motschnig (2022, p. 1) presented "a new method for designing a *course* that is suitable for teaching data science". The latter paper further focused "on the *design* of data science courses" for non-computer science students, the aim of which was to implement the practical considerations and findings suggested by Velaj, et al. (2022, p. 2)

The purpose of the journal article on higher learning research communications by Russell (2021, p. 14) was "to comprehensively describe and justify the case" Design, Development, Implementation, and Support (DDIS) "of an approach for the integration of synchronous virtual meetings" for supporting non-traditional online doctoral candidates.

Synchronous and Asynchronous Learning Approaches

The qualitative study reported on in an international journal article on educational technologies in higher education by Heilporn, Lakhal and Bélisle (2021, p. 1) provided an examination of teachers' strategies to foster "student *engagement* in blended learning (BL), i.e., blended, blended online, and blended synchronous courses that combine *synchronous and asynchronous*" *learning approaches*.

Theme 6: Technology Integration in Various Disciplines

In the *Handbook of Research on User Experience in Web 2.0 Technologies and Its Impact on Universities and Businesses*Pelet (2021a) indicated that as "various areas of discipline continue to progress into the digital age, diverse modes of technology are being experimented with and ultimately implemented into common practices".

The introductory chapter by Pelet (2021b, p. 1) to the latter book designated that the design of interfaces had "become an essential dimension of companies' digital strategies, aiming at enhancing user experiences through" user experience goals.

Theme 7: Educational Policy and Ethics

7.1 Technology Policy in Education

Digital Literacy and Inclusivity

The purpose of the chapter by Van Heerden and Goosen (2023a, p. 73) was "to provide research on issues from a curriculum transformation perspective regarding teaching" open and distance e-learning students in an information and communication technology context "and the implications of COVID-19" for fostering diversity and *inclusivity*.

7.2 Ethical Considerations in Educational Technologies

Ethical considerations related to data management and research integrity in the context of e-schools, community *engagement* and *educational technologies* (Goosen, 2018) should be implemented.

7.3 Assessment and Accreditation

Online Assessment Strategies

The journal article by Goosen and Van Heerden (2018) provided information and communication technology tools and tips with regard to the assessment of students in higher education, the conference paper by Van Heerden and Goosen (2019) described how assessments were used in an open distance e-learning environment to promote self-directed learning, and the conference paper by Van Heerden and Goosen (2021a) portrayed students' perceptions of e-assessment in the context of COVID-19 in the case of the University of South Africa (UNISA).

"The principal aim of the research reported on in" the *lecture notes in networks and systems* article by Van Heerden and Goosen (2023b, p. 827) "was investigating the assessment submission rates of a first-year programming module at an African Open and Distance e-Learning" university.

Quality Assurance in Digital Education

Goosen and Van Heerden (2019a) were promoting research-based opportunities for first year programming learners in terms of relevant and quality IT education.

A journal article by Nesprava, et al. (2023, p. 247) dealt with the formation of the "communicative competencies of applicants for higher education in the context of distance learning from the perspective of neurosciences."

The research reported on by Maulana, Anita and Putra (2022, p. 139) aimed to investigate how English as a Foreign Language (EFL) students applied "critical thinking in speaking activities and to explore the levels of critical thinking achieved by EFL students".

Theme 8: Global and Cultural Perspectives

8.1 International Collaborations in Education

The journal article on occupational therapy education by Todorova, et al. (2022, p. 1) presented "the products and evaluation results" from the development and implementation of *international* "Cooperative Online Peer-assisted and Intercultural Learning in Occupational Therapy" (COPILOT).

The model presented in an *Irish journal* article on *academic practice*, the "Partner Co-hosted Model (PCM), evolved over many years" (Gillespie, Doyle, Jiang, & Humble, 2022, p. 2). Using the latter model had led to meaningful and sustainable international *engagement* and joint academic activity between two institutions.

Cross-Border Online Learning Initiatives

The lecturers involved "facilitated an in-depth reflection on" a virtual client briefed communication project *across borders* and the case study indicated "that although learning outcomes online" were 'virtually' "the same, the student experience" was "inferior to such face-to-face projects" (Duarte & Riedl, 2021, p. 190).

MAIN FOCUS OF THE CHAPTER

Issues, Problems

This section of the chapter will present the authors' perspectives on the issues, problems, etc., as these relate to the main theme of the book on Mobile Platforms, Designs, and Applications for Web3, and arguments supporting the authors' position on Reducing Students' Cognitive Load by using Online Meetings and Recordings for Support. It will also compare and contrast with what had been, or is currently being, done as it relates to the specific topic of the chapter.

Outcomes

For this module, students have to master several outcomes:

- Demonstrate a clear understanding of programming 'problem statements' as stated by computer users in various industries.
- Students apply fundamental programming principles for the development of a computer-based program.
- Students apply object-oriented program development tools for the development of a working computer-based program.
- Students apply object-oriented programming language to develop a solution specific to and, to the satisfaction of, the client.

Even though all registered students at the university can access Microsoft Office 365 and Moodle is now integrated with Microsoft Teams, this plug-in is not available to lecturers. Currently, a module team is created, and students are added manually to the team by the lecturer.

Online meetings have been implemented in this module since 2011 and the lecturer has presented at international and national conferences on the subject. Throughout the years the following concerns have been logged in relation to the online meetings:

1. Attendance of online meetings has consistently been below 10% of registered students.
2. Regardless of the time online meetings are scheduled, weekday morning, afternoon, evening, or weekend, the time does not suit most students.
3. Students do not have data to attend online meetings.
4. Students "forget" that they must attend online meetings.
5. Students expect the online meetings to have a face-to-face class format.

Meeting invitations are sent to the students via Teams to their student email accounts when the meeting is created. Students can add the meeting invitations to their Outlook email calendars. The meeting invitations are added to the Announcement communication repository and shared on the module Telegram group in an attempt to ensure students are aware of meetings. Students joining the Telegram group are also reminded a day before the meeting.

The first online meeting for the module is hosted by the lecturer. During the meeting, the lecturer addresses well-known issues to assist the students in successfully completing the module. Students are given ample time throughout the presentation to ask questions about the module presentation, the module content, and the assessment practices and procedures.

The module e-tutors host weekly meetings with the students. The purpose of an e-tutor is to provide academic support and guidance to students enrolled in online courses. E-tutors are typically experienced educators who are trained to provide online tutoring services and support students in their academic endeavors.

E-tutors are an important resource for students because they can provide personalized support and help students overcome the challenges of online learning. By providing academic guidance and support, e-tutors can help students achieve their academic goals and succeed in their courses. It is not the purpose of an e-tutor to create, design, or present course content, as this is typically the responsibility of the lecturer. Similarly, it is not the purpose of an e-tutor to perform administrative tasks, such as managing student records, assessment records, or technical problems, as this is typically the responsibility of university staff in administrative roles.

Theme 1: Digital Learning and Pedagogy

1.1 Online and Blended Learning

Time management is "a very important aspect of online and blended learning" (Cox, Alexander, West, Abzhaparova, & Hill, 2023, p. 503). According to a journal article on geography in higher education by the latter authors, the "key element to good time management" and how to thrive "*when studying online* is to create a schedule", because it helps one "not only with completing work" on time (Cox, et al., 2023, p. 504), but steps can also be taken to manage one's "time effectively *when studying online*".

Technology-Enhanced Active Learning

As university teachers, Barken, et al. (2023, p. 1) could not "always satisfy students' wishes and requirements for" the university campus as a smart *technology-enhancedactive learning* arena. "In many cases, the common teaching equipment on campus and the personal teaching equipment of many university teachers are obsolete."

The objective of the research paper presented by Boonchutima, Chongkolrattanaporn and Kongchan (2023, p. 2) at the IEEE Region 10 Conference (TENCON) "was to enhance content recognition and application among 23 first-year master's degree international students in the Strategic Planning and Evaluation for Integrated Communications Course at the Faculty of Communication Arts." The latter authors implemented cognitive load theory in online education by leveraging interactive media, testing and interaction to enhance *engagement* and active learning.

Cognitive load can be impacted in both positive and negative ways by online teaching and learning sessions. By introducing additional distractions, such as technological issues, poor internet connection, or other disruptions that can take focus away from the current learning activity, these sessions have the potential to raise the cognitive load. However, online meetings can also lessen the cognitive load by giving students easy access to digital resources such as educational videos, multimedia content, and interactive simulations that can assist and reinforce learning.

An e-journal article by Sulistyarini (2022, p. 166) provided an analysis of the cognitive aspects related to test techniques in Islamic education and learning. "Assessment activities in schools are part of the learning process to reflect an understanding of individual students and measure progress."

1.2 Pedagogical Innovation

Flipped Classroom Models

The e-tutors in this module implement a flipped classroom to support students by following these steps:

- **Assign pre-recorded video lectures:** The lecturer had created pre-recorded video lectures on concepts from the prescribed book. Students are required to watch these before the online meeting. This allows students to watch and learn at their own pace, giving them the opportunity to revisit challenging topics and formulate questions for the e-tutors to address during the online meetings.

- **Assign readings:** Students should read the provided online articles and textbook chapters that further explain programming concepts along with the pre-recorded video lectures. Should students require further clarification, they should ask for assistance from the e-tutor during the online meeting.
- **Set up a discussion forum:** For each chapter, students can ask questions, share their thoughts, and engage in online discussion forums related to the pre-recorded video lectures and readings. The e-tutors monitor the forums for questions that can be addressed both in the forum and during the online meeting.
- **Assign hands-on exercises:** During the actual online meeting, e-tutors explain hands-on programming exercises that allow students to apply the concepts they learned in the pre-recorded lectures and readings. E-tutors also provide *feedback* on students' work and offer additional explanations or guidance as needed.
- **Provide additional resources:** E-tutors also provide additional resources, such as online tutorials, programming **tools**, and other learning materials, to help students further develop their programming skills.

A flipped classroom model encourages students to participate actively in their learning experience. During online meetings, they participate in online discussions, group projects, and other interactive activities with peers, lecturers, and e-tutors after working alone with the instructional materials. Encouraging students to actively engage during the online meetings and develop their own knowledge and meaning supports constructivist learning. Students can increase their understanding and internalization of the concepts they are studying by having meaningful interactions with peers, lecturers, and e-tutors.

Nevertheless, implementing the flipped classroom idea in a fully online program presents some challenges. Learning might be hindered by technical problems, such as slow internet access or trouble using digital resources. Furthermore, it may be difficult for students who lack self-motivation or have restricted access to technology to interact with the course materials and participate completely in group learning activities.

Flipped classroom online sessions could be categorized within several categories in the taxonomy of educational objectives by Bloom (1956), based on the particular learning goals and assessment criteria. Online meetings can foster students' critical thinking, problem-solving, and creative abilities by allowing them to participate in higher-order thinking exercises.

- **Knowledge:** Using a flipped classroom approach, students can get a basic grasp of a subject before the online meeting, which frees up more time for higher-order thinking activities. During the online meeting, this can aid students in remembering and identifying basic concepts and terminology.
- **Comprehension:** Discussions and exercises that assist students in gaining an increased understanding of the material are facilitated through online sessions. Students participate in group discussions, examine case studies, and work together to solve coding challenges during online meetings. In doing so, they improve their comprehension of the subject matter and are able to use concepts and principles towards solutions for difficulties.
- **Application:** Through online sessions, students are assisted in applying the concepts and principles they have learnt to their practical assessments. This helps students apply programming concepts to practical applications.
- **Analysis:** Students are guided in analyzing and interpreting information through online meetings. Students get the ability to think critically and assess the advantages and disadvantages of various methods for tackling programming challenges as a result.
- **Synthesis/Creation:** Through online meetings, students are also guided in producing original works for their project-based assessments. In order to develop something new, this helps students in synthesizing and applying what they have learned.

Microsoft Teams live transcription is activated during all online meetings; this is the process of transcribing spoken words into written text in real time as they are being spoken. Live transcription is especially helpful for people with hearing impairments, as it allows them to follow along with spoken conversations or presentations in real-time. It is also useful for non-native speakers who struggle to keep up with fast-paced conversations or presentations in a second language.

All the online meetings are recorded. Recording the online meetings allows students to review and reinforce the material covered during the session. They can go back and re-watch parts that were unclear or that they may have missed during the live session. The recordings ensure that students who were unable to attend the live session due to scheduling conflicts or other reasons can still access the material and receive the same level of support as those who attended.

The recordings also allow the lecturer and e-tutors to review their own performance and identify areas where they can improve. They can also use the recordings to assess the effectiveness of their teaching methods and adjust them accordingly. Recording the sessions provides a record of what was covered and what support was provided to each student. This can be useful for tracking student progress, evaluating the effectiveness of the e-tutoring program, and addressing any concerns or issues that may arise.

The recordings of the meetings are downloaded from Microsoft Teams, as it has been found that recordings expire or become unavailable at certain points for unknown reasons. The downloaded recordings are uploaded to the lecturer's Microsoft OneDrive account. The Moodle book resource is used to upload the meeting recordings. Some advantages of the book resource are:

- Several connected pages with a table of contents – a bit like a mini website
- Displays neatly on the course page, saving space
- Ability to include text, images, links, sound, and video
- Easy to update if the information changes (no need to delete and re-upload a file!)

Project-Based and Experiential Learning

The conference paper and journal article by Goosen and Van Heerden (2013a) and (2013b) respectively described project-based learning and assessment influencing the pass rates of an ICT module in the context of an ODL institution.

1.3 Learner Engagement and Motivation

"The COVID-19 pandemic required a complete transition to online teaching. With valid concerns of a potential decrease in student *engagement*, it was necessary to focus on the most effective learning strategies and reduce cognitive load" (Collins, 2021, p. 1524). At the 44th international convention on information, communication and electronic technology, the latter author explained how the "software engineering professional practice postgraduate module at" the University College of London was redesigned to increase such *engagement.*

Peer Interaction and Collaborative Learning

Online meetings allow for real-time collaboration between students and lecturers/e-tutors. Collaborative work is an essential aspect in the programming field, and online meetings provide a platform for students to work together, share ideas, and learn from each other. Students can also review the recorded online meetings, which can help them catch up on missed tutor sessions or review difficult concepts, this flexibility allows them to learn at their own pace. This can be especially helpful for students struggling with certain concepts or needing extra time to process information. Joining the online sessions can help remote students broaden their knowledge and skills beyond the printed or multimedia study material. The online meetings and their recordings are essential tools for programming students. They provide accessibility, collaboration, time management, resource sharing, and flexibility, which can help students succeed in their programming studies. As technology continues to advance, online meetings will become an even more critical part of the programming education landscape.

Online meetings can enhance constructivist learning by allowing students to participate in group projects, discussions, and collaborative learning activities with peers, instructors, and e-tutors. Online meetings can also make it easier for students to access technology-enhanced learning environments, which let them explore ideas and concepts through interactive simulations and other online tools.

However, because these reduce the social contact and interpersonal relationships necessary for collaborative learning, online meetings can also provide difficulties for constructivist learning. In addition, attending meetings virtually may lead to a more passive learning environment in which students merely take information rather than actively create their own knowledge. It's critical that lecturers and online instructors understand these effects and create online courses that successfully support and improve learning objectives.

The purpose of an international journal article on management, knowledge and learning by Qafzezi (2023, p. 1) was "to discuss the necessity for the" internationalization of Albanian Higher education Institutions (HEIs), "in light of the recent changes that HEIs in Albania" were undergoing, as well as online collaborative learning in higher education in Albania, together with necessary innovations in this regard.

Feedback and Assessment Strategies

E-tutors can provide a variety of services to students, such as:

- Clarifying course content and helping students to better understand difficult concepts.
- Providing feedback on assignments and assessments to help students improve their performance.
- Offering study strategies and time management guidance to help students stay organized and focused.
- Facilitating online discussions and helping to build a sense of community among students in the online environment.

Theme 3: Digital Collaboration and Communication

3.1 Online Communities and Social Learning

The Role of Social Media in Education

"Social media advertising effectiveness is a fundamental **issue** that remains poorly examined in academic research. The aim of" the research reported on in an international journal article on technology and human interaction by Pelet and Ettis (2022, p. 1) was to investigate the role of perceived originality, liking, credibility, irritation, intrusiveness, and destination.

3.2 Online Teamwork and Collaboration

Collaborative Tools and Platforms

According to the journal article on group decision and negotiation by Cheng, et al. (2023, p. 749), the "recent outbreak of COVID-19 posed discontinuous disruption to traditional learning modes worldwide. In order to keep social distance, online collaborative learning" had "become a necessity during the" COVID-19 period. The latter authors were investigating students' satisfaction with online collaborative learning using an expectation-confirmation model.

An autonomous intelligent systems journal article by Wang and Li (2023, p. 1) indicated that in "response to the impact of COVID-19, the manufacturing industry and academic industrial research have largely shifted to online or hybrid conference formats. The sudden change has posed challenges for researchers and teams to adapt" to. The latter authors therefore suggested remote collaborative process optimization in research and the design of industrial manufacturing.

Group Projects and Peer Assessment

The chapter by Van Heerden and Goosen (2020a) was promoting the growth of fourth industrial revolution information communication technology students and described the implications of open and distance e-learning in this regard.

Virtual Team Dynamics and Success Factors

UNISA offers courses to students who, due to a variety of factors, including distance, disability, or other obligations, are unable to attend in-person classes. As long as students have an internet connection, students studying at UNISA can join in online meetings from any location across the globe.

A journal article on problem-based learning in higher education by Kelly, Conway, Harney and McKeague (2022, p. 1) provided "a narrative review of the crucial elements for" temporary transitions to "online Problem Based Learning (PBL) and a reflective overview of factors to consider when temporarily moving to online tutorials, forming a practical guide" with advice for (e-)tutors, learners and "educators in the health professions and beyond."

The study reported on by Nussli, Oh and Davis (2024, p. 62) in a journal article on e-learning and digital media was designed for capturing "the successes and failures during pandemic teaching at a" teachers' college in Switzerland. An investigation was conducted into the experiences of five undergraduate university students and their perceptions of their faculty's emergency remote teaching approaches.

3.3 Digital Communication and Multimedia

Video Conferencing and Webinars

"While *videoconferencing* is prevalent, concurrent participation channels are limited. People experience challenges keeping up with the discussion, and misunderstanding frequently occurs" (Chen, Li, Liu, Fowler, & Wang, 2023, p. 1). As part of the proceedings of the ACM on human-computer interaction the latter authors introduced 'MeetScript' for designing transcript-based interactions to support active participation in group video meetings.

Digital Storytelling and Visual Communication

The study reported on by Widiartha, Hwang, Yoon and Pratiwi (2023, p. 439) in an international journal article on informatics visualization discussed "learning strategies resilience that can be used to improve learning outcomes during the current pandemic circumstances, which have limitations in face-to-face learning." A systematic literature review by the latter authors provided an analysis of the resilience of the education system in higher education due to the COVID-19 pandemic in Indonesia.

Podcasts, Blogs, and Multimedia Content Creation

Van Heerden and Goosen (2012) reported on the use of *vodcasts* to teach programming in an ODL environment.

Theme 8: Global and Cultural Perspectives

8.3 Education in Crisis and Conflict Zones

A European Conference on e-Learning (ECeL) paper towards hybrid learning in higher education in the wake of the COVID-19 crisis by Gnaur, Hindhede and Andersen (2020, p. 205) indicated that digital "transformation is considered a major change process that takes time and often meets employee resistance and avoidance."

When Kireyev and Zhabotynska (2020, p. 222) described how the COVID-19 pandemic had "made radical adjustments to the organization of the educational process in higher education institutions" and most "governments around the world, including" the Ukraine, the modern tools for the implementation of distance learning the latter authors portrayed as one of the collective monographs in a book on pedagogy in modern conditions, the Ukraine was not yet a *conflict zone*.

Education in Emergency Settings

An "Integrated Multidisciplinary Project at the Kulliyyah of Architecture and Environmental Design (KAED), International Islamic University Malaysia (IIUM), generally requires students to solve relevant real problems related to the built environment" (Bahrudin, Rahim, & Alias, 2022, p. 38). A design ideals journal article by the latter authors reported on online learning experiences of an integrated multidisciplinary course during the COVID-19 pandemic.

Programming courses teaching methods before, during, and after the COVID-19 pandemic was the focus of a paper by Moosa and Bahaaudeen (2023, p. 1) at the International Conference on IT *Innovation* and Knowledge Discovery (ITIKD. "During the pandemic of COVID-19 educational institutions" adopted "online teaching and learning mechanisms. This" "led to some challenges in teaching programming courses as" these are considered to be some "of the most difficult disciplines."

A survey-based study on smart education, as well as the opportunities and challenges induced by the COVID-19 pandemic reported on by Choi, Song and Zaman (2020, p. 1) at the International Smart Cities Conference (ISC2) indicated that the "viability of online education and comparisons of modes of education have long been a topic in educational study."

The chapter by Ngugi and Goosen (2021) considered *innovation*, entrepreneurship, and sustainability for ICT students towards the post-COVID-19 era.

SOLUTIONS AND RECOMMENDATIONS

This section of the chapter will discuss solutions and recommendations in dealing with the issues or problems presented in the preceding section.

Students who pass this module should be able to develop logical programming skills and could extend this knowledge and skills into adding interactivity through object-oriented programming to many programs and its assessment in the context of computer-based programming. Students are equipped to think conceptually to recognize the design rules, techniques, and components to compose a solution.

Qualified students are able to express their logical thinking skills and creativity to society through the design and development of functional working computer-based programs, in industry process systems and organizational information systems, to specific standards (such as user-friendly, robust, solution specific, and to the satisfaction of the client).

Theme 4: Technology and Learning Environments

4.2 Digital Learning Spaces and Infrastructure

Learning Management Systems

The coference paper by Goosen and Van Heerden (2015) discussed e-learning management system technologies for teaching programming at a distance.

Cloud-Based Learning Solutions

For "institutions to effectively implement cloud" technologies to support distance learning, and in the context of optimizing such educational delivery, the journal article by Ahmad (2023, p. 42) could "understand how this technology not only facilitates learning but also" suggested cloud-based solutions for effective distance learning.

Abdulsaeed, et al. (2019, p. 106) presented work on the adoption of cloud-based solutions for e-learning technologies, their relative perspectives for higher education and its usage in a real-world "environment, so that the overall" context of education, academia and learning could be consolidated.

When using cloud-based *Learning Management Systems* (LMS), many "fundamental cloud-based learning platforms are" potential solutions (Malhi, Iqbal, Nabi, & Malhi, 2020, p. 165). E-learning based on cloud computing for educational institutions are vulnerable to security issues and "threats to e-learning systems in addition to cloud-based e-learning security threats" (Malhi, et al., 2020, p. 166).

An evaluation by Nepali (2017, p. 36) contained information about a Graphics Processing Unit (GPU) "service provider for deep learning" and the scalability of deep learning in the cloud, which are providing different kinds of deep learning solutions.

At the offshore technology conference Asia, Wen, Dobson and Hvaara (2020) suggested Mesh learning as a cloud and edge–based computing network "for deploying machine learning solutions in an industrial internet of things" and providing data–driven solutions to the oil and gas industry.

"When it comes to clinical" cloud and machine learning based solutions for healthcare and prevention, "AI cloud computation aims to bring together cloud-based processing systems with the ML skills of AI in order to make interconnected, smart health coverage" possible (Jumani, Siddique, & Laghari, 2023, p. 173). The latter chapter appeared in a book on the *requirements,challenges, solutionsand practices* related to *Image Based Computing for Food and Health Analytics (IBCFHA).*

Many "modern machine learning solutions are already implemented in cloud services" (Tadejko, 2020). "Machine Learning as a Service (MLaaS) is a general definition of various cloud-based" cognitive services based on machine learning methods in architecture of modern knowledge management solutions. Towards software development, the latter chapter formed part of a book on data-centric business and applications.

A questionnaire was sent to 534 students, who were registered for the module ICT1512 – Introduction to Interactive Programming in 2023. 139 students responded to the questionnaire. Of the respondents, 76 students passed the module and 63 students failed.

A total of 21 online meetings were held on a Saturday afternoon between 13:00 and 15:00 throughout 2023. E-tutors reported that attendance was between 5% and 10% of students registered for the module.

Figure 1. Please indicate how many online meetings you attended (Van Heerden)

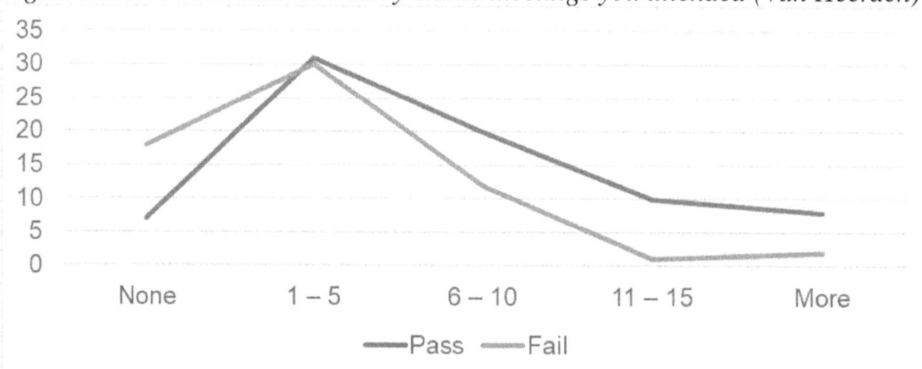

Eighteen (29%) of the respondents who failed this course did not attend any of the online meetings, compared to only seven (9%) of the respondents who passed (see Figure 1). On the other side of the spectrum, only three (5%) of the respondents who failed this course attended eleven or more of the meetings, compared to eighteen (24%) of those who passed.

Figure 2. Please indicate how many of the online meeting recordings you watched (Van Heerden)

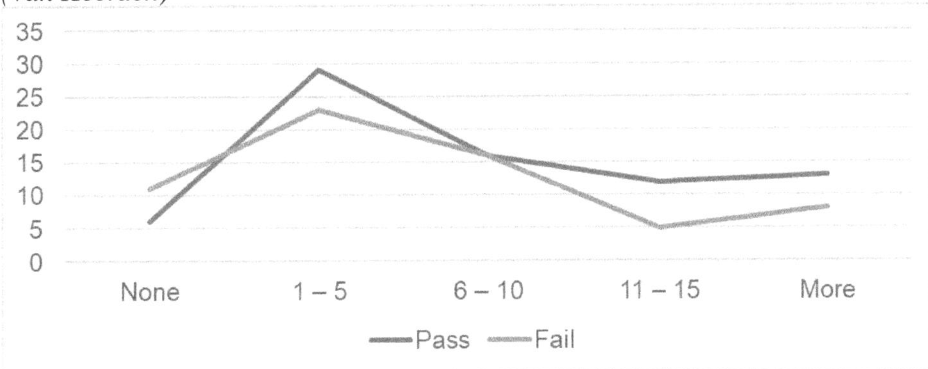

Eleven (17%) of the respondents who failed this course did not watch any of the online meeting recordings, compared to only six (8%) of the respondents who passed (see Figure 2). On the other side of the spectrum, thirteen (21%) of the respondents who failed this course watched eleven or more of the meeting recordings, compared to 25 (33%) of those who passed.

Figure 3. The online meetings were crucial to my success in the module (Van Heerden)

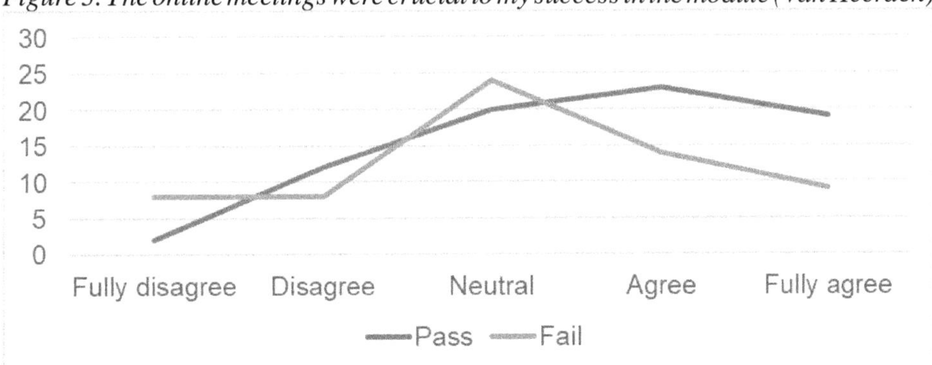

More than half of the respondents who passed (42; 55%) agreed or fully agreed that the virtual team meetings are seen as *crucial* success factors *in the module*, compared to just over a third (23; 36%) of those who failed (see Figure 3).

Figure 4. I understand meeting times cannot be scheduled to suit my personal preference as there are 600+ students in my class (Van Heerden)

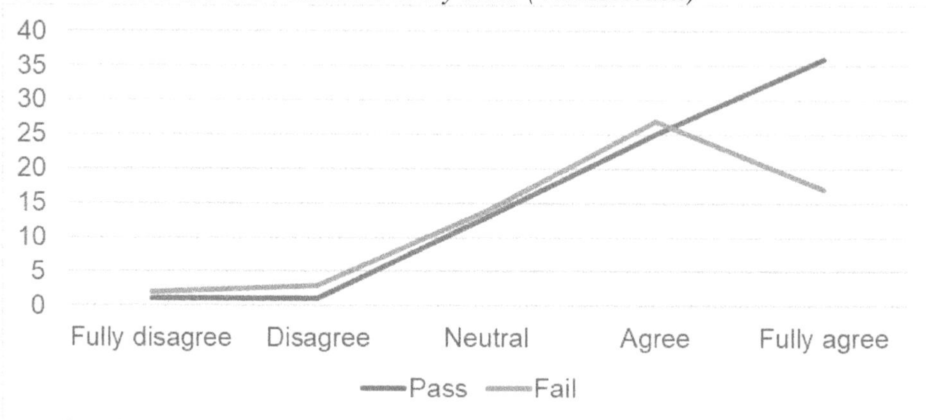

Almost half of the respondents who passed (36; 47%) fully agreed that they *understand meeting times cannot be scheduled to suit* their *personal preference as there are 600+ students in* the *class*, compared to 27 (43%) of those who failed that agreed with the statement. (see Figure 4).

Figure 5. I experienced difficulties connecting to the MS Teams meetings because of my data connection (Van Heerden)

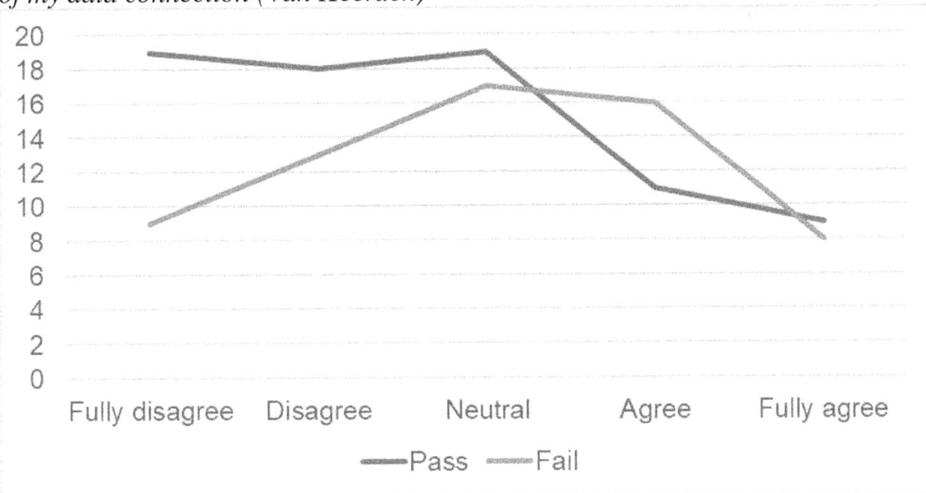

Around a quarter each of the respondents who passed (19; 25%) fully agreed, (18; 24%) agreed and (19; 25%) adopted a neutral stance with regard to the statement '*I experienceddifficultiesconnecting to the MS Teams meetings because of my data connection*' (see Figure 5). The responses of students who failed (again, around a quarter each) were more clustered around neutral: thirteen (21%) agreed, 17 (27%) adopted a neutral stance and sixteen (25%) disagreed.

Figure 6. Attending an online MS Teams meeting does not increase the productivity of my studies (Van Heerden)

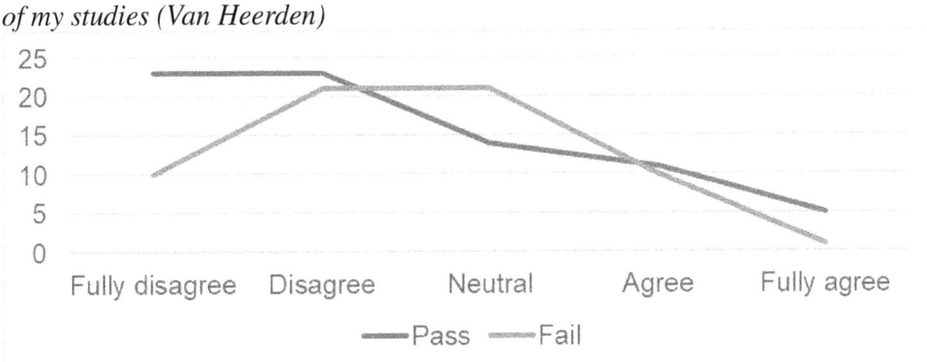

While groups of 23 (30%) each of respondents who passed fully disagreed or disagreed that *attending an online MS Teams meeting* did *not increase the productivity of* their *studies*, the responses of students who failed were again more shifted towards neutral, with a third each (21; 33%) disagreeing or adopting a neutral stance (see Figure 6).

Figure 7. I wanted to participate in the MS Teams meetings (Van Heerden)

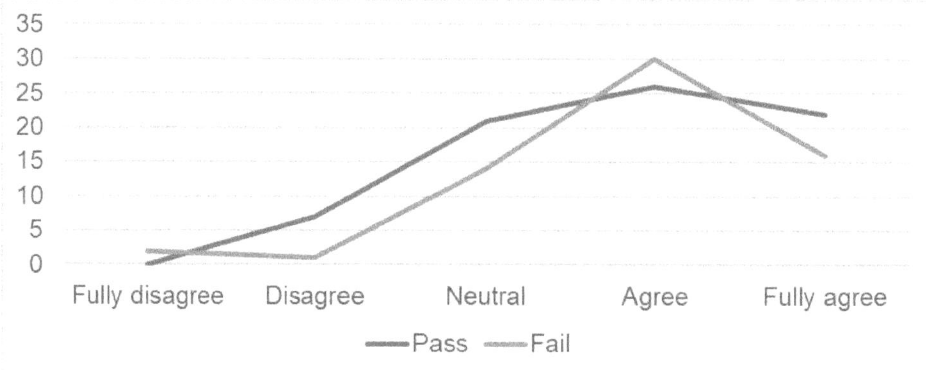

Whereas only seven (9%) of the respondents who passed disagreed and none fully disagreed that they *wanted to participate in the MS Teams meetings*, almost half of the respondents who failed (30; 48%) agreed with this statement and another quarter of them (16; 25%) fully agreed (see Figure 7).

Figure 8. The online meeting recordings were crucial to my success in the module (Van Heerden)

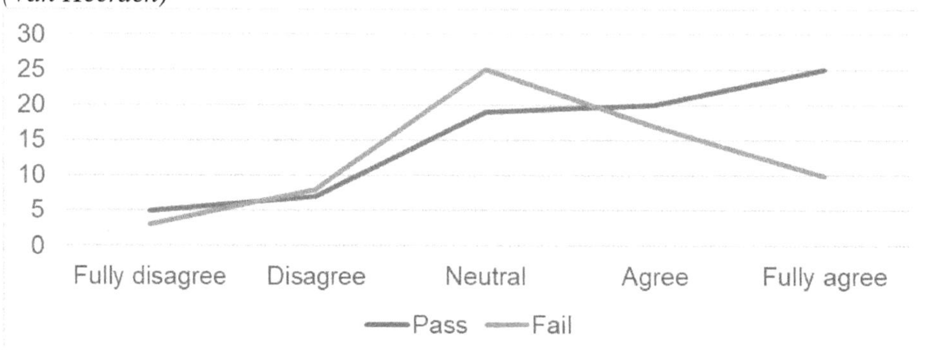

Although a quarter (19;25%) of the respondents who passed were neutral with regard to *the* virtual team *meeting recordings* being *crucialsuccess* factors *in the module* and a third of them (25;33%) fully agreed with the statement, 25 (40%) of the respondents who failed were neutral with regard to the statement and only ten (16%) of them fully agreed (see Figure 8).

Figure 9. The online meetings do not address my questions related to the module content (Van Heerden)

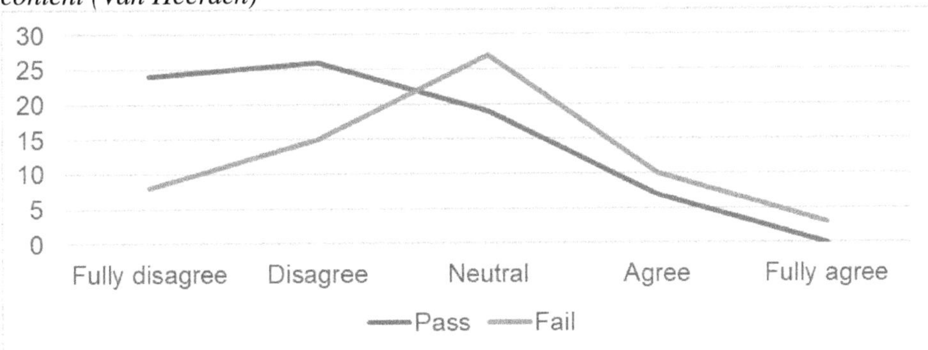

Only seven (9%) of the respondents who passed agreed and none fully agreed that *the online meetings* did *not address* their *questions related to the module content*, with around a third of them each fully disagreeing (24;32%) or disagreeing (26;34%) (see Figure 9). Almost half of the respondents who failed (27;43%) adopted a neutral stance and almost a quarter (15;24%) disagreed.

Figure 10. I do not like attending online classes where lecturers/e-tutors explain academic work (Van Heerden)

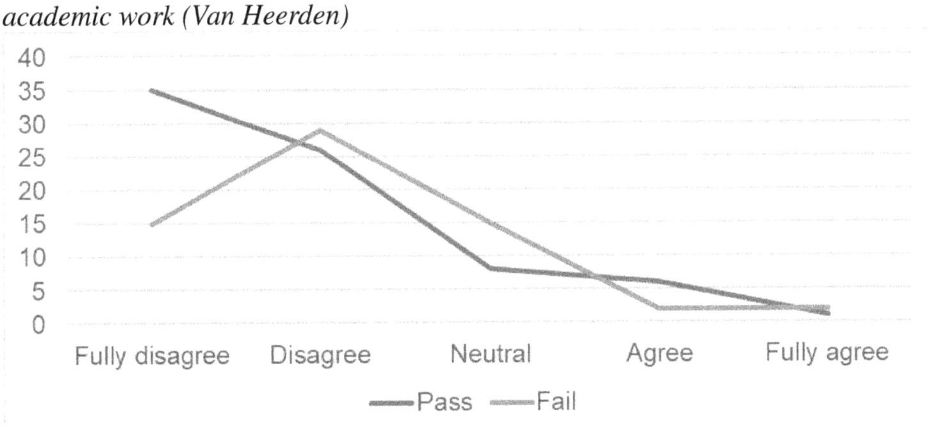

Despite the fact that almost half of the respondents who passed (35; 46%) fully disagreed that they did *not like attendingonline classeswhere lecturers/e-tutors explain academic work*, the same percentage of the respondents who failed (29;46%) disagreed with this statement, while almost a quarter each (15;24%) fully disagreed or adopted a neutral stance (see Figure 10).

Figure 11. I prefer watching recorded lessons to attending online classes (Van Heerden)

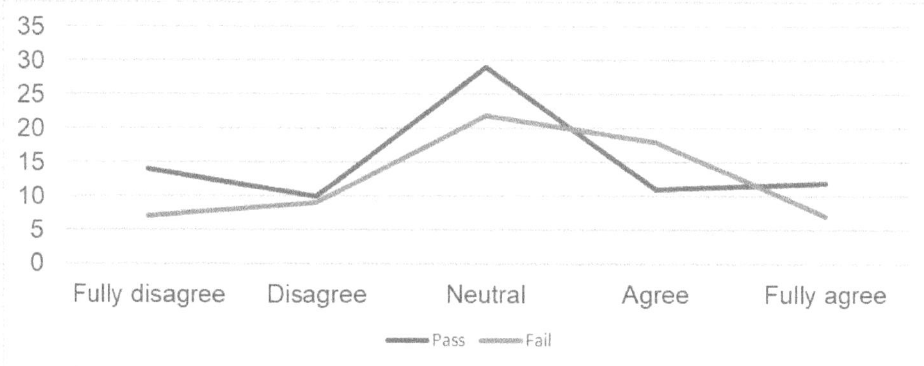

Figure 11 shows the results for the only item where the majority of respondents, irrespective of having passed (29;38%) or failed (22;35%), adopted a neutral stance on preferring to watch *recorded lessons to attendingonline classes*. It is also interesting to note that almost a third of the respondents who failed (18; 29%) agreed with this statement.

Figure 12. I understand that this is an online university without classes. Online meetings are scheduled to assist with work I do not understand (Van Heerden)

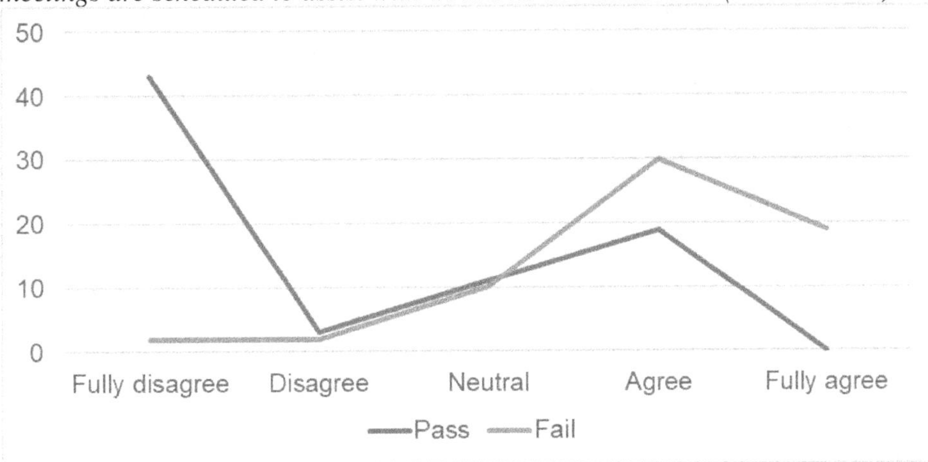

Whilst more than half of the respondents who passed (43; 57%) fully disagreed that they *understand that this is an online university without classes. Online meetings are scheduled to assist with work* they did *not understand*, almost half of the respondents who failed (30;48%) agreed with this statement (see Figure 12)!

Recommendations

In line with the theme discussed earlier in this section, Naidu, Najah, Saqib, Swathi and Pandey (2023, p. 1) were transforming e-learning through cloud-based interactive multimedia authoring solutions, and considered the impact of these "on the overall teaching and learning process." The conference paper by the latter authors finally made recommendations on "a framework, which can be implemented along with various cloud-based authoring solutions."

FUTURE RESEARCH DIRECTIONS

This section of the chapter will discuss future and emerging trends, as well as provide insights about the future of the theme of the book on Mobile Platforms, Designs, and Applications for Web3 from the perspective of the chapter focus on Reducing Students' Cognitive Load by using Online Meetings and Recordings for Support. The viability of a paradigm, model, implementation issues of proposed programs, etc., may be included in this section. If appropriate, this section will suggest future research directions within the domain of the topic.

As "instruction can happen at any time and for a variety of reasons," Lahcen, Mohapatra and Chen (2020, p. 8) wanted to share their perspectives on, and looked forward to, investigating prioritizing strategies for a better transition to remote instruction "in the future, using better methodology".

The journal article by Van Heerden and Goosen (2021b) asked questions about the future of information and communication technology courses.

Theme 2: Emerging Technologies in Education

2.2 Augmented and Virtual Reality

"While it is appealing to consider the potential benefits of incorporating virtual exchange and other technology-based tools when designing a learning experience, it is irresponsible to assume that technology in-and-of itself has the power to improve learning outcomes." A journal article on virtual exchange by Sims (2022, p. 133) provided a practice report on the utilization of research-based principles to support and assess learning outcomes when teaching critical thinking and cultural intelligence via virtual exchange.

Theme 4: Technology and Learning Environments

4.2 Digital Learning Spaces and Infrastructure

Virtual Learning Environments

The study reported on in an international journal article on emerging technologies in education by Songkram, Songkram, Chootongchai and Samanakupt (2021, p. 34) "examined the development of learning and innovation skills among students in the *virtual learning environment* provided by" a smart classroom.

Goosen and Van Heerden (2016) discussed e-*learning environment* tools to address online and open distance education context challenges.

Theme 9: Future Trends and Research Methodologies

"The year 2020 began with grand ideas about building future higher education. Thereafter universities" had "been through a constant swirl of uncertainties and" confusion as these responded "to a novel suite of radically reconfigured fundamentals and prospects" (Coates, Xie, & Hong, 2021, p. 166). A journal article on studies in higher education by the latter authors was engaging transformed fundamentals to design global hybrid higher education.

An entry by Pelet, Belda and Arezki (2023, p. 31) in the *Encyclopedia of Data Science and Machine Learning* indicated that the use of Artificial Intelligence (AI) "is the key to profound changes" and predicting emerging trends in vegetation dynamics "in Africa. It creates as many opportunities as challenges, and to achieve this, foreign capital is welcome."

9.1 Future Trends in Educational Technologies

Emerging Technologies and Their Impact

The paper published from the 17th international conference on Computer Sciences and Information Technologies (CSIT) by Miroshnyk, Matviy, Halaz and Bahlai (2022, p. 260) examined modern emerging trends in the development and use of online platforms for "distance learning. The prerequisites for the transition to distance education in the conditions of the COVID-19 pandemic" were outlined.

Educational Horizons and Technological Advancements

Goosen and Van Heerden (2017) showed how to go beyond the *horizon* of learning programming with *educational* technologies.

CONCLUSION

This section of the chapter will provide a discussion of the overall coverage of the chapter and concluding remarks.

Best practices in online course design and online learning implemented in the module discussed in this chapter are appreciated by student respondents who pass. A blend of synchronous and asynchronous learning approaches is applied through the presentation of online meetings and recordings of these. The flipped classroom model employed further adds to the project-based learning effected.

Virtual Team Dynamics and Success Factors

Respondents who passed agreed that the virtual team meetings and the recordings of these are seen as crucial success factors in the module.

Textual data analysis had

"become a popular method for examining complex human behavior in various fields, including psychology, psychiatry, sociology, computer science, data mining, forensic sciences, and communication studies. However, identifying the most relevant textual parameters for analyzing complex behavior is still a challenge."

Against the background of *psychology research and behavior management*, textual analysis methods as mentioned in the recent study by Uludag (2024, p. 1139) exploring the association between textual parameters and psychological and cognitive factors can be used for personalized education.

"The development of technologies for predicting personality behavior is one of the priority directions for improving the diagnostic apparatus of psychology. The integration of information technologies" can be one of the methods of social network texts analysis for a psychometric model of personal behavior as described by Prokopyev, Ustin, Gafarov and Popov (2024, p. 1) in their *BIO Web of Conferences* paper.

The aim of the study reported on by Namkoong, Park, Lee and Park (2024, p. 1) in a *behavior* and *information technology* journal article was "to verify the causal relationship between the nonverbal immediacy" behavior "(NIB) of an artificial intelligence … agent for mental health counselling and user satisfaction" with regard to serial mediation of positive expectancy violation and rapport.

REFERENCES

Abdulsaeed, A., Burhanuddina, M., Ismaelb, M., Abd Ghania, M. K., Elzamly, A., & Doheir, M. (2019). Adoption of cloud based solutions for E-learning technologies and their relative perspectives for higher education. *Revista Aus*, *26*(10), 105–114.

Ahmad, A. (2023). Optimizing Educational Delivery: Cloud-Based Solutions for Effective Distance Learning. *Jurnal Sistem Informasi dan Teknik Informatika (JAFOTIK) [Journal of Information Systems and Informatics Engineering]*, *1*(2), 41-46.

Archambault, L., Leary, H., & Rice, K. (2022). Pillars of online pedagogy: A framework for teaching in online learning environments. *Educational Psychologist*, *57*(3), 178–191. DOI: 10.1080/00461520.2022.2051513

Bahrudin, F. I., Rahim, A. A., & Alias, N. U. (2022). Online Learning Experiences for Integrated Multidisciplinary Course During the Covid-19 Pandemic. *Design Ideals Journal*, *4*(2), 38–44.

Barken, T. L., Bonacina, S., Bostad, R., Gabarron, E., Garcia, B., Haddeland, K., Hanssen, Ø., Hartvigsen, E., Hartvigsen, G., Hejlesen, O., Henriksen, A., Horsch, A., Iversen, A., Jaccheri, L., Johannessen, E., Johnsen, H. M., Martinez, S. G., Martinez Millana, A., Pelagatti, S., & Årsand, E. (2023). University campus as a smart technology-supported active learning arena. *Septentrio Reports*, (1). Advance online publication. DOI: 10.7557/7.7222

Bloom, B. S. (Ed.). (1956). Taxonomy of educational objectives: Vol. 1. *Cognitive domain*. David McKay.

Boonchutima, S., Chongkolrattanaporn, T., & Kongchan, W. (2023, October). Cognitive Load Theory in Online Education: Leveraging Interactive Media, Testing, Interaction and to Enhance Engagement and Active Learning. *Region 10 Conference (TENCON)* (pp. 2-9). IEEE.

Chen, X., Li, S., Liu, S., Fowler, R., & Wang, X. (2023, October). MeetScript: Designing Transcript-based Interactions to Support Active Participation in Group Video Meetings. *Proceedings of the ACM on Human-Computer Interaction, 7*(CSCW2), 1-32. DOI: 10.1145/3610196

Cheng, X., Bao, Y., Yang, B., Chen, S., Zuo, Y., & Siponen, M. (2023). Investigating Students' Satisfaction with Online Collaborative Learning During the COVID-19 Period: An Expectation-Confirmation Model. *Group Decision and Negotiation*, *32*(4), 749–778. DOI: 10.1007/s10726-023-09829-x PMID: 37304175

Choi, B. Y., Song, S., & Zaman, R. (2020, September). Smart Education: Opportunities and challenges induced by COVID-19 pandemic:[A survey-based study]. *International Smart Cities Conference (ISC2)* (pp. 1-8). IEEE. DOI: 10.1109/ISC251055.2020.9239063

Coates, H., Xie, Z., & Hong, X. (2021). Engaging transformed fundamentals to design global hybrid higher education. *Studies in Higher Education*, *46*(1), 166–176. DOI: 10.1080/03075079.2020.1859683

Collins, G. J. (2021, September). Redesigning a Postgraduate Software Engineering Module to Increase Engagement. *44th International Convention on Information, Communication and Electronic Technology (MIPRO)* (pp. 1524-1529). IEEE. DOI: 10.23919/MIPRO52101.2021.9597084

Cox, W., Alexander, A., West, H., Abzhaparova, A., & Hill, J. (2023). How to thrive when studying online. *Journal of Geography in Higher Education*, *47*(3), 502–511. DOI: 10.1080/03098265.2022.2087214

Duarte, A., & Riedl, K. (2021). "Virtually" the same learning outcomes. A case study of a virtual client briefed communication project across borders. *ICONO 14, Revista de comunicación y tecnologías emergentes [Journal of Communication and Emerging Technologies], 19*(2), 189-211.

Gillespie, B., Doyle, P., Jiang, Z., & Humble, D. (2022). Sustainable international engagement using a partner co-hosted teaching model. *Irish Journal of Academic Practice*, *10*(1), 1–13. DOI: 10.21427/as8x-eq43

Gnaur, D., Hindhede, A. L., & Andersen, V. H. (2020, October). Towards hybrid learning in higher education in the wake of the COVID-19 crisis. *European Conference on e-Learning* (pp. 205-211). Academic Conferences International Limited.

Goosen, L. (2018). Ethical Data Management and Research Integrity in the Context of e-Schools and Community Engagement. In Sibinga, C. (Ed.), *Ensuring Research Integrity and the Ethical Management of Data* (pp. 14–45). IGI Global., DOI: 10.4018/978-1-5225-2730-5.ch002

Goosen, L., & Van Heerden, D. (2013a). Project-Based Assessment Influencing Pass Rates of an ICT Module at an ODL Institution. In E. Ivala (Ed.), *Proceedings of the 8th International Conference on e-Learning.* 1, pp. 157-164. Cape Town: Academic Conferences and Publishing.

Goosen, L., & Van Heerden, D. (2013b). Project-based learning and assessment of an IT module in an ODL context. [SAJHE]. *South African Journal of Higher Education*, *27*(6), 1430–1443.

Goosen, L., & Van Heerden, D. (2015). e-Learning Management System Technologies for Teaching Programming at a Distance. In C. Watson (Ed.), *Proceedings of the 10th International Conference on e-Learning (ICEL)* (pp. 116 - 126). Nassua: Academic Conferences and Publishing International. Retrieved from https://scholar.google.co.za/scholar?oi=bibs&cluster=16255326938393691479&btnI=1&hl=en

Goosen, L., & Van Heerden, D. (2016). e-Learning Environment Tools to Address Online and Open Distance Education Context Challenges. In R. M. Idrus, & N. Zainuddin (Ed.), *Proceedings of the 11th International Conference on e-Learning (ICEL)* (pp. 275 - 284). Kuala Lumpur, Malaysia: Academic Conferences and Publishing International.

Goosen, L., & Van Heerden, D. (2017). Beyond the Horizon of Learning Programming with Educational Technologies. In U. I. Ogbonnaya, & S. Simelane-Mnisi (Ed.), *Proceedings of the South Africa International Conference on Educational Technologies* (pp. 78 - 90). Pretoria: African Academic Research Forum.

Goosen, L., & Van Heerden, D. (2018). Assessment of Students in Higher Education – Information and Communication Technology Tools and Tips. *Progressio, 40*(1), #4704 23 pages. DOI: 10.25159/0256-8853/4706

Goosen, L., & Van Heerden, D. (2019a). Promoting Research-Based Opportunities for First Year Programming Learners: Relevant and Quality Information Technology Education. In Govender, N., Mudaly, R., Mthethwa, T., & Singh-Pillay, A. (Ed.), *Proceedings of the 27th Conference of the Southern African Association for Research in Mathematics, Science and Technology Education (SAARMSTE)* (pp. 215 - 228). Durban: University of KwaZulu-Natal.

Goosen, L., & Van Heerden, D. (2019b). Student Support for Information and Communication Technology Modules in Open Distance Environments: Towards Self-Directed Learning. In Van Wyk, M. M. (Ed.), *Student Support Toward Self-Directed Learning in Open and Distributed Environments* (pp. 26–58). IGI Global., DOI: 10.4018/978-1-5225-9316-4.ch002

Heilporn, G., Lakhal, S., & Bélisle, M. (2021). An examination of teachers' strategies to foster student engagement in blended learning in higher education. *International Journal of Educational Technology in Higher Education, 18*(1), 1–25. DOI: 10.1186/s41239-021-00260-3 PMID: 34805484

Jumani, A. K., Siddique, W. A., & Laghari, A. A. (2023). *Cloud and Machine Learning Based Solutions for Healthcare and Prevention. Image Based Computing for Food and Health Analytics: Requirements, Challenges, Solutions and Practices (IBCFHA)*. Springer International Publishing.

Kelly, D., Conway, C., Harney, S., & McKeague, H. (2022). Temporary Transitions to Online Problem-Based Learning: Advice for Tutors and Learners. *Journal of Problem Based Learning in Higher Education*, *10*(1), 1–19. DOI: 10.54337/ojs.jpblhe.v10i1.6362

Kireyev, I. V., & Zhabotynska, N. V. (2020). Modern tools for the implementation of distance learning. In *Pedagogy in modern conditions: collective monograph* (pp. 222-225). Boston: Primedia eLaunch. DOI: 10.46299/ISG.2020.MONO.PED.III

Lahcen, R. A., Mohapatra, R., & Chen, B. (2020, November 16). Prioritizing strategies for a better transition to remote instruction. *EDUCAUSE Review*. Retrieved from https://er.educause.edu/articles/2020/11/prioritizing-strategies-for-a-better-transition-to-remote-instruction

Malhi, M. S., Iqbal, U., Nabi, M. M., & Malhi, M. A. (2020). E-learning based on cloud computing for educational institution: Security issues and solutions. *International Journal of Electronics and Information Engineering*, *12*(4), 162–169.

Maulana, R., Anita, F., & Putra, M. I. (2022, June). EFL Students' Critical Thinking in Speaking Activities. *Jurnal Pendidikan Bahasa*, *11*(1), 139–152. DOI: 10.31571/bahasa.v11i1.3528

Miroshnyk, R., Matviy, I., Halaz, L., & Bahlai, I. (2022, November). Trends in the Development of Online Platforms for Distance Learning. *17th International Conference on Computer Sciences and Information Technologies (CSIT)* (pp. 260-264). IEEE. DOI: 10.1109/CSIT56902.2022.10000065

Moosa, J., & Bahaaudeen, A. (2023, March). Programming courses Teaching methods Before, During, and After COVID-19 Pandemic. *International Conference on IT Innovation and Knowledge Discovery (ITIKD)* (pp. 1-5). IEEE. DOI: 10.1109/ITIKD56332.2023.10099736

Naidu, V. R., Najah, S., Saqib, M., Swathi, R., & Pandey, N. (2023). Transforming E-Learning through Cloud-Based Interactive Multimedia Authoring Solutions. *SHS Web of Conferences. 156*. EDP Sciences. DOI: 10.1051/shsconf/202315609001

Namkoong, M., Park, Y., Lee, S., & Park, G. (2024). Effect of AI counsellor's nonverbal immediacy behaviour on user satisfaction: Serial mediation of positive expectancy violation and rapport. *Behaviour & Information Technology*, •••, 1–17. DOI: 10.1080/0144929X.2024.2367691

Nepali, S. (2017). *Evaluation of GPU based Cloud Solutions (Scalability of Deep Learning in the Cloud)*. (Master thesis). University of Oslo.

Nesprava, M., Zarishniak, I., Koropetska, O., Kurinna, A., Syvash, S., & Sushchenko, L. (2023). Formation of Communicative Competencies of Applicants for Higher Education in the Context of Distance Learning. *Revista Romaneasca pentru Educatie Multidimensionala [Romanian Journal for Multidimensional Education], 15*(1), 247-260.

Ngugi, J. K., & Goosen, L. (2021). Innovation, Entrepreneurship, and Sustainability for ICT Students Towards the Post-COVID-19 Era. In Carvalho, L. C., Reis, L., & Silveira, C. (Eds.), *Handbook of Research on Entrepreneurship, Innovation, Sustainability, and ICTs in the Post-COVID-19 Era* (pp. 110–131). IGI Global., DOI: 10.4018/978-1-7998-6776-0.ch006

Nussli, N., Oh, K., & Davis, J. P. (2024). Capturing the successes and failures during pandemic teaching: An investigation of university students' perceptions of their faculty's emergency remote teaching approaches. *E-Learning and Digital Media, 21*(1), 42–69. DOI: 10.1177/20427530221147112

Pelet, J.-E. (Ed.). (2021a). *Handbook of Research on User Experience in Web 2.0 Technologies and Its Impact on Universities and Businesses.* IGI Global., Retrieved from https://www.igi-global.com/book/handbook-research-user-experience-web/244230 DOI: 10.4018/978-1-7998-3756-5

Pelet, J.-É. (2021b). Introduction to the Book: User Experience in Web 2.0 Technologies and Its Impact on Universities and Businesses. In *Handbook of Research on User Experience in Web 2.0 Technologies and Its Impact on Universities and Businesses* (pp. 1-18). IGI Global.

Pelet, J. É., Belda, S., & Arezki, D. (2023). Use of AI in Predicting Trends in Vegetation Dynamics in Africa. In *Encyclopedia of Data Science and Machine Learning* (pp. 31–56). IGI Global.

Pelet, J. É., & Ettis, S. A. (2022). Social media advertising effectiveness: The role of perceived originality, liking, credibility, irritation, intrusiveness, and Ad destination. [IJTHI]. *International Journal of Technology and Human Interaction, 18*(1), 1–20. Advance online publication. DOI: 10.4018/IJTHI.2022010106

Prokopyev, N., Ustin, P., Gafarov, F., & Popov, L. (2024). Methods of social network texts analysis for a psychometric model of personal behavior. *BIO Web of Conferences. 116.* EDP Sciences. DOI: 10.1051/bioconf/202411606010

Qafzezi, E. (2023). Online Collaborative Learning in Higher Education in Albania: Some Necessary Innovations. *International Journal of Management. Knowledge and Learning, 12.* Advance online publication. DOI: 10.53615/2232-5697.12.S1-11

Rusli, M. (2020). The effects of various modes of online learning on learning results. *International Journal of Advanced Computer Science and Applications, 11*(4), 100–105. DOI: 10.14569/IJACSA.2020.0110414

Russell, D. L. (2021). Design, Development, Implementation, and Support (DDIS): Supporting Online Nontraditional Doctoral Candidates. *Higher Learning Research Communications, 11*(1), 14–26. DOI: 10.18870/hlrc.v11i1.1186

Sims, L. (2022). Teaching critical thinking and cultural intelligence via virtual exchange: A practice report on the utilization of research-based principles to support and assess learning outcomes. *Journal of Virtual Exchange, 5*, 133–143. DOI: 10.21827/jve.5.38804

Songkram, N., Songkram, N., Chootongchai, S., & Samanakupt, T. (2021). Developing students' learning and innovation skills using the virtual smart classroom. [iJET]. *International Journal of Emerging Technologies in Learning, 16*(4), 34–51. DOI: 10.3991/ijet.v16i04.15221

Sulistyarini, W. (2022). Analysis of Cognitive Aspects of Test Techniques in Islamic education Learning. *EDUKASI: Jurnal Pendidikan Islam (e-Journal), 10*(2), 166-190.

Tadejko, P. (2020). Cloud cognitive services based on machine learning methods in architecture of modern knowledge management solutions. In *Data-Centric Business and Applications: Towards Software Development* (Vol. 4, pp. 169-190). Springer. Retrieved from https://link.springer.com/chapter/10.1007/978-3-030-34706-2_9

Todorova, L., Fattinger, E., Url, E., Vandemaele, S., Pott, U., Strebel, H., Merklein de Freitas, C., Christopher, A., Hendriks, S., & Prellwitz, M. (2022). COPILOT – Development and Implementation of International Cooperative Online Intercultural Learning. *Journal of Occupational Therapy Education, 6*(2). Advance online publication. DOI: 10.26681/jote.2022.060219

Uludag, K. (2024). Exploring the Association Between Textual Parameters and Psychological and Cognitive Factors. *Psychology Research and Behavior Management, 17*, 1139–1150. DOI: 10.2147/PRBM.S460503 PMID: 38505355

Van Heerden, D., & Goosen, L. (2012). Using Vodcasts to Teach Programming in an ODL Environment. *Progressio, 34*(3), 144–160.

Van Heerden, D., & Goosen, L. (2020a, July). Promoting the Growth of Fourth Industrial Revolution Information Communication Technology Students: The Implications of Open and Distance e-Learning. In Buckley, S. B. (Ed.), *Promoting Inclusive Growth in the Fourth Industrial Revolution* (pp. 118–147). IGI Global., DOI: 10.4018/978-1-7998-4882-0.ch005

Van Heerden, D., & Goosen, L. (2020b, December). Information and Communication Technologies to Change Education. In M. Motseke, M. Chitiyo, U. I. Ogbonnaya, O. C. Dada, & G. Charles-Ogan (Ed.), *Proceedings of the South Africa International Conference on Education* (pp. 241-250). Pretoria: African Academic Research Forum.

Van Heerden, D., & Goosen, L. (2021a). Students' Perceptions of e-Assessment in the Context of Covid-19: The Case of UNISA. In M. Qhobela, M. M. Ntsohi, & L. G. Mohafa (Ed.), *Proceedings of the 29th Conference of the Southern African Association for Research in Mathematics, Science and Technology Education (SAARMSTE)* (pp. 291-305). Maseru, Lesotho: SAARMSTE.

Van Heerden, D., & Goosen, L. (2021b). The Future of Information and Communication Technology Courses? (K. Arai, Ed.) *Lecture Notes in Networks and Systems, 285*, 507-526. DOI: 10.1007/978-3-030-80129-8_36

Van Heerden, D., & Goosen, L. (2023a). The Implications of COVID-19 for Fostering Diversity and Inclusion Through Curriculum Transformation: Teaching Open and Distance E-Learning Students. In Tabane, C., Diale, B., Mawela, A., & Zengele, T. (Eds.), *Fostering Diversity and Inclusion Through Curriculum Transformation* (pp. 73–100). IGI Global. DOI: 10.4018/978-1-6684-6995-8.ch005

van Heerden, D., & Goosen, L. (2023b). Investigating the Assessment Submission Rates of a First Year Programming Module at an African Open and Distance e-Learning University. (K. Arai, Ed.) *Lecture Notes in Networks and Systems, 739*, 827–847. DOI: 10.1007/978-3-031-37963-5_57

Van Heerden, D., & Goosen, L. (2019, November 7 - 8). Assessments Used in an Open Distance e-Learning Environment to Promote Self-Directed Learning. In R. Ørngreen, M. Buhl, & B. Meyer (Ed.), *Proceedings of the 18th European Conference on e-Learning (ECEL 2019)* (pp. 593 - 602). Copenhagen: Academic Conferences and Publishing International Limited. DOI: 10.34190/EEL.19.003

Velaj, Y., Dolezal, D., Ambros, R., Plant, C., & Motschnig, R. (2022, October). Designing a Data Science Course for Non-Computer Science Students: Practical Considerations and Findings. *Frontiers in Education (FIE) Conference* (pp. 1-9). IEEE.

Wang, S., & Li, Q. (2023). Remote collaborative process optimization in research and design of industrial manufacturing. *Autonomous Intelligent Systems, 3*(10), 10. Advance online publication. DOI: 10.1007/s43684-023-00056-4

Wen, T., Dobson, E., & Hvaara, R. (2020, October). Mesh Learning: A Cloud and Edge–based Computing Network Providing Data–Driven Solutions to the Oil and Gas Industry. *Offshore Technology Conference Asia.* OnePetro. Retrieved from DOI: 10.4043/30365-MS

Widiartha, I. B., Hwang, J. S., Yoon, H. Y., & Pratiwi, O. N. (2023). Analysis of Resilience of Education System in Higher Education Due to Covid-19 Pandemic in Indonesia: A Systematic Literature Review. [JOIV]. *JOIV: International Journal on Informatics Visualization*, *7*(2), 439–445. DOI: 10.30630/joiv.7.2.1814

Chapter 8
Mapping Cultures Together Online Heritage Initiatives

Munir Ahmad
https://orcid.org/0000-0003-4836-6151
Survey of Pakistan, Pakistan

Maida Maqsood
Government College Women University, Sialkot, Pakistan

ABSTRACT

The digital landscape is transforming cultural heritage preservation. Online mapping initiatives, like UNESCO's GIS and Historypin's community-driven maps, are fostering engagement and accessibility. Europeana's digital library and CyArk's 3D preservation empower us to explore and safeguard heritage across time and space. By catering to diverse heritage types (tangible and intangible), these platforms offer valuable tools for education and global exchange. With the integration of Web3 technologies, these initiatives can further enhance their impact. Decentralized networks enable more equitable access to digital heritage, preventing gatekeeping and censorship. Blockchain can ensure transparent and immutable records of heritage artifacts, addressing ethical concerns related to digital representation. Additionally, the tokenization of cultural assets offers allowing communities to retain control over their heritage. However, the adoption of Web3 also necessitates careful consideration of data sovereignty and digital rights to ensure inclusive and responsible cultural preservation.

DOI: 10.4018/979-8-3693-2973-3.ch008

INTRODUCTION

Cultural heritage represents the tangible and intangible aspects of a community or society passed down through generations. It encompasses traditions, languages, folklore, artifacts, and historic sites. Preserving and promoting cultural heritage fosters a sense of identity, belonging, and understanding between communities. The cultural heritage is spread around the world, however, Zhang et al. (2024) argued that China boasts a vast treasure trove of cultural heritage resources (CRH). These resources span a remarkable timeframe, existing across diverse geographical regions. These resources embody a rich tapestry of functions and reflect dynamic cultural exchanges between various ethnicities throughout history. The cultural heritage has a direct relationship with tourism development. Luekveerawattana (2024) found that cultural heritage tourism thrives on innovation when it respects traditions, offers modern facilities, sets the right prices, and employs a skilled team. All these aspects significantly contribute to innovative practices.

The integration of Augmented Reality (AR) with cultural heritage has emerged as a valuable approach for bringing history to life and facilitating learning. Yoo & Yu (2024) found that integrating key information visually and repeatedly within the AR experience itself is a superior presentation method for cultural heritage AR applications. Similarly, Izaguirre et al. (2024) found that Virtual Reality (VR) holds significant promise for both research and safeguarding tangible and intangible heritage. Moreover, G. Li et al. (2024) found that well-designed VR experiences with clear information, smooth functionality, and beautiful visuals lead to happy and loyal visitors. VR can even create a sense of "flow" for visitors, making them more engaged and enthusiastic. By making collections accessible globally, VR expands museums' reach and influence. They argued that museums need smart information management and marketing to get the most out of VR.

In today's digital age, online heritage initiatives play a crucial role in mapping and sharing cultural heritage with a wider audience. Online heritage mapping initiatives offer several advantages over traditional methods of documenting and showcasing cultural heritage. These initiatives increase accessibility by making cultural heritage accessible to a global audience, transcending geographical boundaries (Avgousti et al., 2024; Bogdanova et al., 2020; Markellou, 2023). These initiatives provide interactive maps that allow users to explore heritage sites, stories, and traditions engagingly (Bikakis et al., 2023; Rees et al., 2023). Moreover, online platforms can empower local communities to contribute their knowledge and perspectives on cultural heritage (Blaschitz et al., 2022; Freitag & Camargo-Borges, 2024). Additionally, mapping cultural heritage fosters dialogue and understanding between communities with diverse traditions. Orphanidou et al. (2024) noted that by exploring cultural heritage through digital platforms, learners develop the ability to navigate the digital world effectively, leading to a more resilient and engaged learning experience.

Against this backdrop, this chapter aims to analyze the role of online heritage mapping initiatives in preserving and promoting cultural heritage. To achieve this, the chapter is divided into thematic sections. Section 2 explores the concept of digital heritage preservation and the various online heritage mapping initiatives, highlighting their benefits. Section 3 delves deeper through case studies of four such initiatives. This section analyzes the methodologies employed by these platforms, the types of cultural heritage documented (tangible or intangible), and the impact these initiatives have on communities and audiences.

DIGITAL HERITAGE PRESERVATION

Heritage Preservation

Culture is a part of the self-identity of people and can be viewed as the primary and most defining type of heritage. If implemented it provides a means of knowing the history and the development of our societies. Heritage conservation is the process of putting and keeping structures, things, places, and landscapes that have values of cultural, historical, or natural significance to future generations (de la Torre, 2013; Jokilehto, 1999). It's a multifaceted endeavor that encompasses various approaches. It includes documenting cultural monuments meticulously by photographing them, by using laser scans, or by using 3D models. Some organizations such as CyArk are quite active in this, creating copies that may prove of value in the future for reference or restoration (Klinke et al., 2018; Statham, 2019). Heritage conservation means the constant care and endeavor made towards maintaining the cultural heritage sites and even the property. It encompasses processes like rehabilitation, conservation, and management of conditions that could lead to dilapidation. Moreover, it involves protecting artifacts and structures that signify a certain society from aspects such as deterioration, weather conditions, vandalism, and abandonment among others. Another important aspect is that legal norms and international cooperation should be used in this regard. It is crucial to ensure the public is informed about the necessity of conservation of historical features.

Historypin and other applications encourage active community participation to ensure that the community feels responsible for the content of the site. Cultural heritage can be reclaimed and made more identifiable for a broader audience. For example, a digital archive, called Europeana, granted access to millions of views of European museums and libraries' digitized objects (Baggett & Gibbs, 2014; Capurro et al., 2023; Capurro & Severo, 2023; Perić et al., 2021; Yuen & Leslie,

2024). Heritage conservation is essential in economic social and cultural compensation whereby heritage plays the important role of strengthening the feeling of identification with some group, culture, either minority or indigenous. Moreover, historical landmarks and relics increase the tourism potential, thus having a positive effect on the generation of earnings and employment in that particular region (Labadi et al., 2021; Udeaja et al., 2020; Woodward & Cooke, 2022). In addition, the study of cultural assets is beneficial to archaeologists, historians, and many other researchers to learn and understand the past. The integration of cultural heritage conservation into the developmental agenda, adds value in the respect that it is more comprehensive, whereby the best interests of the future generation are taken into consideration (Udeaja et al., 2020; Woodward & Cooke, 2022).

Online Heritage Mapping Initiatives

Web-based heritage mapping is the process of developing and making use of the internet and digital technologies to discover, record, and disseminate heritage information. Here are some examples of prominent online heritage mapping initiatives.

- UNESCO World Heritage Centre is dedicated to mapping and providing comprehensive information on the World Heritage Sites throughout the world, using GIS technologies. This center (https://whc.unesco.org/en/) has a website that helps in mapping and monitoring World Heritage Sites all over the world, and is able to provide data as well as spatial inferences.
- Historypin is a culture mapping website (https://www.historypin.org/en/) that lets the users add history photos, videos, and stories to maps so that the culture history can be easily represented.
- Europeana is an online facility (https://www.europeana.eu/en) that offers wide public access to millions of items digitized and made available from museums, galleries, libraries, and archives in Europe and the collections featured here give an insight into Europe's cultural history.
- CyArk (https://www.cyark.org/) specializes in documenting cultural heritage through the use of the digital process, whereby it is involved in the documentation of cultural sites and producing detailed and lively virtual models and tours to ensure that landmarks are safeguarded.
- Arches is an informal and freely available system (https://www.archesproject.org/) with tools for surveying and cataloging CH objects which has been created in collaboration with the Getty Conservation Institute and the World Monuments Fund.

- OpenHeritage 3D (https://openheritage3d.org/) is an interdisciplinary technology platform for sharing relevant digitized models of cultural heritage sites for analysis, protection, and education purposes.
- Google Arts & Culture is a platform (https://artsandculture.google.com/) to browse art and culture from around the world. It offers virtual tours of museums and historical sites, along with images and videos of artworks. You can also find games and quizzes to test your art knowledge.

Benefits of Online Heritage Mapping Initiatives

These initiatives offer a variety of benefits that include:

Increased Accessibility

Digital methods help disseminate information on cultural heritage to people who could otherwise not access such information due to some geographical restrictions. World history and different periods can be studied by anyone who has internet access. Stories can be even experienced through various virtual tours, visiting different places, and viewing different artifacts. This especially proves crucial in situations in which the field location is far detached or can easily be destabilized (Corns et al., 2024; Maietti, 2022; Rueda Márquez de la Plata et al., 2023).

Enhanced Documentation

Technological tools such as GIS and 3-dimensional modeling facilitate the creation of documentation of cultural heritage sites. These technologies offer high-resolution details and relational context, thus have a higher level of depth in interpreting these landmarks (De Reu et al., 2013; Masciotta et al., 2021). For example, Donato & Giuffrida (2019) investigated the Scalea castle in Calabria, Italy, as part of a larger project on Tyrrhenian coast castles. A variety of survey methods including historical research, drone photogrammetry, traditional architectural surveying tools, and differential GPS were used to study the castle. This data helped create a 3D model and a new digital map of the site. The drone survey captured high-resolution photos of the entire castle site and was a cost-effective method. The 3D model is useful for measurements, education, and revealing new information, such as the possibility of unknown structures. Analyzing the construction phases based on the masonry revealed a Norman quadrangular tower as the oldest part, followed by a Swabian phase, an Angevin period, and late medieval additions. New technologies like digital photogrammetry, used in combination with traditional methods, improve the accuracy and detail of documentation for historical buildings, including archaeological and historical elements. This allows researchers to date construction methods with more precision.

Community Engagement

In some of the projects being implemented on the internet including Historypin participants can upload old pictures, history, and stories from their communities. This process ensures that all cultures embrace the responsibility and ownership of antiques. For example, Mutibwa et al. (2020) examined how community-led digital engagement with heritage can promote active citizenship by encouraging responsibility for shared cultural heritage and fostering lasting relationships between local heritage groups and national museums. The authors conducted a pilot project, Science Museum: Community-in-Residence, that revealed significant structural and logistical challenges even before incorporating digital tools, despite pre-existing ties between the community groups and the Science Museum in London. They found that facilitating face-to-face dialogue between the museum and community groups was crucial in defining effective digital co-curation parameters. Liang et al. (2021) conducted a systematic literature review to provide a detailed understanding of social media functionalities and their impact on sustainable urban development. The study concluded that social media platforms can enable a broader range of stakeholders to participate in cultural heritage management decisions and should be widely adopted to encourage global citizen involvement.

Improved Monitoring and Preservation

Cultural heritage sites can be periodically observed through the platforms, and any activity or change in the status of the heritage can be noticed therefore it would be easier to take necessary precautions.(Y. Li et al., 2023) noted that 3D LiDAR technology combined with 3D scanning, high-precision measurement, and reconstruction, has improved the methods and quality of heritage preservation. Integrated with technologies such as 3D printing, digital mapping, IoT, machine learning, intelligent sensors, close-range photogrammetry, infrared detection, stress wave tomography, material analysis, XR technology, and reverse engineering, 3D LiDAR provides significant advantages in real-time monitoring, digitization, geological and environmental data collection, deformation and weather monitoring, system health detection, and digital reproduction of built heritage.

Educational Resources

Online heritage maps are extremely beneficial educative tools since they can enhance learning among students and historians, especially where physical maps cannot be produced. For example, Okanovic et al. (2022) explored natural interaction and interaction using VR/AR (eXtended Reality) for cultural heritage presentations and found that these applications can educate and entertain users with stories brought to life. Similarly, Jadresin Milic et al. (2022) offered valuable tools for educators to use heritage buildings as a way to teach history in a fresh and engaging way.

CASE STUDIES

UNESCO World Heritage Centre

The Centre of the World Heritage of UNESCO (https://whc.unesco.org/) is the core of the World Heritage Convention, which is an important intergovernmental agreement adopted by UNESCO in 1972. This organization acts as the focal point for all issues surrounding World Heritage Sites, which are the natural and cultural property considered as having significant universal-cultural significance for humanity.

The word heritage centre assists the member nation countries in the selection of sites to be considered for listing as world heritage sites. This involves assessing cultural and natural properties against the stipulations of the convention in terms of set parameters. Moreover, the centre plays a critical role in helping countries with preparing nominations for listing on the World Heritage List. This includes the preparation of a documentation procedure addressing the justification and the management plan for the particular site. Furthermore, After the inscription, the centre has various roles that support the conservation of World Heritage sites. It involves offering help in that area in terms of expertise, funding, and encouragement to other countries in the conservation of such cultural and natural assets. Furthermore, the World Heritage Centre has the role of supervising the status of the World Heritage sites in terms of conservation. The centre incorporates reliable, modern Geographic Information Systems (GIS) technologies for mapping and surveillance. This way, they can follow the alterations and monitor risks, which is crucial for maintaining the sustainability of the invaluable landmarks. Thus, the centre provides detailed information and location-based representation of World Heritage Sites through GIS technologies. This data is useful for both the researchers, the wildlife and nature conservation organizations as well as the broader society to gain a better understanding of these unique areas (Bertacchini et al., 2024; Falk & Hagsten, 2024; Rezaei et al., 2024).

Through the dedicated effort of the UNESCO World Heritage Centre, there are currently over 1,199 World Heritage Sites documented worldwide, up to May 2024. Out of which, 933 cultural, 227 natural, and 39 mixed cultural and natural sites exist across 168 countries. Cultural and natural heritage are well represented in the WHL with examples like the Great Wall of China, the Pyramids of Giza, Machu Picchu City, and even physical geographic structures like the Grand Canyon (UNESCO World Heritage Centre, 2024). This indicates that the Centre has a very important mandate of encouraging international cooperation and delivering necessary support that ensure the preservation of numerous items for future generations.

A major feature of the UNESCO World Heritage is that the centre uses GIS to track the World Heritage sites globally (https://whc.unesco.org/en/wh-gis/). This initiative integrates satellite imagery, history data, and geospatial analysis to provide detailed datasets and spatial representations as can be seen from Figure 1. It also plays a vital role in preserving the heritage related to culture and nature throughout the world by giving an opportunity to the stakeholders to get real-time information for their decision-making purposes.

As an example of the work of the UNESCO World Heritage Centre, we see the possibilities of GIS technologies for culture saving. Using geospatial data in the development of the initiative, there is improved surveillance, protection, efficient management, and sharing of information regarding heritage sites to the relevant international stakeholders which include governments, researchers, and conservationists. The extensive database and interactive maps provided by UNESCO are very useful for promoting awareness and mobilizing resources necessary for the conservation of cultural heritage (Bertacchini et al., 2024; Falk & Hagsten, 2024; Huttunen, 2024; Khalaf, 2024; Pinheiro & Martins, 2024).

Figure 1. World heritage online map platform (https://whc.unesco.org/en/wh-gis/)

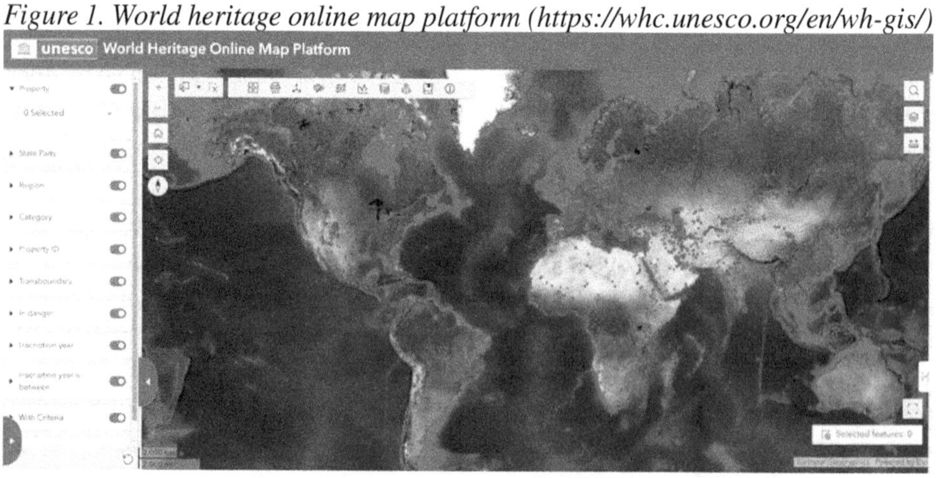

Historypin: Community-Driven Heritage Mapping

Historypin is a social media website (https://www.historypin.org/en/) where users give voice to the past by 'pinning' content such as photographs, videos, and text messages directly to maps and creating a history of our world as can be evident from Figure 2. It makes for an effective bottom-up approach to heritage mapping since people and aggregates get the chance to input their views of things or information. Historypin is a distinctive online tool that opens a door for any person to play an active role in collecting and composing history. In contrast to other repositories, Historypin is not formed only by its administration but by its members. It is open to everyone and all one requires is to upload history-related photos, videos, and potential stories. This makes it possible to obtain a paradigm that different and can encompass vast information hence making the method to be richer and more objective. It is not about big history embraced by conventional history books only, it is about the real history of people's lives, their stories, and memories (Baggett & Gibbs, 2014). One of the most prominent aspects of the Historypin is the fact that all the content is geolocated. Similarly, when the users upload their historical data, they can anchor the document and position it at a particular point of the map. This lets the user experience historic events in terms of space, to see how they occurred in a certain area (Yuen & Leslie, 2024). Think of having past street view photos of your neighborhood that can be laid over current maps thus creating history physically.

Historypin is more than just a database with content that has been proven historically accurate. It positively promotes the practice of narration as well as it supports the creation of the feeling of historical memory. To support the images uploaded by users, they can also provide captions and descriptions as a form of narrative on their images. This makes it easier to have an interesting presentation of historical information, where users can share their stories and appreciate more what is happening in their local history. Historypin also helps to create a more connected approach to the past by incorporating different points of view. This way the platform enables the users to find not only the official history, or the significant events of a certain period or country, but also the history of ordinary people and their stories which are not mentioned in history books. With historypin, the interpretation of the past is a more collective one, which will make more people aware of the many segments and the richness of the past.

Figure 2. Historypin (https://www.historypin.org/en/explore/geo/)

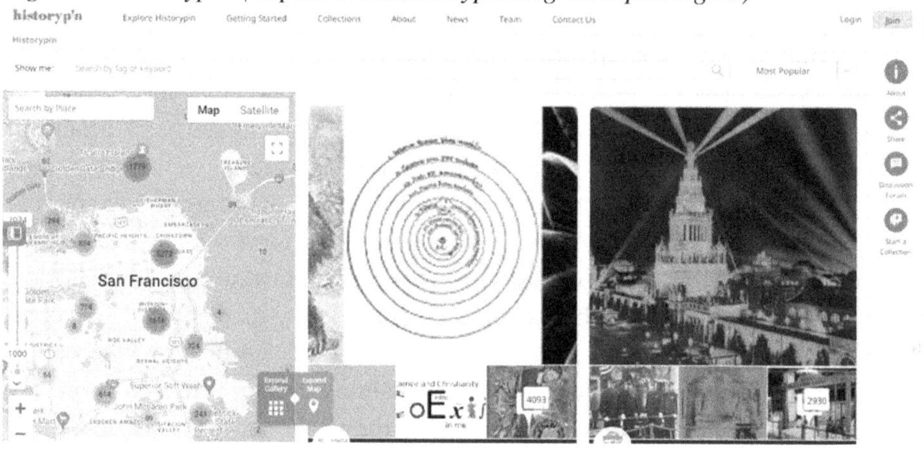

Europeana: A Gateway to Europe's Cultural Riches

Europeana is a one-stop shop for any culture lover who wants to discover the wealth of European cultures. It serves as an access portal to millions of digitalized collections from a vast network of over 3,600 museums, galleries, libraries, and archives in Europe (https://www.europeana.eu/en). It helps to discover Europe's Art treasures by some of the most famous artists ever to exist like the Renaissance masters Michelangelo, Leonardo Da Vinci, modern and contemporary artists, and many others as can be seen from Figure 3. Moreover, the platform gives the option to explore documents which include manuscripts and letters to learn more about the political, social, cultural development of Europe. Experience the past and the present of Europe with the help of photographs and maps is also provided (Capurro & Severo, 2023; Silva & Terra, 2024).

Europeana is not just about offering access to digital objects but it does much more than that. It helps to locate particular items quickly and easily by selecting the relevant keywords, dates, categories, or contributing institutions. It offers specializations as thematic and historical, which gives the viewer a specific and knowledgeable perspective on European art. To make the learning of European history and culture more fun for teachers and students, they can use lesson plans, fun activities, and other teaching aids. Moreover, Developers can leverage Europeana's API to integrate its content into their own applications and educational tools.

Europeana serves as a vital bridge, connecting people around the world with the vast cultural heritage of Europe. Whether you're a seasoned history buff, a curious student, or simply someone with an appreciation for art and culture, Europeana offers a wealth of resources to explore, learn, and be inspired by Europe's rich tapestry of history and creativity. Europeana indicates how collections and objects of cultural importance can be mobilized and presented on a continental level through the use of digital technology. It also helps in promoting the European cultural identity and contributes towards public awareness and academic work by offering an easily accessible platform through Europeana. The centralized files coupled with the effective layout of the flow make this platform beneficial for scholars, educators, or cultural lovers (Borin & Donato, 2023; Capurro et al., 2023; Silva & Terra, 2024).

Figure 3. Europeana (https://www.europeana.eu/en)

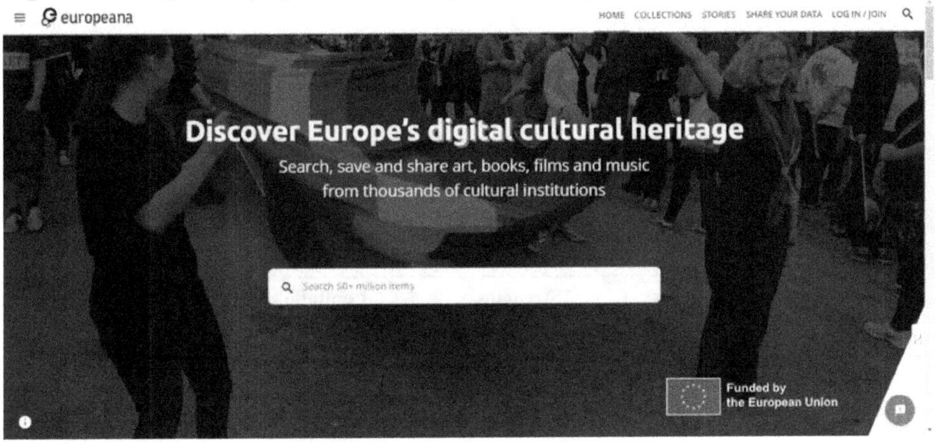

CyArk: Guardians of Culture in the Digital Age

CyArk (https://www.cyark.org/) stands at the forefront of a revolutionary movement: preserving cultural heritage sites for the future through digital archiving. This non-profit organization employs up-to-date technologies such as 3D scanning, subsequently offering broader access to individuals and supporting the safeguarding of the most valuable sites globally through accurate recreations and virtual tours. CyArk's main function is to maintain a digital record of significant structures and sites utilizing precise hi-definition technologies. With the help of accurate lasers, CyArk provides rather detailed 3D models in the field of cultural heritage. It can scan detailed features, surface morphology, and shapes, thus giving a digital survey of the site (Klinke et al., 2018).

To show the exact beauty of the sites, high-resolution and dynamic range photography is used to capture and reproduce the color, lights, and weathering of the monuments. The captured data is then processed through the computer and reconstructed in fine detail in 3D. These models enable audiences to interact virtually with the sites, move between them, as well as contemplate the architectural design. Outfitting these structures with 3D cameras, CyArk produces mesmerizing images that enable online individuals to virtually visit these cultural heritages. This is particularly useful for sites that are situated in remote areas. These digital assets are kept in a public database located on CyArk website, where everyone can find 3D models, data, and educational materials provided by the company. It helps the researchers, educators, or any other interested individual to gain more information about such cultural assets. By showcasing the beauty and fragility of cultural heritage sites, CyArk raises global awareness about the importance of preservation efforts.

Methodologies Employed

Table 1 shows the methodologies employed in these case studies along with the strengths and weaknesses of these online platforms.

Table 1. Methodologies

Online Initiative	Methodologies	Strengths	Limitations	Suitability for Heritage Documentation
UNESCO World Heritage Centre	GIS technologies	Real-time data, spatial visualization, comprehensive monitoring	Data accuracy, interoperability issues, ethical concerns	Suitable for documenting tangible heritage sites
Historypin	Crowd-sourced mapping, digital storytelling	Community engagement, diverse perspectives, user-generated content	Authenticity, reliability of content, digital literacy	Suitable for documenting both tangible and intangible heritage
Europeana	Digital archives, multimedia resources	Extensive collection, centralized access, educational value	Equitable representation, digital divide	Suitable for documenting a wide range of cultural artifacts and practices
CyArk	3D documentation, virtual tours	Detailed preservation, immersive experiences, and protection of at-risk sites	High cost, technical complexity, ethical considerations	Suitable for detailed documentation of tangible heritage sites

Table 1 offers a comparative analysis of online platforms for heritage documentation. Each platform utilizes a distinct methodology, like GIS or crowd-sourcing, with inherent strengths and weaknesses. While some excel at real-time data or community engagement, others provide vast archives or detailed 3D preservation. Ultimately, the best platform depends on the type of heritage being documented, with tangible sites benefiting from spatial data and 3D models, and intangible heritage flourishing with crowd-sourced narratives.

Types of Cultural Heritage Documented

Table 2 shows the Types of Cultural Heritage Documented in these case studies.

Table 2. Types of cultural heritage documented

Online Initiative	Types of Cultural Heritage Documented	Examples of Tangible Heritage	Examples of Intangible Heritage
UNESCO World Heritage Centre	Tangible heritage	Historical sites, natural landmarks	-
Historypin	Tangible and intangible heritage	Photos, and videos of historical places	Oral histories, personal stories, community events
Europeana	Tangible and intangible heritage	Artifacts, artworks, books, archives	Folklore, traditions, cultural practices
CyArk	Tangible heritage	Heritage landmarks, architectural sites	-

The table summarizes the types of cultural heritage documented by various online initiatives. Online initiatives documented a variety of cultural heritage, with some focusing on tangible aspects like historical sites and artifacts (UNESCO, CyArk), while others embraced both tangible and intangible heritage (Historypin, Europeana). Historypin captured intangible heritage through oral histories and community events, while Europeana included folklore and traditions.

Impact on Communities

Table 3 shows the Impact of these case studies on Communities and Audiences

Table 3. Impact on communities

Online Initiative	Impact on Communities and Audiences	Contributions to Cultural Preservation	Community Engagement	Social, Cultural, and Economic Benefits
UNESCO World Heritage Centre	Enhances global awareness and conservation efforts	Provides data for informed conservation	Facilitates collaboration among stakeholders	Protects heritage, promotes tourism, educational value
Historypin	Fosters local involvement and collective memory	Empowers communities to share their heritage	Encourages participation through storytelling	Strengthens community bonds, educational engagement
Europeana	Increases accessibility to European cultural heritage	Centralized repository for preservation	Engages diverse audiences through digital access	Promotes cultural diversity, supports research and education
CyArk	Protects and shares endangered cultural sites	Digitally preserves at-risk heritage	Provides immersive experiences to a global audience	Protects cultural sites, promotes virtual tourism, educational value

Table 3 highlights these online platforms' positive impact on communities and audiences. All contribute to cultural preservation through data collection, collaboration tools, and accessibility. Historypin fosters local participation and storytelling, while CyArk focuses on safeguarding endangered sites. Overall, these platforms strengthen community bonds, promote cultural exchange, and offer educational opportunities for a global audience.

ONLINE HERITAGE AND WEB3 BENEFITS

Web3, often used as a term for the subsequent development of the internet, is different from the Web2 environment where most platforms are controlled by large tech companies and governments. Web3 is grounded on blockchain, which is a public and open database that deals with data storage in a peer-to-peer network of computers or nodes. Web3 is a state where users are dealing directly with each other through P2P systems and, therefore, enjoying more secure and private connections. Blockchain also brings the idea of a record that cannot be changed which guarantees the reliability of data. Another component of Web3 is smart contracts which are contracts that automatically fulfil the conditions of the agreement, with the terms of the contacts directly written in code. These contracts run and perform themselves, in the contractual relations established, where certain conditions are provided; and thus, third party involvement, and possibilities of conflict, are also minimized. Web3 also gives users more control over their digital persona and information; it properties the idea of self-sovereign identity in which users control their identities using cryptographic keys for privacy and security. Further, Web3 is associated with the tokenization of assets such that assets like cryptocurrencies and Non-Fungible Tokens (NFTs), are 'tokens' that can symbolize ownership rights. These tokens give rise to a decentralized market economy, allowing users to buy, sell, and even invest in digital assets. In addition, Web3 has effects on decentralization by using Decentralized Autonomous Organizations (DAOs); in which the power of decision-making is divided and distributed and all members of the organization, whose tokens belong to them, are supposed to make decisions collectively and not autocratically. It also creates physical security since this new internet paradigm is not a centralized network and therefore not easily compromised. In the following aspects, Web3 can be helpful for online heritage initiatives.

Decentralization and Ownership

The concept of Web3 rests on decentralization which means that rather than having a single or few authorities controlling various aspects of the subordinate, there is a network of participants who are involved in the control as well as governance of the various aspects of the subordinate. For the online heritage initiatives what it means is that the platforms can exist as networks without the prospect of being regulated or even shut down by a specific authority, which can be a government, corporation, or institution. This therefore alleviates control of cultural assets from central powers and put it in the hands of communities, to protect, exhibit, and share their culture as they see fit. This is especially so if the heritage involves Indigenous populations and other vulnerable groups that have always been left out in matters of heritage. It empowers communities to protect their traditions in a way that makes them independent and protects them from exploitation.

Immutable Records and Transparency

Probably the greatest strength of Web3 is the application of blockchain technology for the development of tamper-proof and transparent records. This means when cultural heritage information or data in this case digital artifacts, records, and or intangible assets are placed on the blockchain they cannot be changed or deleted. It helps in maintaining the irrefutable integrity and veracity of the data to prevent its modification from any unauthorized person or external influence. This level of transparency is essential for online heritage initiatives since, in such cases, the history of the artifacts is documented in full accordance with the facts. Moreover, smart contracts – the contracts which are enforced through software designed to automatically execute the terms of the contract when the conditions for execution are satisfied – may be used in some aspects such as permissions regarding access, usage rights and distributions of the revenues. It ultimately helps to prevent bias, arbitrary decisions, and even human error in the management of digital heritage assets.

Tokenization and Funding

Web3 establishes the notion of tokenization and, in the case of culture, cultural assets may be minted in the form of NFTs. Tokenization enables heritage projects to seek funds and or create a conveyable value that can be exchanged for such tokens which are equivalent to ownership or access rights to a particular cultural asset. This creates new opportunities for the development of financing as it engulfs purchasing the object to save it from degradation with the further right of ownership. Also, with decentralized crowdfunding platforms people can collect donations to fund their projects from all over the world, and all the collected funds will be recorded on the blockchain. Besides making funding more democratic, it also ensures that the accumulation of money for heritage projects is constant and can be maintained as the projects will be earning it. The distribution of the money to those involved is also ensured to be fair.

Interoperability and Collaboration

From the very nature of decentralization, Web3 contributes to a higher level of integration between the various online heritage projects and tools. This has the implications that heritage data in digital formats remained more open for sharing and linking, thus can provide a 'wired' connection of global cultural information. Such interoperability also enables different organizations, researchers, and communities globally to combine efforts and share resources with similar focus on preservation projects. For instance, a digital library in Europe may well be synchronized with a three-dimensional preservation project in Asia as a way enriching culture and extending its reach to yield more information to the entire universe. In addition, they are inherently more decentralized and therefore open to people, not limited in any way by geography or political systems. It will also make sure that heritage schemes can go to the many diverse users for convergence of digital heritage, and come up with psychologically inclusive frames on how the heritage might be achieved.

Enhanced Security and Privacy

The new concept of web3 is more secure and privacy-preserving than web2 and is important for preserving cultural assets. This is because in a distributed ledger, all information is shared among the nodes in the network and no single node controls the information, meaning that no information would be lost no matter the issue with the servers. This also helps in ensuring that the integrity of the assets that are considered to be of heritage value digitally has been maintained in the long run. Moreover, Web3 allows those communities to own data about them and decide who may collect it and how it will be used. This is especially relevant in the case of safeguarding cultural heritage and avoiding abuses of indigenous and local people's privacy and jurisdiction of their countries. Finally, through data sovereignty, Web3 guarantees that the cultural data is owned by the community in question and that they have the right knowledge to make some decisions regarding the data.

New Forms of Engagement

With Web3 technologies, the possibilities for experiencing and exploring cultural heritage innovate in a very unique manner. Utilizing Web3 integration with virtual reality (VR) and the metaverse, cultural heritage can be given incredible ways of representation where users can interact with narratives in detail, such as exploring heritage sites and collections in full. Such experiences can make history much more tangible and thus endless fascination and more compelling to younger generations and the public. Also, Web3 enables new types of organizations, such as DAOs, which represent groups of individuals following the rules defined by the usage of smart contracts. The idea of the DAO could be applied to the administration of online heritage projects, where the communities and stakeholders themselves would have a say in how the resources would be spent. This decentralizes power to govern cultural heritage to the population to where the cultural heritages belong.

Ethical and Inclusive Representation

An overarching concern that has emerged about the preservation of digital heritage is the issue of how cultural representations are ethical. By way of mitigating this problem, Web3 will make it possible for communities to own the narrative about their cultural heritage to a larger extent. Here, decentralized media networks and distributed ledgers empower people to contribute to the narration of their cultures in the ways that resonate with the values, beliefs and historical experiences of their communities. Also, Web3 brings fairness by reducing exclusion or restrictions to minorities or those in the lower demographic categories. By decentralizing such tools and platforms, Web3 guarantees that more voices in the cultural landscape are represented and that as many stories as possible are kept safe for posterity. This leads to a more diverse representation in cyberspace and more equal treatment for all cultures trying to enter cyberspace.

CONCLUSION

Online heritage mapping initiatives are revolutionizing the way we document, preserve, and share cultural heritage. These platforms offer increased accessibility, foster engagement, empower communities, and promote cross-cultural understanding. UNESCO utilizes GIS to monitor World Heritage Sites. Historypin fosters community engagement through user-contributed stories and photos on interactive maps. Europeana offers a vast digital library of European cultural artifacts. CyArk specializes in the 3D preservation of endangered sites, enabling virtual exploration. Each platform caters to specific heritage types (tangible or intangible) and offers strengths like real-time data or community involvement, making them valuable tools for cultural preservation and education on a global scale.

The success of these initiatives highlights the potential of digital technologies for cultural preservation and education. However, challenges remain such as ensuring equitable access to technology and promoting digital literacy within communities is crucial for inclusive participation. Furthermore, safeguarding sensitive cultural information and addressing potential ethical concerns regarding the online representation of heritage require ongoing attention.

Looking ahead, online heritage mapping can be further enhanced by integrating new technologies like virtual reality (VR) and augmented reality (AR). These technologies can create immersive experiences that bring cultural heritage to life for a wider audience. Additionally, fostering collaboration between cultural institutions, communities, and technology developers holds immense potential for the future of online heritage mapping. By harnessing the power of digital tools, we can build a more comprehensive and inclusive record of our shared cultural heritage for generations to come.

REFERENCES

Avgousti, A., Papaioannou, G., & Hermon, S. (2024). Enhancing Online Accessibility of Digitized Artifacts from Small Museum Collections in Cyprus: An Empirical Evaluation of the CyprusArk Solution. *Journal on Computing and Cultural Heritage*, *17*(3), 1–24. Advance online publication. DOI: 10.1145/3648229

Baggett, M., & Gibbs, R. (2014). Historypin and Pinterest for Digital Collections: Measuring the Impact of Image-Based Social Tools on Discovery and Access. *Journal of Library Administration*, *54*(1), 11–22. Advance online publication. DOI: 10.1080/01930826.2014.893111

Bertacchini, E., Revelli, F., & Zotti, R. (2024). The economic impact of UNESCO World Heritage: Evidence from Italy. *Regional Science and Urban Economics*, *105*, 103996. Advance online publication. DOI: 10.1016/j.regsciurbeco.2024.103996

Bikakis, N., Giannopoulos, G., Sidiropoulos, N., Flouda, C., Doupas, A., Giouli, V., Karioris, P., Botini, P., Vacalopoulou, A., & Stainhaouer, G. (2023). Exposing Geospatial Cultural Heritage Content in Map-based Applications. *CEUR Workshop Proceedings*, •••, 3379.

Blaschitz, E., Mayr, E., & Oppl, S. (2022). Too Low Motivation, Too High Authority? Digital Media Support for Co-Curation in Local Cultural Heritage Communities. *Multimodal Technologies and Interaction*, *6*(5), 33. Advance online publication. DOI: 10.3390/mti6050033

Bogdanova, G., Todorov, T., & Noev, N. (2020). Accessibility testing of digital cultural heritage. *Digital Presentation and Preservation of Cultural and Scientific Heritage, 10 2020-September*. DOI: 10.55630/dipp.2020.10.16

Borin, E., & Donato, F. (2023). Financial Sustainability of Digitizing Cultural Heritage: The International Platform Europeana. *Journal of Risk and Financial Management*, *16*(10), 421. Advance online publication. DOI: 10.3390/jrfm16100421

Capurro, C., Plets, G., & Verheul, J. (2023). Digital heritage infrastructures as cultural policy instruments: Europeana and the enactment of European citizenship. *International Journal of Cultural Policy*. Advance online publication. DOI: 10.1080/10286632.2023.2193401

Capurro, C., & Severo, M. (2023). Mapping European Digital Heritage Politics: An Empirical Study of Europeana as a Web-based Network. *Heritage & Society*, 1–21. Advance online publication. DOI: 10.1080/2159032X.2023.2266801

Corns, A., Davidson, L., Namberi, S., O Reilly, R., & Shaw, R. (2024). Developing enhanced and enriched 3d models of cultural heritage assets as part of the eu co-funded 5dculture project. *International Archives of the Photogrammetry, Remote Sensing and Spatial Information Sciences - ISPRS Archives, 48*(2). DOI: 10.5194/isprs-archives-XLVIII-2-W4-2024-157-2024

de la Torre, M. (2013). Values and Heritage Conservation. *Heritage & Society, 6*(2), 155–166. Advance online publication. DOI: 10.1179/2159032X13Z.00000000011

De Reu, J., Plets, G., Verhoeven, G., De Smedt, P., Bats, M., Cherretté, B., De Maeyer, W., Deconynck, J., Herremans, D., Laloo, P., Van Meirvenne, M., & De Clercq, W. (2013). Towards a three-dimensional cost-effective registration of the archaeological heritage. *Journal of Archaeological Science, 40*(2), 1108–1121. Advance online publication. DOI: 10.1016/j.jas.2012.08.040

Donato, E., & Giuffrida, D. (2019). Combined methodologies for the survey and documentation of historical buildings: The castle of scalea (cs, italy). *Heritage, 2*(3), 2384–2397. Advance online publication. DOI: 10.3390/heritage2030146

Falk, M. T., & Hagsten, E. (2024). Factors with ambiguous qualities for Cultural World Heritage Sites. *Journal of Cultural Heritage, 66*, 384–391. Advance online publication. DOI: 10.1016/j.culher.2023.12.009

Freitag, A. M., & Camargo-Borges, C. (2024). The Digital Bow: Exploring the Potential of Digital Presence for Indigenous Community-Based Tourism in Brazil. *Tourism Planning & Development, 21*(6), 755–772. Advance online publication. DOI: 10.1080/21568316.2024.2307974

Huttunen, M. (2024). Heritage for sustainable peace: The politics of contested histories and the Nanjing controversy at UNESCO. *Frontiers in Political Science, 6*, 1249745. Advance online publication. DOI: 10.3389/fpos.2024.1249745

Izaguirre, J. I., Ferrari, A. A., & Acuto, F. A. (2024). Exploring cultural heritage and archaeological research from a VR-based approach. *Digital Applications in Archaeology and Cultural Heritage, 32*, e00318. Advance online publication. DOI: 10.1016/j.daach.2024.e00318

Jadresin Milic, R., McPherson, P., McConchie, G., Reutlinger, T., & Singh, S. (2022). Architectural History and Sustainable Architectural Heritage Education: Digitalisation of Heritage in New Zealand. *Sustainability (Basel), 14*(24), 16432. Advance online publication. DOI: 10.3390/su142416432

Jokilehto, J. (1999). A century of heritage conservation. *Journal of Architectural Conservation*, *5*(3), 14–33. Advance online publication. DOI: 10.1080/13556207.1999.10785249

Khalaf, R. W. (2024). Adopting a Holistic Approach to Cultural and Natural Heritage Protection Under the UNESCO World Heritage Convention. In *Law and Visual Jurisprudence* (Vol. 12). DOI: 10.1007/978-3-031-47347-0_7

Klinke, H., Surkemper, L., & Underhill, J. (2018). In Conversation with CyArk: Digital Heritage in the 21st Century. *International Journal for Digital Art History*, *0*(3). https://journals.ub.uni-heidelberg.de/index.php/dah/article/view/49914

Labadi, S., Giliberto, F., Rosetti, I., Shetabi, L., & Yildirim, E. (2021). Heritage and the sustainable development goals: Policy guidance for heritage and development actors. In *International Council on Monuments and Sites - ICOMOS.*

Li, G., Lin, S., & Tian, Y. (2024). Immersive Museums in the Digital Age: Exploring the Impact of Virtual Reality on Visitor Satisfaction and Loyalty. *Journal of the Knowledge Economy*. Advance online publication. DOI: 10.1007/s13132-024-01782-7

Li, Y., Zhao, L., Chen, Y., Zhang, N., Fan, H., & Zhang, Z. (2023). 3D LiDAR and multi-technology collaboration for preservation of built heritage in China: A review. *International Journal of Applied Earth Observation and Geoinformation*, *116*, 103156. Advance online publication. DOI: 10.1016/j.jag.2022.103156

Liang, X., Lu, Y., & Martin, J. (2021). A review of the role of social media for the cultural heritage sustainability. *Sustainability (Basel)*, *13*(3), 1055. Advance online publication. DOI: 10.3390/su13031055

Luekveerawattana, R. (2024). Enhancing innovation in cultural heritage tourism: Navigating external factors. *Cogent Social Sciences*, *10*(1), 2301813. Advance online publication. DOI: 10.1080/23311886.2024.2301813

Maietti, F. (2022). Digital Documentation for Enhancement and Conservation of Minor or Inaccessible Heritage Sites. In *Contributions to Management Science*. DOI: 10.1007/978-3-031-14121-8_8

Markellou, M. (2023). Cultural Heritage Accessibility in the Digital Era and the Greek Legal Framework. *International Journal for the Semiotics of Law*, *36*(5), 1945–1969. Advance online publication. DOI: 10.1007/s11196-023-10027-w

Masciotta, M. G., Morais, M. J., Ramos, L. F., Oliveira, D. V., Sánchez-Aparicio, L. J., & González-Aguilera, D. (2021). A Digital-based Integrated Methodology for the Preventive Conservation of Cultural Heritage: The Experience of HeritageCare Project. *International Journal of Architectural Heritage*, *15*(6), 844–863. Advance online publication. DOI: 10.1080/15583058.2019.1668985

Mutibwa, D. H., Hess, A., & Jackson, T. (2020). Strokes of serendipity: Community co-curation and engagement with digital heritage. *Convergence (London)*, *26*(1), 157–177. Advance online publication. DOI: 10.1177/1354856518772030

Okanovic, V., Ivkovic-Kihic, I., Boskovic, D., Mijatovic, B., Prazina, I., Skaljo, E., & Rizvic, S. (2022). Interaction in eXtended Reality Applications for Cultural Heritage. *Applied Sciences (Basel, Switzerland)*, *12*(3), 1241. Advance online publication. DOI: 10.3390/app12031241

Orphanidou, Y., Efthymiou, L., & Panayiotou, G. (2024). Cultural Heritage for Sustainable Education Amidst Digitalisation. *Sustainability (Basel)*, *16*(4), 1540. Advance online publication. DOI: 10.3390/su16041540

Perić, B. Š., Šimundić, B., Muštra, V., & Vugdelija, M. (2021). The role of unesco cultural heritage and cultural sector in tourism development: The case of EU countries. *Sustainability (Basel)*, *13*(10), 5473. Advance online publication. DOI: 10.3390/su13105473

Pinheiro, A. J., & Martins, H. (2024). The World Heritage Classification in Urban Tourism Destinations: Perspectives for the City of Porto, Portugal. *Advances in Science. Technology and Innovation*. Advance online publication. DOI: 10.1007/978-3-031-49536-6_16

Rees, G., Hunt, A., Vitale, V., Horgan, J., & Strachan, P. (2023). Discovering the local in national cultural heritage collections. How web maps can help the UK public engage with their 'own places.'. *Information Communication and Society*, *26*(15), 2885–2903. Advance online publication. DOI: 10.1080/1369118X.2022.2113819

Rezaei, N., Nofre, J., & Ghaderi, Z. (2024). World heritage classification and tourism: Divergent trajectories in Marrakech Medina (Morocco) and M'Zab Valley (Algeria). *Journal of Heritage Tourism*, *19*(1), 111–128. Advance online publication. DOI: 10.1080/1743873X.2023.2259509

Rueda Márquez de la Plata, A., Cruz Franco, P. A., & Ramos Sánchez, J. A. (2023). Applications of Virtual and Augmented Reality Technology to Teaching and Research in Construction and Its Graphic Expression. *Sustainability (Basel)*, *15*(12), 9628. Advance online publication. DOI: 10.3390/su15129628

Silva, A. L., & Terra, A. L. (2024). Cultural heritage on the Semantic Web: The Europeana Data Model. *IFLA Journal*, *50*(1), 93–107. Advance online publication. DOI: 10.1177/03400352231202506

Statham, N. (2019). Scientific rigour of online platforms for 3D visualisation of heritage. *Virtual Archaeology Review*, *10*(20), 1–16. DOI: 10.4995/var.2019.9715

Udeaja, C., Trillo, C., Awuah, K. G. B., Makore, B. C. N., Patel, D. A., Mansuri, L. E., & Jha, K. N. (2020). Urban heritage conservation and rapid urbanization: Insights from Surat, India. *Sustainability (Basel)*, *12*(6), 2172. Advance online publication. DOI: 10.3390/su12062172

UNESCO World Heritage Centre. (2024). *World Heritage Site*. https://whc.unesco.org/en/list

Woodward, S. C., & Cooke, L. (2022). World Heritage and the Sustainable Development Goals. In *World Heritage*. DOI: 10.4324/9781003044857-12

Yoo, E., & Yu, J. (2024). Evaluating the Impact of Presentation on Learning and Narrative in AR of Cultural Heritage. *IEEE Access : Practical Innovations, Open Solutions*, *12*, 25876–25887. Advance online publication. DOI: 10.1109/ACCESS.2024.3365696

Yuen, Y. L. E., & Leslie, C. A. (2024). Enriching Museum Student Users' Curriculum Interpretation, Learning, and Worldview through Digital Archive Approach with HistoryPin. *The International Journal of the Inclusive Museum*, *17*(1), 23–48. Advance online publication. DOI: 10.18848/1835-2014/CGP/v17i01/23-48

Zhang, K., González del Valle-Brena, A., Ramos Riera, I., & Zhao, J. (2024). Ancient routes, new gateways: A systematic literature review of China's cultural route heritage. *Journal of Cultural Heritage Management and Sustainable Development*, *14*(2), 266–281. Advance online publication. DOI: 10.1108/JCHMSD-06-2021-0114

Chapter 9 Neurocognitive Learning Design and Multiclass Algorithms: Academic and Business User Experience in Web 3.0

C. V. Suresh Babu
https://orcid.org/0000-0002-8474-2882
Hindustan Institute of Technology and Science, India

P. M. Akshara
https://orcid.org/0009-0004-8498-0196
Hindustan Institute of Technology and Science, India

Dhanush Harsha
Hindustan Institute of Technology and Science, India

Iniyavan M. Afeef
Hindustan Institute of Technology and Science, India

J. Jowin
Hindustan Institute of Technology and Science, India

ABSTRACT

The study aims to display the application of multiclass algorithms in machine learning for educational settings, particularly for skill assessment, learning style prediction, and peer recommendation. The method of skills assessment uses the RandomForestClassifier model to forecast learners' skill proficiency by using a mock dataset that represents the learners having different skill levels. The module

DOI: 10.4018/979-8-3693-2973-3.ch009

of learning style prediction employs the model to categorize all students into their cognitive preference spectrum according to the dataset which contains their neurocognitive attributes and learning preferences. Through Peer recommendation, the system suggests to the study partners that students typically will be matched together with similar standards, interests, and learning styles. The study stresses the utility of personalized learning freed by multi-class algorithms for students to be assessed on basic skills, their learning patterns to be predicted as well as promotion of cooperative learning which eventually results in improvement of the learning experience and academic success.

1. INTRODUCTION

The neurocognitive approach to learning design is also another way of assimilating cognitive science and neuroscience principles into instructional strategies. This strategy aims at understanding how the brain processes information and learns thus as a basis for improved rapid training. They include fundamental elements such as cognitive processes assessment, execution, and analysis; personality traits identification; neuroscience; self-regulation of learning; and technology integration. Neurocognitive insights must be transformed into everyday use and there should be a mindset of continuous improvement. By making learning interactive and adaptive to all learners it captures the natural functioning of the brain paving the way for an enhanced learning experience based on neurocognitive principles. Through this method, retention, comprehension, and achievement in academic tasks are increased leading to the creation of a new level of schooling that does not focus on one group of students only. Nevertheless, ethical issues are also involved in them along with individual variation and intricate cognitive aspects.

According to (Rose & Strangman, 2007)Universal Design for Learning is an approach that allows for individual differences in curriculum. The approach suggests that cognition and learning have three neural networks namely recognition, strategic, and affective networks. These networks influence how individuals learn since they differ from one person to another. This framework uses this perspective to design flexible, technology-rich curricula that are responsive to a wide range of student's needs, ensuring that the curriculum fits the individual.

Challenges to neurocognitive interventions in education emanate from misconceptions, lack of generalizability, and resource demands. Understanding the long-term effects and unintended consequences remains poorly known while uniform guidelines are absent. A dynamic nature of learning means something that works in one case may not be valid in another context. To deal with these problems a balanced approach, a collaboration between educators, cognitive scientists as well as technologists, and ongoing evaluation of neurocognitive-informed designs is necessary. By analyzing individual neurocognitive data machine learning algorithms can tailor learning experiences to provide real-time adjustments that improve the quality of feedback (Suresh Babu, C. V. & Praveen, S. 2023). The integration of the neurocognitive aspects into the design of learning creates problems, namely, various individual factors, data privacy, and ethics, in real-time adaptation, in the interpretation of AI models and their generalization across domains, and finally, the limited amount of neurocognitive data. Multiclass algorithms can be explored with the purpose of creating personalized learning paths, examining individual learner data, and practicing privacy-preserving approaches. In a real-world setting, interactive online learning models can be utilized to analyze real-time neurocognitive data. The human-understandable AI models can offer knowledge of what goes into the decision-making process, which enables educators to trust the system's proposals. The application of transfer learning can help neurocognitive principles be generalized across different domains. The issue of having less neurocognitive data can be answered by using techniques like data augmentation and semi-supervised learning. Respecting the ethical issues, transparency, and keeping the principles updated based on the empirical evidence becomes essential for the integration of neurocognitive principles into educational technology.

The chapter will demonstrate that learning design will be positively affected if neurocognitive factors are added. Multi-class algorithms in machine learning can handle challenges such as individual differences as well as ethical considerations creating a way to tailor learning paths specifically for each student. They allow for real-time reconfigurability, predictive analytics, and data-driven intelligence, thus promoting ethical practice and continuous improvement.

2. LITERATURE REVIEW

Although some educators can find 'brain science' an inapplicable subject to education, thorough cognitive science knowledge is still vital for educational departments. Along with modern science, they reveal the enormous role of biology in humans' experience and performance, that way provides educators with improved knowledge about how the brain can learn, which might help them subsequently create optimal conditions for learning. Neuroscience also has biomarkers of risk unique to education, and it provides innovative formulas to test interventions as well. (Goswami, 2008b). Such as diffusing understanding of how learning and performance are performed by the human brain i.e. mingling brain imaging techniques and knowing in cognitive psychology. (*An Efficient Approach for Multiclass Student Performance Prediction Based Upon Machine Learning*, 2019b)

Breakthrough in neuroscience plays a fateful role in education since it contributes to the improvement of learning and eliminates the vulnerability to biological and environmental factors. (*Multiclass Prediction Model for Student Grade Prediction Using Machine Learning*, 2021b)

The main goal for neuroscience researchers is diagnosing the learning process and exploring neural conditions that make learning for some people more effortless than for others. This information will suggest the drivers of changes and the best place for our educational intervention in that particular community. (*Neuroscience in Education*, n.d.)

It is the biological approach that will not be the replacement for sociological, psychological, or cultural analyses of education because it is a means of research for them and elicits the overall learning system. Neuroscience as a future trend is not all about the info we cannot understand, the learning capacity that enables us to go beyond the evolution limitations and see such phenomena as brain remodeling up to the detail and made known. (Forstmann & Wagenmakers, 2015b)

Network science helps realize the underlying theory, computational work, and empirical experimentation concepts that can be used to understand the structure and function of the human brain in an advanced way in simpler words and with basic mathematical patterns, Network neuroscience is now developing very fast and has already given very significant insight in the human structural connectivity as well as functional changes at rest, dynamics of networks and their variations between different groups of the patients and healthy persons. (Medaglia et al., 2015b)

In education neuroscience, we can use the teachings from research to make informed decisions in curriculum development which creates meaningful learning enabling students to go through the process of character development as wisdom/ enhanced consciousness becomes the end goal. Educational neuroscience knowledge can be successfully applied to teaching centers and learner communication through brainstorming ideas effectively. It also can help promote equal treatment and education by using or creating an appropriate teaching strategy, framework, and learning material. (Geake & Cooper, 2003b)

A social species is a group of individuals that is organized above the individual and they operate as a whole. This structure implies that social neuroscience is about examining the biological means that lead to these social organizations, processes, or behaviors. This activity being multidisciplinary and taking advantage of contemporary methodologies and comparative studies leads to integration analysis. The sphere of social neuroscience gives the basis for the brain and nervous system functions definition and takes into account the critical societal impact that needs to be researched. (Cacioppo & Decety, 2011b)

Neurological cognitive science is being excited by network theory and large data, with the appearance of brain scanning, analytical methods and progressively compute power. In the case of these anticipations, the role of the brain is the least complex since it is null in the origin of these functions during human development. Contrary to the growing debate about developmental cognitive neuroscience, the maturities of this field have also brought along new problems and deep sinks that have halted learning progress. (Fair et al., 2021b)

Deciphering the mysteries of the brain demands the employment of techniques, methods, and approaches from several disciplines in the fields of biology, psychology, chemistry, physics, and mathematics. The nub of the problem is to unearth the intricate system of connections in the brain that corresponds to the complex behaviors and functions, e.g. thoughts, memory, action, and emotion. Realizing the above mandates necessitates the sustained and articulate collection and fusion of massive data sets from divergent domains in time and space. (Akil et al., 2011b)

Neuroinformatics approaches, for example, connectomics, seek to get a comprehensive picture of neuronal connectivity patterns either at a level of macroscopic units or microscopic ones. The essence of the NIF (Neuroscience Information Framework) is about the whole field of neuroscience, as well as showing how this new substance can improve the existing knowledge and databases. (Barber et al., 2013b)

Although it can be challenging they need to get a more understandable language and means of communicating experimental research to educators that are applicable in the education sector as well. Moreover, they should focus on increasing professional development for educators. Lastly, classrooms should work with systemic problems and propose solutions instead of just solving them. (Ablin, 2008b)

3. THEORETICAL FRAMEWORK

The neurocognitive ability of human beings varies from person to person due to factors like genetics, structure of the brain, early life experiences, nutrition, access to education, supportive relationships, learning and adaptation skills, etc. A personalized learning model is an excellent source of getting personalized educational experiences, according to the specific needs and abilities of students. The system recognizes the strengths and weaknesses thereby adapting to the content and pace, designs personalized learning paths, and offers instant feedback promoting collaboration and communication.

(Adorni and Koceva,2016) they designed a personalized learning path for each student, depending on their knowledge. They used a method based on Education Concept Mapping (ECM) to do this. Hence, the students gain through this practice of self-assessment to reduce cognitive dissonance by being clear on the level of their understanding of the materials and the learning objectives and striving to get rid of any misunderstanding.

(Nacim Yanes et al., 2020) The article suggests a system, which may enable teachers, to improve their courses. It collects data from different places then processes the data to find what needs to be learned and makes use of smart computer programs to review the processed data. It provides teachers with what actions they can do to improve their courses, and accordingly change the way they teach. It may also provide specific counseling based on a teacher's subject of teaching, experience, and what the students need. It always assesses its own recommendation's quality and builds up the learning process around it.

Learning happens through neurocognitive pathways since memory, attention, problem-solving, and mode of cognitive processing contribute to how we remember and what we finally end up having acquired through the process. Memory is very important because it holds what you already know and what you want to know or what you were taught. Thus having a strong memory helps you recollect, recall, and reuse the facts concepts, and useful skills. Attention is one of the keys to staying concentrated on educational activities including reading, writing, mathematics, etc. Individuals who have mastered attentional control can stay focused, and it has a great impact on their learning process. Executive functions are abilities such as planning, organization, problem-solving, and self-regulation, which are in the hierarchy of thinking processes. Children and young people with developed executive functions are easily able to work through more complex learning tasks and struggle less with planning, initiation of a task, and monitoring of their progress. People with poor executive skills on the other hand find these learning tasks more difficult to perform. One more factor that distinguishes us cognitively is our styles of thinking, for instance, analytical vs. holistic thinking or visual vs. verbal processing styles, with which we approach and comprehend information differently. To quantify and examine the accuracy of these factors, an educator or a researcher may use different techniques and tools. Memory assessments consist of tests that assess recall, recognition, as well as spatial memory, focused attention which requires sustained attention, selective attention, and attention assessment which draws mainly on select standardized assessments or behavioral observations, and cognitive styles use various methods including self-report inventories, behavioral observations, or neuroimaging techniques.

The application of neurocognitive factors into educational design means that educational institutions should develop teaching programs and activities that consider the students' skills and psychological peculiarities. This includes developing instructional interventions based on techniques eager to memory strengthening, to help me stay on track as well as scaffold executive function skills and fit diverse cognitive styles. Offering learners the chance to engage actively through a multi-sensory learning process, receiving regular feedback, and being able to self-reflect are some of the support methods that nurture neurocognitive development and not only aid all learners but help achieve the best outcomes as well.

(Del Moral et al., 2022) The paper discusses a three-class problem by using the variables. It goes through the differences behind the excellent algorithms that are applied for the multi-class cleaning up. If the types diversity increases, the performance for all methods deteriorates, but it is not the case for the one-on-one approach. The precision answer is based on the single correct encoding of the class heterogeneity which leads to better decomposition of the multi-class problem. The results can include higher effects of classification and a shorter time to train and evaluate. This work employs synthetic and simple classifier data matrices to represent the effects of non-uniformity and then shows how a design-time similar dataset creates these patterns under genuine learning algorithms in addition to conversion for training processes (Suresh Babu, C. V., Suruthi, G., et. al. 2024b). Researchers investigate how to denote the heterogeneity over different decision boundaries, in addition, they are using it to break down the multi-class problem. The results indicate the existence of a noticeable advance over both neighborhoods constructed by state-of-the-art decomposition methods that do not assume the heterogeneity of the decision borders to exist.

Input data in a multiclass classification system are features (commonly the neurocognitive basis) and categorical labels (most likely the learning style). Data preparation includes normalization, feature scaling, and filling out the missing values to make it suitable for the algorithm. The feature extraction is not directly reflected in the supplied program, but in the practical world, it may be used to extract valuable data from unprocessed data or this may also be used to transform the features into a representation, which can be understood more easily by algorithms.

The centricity of the system is comprised of the multiclass classification model, like the RandomForestClassifier utilized in the provided program. The other mentioned algorithmic techniques include Support Vector Machines (SVM), Gradient Boosting, Neural Networks, and k-nearest Neighbors (k-NN). In this case, the algorithms can distribute the cases depending on their input data between different classes (Suresh Babu, C. V., Sudhir Manoharan et al, 2024).

During the training process, the model with multiclass classification works on the input data by changing the parameters of the model and trying to minimize a particular loss function at all times. Using a trained Randomforestclassifier we can predict learning styles (Visual, Auditory, Kinaesthetic) for the test set, based on their neurocognitive skills.

The result of the multiclass classification model is evaluated by metrics like accuracy, precision, recall, F1 score, and so on. The final result is the learning style prediction of the test instances for your future analysis or visualization or informing your educational interventions which are supposed to suit every learner according to their preferences and needs.

4. METHODOLOGY

Skill assessment:

The program is modeled to predict the proficiency level of a student using the multiclass algorithm. A simulated dataset is produced with NumPy. The dataset is split into features X representing skill levels and targets y indicating levels of proficiency. Finally, a RandomForestClassifier model is trained on the features and targets using fit() function.

Implementation of a learner engagement simulation is done by the development of a random learner skill profile. The model forecasts the student's proficiency level according to the image of their skill profile. A horizontal bar chart graph is used to showcase a learner's skill profile, with skill on the y-axis and skill levels on the x-axis.

The expected proficiency level is displayed on the console. This technique permits the imitation of learner involvement and the foresight of proficiency levels as per skills is made possible by the RandomForestClassifier model.

- **Source code:**

```
skill assessment

import numpy as np

import pandas as pd

from sklearn.ensemble import RandomForestClassifier

import matplotlib.pyplot as plt
```

```
# Generate simulated dataset with features (skills) and tar-
get (proficiency levels)

np.random.seed(0)

n_samples = 1000

n_skills = 10

skills = ['Skill_' + str(i) for i in range(1, n_skills + 1)]

proficiency_levels = ['Novice', 'Intermediate', 'Expert']

data = pd.DataFrame(np.random.randint(0, 100, size=(n_sam-
ples, n_skills)), columns=skills)

data['Proficiency'] = np.random.choice(proficiency_levels,
size=n_samples)

# Split data into features (X) and target (y)

X = data.drop(columns='Proficiency')

y = data['Proficiency']

# Train RandomForestClassifier model

model = RandomForestClassifier()
```

```
model.fit(X, y)

# Simulate learner engagement

learner_skills = np.random.randint(0, 100, size=(1, n_
skills))

learner_proficiency = model.predict(learner_skills)

# Plot learner skill profile

plt.figure(figsize=(10, 6))

plt.barh(skills, learner_skills.flatten(), color='light-
blue', label='Learner Skills')

plt.xlabel('Skill Level')

plt.ylabel('Skills')

plt.title('Learner Skill Profile')

plt.legend()

plt.grid(axis='x')

plt.show()
```

```
# Print predicted proficiency level

print('Predicted Proficiency Level:', learner_proficien-
cy[0])
```

- **Prediction of learning style:**

This program seeks to develop a multiclass model that uses neurocognition assessments to predict learners' preferred learning styles. The neurocognitive skills of students and their compatible learning styles are compiled in a dataset that undergoes this technique. The dataset is then split into features comprising (neurological skills) and target variables (learning styles). A Random Forest Classifier is trained on the training set to combat the task of learning style prediction. The model's performance is assessed on the test set, and the simulated and real learning styles are presented side by side in the form of histograms.

A CSV file is used as a source of storage, and training and testing datasets are separated by a function from the scikit-learn package, train_test_split. Thus, with the trained model, we can predict the learning styles for the test set, with the result of the prediction saved under the y_pred variable. The numerical values are set to the learning style name of the given label (Visual, Auditory, or Kinaesthetic). A histogram is used for this aspect to inform the distribution of predicted and actual learning styles. Therefore, it becomes easier to compare the two sets of data.

This method helps to forecast as well as to make a judgment concerning the learning styles depending on the capacity of students' neurocognitive skills using the multiclass classification model. Plotted results of the model show how the predicted and actual learning styles are matched, therefore we have visual knowledge about the performance and accuracy of the model toward finding the students' learning preferences.

- **Dataset:**

The dataset constitutes six cognitive abilities and a range of 0-100 which are responsible for defining the different learning styles of individuals. It also applies to a kind of variable that is categorical and overrides learning styles according to visual, auditory, and kinesthetic classifications. The data proposed for this research is for monitoring the interaction between cognitive abilities and learning manners and drawing the patterns for the prediction of learning style.

Table 1.

memory	attention	problem_solving	creativity	logical_thinking	communication	learning_styles
80	75	85	70	80	75	1
70	85	80	65	75	80	2
75	70	90	75	85	70	3
85	80	75	85	70	80	1
80	75	85	70	80	75	2
70	85	80	65	75	80	3
75	70	90	75	85	70	1
85	80	75	85	70	80	2
80	75	85	70	80	75	3
70	85	80	65	75	80	1

- Source code:

```
import numpy as np

import pandas as pd

from sklearn.model_selection import train_test_split

from sklearn.ensemble import RandomForestClassifier

import matplotlib.pyplot as plt

# Define the neurocognitive skills

neurocognitive_skills = ['memory', 'attention', 'problem_
solving', 'creativity', 'logical_thinking', 'communication']
```

```
# Load the dataset (replace 'dataset.csv' with your dataset file)

data = pd.read_csv('dataset.csv')

# Split the dataset into features (X) and target (y)

X = data[neurocognitive_skills]

y = data['learning_styles'] # Replace 'learning_style' with the target variable in your dataset

# Split the data into training and testing sets

X_train, X_test, y_train, y_test = train_test_split(X, y, test_size=0.2, random_state=42)

# Train the multiclass classification model (Random Forest Classifier)

model = RandomForestClassifier()

model.fit(X_train, y_train)

# Predict the learning styles for the test set

y_pred = model.predict(X_test)
```

```
# Mapping for numerical labels to learning styles

label_mapping = {1: 'Visual', 2: 'Auditory', 3: 'Kinaesthet-
ic'}

# Replace numerical labels with learning styles in y_pred
and y_test

y_pred_labels = [label_mapping[label] for label in y_pred]

y_test_labels = [label_mapping[label] for label in y_test]

# Plot histograms of predicted and actual learning styles

plt.figure(figsize=(10, 5))

plt.subplot(1, 2, 1)

plt.hist(y_pred_labels, bins=np.arange(len(np.unique(y))) -
0.5, alpha=0.5, color='blue', label='Predicted')

plt.xticks(rotation=45)

plt.xlabel('Learning Style')

plt.ylabel('Frequency')

plt.title('Predicted vs Actual Learning Styles')
```

```
plt.legend()

plt.subplot(1, 2, 2)

plt.hist(y_test_labels, bins=np.arange(len(np.unique(y))) -
0.5, alpha=0.5, color='green', label='Actual')

plt.xticks(rotation=45)

plt.xlabel('Learning Style')

plt.ylabel('Frequency')

plt.title('Predicted vs Actual Learning Styles')

plt.legend()

plt.tight_layout()

plt.show()
```

- **Peer recommendation:**

This program is established in a way that promotes peer-to-peer learning by determining a peer's competencies and skills and further narrowing it down to direct inquiry. It uses a data set containing student's information related to their present adaptation levels, interests, and learning approach. In this case, the program imports data from a file 'dataset.csv', and the function `recommend_peer_profiles(student_id,skill_level)` is created to provide a list of recommended peers for students based on their skill level. The function is in favor of profiling the data set and searching for student profiles that are close to the level of the input student's level and the student's profile is not presented on the list. The function produces a DataFrame, which contains the recommended peer profile. Primarily, the app asks students to input their student ID number and their skill level. The function called on the interface will be `recommend_peer_profiles` with all given information and it will return the list of peer profiles. In case of the matches, the program prints out the recommended profiles; if no matches are found, then a message specifying "no matching profiles" is shown.

When the program is carried out, the main function is executed first, which requires the user to pick his student ID, followed by showing his skill level. The curriculum does more than just provide students with a platform where they can unravel their passions and discover others like them. It also creates a cohesive environment in which students can work with individuals who possess similar levels of skills and thus, have an opportunity for collaboration.

Table 2. Dataset

Student_ID	Skill_Level	Interest	Learning_Preference
1	Intermediate	Programming	Visual
2	Intermediate	Data Science	Kinaesthetic
3	Advanced	Mathematics	Auditory
4	Intermediate	Data Science	Visual
5	Beginner	Programming	Kinaesthetic
6	Advanced	Mathematics	Visual
7	Beginner	Data Science	Auditory
8	Intermediate	Mathematics	Visual
9	Advanced	Programming	Auditory
10	Beginner	Programming	Kinaesthetic

- Source code:

```
import pandas as pd


# Read the dataset
```

```
df = pd.read_csv('dataset.csv') # Replace 'your_dataset.csv' with the path to your dataset file

def recommend_peer_profiles(student_id, skill_level):

# Filter the dataset to find similar skill levels

similar_profiles = df[df['Skill_Level'] == skill_level]

# Remove the current student from the list

similar_profiles = similar_profiles[similar_profiles['Student_ID'] != student_id]

return similar_profiles[['Student_ID', 'Skill_Level', 'Interest', 'Learning_Preference']]

def main():

# Ask the user for student ID and skill level

student_id = input("Enter your Student ID: ")

skill_level = input("Enter your Skill Level: ")

# Recommend peer profiles based on skill level
```

```
recommended_profiles = recommend_peer_profiles(student_id,
skill_level)

# Print recommended profiles

if not recommended_profiles.empty:

print("\nRecommended peer profiles based on similar skill
level:")

print(recommended_profiles)

else:

print("\nNo peer profiles found with similar skill level.")

if __name__ == "__main__":

main()
```

5. FINDINGS AND RESULTS

- **Skill assessment:**

The learner's proficiency level is inversely proportional to the jump in their skill levels here. It makes a virtual dataset of people and the skill level of every one of them is random, they are matched with proficiency levels like Novice, Intermediate, or Expert. Eventually, as the RandomForestClassifier model is trained by this dataset, it simulates the probability skill distribution of a learner with random switching levels. The next step is the learner's proficiency level prediction using this model and the creation of his skill profile in a horizontal bar chart.

Figure 1. Skill assessment result

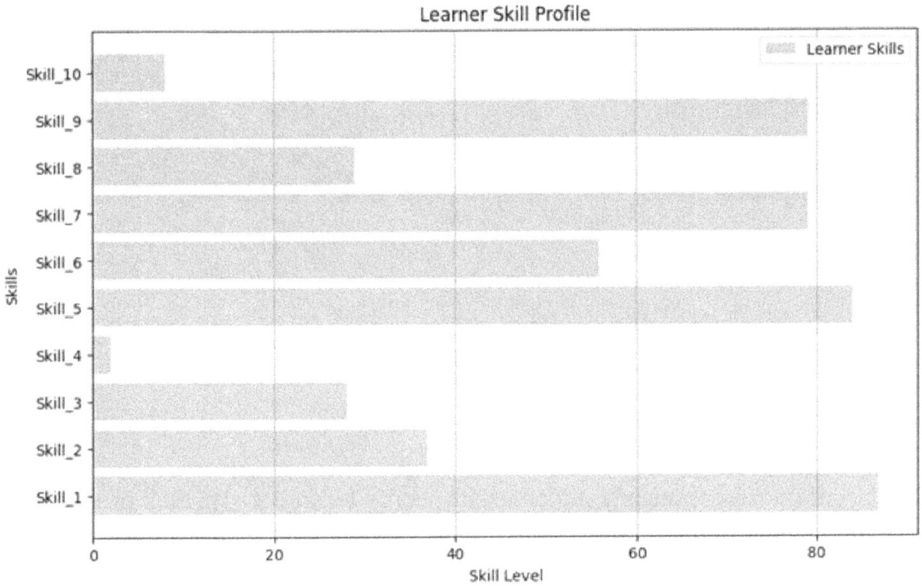

- **Learning style prediction:**

This program facilitates the recognition of the way students ideally would like to learn and measure it using a usual classifier called the Random Forest Classifier. Harmonize with a database expounding on students' neurocognitive characteristics and their mode of learning. Eventually, after it does training on parts of the data, the model is then checked on how it predicts learning styles for the other information it has not yet been exposed to. Ultimately a graph goes out which has two histograms showing the facts: what has been predicted concerning learning styles versus what has been observed. This shows what scope the model has in categorizing the learning preferences of students and how well it can do it

Figure 2. Prediction of learning style

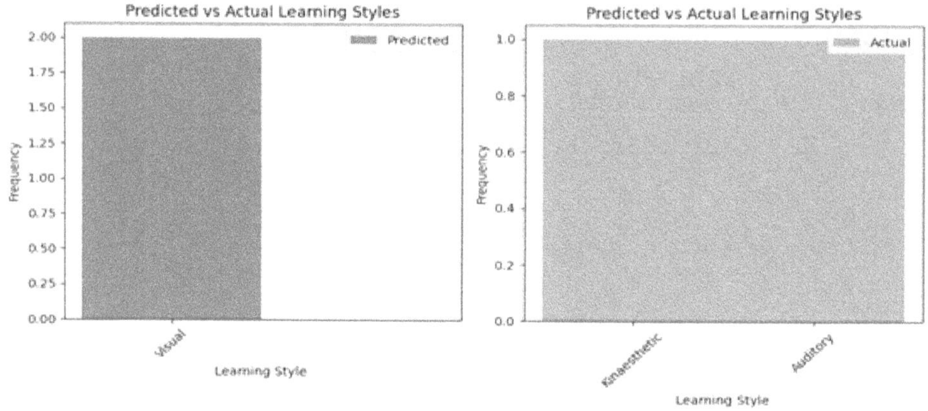

- Peer recommendation:

The program recommends students with peers who are equal in their proficiency, have similar interests and would like to assume the same study patterns as themselves. Here, a set of data is utilized to pick peers with the same standard levels, failing to consider the learner as well. Next, the course suggests study partners by showing the grantee's IDs along with proficiency level, major, interest, and preferred learning style. The text to the user is that there is no matching profile available when there are no appropriate competent partners identified. The program when they have one-to-one feedback with each student and individualizes suggestions of collaborative learning based on the student's proficiency level.

Figure 3. Peer recommendation based on similar skill level

```
Enter your Student ID: 21
Enter your Skill Level: Beginner

Recommended peer profiles based on similar skill level:
    Student_ID Skill_Level      Interest Learning_Preference
4            5    Beginner   Programming        Kinaesthetic
6            7    Beginner  Data Science            Auditory
9           10    Beginner   Programming        Kinaesthetic
14          15    Beginner   Mathematics        Kinaesthetic
17          18    Beginner  Data Science              Visual
21          22    Beginner  Data Science              Visual
23          24    Beginner  Data Science            Auditory
28          29    Beginner   Programming              Visual
32          33    Beginner   Programming              Visual
34          35    Beginner   Mathematics        Kinaesthetic
37          38    Beginner   Mathematics              Visual
40          41    Beginner   Programming              Visual
43          44    Beginner  Data Science              Visual
46          47    Beginner  Data Science              Visual
49          50    Beginner  Data Science              Visual
```

6. CONCLUSION

Machine learning methods, such as the multiclass approach, are doing miracles when education specialists implement them to find solutions to various difficulties that education throws at them. This lets algorithms provide for the formation of individual-focused learning paths that consider learner diversity which might include variation in the way students learn and actualize new information. By doing so, it becomes a guarantee that every student receives the help he/she needs to interact most appropriately with the subject and do much better at understanding.

Multiclass algorithms have a prominent role in collaborative learning and this is visible when it groups students into classes with peers who are at the same skill level or who understand the concepts with similar efficiency. This creates feelings of community including support and peer learning where they can socialize and learn in a fun but respectful way. It is not until the real qualities of multiclass algorithms are laid bare that you begin to appreciate their versatility and adaptability. They can handle various learning styles, cognitive abilities of individuals with ease, and hence they are considered an invaluable asset to educators. By relying on the predictive power of these algorithms, schools and universities can also help direct resources correctly, adjusting the didactic process to the different student aptitudes, and creating a collaborative learning atmosphere that straightens educating effectiveness. Implementation of multiclass algorithms into the school process is a major change that takes into account a different view of what the teaching and learning process is. Through the application the data-driven insights and predictive modeling, educators can differentiate, promote mutual understanding among students, and consequently notice and celebrate achievement of learning. Programs, with these timely additions, will surely be the ones to help the education field with its advancement and progress that will finally be rapid and effective.

7. FUTURE DIRECTIONS FOR RESEARCH

In the last few years, the integration of machine-learning systems has been changing the way education is done, bringing about new possibilities to improve learning and teaching momentums. By adopting personalized learning paths, adaptive testing systems, cross-domain transfer learning, social and emotional learning (SEL) support, and ethical thinking, there are many ways education can be put on the path of positive change.

In collaboration with the teaching process with the assistance of machine learning technologies, tutors can adjust lessons to the level of student readiness, maintain motivation, and thereby develop academic success. The adoption of these systems involves the use of algorithms that check on core cognitive processes and purposefully endeavor to achieve great educational outcomes(Li et al., 2020).

When machine learning is combined with social and emotional learning (SEL), end-to-end solutions are created which lets the systems identify and address the social and emotional needs of students (Zhong et al., 2021). Adaptive assessment systems soar in flying higher among innovation elements in education, readapting assessment tasks driven by current performance data of students and the inferred mental capabilities. Furthermore, this approach offers more precision during the assessment and adds information about the learning journey and what needs to be improved (Diao et al., 2019).

Interdisciplinary transfer learning, in which knowledge in post-secondary settings is made consistent with other domains, holds out the hope that education would not be limited to academic and disciplinary issues, therefore, offering a feasible solution to the paucity of resources. Engaging in the interplay of knowledge and skills acquired from different domains, learners can master the ability of interdisciplinary (i.e., across subjects) competence that works miracles in the dynamic world of today (Pan and Yang, 2010). The area of applied linguistic studies is developing such methods as experiments, advanced surveys, and computer modeling, to name but a few, and it is these methods that help to overcome linguistic difficulties and benefit modern society. The writers state that the solutions are possible only if public attention is directed towards doing the hard and sincere work with philosophical challenges like objectivity and bias(Glass, 2006b). Lastly, the developers of the documentary emphasize the importance of big data and artificial intelligence in various aspects of education which include research and policy-making, as well as industry (Suresh Babu C.V., 2023). Big data and AI technology in education have made very noteworthy changes in the areas of evaluation, individualized instruction, and precision learning. On the other hand, this educational theme points to the significance of avoiding over-generalizing the use of educational analytics findings. The pattern clarifies that governments should provide lifelong learning, establish teacher training programs, and shield individual data. The text also discusses the exchange of relations between academia and industry so that the emerging technologies are guided well by applicable theories and ideas and are successfully checked through empirical proof. In addition, they propose a dialogue between "cold" people and "warm" humanity to find a middle ground for respect between teachers and students on this and other topics and technology in teaching and learning. (Luan et al., 2020b)

REFERENCES

Yanes, N., Mostafa, A. M., Ezz, M. and Almuayqil, S. N. (2020). "A Machine Learning-Based Recommender System for Improving Students Learning Experiences," in IEEE Access, vol. 8, pp. 201218-201235, doi: 10.1109/ACCESS.2020.3036336.

Ablin, J. L. (2008). Learning as problem design versus problem solving: Making the connection between cognitive neuroscience research and educational practice. *Mind, Brain, and Education/Mind. Mind, Brain and Education : the Official Journal of the International Mind, Brain, and Education Society*, *2*(2), 52–54. DOI: 10.1111/j.1751-228X.2008.00030.x

Adorni, G., & Koceva, F. (2016). Educational Concept Maps for Personalized Learning Path Generation. In Lecture notes in computer science (pp. 135–148). DOI: 10.1007/978-3-319-49130-1_11

Akil, H., Martone, M., & Van Essen, D. C. (2011). Challenges and Opportunities in mining Neuroscience data. *Science*, *331*(6018), 708–712. DOI: 10.1126/science.1199305 PMID: 21311009

Jain, A. and Solanki, S. (2019). "An Efficient Approach for Multiclass Student Performance Prediction based upon Machine Learning," 2019 International Conference on Communication and Electronics Systems (ICCES), Coimbatore, India, pp. 1457-1462, doi: 10.1109/ICCES45898.2019.9002038.

Cacioppo, J. T., & Decety, J. (2011). Social neuroscience: Challenges and opportunities in the study of complex behavior. *Annals of the New York Academy of Sciences*, *1224*(1), 162–173. DOI: 10.1111/j.1749-6632.2010.05858.x PMID: 21251011

Challco, G. C., Bittencourt, I. I., & Isotani, S. (2020). Can Ontologies Support the Gamification of Scripted Collaborative Learning Sessions? In: Bittencourt, I., Cukurova, M., Muldner, K., Luckin, R., Millán, E. (eds) Artificial Intelligence in Education. AIED 2020. Lecture Notes in Computer Science(), vol 12163. Springer, Cham. https://doi.org/DOI: 10.1007/978-3-030-52237-7_7

Del Moral, P., Nowaczyk, S., & Pashami, S. (2022). Why is multiclass classification hard? *IEEE Access : Practical Innovations, Open Solutions*, *10*, 80448–80462. DOI: 10.1109/ACCESS.2022.3192514

Fair, D. A., Dosenbach, N. U., Moore, A. H., Satterthwaite, T. D., & Milham, M. P. (2021). Developmental cognitive neuroscience in the era of networks and big data: Strengths, weaknesses, opportunities, and threats. *Annual Review of Developmental Psychology*, *3*(1), 249–275. DOI: 10.1146/annurev-devpsych-121318-085124

Forstmann, B. U., & Wagenmakers, E. (2015). An Introduction to Model-Based Cognitive Neuroscience. In *Springer eBooks*. https://doi.org/DOI: 10.1007/978-1-4939-2236-9

Shukla, A. K., Chowdury, M. A. M., Nath, R. and Muhuri, P. K. (2021). "Fuzzy Reliability Redundancy Allocation Problem Using Multi-factorial Evolutionary Algorithm," 2021 IEEE International Conference on Systems, Man, and Cybernetics (SMC), Melbourne, Australia, 2021, pp. 2512-2517, doi: 10.1109/SMC52423.2021.9658908.

Geake, J., & Cooper, P. (2003). Cognitive Neuroscience: Implications for education? *Westminster Studies in Education*, *26*(1), 7–20. DOI: 10.1080/0140672030260102

Goswami, U. (2008). Principles of Learning, Implications for Teaching: A Cognitive Neuroscience perspective. *Journal of Philosophy of Education*, *42*(3–4), 381–399. DOI: 10.1111/j.1467-9752.2008.00639.x

Koenig, N., Anzelmi, G., Naso, D., Nienhaus, M., & Grasso, E. "An Improved IDIM Technique for Sensorless Control of Single-Phase Electromagnetic Drives," 2019 IEEE 10th International Symposium on Sensorless Control for Electrical Drives (SLED), Turin, Italy, 2019, pp. 1-6, DOI: 10.1109/SLED.2019.8896303

Medaglia, J. D., Lynall, M., & Bassett, D. S. (2015). Cognitive Network Neuroscience. *Journal of Cognitive Neuroscience*, *27*(8), 1471–1491. DOI: 10.1162/jocn_a_00810 PMID: 25803596

S. D. A. Bujang et al., "Multiclass Prediction Model for Student Grade Prediction Using Machine Learning," in IEEE Access, vol. 9, pp. 95608-95621, 2021, doi: 10.1109/ACCESS.2021.3093563.

Suresh Babu, C. V. (2023). *Artificial Intelligence and Expert Systems*. Anniyappa Publications.

Suresh Babu, C. V., & Praveen, S. (2023). Swarm Intelligence and Evolutionary Machine Learning Algorithms for COVID-19: Pandemic and Epidemic Review. In Suresh Kumar, A., Kose, U., Sharma, S., & Jerald Nirmal Kumar, S. (Eds.), *Dynamics of Swarm Intelligence Health Analysis for the Next Generation* (pp. 83–103). IGI Global., DOI: 10.4018/978-1-6684-6894-4.ch005

Suresh Babu, C. V., Suruthi, G., Indhumathi, C., & Sushruth, S. (2024b). Integrated approach for network intrusion detection: Combining KNN algorithm, Karhunen-Loève transform, and genetic algorithm optimization. In Metaheuristic and machine learning optimization strategies for complex systems (p. 21). DOI: 10.4018/979-8-3693-7842-7.ch002

SureshBabu. C. V., Sudhir Manoharan., L., G. K., & V., S. K. (2024). Application of Support Vector Machine Algorithm in Automated Lending Protocols for Decentralized Finance Platforms. In L. Vardari & I. Qabrati (Eds.), Decentralized Finance and Tokenization in FinTech (pp. 1-20). IGI Global. DOI: 10.4018/979-8-3693-3346-4.ch001

Tam, N. T., Hoang, V., Bình, H. T. T., & Vĩnh, L. T. (2022). Multi-objective teaching–learning evolutionary algorithm for enhancing sensor network coverage and lifetime. *Engineering Applications of Artificial Intelligence*, *108*, 104554. DOI: 10.1016/j.engappai.2021.104554

Chapter 10
Value Co-Creation of Design in the Internet Economy

Balaji Gopalan
https://orcid.org/0000-0002-1082-5597
Jain University, India

Ravishankar S. Ulle
https://orcid.org/0009-0008-1011-8738
Jain University, India

S. Yogananthan
https://orcid.org/0009-0007-5583-0924
Jain University, India

ABSTRACT

In today's internet economy and Web 3.0, firms are using virtual Internet portals for co-design. Product design by firms have focused predominantly on the significance of product aesthetics. Virtual co-design by firms are moving towards new product design using creative themes to focus on the aesthetics of design in association with a product function. Firms are integrating the internet for co-design, customization and the personalization of products and web portals are facilitating the personalization and customization of ideas, concepts and designs and are co-creating value for firms. Firms today have become agents of change and are adding value to professions and vocations. Today, firms acknowledge the fact that products can be designed virtually.

DOI: 10.4018/979-8-3693-2973-3.ch010

1 INTRODUCTION

Various industry sectors have been using computer-aided design (CAD) for many years. Today, Designer 3D software is being used for simulations and designs in a number of product sectors, including the fashion and textile industries. Interactive design software has made it easy and feasible to create clothing with an almost perfect fit (Wolff et al., 2023). Software like NedGraphics, Optitex, Accumark 3D, VStitcher, Clo3D, and a few others are being utilized by textile companies to personalize fabric designs with colors, textures, avatars, and sizing (Särmäkari 2023). Today, manufacturers across industries integrate product design with supply chain management, production, and logistics systems.

Further, the internet economy today facilitates even small and medium industries to expand internationally with the support of information technology, new business logic, online payment transactions, service conveniences and other IT enabled services (Bell and Loane 2010; Mainardes et al. 2017; Grover and Kohli 2012; Oh and Teo 2010; Rai et al. 2012). CAD has made it easier for designer firms to create designs more cost effectively and with design flexibility from design repositories before actually making a product (Arrighi and Mougenot 2019). Take the example of the Kansei engineering approach. In the Kansei engineering approach to virtual design of kitchens using software, designers can source millions of kitchen design configurations that incorporate emotions, lifestyles and kitchen engineering (Nagamachi 2010). In other areas such as home décor, designer software such as UNITY have facilitated customized designing of walls, windows, decorative elements, tapestry and flooring (Arrighi and Mougenot 2019).

In the example of Nike ID's successful experiment with customers in providing a web portal for co-designing shoes, the flexibility of designing products allowing customers to personalize designs for functionality, texturing, design and aesthetics multiplies the probabilities and combinations of product design. Fan-based networks and online marketplaces (Healy and McDonagh 2013; Kim et al. 2008) are playing a greater role in promoting brands with a focus on customized designs and personalized products and services (Füller and Matzler 2007) greatly increasing the value of the firm (Du et al. 2006) and brands. The flexibility of configurable settings in internet portals for product designs is found to have a positive effect on product quality (Trentin et al. 2012). For designer firms, the ability to configure designs using software has enhanced design problem solving and better visualization of design simulations (Füller and Matzler 2007; Anna 2018; Arrighi and Mougenot 2019; Boldt and Carvalho 2018). This also aligns inter-intra firm coordination between manufacturing, logistics and supply chain management (Sanders and Stappers 2008; Dell'Era and Verganti 2009; Schiavone et al., 2020; Rai et al. 2012).

Small and medium industries facilitated by today's internet economy are expanding into markets providing opportunities for making businesses more profitable (Bell and Loane 2010; Ceccagnoli et al. 2012; Gray et al. 2011; Grover and Kohli 2012). In the area of online shopping, entrepreneurship and start-ups with new business logic have emerged from the socio-technological phenomenon of the internet economy (Lechner and Hummel 2002; Alexiou 2018; Au et al. 2009; Bouncken and Reuschl 2018; Dell'Era and Verganti 2009; Bughin et al. 2011). This experience of the socio-technological phenomenon is shared by hybrid commerce delivery systems (Oh and Teo, 2010).

2 LITERATURE REVIEW, AIMS AND OBJECTIVES

Brands such as Nike, Lectra's Accumark-3D, V-Stitcher, Clo and Optitex have successfully integrated design, manufacturing and supply chain management facilitating the entire design process for designing a range of products such as shoes or an entire clothing line. Designer software today support firms with a configurable design database, technical design tracking, customization and simulation, product and service information, pricing, order fulfillment and service conveniences. This has resulted in the personalization of designs, loyalty for firms and optimization of costs that exceeds the value of the brand and facilitates production economics (Boldt and Carvalho 2018; Du et al. 2006; Yang et al. 2017; Oh and Teo 2010; Zeithaml 1988; Tellis and Gaeth 1990; Füller and Matzler 2007; Arrighi and Mougenot 2019; Trentin et al. 2012). Further, today's hybrid commerce delivery systems such as online shopping along with social networks have added value by integrating various geographies, demography and themes in terms of improved portfolios for design selection, customization and reviews (Messinger et al. 2009, Arrighi and Mougenot 2019; Agarwal et al. 2008; Colliander and Dahlén 2011). For example, in a study on the furniture industry, survey responses confirmed that 50% of product preferences depend on price, 20% on deliveries, 20% on customization and 10% on the time required to customize the product (Lihra et al. 2012).

3. RESEARCH PROBLEM

It has been a challenge to integrate creative industries from the disorganized sector in India directly into online shopping. Popular online shopping portals have begun partnering with many artisans, weavers, textile industries and home decor experts who have become shareholders in the business. Ethnic products are becoming more popular in online shopping portals and customers now browse online shopping portals in their own local languages. Online shopping now offers customers the option of buying either ready-made, customized or co-designed products. In terms of comprehending the research problem, this paper examines the economics of online shopping portals and how they may promote, modernize and integrate ethnic goods manufacturers, disorganized sectors and cottage industries across India by mobilizing the innovativeness, efficacy and market knowledge of cultural and ethnic products for the internet economy.

Research questions identified:

1) What is the demand for customized products in online shopping portals?
2) What is the demand for customizing designs in online shopping portals?
3) How successful are online shopping portals in delivering customized products?
4) How can product customization improve brand value in online shopping portals?

Research Methodology

The research methodology and theory in this study explores 30 years of research on value co-creation between customers and firms in the internet economy and evaluates 135 survey responses covering various industries.

1) Objective of the study:
    a) To study the elements of online web portals facilitating value co-creation.
    b) To study the co-creation of design in successful online shopping portals.
    c) To study how customers can be integrated for the co-design of brands.
2) Survey Questionnaire: A survey was administered to gather responses of customer experiences in co-creating products with firms. As wide variance is expected in the data collected and abstractness of attributes that facilitate co-creation, this study utilizes analytics in the best way to study value co-creation processes between firms and customers.
3) Theory: This study is theoretically anchored on identifying various customer attributes of value co-creation relevant for businesses who intend to integrate customers in the co-design of products.

4. SIGNIFICANCE AND CONTRIBUTION OF THE STUDY

(a) It opens new theoretical discussions about the specific attributes of value co-creation that brands can use to enhance the experience of product customization in online shopping portals. Many brands have successfully facilitated this experience for the customer. Online shopping portals now facilitate the customization of product designs and its integration into production, logistics and supply chain management. The issues with online shopping portals facilitating customized product design for customers is that they are limited to certain international brands. The context can be applied to different regions, cultures and traditions to facilitate the economic growth of cottage industries in countries where professions associated with arts and crafts are disappearing. This could provide enormous opportunities for employment and preservation of indigenous cultures.

(b) Significantly, regionalization of online shopping portals is inevitable and supporting local markets that are transitioning into the internet economy facilitates greater integration and support for local businesses, traditions and cultures in India. According to a study, the handloom industry from the rural areas of India employs about three million people and is the second largest employer (K and T, 2024). Around 24% working in the handloom sector were earning an income ranging from Rs. 10,000 to Rs. 20,000 and sometimes 54% of families were earning double the amount. People are willing to spend in online shopping portals on ethnic products such as sarees for comfort, fit, patriotism, uniqueness, money's worth, variety and designs, cash on delivery, delivery time, packaging, returnable items, attractive discounts, and convenience. In India, the Ministry of Textiles and the National Handloom Development Programme supports the handloom industry and it was estimated that the total handloom exports for the years 2019-2020 was worth US $315.62 million (Attri and Bairagi 2022). The handicraft industry was expected to grow by 20% with an estimated export value of $3.5 billion that includes woodwares, metalware, embroidered, handprinted textiles, fabrics, jewellery, and crocheted goods. Online shopping portals along with social media now support entrepreneurs, creative professionals, hobbyists and boutique owners. In the handicrafts industry, businesses to sustain supply chain resilience need to focus on supply chain management in terms of cost optimization, product differentiation, raw material management, partnerships, ownership, franchising and financial management (Yadav and Tripathi 2024).

5. DATA ANALYSIS

A survey questionnaire helped facilitate responses from 135 managers from various industries across India who explained the relevance of the internet economy and the role of the customer in terms of improving products and services. A Likert scale was used to collect the data. Structural equation modeling was used to study how social, economic and intellectual motivation between customers and firms facilitate the value co-creation process. The analysis intends to identify the attributes and qualities of value co-creation that may be integrated within online shopping portals for customizing the product, design and experience while purchasing products.

6 BACKGROUND STUDY

Various professions and vocations utilize the internet and mobile technologies for work-life balance, entertainment, knowledge, shopping and services (Gray et al. 2011; Höflich et al. 2010; Wagner and Majchrzak 2006; Gordon and Silva 2011; Brynskov et al. 2018). Online shopping portals with a greater customer reach now facilitates a quality experience for the customer who purchase products based on ratings in social commerce networks (Schlosser et al. 2006; Stephen and Toubia 2010; Rafaeli and Noy 2002; Riegner, 2007; Lechner and Hummel 2002; Oh and Teo 2010). The most transformative experience for the customer is that of online shopping portals facilitating a unique experience of customizing the design of products before purchase.

6.1 Virtual Design for Co-Creation

Figure 1. Design quadrant

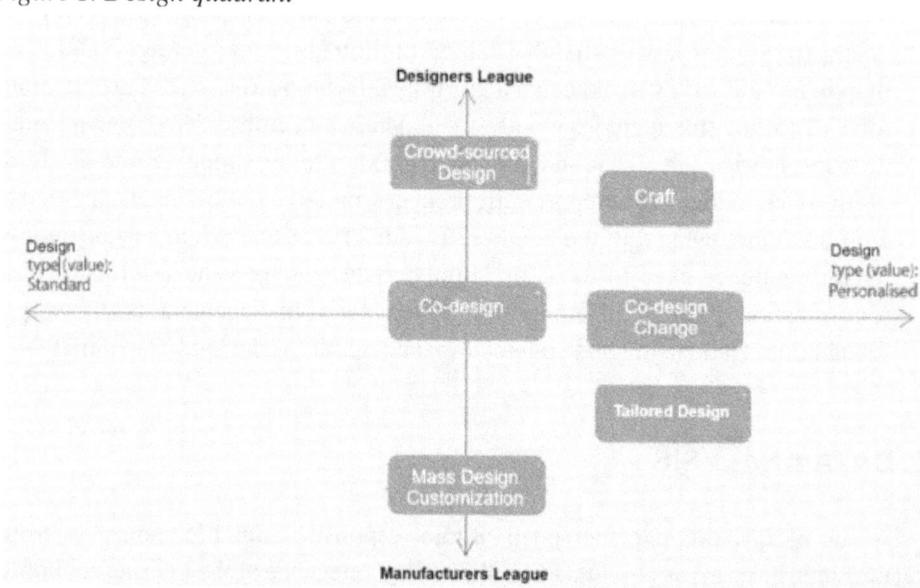

Figure 1 above shows the design quadrant and the customization of product designs for various needs. Designer software such as V-Stitcher, Clo3D, Lectra's Accumark-3D, and Optitex have demonstrated personalized and customized designing of garments and clothing. Manufacturer's use of design software to enhance product configuration leading to improved product quality (Trentin et al. 2012) has demonstrated its use in the fashion and textile industry for designs and simulations. Prahalad and Ramaswamy (2003) explained the use of the product space, design space and the experience space to create environments for customers to co-design products with firms. This is shown in Figure 2 below.

Figure 2. Locus of co-creative design excellence (Prahalad and Ramaswamy 2003)

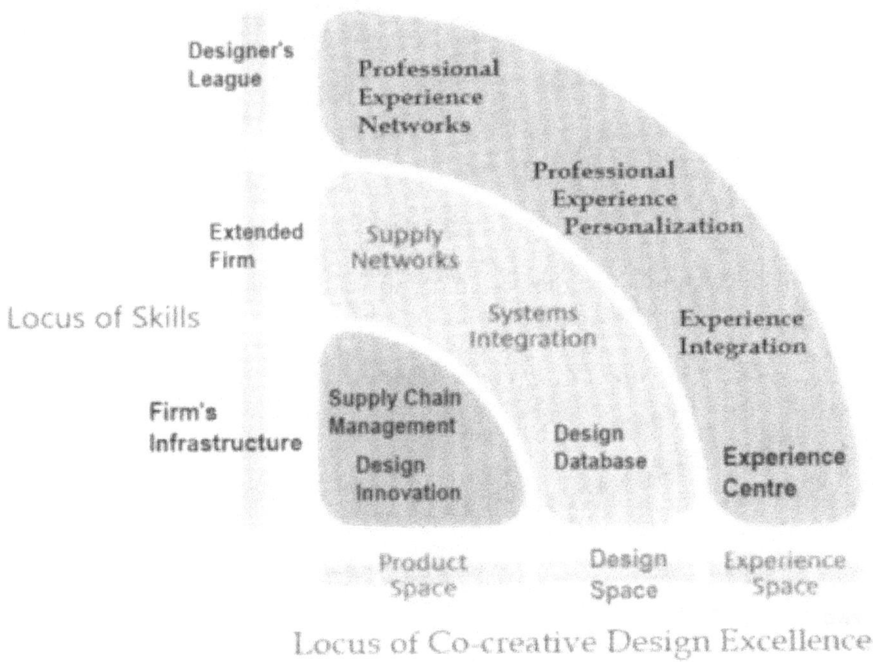

Figure 3. Customization of design fabrics (Woodbridge 2024)

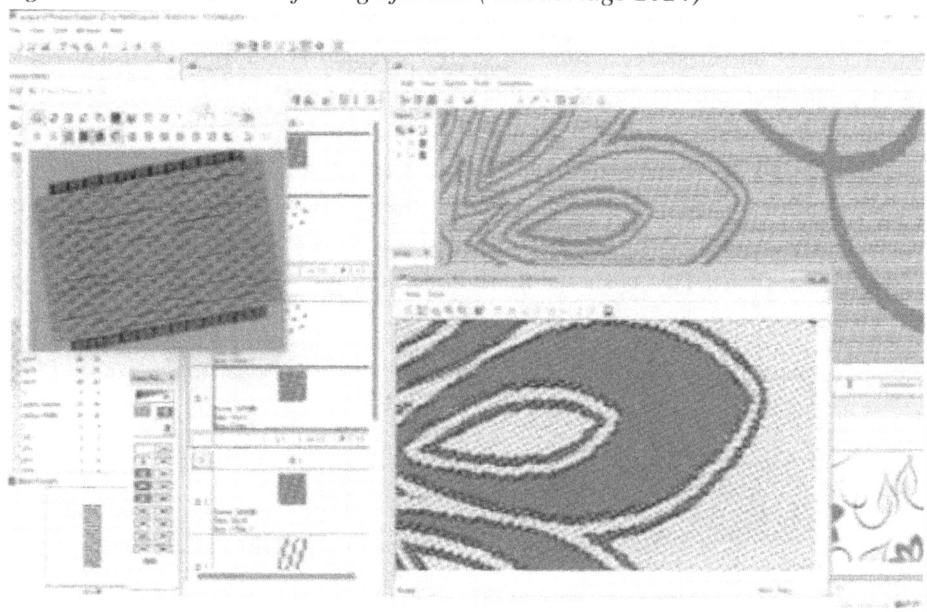

Figure 3 above shows how the design of fabrics can be customized for apparel.

Figure 4. Design of apparel (Wolff et al. 2023)

Figure 5. Design of apparel (Boldt and Carvalho 2018)

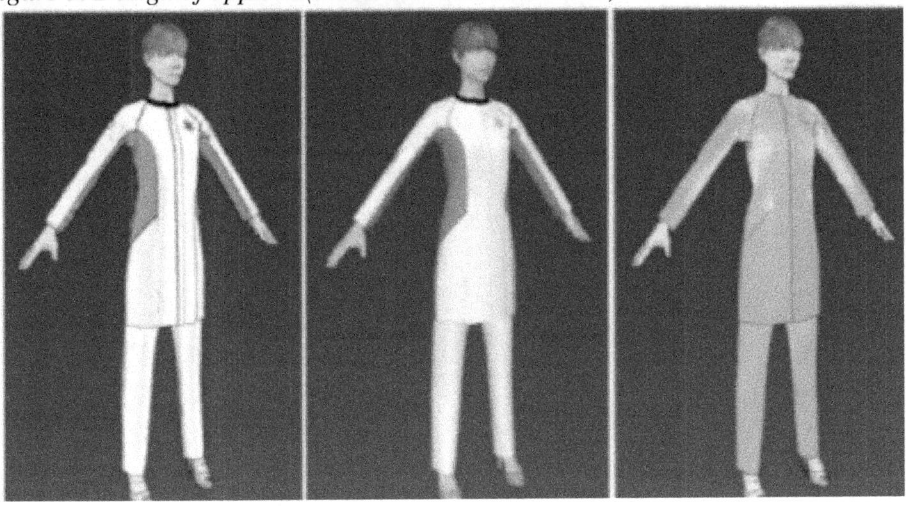

Figure 4 and Figure 5 above show how the design of apparel can study the fit and evaluate design comfort. 3D Designer software now facilitates (1) integrated and configurable designs, (2) value creation intensity and (3) optimized prototype design (Arrighi and Mougenot 2019; Boldt and Carvalho 2018).

Figure 6. Customization of apparel designs (Accumark-3D. A Lectra Company. August 2021)

The above Figure 6 shows how apparel designs can be customized and integrated with supply chain management within no time. The next Figure 7 shows how in garment design projects, complicated applications of designer software and flat patterns are transformed from technical 2D designs for finalized renderings in 3D.

Figure 7. Garment design projects (Clo3D. August 2021)

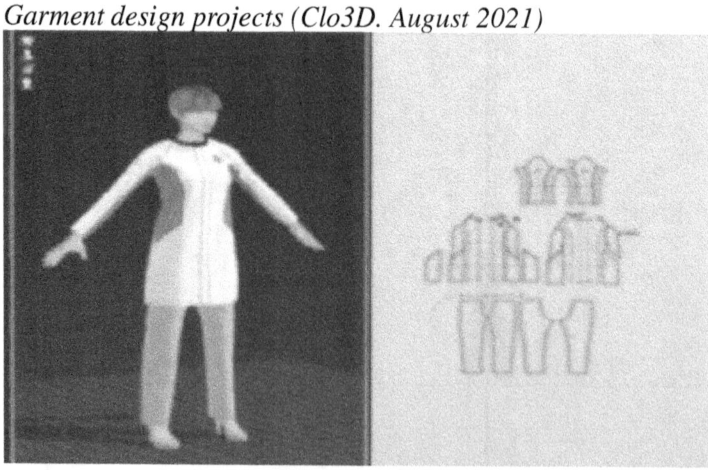

Figure 8. Clo3D effect on manufacturing (Clo3D. August 2021)

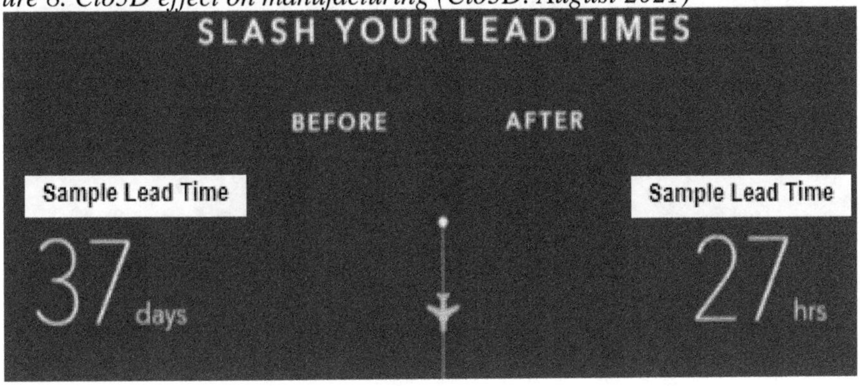

Figure 8 above shows how Clo3D has reduced the manufacturing lead time from 37 days to about 27 hours, a significant and huge saving in time and money for apparel industries. Figure 9 shows how Clo3D has integrated apparel design processes such as designing, tacking, sewing and selection of fabrics and has drastically reduced design time before production.

Figure 9. Clo3D effect on apparel design (Clo3D. August 2021)

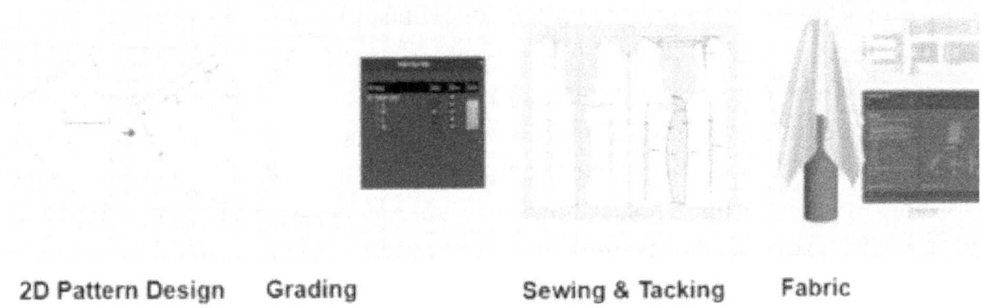

Figure 10. Opitex effect on design time and costs (Optitex. August 2021)

Figure 10 above shows how Optitex has reduced the design time and costs in manufacturing apparel with its software.

Nike's NIKEiD online shopping portal lets customers design shoes and sneakers in real time before purchase. Nike is one company, that recognizes the potential of using online customization interfaces, focusing on the development of online customization platforms. This is shown in Figure 11 below. Shoppers on NIKEiD are now able to design shoes with a selection of colors, textures, and visualizations before purchase. Co-design on Internet shopping portals is a win-win for both manufacturers and shoppers and facilitates the intensity in designing, customization, and aesthetics. New technologies and internet portals crowdsource design needs across the Internet economy and overcomes physical constraints (Oliveira and Cunha 2019).

Figure 11. NIKEiD (NIKE. August 2021)

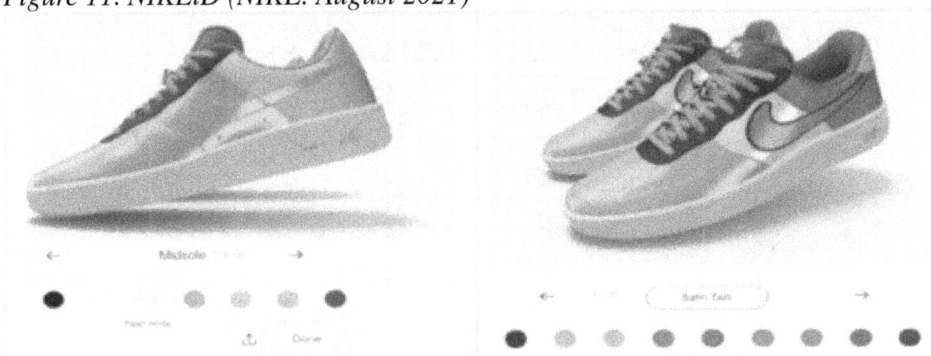

Online internet design portals like NikeID are facilitating customized designer shoes. Another example is Zalando's algorithm used for customizing sneakers shown in Figure 12.

Figure 12. Zalando's algorithm (Foiasi et al. 2023)

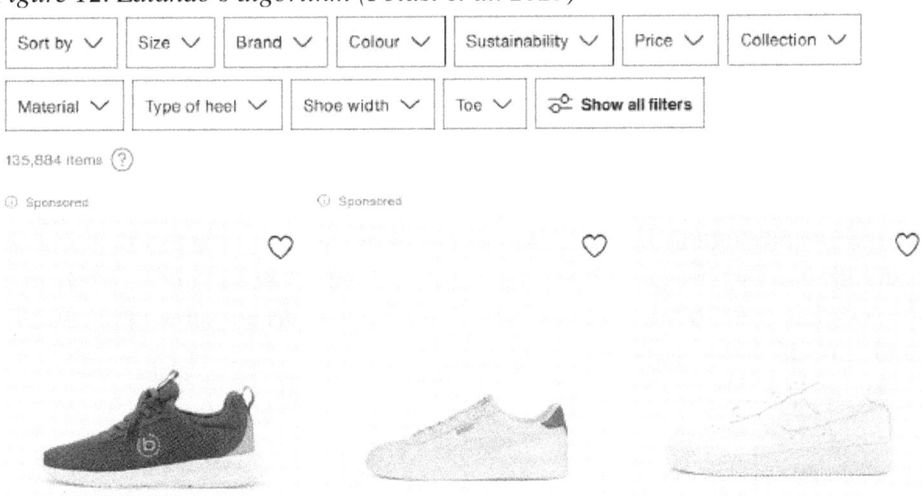

Co-designing in online portals now facilitates design exploration, selection, simulation of product features for design customization (Nachtigall et al. 2020). Online design interfaces facilitate a variety of processes for product design. This is shown in Figure 13 below.

Figure 13. Online design interfaces (Nachtigall et al. 2020)

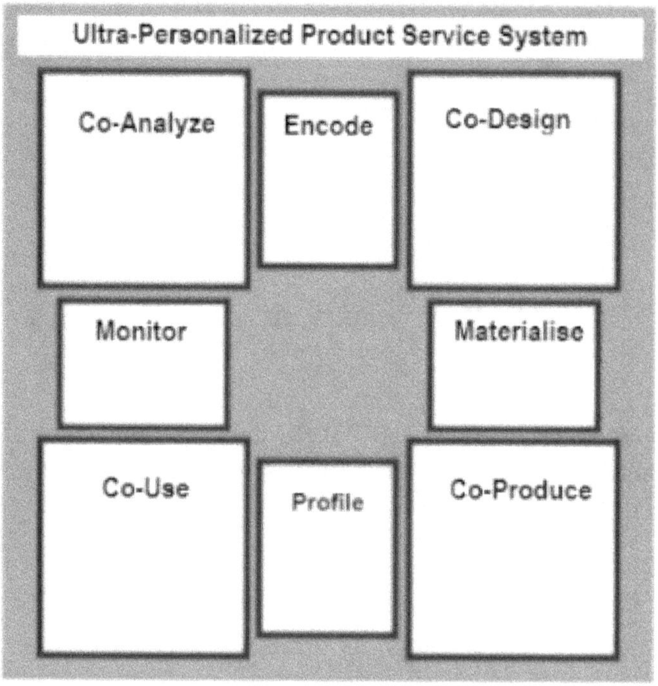

LEGO's Digital Designer web portal lets fans create and share different themes of Lego designs across different age groups around the world. This has resulted in successful co-branding and value co-creation. This reiterates the fact that product customization by fans can enhance the value of the product and the brand (Kim et al. 2008; Du et al. 2006). A few popular fan made designs are shown in Figure 14 and Figure 15.

Figure 14. Fan-made designs (LEGO. August 2021)

Figure 15. Fan-made designs (Isa and Liem 2021)

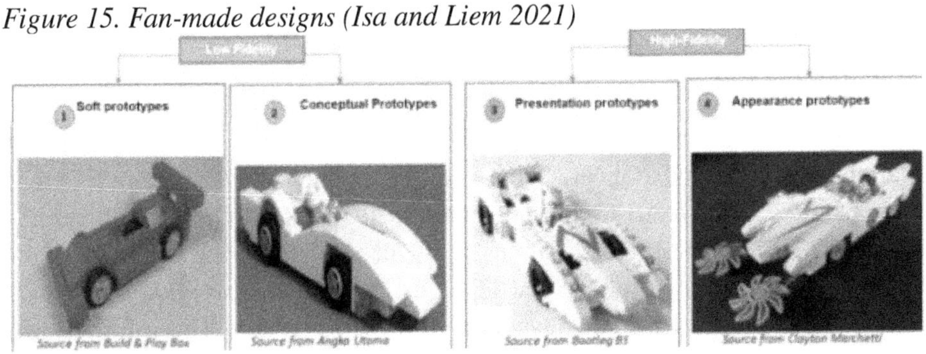

Firms online are able to better facilitate co-production and co-evolution in the design of products and services (Hine 2005:93; Anna, 2018; Dalhuizen et al. 2019; Dell'Era and Verganti 2009; Kohler et al. 2011). Automobile companies such as the Mini Cooper facilitate online customization of car designs for customers to decide and select the color, roofing, wheels, upholstery, surface and transmission mechanisms. This is shown in the next Figure 16.

Figure 16. Mini Cooper (MiniUSA. August 2021)

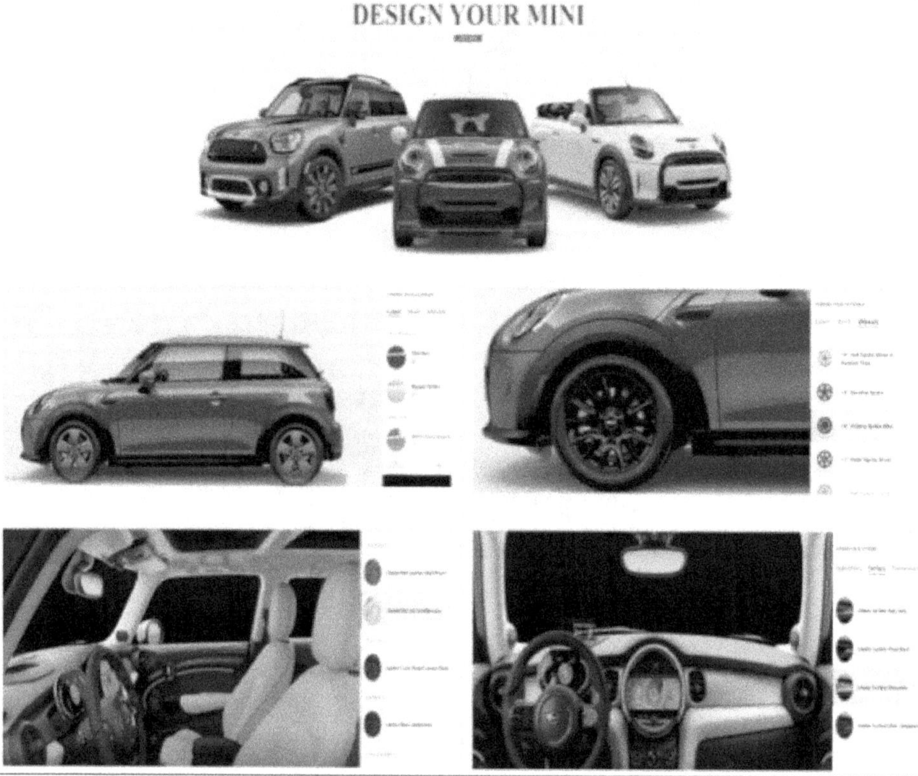

This is the result of online portals offering virtual design with the enhanced experience (Sanders and Stappers 2008) and convenience of customizing different design features of a product (Schiavone et al. 2020; Verma et al. 2012; Zomerdijk and Voss 2010). In the fragrance industry of incense sticks, the Cycle brand of incense lets customers customize and select incense aromas based on experience preferences, fragrance selection, quantity and special occasions. This is also shown in Figure 17 below.

Figure 17. Cycle brand (Cycle Brand. August 2021)

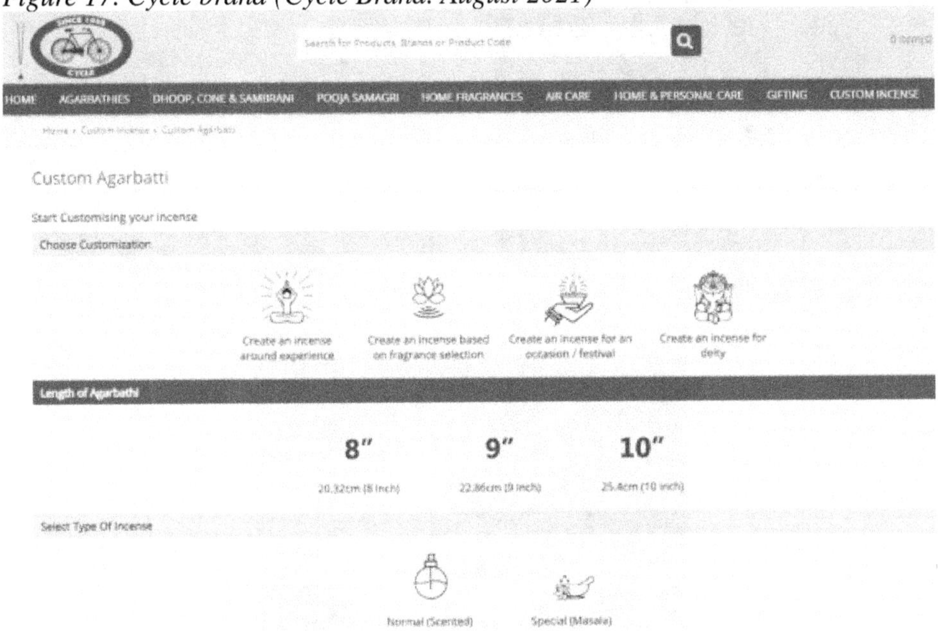

In the use of landscape designing software (shown in figure), three-dimensional geometry and laser scanning can project spatial models from cameras onto ductile clay supports on worktables. Further, the GIS (Geographic Information Systems) simulations can facilitate study of the geographical terrain, land erosion, visibility and traveling time. The simulations provide an opportunity for designers to use GIS simulations in the landscaping, planning and designing of urban spaces to enrich the planners navigating and understanding complex and dynamic terrain-based databases (Ishii et al. 2004). This is shown in Figure 18.

Figure 18. GIS simulations (Ishii et al. 2004)

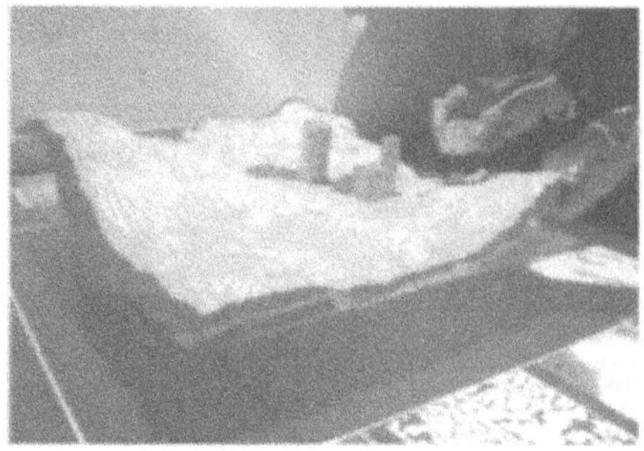

Camera scanners that were used to scan surface geometry were able to scan surfaces in seconds resulting in scanned real-time surface picturization that was resampled into x, y and z co-ordinates and converted into a GIS readable format.

6.2 New Products and Services

With Web 2.0 and the growth of the internet economy, IT business logic for business processes, integration of social commerce networks and inter and intra firm capabilities of industries is changing businesses, expanding operations, product and portfolio management (Bell and Loane 2010; Bughin et al. 2011; Grover and Kohli 2012; Rai et al. 2012; Stephen and Toubia 2010; Agarwal et al. 2008). Therefore, industry collaboration and integration of IT business logic in the internet economy facilitates economic growth and product and service lifecycle management (Anna 2018; Au et al. 2009; Bouncken and Reuschl 2018; Daalhuizen et al. 2019; Dell'Era and Verganti 2009; Gummesson 2008; Ketonen and Valkokari 2019; Omachonu and Einspruch 2010). The internet economy now facilitates businesses to invite firms and customers for co-designing and personalization across inter-firm projects more effectively (Arrighi and Mougenot 2019; Au et al. 2009; Kohler et al. 2011; Sanders and Stappers 2018; Schiavone et al. 2020; Verma et al. 2012; Zomerdijk and Voss

2010). This encourages new product and service design, improvements, upgrades and business management.

In the case of 3D manufacturing that is transforming engineering and other fields, product designing involving the processes of thermodynamic curing, sintering, melting, solidification, phase transformation and binding of material are being optimized and simplified for production (Kang et al. 2018). Manufacturing and the integration of CNC machines with 3D printing and classified composable and reusable additive manufacturing processes for printing a variety of products has become a reality. Database management for 3D manufacturing to configure and generate product assemblies for a range of products based on product classification significantly optimizes costs, improves quality management, productivity and efficiency. This is shown in Figure 19.

Figure 19. Database management

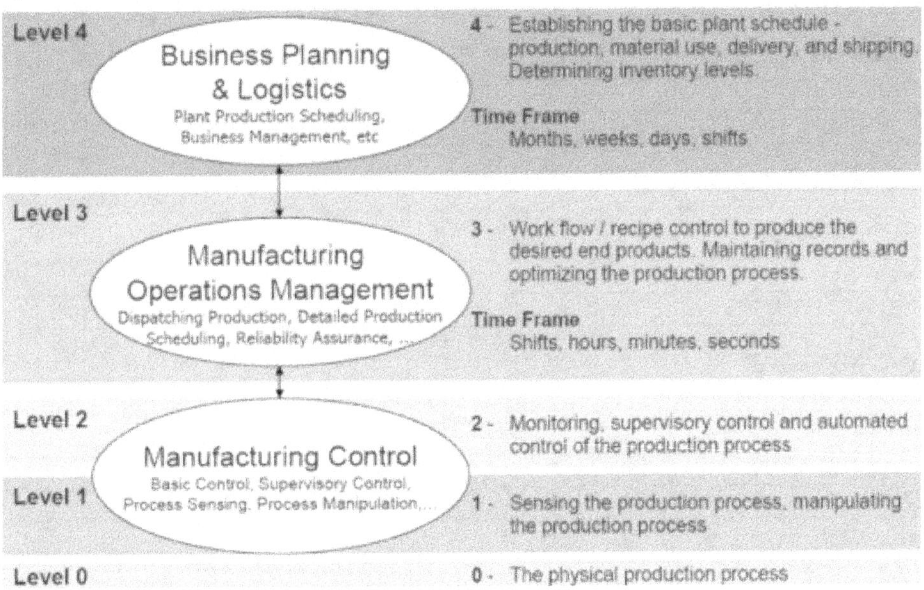

It is now possible for firms to integrate scientific knowledge, product portfolio management with inter-firm manufacturing and the internet economy for projects, economic growth and market needs more effectively (Hine 2005; Grover and Kohli 2012; Bell and Loane 2010; Frey et al. 2011; Nagamachi 2010; Rai et al. 2012; Rindfleisch and Im, 2019; Füller and Matzler 2007). A simulation of a manufacturing model is shown in Figure 20. The profitability may depend on the constraints of resources such as labor, raw material, variable costs, inventory carrying costs and equipment costs.

Figure 20. Simulation of manufacturing model (Albright and Winston 2013)

Simulation of a fixed cost apparel manufacturing model					
Input data on products					
	Shirts	Shorts	Pants	Skirts	Jackets
Labor hours/unit	2	1	6	4	8
Cloth (sq. yd.)/unit	3	2.5	4	4.5	5.5
Selling price/unit	$35	$40	$65	$70	$110
Variable cost/unit	$5	$5	$15	$15	$25
Fixed cost for equipment	$1,500	$1,200	$1,600	$1,500	$1,600
Production plan, constraints on capacity					
	Shirts	Shorts	Pants	Skirts	Jackets
Rent Equipment	0	1	0	0	1
Units produced	0	2000	0	0	1000
Logical upper limit	0.00	4200.00	0.00	0.00	1250.00
Constraints on resources					
	Resource used		Available		
Labor hours	10000.00		10000		
Recycled Cloth (unit)	10500.00		10500		
Monetary outputs					
Revenue	$190,000				
Variable cost	$35,000				
Fixed cost for equipment	$2,800				
Profit	$152,200				

Kraft foods, one of the largest food and beverage companies in the world invited customers and co-created 48 diet brand entrees, snacks, and frozen foods and generated sales worth about $100 million (Communistudy 2007). Kraft Foods' success is shown in Figure 21.

Figure 21. Kraft Food's (Communispace July 2013)

Another example is how IKEA's Home Planner software and furniture solutions invites customers to design and save kitchen plans on the internet and visit a local IKEA store to finalize the design and complete a purchase. Figure 22 and Figure 23 talks about IKEA's Home Planner and Furniture Design portal.

Figure 22. IKEA's home panner and furniture design portal (IKEA Group. July 2013)

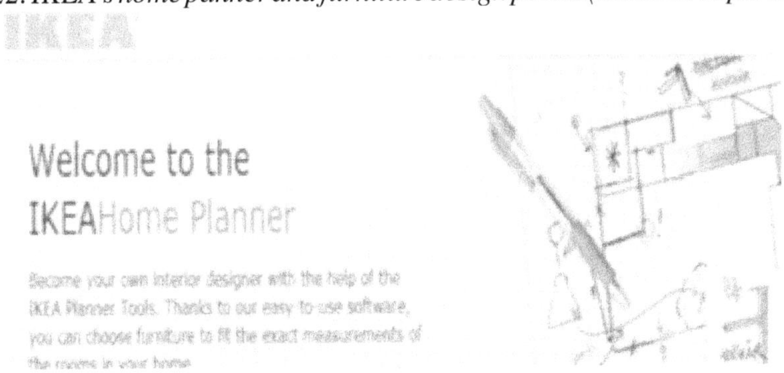

Figure 23. IKEA's home panner and furniture design portal

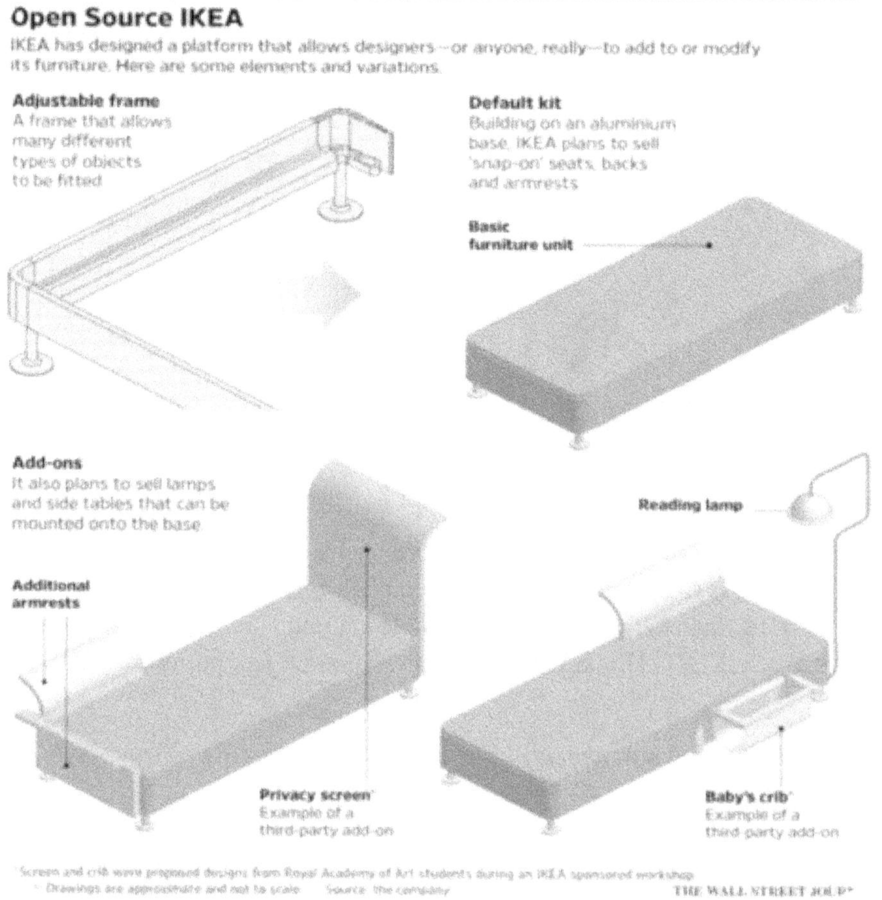

An example of IKEA's open-source furniture solutions. Source: Harvard Business School

Figure 24 visualizes the system of interface design for online design portals and considerations for the customization of apparels.

Figure 24. Interface design system (Li and Chen 2018)

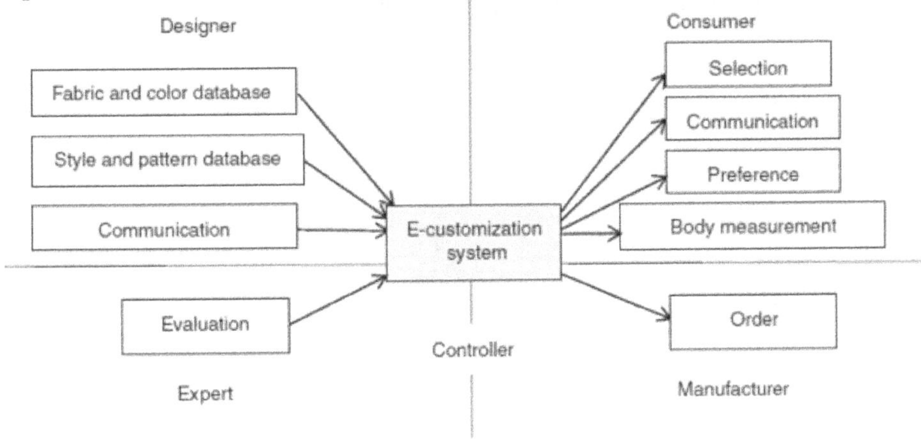

Users now are able to create designs by (1) integrating various design processes, (2) multiply design activity and simulation and (3) govern and optimize the designs (Arrighi and Mougenot 2019; Boldt and Carvalho 2018). In logistics and supply chain management, firms have an advantage when they utilize IT to improve the efficiency of inter-firm capabilities across the industry (Rai et al. 2012; Grover and Kohli 2012).

7.0 RESULTS, SUMMARY AND CONCLUSIONS

Value co-creation is a paradigm integrating firms and customers in online portals to design, personalize and customize products and services for the needs of brands. To study the application of value co-creation by the industry for integrating customers and firms into the process of co-designing products and services, a survey was completed to discuss about the managerial experiences across many industries. Using Structural Equation Modeling to analyze the data collected from 135 managers from across various industry sectors in India and with a comprehensive analysis of publications on value co-creation, the attributes of value co-creation processes that add value to firms and customers were identified as social, economic and intellectual motivation. Intellectual motivation of customer interaction, customer efficacy, customer innovation along with the economic motivation attributes such as customer income and incentives, market knowledge, problem-solving and learning, customer productivity in networking, and the value creation in social networks are very significant. These attributes of social, economic and intellectual motivation need to be integrated into the product, design and experience space within online shopping portals to enhance value co-creation processes for both the customer and the firm. The Structural Equation Modeling is shown in Figure 25.

Figure 25. Structural equation modeling (Gopalan 2019)

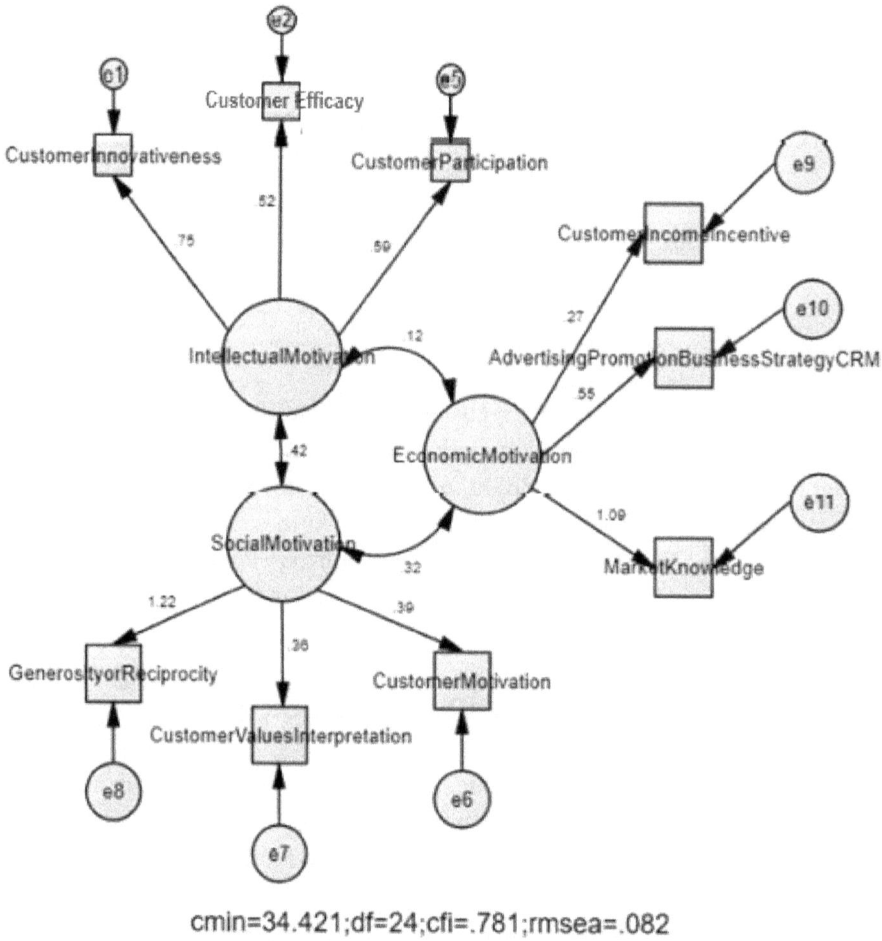

Figure 26 elaborates on integrating Social, Economic and Intellectual Motivation with Co-design utilizing the locus of skills and the locus of co-creative design

Figure 26. Integrating social, economic and intellectual motivation (Prahalad and Ramaswamy 2003)

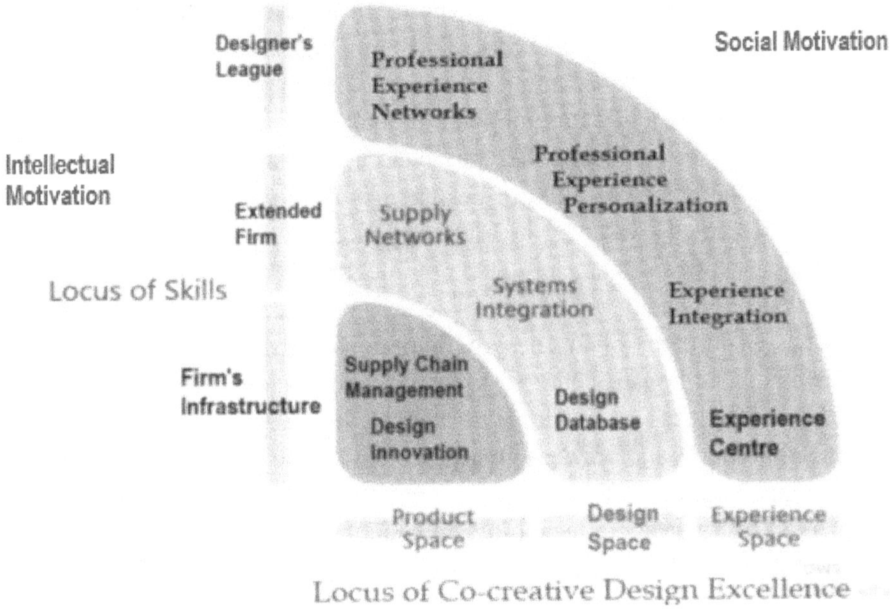

The locus of co-creative design excellence and the locus of skills inclusive of social networks of wisdom when integrated with the social, economic and intellectual motivation of customers utilizing the product space, design space and experience space within online shopping portals enhances the experience of product customization for the customer and adds unique brand value for the firm. Socio-technical design of ICT for design projects improves the quality of interactivity between customers and technology when it facilitates ease of product configuration and simulation for better quality products. Designer software needs to integrate various design processes, multiply design activity and improve the governance of the design for optimization. The use of designer 3D software has made entries into various product categories including the fashion and textile industry for designs and simulations. Online shopping now integrates designer software for customers to co-design products on the internet before purchase.

Today, the internet economy is facilitating even small and medium industries to expand internationally supported by information technology, new business logic, online payment transactions and other IT enabled services. Firms online are able to better facilitate co-production and co-evolution in the design of products and services. Computer aided designing has made it easier for designer firms to create designs more cost effectively before actually making a product saving a lot of resources and investments.

The designing of products with a flexibility in functionality, texturing, design and aesthetics multiplies the probabilities and combinations of product design. This method of using a product configurator is found to have a positive effect on product quality. The IT infrastructure that supports these businesses depends on a configurable design database, technical design versions, customization and simulation. This has resulted in the personalization of designs, loyalty for firms and optimization of costs that exceeds the value of the brand and facilitates production economics.

3D Designer software has facilitated (1) integrated and configurable designs, (2) value creation intensity and (3) optimized prototype design. For firms, this has enhanced design problem solving, design simulations and also co-ordination of inter-firm capabilities for logistics and supply chain management. Fan-based networks and online marketplaces are playing a greater role in the design of customized and personalized products and services greatly increasing the value of the firm. In the area of online shopping, entrepreneurship and start-ups with new business logic have emerged from the socio-technological phenomenon of the internet economy. Today's employed mobile and Internet subscribers utilize IT to organize themselves via emails, mobile phones and subscribed services. With Web 2.0 and the growth of the internet economy, IT business logic for business processes, integration of social commerce networks and inter and intra firm capabilities of industries is changing businesses, expanding operations, product and portfolio management. Therefore, industry collaboration and integration of IT business logic in the internet economy facilitates economic growth.

Table 1. Data sharing agreement

Availability of Data	Data Availability Statement	Policy
Data openly available in a public repository that does not issue DOIs	The data that support the findings of this study are openly available on Google Sheet at https://docs.google.com/spreadsheets/d/1trA5DbRc2ns3WUUdTwsO86SEVYC4hNyETBJH-z0AhXg/edit?usp=sharing Click this link for data access	All

REFERENCES

Agarwal, R., Gupta, A. K., & Kraut, R. (2008). The interplay between digital and social networks. *Information Systems Research, 19*(3), 243–252. DOI: 10.1287/isre.1080.0200

Alexiou, M. (2018). Modeling guided tour participants' experiences. *International Journal of Culture, Tourism and Hospitality Research, 12*(3), 257–276. DOI: 10.1108/IJCTHR-10-2017-0104

Anna, L. (2018). Value creation by engaging customers in the process of product and business design in a virtual environment. Handel Wewnetrzny, (375), 160-168. Retrieved from https://search-proquest-com.proxy.uwasa.fi/docview/2129933661?accountid=14797

Arrighi, P.-A., & Mougenot, C. (2019). Towards user empowerment in product design: A mixed reality tool for interactive virtual prototyping. *Journal of Intelligent Manufacturing, 30*(2), 743–754. DOI: 10.1007/s10845-016-1276-0

Attri, R., & Bairagi, R. (2022). Guthali – challenges in marketing Indian handicrafts and handloom. *Emerald Emerging Markets Case Studies, 12*(1), 1–23. DOI: 10.1108/EEMCS-09-2021-0298

Au, Y. A., Carpenter, D., Chen, X., & Clark, J. G. (2009). Virtual organizational learning in open source software development projects. *Information & Management, 46*(1), 9–15. DOI: 10.1016/j.im.2008.09.004

Bell, J., & Loane, S. (2010). New-wave' global firms: Web 2.0 and SME internationalisation. *Journal of Marketing Management, 26*(3/4), 213–229. DOI: 10.1080/02672571003594648

Boldt, R., & Carvalho, M. (2018). Virtual prototyping as an evaluation method for functional clothing. *IOP Conference Series. Materials Science and Engineering, 460*(1), 012040. Advance online publication. DOI: 10.1088/1757-899X/460/1/012040

Bouncken, R. B., & Reuschl, A. J. (2018). Coworking-spaces: How a phenomenon of the sharing economy builds a novel trend for the workplace and for entrepreneurship. *Review of Managerial Science, 12*(1), 317–334. DOI: 10.1007/s11846-016-0215-y

Brynskov, M., Heijnen, A., Balestrini, M., & Raetzsch, C. (2018). Experimentation at scale: Challenges for making urban informatics work. *Smart and Sustainable Built Environment, 7*(1), 150–163. DOI: 10.1108/SASBE-10-2017-0054

Bughin, J., Byers, A. H. and Chui, M. (2011). How social technologies are extending the organization. *McKinsey Quarterly Report.*

Colliander, J., & Dahlén, M. (2011). Following the Fashionable Friend: The Power of Social Media - Weighing the Publicity Effectiveness of Blogs versus Online Magazines. *Journal of Advertising Research, 51*(1), 313–320. DOI: 10.2501/jar-51-1-313-320

Daalhuizen, J., & Timmer, R. Martijn van, d. W., & Gardien, P. (2019). An architecture of design doing: A framework for capturing the ever-evolving practice of design to drive organizational learning. *International Journal of Design*, 13(1), 37-52. Retrieved from https://search-proquest-com.proxy.uwasa.fi/docview/2226896677?accountid=14797

Dell'Era, C., & Verganti, R. (2009). Design-driven laboratories: Organization and strategy of laboratories specialized in the development of radical design-driven innovations. *R & D Management, 39*, 1–1.

Du, X., Jiao, J., & Tseng, M. (2006). Understanding customer satisfaction in product customization. *International Journal of Advanced Manufacturing Technology, 31*(3–4), 396–406. DOI: 10.1007/s00170-005-0177-8

Foia i, T., Pantazi-Băjenaru, M., & Gurău, D. (2023). Personal Design, the New Fashion Trend with Applications of Innovative Technologies. Leather & Footwear Journal. *Revista de Pielarie - Încaltaminte, 23*(3), 199–208. DOI: 10.24264/lfj.23.3.5

Frey, K., Lüthje, C., & Haag, S. (2011). Whom Should Firms Attract to Open Innovation Platforms? The Role of Knowledge Diversity and Motivation. *Long Range Planning, 44*(5–6), 397–420. DOI: 10.1016/j.lrp.2011.09.006

Füller, J., & Matzler, K. (2007). Virtual product experience and customer participation—A chance for customer-centred, really new products. *Technovation, 27*(6–7), 378–387. DOI: 10.1016/j.technovation.2006.09.005

Gopalan, B. (2019). 'A Study on Variables, Technology Facilitators and Measures of Value Co-creation for Management', Acta Wasaensia 417, Doctoral dissertation, University of Vaasa. Vaasan yliopisto.

Gopalan, B., & Kohtamäki, M. (2017). Customer-The Value Co-Creator. *International Journal of Scientific & Technology Research*, Volume 6 – Issue 4, April 2017 Edition. ISSN 2277-8616.

Gordon, E., & Silva, A. (2011). *Net Locality: Why Location Matters in a Networked World.* Wiley-Blackwell. DOI: 10.1002/9781444340679

Gray, P. H., Parise, S., & Iyer, B. (2011). Innovation Impacts of using Social Bookmarking Systems. *Management Information Systems Quarterly*, *35*(3), 629–643. DOI: 10.2307/23042800

Grover, V. and Kohli, R. (2012). Cocreating IT Value: New Capabilities and Metrics for Multifirm Environments. *MIS Quarterly (36, 1), pp. 225-232.*

Gummesson, E. (2008). Extending the service-dominant logic: From customer centricity to balanced Centricity. *Journal of the Academy of Marketing Science*, *36*(1), 15–17. DOI: 10.1007/s11747-007-0065-x

Gummesson, E., & Mele, C. (2010). Marketing as value co-creation through network interaction and resource integration. *Journal of Business Market Management*, *4*(4), 181–198. DOI: 10.1007/s12087-010-0044-2

Hine, C. (2005). Internet Research and the Sociology of Cyber-Social-Scientific Knowledge. *The Information Society*, *21*(4), 239–248. DOI: 10.1080/01972240591007553

Höflich, J. R., Kircher, G. F., and Linke, C. (2010). Mobile Media and the Change of Everyday Life. *Frankfurt, DEU: Peter Lang AG, 2010. ProQuest ebrary. Web. 10 November 2014.* Copyright © 2010. Peter Lang AG. All rights reserved.

IKEA HOME PLANNER. Ikea.com, n.d. Web. 19 Dec. 2014. <https://www.ikea.com/ms/en_JP/rooms_ideas/splashplanners.html>

Innovation Management / Crowdsourcing / Challenges / Competitions. Innocentive.com, n.d. Web. 19 Dec. 2014. <https://www.innocentive.com/>

Isa, S. S., & Liem, A. (2021). Exploring the role of physical prototypes during co-creation activities at LEGO company using case study validation. *CoDesign*, *17*(3), 330–354. DOI: 10.1080/15710882.2020.1715443

Ishii, H., Ratti, C., Piper, B., Wang, Y., Biderman, A., & Ben-Joseph, E. (2004). Bringing clay and sand into digital design — Continuous tangible user interfaces. *BT Technology Journal*, *22*(4), 287–299. https://www.proquest.com/scholarly-journals/bringing-clay-sand-into-digital-design-continuous/docview/215203715/se-2?accountid=177896. DOI: 10.1023/B:BTTJ.0000047607.16164.16

K, A. and T, R. (2024), "Beyond the loom: understanding handloom product purchase motivations using the extended theory of planned behavior", Research Journal of Textile and Apparel, Vol. ahead-of-print No. ahead-of-print. DOI: 10.1108/RJTA-01-2024-0019

Kang, H. S., Noh, S. D., Son, J. Y., Kim, H., Park, J. H., & Lee, J. Y. (2018). The FaaS system using additive manufacturing for personalized production. *Rapid Prototyping Journal*, *24*(9), 1486–1499. DOI: 10.1108/RPJ-11-2016-0195

Ketonen-Oksi, S., & Valkokari, K. (2019). Innovation ecosystems as structures for value co-creation. *Technology Innovation Management Review*, *9*(2), 25–35. https://search-proquest-com.proxy.uwasa.fi/docview/2197276312?accountid=14797. DOI: 10.22215/timreview/1216

Kim, J. W., Choi, J., Qualls, W., & Han, K. (2008). It takes a marketplace community to raise brand commitment: The role of online communities. *Journal of Marketing Management*, *24*(3/4), 409–431. DOI: 10.1362/026725708X306167

Kraft Customer Co-creation Case Study / Communispace. Communispace.com, n.d. Web. 19 Dec. 2014. <http://www.communispace.com/Kraft-South-Beach-Diet-case-study/>

Lechner, U., & Hummel, J. (2002). Business models and system architectures of virtual communities: From a sociological phenomenon to peer-to-peer architectures. *International Journal of Electronic Commerce*, *6*(3), 41–53. DOI: 10.1080/10864415.2002.11044242

Lego Digital Designer. Lego.com, n.d. Web. 19 Dec. 2014. http://ldd.lego.com/en-us/

Li, P., & Chen, J.-H. (2018). A model of an e-customized co-design system on garment design. *International Journal of Clothing Science and Technology*, *30*(5), 628–640. DOI: 10.1108/IJCST-01-2018-0011

Lihra, T., Buehlmann, U., & Graf, R. (2012). Customer preferences for customized household furniture. *Journal of Forest Economics*, *18*(2), 94–112. DOI: 10.1016/j.jfe.2011.11.001

Magazines, F. Flipboard.com, n.d. Web. 19 Dec. 2014. <https://about.flipboard.com/magazines/>

Mainardes, E. W., Teixeira, A., & Romano, P. C. S. (2017). Determinants of co-creation in banking services. *International Journal of Bank Marketing*, *35*(2), 187–204. https://search-proquest-com.proxy.uwasa.fi/docview/1868279930?accountid=14797. DOI: 10.1108/IJBM-10-2015-0165

Messinger, P. R., Stroulia, E., Lyons, K., Bone, M., Niu, R. H., Smirnov, K., & Perelgut, S. (2009). Virtual worlds - past, present, and future: New directions in social computing. *Decision Support Systems*, *47*(3), 204–228. DOI: 10.1016/j.dss.2009.02.014

Nachtigall, T., Mironcika, S., Tomico, O., & Feijs, L. (2020). Designing ultra-personalized product service systems. *CoDesign*, *16*(4), 274–292. DOI: 10.1080/15710882.2020.1842454

Nagamachi, M. (2010). *Kansei/affective engineering*. CRC Press.

NikeID Customize Shoes and Accessories. Nike.com, n.d. Web. 19 Dec. 2014. https://www.nike.com/us/en_us/c/nikeid

Oh, L. and Teo, H. (2010). Consumer value co-creation in a hybrid commerce service-delivery system. *International Journal of Electronic Commerce (14:3), pp. 35-62.*

Oliveira, N., & Cunha, J. (2019). Co-design and Footwear: Breaking Boundaries with Online Customization Interfaces. *The International Journal of Visual Design*, *13*(1), 1–26. DOI: 10.18848/2325-1581/CGP/v13i01/1-26

Omachonu, V. K., & Einspruch, N. G. (2010). Innovation in healthcare delivery systems: A conceptual Framework. *The Innovation Journal*, *15*(1), 1–20.

Ozuem, W., Howell, K. E., & Lancaster, G. (2008). Communicating in the new interactive marketspace. *European Journal of Marketing*, *42*(9/10), 1059–1083. DOI: 10.1108/03090560810891145

Pikkarainen, M., Huhtala, T., Kemppainen, L., & Häikiö, J. (2019). Success factors for data–driven service delivery networks. *Journal of Innovation Management*, *7*(4), 14–46. DOI: 10.24840/2183-0606_007.004_0003

Prahalad, C. and Ramaswamy, V., (2003). The New Frontier of Experience Innovation. MIT Sloan Management Review (44:4), pp. 12-18.

Rafaeli, S. & Noy, A. (2002). Online auctions, messaging, communication and social facilitation: A simulation and experimental evidence. *European Journal of Information Systems*, 11(3), 196-196-207.

Rai, A., Pavlou, P., Im, G., and Du, S. (2012). Interfirm IT capability profiles and communications for cocreating relational value: Evidence from the logistics industry. *MIS Quarterly (36:1), pp. 233-262.*

Riegner, C. (2007). Word of mouth on the web: The impact of Web 2.0 on consumer purchase decisions. *Journal of Advertising Research*, *47*(4), 436–447. DOI: 10.2501/S0021849907070456

Rindfleisch, A., & Im, S. (2019). Enhancing customer centricity via 3D printing. Handbook on Customer Centricity. Robert Palmatier, Christine Moorman, and Ju-Yeon Lee, (Eds), Edward Elgar, New York.

Romero, D., & Molina, A. (2011). Collaborative networked organizations and customer communities: Value co-creation and co-innovation in the networking era. *Production Planning and Control*, *22*(5-6), 447–472. DOI: 10.1080/09537287.2010.536619

Sanders, E. B. N., & Stappers, P. J. (2008). Co-creation and the new landscapes of design. *CoDesign*, *4*(1), 1, 5–18. DOI: 10.1080/15710880701875068

Särmäkari, N. (2023). Digital 3D Fashion Designers: Cases of Atacac and The Fabricant. *Fashion Theory*, *27*(1), 85–114. DOI: 10.1080/1362704X.2021.1981657

Schiavone, F., Leone, D., Sorrentino, A., & Scaletti, A. (2020). Re-designing the service experience in the value co-creation process: An exploratory study of a healthcare network. *Business Process Management Journal*, *26*(4), 889–908. DOI: 10.1108/BPMJ-11-2019-0475

Schlosser, A. E., White, T. B. and Lloyd, S. M. (2006). Converting Web Site Visitors into Buyers: How Web Site Investment Increases Consumer Trusting Beliefs and Online Purchase Intentions. *Journal of Marketing* (70:2), pp.133-148.

Stephen, A. T., & Toubia, O. (2010). Deriving Value from Social Commerce Networks. *JMR, Journal of Marketing Research*, *47*(2), 215–228. DOI: 10.1509/jmkr.47.2.215

Tellis, G. J., & Gaeth, G. J. (1990). Best value, price-seeking, and price aversion: The impact of information and learning on consumer choices. *Journal of Marketing*, *54*(2), 34–45. DOI: 10.1177/002224299005400203

Trentin, A., Perin, E., & Forza, C. (2012). Product configurator impact on product quality. *International Journal of Production Economics*, *135*(2), 850–859. DOI: 10.1016/j.ijpe.2011.10.023

Verma, R., Teixeira, J., Patrıcio, L., Nunes, N. J., Nobrega, L., Fisk, R. P., & Constantine, L. (2012). Customer experience modeling: From customer experience to service design. *Journal of Service Management*, *23*(3), 362–376. DOI: 10.1108/09564231211248453

Wagner, C., & Majchrzak, A. (2006). Enabling Customer-Centricity Using Wikis and the Wiki Way. *Journal of Management Information Systems*, *23*(3), 17–43. DOI: 10.2753/MIS0742-1222230302

Wolff, K., Herholz, P., Ziegler, V., Link, F., Brügel, N., & Sorkine, H. O. (2023). Designing Personalized Garments with Body Movement. *Computer Graphics Forum*, *42*(1), 180–194. DOI: 10.1111/cgf.14728

Woodbridge, J. (2024). Digital Innovations In Computer-Aided Design Software For Weaving: CAD developers are able to react to client's needs and also anticipate future needs to offer the textile industry the tools it requires for modern production. *Textile World*, *174*(1), 32–35.

Yadav, U.S. and Tripathi, R. (2024), "Impact of innovation, entrepreneurial orientation and entrepreneurial leadership on supply chain resilience in handicraft industry: moderating role of supply chain orientation", Benchmarking: An International Journal, Vol. ahead-of-print No. ahead-of-print. DOI: 10.1108/BIJ-09-2023-0615

Yang, S., Song, Y., Chen, S., & Xia, X. (2017). Why are customers loyal in sharing-economy services? a relational benefits perspective. *Journal of Services Marketing*, *31*(1), 48–62. DOI: 10.1108/JSM-01-2016-0042

Zeithaml, V. A. (1988). Consumer perceptions of price, quality, and value: A means-end model and synthesis of evidence. *Journal of Marketing*, *52*(3), 2–22. DOI: 10.1177/002224298805200302

Zomerdijk, L. G., & Voss, C. A. (2010). Service design for experience-centric services. *Journal of Service Research*, *13*(1), 67–82. DOI: 10.1177/1094670509351960

Chapter 11
Advanced Human-Machine Interfaces for User Experience and Interaction in Information Applications

Sanjay Taneja
https://orcid.org/0000-0002-3632-4053
Graphic Era University, India

Reepu Reepu
https://orcid.org/0000-0002-5607-9825
Chandigarh University, India

Mandeep Singh
https://orcid.org/0000-0001-9520-8610
Chandigarh University, India

ABSTRACT

This chapter explores the advancements in human-machine interfaces (HMIs) and their potential to enhance user experience and interaction in information applications, particularly within Web3 environments. As decentralized technologies like blockchain and dApps grow, interface design becomes crucial for improving user engagement and usability. The paper examines the latest developments in HMIs, such as natural language processing, gesture recognition, augmented reality (AR), and virtual reality (VR), and their impact on Web3 applications. These technologies offer innovative ways to enhance user experience by providing more intuitive and

DOI: 10.4018/979-8-3693-2973-3.ch011

immersive interactions in decentralized systems. Additionally, the paper discusses the challenges of implementing advanced HMIs in Web3, including issues of compatibility with blockchain protocols and the need for seamless user experiences.

INTRODUCTION TO USER EXPERIENCE AND INFORMATION APPLICATIONS

User experience refers to the overall interaction and satisfaction that users have when using a product or service. It encompasses the emotional, cognitive, and behavioral aspects of the user's interaction with the system.

Enhancing user experience and interaction in information applications has become crucial in today's digital landscape. As more and more people rely on information applications for various tasks and activities, it is essential to ensure that these applications are designed in a way that provides a seamless and enjoyable user experience. There has been a growing interest in both academia and industry regarding user experience, as reflected in the increasing number of publications and companies transitioning towards user-centric design (Dabouis et al., 2023).

User experience plays a vital role in the success of information applications. If the user experience is poor, users may become frustrated, lose interest, and be less inclined to use the application. To address this challenge, advanced human-machine interfaces have been developed to enhance user experience and interaction in information applications.

These interfaces utilize innovative technologies and design principles to create intuitive, efficient, and engaging user experiences.

Factors Affecting User Experience and Interaction

Several factors contribute to the overall user experience and interaction in information applications. These factors include branding, usability, and the interface design (Fajar & Legowo, 2018).

Branding plays an important role in shaping the user experience. It covers all elements related to the design and visual aspects of a website or application. A visually appealing and cohesive branding can create a positive impression on users and enhance their overall experience.

Usability is another critical factor in enhancing user experience and interaction. It refers to the ease of use of the application and how well it allows users to achieve their goals. A usable information application is intuitive, efficient, and minimizes the cognitive effort required of users. Effective usability involves factors such as learnability, appropriateness, recognizably, portability, user error protection, user interface aesthetics, and accessibility (Brdnik et al., 2022). The design and interface of an information application also significantly impacts user experience and interaction.

The design of an information application includes aspects such as layout, navigation, typography, color scheme, and visual hierarchy. These design elements should be carefully considered to ensure that they are visually appealing, easy to understand and navigate, and enhance the overall user experience. In addition to branding, usability, and interface design, the quality of information provided by the application is also crucial for user experience. The information architecture and content design of the application play a vital role in shaping users' perceptions of the credibility and quality of the application. Users rely on accurate and relevant information to make informed decisions or complete tasks efficiently. Without accurate and reliable information, users may become frustrated or lose trust in the application, leading to a negative user experience. In addition to these factors, there are 'deeper' aspects that can also significantly impact the user experience (Gibson & Martinez-Maldonado, 2017).

Understanding Human-Machine Interfaces

Figure 1. Understanding human-machine interfaces (Gibson & Martinez-Maldonado, 2017)

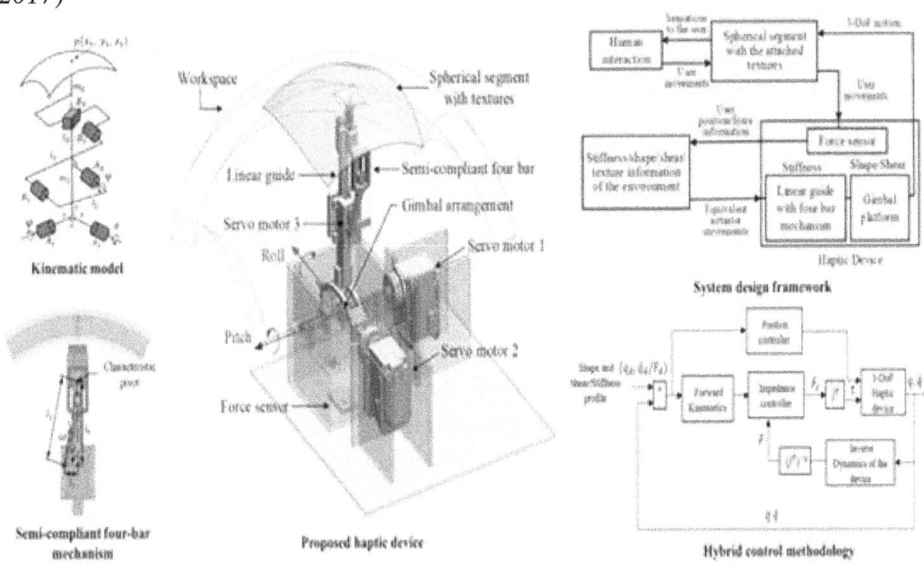

To enhance user experience and interaction in information applications, it is important to understand the concept of human-machine interfaces. Human-machine interfaces refer to the means by which humans interact with machines, such as computers or software applications. These interfaces can be physical, such as keyboards or touchscreens, or they can be virtual, such as graphical user interfaces or voice recognition systems. Research has shown that advanced human-machine interfaces can greatly enhance user experience and interaction in information applications. Studies have shown that advanced human-machine interfaces, such as natural language processing and gesture recognition, can make the interaction with information applications more intuitive and efficient. By utilizing advanced human-machine interfaces, information applications can provide a more natural and seamless user experience. Advantages of Advanced Human-Machine Interfaces include improved ease of use, increased productivity, and enhanced decision-making capabilities.

Improved Ease of Use: Advanced human-machine interfaces can simplify the interaction between users and information applications.

These interfaces can eliminate the need for complex commands or navigation, allowing users to interact with the application in a more intuitive and natural way.

Increased Productivity: Advanced human-machine interfaces can streamline tasks and processes, allowing users to complete them more quickly and efficiently. For example, the use of voice recognition technology in a virtual assistant application can enable users to perform tasks simply by speaking commands, eliminating the need for manual input or navigating through complex menus.

Enhanced Decision-Making Capabilities: Advanced human-machine interfaces can provide users with more relevant and actionable information, allowing them to make better decisions.

For example, a weather forecasting application with an advanced human-machine interface could provide real-time weather updates, personalized recommendations based on user preferences, and interactive visual displays of weather patterns.

The Role of Advanced Interfaces in Enhancing User Experience

Advanced human-machine interfaces play a crucial role in enhancing user experience in information applications. These interfaces provide users with a more intuitive and seamless interaction, leading to improved ease of use.

By incorporating natural language processing and gesture recognition technology, advanced interfaces can eliminate the need for complex commands or navigation, allowing users to interact with information applications in a more natural and effortless manner. This not only reduces the learning curve for new users but also enhances the overall usability of the application, leading to higher user satisfaction. Moreover, advanced interfaces also contribute to increased productivity. By streamlining tasks and processes, these interfaces enable users to complete their work more efficiently. For example, a healthcare information application with an advanced human-machine interface can simplify the process of accessing patient records and inputting data, allowing healthcare professionals to spend more time on patient care rather than administrative tasks. Furthermore, advanced interfaces can enhance decision-making capabilities by providing users with relevant and actionable information. For instance, a financial analytics application with an advanced human-machine interface can analyze complex financial data and provide users with interactive visualizations and personalized recommendations for investment strategies. Overall, advanced human-machine interfaces are essential for enhancing user experience and interaction in information applications (Lehoux, 2004).

CURRENT CHALLENGES IN INFORMATION APPLICATION INTERACTIVITY

Despite the benefits of advanced human-machine interfaces, there are several challenges that need to be addressed in order to fully enhance user experience and interaction in information applications.

One of the key challenges is the need to make a quantitative economic case for designing and implementing advanced interfaces. Prospective industry users of these technologies often require concrete evidence of the return on investment before adopting advanced human-machine interfaces. This notion has gained impetus over the last 20 years with the growth of information technology and research into Human-Computer Interface. Research into Human-Computer Interface has shown that a well-designed interface can significantly impact workers' efficiency. Additionally, the development of new industrial service solutions brings about the need for advanced human-machine interfaces. These interfaces should not only improve user experience and interaction but also generate affect, efficiency, satisfactory interactions, and guarantee learning processes in complex systems like industrial machinery (Zabalo et al., 2018). Another challenge is ensuring that human-machine interfaces provide information in the most user-friendly way possible (Kari & Steinert, 2021). Studies have shown that users' perception of an interface's usability and ease of use greatly affects their overall experience and satisfaction. To address these challenges and enhance user experience and interaction in information applications, researchers and developers need to focus on several key areas.

Firstly, there is a need for further research and development in advanced human-machine interfaces to ensure their effectiveness and usability.

This can be achieved through the use of advanced technologies such as natural language processing, machine learning, and data visualization. These technologies can enable interfaces to better understand and respond to user input, adapt to individual preferences, and present information in a clear and intuitive manner. Furthermore, the design of advanced human-machine interfaces should also take into account the specific tasks, goals, plans, and problem domain of the users (Hou et al., 2011). By considering these factors, interfaces can be tailored to meet the needs of users and provide them with the most relevant and useful information. Secondly, the evaluation of advanced human-machine interfaces is crucial in determining their effectiveness and impact on user experience.

RESEARCH METHODOLOGY: STUDYING INTERFACE USER INTERACTION

To study the user interaction with advanced human-machine interfaces, a combination of research methodologies can be utilized. One possible approach is to conduct usability testing, where participants are given specific tasks to perform using the interface while their interactions and feedback are observed and recorded. Usability testing can provide valuable insights into how users navigate through the interface, whether they encounter any difficulties or frustrations, and how effectively they are able to accomplish their tasks. Another approach is to use eye-tracking technology, which can provide detailed information about where users look and focus their attention while interacting with the interface. This information can help identify areas of the interface that may need improvement or optimization.

Techniques for Improving User Interaction

There are several techniques that can be employed to enhance user interaction in information applications through advanced human-machine interfaces. One approach is the use of natural language processing to enable users to interact with the interface using their own words and sentences. This can make the interaction more intuitive and user-friendly, as users can communicate in a way that feels natural to them. Another technique is the incorporation of machine learning algorithms to adapt the interface based on user preferences and behavior. These algorithms can analyze user data and make personalized recommendations or adjustments to the interface, improving the user experience over time. Additionally, the use of advanced visualization techniques can also enhance user interaction. For example, the incorporation of interactive and dynamic visualizations can help users better understand complex information and make more informed decisions.

Figure 2. (Hou et al., 2011)

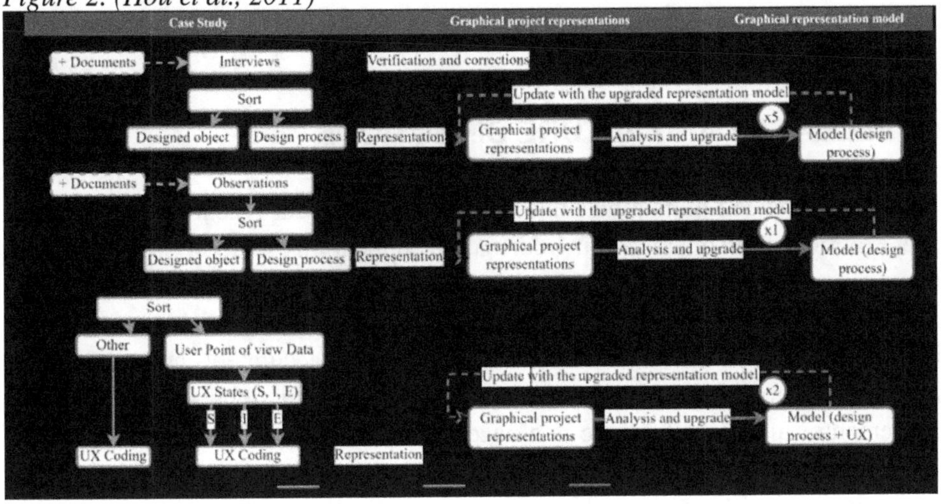

Evaluating the Effectiveness of Human-Machine Interfaces

The evaluation of the effectiveness of human-machine interfaces is crucial in ensuring that they meet the needs and expectations of users. There are several evaluation methods that can be utilized to assess the effectiveness of human-machine interfaces. One commonly used method is user-centered evaluations, which involves gathering feedback and insights directly from users. This can be done through techniques such as questionnaires, interviews, and observations of user behavior. Another approach is the use of cognitive psychology and interaction design principles to evaluate usability.

CASE STUDIES: SUCCESSFUL APPLICATIONS OF ADVANCED HUMAN-MACHINE INTERFACES

There have been several successful applications of advanced human-machine interfaces in enhancing user experience and interaction in information applications.

One notable example is the use of gesture recognition technology in gaming consoles such as the Nintendo Wii. This technology allows users to control the game using natural gestures, making the gaming experience more immersive and enjoyable. Another successful application is in virtual reality systems, where users can interact with a simulated environment using a combination of gesture recognition, voice interaction, and haptic feedback. These advanced interfaces have revolutionized industries such as architecture, healthcare, and education by providing users with immersive and interactive experiences.

CHALLENGES AND FUTURE DIRECTIONS

While advanced human-machine interfaces offer great potential in enhancing user experience and interaction in information applications, there are still challenges that need to be addressed for further improvement.

One major challenge is the development of accurate and reliable gesture recognition systems. These systems need to be able to accurately interpret a wide range of gestures and differentiate between intended user actions and unintentional movements. Additionally, there is a need for more research on the usability and user experience of augmented reality interfaces. To overcome these challenges, researchers and designers need to collaborate and continue to explore innovative approaches. Furthermore, the evaluation of usability and user experience in advanced human-machine interfaces is an ongoing research area. There is a need for further research to develop effective methods of evaluating the usability and user experience of these interfaces.

FUTURE TRENDS IN HUMAN-MACHINE INTERFACE TECHNOLOGY

Future trends in human-machine interface technology are promising and hold great potential for enhancing user experience and interaction in information applications.

One of the future trends is the development of natural user interfaces that rely on intuitive and natural behaviors, such as gestures.

These interfaces allow users to interact with machines in a more intuitive and seamless way, mimicking human-human interaction. Another trend is the integration of multiple modalities in human-machine interfaces.

This includes combining gesture recognition, voice interaction, virtual reality, augmented reality, and haptic interaction to create a more immersive and interactive experience (Deebak & Al-Turjman, 2021). By incorporating these different modalities, users can interact with information applications in a more intuitive and natural manner. Furthermore, the use of haptic interfaces is also a future trend in human-machine interface technology. Haptic interfaces stimulate the human senses through touch sensations, allowing users to qualitatively perceive and manipulate virtual or remote environments (Pediredla et al., 2021).

Impact of Enhanced User Experience on Information Application Adoption

The enhanced user experience and interaction facilitated by advanced human-machine interfaces have a significant impact on the adoption of information applications. When users are able to interact with information applications seamlessly and intuitively, they are more likely to engage with and adopt these applications. This, in turn, leads to increased efficiency and productivity in performing tasks and achieving desired outcomes. Moreover, the enhanced user experience also contributes to improved satisfaction and enjoyment, which can further encourage users to continue using the information applications. ## Challenges and Considerations in Designing Advanced Human-Machine Interfaces Designing advanced human-machine interfaces entails various challenges and considerations.

One challenge is the need to ensure compatibility and interoperability across different devices and platforms. As technology advances and new devices come into the market, it becomes essential for advanced human-machine interfaces to be compatible with a range of devices and platforms. Another challenge is the need to provide a realistic and immersive experience to users. This can be achieved through the use of technologies such as computer graphics, virtual reality, and augmented reality. However, the insufficiency of rendering various haptic modalities can limit the realism and effectiveness of these interfaces.

CONCLUSION: ADVANCING INTERACTION FOR BETTER USER EXPERIENCE

In conclusion, advanced human-machine interfaces play a crucial role in enhancing user experience and interaction in information applications.

These interfaces, such as gesture recognition, voice interaction, virtual reality, augmented reality, and haptic interaction, offer more intuitive and natural ways for users to interact with information applications. Through the use of advanced technologies like computer graphics, virtual reality, and augmented reality, these interfaces provide a more immersive and realistic experience for users in virtual or remote environments. Additionally, the design of effective and efficient human-machine interfaces is essential for overall system performance, as it allows users to quickly understand and interact with the technology in a smooth and efficient manner (Hou et al., 2011). Moreover, the design of advanced human-machine interfaces must prioritize compatibility and interoperability across different devices and platforms to ensure that users can seamlessly engage with these applications regardless of the device they are using. Furthermore, the challenges in designing advanced interfaces, such as ensuring compatibility and providing a realistic experience, must be addressed to maximize the benefits of these interfaces. Through addressing these challenges, the field of human-machine interfaces can continue to advance and provide users with a more intuitive, immersive, and satisfying experience. In today's rapidly changing world, the significance of accurate weather forecasts cannot be overstated. Overall, enhancing user experience and interaction in information applications through advanced human-machine interfaces is crucial for improving the usability and effectiveness of these applications.

In conclusion, advanced human-machine interfaces have the potential to greatly enhance user experience and interaction in information applications.

By utilizing technologies such as gesture recognition, voice interaction, virtual reality, augmented reality, and haptic interaction, these interfaces offer more intuitive and natural ways for users to interact with information applications. These interfaces provide a more immersive and realistic experience in virtual or remote environments, improving the overall user experience.

REFERENCES

Mónica Faria, B., Vasconcelos, S., Paulo Reis, L. and Lau, N. (2012). A Methodology for Creating Intelligent Wheelchair Users' Profiles. In Proceedings of the 4th International Conference on Agents and Artificial Intelligence - Volume 2: ICAART; ISBN 978-989-8425-95-9; ISSN 2184-433X, SciTePress, pages 171-179. DOI: 10.5220/0003749701710179. DOI: 10.3390/s22155830 PMID: 35957387

Brdnik, S., Heričko, T., & Šumak, B. (2022). Intelligent User Interfaces and Their Evaluation: A Systematic Mapping Study. *Sensors (Basel)*, *22*(15), 5830. DOI: 10.3390/s22155830 PMID: 35957387

Dabouis, B., Boccara, V., & Yannou, B. (2023). Retrospective coding of the ux design process for ux design enhancement in design agencies. *Proceedings of the Design Society*, *3*, 3105–3114. DOI: 10.1017/pds.2023.311

Deebak, B. D., & Al-Turjman, F. (2021). Digital-twin assisted: Fault diagnosis using deep transfer learning for machining tool condition. *International Journal of Intelligent Systems*, *37*(12), 10289–10316.

Fajar, A. N., & Legowo, N. (2018). Services modeling based on soa and bpm for information system flexibility improvement. [IJECE]. *International Journal of Electrical and Computer Engineering*, *8*(4), 2451. DOI: 10.11591/ijece.v8i4.pp2451-2455

Gibson, A., & Martínez-Maldonado, R. (2017). That dashboard looks nice, but what does it mean? *Proceedings of the 29th Australian Conference on Computer-Human Interaction*. DOI: 10.1145/3152771.3156171

Hou, M., Zhu, H., Zhou, M., & Arrabito, G. G. (2011). Optimizing operator–agent interaction in intelligent adaptive interface design: A conceptual framework. *IEEE Transactions on Systems, Man, and Cybernetics. Part C, Applications and Reviews*, *41*(2), 161–178. DOI: 10.1109/TSMCC.2010.2052041

Kari, R., & Steinert, M. (2021). Human factor issues in remote ship operations: Lesson learned by studying different domains. *Journal of Marine Science and Engineering*, *9*(4), 385. DOI: 10.3390/jmse9040385

Lehoux, P. (2004). Patients' perspectives on high-tech home care: A qualitative inquiry into the user-friendliness of four technologies. *BMC Health Services Research*, *4*(1), 28. Advance online publication. DOI: 10.1186/1472-6963-4-28 PMID: 15462682

Pediredla, V. K., Chandrasekaran, K., Annamraju, S., & Thondiyath, A. (2021). Design, analysis, and control of a 3-dof novel haptic device displaying stiffness, texture, shape, and shear. *IEEE Access : Practical Innovations, Open Solutions*, *9*, 72055–72065. DOI: 10.1109/ACCESS.2021.3079175

Zabalo, E. A., Erle, G. L., & Gerrikagoitia, J. K. (2018). *Evaluating the human machine interface experience in industrial workplaces*. Electronic Workshops in Computing., DOI: 10.14236/ewic/HCI2018.93

Chapter 12
Chatbots as Learning Companions Exploring Ethical Dimensions of AI in Education

Maida Maqsood
Government College Women University Sialkot, Pakistan

Hafsa Hamid Butt
Minhaj University, Lahore, Pakistan

Muhammad Awais Ali
https://orcid.org/0009-0007-3223-7140
Bahria University, Pakistan

Caleb Chidozie Chinedu
https://orcid.org/0000-0002-0548-3297
Universiti Tun Hussein Onn Malaysia, Malaysia

Munir Ahmad
https://orcid.org/0000-0003-4836-6151
Survey of Pakistan, Pakistan

ABSTRACT

The purpose of this chapter is to examine the ethical concerns and benefits associated with the integration of Artificial Intelligence (AI), particularly chatbots, in education. A comprehensive literature review was conducted to identify and analyze ethical considerations related to AI in education. The applicability of the web3 application in the identification and analysis of ethical concerns of AI chatbots is also

DOI: 10.4018/979-8-3693-2973-3.ch012

explored. The findings revealed a spectrum of ethical concerns spanning fairness, transparency, privacy, autonomy, and educational inequality. Ethical concerns also include the misuse of private data, algorithmic biases, surveillance, and threats to job security. Conversely, the benefits of AI in education encompass improved learner experiences, enhanced teaching efficiency, and personalized learning opportunities. Chatbots, in particular, demonstrate potential in fostering engagement, increasing interest in subjects, and offering immediate support to students.

INTRODUCTION

Web 3, otherwise called Web 3. 0, signifies the next revolution of the internet that was proposed, centering on decentralization, the empowerment of the users, and the integration of blockchain technologies (Cheng 2024; Albreem et al. 2021). Unlike the predecessors of the web, Web 3 is focused on how data is managed and what services need to be provided in a different way. Chatbots – the programs that are designed to answer questions and ask questions back and that are a similitude of conversational talks – can be marked as a prominent profiting part of and contributor to the Web 3 world. By integrating chatbots into Web 3, now the conversational agents can function on the networks that provide decentralization, so the conversational agents can operate in a transparent and secure way through the use of blockchain and smart contracts. It can pave the way for safer, user-based data interactions, customized experiences, and automation of transactions and services.

Chatbots and related algorithms can simulate human interactions and generate human-like text (Ahmad et al. 2024). Chatbots have multiple applications in the education sector. Chatbots are mainly designed on a web platform to teach computer science, language, general education, and a few other fields such as engineering and mathematics (Kuhail et al. 2023). Chatbots can serve as engaging and responsive conversational learning tools in teaching basic concepts and providing educational resources. Chatbots show the potential to assist students in learning basic content interactively and confidentially (Chen et al. 2023). Chatbot technologies can provide instant interaction and support to students outside of class (Y. T. Lin and Ye 2023).

Chatbots may be used in education to deliver pedagogical content and assess, enhancing the attraction of technology and gaining students' trust (Georgescu 2018). In education, Chatbots can enhance student learning and improve services (Pérez, Daradoumis, and Puig 2020). AI-powered chatbots can offer homework and study assistance by providing detailed feedback, explanations, and step-by-step solutions to students' questions and assignments. AI chatbots can contribute to skills development by offering writing suggestions, problem-solving guidance, and facilitating group discussions and debates (Labadze, Grigolia, and Machaidze 2023). Chatbots in education can fill the gap in resources and address logistics and diversified issues faced by normal classes (Gowda et al. 2021). Thus, the application of Chatbots in education can potentially reduce costs and supplement teacher instruction in transformative ways (Riel 2020).

AI chatbots offer immediate support by answering questions, offering explanations, and providing additional resources in educational settings. Chatbots provide correct answers to students using natural language processing techniques and domain-specific ontologies (Clarizia et al. 2018). Children can internalize computers' intelligent tools and use them as cognitive ones, leading to improved reading comprehension and essay writing (Salomon 1988). Educators benefit from AI chatbots through time-saving assistance and improved pedagogy. Chatbots can be valuable tools in the teaching/learning process by providing information about courses, procedures, and school services (Mendoza et al. 2020). However, besides many useful applications of chatbots, teachers' acceptance of chatbots depends on factors like perceived ease of use, perceived usefulness, and their age and digital skills (Chocarro, Cortiñas, and Marcos-Matás 2023).

Ethical considerations surrounding the introduction of chatbots as a means for application into education in the AI domain call to mind very serious issues regarding privacy and data security. As such it is necessary for educational institutions and developers of AI to implement strict data protection policies in their fight against the above risks (Figueira 2017). Bias and fairness in the domain of AI-driven chatbots for learning lead to an array of profound ethical dilemmas that necessitate a rigid review, as well as preventive control. While presumable, the algorithms of intelligent chatbots may offer custom-tailored learning experiences that are specific to individual learners unknowingly amplify and reinforce preconceived biases. Widespread in deprived societies, this may lead to discriminatory treatment and an unsympathetic attitude towards students accordingly (Crawford and Calo 2016).

According to Solon Barocas, Moritz Hardt (2020), if the training data is not diverse and incorporates historical biases; then it is highly likely that the AI system will learn about known biases as well as reflect those in its functions or evaluations. For instance, a chatbot trained mainly based on data collected from a specific demographic might perform below par when talking to students of other backgrounds thus causing injustice and discrepancies in teaching aid provision. To address the issue of potential bias, it is crucial that AI producers and educators create programs that are aimed at detecting as well as diminishing biases in systems under consideration. Educators should support the provision of knowledge and skills that help students evaluate AI-generated results with objectivity. This encompasses understanding the algorithms that fuel these tools, the nature of the data they use, and ethics as well as the privacy implications it creates (Payton and Hague 2010).

Facing the rapid technological advancement and highly volatile area of artificial intelligence as applied to education, it is beneficial to evaluate the ethical dimensions of the use of chatbots being learning companions in education. The primary objectives of this chapter are to delve into scholarly literature to identify and evaluate ethical concerns surrounding the use of AI in education, conduct a thorough analysis of its benefits, and propose recommendations to mitigate these ethical concerns. Another objective is to explore the applicability of web3 to identify and evaluate ethical concerns. In pursuit of these objectives, the chapter is structured into distinct sections.

LITERATURE REVIEW

Key technological concepts in chatbot technology include pattern matching, AI Markup Language (AIML), latent semantic analysis (LSA), and natural language processing (NLP). Chatbots can be classified based on various criteria such as knowledge domain, service provided, goals, input processing, response generation method, human aid, and development platform permissions. Chatbots, driven by machine learning and AI, are positioned as the future of conversational services, yet their development confronts hurdles in programming and integrating AI and NLP. These virtual entities, exemplified by cloud-based services like IBM Watson, Microsoft Bot, AWS Lambda, and Heroku, leverage machine learning and AI (Rahman, Al Mamun, and Islam 2018).

The design and development of chatbots involve understanding user requirements, implementing accurate knowledge representation, and selecting appropriate response-generation strategies. Looking ahead, chatbots are expected to continue evolving, becoming more sophisticated and integrated into daily life, offering seamless interactions and significant benefits for users and businesses alike (Adamopoulou and Moussiades 2020). There is a challenge in addressing bias and fairness concerns in modern chatbot design, attributed to factors like large training data, model sizes, and interpretability issues (Xue et al. 2024). Moreover, future challenges in chatbot development include enhancing system stability, adding new functionalities, and collecting user feedback, which are categorized into system-related, functionality-related, and user-related challenges (Calvaresi et al. 2023).

ChatGPT, developed by OpenAI, has gained popularity since its launch in November 2022, demonstrating its ability to produce various forms of text. It holds promise for positively impacting academia and libraries by improving various services such as search, reference, cataloging, metadata generation, and content creation. However, ethical considerations like privacy and bias need addressing, prompting professionals to explore responsible integration of ChatGPT to enhance efficiency and knowledge dissemination (Lund and Wang 2023). ChatGPT garnered significant attention on Twitter and in the news, with discussions spanning various topics and reactions, including speculation about its potential to replace platforms like StackOverflow for coding queries due to its effective code-writing capabilities. In this context, Taecharungroj (2023) used t-SNE visualization to analyze Twitter discussions about ChatGPT, revealing insights into its functionalities and potential impacts. Four key issues highlighted by the author include job evolution, changes in the technological landscape, the quest for artificial general intelligence, and ethical considerations in AI progress. Similarly, AlZu'bi et al. (2024) constructed and trained a text classification model for a chatbot using Python, on customer survey responses, with the extra trees' classifier proving most effective at 90% accuracy, underscoring the importance of text preprocessing and classifier selection.

Chatbots have rapidly evolved, becoming extensively utilized across various fields such as marketing, education, healthcare, entertainment, and more, offering numerous advantages for users and developers alike. They have seen significant development since their inception, with notable advancements in technology and adoption across diverse sectors. Users engage with chatbots primarily for productivity enhancement, entertainment, social interaction, and novelty exploration. For example, chatbots are increasingly popular in business and healthcare, driven by the widespread use of apps and advancements in AI technologies. They operate on a three-layer architecture incorporating NLP, NLU, and Decision engine, with AI achieved through Recurrent Neural Network (RNN) and Long Short-Term Memory (LSTM) as demonstrated by Borah et al. (2019).

Chatbots powered by AI and natural language processing significantly impact education. Traymbak et al. (2024) conducted a bibliometric analysis using VOS viewer software and examined 49 papers from 2005 to 2023 with the keyword "chatbot in education." Findings revealed an average of 30.76 citations per year and 10.67 citations per author, demonstrating sustained interest. The study emphasized the significant interest and influence of chatbots in education through citation metrics and author analysis. Similarly, an analysis of journal publications on artificial intelligence technology in educational research conducted by Karaca and Kılcan (2023) revealed a significant increase in recent years, with notable contributions from key nations like the United States, China, and Spain. Türkiye and Russia are among the most productive nations but lack international collaboration. Journal articles primarily focus on subjects such as dropout rates, chatbots, language learning, student involvement and performance, e-learning, and collaborative learning. Moreover, Ramandanis and Xinogalos (2023) conducted a systematic literature review to analyze development methodologies and evolution of chatbots in educational settings over the past 5 years, leveraging the PRISMA framework. The review noted that various studies have explored chatbots' impact across different educational domains, including language learning, tutoring, and student support, both in traditional and online learning environments. Research has also delved into personalized design approaches to cater to individual learner needs. Understanding user behavior and perceptions remains pivotal for optimizing chatbot functionality in educational contexts.

Okonkwo and Ade-Ibijola (2021) explored the evaluation of intelligent personal assistants such as Amazon Alexa, Google Assistant, Microsoft Cortana, and Apple Siri for assisting the elderly, along with the development of Omniman, a mobile assistive robot for intralogistics applications. Chatbots are examined as both passing trends and valuable pedagogical tools in education, with specific applications ranging from medical consultant systems to data-driven educational chatbots and tools like Bookbuddy for interactive language lessons. Moreover, chatbots are extensively utilized in education to foster student engagement with learning materials, as highlighted by Wan Hamzah et al. (2021) which specifically investigated the use of a Chatbot for querying Web Programming content. Employing learning analytics methods, the research analyzed the interactions between students and the Chatbot, revealing a notable success rate in the Chatbot's responses to student queries. Moreover, students exhibited a clear preference for learning content about PHP, SQL, and HTML. The Chatbot's responses were iteratively updated based on proposed actions to further improve success rates.

Liu, Subbareddy, and Raghavendra (2022) presented an AI-based chatbot intended to enrich students' learning experience in higher education by evaluating their responses, offering insights for skill enhancement, and aiming to boost thinking ability and expectations. Utilizing concept mapping, the system enhanced students' understanding of specific subjects, while simulation results compared its efficacy with traditional methods based on factors such as assessment ratio and active learning factor.

The use of chatbot can be witnessed in many forms of the education. For example, McAlister, Alhabash, and Yang (2024) delved into the role of ChatGPT, in marketing education and highlighted its utility in advertising and marketing communications education. It addressed concerns surrounding AI technologies in education and scholarship, advocating for their integration, while also proposed guidelines for best practices and ethical considerations in their use. Additionally, it suggested a research agenda to deepen understanding of AI's impact on advertising and marketing education. Similarly, Corrêa et al. (2023) demonstrated the development of Lhia, a smart chatbot in addressing breastfeeding education and human milk donor recruitment, offering potential support in contexts with low exclusive breastfeeding rates and insufficient human milk stocks in Brazil. The study involved a co-design methodology with health professionals, utilizing deep learning-based natural language processing pipelines to classify user intents, resulting in a 93% accuracy rate.

Lhia's architecture, built on the Rasa platform, facilitated intent recognition, action processing, event scheduling, and database management.

Chatbots in medical education are being explored due to disruptions caused by the COVID-19 pandemic, aiming to augment remote teaching. Kaur et al. (2021) conducted a thematic analysis of focus groups that revealed five main themes: chatbot use as a clinical simulation tool, revision tool, suitability by medical school year group, standardization of education and assessment, and challenges of use and implementation. Participants highlighted the potential benefits of chatbots in practicing clinical skills and pharmacology, as well as for information retrieval and revision. The differential usefulness of chatbots was noted across medical school year groups, with first-year students seen as potentially benefiting more. Participants who haven't used chatbots in medical education fear that substituting them for real patients would hinder their learning and put them at a disadvantage compared to those with more patient exposure. The study also highlighted the potential of integrating chatbots into medical curricula, especially in earlier years, to supplement traditional methods and enhance learning opportunities. The study concluded that chatbots are underutilized in British medical education and suggested their integration to promote self-learning, enhance competence, and improve patient safety.

ChatGPT's conversational and programming abilities, coupled with the OPTIMAL model, can enhance communication for scientific data analysis education in bioinformatics as noted by Shue et al. (2023). Practical considerations, such as clear prompt definition and understanding of key concepts, facilitated the iterative process of refining prompts and code through chatbot interactions, resulting in clear prompts and reference code beneficial for beginners. Similarly, AI-Chatbots, exemplified by ChatGPT, offer versatile applications in nursing education, aiding in drafting course materials and facilitating personalized self-paced learning, as well as providing opportunities for problem-based learning as noted by Tam et al. (2023). The study also finds that AI-Chatbots show promise in streamlining administrative tasks in nursing, potentially alleviating healthcare worker shortages and burnout, while also assisting in socially supporting patients for therapeutic purposes. Moreover, they can help overcome technical barriers in nursing informatics, increasing accessibility for individuals without technical backgrounds. However, concerns regarding over-reliance leading to plagiarism and limited critical thinking skills among students are notable. To address these, educators must provide clear guidelines emphasizing critical thinking and proper citation.

Traditional biology classrooms often lack sufficient teacher-student interaction, potentially impeding learning. Introducing suitable learning tools beyond class time can aid in reinforcing biology knowledge. Y. T. Lin and Ye (2023) introduced a biology learning chatbot system to facilitate out-of-class learning. A quasi-experiment involving 34 grade 7 students demonstrated the chatbot's positive impact on biology learning achievements. Whereas, Thorat et al. (2024) noted that use of chatbot in dental education offers personalized learning pathways tailored to individual students' needs and preferences, enhancing clinical reasoning and communication skills through integration into virtual patient simulation scenarios. With 24/7 accessibility and multilingual support, it can promote inclusivity and breaks down language barriers. Serving as an interactive dental dictionary, chatbot can provides instant access to terminology and definitions, facilitating evidence-based learning by offering a vast repository of research papers and literature.

Chatbots emerged as promising tools for health education and engagement, capable of providing early health advice and supporting preventive care. Mokmin and Ibrahim (2021) evaluated a health chatbot's usefulness, performance, and technology acceptance among undergraduate students, with 73.3% of respondents finding it helpful in understanding health issues and engaging in conversation. The chatbot demonstrated a low exit rate, indicating user engagement, while highlighting the importance of health literacy, especially among Malaysian youth facing challenges with non-communicable diseases and health education.

Chatbot technology is increasingly integrated into higher educational institutions. For example, Madhavan et al. (2023) demonstrated implementing chatbots in higher education in India to enhance student interactions and services. Utilizing Python, Flask Framework, PyTorch, NLTK, HTML, CSS, and JavaScript, the authors demonstrated the use of a chatbot system to provide academic guidance, personalized recommendations, and career path assistance to students. Similarly, universities are embracing AI tools such as chatbots to enhance educational services, as evidenced by a bibliometric analysis conducted by Chamorro-Atalaya et al. (2023) covering 210 manuscripts from 2013 to 2023, indicating a growing trend in scientific production. These chatbots primarily target improving academic performance, administrative management, and overall university well-being. The authors noted that there's a notable gap in research concerning student satisfaction with chatbot usage, as well as the absence of a regulatory framework for their application in universities.

Moreover, Polyportis and Pahos (2024) explored various factors influencing the adoption of ChatGPT in higher education, covering areas such as the role of meta-UTAUT factors, perceived anthropomorphism, and perceived intelligence in chatbot-based services. The authors noted that studies examined various aspects of the use of chatbots in higher education such as the responsible use of ChatGPT and innovation in higher education, consumer response to radical versus incremental product design, ethical principles for AI in education, the effect of AI chatbot empathy on willingness to donate and understand consumer adoption of mobile payments. Furthermore, Essel et al. (2022) focused on the impact of chatbots in Ghanaian higher education and revealed that students interacting with the chatbot demonstrated improved academic performance compared to those engaging with the course instructor. Additionally, data from focus groups within the experimental cohort indicated confidence in the chatbot's integration into the course.

A study conducted by Al-Abdullatif, Al-Dokhny, and Drwish (2023) with 60 Saudi postgraduates revealed that Bashayer (chatbot) users exhibited heightened motivation and employed more cognitive and metacognitive strategies compared to controls. Using a quantitative quasi-experimental design, it divided Saudi postgraduates into control and experimental groups. Measurement utilized the Motivated Strategies for Learning Questionnaire (MSLQ), assessing motivation and learning strategies. The findings indicated significantly higher motivation and better learning strategies in the experimental group, paving the way for improved cognitive and metacognitive learning among postgraduates.

Universities commonly offer counseling services and information to prospective students via direct visits, phone calls, or social media, but increased visitor traffic often results in longer wait times and reduced satisfaction due to limited officer availability, typically during business hours. Implementing chatbots can mitigate this issue by efficiently addressing frequently asked questions. Aloqayli and Abdelhafez (2023) developed and tested a chatbot for higher education admission using the Botsify platform by engaging postgraduate students. The chatbot's performance was evaluated using the Chatbot Usability Questionnaire (CUQ) and Confusion Matrix, revealing effective question answering with a 91% accuracy rate. Similarly, Bilquise, Ibrahim, and Salhieh (2023) examined university students' willingness to adopt academic advising chatbots, focusing on functional, socio-emotional, and relational factors influencing chatbot acceptance. Integrating various technology acceptance models into an educational context, data was collected from 207 university students in the UAE via a questionnaire survey, employing PLS-SEM causal modeling for hypothesis testing. Results indicated that perceived ease of use and social influence significantly impact chatbot acceptance, while perceived usefulness, autonomy, and trust did not significantly influence acceptance.

Chatbot technology has demonstrated a good impact on learning outcomes. For example, Deng and Yu (2023) demonstrated a medium-to-high effect on overall learning outcomes in sustainable education, with significant improvements noted in explicit reasoning, learning achievement, knowledge retention, and learning interest. While no significant differences were found in critical thinking, learning engagement, and motivation compared to traditional methods, moderator analyses indicated varying effect sizes based on chatbot roles without significant differences in learning outcomes. It is also noted that intervention duration and learning content also do not significantly impact effectiveness. Similarly, Al-Abdullatif (2023) delved into students' perceptions and acceptance of chatbots in learning activities, recognizing their increasing importance in education as technology evolves. Integrating the Technology Acceptance Model (TAM) and the Value-Based Adoption Model

(VAM), the study involved 432 participants in an online survey. Key findings revealed that drivers of chatbot acceptance include perceived usefulness, ease of use, attitude, enjoyment, and value, while perceived risk did not significantly predict chatbot acceptance.

Chatbots and Web3

Web3 can solve several problems and issues with conventional, centralized AI systems. Compared with the traditional architecture of chatbot systems, in which user information is collected, stored, and regulated by centralized organizational entities at the message level, this would be fundamentally problematic in terms of privacy and abuse of power. In this context, Web3 can enable users to own and manage data through the help of decentralized storage solutions and the use of blockchains (Bamakan and Far 2024). For instance, students using educative chatbots engaging in learning can upload their learning data into a blockchain, and such data is safe, personal, and only retrievable with permission from such students. Such decentralized control is very important to safeguard student's privacy and gain their trust in the AI systems.

Moreover, centralized AI systems provide decision-making results and information processing in a 'closed format, 'that is, the decision-making of chatbots is not transparent. Whereas, transparency is one of Web3's key characteristics (Razzaq 2024). Using blockchains the decision-making processes of the chatbots can be made fully explainable and traceable. For instance, if a chatbot recommends a student a learning model, the rationale embedded in that model can be audited on the blockchain.

In the traditional systems governance of chatbot systems is done by one organization and this may at times act in the best interest of all the users hence becoming biased or unethical. Through Web3, the governing of chatbots can be done through a decentralized autonomous organization in which the chatbot and its development and management can be collectively controlled by educators, students, and developers (Li and Chen 2024). This democratic approach guarantees that the application of the chatbot, its behavior, and its development, correspond to the standards of the community that it belongs to prevent users from any prejudice or the application of any unethical approaches.

Centralized systems have low motivation for the community to get engaged in the evolution and advancement of chatbots and thus have a limited variety of inputs. Web3 can incorporate the use of tokens, making more stakeholders contribute to the improvement of the chatbot (Li and Chen 2024). For instance, the educators and developers may be rewarded the tokens with the help of contributing to the knowledge base in the chatbot or enhancing the algorithms used in the platform.

This incentivization results in faster evolution and growth of the chatbot because many people will be chipping in with their ideas regarding the chatbot to make it more useful in the provision of education.

The main downside combined with having centralized chatbots is censorship and the issue of single points of failure, that is, the system can simply be turned off or manipulated at the discretion of the controlling entity. Other benefits of Web3 are that chatbot systems are less prone to failure and censorship due to decentralization. When a chatbot is hosted in a decentralized environment, the infrastructure cannot be nullified or manipulated by any one authority, this means that the users will be able to continue to engage with the chatbot freely and without prejudice, this is particularly important in learning institutions where freedom of information and expression is paramount.

METHODOLOGY

To comprehensively explore the ethical concerns surrounding the use of Artificial Intelligence (AI) in education, and to conduct a thorough benefits analysis, a review of scholarly literature was undertaken. The evaluation framework is partially inspired by AI 4People's ethical framework (Floridi et al. 2022) is composed of four steps.

- **Identification of Ethical Concerns**

In this step, articles, research papers, and academic publications addressing ethical concerns associated with the use of AI and chatbots in education are explored to identify ethical concerns. Moreover, how web3 applications support the identification of ethical concerns is also explored.

- **Analysis of Ethical Concerns**

In the second step, the identified ethical concerns are critically evaluated and categorized, considering their implications for educational practices, student well-being, and institutional integrity. Special attention is paid to recurring themes such as fairness, transparency, privacy, bias, and accountability. Further, the applicability of web3 for the analysis of ethical concerns is also described.

- **Assessment of Benefits**

In this step, the benefits associated with the integration of AI, particularly chatbots, in education are analyzed and reported accordingly. In this step, the connectivity of web3 applications with the benefits is also presented.

- **Recommendations Development**

Based on the synthesized findings, recommendations for ethical mitigation and responsible implementation of AI technologies in education are formulated. In addition, how web3 applications are suitable for developing recommendations is explored.

FINDINGS

The findings of the study revealed a multitude of ethical concerns and benefits associated with the integration of Artificial Intelligence (AI), particularly chatbots, in education. This section presented the findings of the study based on the methodology described in the previous section.

Identification of Ethical Concerns

A literature review was conducted to identify the ethical concerns, as outlined below. Figure 1 illustrates the detailed categorization of the identified ethical concerns into seven categories.

The advent of Artificial Intelligence (AI) technology raises a plethora of ethical considerations, a topic currently under consideration by various entities spanning from grassroots organizations in civil society to prominent corporations and governmental bodies. Green (2018) highlighted twelve ethical concerns of AI such as "function, transparency, evil use, good use, bias, unemployment, socio-economic inequality, moral automation and human de-skilling, robot consciousness and rights, dependency, social-psychological effects, and spiritual effects". These concerns may have applicability in various domains including education. Similarly, Holmes et al. (2022) identified fairness, accountability, transparency, bias, autonomy, agency, and inclusion as ethical challenges of employing AI in education. Whereas, AI ethics in education included transparency, justice, fairness, equity, non-maleficence, responsibility, and privacy as noted by Yu and Yu (2023).

Misuse of private data or surveillance of people's lives is endorsed by Klimova, Pikhart, and Kacetl (2023). Jobin, Ienca, and Vayena (2019) revealed a global convergence emerging around five ethical concerns such as transparency, justice and fairness, non-maleficence, responsibility, and privacy. Bu (2022) noted that educational AI poses three key ethical risks such as data security, deconstructing teacher-student roles and educational inequality, and alienation from educational goals. AI systems can amplify existing systemic biases and discrimination within societies, thereby perpetuating privacy, autonomy, and surveillance concerns, particularly for students belonging to marginalized and underserved groups (Akgun and Greenhow 2022). The three most prominent ethical concerns associated with the use of instructional technology in education are copyright, learner privacy, and accessibility as endorsed by H. Lin (2007).

AI in education has great potential, but clear regulations are needed to ensure ethical and fair use, including ethical concerns such as fairness, bias, equity, inclusion, data transparency, and collaborative approaches between disciplines (Caccavale et al. 2022). AI in education may promote learning but may present limited or untruthful information to students, potentially conflicting with the values of Fairness, Accountability, Transparency, and Ethics (FATE) (Sjödén 2020). Reiss (2021) noted that AI in education has the potential to enrich student learning and complement teachers' work, while also enabling a straddle between school and home, but risks becoming less social. AI in education faces ethical concerns related to algorithmic biases, uneven implementation, and differential access, as well as the need to establish ethical parameters between AI and students (Papa and Jackson 2021).

The most prevalent ethical principles of AI are transparency, justice and fairness, responsibility, non-maleficence, and privacy (Zhou et al. 2020). Concerns about algorithmic systems' fairness, bias, transparency, access, participation, and discrimination are underlying issues in AI Ethics (Hoffmann et al. 2018). AI in education raises ethical concerns related to surveillance, exacerbated social inequality, and threats to job security (Huang, Samek, and Shiri 2021). Chatbots pose ethical challenges linked to AI applications and raise concerns about the ethical implications of automating online conversational processes and integrating AI (Murtarelli, Gregory, and Romenti 2021).

Incorporating code reviews and social coding platforms into software engineering education is beneficial but faces challenges like steep learning curves and privacy considerations (Farah et al. 2022). Ethical concerns associated with robot teachers include privacy, attachment, deception, loss of human contact, and control and accountability (Sharkey 2016). Despite the potential benefits of AI systems like chatbots in research, ethical concerns such as bias in data, lack of context understanding, and potential misuse raise significant challenges (Kooli 2023). Ethical considerations regarding AI in education involve data privacy, bias reinforcement, and the digital divide (Ifelebuegu, Kulume, and Cherukut 2023). The use of ChatGPT raises questions about plagiarism detection and the authenticity of student work (Gill et al. 2024).

Web3 and Identification of Ethical Concerns

Ethical concerns can be addressed by web3 applications through the use of databases and the blockchain system. For example, a decentralized library could be formed using the blockchain, where articles, research papers, and academic publications can be stored, and work history is marked and is difficult to forge. This method helps reduce the centralization of power so that one individual or agency cannot delete or twist around information. Moreover, these repositories could be run by DAOs, which means that, for instance, educators, researchers, or students could vote on which ethical issues should be addressed first. One could be a Decentralized Autonomous Organization that is used to have educators submit and vote on the most crucial issues about AI biases in grading.

Figure 1. Detailed categorization of the identified ethical concerns

Assessment of Ethical Concerns

A detailed assessment of identified ethical concerns is performed in this section.

Fairness, Justice, and Equity

The use of chatbots in education should ensure providing equal opportunities and treatment to all students without any biases or preferential treatment, regardless of their background or circumstances (Devillers, Fogelman-Soulié, and Baeza-Yates 2021). Failure to uphold fairness can lead to resentment and hinder students' motivation to learn. Therefore, to bring fairness to the use of chatbots in education, regular audits of chatbot interactions, diverse training datasets, and continuous monitoring for potential biases, are essentially required.

The implementation of chatbots should align with principles of justice, ensuring equal opportunities for all students and fair treatment and consequences for all stakeholders (Cachat-Rosset and Klarsfeld 2023). Lack of justice may result in disillusionment and distrust among students, educators, and administrators. Therefore, regular assessments of chatbot interventions to identify and rectify any instances of injustice are required.

Chatbots should contribute to educational equity necessitates addressing disparities by providing equal resources and assistance to all students, regardless of background. Failure to achieve equity can perpetuate systemic injustices and widen educational gaps. It is required to implement features that address the specific needs of diverse student populations and regularly assess the impact on equitable access.

Transparency and Accountability

Users should be aware that they are interacting with chatbots, and the system's functionalities should be transparent (Cachat-Rosset and Klarsfeld 2023; Men, Zhou, and Sunny Tsai 2022). Transparency in educational processes fosters trust and understanding among stakeholders. Lack of transparency can lead to suspicion and undermine confidence in the education system. Communication of the role of chatbots in education should be clear to provide information on their limitations, and offer transparency in decision-making processes.

Clear accountability mechanisms should be in place for the actions and decisions made by chatbots. Holding individuals and institutions accountable for their actions and decisions is essential for maintaining integrity and promoting improvement. Without accountability, there is a risk of irresponsibility and negligence in educational practices. Thus, it is necessary to establish protocols for addressing errors and ensure that accountability rests with both the developers and the educational institution.

Bias and Discrimination

Efforts should be made to mitigate biases in chatbot interactions, ensuring fair treatment of all students (Zabel and Otto 2021). Addressing bias in education requires recognizing and mitigating implicit biases that may affect decision-making and interactions. Failure to address bias can perpetuate inequalities and undermine the credibility of educational institutions. Regular assessment and addressing biases in chatbot algorithms, diversifying training data, and involving diverse teams in the development process, can help to mitigate bias concerns. Including bias detection mechanisms in the development process and conducting ongoing assessments can address algorithmic biases.

Chatbots should not discriminate against students based on characteristics such as race, gender, or socioeconomic status (Illescas, Ortega, and Jadán-Guerrero 2023; Feine et al. 2020). Eliminating discrimination involves creating inclusive environments where all individuals are treated with respect and dignity. Discriminatory practices can marginalize certain groups and hinder their academic and personal development. Implementing strict guidelines against discriminatory behavior and regular monitoring of chatbot interactions for potential discriminatory actions can help address discrimination concerns in the use of AI in education.

Autonomy, Agency, and Responsibility

Students' autonomy should be respected in interactions with chatbots (Nguyen, Sidorova, and Torres 2022). Respecting students' autonomy enables them to make informed choices and take ownership of their learning journey. Limiting autonomy diminishes students' sense of agency and inhibits their ability to develop critical thinking skills. To handle these, it is recommended to provide options for students to control their interactions with chatbots, allowing them to opt out or customize their experiences.

Fostering agency empowers students to act independently and advocate for their needs (Fanni et al. 2023). Students should have a sense of agency in their educational experiences, even when using chatbots. Lack of agency undermines students' motivation and engagement in learning activities. Involving students in the design and feedback process for chatbots can allow them to provide input on features and functionalities.

Educational institutions and developers should take responsibility for the impact of chatbots on student learning (McNealy 2023). Promoting responsibility encourages students to fulfill their obligations and contribute positively to the learning community. Neglecting responsibility leads to apathy and disengagement from educational pursuits. It is required to establish clear lines of responsibility, with mechanisms for addressing issues and ensuring ongoing improvement.

Users should have control over their interactions with chatbots, and accountability measures should be clearly defined. Balancing control and accountability ensures that decision-making processes are transparent and fair. Excessive control stifles innovation and creativity, while insufficient accountability breeds mistrust and resentment. Implementing features that allow users to control and understand how chatbots influence their educational experiences, can help to address this ethical concern.

Privacy and Data Security

Chatbots should prioritize user privacy, ensuring that personal information is handled securely (Hasal et al. 2021; Yang et al. 2023). Protecting individuals' privacy safeguards their personal information and promotes trust in educational institutions. Violating privacy rights can erode confidence and may lead to legal and ethical repercussions. To handle this, implement robust data protection measures, including encryption and secure storage, and clearly communicate privacy policies to users.

Learner privacy should be a top priority, safeguarding sensitive information from unauthorized access. Safeguarding learner privacy involves respecting students' rights to confidentiality and autonomy over their personal data. Breaching learner privacy can undermine trust and may deter students from engaging in educational activities. So, to handle this concern, regularly review and update privacy policies, conduct privacy impact assessments, and provide users with control over their data.

Stringent data security measures should be in place to prevent unauthorized access or data breaches (Yang et al. 2023). Ensuring data security prevents unauthorized access and misuse of sensitive information. Neglecting data security exposes individuals to identity theft and compromises the integrity of educational systems. Regularly updating security protocols, conducting security audits, and ensuring compliance with data protection regulations, are necessary to address this concern. Chatbots should not be used to exploit or misuse private data for any purpose. Misusing private data can violate individuals' rights and undermine the credibility of educational institutions. Preventing misuse requires robust policies and enforcement mechanisms.

Educational Inequality and Access

The introduction of chatbots should not contribute to the deconstruction of essential teacher-student roles. Reimagining teacher-student roles fosters collaborative and participatory learning environments (Kooli 2023). However, deconstruction must not undermine the expertise and authority of educators or marginalize student voices. It is required to clearly define the role of chatbots as supplementary and collaborative tools, ensuring that they complement rather than replace teachers.

Chatbots should actively contribute to reducing educational inequalities rather than exacerbating them. Addressing educational inequality requires systemic reforms and targeted interventions to address socioeconomic disparities and structural barriers. Ignoring educational inequality perpetuates cycles of disadvantage and limits opportunities for marginalized communities. Therefore, it is essential to implement features that address the specific needs of underprivileged students, promote accessibility, and provide equal opportunities for all.

Chatbots should align with educational goals and not contribute to students feeling alienated from the learning process. Alienation from educational goals signifies a disconnect between students' aspirations and institutional objectives. Realigning educational goals with students' interests and needs enhances motivation and engagement. To address this, it is suggested to regularly assess the impact of chatbots on students' engagement and satisfaction, making adjustments as needed.

Access to educational resources facilitated by chatbots should be equitable, avoiding differential access based on factors like socioeconomic status. Neglecting differential access exacerbates educational inequalities and perpetuates cycles of disadvantage. Closing gaps in access to educational resources and opportunities requires proactive measures to bridge the digital divide, to address socio-economic disparities and systemic barriers to ensure that all students have equal access to chatbot-supported resources.

The use of chatbots should not pose threats to the job security of educational professionals. Recognizing threats to job security acknowledges the challenges faced by educators in evolving educational landscapes. Proactively supporting educators through professional development and job security measures promotes stability and innovation. To handle this, clearly communicate the role of chatbots as supportive tools, and involve educators in the development and implementation process to ensure collaboration rather than replacement.

Chatbots should actively work to minimize social inequality within educational settings. Mitigating exacerbated social inequality necessitates targeted interventions and systemic reforms to address root causes and promote social justice. Ignoring social inequality perpetuates cycles of disadvantage and undermines the principles of fairness and equity.

Collaboration and Ethical Use

Promoting interdisciplinary collaboration can enrich learning experiences and foster holistic understanding (Følstad et al. 2021). However, collaboration must be equitable and respectful of diverse perspectives. Recognizing the importance of context understanding ensures that educational interventions are responsive to students' backgrounds and experiences. Neglecting context understanding may lead to culturally insensitive practices and inequitable outcomes.

Anticipating potential misuse of educational technologies requires proactive measures to address ethical concerns and safeguard students' well-being. Ethical guidelines and oversight mechanisms help mitigate risks and promote responsible use. Acknowledging the importance of human contact underscores the value of interpersonal relationships in education. Balancing technological advancements with human interaction preserves empathy and fosters meaningful connections in learning environments.

Web3 and Assessment of Ethical Concerns

During the analysis phase, Web3 can contribute to a more critical and distributed exploration of ethical issues via collective platforms with the help of smart contracts. These platforms could potentially enable worldwide domain experts to tag ethical issues as well as the categorization of such concerns into various categories and these records formed what could be described as an immutable ledger on a blockchain. For example, the Web3 platform can be created to include educators and ethicists who sort out the problems with the AI chatbot, such as privacy or bias. Contributors could be paid back for their analysis via tokens and this way, the process would be incentivized as well as free from bias. Apart from making sure that there is a comprehensive assessment of these ethical issues, this decentralized method makes it easy to track how these issues were assessed.

Benefit Analysis

Chatbots are increasingly employed in education to aid students as virtual tutors in various subject areas. The benefits of AI in education include many dimensions that are discussed below and summarized in Figure 2.

AI in education improves learners' experience and overall quality of learning by automating tasks and leveraging machine learning and adaptability. The role of Artificial Intelligence techniques is increasingly significant in educational settings, particularly in special education (Hopcan et al. 2022). These are also increasingly used in early childhood education (ECE) to enhance learning and development among young children (Su and Yang 2022). AI can transform specialized education as well. For example, nursing education can be supported by artificial intelligence, including administration, clinical care, education, policy, and research (Buchanan et al. 2021). Similarly, chatbots can foster engagement and increase interest in basic CS concepts (Benotti, Martínez, and Schapachnik 2014). Chatbot can introduce high school students to computer science concepts through programming chatbots, with automatic formative assessment and improved task completion rates (Benotti, Martínez, and Schapachnik 2018).

AI can enhance teachers' roles in designing and facilitating AI-enabled teaching and learning (Lameras and Arnab 2022). Chatbots showed the potential to assist students in learning basic content interactively and confidentially (Chen et al. 2023). Chatbots in education can focus on managing communication and providing correct answers to students using natural language processing techniques and domain-specific ontologies (Clarizia et al. 2018). Chatbots can assist users in learning and potentially reduce feelings of isolation and detachment in E-Learning platforms (Wu et al. 2020). Chatbots can enhance traditional course teaching by addressing five principles of Chickering and Gamson's Seven Principles for Good Teaching (Gonda et al. 2018). Chatbots can also be used in educational contexts to respond to students' questions and contribute to assistance automation in the learning context (Oliveira et al. 2019). They can effectively improve the learning and P2P evaluation process in a MOOC, with 90% of learners encouraging their use in future courses (Pereira et al. 2019).

Chatbot technologies can provide instant interaction and support to students outside of class (Y. T. Lin and Ye 2023). Coaching is recognized as a significant tool for reflecting learning processes in higher education. Digital media and AI-based technologies like chatbots can support self-coaching processes (Mai, Neef, and Richert 2022). The e-JAVA chatbot project utilizes rule-based techniques to address computational problems and offers instant responses to template-based questions. The primary aim of the e-JAVA chatbot project is to support students in solving JAVA programming language problems effectively (Mad Daud 2020). Low student engagement and motivation in online classes are significant issues. The chatbot can improve student engagement by employing instructor immediacy techniques and providing 24/7 availability for student inquiries (Jasin et al. 2023).

Chatbots in smart schools can prevent student and instructor absences and safeguard their health, influenced by factors like performance expectation, effort expectation, social influence, and health and safety (Rukhiran, Phaokla, and Netinant 2022). Chatbots can improve learners' emotional confidence and strengthen their self-efficacy for skill learning (Zhang et al. 2022). Chatbots can serve as an extra-school tool to carry out academic and administrative tasks and facilitate communication between middle-school students and academic staff (Mendoza et al. 2022). Chatbots can be integrated into both online and face-to-face content to augment challenges encountered in teaching (Gonda and Chu 2019). Even, AI-powered chatbots are effective e-learning tools for students learning complex software like AutoCAD.

AI chatbots can offer immediate support by answering questions, offering explanations, and providing additional resources in educational settings. Educators can benefit from AI chatbots through time-saving assistance and improved pedagogy. AI-powered chatbots can offer homework and study assistance by providing detailed feedback, explanations, and step-by-step solutions to students' questions and assignments. AI chatbots can contribute to skills development by offering writing suggestions, problem-solving guidance, and facilitating group discussions and debates (Labadze, Grigolia, and Machaidze 2023).

AI chatbots like ChatGPT play a crucial role in personalized learning and can benefit educational institutions at all levels, from elementary schools to universities. ChatGPT can assist educators in creating instructional content, offering suggestions, and acting as an online educator to learners by answering questions, promoting group work, and transforming education through smartphones and IoT gadgets (Gill et al. 2024).

Web3 and Benefit Analysis

Web3 can complement the evaluation of the advantages linked to the implementation of AI and chatbots in education by means of Decentralized and Community-Based assessment. For instance, a Web3-based platform could let students, teachers, and developers submit the values of the AI tools for consideration, such as personalization of learning, accommodation of students with disabilities, etc. Wide participation could be motivated through the issue of tokens in that, of benefits got from the blockchain, none can be fully blinded and understood from the perspective of one institution or group. Such decentralized review system would serve to build a more holistic and objective picture as to how these AI technologies are benefiting education and where are they lacking or perhaps failing.

Figure 2. Benefit analysis

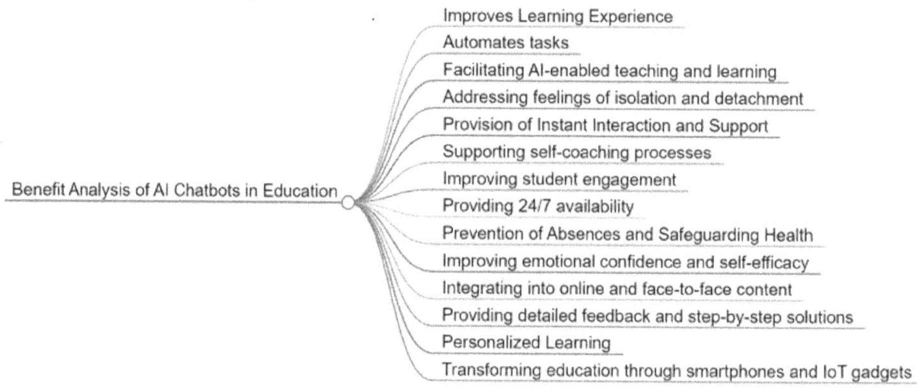

Recommendations for Ethical Mitigation

In today's educational landscape, the integration of AI-driven technologies, particularly chatbots, presents both opportunities and ethical challenges. To navigate this terrain responsibly, a multifaceted approach is necessary, combining robust data protection measures like encryption and anonymization with transparency and accountability mechanisms within chatbot algorithms.

Critical thinking skills are paramount, encouraging students to question and evaluate chatbot responses independently. Concurrently, bias detection algorithms and algorithmic auditing techniques can play a pivotal role in identifying and mitigating biases in chatbot training data, ensuring equitable treatment for all students. A comprehensive framework for ethical AI in education, as advocated by Holmes et al. (2022), underlines the importance of interdisciplinary collaboration and stringent guidelines in addressing complex ethical issues and ensuring student learning. Klimova, Pikhart, and Kacetl (2023) stress the need for ethical principles in AI-driven mobile apps, emphasizing algorithm vigilance and collaborative research.

Redefinition of teachers' fundamental duties, the instruction of students in the sensible use of AI, and the promotion of effective regulation of AI's deployment in education are advocated by Bu (2022) as countermeasures. Whereas, Wang (2021) suggested that while AI-driven decision-making may challenge moral values, human judgment guided by ethics remains paramount. Chatbots in education, as highlighted by Savin-Baden, Tombs, and Bhakta (2015), require truthfulness, personalization, and emotional engagement to enhance online learning, but their integration may undermine traditional notions of learning and higher education. Kooli (2023) underscored the importance of critically evaluating chatbot-provided information and verifying it before use, while Gill et al. (2024) emphasized the need for educators and institutions to understand ChatGPT's capabilities, develop guidelines and training programs to effectively utilize ChatGPT while maintaining academic standards as well as update academic regulations accordingly.

Web3 and Recommendations for Ethical Mitigation

Web3 can make the processes of creating ethical guidelines for AI usage in learning more open and engaging, which is crucial when creating a set of recommendations to follow. For instance, a DAO can be created to collect opinions from students, teachers, developers, and ethicists. These stakeholders could suggest, discuss and, in some cases, cast their vote regarding recommendations that should guide this process thus having the guidelines set a reflection of the community's consensus. An example could be an initiative in a DAO environment to have teachers' discussions on the use of AI in classes, for example, on ways and means of protecting data or addressing biases in algorithms. If some of these recommendations are to be implemented, smart contracts could help enforce them right from the educational platforms.

Building upon these insights, the following recommendations emerge:

- Implement bias detection mechanisms and regular audits to identify and address biases in chatbot algorithms. Ensure diverse representation in dataset creation and algorithm development.
- Strengthen data encryption, access controls, and user consent mechanisms to safeguard student privacy and prevent unauthorized data access.
- Develop strategies to bridge the digital divide and ensure equitable access to chatbot-supported educational resources and assistance for all students.
- Provide educators with training and resources to effectively integrate chatbots into the learning environment and maintain a balance between technology-mediated and human interactions.
- Establish clear ethical guidelines and governance frameworks for the development, deployment, and use of chatbots in education, with mechanisms for accountability and transparency.
- Regularly evaluate the impact of chatbots on student learning outcomes, engagement, and satisfaction. Use feedback and data insights to refine chatbot functionalities and address emerging challenges.

IMPLICATIONS AND LIMITATIONS

Incorporating AI, including chatbots, into the education field is most certainly a powerful factor that can lead to numerous implications that can cause an improvement in the teaching and learning cycle. The AI chatbots can give the chance where a student learner can get personalized features but at an individual level. This may lead to the enhancement of academic achievements and engagement as students are empowered to learn better when supported in such a way as to suit their own unique requirements. Chatbots can envisage helping educators in administration responsibilities such as inputting daily attendance and providing feedback for students' work at once. Teachers no longer get into investigating the basic, direct facts, which allows them to focus their time on the complex and interactive elements of education. Through this process, teachers can enable students to have a richer learning experience. AI chatbots can provide a wide possibility of customized resources and buffers which is welcome primarily to special education and early childhood education hence, to ensure students receive full attention and achieve success.

Chatbots, as tools well-planned and executed can function as a democratizing factor in education with equal opportunities resulting for all. It includes even those from marginalized families. The AI system, which brushes the inequality of educational opportunities, brings reinforcement for backward children. In this way, it can be a stimulus for them to confront educational inequality. This is more of a critical factor because all students should be provided with the utmost resources as well as facilities at their disposal and should have people who are able to assist them to be able to perform well in their studies in spite of the fact that their socioeconomic status could be poor.

At the same time, AI in education is raising meaningful issues of privacy and ethical concerns in general. Achieving this involves various data protection measures, such as encryption and secure storage which increases the confidence in institutions. Also, it is equally to consider ethical uses of data so that students can be made quality AI systems that do not misuse or exploit student information. Transparency about the role of the chatbots and areas where their strengths and weaknesses are, as well as having set accountability structures, can assist in garnering trust and credibility among all education institution key actors.

The AI introduction in terms of the teacher-student relationship is manifested as well. AI should adjunct, not decussate, educators. Suitable training and using teachers in AI implementation would leverage the sense of collaboration and innovation among the teachers who are then enabled to harness the technology and not the other way round, whereby the roles of the teachers are jeopardized. While tech is growing fast, still ensuring human communication besides technological innovations is essential to maintain empathy and a relationship in the field of education which are vital for efficient teaching and education.

It should be noted that although the advantages are compelling, the weaknesses have to be dealt with as well. Implementing AI brings along implementation challenges such as resource constraints and the proper training of educators can hamper the efficient adoption in education settings. Yet privacy and other ethical concerns are present such as data security risks and data bias thus the community should remain vigilant round the clock to tackle them. AI's integration may also spark a debate among educators concerning unemployment as a clear message regarding AI's supportive role in this process should be communicated.

The digital gap can aggravate the issues behind educational inequalities, it excludes those students who lack technology to have equitable access. The subsequent question here is how to deal with this. The answer might be in reaching for the targeted actions aiming to provide the benefit of AI to all children. Resource inequities in the allocation of funds may result in understaffed schools that are ultimately unable to use AI in the best manner and hence, the difference between well-sourced and under-sourced schools eventually becomes too huge. Autonomy of the students and giving them agency over their learning experiences should be the prime focus in order to avoid the danger of dependency and independence. The creation of ethical standards and governmental structures as key components of the system of AI usage in education are amongst the most difficult but necessary tasks to be performed. Constantly upgrading and amending of the above frameworks are imperative to not only confront the new challenges but also make sure that AI is used wisely in education.

CONCLUSION

The integration of Artificial Intelligence (AI), particularly chatbots, in education, presents a myriad of ethical concerns and benefits, as revealed by the comprehensive findings of this study. Through a thorough literature review and analysis, the study identified a spectrum of ethical considerations spanning fairness, transparency, privacy, autonomy, and educational inequality.

Ethical concerns surrounding the use of AI in education include the misuse of private data, algorithmic biases, surveillance, and threats to job security. These concerns underscore the importance of establishing clear regulations and guidelines to ensure the ethical and fair use of AI technologies in educational settings. On the other hand, the benefits of AI in education are significant and multifaceted. AI technologies, including chatbots, have the potential to enhance learners' experiences, improve teaching efficiency, and provide personalized learning experiences. They can foster engagement, increase interest in subjects, and offer immediate support to students both inside and outside the classroom.

To address the ethical concerns associated with AI in education, a multifaceted approach is necessary. This includes implementing robust data protection measures, ensuring transparency and accountability in chatbot algorithms, and promoting critical thinking skills among students to evaluate AI-generated responses independently. Furthermore, it is essential to bridge the digital divide, provide training for educators, and establish clear ethical guidelines and governance frameworks for the development and deployment of AI technologies in education.

By integrating these recommendations into educational practices, stakeholders can harness the benefits of AI-driven technologies while upholding ethical standards and promoting meaningful learning experiences for all students. It is imperative for educators, policymakers, and technology developers to collaborate and ensure that AI in education serves the best interests of learners and upholds ethical principles.

REFERENCES

Adamopoulou, E., & Moussiades, L. (2020). An Overview of Chatbot Technology. In *IFIP Advances in Information and Communication Technology* (Vol. 584). IFIP., DOI: 10.1007/978-3-030-49186-4_31

Ahmad, M., Muhammad, K. H. N., Mobo, F. D., Tahir, M. W., & Akram, M. (2024). Navigating the Journey: How Chatbots Are Transforming Tourism and Hospitality. In Darwish, D. (Ed.), *Design and Development of Emerging Chatbot Technology* (pp. 236–255). IGI Global., DOI: 10.4018/979-8-3693-1830-0.ch014

Akgun, S., & Greenhow, C. 2022. "Artificial Intelligence (AI) in Education: Addressing Societal and Ethical Challenges in K-12 Settings." In *Proceedings of International Conference of the Learning Sciences, ICLS.*

Al-Abdullatif, A. M. (2023). Modeling Students' Perceptions of Chatbots in Learning: Integrating Technology Acceptance with the Value-Based Adoption Model. *Education Sciences, 13*(11), 1151. Advance online publication. DOI: 10.3390/educsci13111151

Al-Abdullatif, A. M., Al-Dokhny, A. A., & Drwish, A. M. (2023). Implementing the Bashayer Chatbot in Saudi Higher Education: Measuring the Influence on Students' Motivation and Learning Strategies. *Frontiers in Psychology, 14*, 1129070. Advance online publication. DOI: 10.3389/fpsyg.2023.1129070 PMID: 37255522

Albreem, M. A., Sheikh, A. M., Alsharif, M. H., Jusoh, M., & Mohd, N. M. Y. (2021). Green Internet of Things (GIoT): Applications, Practices, Awareness, and Challenges. *IEEE Access : Practical Innovations, Open Solutions, 9*, 38833–38858. Advance online publication. DOI: 10.1109/ACCESS.2021.3061697

Aloqayli, A., & Abdelhafez, H. (2023). Intelligent Chatbot for Admission in Higher Education. *International Journal of Information and Education Technology (IJIET), 13*(9), 1348–1357. Advance online publication. DOI: 10.18178/ijiet.2023.13.9.1937

AlZu'bi, S., Mughaid, A., Quiam, F., & Hendawi, S. (2024). Exploring the Capabilities and Limitations of Chatgpt and Alternative Big Language Models. *Artificial Intelligence and Applications (Commerce, Calif.), 2*(1), 28–37. DOI: 10.47852/bonviewAIA3202820

Bamakan, Seyed Mojtaba Hosseini, and Saeed Banaeian Far. 2024. "Distributed and Trustworthy Digital Twin Platform Based on Blockchain and Web3 Technologies." *Cyber Security and Applications*, 100064.

Barocas, S., Hardt, M., & Narayanan, A. (2020). *Fairness in Machine Learning Limitations and Opportunities*. Book.

Benotti, L., Martínez, M. C., & Schapachnik, F. 2014. "Engaging High School Students Using Chatbots." In *ITICSE 2014 - Proceedings of the 2014 Innovation and Technology in Computer Science Education Conference*. DOI: 10.1145/2591708.2591728

Benotti, L., Martínez, M. C., & Schapachnik, F. (2018). A Tool for Introducing Computer Science with Automatic Formative Assessment. *IEEE Transactions on Learning Technologies*, *11*(2), 179–192. Advance online publication. DOI: 10.1109/TLT.2017.2682084

Bilquise, G., Ibrahim, S., & Sa'Ed, E. M. S. (2023). Investigating Student Acceptance of an Academic Advising Chatbot in Higher Education Institutions. *Education and Information Technologies*. Advance online publication. DOI: 10.1007/s10639-023-12076-x

Borah, B., Pathak, D., Sarmah, P., Som, B., & Nandi, S. 2019. "Survey of Textbased Chatbot in Perspective of Recent Technologies." In *Communications in Computer and Information Science*. Vol. 1031. DOI: 10.1007/978-981-13-8581-0_7

Bu, Q. (2022). Ethical Risks in Integrating Artificial Intelligence into Education and Potential Countermeasures. *Science Insights*, *41*(1), 561–566. Advance online publication. DOI: 10.15354/si.22.re067

Buchanan, C., Howitt, M. L., Wilson, R., Booth, R. G., Risling, T., & Bamford, M. (2021). *"Predicted Influences of Artificial Intelligence on Nursing Education: Scoping Review." JMIR Nursing*. JMIR Publications Inc., DOI: 10.2196/23933

Caccavale, F., Gargalo, C. L., Gernaey, K. V., & Krühne, U. 2022. "To Be Fair: Ethical and Fair Application of Artificial Intelligence in Virtual Laboratories." In *SEFI 2022 - 50th Annual Conference of the European Society for Engineering Education, Proceedings*. DOI: 10.5821/conference-9788412322262.1398

Cachat-Rosset, G., & Klarsfeld, A. (2023). Diversity, Equity, and Inclusion in Artificial Intelligence: An Evaluation of Guidelines. *Applied Artificial Intelligence*, *37*(1), 2176618. Advance online publication. DOI: 10.1080/08839514.2023.2176618

Calvaresi, D., Eggenschwiler, S., Mualla, Y., Schumacher, M., & Calbimonte, J. P. (2023). Exploring Agent-Based Chatbots: A Systematic Literature Review. *Journal of Ambient Intelligence and Humanized Computing*, *14*(8), 11207–11226. Advance online publication. DOI: 10.1007/s12652-023-04626-5

Chamorro-Atalaya, O., Olivares-Zegarra, S., Sobrino-Chunga, L., Guerrero-Carranza, R., Vargas-Diaz, A., Huarcaya-Godoy, M., Rasilla-Rovegno, J., Suarez-Bazalar, R., Poma-Garcia, J., & Cruz-Telada, Y. (2023). Application of the Chatbot in University Education: A Bibliometric Analysis of Indexed Scientific Production in SCOPUS, 2013-2023. *International Journal of Learning, Teaching and Educational Research*, *22*(7), 281–304. Advance online publication. DOI: 10.26803/ijlter.22.7.15

Chen, Y., Jensen, S., Albert, L. J., Gupta, S., & Lee, T. (2023). Artificial Intelligence (AI) Student Assistants in the Classroom: Designing Chatbots to Support Student Success. *Information Systems Frontiers*, *25*(1), 161–182. Advance online publication. DOI: 10.1007/s10796-022-10291-4

Cheng, S. (2024). Applications of Web 3.0. In *Web 3.0: Concept, Content and Context* (pp. 109–145). Springer. DOI: 10.1007/978-981-99-6319-5_5

Chocarro, R., Cortiñas, M., & Marcos-Matás, G. (2023). Teachers' Attitudes towards Chatbots in Education: A Technology Acceptance Model Approach Considering the Effect of Social Language, Bot Proactiveness, and Users' Characteristics. *Educational Studies*, *49*(2), 295–313. Advance online publication. DOI: 10.1080/03055698.2020.1850426

Clarizia, F., Colace, F., Lombardi, M., Pascale, F., & Santaniello, D. (2018). Chatbot: An Education Support System for Student. In. Lecture Notes in Computer Science: Vol. 11161. *Including Subseries Lecture Notes in Artificial Intelligence and Lecture Notes in Bioinformatics)*. LNCS., DOI: 10.1007/978-3-030-01689-0_23

Corrêa, J. S., Pereira de Araújo Neto, A., Rebouças Pinto, G., Daniel Batista Lima, L., & Soares Teles, A. (2023). Lhia: A Smart Chatbot for Breastfeeding Education and Recruitment of Human Milk Donors. *Applied Sciences (Basel, Switzerland)*, *13*(12), 6923. Advance online publication. DOI: 10.3390/app13126923

Crawford, K., & Calo, R. (2016). There Is a Blind Spot in AI Research. *Nature*, *538*(7625), 311–313. Advance online publication. DOI: 10.1038/538311a PMID: 27762391

Daud, M., & Hawa, S. (2020). E-JAVA Chatbot for Learning Programming Language: A Post-Pandemic Alternative Virtual Tutor. *International Journal of Emerging Trends in Engineering Research*, *8*(7), 3290–3298. DOI: 10.30534/ijeter/2020/67872020

Deng, X., & Yu, Z. (2023). *A Meta-Analysis and Systematic Review of the Effect of Chatbot Technology Use in Sustainable Education*. Sustainability., DOI: 10.3390/su15042940

Devillers, L., Fogelman-Soulié, F., & Baeza-Yates, R. (2021). AI & Human Values: Inequalities, Biases, Fairness, Nudge, and Feedback Loops. In. Lecture Notes in Computer Science: Vol. 12600. *Including Subseries Lecture Notes in Artificial Intelligence and Lecture Notes in Bioinformatics)*. LNCS., DOI: 10.1007/978-3-030-69128-8_6

Essel, H. B., Vlachopoulos, D., Tachie-Menson, A., Johnson, E. E., & Baah, P. K. (2022). The Impact of a Virtual Teaching Assistant (Chatbot) on Students' Learning in Ghanaian Higher Education. *International Journal of Educational Technology in Higher Education, 19*(1), 57. Advance online publication. DOI: 10.1186/s41239-022-00362-6

Fanni, R., Steinkogler, V. E., Zampedri, G., & Pierson, J. (2023). Enhancing Human Agency through Redress in Artificial Intelligence Systems. *AI & Society, 38*(2), 537–547. Advance online publication. DOI: 10.1007/s00146-022-01454-7 PMID: 35692234

Farah, J. C., Spaenlehauer, B., Sharma, V., Rodriguez-Triana, M. J., Ingram, S., & Gillet, D. 2022. "Impersonating Chatbots in a Code Review Exercise to Teach Software Engineering Best Practices." In *IEEE Global Engineering Education Conference, EDUCON*, 2022-March:1634–42. IEEE Computer Society. DOI: 10.1109/EDUCON52537.2022.9766793

Feine, J., Gnewuch, U., Morana, S., & Maedche, A. (2020). Gender Bias in Chatbot Design. In. Lecture Notes in Computer Science: Vol. 11970. *Including Subseries Lecture Notes in Artificial Intelligence and Lecture Notes in Bioinformatics)*. LNCS., DOI: 10.1007/978-3-030-39540-7_6

Figueira, C. (2017). A Joint Communication to the European Parliament and the Council: Towards an EU Strategy for International Cultural Relations, by the European Commission, 2016. *Cultural Trends, 26*(1), 81–85. DOI: 10.1080/09548963.2017.1274371

Floridi, L, J Cowls, M Beltrametti, and others. 2022. "AI 4People's Ethical Framework for a Good AI Society: Opportunities, Risks, Principles, and Recommendations (2020)."

Følstad, A., Araujo, T., Effie, L. C. L., Brandtzaeg, P. B., Papadopoulos, S., Reis, L., & Baez, M.. (2021). Future Directions for Chatbot Research: An Interdisciplinary Research Agenda. *Computing, 103*(12), 2915–2942. Advance online publication. DOI: 10.1007/s00607-021-01016-7

Gill, S. S., Xu, M., Patros, P., Wu, H., Kaur, R., Kaur, K., Fuller, S., Singh, M., Arora, P., Parlikad, A. K., Stankovski, V., Abraham, A., Ghosh, S. K., Lutfiyya, H., Kanhere, S. S., Bahsoon, R., Rana, O., Dustdar, S., Sakellariou, R., & Buyya, R. (2024). Transformative Effects of ChatGPT on Modern Education: Emerging Era of AI Chatbots. *Internet of Things and Cyber-Physical Systems*, *4*, 19–23. Advance online publication. DOI: 10.1016/j.iotcps.2023.06.002

Gonda, D. E., & Chu, B. 2019. "Chatbot as a Learning Resource? Creating Conversational Bots as a Supplement for Teaching Assistant Training Course." In *TALE 2019 - 2019 IEEE International Conference on Engineering, Technology and Education*. DOI: 10.1109/TALE48000.2019.9225974

Gonda, D. E., Luo, J., Wong, Y. L., & Lei, C. U. 2018. "Evaluation of Developing Educational Chatbots Based on the Seven Principles for Good Teaching." In *Proceedings of 2018 IEEE International Conference on Teaching, Assessment, and Learning for Engineering, TALE 2018*. DOI: 10.1109/TALE.2018.8615175

Gowda, M. P. C., Srivastava, A., Chakraborty, S., Ghosh, A., & Raj, H. 2021. "Development of Information Technology Telecom Chatbot: An Artificial Intelligence and Machine Learning Approach." In *Proceedings of 2021 2nd International Conference on Intelligent Engineering and Management, ICIEM 2021*. DOI: 10.1109/ICIEM51511.2021.9445354

Green, B. P. (2018). Ethical Reflections on Artificial Intelligence. *Scientia et Fides*, *6*(2), 9. Advance online publication. DOI: 10.12775/SetF.2018.015

Hamzah, W., Wan, M. A. F., Ismail, I., Yusof, M. K., Syarilla, I. M. S., & Yacob, A. (2021). Using Learning Analytics to Explore Responses from Student Conversations with Chatbot for Education. *International Journal of Engineering Pedagogy*, *11*(6), 70–84. Advance online publication. DOI: 10.3991/ijep.v11i6.23475

Hasal, M., Nowaková, J., Saghair, K. A., Abdulla, H., Snášel, V., & Ogiela, L. 2021. "Chatbots: Security, Privacy, Data Protection, and Social Aspects." In *Concurrency and Computation: Practice and Experience*. Vol. 33. DOI: 10.1002/cpe.6426

Hoffmann, A. L., Roberts, S. T., Wolf, C. T., & Wood, S. (2018). Beyond Fairness, Accountability, and Transparency in the Ethics of Algorithms: Contributions and Perspectives from LIS. *Proceedings of the Association for Information Science and Technology*, *55*(1), 694–696. Advance online publication. DOI: 10.1002/pra2.2018.14505501084

Holmes, W., Porayska-Pomsta, K., Holstein, K., Sutherland, E., Baker, T., Shum, S. B., Santos, O. C., Rodrigo, M. T., Cukurova, M., Bittencourt, I. I., & Koedinger, K. R. (2022). Ethics of AI in Education: Towards a Community-Wide Framework. *International Journal of Artificial Intelligence in Education*, *32*(3), 504–526. Advance online publication. DOI: 10.1007/s40593-021-00239-1

Hopcan, S., Polat, E., Ozturk, M. E., & Ozturk, L. (2022). Artificial Intelligence in Special Education: A Systematic Review. *Interactive Learning Environments*. Advance online publication. DOI: 10.1080/10494820.2022.2067186

Huang, C., Samek, T., & Shiri, A. (2021). AI and Ethics: Ethical and Educational Perspectives for LIS. *Journal of Education for Library and Information Science*, *62*(4), 351–365. Advance online publication. DOI: 10.3138/jelis-62-4-2020-0106

Ifelebuegu, A. O., Kulume, P., & Cherukut, P. (2023). Chatbots and AI in Education (AIEd) Tools: The Good, the Bad, and the Ugly. *Journal of Applied Learning and Teaching*, *6*(2).

Illescas, C., Ortega, T., & Jadán-Guerrero, J. 2023. "Gender Bias in Chatbots and Its Programming." In *Smart Innovation, Systems and Technologies*. Vol. 337 SIST. DOI: 10.1007/978-981-19-9099-1_33

Jasin, J., Ng, H. T., Atmosukarto, I., Iyer, P., Osman, F., Peng, Y. K. W., Pua, C. Y., & Cheow, W. S. (2023). The Implementation of Chatbot-Mediated Immediacy for Synchronous Communication in an Online Chemistry Course. *Education and Information Technologies*, *28*(8), 10665–10690. DOI: 10.1007/s10639-023-11602-1 PMID: 36779194

Jobin, A., Ienca, M., & Vayena, E. (2019). The Global Landscape of AI Ethics Guidelines. *Nature Machine Intelligence*, *1*(9), 389–399. Advance online publication. DOI: 10.1038/s42256-019-0088-2

Karaca, A., & Kılcan, B. (2023). The Adventure of Artificial Intelligence Technology in Education: Comprehensive Scientific Mapping Analysis. *Participatory Educational Research*, *10*(4), 144–165. Advance online publication. DOI: 10.17275/per.23.64.10.4

Kaur, A., Singh, S., Chandan, J. S., Robbins, T., & Patel, V. (2021). Qualitative Exploration of Digital Chatbot Use in Medical Education: A Pilot Study. *Digital Health*, *7*, 20552076211038151. Advance online publication. DOI: 10.1177/20552076211038151 PMID: 34513002

Klimova, B., Pikhart, M., & Kacetl, J. (2023). Ethical Issues of the Use of AI-Driven Mobile Apps for Education. *Frontiers in Public Health, 10*, 1118116. Advance online publication. DOI: 10.3389/fpubh.2022.1118116 PMID: 36711343

Kooli, C. (2023). Chatbots in Education and Research: A Critical Examination of Ethical Implications and Solutions. *Sustainability (Basel), 15*(7), 5614. Advance online publication. DOI: 10.3390/su15075614

Kuhail, M. A., Alturki, N., Alramlawi, S., & Alhejori, K. (2023). Interacting with Educational Chatbots: A Systematic Review. *Education and Information Technologies, 28*(1), 973–1018. Advance online publication. DOI: 10.1007/s10639-022-11177-3

Labadze, L., Grigolia, M., & Machaidze, L. (2023). Role of AI Chatbots in Education: Systematic Literature Review. *International Journal of Educational Technology in Higher Education, 20*(1), 56. DOI: 10.1186/s41239-023-00426-1

Lameras, P., & Arnab, S. (2022). Power to the Teachers: An Exploratory Review on Artificial Intelligence in Education. *Information (Basel), 13*(1), 14. Advance online publication. DOI: 10.3390/info13010014

Li, S. and Yan, C. (2024). "Governing Decentralized Autonomous Organizations as Digital Commons." *Journal of Business Venturing Insights* 21. .DOI: 10.1016/j.jbvi.2024.e00450

Lin, H. (2007). The Ethics of Instructional Technology: Issues and Coping Strategies Experienced by Professional Technologists in Design and Training Situations in Higher Education. *Educational Technology Research and Development, 55*(5), 411–437. Advance online publication. DOI: 10.1007/s11423-006-9029-y

Lin, Y. T., & Jian, H. Y. (2023). Development of an Educational Chatbot System for Enhancing Students' Biology Learning Performance. *Wangji Wanglu Jishu Xuekan, 24*(2), 275–281. DOI: 10.53106/160792642023032402006

Liu, L., Subbareddy, R., & Raghavendra, C. G. (2022). AI Intelligence Chatbot to Improve Students Learning in the Higher Education Platform. *Journal of Interconnection Networks, 22*(Supp02), 2143032. Advance online publication. DOI: 10.1142/S0219265921430325

Lund, B. D., & Wang, T. (2023). Chatting about ChatGPT: How May AI and GPT Impact Academia and Libraries? *Library Hi Tech News, 40*(3), 26–29. Advance online publication. DOI: 10.1108/LHTN-01-2023-0009

Madhavan, G., Mythily, M., Sharon, R., & Isaac Ritharson, P. 2023. "Chatbots Embracing Artificial Intelligence Solutions to Assist Institutions in Improving Student Interactions." In *Proceedings of the International Conference on Circuit Power and Computing Technologies, ICCPCT 2023*. DOI: 10.1109/ICCPCT58313.2023.10245835

Mai, V., Neef, C. & Richert, A. (2022). "Clicking vs. Writing"—The Impact of a Chatbot's Interaction Method on the Working Alliance in AI-based Coaching. Coaching Theor. Prax. 8, 15–31. https://doi.org/10.1365/s40896-021-00063-3DOI: 10.1108/LHTN-01-2023-0009

McAlister, A. R., Alhabash, S., & Yang, J. (2024). Artificial Intelligence and ChatGPT: Exploring Current and Potential Future Roles in Marketing Education. *Journal of Marketing Communications*, *30*(2), 166–187. Advance online publication. DOI: 10.1080/13527266.2023.2289034

McNealy, J. E. (2023). "Who's Liable?: Agency and Accountability in Human–Machine Communication." In *The Sage Handbook of Human–Machine Communication*. DOI: 10.4135/9781529782783.n52

Men, L. R., Zhou, A., & Wan, H. S. T. (2022). Harnessing the Power of Chatbot Social Conversation for Organizational Listening: The Impact on Perceived Transparency and Organization-Public Relationships. *Journal of Public Relations Research*, *34*(1–2), 20–44. Advance online publication. DOI: 10.1080/1062726X.2022.2068553

Mendoza, S., Hernández-León, M., Sánchez-Adame, L. M., Rodríguez, J., Decouchant, D., & Meneses-Viveros, A. (2020). Supporting Student-Teacher Interaction through a Chatbot. In. Lecture Notes in Computer Science: Vol. 12206. *Including Subseries Lecture Notes in Artificial Intelligence and Lecture Notes in Bioinformatics)*. LNCS., DOI: 10.1007/978-3-030-50506-6_8

Mendoza, S., Sánchez-Adame, L. M., Urquiza-Yllescas, J. F., González-Beltrán, B. A., & Decouchant, D. (2022). A Model to Develop Chatbots for Assisting the Teaching and Learning Process. *Sensors (Basel)*, *22*(15), 5532. Advance online publication. DOI: 10.3390/s22155532 PMID: 35898035

Mokmin, N. A. M., & Ibrahim, N. A. (2021). The Evaluation of Chatbot as a Tool for Health Literacy Education among Undergraduate Students. *Education and Information Technologies*, *26*(5), 6033–6049. Advance online publication. DOI: 10.1007/s10639-021-10542-y PMID: 34054328

Murtarelli, G., Gregory, A., & Romenti, S. (2021). A Conversation-Based Perspective for Shaping Ethical Human–Machine Interactions: The Particular Challenge of Chatbots. *Journal of Business Research*, *129*, 927–935. Advance online publication. DOI: 10.1016/j.jbusres.2020.09.018

Nguyen, Q. N., Sidorova, A., & Torres, R. (2022). User Interactions with Chatbot Interfaces vs. Menu-Based Interfaces: An Empirical Study. *Computers in Human Behavior, 128*, 107093. Advance online publication. DOI: 10.1016/j.chb.2021.107093

Okonkwo, Chinedu Wilfred, and Abejide Ade-Ibijola. (2021). "Chatbots Applications in Education: A Systematic Review." *Computers and Education: Artificial Intelligence*. .DOI: 10.1016/j.caeai.2021.100033

Oliveira, J. D. S., Espindola, D. B., Barwaldt, R., Luciano, M. I. R., & Pias, M. (2019). "IBM Watson Application as FAQ Assistant about Moodle." In *Proceedings - Frontiers in Education Conference, FIE*. Vol. 2019-October. DOI: 10.1109/FIE43999.2019.9028667

Papa, R., & Jackson, K. M. (2021). "Enduring Questions, Innovative Technologies: Educational Theories Interface with AI." In *Intelligent Computing - Proceedings of the 2021 Computing Conference*. DOI: 10.1007/978-3-030-80126-7_51

Payton, S., & Hague, C. (2010). *Digital Literacy in Practice: Case Studies of Primary and Secondary Classrooms*. Futurelab.

Pereira, J., Fernández-Raga, M., Osuna-Acedo, S., Roura-Redondo, M., Almazán-López, O., & Buldón-Olalla, A. (2019). Promoting Learners' Voice Productions Using Chatbots as a Tool for Improving the Learning Process in a MOOC. *Technology, Knowledge and Learning, 24*(4), 545–565. Advance online publication. DOI: 10.1007/s10758-019-09414-9

Pérez, J. Q., Daradoumis, T., & Joan, M. M. P. (2020). Rediscovering the Use of Chatbots in Education: A Systematic Literature Review. *Computer Applications in Engineering Education, 28*(6), 1549–1565. Advance online publication. DOI: 10.1002/cae.22326

Polyportis, A., & Pahos, N. (2024). Understanding Students' Adoption of the ChatGPT Chatbot in Higher Education: The Role of Anthropomorphism, Trust, Design Novelty and Institutional Policy. *Behaviour & Information Technology*. Advance online publication. DOI: 10.1080/0144929X.2024.2317364

Rahman, A. M., Abdullah, A. M., and Alma, I. (2018). "Programming Challenges of Chatbot: Current and Future Prospective." In *5th IEEE Region 10 Humanitarian Technology Conference 2017, R10-HTC 2017*. Vol. 2018-January. DOI: 10.1109/R10-HTC.2017.8288910

Ramandanis, D., & Xinogalos, S. (2023). *Designing a Chatbot for Contemporary Education: A Systematic Literature Review*. Information., DOI: 10.3390/info14090503

Razzaq, A. (2024). A Web3 Secure Platform for Assessments and Educational Resources Based on Blockchain. *Computer Applications in Engineering Education, 32*(1), e22677. Advance online publication. DOI: 10.1002/cae.22677

Reiss, M. J. (2021). The Use of AI in Education: Practicalities and Ethical Considerations. *London Review of Education, 19*(1). Advance online publication. DOI: 10.14324/LRE.19.1.05

Riel, J. 2020. "Essential Features and Critical Issues with Educational Chatbots: Toward Personalized Learning via Digital Agents." In *Handbook of Research on Modern Educational Technologies, Applications, and Management (2 Vol.)*. DOI: 10.4018/978-1-7998-3476-2.ch015

Rukhiran, M., Phaokla, N., & Netinant, P. (2022). Adoption of Environmental Information Chatbot Services Based on the Internet of Educational Things in Smart Schools: Structural Equation Modeling Approach. *Sustainability (Basel), 14*(23), 15621. Advance online publication. DOI: 10.3390/su142315621

Salomon, G. (1988). AI in Reverse: Computer Tools That Turn Cognitive. *Journal of Educational Computing Research, 4*(2), 123–139. Advance online publication. DOI: 10.2190/4LU7-VW23-EGB1-AW5G

Savin-Baden, M., Tombs, G., & Bhakta, R. (2015). Beyond Robotic Wastelands of Time: Abandoned Pedagogical Agents and New Pedalled Pedagogies. *E-Learning and Digital Media, 12*(3–4), 295–314. Advance online publication. DOI: 10.1177/2042753015571835

Sharkey, A. J. C. (2016). Should We Welcome Robot Teachers? *Ethics and Information Technology, 18*(4), 283–297. Advance online publication. DOI: 10.1007/s10676-016-9387-z

Shue, E., Liu, L., Li, B., Feng, Z., Li, X., & Hu, G. (2023). Empowering Beginners in Bioinformatics with ChatGPT. *Quantitative Biology, 11*(2), 105–108. Advance online publication. DOI: 10.15302/J-QB-023-0327 PMID: 37378043

Sjödén, B. (2020). When Lying, Hiding and Deceiving Promotes Learning - A Case for Augmented Intelligence with Augmented Ethics. In. Lecture Notes in Computer Science: Vol. 12164. *Including Subseries Lecture Notes in Artificial Intelligence and Lecture Notes in Bioinformatics)*. LNAI., DOI: 10.1007/978-3-030-52240-7_53

Su, J., & Yang, W. (2022). *"Artificial Intelligence in Early Childhood Education: A Scoping Review." Computers and Education: Artificial Intelligence*. Elsevier B.V., DOI: 10.1016/j.caeai.2022.100049

Taecharungroj, V. (2023). 'What Can ChatGPT Do?' Analyzing Early Reactions to the Innovative AI Chatbot on Twitter. *Big Data and Cognitive Computing*, *7*(1), 35. Advance online publication. DOI: 10.3390/bdcc7010035

Tam, W., Huynh, T., Tang, A., Luong, S., Khatri, Y., & Zhou, W. (2023). Nursing Education in the Age of Artificial Intelligence Powered Chatbots (AI-Chatbots): Are We Ready Yet? *Nurse Education Today*, *129*, 105917. Advance online publication. DOI: 10.1016/j.nedt.2023.105917 PMID: 37506622

Thorat, V. A., Rao, P., Joshi, N., Talreja, P., & Shetty, A. (2024). The Role of Chatbot GPT Technology in Undergraduate Dental Education. *Cureus*. Advance online publication. DOI: 10.7759/cureus.54193 PMID: 38496058

Traymbak, S., Sharma, M., Anand, A., & Shukla, A. (2024). Chatbot Technology in the Education Sector: A Bibliometrics Analysis Using VOS Viewer. *International Journal of System Assurance Engineering and Management*. Advance online publication. DOI: 10.1007/s13198-023-02230-6

Wang, Y. (2021). Artificial Intelligence in Educational Leadership: A Symbiotic Role of Human-Artificial Intelligence Decision-Making. *Journal of Educational Administration*, *59*(3), 256–270. Advance online publication. DOI: 10.1108/JEA-10-2020-0216

Wu, E. H. K., Chun, H. L., Ou, Y. Y., Chen, Z. L., Wei, K. W., & Chi, Y. C. (2020). Advantages and Constraints of a Hybrid Model K-12 E-Learning Assistant Chatbot. *IEEE Access : Practical Innovations, Open Solutions*, *8*, 77788–77801. Advance online publication. DOI: 10.1109/ACCESS.2020.2988252

Xue, J., Wang, Y.-C., Wei, C., Liu, X., Woo, J., & Jay Kuo, C.-C. (2024). Bias and Fairness in Chatbots: An Overview. *APSIPA Transactions on Signal and Information Processing*, *13*(2). Advance online publication. DOI: 10.1561/116.00000064

Yang, J., Chen, Y. L., Por, L. Y., & Ku, C. S. (2023). *A Systematic Literature Review of Information Security in Chatbots*. Applied Sciences., DOI: 10.3390/app13116355

Yu, L., & Yu, Z. (2023). Qualitative and Quantitative Analyses of Artificial Intelligence Ethics in Education Using VOSviewer and CitNetExplorer. *Frontiers in Psychology*, *14*, 1061778. Advance online publication. DOI: 10.3389/fpsyg.2023.1061778 PMID: 36968737

Zabel, S., & Otto, S. (2021). Bias in, Bias Out – the Similarity-Attraction Effect Between Chatbot Designers and Users. In. Lecture Notes in Computer Science: Vol. 12764. *Including Subseries Lecture Notes in Artificial Intelligence and Lecture Notes in Bioinformatics)*. LNCS., DOI: 10.1007/978-3-030-78468-3_13

Zhang, C., Li, G., Hashimoto, H., & Zhang, Z. 2022. "Digital Transformation (DX) for Skill Learners: The Design Methodology and Implementation of Educational Chatbot Using Knowledge Connection and Emotional Expression." In *IEEE Global Engineering Education Conference, EDUCON*. Vol. 2022-March. DOI: 10.1109/EDUCON52537.2022.9766384

Zhou, J., Chen, F., Berry, A., Reed, M., Zhang, S., & Savage, S. 2020. "A Survey on Ethical Principles of AI and Implementations." In *2020 IEEE Symposium Series on Computational Intelligence, SSCI 2020*. DOI: 10.1109/SSCI47803.2020.9308437

Chapter 13
Gamification of Learning to Boost Students' Motivation and Study Engagement

Laila Zeroual
Abdelmalek Essaâdi University, Morocco

ABSTRACT

First introduced in the early 2010s, the term "gamification" is now widely used. It has been implemented in fields as varied as marketing and healthcare or crowd-sourcing. Here, the authors focus on its use in education. Today, many students lack motivation and show little interest for learning in class. Given the choice, many would rather play video games than read a book or complete an assignment. This study was conducted to identify the potential effects of gamification on learner motivation and engagement. The study was carried out involving students enrolled at a Moroccan university. The major findings of the study showed that gamification had a positive effect on students' lives. This was shown by their greater motivation to learn and their commitment to taking part in the games.

DOI: 10.4018/979-8-3693-2973-3.ch013

INTRODUCTION

First introduced in the early 2010s, the term "gamification" is now widely used. It has been implemented in fields as varied as marketing and healthcare (Huotari and Hamari, 2017; Wilson and McDonagh, 2014), or crowdsourcing (Venhuizen et al., 2013). Here, we focus on its use in education (Kapp, 2012).

Today, many students lack motivation and show little interest for learning in class. Given the choice, many would rather play video games than read a book or complete an assignment.

New generations of learners (generations Z and Alpha) are raising the need for new pedagogical strategies and tools. In the literature, we find the components that define this new generation of learners (Hamel, 2021): motivation by affect, need for recognition, difficulty in accepting constructive criticism, diminished sense of responsibility, few links between effort and result, "zapping" phenomenon, hyper-connected and socializing via screens, search for immediacy, generations evolving in an environment of technological objects. More and more, learners find themselves drawn in by their phones, social media or even games.

One possible way of making education more relevant to real-life skills and more engaging for learners is through gamification. Simulators were initially developed by large companies to train staff in complex situations that would be difficult to handle in the real world, and have been the cornerstone in the evolution of digital technologies, particularly in the world of video games. Widely adopted and acclaimed by our modern society, games and simulations have emerged as communication and awareness-raising tools in the form of educational games.

As Prensky (2001) argues, whilst there is no magic recipe, educators can design the perfect mix of education and entertainment to suit their students' needs and context, as validated by a number of other research studies. an entire educational module becomes a game. It is based on the use of digital technologies, particularly from the world of video games. However, gamification is a demanding approach for educators, and an engaging one for learners. Meanwhile, the researcher has enthusiastically presented the solution to learner disengagement through the combination of education and entertainment; thus, the term edutainment takes its place,

In our study, we are focusing on games with a learning objective. Learning through play, or ludopedagogy (Wareham-Morris & McGowan, 2018) learning is learner-centred and offers opportunities to the learner for specific tasks that require propositional and functional knowledge to succeed in learning objectives (Eaton, 2017).

By reallocating the notion of "gamification" to the teaching or educational sector, we aim to verify its influence on learners' motivation and engagement via their responses to the various questions in the administered survey and the results of the statistical tests used.

To gain an understanding of this causal relationship, we will first introduce the concept of gamification, then focus on the raltion between our three basic notions of gamification, motivation and engagement. Next, we shall outline the interest of our subject and the research methodology we adopted. Finally, we will discuss the results of our quantitative study.

CONCEPTUALIZING GAMIFICATION

While gamification is not a new concept, the term itself was introduced in the 2000s (Brühlmann, 2017; Yang et al., 2017). At the time, the term didn't attract much attention. It was only a few years later, from 2010 onwards, that it became increasingly popular (Huotari and Hamari, 2012; Robson et al., 2015).

Gamification is a very broad concept, the idea being to use game and game-design elements (reward, points, levels, resources, missions, characters or avatar, progression, challenges, feedback, collaboration, luck ...) in non-game contexts (Deterding et al., 2011).

The most straightforward definition of gamification refers to the use of game elements in a non-game context (Dale, 2014, González et al., 2016; Attali and Arieli-Attali, 2015;) . This very broad definition makes it possible to cover a large number of forms of play, including the use of narrative, competition (e.g., points and scoreboards) or rewards (e.g., badges, experiences).

Zichermann and Cunningham (2011) define gamification as "using game thinking and game mechanics to engage users and solve problems". Gamification is a process that can be implemented to meet certain objectives, which will vary from one organization to another.

Huotari and Hamari (2017) According to them, "gamification refers to a process that enhances a service with suggestive capabilities for gamified experiences, with the aim of supporting overall user value creation" (p. 25). This definition emphasizes the purpose of gamification rather than the method.

We can therefore draw a conclusion stating that there is no consensus on the definition of gamification among researchers. For Kapp (2012) pedagogical strategy is altered to fit game elements in which, instead of learning objectives, the teacher of a gamified classroom will present a challenge or quest that players must undertake to lead them to the learning experience.

In other words, a game is a system of action shaped by predefined rules, with variable and measurable outcomes, scenarios, options and efforts, in which the player feels involved and takes action, rather than just being a passive learner (Juul, 2005). The immersive capacity of games has earned them a place in the world of education, and "within the range of active pedagogies, they offer a privileged means of involving learners, notably through immersion in a realistic universe" (Sanchez E, 2019).

Gamification can provide learners with ongoing opportunities to improve their knowledge through spontaneous feedback while academic tasks are instilled throughout the gaming experience (Imed Bouchrika et al 2019). Folmar's (2015) gamification characterization captured an important idea in the application of gamification in learning and other fields: game thinking. Folmar described gamification as the use of game thinking and game mechanics for non-game purposes.

Connecting Gamification to Motivation and Engagement

LTwo closely related and often overlapping concepts in the fields of intrinsic motivation and cognitive engagement are motivation and engagement (Guthrie, Willinger and You, 2012). Despite this strong link between motivation and engagement, the two terms are not synonymous, and the presence of one does not necessarily mean that the other will emerge. As explained by Appleton, Christenson, Kim and Reschly (2006), motivation and engagement are important in learning, but they need to be kept separate as independent concepts.

The consensus among researchers is that gamification has effects on learning and the enhancement of the learning objective, although these are difficult to demonstrate. These effects mainly concern engagement and motivation.

Engagement

Over the years, the concept of engagement has become increasingly present in various disciplines such as education and psychology (Vivek et al., 2014). Authors such as Pomerantz (2006), Downer, Rimm-Kaufman and Pianta (2007) define engagement as a concept with a behavioral dimension. Van Doorn et al (2010) highlight the behavioral manifestation. This behavioral dimension is in most cases prescribed, but some add the cognitive and/or emotional, or even social dimension (Vivek et al., 2014).

Engagement is defined as "the intensity of an individual's involvement and connection with an organization's services and/or activities, which is initiated either by the consumer or by the organization" (Vivek et al., 2012, p. 133).

Other researchers have focused on observable aspects of engagement such as learners' behaviors, their effort and dedication in completing schoolwork, as well as their levels of participation and attendance (Ryan, 2000).

In addition, gamification is considered an experience facilitator (Yang et al., 2017). An enjoyable and successful experience will lead to a state of flow (Hamari & Koivisto, 2014). Commitment is the potential outcome of a successful experience (Leclercq et al., 2017). Gamification is one of the facilitating mechanisms that have been introduced to improve the experience, and in the long term, engagement (Robson et al., 2015).

Prensky (2001), game features can provide the entertainment part of the game. a pedagogical design needed to engage learners. Borrowing game elements and incorporating them into the classroom environment can facilitate engagement.

Indeed, Kuh (2009) has historically tracked the concept of engagement, from its meaning in terms of the time learners spend on the task, to the outcome and achievement of learning, the quality of student effort, student interaction and immersion in the learning experience, and finally, his own definition, to the quality and effort learners invest in an authentic activity. It is worth noting that the common theme in all the definitions discussed by Kuh (2009) is the visible aspect of engagement as manifested in learners' behavior towards the learning experience, and in the quality and time invested in the learning task. However, assimilating engagement with time on task is unfair if we wish to fully grasp the significance of the term.

In many studies, students' levels of engagement increased considerably after the introduction of game elements. From the perspective that engagement is the prospect of a long-term relationship (Leclercq et al., 2017), Hofacker et al. (2016) mention that motivations are key. As a result, a person will be more inclined to be engaged if he or she is motivated to participate in the experience.

H2: Gamification is positively related to study engagement.

Motivation

Although gamification has become an increasingly popular practice (Yang et al., 2017), implementing gamification mechanisms simply because they work in other organizations is not advisable. First and foremost, it's important to understand what motivates learners to take part in these interactions (Hamari et al., 2014). Then mechanisms can be put in place to address them (Poncin et al., 2017).

Indeed, more and more studies show that people learning through a game are more motivated, learn faster and understand better (Panagiotis, 2016). The study by (Sanchez & Gómez Trigueros, 2019) also shows a positive effect of gamification on motivation in terms of interest and fun.

Thus, the study by Alomari et al. (2019) reviewed several gamification techniques that can be used in different university courses. The results showed the role of certain game elements such as points, badges and leaderboards in effective learning and in keeping learners motivated and engaged.

Baptista, (2019) shows at least 21 improvements of gamification on the task. These include fun, 65 a sense of usefulness, intention to do the task again, attitude, learning opportunities, and socialization.

The ambition of this type of training is to make use of playful resources to place learners at the heart of the learning process, making them actors in their own training and encouraging them to take an active role in consolidating their knowledge.

By facilitating the acquisition of skills within a heterogeneous class, while creating commitment and maintaining motivation among learners so that they persevere and progress in their learning (Perrenoud, 2015 et al.)

The relationship between intrinsic and extrinsic motivation. At a theoretical level, gamification is largely based on the use of extrinsic rewards: badges, experience, points, upward or downward comparisons with others, or positive feedback. According to cognitive appraisal theory (Deci & Ryan, 1985), external events modify intrinsic motivation (i.e., doing this because I want to, not because I have to), depending on the event's controllability. If the event, e.g. the reward, serves the information it conveys, it will tend to make the player feel competent and in control of the game, increasing intrinsic motivation. However, rewarding the player in a controlling way, forcing him to play in a certain way or at a pace that doesn't suit him, will make him feel powerless and incompetent, reducing his intrinsic motivation. Furthermore, giving extra rewards to a task that is interesting in itself reduces motivation to do it (Deci & Ryan, 2000). So, we need to be very careful about using gamification for rewards, at the risk of reducing participants' intrinsic motivation.

Malone (1980), in his work on intrinsic motivation, states that a situation is considered “challenging” when it involves objectives with uncertain outcomes. It is with this uncertainty that certain gamification mechanisms will play to motivate people. Uncertainty creates suspense, which in turn increases the perceived challenge and hence the enjoyment of a game (Brümann, 2016).

H2: Gamification is positively related to students’ motivation.

MATERIALS AND METHODS

To test our hypotheses, we collected data from a university in Morocco. We began our study by administering a questionnaire to students at bac+3, bac+4 and bac+5 levels, which was then modified several times before reaching a final version that was both correct in form and content. We ensured that their participation was voluntary, following the principle of convenience sampling we adopted, and that their responses would be used solely for research purposes.

We distributed our questionnaire to 300 students and received 230 validated responses. The response rate was **%. The descriptive statistics of the sample is as follows: In terms of gender, 44% are men and 56% are women

To further test the research hypotheses and confirm causal relationships, a latent variable structural equation modeling, partial least squares (PLS) estimation procedure, using SmartPLS3 software, was used, with a double evaluation of the research model components. External and internal.

RESULTS DISCUSSION

Measurement Model / Other Model Test

Reliability and Convergent Validity

Table 2 covers the measurement of item reliability (loading>0.70), construct reliability (C.R.>0.70) and average variance extracted (A.V.E.>0.50)

Table 1. Concept reliability and convergent validity of the measurement model

Constructs	Items	Scores factoriels (Loading)	A.V.E	Fiabilité Composite C.R)
Gamification	GAM1	0,857	0,633	0,897
	GAM2	0,809		
	GAM3	0,787		
	GAM4	0,720		
	GAM5	0,722		
Motivation	MT1	0,820	0,748	0,899
	MT2	0,876		
	MT3	0,893		
Engagement	ENG1	0,868	0,789	0,945
	ENG2	0,851		
	ENG3	0,892		
	ENG4	0,935		

In this table, the survey scales and their internal consistency are presented, showing that for the responses provided, all composite reliability measures were well above the recommended level of 0.70. Reliability scores found ranged from

(0.8 to 0.9) values above the suggested threshold, indicating good internal consistency (Nunnally, J. C.; 1978).

Furthermore, there is adequate convergent validity when the constructs have an average variance extracted (AVE) of at least 0.5 (Fornell, C., & Larcker, D. F.; 1981) and, as shown in the table above, all AVE values are above the threshold value of 0.5 and range between (0.5 and 0.7). Lastly, for most of the scales, item saturation is higher than or equal to (0.7).

Discriminant Validity

Table 3's discriminant validity is based on the assumption that the manifest variable correlates as well with its own latent variable as with the other latent variables, and that each latent variable better explains its own manifest variables. The test is carried out using the criterion proposed by Fornell, C., & Larcker, D. F. (1981) and the “Cross Loading” criterion for manifest variables.

--The criterion of Fornell, C., & Larcker, D. F. (1981). states that a latent variable should better account for the variance of its own manifest variables than for the variance of other latent variables. This means, strictly speaking, that the A.V.E. of a latent variable should be higher than the square of the correlations between the latent variable and all other variables.

--The cross-loading criterion: A manifest variable's contributions to the latent variable attributed to it must be greater than those of all other latent variables.

Table 2. Concept correlation with the square root of the mean variance

	AVE	Gamification	Motivation	Engagament
Gamification	0,633	0,860		
Motivation	0,748	0,733	0,802	
Engagement	0,789	0,643	0,537	0,889

We notice that the results provided meet the Franll and Harcket criterion already presented above and are therefore satisfactory (the factorial weight of a dimension on a given construct is greater than all its factorial weights on the other constructs). This finding is also confirmed by cross-validation.

Hypothesis Testing

Internal model evaluation consists in testing the research hypotheses, by verifying the significance of the causal relationships between the latent variables.

The following table provides a summary of the various hypothesized relationships in our research model, along with the estimated coefficients and their significance.

Table 3. Summary of hypothesis validation results

Hypothesis	β-standardized= Path coefficient	T-Value	P-Value	Hypothesis status
Trust -> Collaboration	0,644	11,676	0,000**	Validated
Training quality -> Service quality	0,590	12,473	0,000**	Validated
Information system quality -> Information quality	0,518	11,522	0,000**	Validated

+P<,15 ;*P<,10 ;**P<,05 ; ***P<,01 / NS: not significant

This table shows the T-values and P-values for the dogene variables in the model.

DISCUSSION

Our research hypotheses were supported by statistically significant results (the results also covered a range of sub-hypotheses). The following section will discuss our research hypotheses, while linking them to previous theoretical studies.

The Effect of Gamification to Study Engagement and Students' Motivation

The main appeal of gamification is that it introduces a playful dimension and a spirit of competition. Not only does it make your training programs more dynamic, it also significantly increases learner engagement. Competition is an effective lever for boosting student motivation and commitment over the long term, simply because it adds a sense of satisfaction and encourages effortless learning. Winning trophies, gaining access to new levels or winning exclusive items are all rewards that create real motivation, even when the exercise is technical and serious. This in turn adds a certain lightness and competitive edge. Whatever the game, the desire to win adds interest. Apply this motivational lever to learning.

Gamification can be used to increase student engagement, change perceptions and behavior, and develop skills through a different approach (Cheong, Flippou and Cheong 2014). Gamification also makes it possible to personalize learning, combat bad stress (de-dramatization of errors) and encourage mutual support. In addition, gamification provides regular feedback, ensuring that training is followed up and, above all, that it is understood. The trainer can have direct feedback on its impact on students, and so fine-tune it to suit any needs, and understand and explore the interaction between various factors in the pedagogical approach (Prieto-Andreu et al., 2022).

For successful learning, pleasure and pedagogy go hand in hand. Pleasure is essential in a gamification process. Playing a game doesn't feel like learning, it feels like having fun. Learners memorize faster when they're having fun.

It's one of the things that keeps video game players engaged and coming back for more. Gamification borrows the playful element from video games not only to win learners' commitment, but also to positively increase their motivation. The combination of high motivation and high task engagement results in successful learning experiences (Davis and McPartland, 2012). gamification is considered an experience facilitator (Yang et al., 2017).

Another very important element is pedagogy. A training course needs to be personalized and individualized so that the learner feels involved. Setting goals for learners to achieve. These objectives can be set by the trainers or by the learners themselves. A reward system can also be put in place.

With gamification, the learner is not in a passive posture: he or she is an actor in the training process, putting into practice what he or she has learned. The theoretical concepts imparted are applied to real-life situations within the framework of the game. This means that the learner internalizes the concepts more quickly, enabling him or her to consolidate what has been learned. What's more, learners can apply the new knowledge they have acquired in the real world, based on situations experienced during game activities. What's more, gamification is a powerful lever for strengthening team cohesion, instilling a spirit of positive competition and promoting teaching quality (Hernández-Fernández et al., 2020; Arufe Giráldez et al., 2022).

CONCLUSION

Gamification has proved to be an effective technique for stimulating engagement and motivation, but in education, further research is required to provide evidence of its benefits on both students' affective states and their learning outcomes.

Most notably, it has contributed to understanding how gamification affects the engagement and learning behavior of university students. Future research could investigate the effect of gamification in various disciplines and universities.

REFERENCES

Alomari, I., Al-Samarraie, H., & Yousef, R. (2019). The Role of Gamification Techniques in *Promoting Student Learning*: A Review and Synthesis. *Journal of Information Technology Education, 18*, 395–417. DOI: 10.28945/4417

Appleton, J. J., Christenson, S. L., Kim, D., & Reschly, A. L. (2006). Measuring cognitive and psychological engagement: Validation of the Student Engagement Instrument. *Journal of School Psychology, 44*(5), 427–445. DOI: 10.1016/j.jsp.2006.04.002

Arufe Giráldez, V., Sanmiguel-Rodríguez, A., Ramos Álvarez, O., & Navarro-Patón, R. (2022). Can gamification influence the academic performance of students? *Sustainability (Basel), 14*(9), 5115. DOI: 10.3390/su14095115

Attali, Y., & Arieli-Attali, M. (2015). Gamification in assessment: Do points affect test performance? *Computers & Education, 83*, 57–63. DOI: 10.1016/j.compedu.2014.12.012

Baptista, G., & Oliveira, T. (2019). Gamification and serious games : A literature metaanalysis and integrative model. *Computers in Human Behavior, 92*, 306–315. DOI: 10.1016/j.chb.2018.11.030

Catteeuw, F. E. F., & Vonderhorst, J. (2007). Employee engagement: Boosting productivity in turbulent times. *Organization Development Journal, 25*(2), 151–157.

Cheong, C., Filippou, J., & Cheong, F. (2014). Toward the gamification of learning: Investigating student perceptions of game elements. *Journal of Information Systems Education, 25*(3), 233.

Dale, S. (2014). Gamification: Making work fun, or making fun of work? *Business Information Review, 31*(2), 82–90. DOI: 10.1177/0266382114538350

Davis, M. H., & McPartland, J. M. (2012). High School Reform and Student Engagement. In Christenson, S. L., Reschly, A. L., & Wylie, C. (Eds.), *Handbook of Research on Student Engagement* (pp. 515–539). Springer US., DOI: 10.1007/978-1-4614-2018-7_25

Deterding, S. (2011, September 15). Gamification Research Network. Retrieved from A Quick Buck by Copy and Paste: http://gamification-research.org/2011/09/a-quick-buck-bycopy-and-paste/

Downer, J. T., Rimm-Kaufman, S. E., & Pianta, R. C. (2007). How do classroom conditions and children's risk for school problems contribute to children's behavioral engagement in learning? *School Psychology Review, 36*(3), 413–432. DOI: 10.1080/02796015.2007.12087938

Eaton, M. (2017). The flipped classroom. *The Clinical Teacher, 14*(4), 301–302. DOI: 10.1111/tct.12685 PMID: 28703501

Folmar, D. (2015). *Game it up: Using gamification to incentivize your library.* Rowman & Littlefield.

Fornell, C., & Larcker, D. F. (1981). Evaluating Structural Equation Models with Unobservable Variables and Measurement Error. *JMR, Journal of Marketing Research, 18*(1), 39. DOI: 10.2307/3151312

González, C. S., Gómez, N., Navarro, V., Cairós, M., Quirce, C., Toledo, P., & Marrero-Gordillo, N. (2016). Learning healthy lifestyles through active videogames, motor games and the gamification of educational activities. *Computers in Human Behavior, 55*, 529–551. DOI: 10.1016/j.chb.2015.08.052

Groh, F. (2012). Gamification: state of the art definition and utilization. In Proceedings of the 4th seminar on Research trends in media information, (pp. 39-46). February 14. Ulm

Guthrie, J. T., Guthrie, A., & You, W. (2012). Instructional Contexts for Engagement and Achievement in Reading. In Christenson, S. L., Reschly, A. L., & Wylie, C. (Eds.), *Handbook of Research on Student Engagement* (pp. 601–634). Springer US., Retrieved from http://link.springer.com/10.1007/978-1-4614-2018-7_29 DOI: 10.1007/978-1-4614-2018-7_29

Hamari, J., & Koivisto, J. (2014). Measuring flow in gamification: Dispositional flow scale-2. *Computers in Human Behavior, 40*, 133–143. DOI: 10.1016/j.chb.2014.07.048

Hernández-Fernández, A., Olmedo-Torre, N., & Peña, M. (2020). Is classroom gamification opposed to performance? *Sustainability (Basel), 12*(23), 9958. DOI: 10.3390/su12239958

Hofacker, C. F., de Ruyter, K., Lurie, N. H., Manchanda, P., & Donaldson, J. (2016). Gamification and Mobile Marketing Effectiveness. *Journal of Interactive Marketing, 34*(1), 25–36. DOI: 10.1016/j.intmar.2016.03.001

Huotari, K., & Hamari, J. (2017). A definition for gamification: Anchoring gamification in the service marketing literature. Electronic Markets, (27/1), p. 21-31.

JUUL J. (2005). *Half-Real: Video Games Between Real Rules and Fictional Worlds*. MIT Press.

Kapp, K. M. (2012). The Gamification of Learning and Instruction: Game-based Methods and Strategies for Training and Education.

Kuh, G. D. (2009). The national survey of student engagement: Conceptual and empirical foundations. *New Directions for Institutional Research*, *2009*(141), 5–20. DOI: 10.1002/ir.283

Leclercq, T., Poncin, I., & Hammedi, W. (2017). The engagement process during value co-creation: Gamification in new product development platforms. *International Journal of Electronic Commerce*, *21*(4), 454–488.

Malone, T. W. (1980). What makes things fun to learn? Heuristics for designing instructional computer games. In *Proceedings of the 3rd ACM SIGSMALL symposium and the first SIGPC symposium on Small systems* (pp. 162–169). ACM. DOI: 10.1145/800088.802839

Mekler, E. D., Brühlmann, F., Tuch, A. N., & Opwis, K. (2017). Towards understanding the effects of individual gamific. elements on intrinsic motivation and performance. *Computers in Human Behavior*, *71*, 525–534. DOI: 10.1016/j.chb.2015.08.048

Nunnally, J. C. (1978). *Psychometric theory* (2nd ed.). McGraw-Hill.

Panagiotis, F., Theodoros, M., Leinfellner, R., & Yasmine, R. (2016). Climbing Up the Leaderboard : An Empirical Study of Applying Gamification Techniques to a Computer Programming Class. *Electronic Journal of e-Learning*, *14*, 94–110.

Perrenoud, P. (2015). Travail réel des enseignants et formation. *Recherches & Educations*, *14*, 205–208.

Pomerantz, N. K. (2006). Student engagement: A new paradigm for student affairs. *The College Student Affairs Journal*, *25*(2), 176–185.

Poncin, I., Garnier, M., Slim Ben Mimoun, M., & Leclercq, T. (2017). Smart technologies and shopping experience: Are gamification interfaces effective? The case of the Smartstore. *Technological Forecasting and Social Change*, *124*, 1–12. DOI: 10.1016/j.techfore.2017.01.025

Prensky, M. (2001). *Digital game-based learning*. McGraw Hill.

Prieto-Andreu, J. M., Gómez-Escalonilla-Torrijos, J. D., & Said-Hung, E. (2022). Gamification, motivation, and performance in education: A systematic review. Rev. Electrón. *Educare (San José)*, *26*, 251–273.

Robson, K., Plangger, K., Kietzmann, J. H., McCarthy, I., & Pitt, L. (2015). Is it all a game? Understanding the principles of gamification. *Business Horizons*, *58*(4), 411–420. DOI: 10.1016/j.bushor.2015.03.006

Robson, K., Plangger, K., Kietzmann, J. H., McCarthy, I., & Pitt, L. (2015). Is it all a game? Understanding the principles of gamification. *Business Horizons*, *58*(4), 411–420. DOI: 10.1016/j.bushor.2015.03.006

Ryan, R. M., & Deci, E. L. (2000). Self-Determination Theory and the Facilitation of Intrinsic Motivation, Social Development, and Well-Being. *The American Psychologist*, *55*(1), 11. DOI: 10.1037/0003-066X.55.1.68 PMID: 11392867

Ryan, R. M., & Deci, E. L. (2000). Self-determination theory and the facilitation of intrinsic motivation, social development, and well-being. *The American Psychologist*, *55*(1), 56–68. DOI: 10.1037/0003-066X.55.1.68 PMID: 11392867

Sánchez, D. O., & Trigueros, I. M. G. (2019). Gamification, social problems, and gender in the teaching of social sciences : Representations and discourse of trainee teachers. *PLoS One*, *14*(6), e0218869. DOI: 10.1371/journal.pone.0218869 PMID: 31242248

Sánchez, D. R., Langer, M., & Kaur, R. (2019). Gamification in the classroom : Examining the impact of gamified quizzes on student learning. *Computers & Education, 103666*. Advance online publication. DOI: 10.1016/j.compedu.2019.10366

Van Doorn, J., Lemon, K. E., Mittal, V., Nab, S., Pick, D., Pirner, P., & Verhoef, P. C. (2010). Customer engagement behavior: Theoretical foundations and research directions. *Journal of Service Research*, *13*(3), 253–266. DOI: 10.1177/1094670510375599

Venhuizen, N. J., Basile, V., Evang, K., & Bos, J. 2013. Gamification for Word Sense Labeling. In *Proceedings of the 10th International Conference on Computational Semantics (IWCS 2013) – Short Papers*, pages 397–403, Potsdam, Germany. Association for Computational Linguistics.

Vivek, S. D., Beatty, S. E., Dalela, V., & Morgan, R. M. (2014). A generalized multidimensional scale for measuring customer engagement. *Journal of Marketing Theory and Practice*, *22*(4), 401–420. DOI: 10.2753/MTP1069-6679220404

Wareham-Morris, K., & McGowan, J. (2018). Gamified Learning : A Rationale for Ludopedagogy and Gamified Classrooms. *Worcester Journal of Learning and Teaching*, *12*, 23–31.

Wilson, A. S., & McDonagh, J. E. (2014). A Gamification Model to Encourage Positive Healthcare Behaviours in Young People with Long Term Conditions. *EAI Endorsed Transactions on Game-Based Learning*, *1*(2), e3. Advance online publication. DOI: 10.4108/sg.1.2.e3

Yang, Y., Asaad, Y., and Dwivedi, Y. (2017). Examining the impact of gamification on intention of engagement and brand attitude in the marketing context, Computers in Human Behavior, Volume 73, Pages 459-469, ISSN 0747-5632, DOI: 10.1016/j.chb.2017.03.066

Zichemann, G. & Cunningham, C. (2011). Gamification by design: Implementing game mechanics in web and mobile apps. CA: O'Reilly Media Inc.

Chapter 14
Advancements in Educational Technology:
Navigating the Landscape of User Experience in Web 3.0

Pankaj Bhambri
https://orcid.org/0000-0003-4437-4103
Guru Nanak Dev Engineering College, India

Sita Rani
https://orcid.org/0000-0003-2778-0214
Guru Nanak Dev Engineering College, India

ABSTRACT

The talk commences with analyzing the influence of user experience in e-learning and the transition from Web 2.0 technologies to the current Web 3.0 paradigm. The chapter delves into the theory and application of designing contemporary ubiquitous interfaces, with a focus on the significance of developing immersive and captivating learning environments. This study delves at the role of serious games and entertainment technologies in improving educational experiences, with a focus on their capacity for facilitating successful learning. The investigation encompasses the utilization of online communities and social media platforms for both business and education, emphasizing the interdependent nature of digital engagements. The chapter explores the importance of human-computer interaction in meeting the varied demands of learners and customers. It highlights the function of interfaces in structuring educational experiences.

DOI: 10.4018/979-8-3693-2973-3.ch014

1.1 INTRODUCTION

The development of educational technology in the era of Web 3.0 is notably impacted by constructivism, social learning theory, and cognitive load theory, all of which make distinct contributions to the overall user experience (Dudley and Kachka, 2019). Constructivism places significant emphasis on the value of interactive and learner-centered environments, wherein users are encouraged to actively construct knowledge by means of personalized and engaging digital experiences.

Language barriers represent an additional noteworthy issue. Localization and multilingual support should be incorporated into Web 3.0 technologies in order to accommodate non-native speakers and users of various dialects (Lave and Wenger, 2019). This promotes inclusivity by guaranteeing that educational materials are readily comprehensible and accessible to a wider range of individuals. It is of the utmost importance that educational technologies are culturally sensitive (Lave and Wenger, 2019).

1.1.1 Transforming Education in the 21st Century: The Role of EdTech

EdTech, short for educational technology, refers to the use of technology to improve and simplify the process of teaching and learning. It encompasses the use of diverse digital technologies, resources, & platforms into educational environments to facilitate instructional goals, involve learners, and enhance educational results (Bhambri and Khang, 2024d). EdTech leverages innovations such as online learning platforms, interactive multimedia, virtual reality, and artificial intelligence to create more dynamic and personalized learning experiences (Chen and Chen, 2018). It aims to address diverse learning styles, foster collaboration, and provide access to educational resources beyond traditional boundaries, making education more inclusive and adaptable to the evolving needs of learners in the 21st century.

1.1.2 Evolution of the Web: From Static Pages to Intelligent Interaction

The progression of web technologies can be classified into three discrete stages: Web 1.0, Web 2.0, and Web 3.0. Web 1.0, sometimes known as the "static web," originated during the early stages of the internet, with a primary emphasis on unidirectional communication, where users were limited to information consumption solely (Means and Neisler, 2019). During this era, websites were static and lacked interactivity, serving as repositories of information without much user engagement. The shift to Web 2.0 marked a transformative period, characterized by dynamic, user-generated content and increased interactivity. This phase saw the rise of social media platforms, blogging, and collaborative online tools that empowered users to actively contribute, share, and interact with content. Web 2.0 laid the foundation for a more participatory and interconnected digital landscape. Web 3.0 endeavours to enhance user experience through the utilisation of advanced technologies such as machine learning, artificial intelligence, and the incorporation of decentralised technologies like blockchain (Evans, 2019).

1.1.3 Importance of User Experience in Educational Technology

The importance of user experience (UX) in educational technology lies at the core of effective learning outcomes and engagement. A positive UX enhances the overall usability and accessibility of educational tools, ensuring that learners can easily navigate, understand, and interact with the content (Aguilar, 2015). Intuitive design and user-friendly interfaces contribute to increased student motivation, as they can focus more on the educational material rather than struggling with the technology itself (Gee, 2019). Moreover, a well-crafted UX considers diverse learning styles and promotes inclusivity, accommodating a broad range of users.

1.1.4 Constructivism, Social Learning Theory, and Cognitive Load Theory

Constructivism highlights the active process of learners constructing knowledge. Based on constructivist concepts, learning is not a passive process of absorbing knowledge, but rather an active process where individuals actively build their understanding of the world via interactions with their surroundings (Bhambri and Khang, 2024e). When considering the use of technology in education, this viewpoint emphasizes the significance of including students in genuine, interactive activities that allow them to investigate, modify, and generate utilizing technical instruments. Instead of seeing technology as a simple tool for delivering information, constructivism promotes the idea that educators should create learning environments that use technology to foster investigation, teamwork, and the creation of knowledge. Constructivism emphasizes the importance of social contact and collaboration in the process of learning. Within the realm of technology integration, this entails acknowledging the capacity of digital platforms and tools to enhance communication, cooperation, and knowledge exchange among students, as well as between students and professors (Bhambri and Khang, 2024a). Through the use of technology, educators can facilitate collaborative learning experiences that enable students to actively construct knowledge through dialogue, negotiation, and collective sense-making. Constructivism emphasizes the significance of offering chances for students to contemplate their learning experiences, establish links between new information and their current comprehension, and participate in metacognitive processes that deepen their understanding of content and improve their capacity to apply knowledge to novel situations. Viewed from this perspective, the incorporation of technology serves not just as a method to provide teaching, but also as a stimulus for engaging, cooperative, and thoughtful learning encounters that are in line with constructivist principles.

Psychologist Albert Bandura's social learning theory states that individuals acquire knowledge and skills by seeing, imitating, and modeling the behaviors, attitudes, and outcomes of others. This theory highlights the significance of social interactions and the influence of the environment in molding behavior. In the context of incorporating technology into education, the social learning theory proposes that students acquire knowledge not only through explicit instruction but also by witnessing how their peers, teachers, and other prominent individuals in their educational setting utilize technology. This implies that the effective incorporation of technology in education should encompass more than just granting access to technology. It should also encompass the creation of chances for collaborative learning, peer teaching, and demonstration of proficient technology utilization (Bhambri et al., 2024a). The social learning theory emphasizes the importance of reinforcement and feedback in the process of learning. Within the realm of incorporating technology into education, this means that students are more inclined to embrace and continue using technology when they receive favorable encouragement and feedback from their social surroundings. Teachers have a vital role in giving helpful feedback and motivation, while peers can provide support and reinforcement through collaborative learning experiences. Through comprehension and implementation of the ideas of the social learning theory, educators have the ability to create learning environments that utilize technology to encourage active participation, collaboration, and ongoing progress, resulting in improved educational results.

As per the Central Limit Theorem, the working memory has a finite capacity, and when it becomes overwhelmed, it hinders the process of learning. Cognitive Load Theory (CLT) categorizes cognitive burden into three distinct types: intrinsic, external, and relevant. Intrinsic cognitive load pertains to the inherent intricacy of the activity, whereas external cognitive load comprises the cognitive strain caused by instructional design components that are unrelated to the learning objectives. Germane cognitive load refers to the mental work required to organize and integrate new knowledge into existing cognitive systems. Through the optimization of instructional design to reduce unnecessary cognitive load and improve relevant cognitive load, educators can effectively promote learning and boost the retention of knowledge. When examining the incorporation of technology in education from the perspective of CLT, it is crucial to assess the impact of technological instruments on cognitive load. The design and deployment of technology can either reduce or increase cognitive burden (Bhambri and Khang, 2024b). Efficiently constructed educational technology can assist in the learning process by offering customized help and minimizing unnecessary mental effort. Nevertheless, inadequately designed technology or an excessive dependence on it might inundate pupils with irrelevant information or intricate interfaces, so augmenting unneeded cognitive load and impeding learning outcomes. Thus, by utilizing the principles of CLT in the development and assessment of educational technology, educators can make well-informed choices on its incorporation, guaranteeing that it improves rather than hinders the learning process.

1.2 FOUNDATIONS OF EDUCATIONAL TECHNOLOGY

Foundations of educational technology encompass the fundamental principles and theoretical underpinnings that guide the integration of technology into the educational landscape (Siemens, 2018). Grounded in pedagogy, psychology, and instructional design, these foundations emphasize the thoughtful and intentional use of technology to enhance teaching and learning. Educational technology foundations include theories such as constructivism, which emphasizes active learning and knowledge construction, and cognitive load theory, which guides the optimal presentation of information (Zawacki-Richter et al., 2016). Additionally, principles from educational psychology, such as motivation and learning styles, play a crucial role in designing technology-driven learning experiences. Comprehending these fundamental principles is crucial for educators or instructional designers to efficiently utilize technology as a tool to assist a wide range of learners, encourage involvement, and facilitate significant educational experiences.

1.2.1 Evolution of Educational Technology: From Radio to AI

Beginning with the advent of educational radio and television in the early 20th century, technological advancements continued to shape educational practices (Al-Azawei et al., 2016). The introduction of multimedia projectors, computers, and educational software in the mid-20th century marked a significant shift towards interactive learning tools. The emergence of the internet in the late 20th century further transformed educational landscapes, leading to the development of online courses, e-learning platforms, and virtual classrooms (Downes, 2018). In recent years, mobile devices, augmented reality, and artificial intelligence have played pivotal roles in shaping the educational technology landscape (Li et al., 2018). This historical evolution reflects a continuous effort to harness technology to improve access to education, enhance instructional methodologies, and adapt to the changing needs of learners in an increasingly digital world.

- **Evolution of Educational Technology (From Traditional Teaching Methods to Digital Integration):** With the emergence of digital technology, specifically computers and the internet, a significant change in perspective started to occur. Digital tools not only improved the effectiveness of administrative work, but also provided interactive learning platforms, multimedia resources, and customized learning experiences. With the progress of digital integration, educational technology has broadened to include a wide range of tools and platforms, such as Learning Management Systems (LMS), virtual classrooms, educational apps, and interactive simulations (Bhambri and Rani, 2024c). These technologies have made education more accessible to people throughout the world by removing geographical limitations and offering high-quality learning materials.
- **Influence of Behaviorism, Constructivism, and Connectivism on Educational Technology:** Behaviorism, a psychological approach that originated in the early 20th century, places emphasis on observable behaviors and the correlations between stimuli and responses in the process of learning. Behaviorism has had a significant impact on the development of computer-based instructional programs and simulations in the field of educational technology. These programs and simulations are designed to give learners quick feedback, which helps to reinforce desired behaviors. For example, educational software frequently integrates gamification aspects, in which learners receive rewards for finishing tasks or reaching milestones, reflecting the ideas of behaviorist reinforcement. Contrarily, constructivism asserts that learning is a dynamic process of creating knowledge by drawing upon previous experiences and engaging in social relationships. Connectivism, within the realm of educational technology, emphasizes the significance of online networks, social media, and digital resources in promoting learning (Bhambri et al., 2024b). Online communities, social learning platforms, and personalized recommendation systems utilize the ideas of connectivism to facilitate learners' access to knowledge, collaboration with peers, and participation in distributed learning networks.

1.2.2 Key Concepts in Educational Technology

Comprehending behaviorism entails acknowledging that human behavior is predominantly influenced by environmental stimuli and reinforcing systems. Behaviorists prioritize the study of behaviors that can be directly observed and the external circumstances that impact them, rather than giving attention to internal cognitive processes. In the field of educational technology, behaviorist ideas are frequently utilized by employing techniques such as operant conditioning. This involves reinforcing desired behaviors through positive feedback or incentives, while discouraging undesirable actions through consequences or withholding reinforcement. By integrating behaviorist ideas into educational technology, educators can design captivating and efficient learning experiences that promote desired behaviors and facilitate the development of skills.

To explore constructivism, one must comprehend that learners actively construct their own knowledge and understanding through interactions with their environment and experiences. In the field of educational technology, constructivist concepts are utilized to promote active learning through the provision of chances for students to participate in practical activities, collaborative projects, and real-world problem-solving assignments.

Utilizing social learning theory in digital educational settings entails acknowledging the significance of social interactions and cooperative learning experiences in the educational process. This method places significant emphasis on the influence of peers, mentors, and communities in determining learning outcomes, drawing upon the theories of Bandura, Vygotsky, and Wenger. Social learning theory can be implemented in digital educational settings by incorporating features such as online discussion forums, group projects, peer feedback mechanisms, and collaborative document editing tools. These technologies enable the exchange of knowledge, collaborative resolution of problems, and the joint creation of understanding among learners (Bhambri and Rani, 2024d).

Cognitive Load Theory (CLT) provides valuable insights into the cognitive processes involved in information processing and proposes strategies to enhance learning experiences, especially in the digital era where excessive information can overwhelm individuals. CLT posits that learners possess a finite ability to process information, and hence, instructional design should focus on properly managing cognitive load to prevent overwhelming learners' cognitive resources. In digital educational settings, this approach can be implemented by delivering information in small, digestible portions, reducing unnecessary cognitive load by removing distractions or irrelevant content, and carefully organizing learning materials to support steady skill development.

Figure 1.1 illustrates the components of the System of Educational Technologies. The figure includes various elements such as hardware, software, network connections, and interactive interfaces. Arrows and labels demonstrate the flow and interaction between these components, highlighting the integrated nature of the educational technology system.

Figure 1. The components of the system of educational technologies

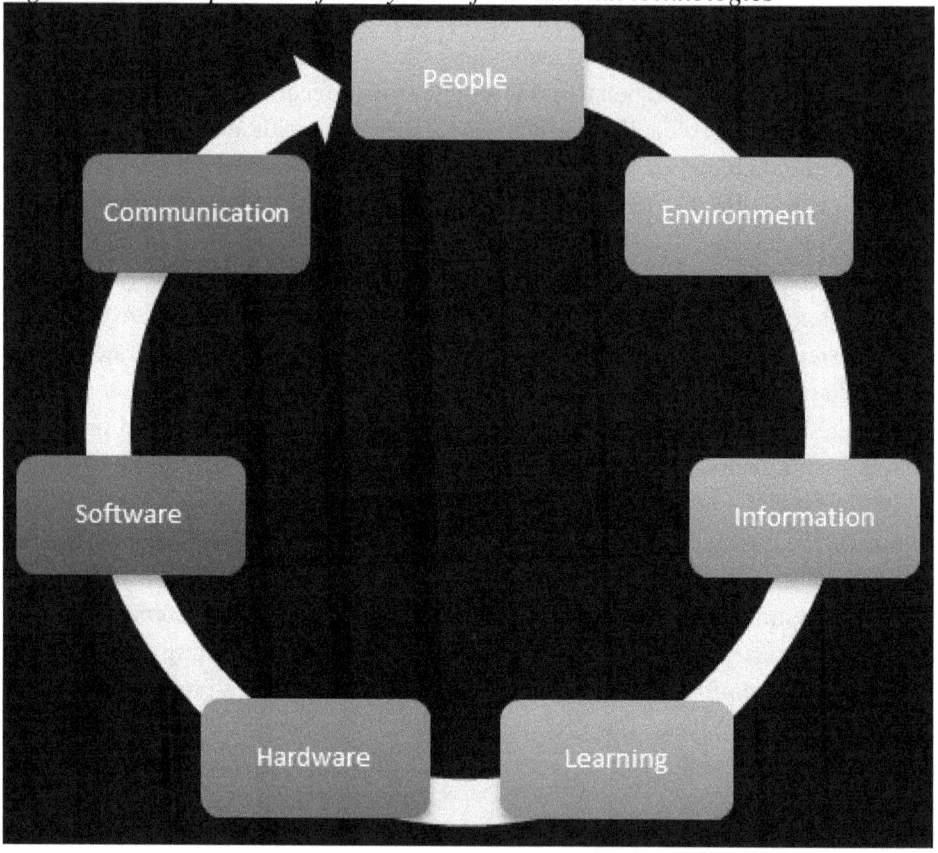

These key concepts provide a foundation for educators, instructional designers, and policymakers to navigate the dynamic landscape of educational technology and its applications in diverse learning environments. Some fundamental concepts include:

- **Digital Literacy:** It refers to the capacity to effectively use, comprehend, and assess technology and data across different situations (Gardner, 2017).
- **Pedagogy:** The art and science of teaching, focusing on instructional methods, strategies, and the overall approach to facilitating learning.
- **Blended Learning:** The integration of conventional in-person teaching with online learning elements, utilizing both tangible and digital instructional resources (Lin et al., 2019).
- **Adaptive Learning:** The use of technology to personalize learning experiences, tailoring content and pacing to meet individual student needs.

- **Gamification:** Incorporating game elements and principles into educational activities to enhance engagement and motivation (Reeves et al., 2017).
- **Flipped Classroom:** Adopting a flipped teaching approach by providing educational material online prior to in-person sessions, and utilizing face-to-face interactions for practical application and discussion.
- **LMS:** An online platform that enables the organization, distribution, and monitoring of educational materials and tasks.
- **Assistive Technology:** Tools and devices designed to support individuals with disabilities, enabling them to engage more effectively in learning activities (West, 2019).
- **Open Educational Resources (OER):** OER encompass educational products such as textbooks or multimedia content that are accessible without cost and can be utilized, altered, and distributed.
- **Augmented Reality (AR) and Virtual Reality (VR):** Immersive technologies refer to technologies that enhance the learning experience by overlaying digital content onto the actual world or by generating simulated environments.

1.2.3 Integration of Technology in Education

By integrating technologies such as whiteboards that are interactive, educational software, internet-based tools, and collaborative platforms, instructors have the ability to establish dynamic and captivating environments for learning (Kirschner and van Merriënboer, 2013). When effectively implemented, technology becomes a powerful enabler, empowering both educators and learners to navigate an ever-evolving educational landscape.

- **Application of Learning Theories in Educational Technology Integration:** The integration of social interaction features such as discussion forums and collaborative projects is informed by social learning theory, which promotes knowledge sharing and peer collaboration. The design of digital materials is guided by cognitive load theory to effectively control cognitive load, thereby enabling learners to efficiently process and retain information. By amalgamating these learning theories, educators can utilize the whole capacity of educational technology to generate captivating, efficient, and individualized learning encounters that accommodate various learning styles and requirements.
- **Strategies for Aligning Technological Tools with Pedagogical Frameworks:** The process of alignment commences with establishing a comprehensive comprehension of instructional objectives, such as cultivating critical thinking or advancing collaborative learning. Teachers should there-

after choose technology resources that align with these objectives, taking into account variables such as accessibility, usability, and suitability for the learning environment. The integration of the selected technologies should be purposeful, taking into account how they can complement current educational techniques and improve student engagement. Professional development and training are essential for educators to acquire the necessary skills and expertise to effectively utilize these tools. Regular assessment and contemplation of the congruity between technology and pedagogy are crucial for continuously improving teaching methods and maximizing learning results.

- **Case Studies Demonstrating Effective Integration of Learning Theories and Technology:** There are numerous case studies that showcase successful integration of learning theories with technology, highlighting creative methods that maximize learning results. For example, a high school science teacher used VR simulations in a constructivist-inspired method to fully engage pupils in intricate scientific ideas. This allowed them to actively investigate and control chemical structures within 3D surroundings. The VR simulations fostered profound comprehension and mastery of concepts by involving students in practical experimentation and exploration. In a social learning setting, an online learning platform incorporates discussion forums and collaborative project spaces, allowing students to participate in peer-to-peer knowledge sharing and the joint creation of understanding. By actively engaging in online communities of practice, learners not only gained knowledge of the subject matter but also cultivated vital skills such as critical thinking, communication, and cooperation, which are crucial for success in the digital era. These case studies exemplify the symbiotic relationship between learning theories and technology, illustrating how deliberate integration may enrich learning experiences and enable students to cultivate a lifetime commitment to learning. By integrating technological tools with pedagogical frameworks and applying the principles of behaviorism, constructivism, social learning theory, and cognitive load theory, educators can establish interactive and efficient learning environments that accommodate various learning styles and needs. This approach ultimately promotes enhanced comprehension and long-term retention of knowledge.

1.2.4 Digital Divide, Language Barriers, and the Need for Culturally-Responsive Educational Technologies

The development and implementation of educational technologies should be culturally responsive to the needs and backgrounds of diverse learners. Culturally responsive educational technologies acknowledge and incorporate students' cultural backgrounds, experiences, and perspectives into the learning process. This approach fosters a sense of belonging and relevance for students, promoting engagement and learning outcomes. Culturally responsive technologies can help address cultural biases and stereotypes embedded in educational materials, ensuring that content is respectful and representative of diverse cultures and identities (Bhambri and Khang, 2024c). To effectively address cultural and contextual considerations in educational technology integration, collaboration among stakeholders is essential. This includes educators, technology developers, policymakers, and community members working together to identify and address barriers to access and effectiveness. Ongoing research and evaluation are needed to assess the impact of technology integration on diverse populations and to refine approaches to ensure inclusivity and cultural responsiveness. By prioritizing equity and cultural sensitivity in the design and implementation of educational technologies, we can strive towards creating learning environments that are accessible, relevant, and empowering for all learners, regardless of their cultural or contextual backgrounds.

1.3 WEB 3.0: A PARADIGM SHIFT

Web 3.0 represents a significant paradigm shift in the digital landscape, emphasizing decentralized, user-centric interactions and a more intelligent, context-aware internet. In the realm of academia and business, this evolution brings forth profound impacts on UX. With the increased emphasis on decentralization and user control in Web 3.0, academic institutions can explore innovative approaches to collaborative learning, research, and knowledge dissemination (Bower et al., 2017). Businesses, on the other hand, are poised to benefit from enhanced customer engagement, personalized services, and improved data security. The user experience in Web 3.0 becomes a pivotal factor, influencing not only how individuals interact with information but also shaping the success of academic initiatives and business ventures. As Web 3.0 unfolds, stakeholders in academia and business must adapt to these changes, embracing the transformative potential of decentralized, user-centric digital experiences.

1.3.1 Understanding Web 3.0 and Its Characteristics

Unlike its predecessors, Web 3.0 focuses on enhancing user experiences through technologies like artificial intelligence, machine learning, and decentralized networks (Becker et al., 2017). The core characteristics of Web 3.0 include semantic understanding, allowing the web to interpret and respond to user queries contextually (Laurillard, 2017). The interoperability of data and services across different platforms and applications is also a central tenet, fostering a more seamless and connected online environment. In essence, Web 3.0 represents a sophisticated and user-centric phase of the internet; where intelligent algorithms, decentralized architectures, and enhanced connectivity converge to redefine how we interact with information and services online.

1.3.2 Implications for Educational Technology

With the integration of advanced technologies like artificial intelligence and blockchain, educational platforms can offer tailored content and adaptive learning paths, catering to individual student needs (Rienties and Kinchin, 2014). Decentralized identity and credentialing systems enabled by Web 3.0 can enhance the security and integrity of educational records, providing a more transparent and verifiable way to validate academic achievements. Smart contracts and blockchain can streamline administrative processes such as enrollment, certification, and resource allocation, reducing bureaucracy and enhancing overall efficiency. Additionally, the interoperability of data across educational platforms fosters seamless collaboration and data sharing, allowing for a more holistic and comprehensive understanding of student progress (Waycott et al., 2017). Overall, Web 3.0 has the potential to revolutionize educational technology, creating a more dynamic, personalized, and transparent learning environment.

1.3.3 User Experience Considerations in Web 3.0

The decentralized nature of Web 3.0, enabled by technologies like blockchain, underscores the importance of ensuring transparent, secure, and intuitive interactions for users navigating through decentralized applications and platforms. Semantic understanding, a key feature of Web 3.0, implies that user interfaces should prioritize contextual relevance, providing personalized and meaningful content (Clark and Mayer, 2016). Interoperability becomes crucial as users engage with a diverse range of platforms, necessitating seamless data and service integration. In navigating this evolving digital landscape, designers and developers must prioritize user empowerment, data privacy, and fluid cross-platform experiences to capitalize on the transformative potential of Web 3.0 and offer users an enhanced, trustworthy, and cohesive online environment.

1.3.4 Limitations and Challenges Associated With Integration of Technologies

Considerable prospects and noteworthy obstacles are presented by the incorporation of cutting-edge technologies into education, including artificial intelligence, blockchain, and immersive technologies. Although AI in education can provide streamlined administrative support and individualized learning experiences, it can also give rise to apprehensions regarding data privacy, algorithmic prejudice, and the dehumanization of the learning process. Effective operation of AI systems frequently necessitates vast quantities of data, which raises concerns regarding data security and student privacy. Without meticulous design and monitoring, AI algorithms have the potential to sustain preexisting biases, thereby resulting in disparities in educational achievements.

To overcome these obstacles, a comprehensive strategy is required. Critical measures for AI include the enforcement of rigorous data protection regulations, the conduction of routine audits to detect and rectify biases, and the maintenance of transparency in the decision-making processes of AI. In addition, educators and students should receive training on the implications of AI tools.

1.3.5 Research Findings and Statistical Evidences

The field of educational technology, particularly in the context of Web 3.0, has received significant attention in recent years. Empirical research, case studies, and statistical evidence all confirm that educational technologies are successful and have a significant influence, especially in the context of Web 3.0. Educational technology have the ability to change education and empower learners globally by expanding access to education, promoting learning outcomes, enabling personalized learning experiences, and preparing students for the future workforce. Although anecdotal evidence suggests its usefulness, empirical data, research findings, case studies, and statistical evidence offer a more definitive knowledge of its influence. Here's an overview of some key points:

- **Improved Access to Education:** An important consequence of educational technologies, particularly in Web 3.0, is their capacity to democratize the availability of education. Studies conducted by reputable institutions such as UNESCO and the World Bank have demonstrated that online learning platforms, digital libraries, and open educational resources (OERs) have effectively reduced the disparity in educational access, especially in distant or underserved regions.

- **Enhanced Learning Outcomes:** Multiple research have shown that incorporating educational technologies into conventional teaching techniques can result in enhanced learning outcomes. An instance of this may be seen in a meta-analysis published in the Journal of Computing in Higher Education, which discovered that the integration of traditional face-to-face training with online components, known as blended learning, led to greater student accomplishment when compared to either solely face-to-face or purely online instruction.
- **Personalized Learning:** Web 3.0 technologies, such as adaptive learning platforms and AI-driven educational tools, provide customized learning experiences that are specifically designed to meet the unique needs and learning preferences of each student. Studies undertaken by esteemed institutions such as the Gates Foundation and the RAND Corporation have demonstrated that implementing individualized learning methods can result in heightened student engagement, motivation, and academic achievement.
- **Data-Driven Decision Making:** Educational technology produce huge quantities of data regarding student performance, involvement, and progress in learning (Spector et al., 2013). Examining this data can offer significant perspectives for educators to customize lessons, identify children who are at risk, and evaluate the efficacy of teaching methodologies. Research has demonstrated that educational institutions that utilize data analytics tools have observed enhancements in student achievements and institutional efficiency.
- **Skill Development for the Future Workforce:** Due to the swift progress of technology, there is an increasing need for those who possess digital literacy and specific expertise. Educational technologies are essential in equipping students with the necessary skills and knowledge to succeed in the future job market. These technologies offer practical learning experiences, foster cooperation, and facilitate the development of skills in coding, robotics, and digital design.
- **Cost-Effectiveness and Scalability:** Although the initial financial commitment to educational technology infrastructure and resources may be significant, research has demonstrated that it can ultimately result in cost reductions for educational institutions. Online courses and virtual classrooms can decrease expenses related to physical infrastructure and enable universities to access a wider audience, hence enhancing scalability.
- **Case Studies and Success Stories:** Various case studies and success stories demonstrate the significant and positive effects of instructional technologies in a wide range of environments, including K-12 schools, higher education institutions, and corporate training programs. For example, platforms like as Khan Academy, Coursera, and Codecademy have successfully reached a vast

number of learners globally and have played a crucial role in making high-quality education accessible to all.

1.4 CURRENT STATE OF EDUCATIONAL TECHNOLOGY IN WEB 3.0

Educational platforms leveraging Web 3.0 technologies aim to enhance learning experiences through decentralized content creation, distribution, and credentialing, reducing reliance on traditional centralized authorities. The semantic understanding capabilities of Web 3.0 contribute to personalized and adaptive learning experiences, tailoring educational content to individual needs (Siemens and Tittenberger, 2009).

1.4.1 Analysis of Existing Educational Technology Platforms

Blockchain technology, a cornerstone of Web 3.0, is increasingly being explored in existing platforms for secure and transparent credential verification. However, interoperability remains a challenge, with many educational technologies struggling to seamlessly integrate with decentralized ecosystems (Steinkuehler and Duncan, 2008). The analysis underscores the need for educational platforms to adapt to the evolving Web 3.0 landscape, emphasizing decentralized structures, semantic intelligence, and secure, transparent credentialing to truly harness the transformative potential of emerging technologies in education.

1.4.2 User Experience Trends in Web 3.0 Education

As Web 3.0 continues to shape the educational landscape, several user experience trends have emerged, redefining how learners engage with content and interact within decentralized educational ecosystems (Bhambri and Rani, 2024a). One notable trend is the emphasis on personalized learning experiences driven by semantic understanding. With intelligent algorithms, educational platforms in Web 3.0 can analyze user behavior, preferences, and learning styles to deliver customized content and adaptive assessments. Decentralized credentialing systems, powered by blockchain, are gaining prominence, ensuring secure, transparent, and verifiable records of academic achievements. Interoperability remains a key focus, allowing seamless integration of educational resources and services across different platforms, providing a cohesive and user-friendly experience (Prensky, 2018). As Web 3.0 education evolves, these user experience trends underscore a commitment to user empowerment, personalization, and technological innovation in the pursuit of more effective and inclusive learning experiences.

1.4.3 Case Studies and Best Practices

The latest developments in the field of educational technology and Web 3.0 for the most up-to-date case studies and best practices are as under:

- **Blockchain in Education:** Holberton School, a project-based alternative to college education, uses blockchain to secure and verify student credentials. Blockchain ensures the integrity of educational records, making it easier for employers to verify graduates' qualifications.
- **Decentralized Learning Platforms:** BitDegree is a blockchain-based platform that incentivizes learning through token rewards. Students can earn tokens by completing courses and use them to access premium content or even receive job offers. This model promotes continuous learning and skill development.
- **VR and AR in Education:** zSpace provides AR and VR solutions for education. It allows students to interact with virtual objects in a 3D space, enhancing their understanding of complex subjects like anatomy or physics. This technology provides an immersive learning experience.
- **Smart Contracts for Credentialing:** The collaboration between MIT Media Lab and Learning Machine resulted in the creation of Blockcerts, a system that use blockchain technology to issue, view, and authenticate academic credentials. Smart contracts ensure the validity of certificates, and graduates have control over sharing their achievements.
- **AI-Powered Personalized Learning:** DreamBox is an adaptive learning platform that uses artificial intelligence to personalize lessons for each student. It adjusts content based on individual progress, ensuring that students receive targeted instruction to meet their unique learning needs.
- **Open Educational Resources (OER) on the Blockchain:** LBRY Credits is a decentralized content-sharing platform that can be applied to educational resources. It allows creators to publish content and be compensated directly by consumers through blockchain-based transactions, eliminating intermediaries.

1.5 ETHICAL AND PRIVACY CONSIDERATIONS

Although blockchain technology provides improved security and transparency for educational transactions, it also gives rise to issues around the permanence of data and the right to have information erased, as well as the possibility of sensitive information being exposed through unchangeable records.

1.5.1 Guidelines

By adhering to the guidelines, educational stakeholders can foster a culture of trust, transparency, and respect for privacy in the development and implementation of technologies within the evolving landscape of Web 3.0. Guidelines for addressing these ethical and privacy concerns in educational technologies within the context of Web 3.0 include:

- **Data Encryption and Decentralized Storage:** Deploy resilient encryption protocols to safeguard confidential information during transmission and storage. Employ decentralized storage solutions that disperse data among several nodes, thereby diminishing the likelihood of singular points of failure and unwanted access.
- **User Consent and Control:** Give utmost importance to obtaining user consent and enable learners to have full control over their personal data. Offer clear and unambiguous policies and consent methods that enable individuals to make well-informed choices regarding the gathering, utilization, and dissemination of their data. Facilitate the ability for users to withdraw their consent and efficiently control their privacy choices.
- **Privacy by Design:** Incorporate privacy considerations into the design and development of educational technologies from the beginning. Implement privacy-preserving concepts such as data minimization, purpose limitation, and user anonymity to reduce the gathering and storage of superfluous personal information.
- **Transparency and Accountability:** Ensure clear and open communication about data practices and the organizations that control them. Develop explicit guidelines and protocols for the management of data, encompassing aspects such as data accessibility, sharing, and retention. Ensure that stakeholders are held responsible for adhering to ethical and regulatory norms by conducting frequent audits and assessments.
- **Ethical Use of AI and Analytics:** Guarantee that the algorithms and analytics utilized in educational technology are created and implemented in an ethical manner. To reduce the possibility of algorithmic bias and prejudice, it is important to regularly assess and examine AI systems for fairness, transparency, and accountability.
- **Education and Awareness:** Encourage the development of knowledge and skills in using digital technology and raise awareness about the rights and responsibilities related to privacy among educators, learners, and other individuals involved. Deliver training and provide tools to enhance users' com-

prehension of the consequences of data privacy and security in educational settings.

1.6 CHALLENGES AND OPPORTUNITIES

Striking a balance between innovation and ethical considerations is crucial. Moreover, addressing the digital divide and ensuring equitable access to these technologies becomes imperative to harness the full potential of educational advancements in the Web 3.0 era (Yilmaz, 2018). Effectively overcoming these hurdles offers the potential to transform education, creating a dynamic and efficient learning environment that accommodates all learning styles and requirements.

1.6.1 Addressing User Experience Challenges in Web 3.0 Education

The decentralized and immersive nature of Web 3.0 offers exciting opportunities to revolutionize educational experiences through enhanced interactivity, personalized learning, and decentralized content creation. However, navigating this landscape also poses challenges such as ensuring seamless integration of emerging technologies, addressing potential accessibility issues, and maintaining data security and privacy (Hrastinski, 2017). Striking a balance between harnessing the full potential of Web 3.0 for education and mitigating its inherent challenges requires a comprehensive approach that involves collaboration between educators, technologists, and policymakers to shape a user-centric and inclusive educational technology ecosystem.

1.6.2 Opportunities for Innovation and Improvement

The rapid evolution of technology offers unprecedented opportunities for enhancing educational experiences through immersive and personalized learning platforms (Koohang et al., 2009). However, with these advancements come challenges such as ensuring accessibility, inclusivity, and addressing potential ethical concerns in the implementation of emerging technologies. The multifaceted landscape of Web 3.0 introduces novel possibilities like blockchain-based educational credentials and decentralized learning ecosystems. Navigating this complex terrain requires a careful balance between leveraging the potential for innovation and addressing the associated challenges to create a seamless and inclusive user experience that fosters effective learning in the digital era.

1.6.3 Balancing Technological Advancements with Pedagogical Goals

While embracing the potential of cutting-edge technologies, it is imperative to ensure that these advancements in educational technology align seamlessly with educational objectives and pedagogical strategies (Dede, 2017). The integration of Web 3.0 technologies should enhance rather than overshadow the learning experience, fostering engagement, collaboration, and critical thinking among students. Striking a harmonious balance between technological tools and pedagogical goals will not only optimize the educational experience but also contribute to the development of a technologically literate and intellectually adept generation capable of navigating the complexities of the modern world (Singh and Bhambri, 2023).

1.6.4 Limitations and Challenges Associated With the Integration of Technologies

Accessing expensive infrastructure and specialist skills is necessary for integrating these new technologies. This creates a digital divide and puts students and communities with minimal resources at a disadvantage (Wiggins and McTighe, 2005). Although blockchain technology presents advantages in terms of ensuring safe authentication and validation of educational credentials, its practical application encounters difficulties with scalability, interoperability, and regulatory frameworks. In order to address these difficulties, it is essential to give priority to fairness and inclusiveness while designing and implementing educational technologies. This entails guaranteeing that technology integration programs are available to all students, irrespective of their socioeconomic status or geographical position. Possible approaches to tackle the digital gap may involve implementing financial assistance programs to facilitate technology access, allocating resources towards the construction of infrastructure in underprivileged regions, and giving comprehensive training and assistance to educators and students to optimize the utilization of these technologies (Bhambri, 2024a). In order to overcome algorithmic bias in AI systems used for educational purposes, it is crucial to implement transparent and responsible algorithm design. Furthermore, continuous monitoring and evaluation should be conducted to discover and rectify any biases that may arise.

Ethical concerns arise when employing AI in education, encompassing matters of data privacy, algorithmic prejudice, and the dehumanization of learning encounters. Blockchain technology provides improved security and transparency for educational credentials and transactions. It encounters challenges in terms of scalability, interoperability, and regulatory compliance. Immersive technologies such as VR and AR necessitate substantial investment in both hardware and software, rendering them unattainable for several educational institutions and learners.

In order to address these difficulties, it is essential to adopt a comprehensive approach. Prioritizing the issue, it is crucial to make collaborative endeavors in order to tackle the digital gap by enhancing the availability of technology and internet connectivity, especially in marginalized groups. This may entail government initiatives, collaborations between the public and commercial sectors, and community-based programs with the goal of offering cost-effective equipment, internet connectivity, and training in digital literacy. It is imperative to prioritize the establishment of interoperability and standards in order to guarantee smooth integration and compatibility among various platforms and systems. Continued research and assessment are necessary to determine the effects of these technologies on teaching and learning outcomes, as well as their implications for fairness, variety, and inclusivity in education.

1.7 DESIGN PRINCIPLES FOR OPTIMAL USER EXPERIENCE

User experience design should prioritize accessibility, intuitiveness, and engagement to facilitate seamless interaction between students and the educational tools (Wang et al., 2015). A responsive and user-friendly interface, combined with clear navigation and thoughtful information architecture, contributes to an environment that fosters learning without unnecessary barriers.

1.7.1 Human-Centered Design in Educational Technology

Human-Centered Design (HCD) in educational technology places the learner at the forefront of the design process, prioritizing their needs, preferences, and overall user experience (Anderson, 2018). This approach recognizes that effective educational technology goes beyond functionality, emphasizing the importance of understanding and catering to the human aspects of learning. HCD involves engaging with educators, students, and other stakeholders to gather insights, empathize with their experiences, and incorporate their feedback into the design process. By adopting HCD principles, educational technology developers can create intuitive interfaces, personalized learning experiences, and adaptive tools that address the diverse needs of learners. This user-centric approach encourages the development of inclusive solutions, considering factors such as accessibility, cultural sensitivity, and different learning styles (Garrison et al., 2016). Ultimately, integrating Human-Centered Design into educational technology ensures that advancements are not only technologically robust but also genuinely enhance the teaching and learning experience, fostering a more engaging, effective, and student-centered educational environment.

1.7.2 Personalization and Adaptive Learning

Personalization involves customizing learning paths, content, and pace to match individual student needs and preferences. Adaptive learning takes this a step further by leveraging technology to dynamically adjust content and activities based on a learner's progress, strengths, and weaknesses. These advancements enable a more student-centric approach, fostering greater engagement and understanding (Johnson et al., 2015). Adaptive learning algorithms can analyze data on students' performance and preferences, providing real-time feedback and suggesting personalized learning materials. This not only accommodates diverse learning styles but also helps address gaps in understanding, promoting a more efficient and effective learning journey. The integration of personalization and adaptive learning in educational technology aligns with the recognition that each student learns differently, optimizing educational outcomes by tailoring the experience to the individual learner's needs (Kay, 2016). As technology continues to evolve, the synergy between personalization, adaptive learning, and educational technology holds immense promise for creating more inclusive, efficient, and effective learning environments.

1.7.3 Accessibility and Inclusivity in Web 3.0 Education

Web 3.0, characterized by increased interactivity, connectivity, and semantic understanding, has the potential to revolutionize education but must be designed with accessibility in mind (Chao and Lo, 2018). Incorporating features such as screen reader compatibility, text-to-speech options, and adjustable font sizes ensures that individuals with visual impairments or learning disabilities can access and engage with educational content (Mishra and Koehler, 2006). By embracing universal design principles, educational technology in Web 3.0 can break down barriers, making education accessible to a broader spectrum of learners and fostering a more equitable and inclusive educational landscape.

1.8 ETHICAL AND PRIVACY CONSIDERATIONS RELATED TO THE USE OF EDUCATIONAL TECHNOLOGIES

The decentralized structure of Web 3.0 brings about intricacies in data ownership and governance, prompting inquiries regarding the individuals or entities that own authority over student data and the manner in which it is being employed. In order to tackle these problems, it is imperative that educational institutions and technology developers give utmost importance to data privacy and security at every stage of the design and implementation process. This entails the adoption of strong encryption mechanisms, the implementation of strict access controls, and the regular performance of audits to guarantee adherence to data protection requirements. Openness plays a crucial role in establishing trust with people.

Algorithmic bias and discrimination are important ethical considerations in the field of educational technologies. AI algorithms utilized in educational applications may unintentionally sustain or intensify preexisting prejudices, resulting in unequal opportunities and outcomes for students from various backgrounds (Bhambri, 2024b). In order to reduce this danger, developers must give importance to ensuring justice and equality in the design of algorithms, by include techniques to identify and reduce prejudice. Teachers should encourage conversations about privacy, data ethics, and digital rights, enabling students to champion their own privacy and make ethical choices in digital settings. By cultivating a culture that promotes ethical utilization of technology in educational institutions, we can guarantee that the advantages of educational technologies are achieved while mitigating the potential hazards to privacy and ethics.

1.9 CASE STUDIES AND EXEMPLARS

Case Studies mentioning the showcase of successful educational technology implementations along with lessons learned from real-world examples and their impact on learning outcomes is mentioned below:

- **VR in Medical Education:** One compelling case study showcases the successful integration of virtual reality in medical education, providing an immersive learning experience for students. A medical school used VR simulations into surgical training, enabling students to engage in realistic virtual environments and rehearse intricate operations. The lessons learned from this implementation highlighted the significant improvement in students' spatial awareness and procedural skills. The impact on learning outcomes was evident, as students who engaged in VR-based training demonstrated increased confidence and proficiency in actual surgical settings (Rana et al., 2024). This case underscores the potential of educational technology to transform traditional learning methods and enhance skill acquisition.
- **Adaptive Learning Platforms in K-12 Education:** Another exemplar focuses on the deployment of adaptive learning platforms in K-12 education. A school district integrated personalized learning technologies that adapt

to individual student needs and pace. The platform collected data on students' progress and adjusted content accordingly, fostering a more tailored educational experience. The lesson learned from this case emphasizes the importance of leveraging data analytics to optimize personalized learning paths. The impact on learning outcomes was notable, with students showing improved academic performance and increased engagement. This case illustrates the potential of adaptive technologies to address diverse learning styles and enhance the overall effectiveness of education.

- **Gamification in Higher Education:** A third case study highlights the implementation of gamification principles in higher education to improve student engagement and collaboration. A university incorporated game elements into coursework, creating a competitive and interactive learning environment (Bhambri and Rani, 2024b). Lessons learned from this case emphasized the need for careful design to balance entertainment and educational goals. The impact on learning outcomes was positive, as students demonstrated increased motivation, participation, and knowledge retention. This case underscores the potential of gamification in fostering a more dynamic and enjoyable learning experience, particularly in the context of higher education.
- **Blockchain in Credentialing and Certification:** Exploring advancements in educational technology within the context of Web 3.0, a case study on blockchain in credentialing and certification provides insights into the secure and transparent validation of academic achievements. By leveraging blockchain technology, educational institutions can issue digital certificates and diplomas, ensuring the integrity and authenticity of credentials. The lessons learned from this implementation highlight the importance of decentralized and tamper-proof systems. The impact on learning outcomes is evident in the increased trust and recognition of digitally verified credentials, streamlining the hiring process for employers and empowering learners with verifiable qualifications.
- **AR for Language Learning:** Lastly, an exemplar in language education demonstrates the successful integration of augmented reality to enhance language learning experiences. Language learning apps utilizing AR technology provide real-world context and immersive language practice. Lessons learned from this case underscore the significance of context-aware learning experiences and user-friendly interfaces. The impact on learning outcomes is substantial, with students achieving higher language proficiency levels through contextual and interactive AR applications. This case illustrates the potential of AR to transform language education and showcases the importance of user experience design in the evolving landscape of educational technology within Web 3.0.

1.10 DISCUSSION

Web 3.0 presents exceptional prospects for improving the distribution, engagement, and assessment of educational content by utilizing advanced technologies like blockchain, artificial intelligence, and augmented reality. The chapter promotes a human-centered approach that fosters inclusivity, accessibility, and flexibility, while acknowledging the relationship between technological improvements and educational aims. The statement emphasizes the importance of consistently coming up with new ideas, working together, and including all relevant parties in order to successfully traverse the ever-changing educational technology landscape. The chapter advocates for collaborative endeavors to fully utilize the capabilities of Web 3.0 in redefining education. It highlights the need of user-centered design principles in achieving its revolutionary potential.

1.11 CONCLUSION

The conclusion emphasizes the necessity for educators, institutions, and EdTech developers to give priority to user experience (UX) considerations while designing and implementing educational technologies in the Web 3.0 environment. As we move forward, one of the key future directions in educational technology involves the increased integration of AI and machine learning (ML) algorithms (Brown and Green, 2016). These technologies will play a pivotal role in personalizing learning experiences, adapting content in real-time to individual student needs, and providing data-driven insights for educators. AI-driven tutoring systems, automated grading, and intelligent learning analytics are expected to become more sophisticated, offering educators valuable tools to enhance instructional strategies. Moreover, AI can assist in identifying learning gaps and recommending targeted interventions, contributing to a more efficient and personalized educational landscape.

1.12 FUTURE DIRECTIONS

The future of education in the context of Web 3.0 is anticipated to witness the rise of decentralized learning environments (Bakshi et al., 2021). Blockchain technology is expected to have a significant impact on ensuring the security of educational data, allowing for transparent verification of credentials, and facilitating direct transactions between peers in the field of education. Utilizing smart contracts on a blockchain can optimize administrative procedures, guaranteeing the legitimacy of academic accomplishments. Moreover, immersive technologies like augmented and virtual reality have the potential to increase interactive and collaborative learning experiences on decentralized platforms. As the education sector embraces the principles of decentralization, the landscape of Web 3.0 education is poised to become more transparent, secure, and inclusive. Anticipated advances in user experience within educational technology include the widespread adoption of AR/VR. These technologies have the potential to revolutionize how students engage with content, offering immersive and interactive learning experiences. AR/VR applications could simulate historical events, dissect virtual organisms, or enable students to explore architectural wonders, providing a level of engagement and understanding not achievable through traditional methods. Improved hardware, such as more affordable and user-friendly VR headsets, is expected to contribute to the broader integration of these technologies in education. As the field progresses, a seamless and intuitive user experience will be paramount, ensuring that AR/VR tools are accessible and effectively contribute to enhanced learning outcomes.

1.13 RECOMMENDATIONS FOR STAKEHOLDERS

Stakeholders, including policymakers, administrators, and investors, should prioritize creating an enabling environment for the integration of educational technology. Establishing clear guidelines and standards for the ethical use of data, ensuring equitable access to technology, and fostering collaboration among diverse stakeholders are essential. Policymakers should consider incentivizing institutions to adopt emerging technologies, while administrators and investors should support initiatives that promote innovation in educational practices. A collaborative approach that involves all stakeholders in shaping the future of education technology will lead to more sustainable and impactful implementations (Anand and Bhambri, 2018). It is important to promote ongoing professional development programs to provide educators with the necessary skills to efficiently incorporate and utilize technology in the classroom. Flexibility and adaptability are crucial, as technology evolves rapidly. Educational institutions ought to formulate comprehensive strategies to fully exploit the potential of technology for learning. This includes investing in infrastructure, ensuring widespread access to devices and high-speed internet, and creating a supportive technological ecosystem. Collaboration with industry partners and ongoing research to identify emerging trends will keep institutions at the forefront of educational innovation. Strategic planning should also include measures for cybersecurity and data privacy to safeguard sensitive information. EdTech developers and designers should prioritize user-centric design principles to create intuitive and accessible educational tools. Understanding the needs of both educators and learners is paramount in developing technology that seamlessly integrates with the learning process. Regular user testing and feedback loops should be integral to the design and development process.

Stakeholders in the educational technology ecosystem should prioritize collaboration, open communication, and shared responsibility to effectively handle ethical and privacy concerns in the changing world of Web 3.0. The involvement of various individuals and groups, including as educators, policymakers, technologists, researchers, and learners, is crucial for creating holistic solutions that effectively combine innovation with ethical considerations and privacy protections.

Key stakeholders in the field of educational technology include educators, technology developers, policymakers, parents, and students. Each of these groups has a significant impact on influencing the future of educational technology. It is imperative for these parties involved to cooperate closely, exchanging knowledge, skills, and assets to tackle the various difficulties and possibilities brought about by technology in the field of education. Effective communication channels promote transparency and trust among stakeholders, allowing them to participate in meaningful discussions and collaboratively determine priorities, objectives, and strategies for utilizing technology to improve learning outcomes (Rani et al., 2024).

REFERENCES

Aguilar, S. J. (2015). Web 3.0 technologies and enhanced learning environments: An analysis of students' perceptions. *International Journal of Educational Technology*, *2*(1), 1–8.

Al-Azawei, A., Parslow, P., & Lundqvist, K. (2016). Investigating the effect of learning styles in a blended e-learning system: An extension of the technology acceptance model (TAM). *Australasian Journal of Educational Technology*, *32*(5), 17–32. DOI: 10.14742/ajet.2741

Anand, A., & Bhambri, P. (2018). Rotation, Scale and Translation Invariant Character Recognition System using Neural Network. I.K.Gujral Punjab Technical University, Jalandhar (M.Tech. thesis).

Anderson, C. A. (2018). Educational Technology and Web 3.0: Transforming Learning Experiences. *Educational Technology Research and Development*, *66*(6), 1323–1336.

Bakshi, P., Bhambri, P., & Thapar, V. (2021). A review paper on wireless sensor network techniques in Internet of Things (IoT). Wesleyan Journal of Research, 14(7), 147-160. Retrieved from https://www.wesleyanjournal.in/

Becker, S. A., Cummins, M., Davis, A., & Freeman, A. (2017). *NMC/CoSN Horizon Report: 2017 K-* (12th ed.). The New Media Consortium.

Bhambri, P. (2024a). Wallets and Transactions. In Darwish, D. (Ed.), *Decentralizing the Online Experience With Web3 Technologies* (pp. 90–106). IGI Global., DOI: 10.4018/979-8-3693-1532-3.ch004

Bhambri, P. (2024b). NFTs: Transforming Digital Ownership in the Web 3 Era. In Darwish, D. (Ed.), *Decentralizing the Online Experience With Web3 Technologies* (pp. 151–167). IGI Global., DOI: 10.4018/979-8-3693-1532-3.ch007

Bhambri, P., & Khang, A. (2024a). Managing and Monitoring Patient's Healthcare Using AI and IoT Technologies. In Khang, A. (Ed.), *Driving Smart Medical Diagnosis Through AI-Powered Technologies and Applications* (pp. 1–23). IGI Global., DOI: 10.4018/979-8-3693-3679-3.ch001

Bhambri, P., & Khang, A. (2024b). AI-Integrated Biosensors and Bioelectronics for Healthcare. In Khang, A. (Ed.), *AI-Driven Innovations in Digital Healthcare: Emerging Trends, Challenges, and Applications* (pp. 82–96). IGI Global., DOI: 10.4018/979-8-3693-3218-4.ch004

Bhambri, P., & Khang, A. (2024c). Machine Learning Advancements in E-Health: Transforming Digital Healthcare. In Khang, A. (Ed.), *Medical Robotics and AI-Assisted Diagnostics for a High-Tech Healthcare Industry* (pp. 174–194). IGI Global., DOI: 10.4018/979-8-3693-2105-8.ch012

Bhambri, P., & Khang, A. (2024d). Biosensor Applications and Principles of Agricultural and Aquacultural Sectors. In Khang, A. (Ed.), *Agriculture and Aquaculture Applications of Biosensors and Bioelectronics* (pp. 1–17). IGI Global., DOI: 10.4018/979-8-3693-2069-3.ch001

Bhambri, P., & Khang, A. (2024e). Challenges and future directions on business intelligence. In Özsungur, F. (Ed.), *Generating entrepreneurial ideas with AI* (pp. 117–146). IGI Global., DOI: 10.4018/979-8-3693-3498-0.ch006

Bhambri, P., & Rani, S. (2024a). Ethical Issues for Climate Change and Mental Health. In Samanta, D., & Garg, M. (Eds.), *Impact of Climate Change on Mental Health and Well-Being* (pp. 178–198). IGI Global., DOI: 10.4018/979-8-3693-2177-5.ch012

Bhambri, P., & Rani, S. (2024b). *Challenges, Opportunities, and the Future of Industrial Engineering with IoT and AI. Integration of AI-Based Manufacturing and Industrial Engineering Systems with the Internet of Things*. CRC Press.

Bhambri, P., & Rani, S. (2024c). Best Practices and Tips for Selecting Chatbots. In Darwish, D. (Ed.), *Design and Development of Emerging Chatbot Technology* (pp. 114–129). IGI Global., DOI: 10.4018/979-8-3693-1830-0.ch007

Bhambri, P., & Rani, S. (2024d). Issues Related to Chatbots. In Darwish, D. (Ed.), *Design and Development of Emerging Chatbot Technology* (pp. 130–147). IGI Global., DOI: 10.4018/979-8-3693-1830-0.ch008

Bhambri, P., Rani, S., & Pareek, P. K. (2024a). Paperless paradigm: Intelligent automation in document and record management. In Darwish, D. (Ed.), *Generating entrepreneurial ideas with AI* (pp. 164–183)., https://www.igi-global.com/book/hyperautomation-business-society/335477

Bhambri, P., Rani, S., & Pareek, P. K. (2024b). Financial innovations: Intelligent automation in finance and insurance sectors. In Darwish, D. (Ed.), *Generating entrepreneurial ideas with AI* (pp. 226–243)., DOI: 10.4018/979-8-3693-3354-9.ch012

Bower, M., Howe, C., McCredie, N., Robinson, A., Grover, D., & Tyack, A. (2017). A design-based research approach to enhancing inquiry-based learning in geography using geospatial technologies. *Learning Environments Research*, *20*(2), 191–210.

Brown, M., & Green, T. (2016). *The essentials of instructional design: Connecting fundamental principles with process and practice*. Routledge.

Chao, T. C., & Lo, H. C. (2018). An exploratory study on applying Web 3.0 tools to conduct e-learning in virtual communities. *Turkish Online Journal of Distance Education, 19*(1), 124–136.

Chen, P. H., & Chen, Y. L. (2018). Integrating Web 3.0 Technologies in Higher Education: A Constructivist Framework. *Journal of Educational Technology & Society, 21*(2), 222–236.

Clark, D., & Mayer, R. E. (2016). *E-learning and the science of instruction: Proven guidelines for consumers and designers of multimedia learning*. John Wiley & Sons. DOI: 10.1002/9781119239086

Dede, C. (2017). Immersive interfaces for engagement and learning. *Science, 317*(5839), 66–69. PMID: 19119219

Downes, S. (2018). Learning networks and connective knowledge. Instructional Technology Forum, 2006(3), 14-27.

Dudley, N. M., & Kachka, M. P. (2019). The role of user experience in educational technology: A literature review. *Educational Technology Research and Development, 67*(1), 97–125.

Evans, C. (2019). The effectiveness of m-learning in the form of podcast revision lectures in higher education. *Computers & Education, 50*(2), 491–498. DOI: 10.1016/j.compedu.2007.09.016

Gardner, H. (2017). *Multiple intelligences: New horizons in theory and practice*. Basic Books.

Garrison, D. R., Anderson, T., & Archer, W. (2016). Critical thinking, cognitive presence, and computer conferencing in distance education. *American Journal of Distance Education, 15*(1), 7–23. DOI: 10.1080/08923640109527071

Gee, J. P. (2019). What video games have to teach us about learning and literacy. [CIE]. *Computers in Entertainment, 1*(1), 20–20. DOI: 10.1145/950566.950595

Hrastinski, S. (2017). Asynchronous and synchronous e-learning. *EDUCAUSE Quarterly, 31*(4), 51–55.

Johnson, L., Adams Becker, S., Estrada, V., & Freeman, A. (2015). *NMC/CoSN Horizon Report: 2015 K-* (12th ed.). The New Media Consortium.

Kay, R. H. (2016). Exploring the use of video podcasts in education: A comprehensive review of the literature. *Computers in Human Behavior*, *28*(3), 820–831. DOI: 10.1016/j.chb.2012.01.011

Kirschner, P. A., & van Merriënboer, J. J. (2013). Do learners really know best? Urban legends in education. *Educational Psychologist*, *48*(3), 169–183. DOI: 10.1080/00461520.2013.804395

Koohang, A., Riley, L., Smith, T., & Schreurs, J. (2009). E-learning and constructivism: From theory to application. *Interdisciplinary Journal of E-Learning and Learning Objects*, *5*(1), 91–109. DOI: 10.28945/3321

Laurillard, D. (2017). *Rethinking university teaching: A conversational framework for the effective use of learning technologies*. Routledge.

Lave, J., & Wenger, E. (2019). *Situated learning: Legitimate peripheral participation*. Cambridge University Press.

Li, L., Wang, Y., & Wang, H. (2018). The impact of instructional design in an online collaborative learning environment. *Computers & Education*, *55*(2), 681–690.

Lin, F. R., Liu, Y. L., & Yuan, S. M. (2019). The impact of user satisfaction with online learning management system on learner performance. *Behaviour & Information Technology*, *38*(2), 125–134.

Means, B., & Neisler, J. (2019). Using technology to support at-risk students' learning. *Journal of Educational Computing Research*, *35*(4), 381–399.

Mishra, P., & Koehler, M. J. (2006). Technological pedagogical content knowledge: A framework for teacher knowledge. *Teachers College Record*, *108*(6), 1017–1054. DOI: 10.1111/j.1467-9620.2006.00684.x

Prensky, M. (2018). *Don't bother me mom—I'm learning!: How computer and video games are preparing your kids for 21st century success and how you can help!* Paragon House.

Rana, R., Bhambri, P., & Chhabra, Y. (2024). Evolution and the Future of Industrial Engineering with the IoT and AI. In *Integration of AI-Based Manufacturing and Industrial Engineering Systems with the Internet of Things* (pp. 19–37). CRC Press.

Rani, S., Bhambri, P., Kaur, J., & Sangwan, Y. S. (2024). Exploring the application domains of ML-based facial emotion recognition systems: Framework, techniques and challenges. In *Second International Conference on Computing and Communication Networks (ICCCN 2022)* (pp. 090008-1–090008-9). AIP Conf. Proc. 2919. https://doi.org/DOI: 10.1063/5.0184852

Reeves, T. C., Herrington, J., & Oliver, R. (2017). *A guide to authentic e-learning*. Routledge.

Rienties, B., & Kinchin, I. M. (2014). Understanding (in) formal learning in an academic development programme: A social network perspective. *Teaching and Teacher Education*, *39*, 123–135. DOI: 10.1016/j.tate.2014.01.004

Siemens, G. (2018). Connectivism: A learning theory for the digital age. *International Journal of Instructional Technology and Distance Learning*, *2*(1), 3–10.

Siemens, G., & Tittenberger, P. (2009). *Handbook of emerging technologies for learning*. University of Manitoba.

Singh, G., & Bhambri, P. (2023). Simulation Analysis of AODV and DSDV Routing Protocols for Secure and Reliable Service in Mobile Adhoc Networks (MANETs). In Integration of AI-Based Manufacturing and Industrial Engineering Systems with the Internet of Things (pp. 205-216). CRC Press.

Spector, J. M., Merrill, M. D., Van Merriënboer, J. J., & Driscoll, M. P. (2013). *Handbook of research on educational communications and technology*. Springer.

Steinkuehler, C., & Duncan, S. (2008). Scientific habits of mind in virtual worlds. *Journal of Science Education and Technology*, *17*(6), 530–543. DOI: 10.1007/s10956-008-9120-8

Wang, S. K., Hsu, H. Y., & Campbell, T. (2015). Using the cloud-based mobile learning environment to support collaborative learning in higher education. *Computers & Education*, *78*, 78–88.

Waycott, J., Sheard, J., Thompson, C., & Clerehan, R. (2017). Making students partners and producers of technology for learning. In *Proceedings of the 22nd annual conference of the Australasian Society for Computers in Learning in Tertiary Education (ASCILITE)* (pp. 839-843).

West, R. E. (2019). Transformative Learning in the Design Studio: A Case Study of Web 3.0 in Architectural Education. *Journal of Educational Technology & Society*, *22*(2), 172–184.

Wiggins, G., & McTighe, J. (2005). *Understanding by design*. ASCD.

Yilmaz, R. (2018). The effects of Web 3.0 technology on learning and teaching: A case study in teacher education. *Journal of Educational Technology & Society*, *21*(2), 222–236.

Zawacki-Richter, O., & Naidu, S. (2016). Mapping research trends from 35 years of publications in Distance Education. *Distance Education*, *37*(3), 245–269. DOI: 10.1080/01587919.2016.1185079

Chapter 15
Designing and Developing a Web3 Mobile Platform:
Integrating Blockchain and AI for Enhanced Functionality, Security, and User Experience

C. V. Suresh Babu
https://orcid.org/0000-0002-8474-2882
Hindustan Institute of Technology and Science, India

Malini Premakumari William
https://orcid.org/0009-0004-6165-2501
Bourntec Solutions, Inc., USA

ABSTRACT

In order to improve functionality, security, and user experience, this chapter examines the design and implementation of a Web3 mobile platform that combines blockchain technology with artificial intelligence (AI). The methodology addresses major issues in usability, security, and scalability by employing an exploratory and developmental approach that prioritizes user-centered design principles and iterative feedback loops. The results show that greater trust and uptake of decentralized technologies are fostered by Web3 applications that are easy to use, safe, and scalable. The chapter emphasizes that in order to remove obstacles and build a strong Web3 ecosystem, stakeholders—including developers, investors, regulatory agencies, and users—must work together. The work's ramifications highlight how crucial it is to resolve present issues in order to fully utilize Web3 technologies'

DOI: 10.4018/979-8-3693-2973-3.ch015

promise to transform digital interactions.

1.0. INTRODUCTION

1.1. Overview of Web3 and Its Significance

Web3, the next evolution of the internet, represents a paradigm shift from the traditional, centralized Web2 framework by decentralizing data and governance through blockchain technology. In this decentralized model, users gain control over their data, identities, and digital assets, removing reliance on centralized platforms and intermediaries (Buterin, 2014). Web3 promotes user autonomy, secure data sharing, and transparency, which are especially valuable for privacy-conscious users and those affected by restrictive data practices. These features mark a fundamental transformation in how digital interactions occur, fostering a participatory ecosystem with digital ownership and peer-to-peer exchanges (Wood, 2020). The convergence of Web3 with advanced technologies such as blockchain, artificial intelligence (AI), and smart contracts enhances user experiences and functionality. Blockchain technology facilitates data integrity and security through immutable ledgers, while AI enriches data analysis, automation, and personalized interactions, addressing diverse user needs dynamically (Kouhizadeh et al., 2021). This chapter will explore how these technologies interact to create a cohesive, user-focused Web3 mobile platform.

1.2. Objectives of the Chapter

This chapter's main goal is to provide an overview of the crucial procedures and factors to be taken into account while creating a Web3 mobile platform that uses blockchain and artificial intelligence to improve usability, security, and functionality. The chapter specifically seeks to offer:

- A thorough grasp of Web3's foundational ideas and architecture, with an emphasis on how blockchain and artificial intelligence work in tandem to produce safe and responsive apps (Singh & Sandhu, 2021).
- Guidance on creating Web3-based decentralized applications (dApps), which demonstrate how the distributed nature of blockchain technology enhances user control and data protection (Nakamoto, 2008).
- An examination of how AI improves Web3 platforms' functionality, namely in the areas of data processing, user interaction, and personalization (Zhang et al., 2022).

- Practical design and development strategies that balance security, privacy, and performance, addressing common challenges faced when integrating blockchain and AI in a mobile platform environment.

1.3. Structure of the Chapter

The chapter is structured to guide readers through the conceptual and technical aspects of building a Web3 mobile platform that incorporates blockchain and AI.

1. **Understanding Web3 Fundamentals**: This section covers the essential components of Web3, including decentralized networks, smart contracts, and user sovereignty principles. Key attributes of Web3 are explored, with an emphasis on their role in enhancing digital trust and transparency (Wood, 2020).
2. **Blockchain Technology in Web3**: Here, we discuss how blockchain supports Web3 platforms, examining its functionalities, from data immutability and decentralized governance to the use of smart contracts for executing automated, secure transactions (Tapscott & Tapscott, 2016).
3. **Integrating AI for Enhanced Functionality**: This part highlights the transformative role of AI in Web3, including its ability to drive intelligent data processing, enhance security, and facilitate more personalized user experiences through predictive analytics and machine learning algorithms (Kouhizadeh et al., 2021).
4. **Design and Development Strategies**: The technical heart of the chapter provides detailed strategies for building a Web3 mobile platform that maintains data security and integrity. Design considerations around user interface (UI) and user experience (UX) in a decentralized application context are covered, as well as methodologies for handling on-chain and off-chain data seamlessly (Zhang et al., 2022).
5. **Challenges and Future Directions**: This concluding section addresses potential technical, regulatory, and scalability challenges associated with Web3 mobile platforms, proposing solutions to address these issues while outlining future research opportunities and advancements in Web3 and blockchain-driven mobile applications (Singh & Sandhu, 2021).

Through this structure, the chapter aims to equip developers, researchers, and technology enthusiasts with the knowledge needed to understand, design, and implement Web3 mobile platforms, paving the way for a more decentralized, secure, and user-focused digital ecosystem.

2.0. BACKGROUND AND CONTEXT

2.1. Current State of Web3 Applications

The evolution of Web3 has catalyzed the development of decentralized applications (dApps) that prioritize user empowerment, privacy, and data ownership. As of 2024, the Web3 ecosystem has witnessed a significant proliferation of applications across various sectors, including finance (DeFi), gaming (GameFi), social media, and supply chain management (Frolov et al., 2023). These applications leverage blockchain technology to create transparent and secure environments where users can interact without intermediaries. Popular platforms such as Ethereum, Polkadot, and Solana serve as the foundational frameworks for these dApps, enabling developers to build innovative solutions that are resistant to censorship and fraud (Khan et al., 2024).

Despite the rapid growth of Web3 applications, adoption remains hindered by usability challenges, particularly for non-technical users. Many users find blockchain technologies complex and cumbersome, which can discourage engagement and hinder mass adoption (Tönnies et al., 2022). Nevertheless, advancements in user interface (UI) and user experience (UX) design are gradually addressing these barriers, facilitating easier navigation and interaction within the Web3 ecosystem (Singh et al., 2023).

2.2. Challenges in Usability, Security, and Scalability

While the promise of Web3 is significant, several challenges threaten its widespread implementation. Usability is a prominent concern; many users struggle with wallet management, private key security, and transaction processes, leading to user frustration and abandonment (Huang et al., 2023). Simplifying these processes while maintaining security is essential for enhancing user engagement and satisfaction.

Security remains another critical issue, especially given the rise of hacks and exploits targeting Web3 applications. The decentralized nature of these platforms can create vulnerabilities, making them attractive targets for malicious actors (Reid et al., 2022). In particular, smart contracts, which automate transactions, can contain bugs or security flaws that, if exploited, could lead to significant financial losses for users and developers alike (Zhang et al., 2023). Consequently, ensuring robust security measures and conducting thorough audits is vital to building trust within the community.

Scalability is also a significant challenge for Web3 applications, as many blockchain networks face limitations in transaction throughput and speed. High gas fees and slow confirmation times can deter users from engaging with decentralized platforms, particularly during peak demand (Swan, 2021). Innovations such as layer-2 solutions and sharding are being explored to enhance scalability and improve the overall user experience, allowing Web3 applications to accommodate a larger user base without compromising performance (Peters et al., 2023).

2.3. Importance of Integrating Blockchain and AI

The integration of blockchain and artificial intelligence (AI) holds immense potential for overcoming the challenges faced by Web3 applications while enhancing functionality and user experience. Blockchain provides a decentralized and secure environment for data storage and transaction processing, while AI brings advanced analytical capabilities and automation to the table. By combining these technologies, developers can create intelligent dApps that adapt to user behaviors, preferences, and needs.

AI can enhance security by enabling real-time monitoring and anomaly detection in blockchain networks, identifying potential threats and vulnerabilities before they can be exploited (Soni et al., 2022). Furthermore, AI-driven algorithms can facilitate personalized user experiences by analyzing data patterns and offering tailored services, thereby increasing user satisfaction and engagement (Gao et al., 2023). The synergy between blockchain's transparency and AI's predictive analytics creates opportunities for innovative solutions across various domains, including finance, healthcare, and supply chain management.

Moreover, the decentralized nature of blockchain can help address concerns about data privacy and bias in AI algorithms. By using decentralized data storage and processing, AI systems can mitigate risks associated with data centralization, enabling fairer and more ethical AI applications (Dufour et al., 2023). Overall, the integration of blockchain and AI is essential for unlocking the full potential of Web3 applications, driving innovation, and fostering a more secure and user-centric digital ecosystem.

3.0. PROBLEM STATEMENT

3.1. Lack of User-Friendly Web3 Applications

Despite the burgeoning interest in Web3 technologies and applications, a significant barrier to widespread adoption remains the lack of user-friendly interfaces and experiences. Most existing Web3 applications, often characterized by complex processes and intricate design layouts, create obstacles for the average user, particularly those without a technical background (Tönnies et al., 2022). A survey conducted by Tiwari et al. (2023) indicates that nearly 70% of potential users express frustration with the usability of Web3 platforms, citing difficulties in navigation, account management, and transaction execution as primary concerns. This lack of user-friendliness not only impedes engagement but also discourages new users from exploring the benefits that decentralized applications can offer (Huang et al., 2023). To bridge the gap between technology and users, there is a critical need for designs that prioritize simplicity and intuitiveness while maintaining the inherent advantages of blockchain technology.

3.2. Key Challenges in Web3 Mobile Platform Development

Table 1. Key challenges in Web3 mobile platform development

Challenge	Description	Impact	Potential Solutions
Complex Interfaces	Web3 applications often have intricate interfaces filled with technical jargon, making navigation difficult for users. Users struggle with wallet setup, transaction signing, and gas fee management.	Leads to user errors (e.g., sending assets to the wrong address) and discourages adoption.	Simplified UI/UX design, better onboarding guides, and intuitive transaction flows.
Security Vulnerabilities	Blockchain-based applications are prone to phishing attacks, smart contract exploits, and private key theft. Losses in DeFi projects exceeded $1 billion in 2022.	Erodes user trust and slows adoption due to fear of asset loss.	Enhanced security protocols, multi-factor authentication, and robust smart contract auditing.
Inefficient Transaction Processing	High transaction fees and slow processing times due to blockchain scalability limitations (e.g., Ethereum gas fee surges).	Causes frustration for users accustomed to instant transactions in traditional systems.	Implementing layer-2 scaling solutions, optimizing consensus mechanisms, and reducing transaction costs.

By addressing these challenges, developers can enhance functionality, security, and user experience in Web3 mobile platforms, fostering broader adoption.

4.0. OBJECTIVES

In this chapter, we delve into the innovative convergence of blockchain technology and artificial intelligence within the realm of Web3 mobile platforms. By exploring the foundational principles of blockchain and assessing cutting-edge Web3 technologies, we aim to outline a roadmap for developing secure, scalable, and user-centric mobile applications. The following objectives guide our exploration and design strategies, providing a structured framework to enhance both functionality and user experience in this evolving digital landscape.

Table 2. Objective and description

Objective	Description
To understand blockchain fundamentals	Provide a comprehensive overview of blockchain technology, including decentralization, consensus mechanisms, smart contracts, and tokenomics to establish a strong theoretical foundation.
To evaluate Web3 technologies	Analyze existing Web3 solutions such as dApps, DeFi, and NFTs, assessing their strengths, weaknesses, and potential for enhancing user experience.
To design intuitive user interfaces	Establish best practices for creating user-friendly interfaces that simplify blockchain interactions and improve accessibility for both technical and non-technical users.
To ensure robust security and privacy	Explore security measures like encryption, multi-signature wallets, and secure smart contract development while addressing privacy concerns in blockchain transactions.
To enhance scalability through AI	Investigate how AI-driven solutions, such as predictive analytics and machine learning, can optimize transaction processing and resource allocation to improve Web3 platform performance.
To expand knowledge in Web3 and blockchain	Contribute to academic and industry discussions by providing insights into emerging trends, challenges, and innovations, fostering further research and development in the field.

These objectives collectively guide the chapter in offering a structured approach to developing a Web3 mobile platform with enhanced functionality, security, and user experience.

5.0. UNDERSTANDING BLOCKCHAIN FUNDAMENTALS

This section delves into the foundational elements of blockchain technology, highlighting its architecture, various types, and practical applications. Understanding these fundamentals is crucial for designing and developing a Web3 mobile platform that integrates blockchain and AI, enabling enhanced functionality, security, and user experience.

5.1. Basics of Blockchain

Decentralized Ledgers

At its core, blockchain is a decentralized ledger technology (DLT) that allows multiple parties to maintain a shared database without the need for a central authority. Each participant, or node, in the network holds a copy of the entire ledger, ensuring that the information is transparent and tamper-proof (Narayanan et al., 2016). This decentralized architecture enhances security by reducing single points of failure, fostering trust among participants and enabling seamless peer-to-peer transactions.

Cryptographic Hashing

Cryptographic hashing is integral to blockchain's security model. Each block in a blockchain contains a unique hash generated by a cryptographic algorithm, which is a fixed-length string produced from the block's contents (Suresh Babu, C. V., Surendar, et. al 2024). This hash is linked to the previous block's hash, creating a secure chain. If an attempt is made to alter a block, its hash will change, leading to a cascade of changes in subsequent blocks, making tampering easily detectable. This feature not only secures the data but also preserves the integrity of the entire blockchain.

Consensus Mechanisms

Consensus mechanisms are essential protocols that allow blockchain participants to agree on the validity of transactions. These mechanisms ensure that all nodes in the network have a consistent view of the ledger. Prominent consensus algorithms include Proof of Work (PoW) and Proof of Stake (PoS). In PoW, miners compete to solve complex mathematical problems to validate transactions, consuming significant computational resources (Swan, 2021). Conversely, PoS allows validators to create new blocks based on the number of coins they hold and are willing to "stake," which is a more energy-efficient method of achieving consensus (Buterin, 2014).

Smart Contracts

Smart contracts are programmable contracts executed automatically when predefined conditions are met. These self-executing contracts are coded into the blockchain, eliminating the need for intermediaries and enabling trustless interactions between parties (Suresh Babu, C. V. & Sanjai Das 2023). For instance, in a real estate transaction, a smart contract could automatically transfer ownership upon the successful completion of payment, streamlining processes and reducing transaction costs.

5.2. Types of Blockchain

Public Blockchain

Public blockchains are open for anyone to join and participate. They are characterized by transparency, as all transactions can be viewed by any user, making them highly secure and decentralized. Examples include Bitcoin and Ethereum, where users can validate transactions and participate in the consensus process. This openness fosters trust but can pose challenges related to scalability and transaction speed (Tapscott & Tapscott, 2016).

Private Blockchain

Private blockchains, in contrast, are restricted to a specific group of users, often within an organization or consortium. This model offers greater control and privacy since only authorized participants can access and manage the network. While private blockchains can process transactions more quickly than public ones, they may sacrifice some degree of decentralization and transparency (Suresh Babu, C. V. & Sanjai Das, 2023).

Consortium Blockchain

Consortium blockchains represent a hybrid model that combines elements of both public and private blockchains. Governed by a group of organizations, these blockchains allow shared control while maintaining some level of privacy. Consortium blockchains are especially relevant in industries such as finance and supply chain management, where multiple stakeholders need to collaborate securely and efficiently (Dinh et al., 2018).

5.3. Use Cases

Supply Chain Management

Blockchain technology has significant applications in supply chain management by enabling transparent tracking of goods from production to delivery. By leveraging blockchain, stakeholders can access real-time data regarding the product's journey, enhancing traceability and authenticity (Kouhizadeh & Sarkis, 2021). This transparency builds consumer trust and can lead to improved efficiency in supply chain operations by minimizing fraud and errors.

Voting Systems

Blockchain can enhance the security and integrity of voting systems by providing a tamper-proof record of votes. Utilizing blockchain for voting ensures that all votes are securely recorded and results are verifiable and transparent, thus reducing the potential for electoral fraud (Cohen et al., 2020). Pilot projects exploring blockchain-based voting systems have demonstrated their feasibility, indicating a promising future for secure elections.

Identity Verification

Blockchain can streamline identity verification processes, allowing individuals to control their digital identities securely. Through decentralized identity solutions, users can store their identity credentials on a blockchain, sharing only the necessary information with service providers (Zhang et al., 2020). This approach not only enhances privacy but also reduces the risk of identity theft, making it a compelling application of blockchain technology.

By grasping these fundamental aspects of blockchain, developers and researchers can effectively harness this technology in designing and developing a Web3 mobile platform that integrates AI, ultimately enhancing functionality, security, and user experience.

6.0. EVALUATING WEB3 TECHNOLOGIES

In the development of a Web3 mobile platform, it is crucial to evaluate the technologies that underpin decentralized systems. This section explores four key components: decentralized applications (dApps), smart contracts, interoperability among blockchains, and governance models, which collectively form the backbone of the Web3 ecosystem.

6.1. Decentralized Applications (dApps)

Architecture and Interaction with Blockchain Networks

Decentralized applications (dApps) are software applications that run on a peer-to-peer network rather than a centralized server. They leverage blockchain technology to ensure transparency, security, and user control over data. The architecture of a dApp typically includes three layers: the user interface, the application logic, and the blockchain layer (Swan, 2021).

The user interface is responsible for interaction with users, often developed using standard web technologies such as HTML, CSS, and JavaScript. The application logic, usually coded in languages such as Solidity or Rust, is where the core functionality resides. Finally, the blockchain layer manages data storage and ensures immutability and transparency.

Interaction with blockchain networks occurs through application programming interfaces (APIs) or directly via smart contracts. For instance, dApps like Uniswap and Cryptokitties interact with the Ethereum blockchain to facilitate decentralized trading and digital asset ownership (Buterin, 2014). This decentralized nature allows users to engage with the platform without intermediaries, enhancing security and fostering trust.

6.2. Smart Contracts

Creation and Execution on Various Blockchains

Smart contracts are self-executing contracts with the terms of the agreement directly written into code. They play a pivotal role in automating processes and facilitating trustless interactions. The creation of smart contracts typically involves defining the contract's rules and conditions using programming languages specific to the blockchain platform, such as Solidity for Ethereum or Vyper for hyperledger Fabric (Suresh Babu, C. V. & Sanjai Das 2023).

Once deployed on a blockchain, smart contracts execute automatically when predetermined conditions are met, eliminating the need for intermediaries. For example, in a decentralized finance (DeFi) application, a smart contract could automatically liquidate collateral if its value falls below a certain threshold (Zohar, 2015). This automation reduces operational risks and enhances efficiency, making smart contracts a cornerstone of Web3 technologies.

Different blockchains offer unique features for smart contract execution. For example, Ethereum is renowned for its robust smart contract capabilities, while newer blockchains like Polkadot and Solana provide enhanced scalability and lower transaction costs. Understanding these differences is crucial for developers aiming to optimize dApps for performance and user experience.

6.3. Interoperability

Interaction and Integration of Different Blockchains and Protocols

Interoperability refers to the ability of different blockchain networks and protocols to communicate and work together. In the context of Web3, interoperability is vital for creating a seamless user experience, enabling users to navigate multiple dApps and platforms without friction (Babu, C. V. Suresh, Sudhir Manoharan, 2024).

Cross-chain communication protocols, such as Polkadot and Cosmos, facilitate interoperability by allowing the transfer of data and assets across different blockchains. For instance, Polkadot's relay chain connects various parachains, enabling them to share information while maintaining their own consensus mechanisms (Wood, 2016). This interconnectedness enhances the overall functionality of Web3 applications, as users can leverage diverse services across multiple platforms.

Moreover, interoperability can mitigate the risk of blockchain fragmentation, where the proliferation of isolated networks hampers user experience and limits the potential of decentralized ecosystems (Babu, C. V. Suresh, Sudhir Manoharan, 2024). Therefore, evaluating interoperability solutions is essential for developers aiming to build robust Web3 applications that foster collaboration among various blockchain technologies.

6.4. Governance Models

Decentralized Autonomous Organizations (DAOs) and Decision-Making in Web3

Governance in Web3 is fundamentally different from traditional governance models, primarily due to the decentralized nature of blockchain technology. Decentralized Autonomous Organizations (DAOs) are a prominent governance model within the Web3 ecosystem. DAOs operate through smart contracts that define the rules for decision-making and fund management, allowing participants to vote on proposals and initiatives (Hassan et al., 2021).

DAOs enable community-driven governance, where stakeholders have a direct say in the direction of the project. This participatory approach fosters a sense of ownership and accountability among members, aligning incentives toward collective success. For example, projects like MakerDAO allow users to participate in governance decisions affecting the DAI stablecoin, influencing monetary policy and risk management (Buterin, 2014).

However, governance in DAOs presents challenges, including potential voter apathy, governance attacks, and the complexity of decision-making processes (Hassan et al., 2021). As Web3 continues to evolve, exploring innovative governance models will be crucial for sustaining user engagement and ensuring effective decision-making within decentralized ecosystems.

7.0. DESIGNING INTUITIVE USER INTERFACES

Creating an intuitive user interface (UI) is critical in the development of a Web3 mobile platform, as it directly influences user engagement and satisfaction. This section explores the essential components of designing user-friendly interfaces, emphasizing user experience (UX), user-centered design, and accessibility.

7.1. User Experience (UX): Creating User-Friendly and Accessible Interfaces

User experience (UX) encompasses all aspects of the user's interaction with a product, particularly focusing on how easy and enjoyable it is to use (Garrett, 2011). In the context of Web3 applications, the complexity of blockchain technology often poses challenges for users unfamiliar with decentralized systems. To counter this, designers must create interfaces that simplify interactions without compromising functionality.

Key elements of effective UX design include clear navigation, coherent information architecture, and visual consistency. According to Nielsen (1994), usability principles such as learnability, efficiency, memorability, and error prevention are crucial for enhancing UX. For instance, incorporating familiar design patterns can help users navigate the application more intuitively.

Furthermore, providing informative tooltips and help guides can assist users in understanding complex processes such as wallet management or transaction signing, fostering a smoother onboarding experience (Suresh Babu, C. V. & Abhinaba Pal. 2023).. As a result, the design must prioritize clarity and simplicity, enabling users to engage confidently with the platform's features.

7.2. User-Centered Design: Incorporating User Feedback to Improve Functionality

User-centered design (UCD) is an iterative design approach that prioritizes the needs, preferences, and limitations of end-users throughout the development process (Norman, 2013). Involving users early and continuously can provide valuable insights into their experiences, allowing designers to refine the interface effectively.

Conducting usability testing sessions with real users can unveil pain points and identify areas for improvement. Techniques such as A/B testing, where different design versions are tested to evaluate user response, can yield data-driven insights (Kahneman, 2011). Additionally, gathering qualitative feedback through surveys or interviews helps designers understand user motivations and preferences, guiding adjustments to UI elements.

An example of user-centered design in practice is the development of Web3 wallets, where user feedback has led to simplified onboarding processes and improved security features. By addressing user concerns about the complexity of managing private keys, designers can enhance the overall user experience and drive adoption (Kim et al., 2021).

7.3. Accessibility: Ensuring Usability for People with Disabilities

Accessibility is a fundamental aspect of UI design that ensures usability for people with disabilities. The Web Content Accessibility Guidelines (WCAG) provide a comprehensive framework for creating accessible web applications, emphasizing the importance of making content perceivable, operable, understandable, and robust (World Wide Web Consortium [W3C], 2018).

To achieve accessibility in Web3 mobile platforms, designers should consider various factors, such as:

1. **Color Contrast**: Ensuring sufficient contrast between text and background colors improves readability for users with visual impairments (Lidwell et al., 2010).
2. **Keyboard Navigation**: Providing keyboard shortcuts and ensuring that all interactive elements are navigable via keyboard enhances usability for users with mobility impairments.
3. **Screen Reader Compatibility**: Designing interfaces that work well with screen readers, including proper labeling of UI elements, can assist users who are blind or have low vision (Rosa et al., 2021).

4. **Alternative Text**: Including descriptive alt text for images and icons ensures that users who rely on assistive technologies can comprehend visual content.

By adhering to accessibility standards, designers can create inclusive Web3 platforms that cater to a diverse range of users, fostering a more equitable digital environment. As the demand for accessible technology continues to grow, integrating accessibility features into the design process is essential for driving widespread adoption of Web3 applications.

8.0. ENSURING ROBUST SECURITY AND PRIVACY

As Web3 applications evolve, ensuring robust security and privacy becomes paramount for user trust and the overall success of decentralized platforms. This section discusses essential security practices, privacy measures, and compliance considerations in the development of a Web3 mobile platform.

8.1. Security Practices: Encryption, Secure Key Management, Regular Audits

Security is a critical component of Web3 applications, which rely heavily on blockchain technology to safeguard user data and transactions. Effective security practices include encryption, secure key management, and regular audits.

1. **Encryption**: Data encryption is vital for protecting sensitive information during transmission and storage. Utilizing strong encryption algorithms, such as AES-256, ensures that data is unintelligible to unauthorized users (Stallings & Brown, 2019). In the context of Web3, both symmetric and asymmetric encryption techniques are employed to secure communication between clients and blockchain networks, ensuring data integrity and confidentiality.
2. **Secure Key Management**: In blockchain applications, cryptographic keys play a crucial role in user authentication and transaction authorization. Proper key management practices, including the use of hardware wallets, multi-signature schemes, and secure key recovery options, can mitigate the risks of key theft and unauthorized access (Kostiainen et al., 2019). The implementation of robust key management protocols is essential for protecting user assets and maintaining the security of the platform.
3. **Regular Audits**: Conducting regular security audits and vulnerability assessments helps identify and mitigate potential threats in Web3 applications. These audits should include code reviews, penetration testing, and risk assessments to ensure

that the application is resilient against attacks (Suresh Babu, C. V. & Abhinaba Pal. 2023).. Additionally, engaging third-party security firms can provide an unbiased evaluation of the platform's security posture, fostering transparency and trust among users.

8.2. Privacy Measures: Zero-Knowledge Proofs, Privacy-Focused Protocols

Privacy in Web3 applications is critical for protecting user data and maintaining confidentiality in transactions. Implementing privacy measures, such as zero-knowledge proofs (ZKPs) and privacy-focused protocols, can enhance user privacy without compromising functionality.

1. **Zero-Knowledge Proofs (ZKPs)**: ZKPs enable one party to prove to another that a statement is true without revealing any additional information. This cryptographic technique is particularly valuable in scenarios where privacy is paramount, such as financial transactions or identity verification (Miers et al., 2013). By utilizing ZKPs, Web3 platforms can allow users to validate their transactions or identities without exposing sensitive data, thereby maintaining privacy while ensuring trust.
2. **Privacy-Focused Protocols**: Several privacy-focused protocols have emerged in the Web3 ecosystem, such as Monero and Zcash, which incorporate advanced cryptographic techniques to provide enhanced privacy features. These protocols utilize ring signatures, stealth addresses, and confidential transactions to obscure transaction details and user identities (Bada et al., 2020). Integrating such privacy protocols into a Web3 mobile platform can help address user concerns about data privacy and enhance the overall user experience.

8.3. Compliance: Regulations Such as GDPR and CCPA

Compliance with data protection regulations is crucial for Web3 platforms to build trust and ensure legal operation. Two prominent regulations that influence data privacy practices are the General Data Protection Regulation (GDPR) and the California Consumer Privacy Act (CCPA).

1. **General Data Protection Regulation (GDPR)**: GDPR establishes stringent guidelines for the collection, storage, and processing of personal data within the European Union. Web3 platforms must ensure that user consent is obtained before processing personal data and provide users with the right to access, rectify, or delete their information (European Commission, 2020). Compliance

with GDPR not only mitigates legal risks but also enhances user trust in the platform.

2. **California Consumer Privacy Act (CCPA)**: The CCPA aims to enhance privacy rights and consumer protection for residents of California. Similar to GDPR, it grants consumers rights regarding their personal data, including the right to know what data is collected and the ability to opt out of data selling (California Legislative Information, 2018). Web3 platforms should implement mechanisms to comply with CCPA requirements, ensuring transparency and user control over their data.

By prioritizing security practices, implementing effective privacy measures, and adhering to regulatory compliance, developers can create a robust Web3 mobile platform that instills confidence in users and supports the sustainable growth of decentralized applications.

9.0. ENHANCING SCALABILITY THROUGH AI

Scalability is a crucial challenge for Web3 applications, particularly as user demand and transaction volumes increase. Integrating artificial intelligence (AI) can significantly enhance scalability by optimizing blockchain operations, enabling predictive capabilities, and automating processes. This section explores scalable solutions, predictive analytics, and automation through AI in the context of Web3 mobile platforms.

9.1. Scalable Solutions: AI Techniques Like Sharding and Layer-2 Solutions

1. **Sharding**: Sharding is a database partitioning technique that improves scalability by distributing data across multiple nodes, allowing for parallel processing of transactions. In blockchain systems, sharding enables the network to handle a larger number of transactions simultaneously, reducing congestion and improving transaction throughput (Suresh Babu, C. V. & Abhinaba Pal. 2023).. AI can enhance the sharding process by intelligently determining how to partition data based on usage patterns and transaction volumes, thereby optimizing performance and resource allocation.
2. **Layer-2 Solutions**: Layer-2 solutions, such as state channels and rollups, are built on top of existing blockchain networks to alleviate scalability issues. These solutions allow for off-chain transactions, reducing the load on the main blockchain while still ensuring security and transparency. AI can facilitate the

management of layer-2 solutions by predicting transaction loads and dynamically adjusting resources to maintain optimal performance (Khan et al., 2021). For example, AI algorithms can analyze historical transaction data to forecast peak usage times, enabling proactive scaling of layer-2 resources.

9.2. Predictive Analytics: Forecasting Trends and Detecting Anomalies in Blockchain Networks

AI-driven predictive analytics can play a significant role in enhancing the scalability of Web3 platforms by providing insights into network behavior and user activities.

1. **Forecasting Trends**: Machine learning algorithms can analyze vast amounts of data from blockchain networks to identify trends and patterns in user behavior, transaction volumes, and market dynamics. By leveraging historical data, AI can forecast future demands, enabling developers to proactively adjust network resources and optimize performance (Chong et al., 2021). This ability to anticipate changes can enhance user experience by ensuring that the platform remains responsive during high-demand periods.
2. **Detecting Anomalies**: AI can also be utilized to detect anomalies within blockchain networks, such as unusual transaction patterns that may indicate fraud or security breaches. Anomaly detection algorithms can analyze transaction data in real time, flagging suspicious activities for further investigation. By identifying and mitigating potential threats quickly, AI can help maintain the integrity and performance of the blockchain network, thereby supporting scalability (Oluoch et al., 2020).

9.3. Automation: AI-Driven Smart Contracts to Streamline Processes

The integration of AI into smart contracts can significantly enhance the efficiency and scalability of Web3 applications by automating various processes.

1. **AI-Driven Smart Contracts**: Traditional smart contracts execute predefined conditions autonomously, but incorporating AI can enable them to adapt and learn from new data. For instance, AI algorithms can analyze external data sources to dynamically adjust contract terms based on real-time market conditions or user behaviors (Babu, C. V. Suresh, Sudhir Manoharan, 2024). This adaptability can improve the efficiency of transactions and reduce the need for manual intervention, thereby streamlining operations.

2. **Streamlining Processes**: AI can automate complex workflows by integrating with smart contracts, reducing the time and effort required to execute transactions. For example, in supply chain management, AI-driven smart contracts can automatically trigger payments and order updates based on real-time inventory levels and shipping statuses (Helo & Shamsuzzoha, 2021). This level of automation not only enhances operational efficiency but also reduces transaction costs, making Web3 platforms more scalable and user-friendly.

10.0. EXPANDING KNOWLEDGE IN WEB3 AND BLOCKCHAIN

As the landscape of Web3 and blockchain technology evolves rapidly, it is imperative for developers, researchers, and practitioners to continuously enhance their knowledge and skills. This section discusses three critical approaches to expanding knowledge in Web3 and blockchain: continuous learning, networking, and gaining hands-on experience through projects and open-source contributions.

10.1. Continuous Learning: Keeping Updated with Latest Developments

The field of Web3 and blockchain is characterized by rapid technological advancements, necessitating a commitment to continuous learning.

1. **Online Courses and Certifications**: Numerous platforms offer specialized courses on blockchain technology, decentralized applications (dApps), and smart contracts. Resources such as Coursera, edX, and Udacity provide courses designed by industry experts, allowing learners to stay abreast of the latest trends and technologies (Peters et al., 2021). Engaging in structured learning can help individuals gain a comprehensive understanding of complex concepts and applications.
2. **Research Papers and Journals**: Academic and industry research continues to produce a wealth of knowledge about blockchain and Web3. Reading peer-reviewed journals, white papers, and conference proceedings can provide insights into emerging technologies and methodologies (Suresh Babu, C. V. & Abhinaba Pal. 2023).. Staying informed about ongoing research can enhance one's understanding of theoretical frameworks and their practical implications.
3. **Webinars and Workshops**: Attending webinars and workshops hosted by industry leaders can be a valuable way to learn about the latest innovations and best practices in Web3 and blockchain. These events often feature case studies,

discussions on regulatory changes, and expert opinions, providing a platform for interactive learning (Mackey et al., 2021).

10.2. Networking: Engaging with Industry Professionals and Communities

Building a professional network is crucial for knowledge expansion and career development in the Web3 and blockchain space.

1. **Industry Conferences and Meetups**: Participating in conferences and local meetups allows individuals to connect with industry professionals, researchers, and enthusiasts. Events like Devcon, Consensus, and local blockchain meetups offer opportunities for networking, collaboration, and knowledge sharing (Krause et al., 2020). These interactions can lead to mentorship opportunities and potential partnerships on projects.
2. **Online Communities and Forums**: Engaging with online communities such as Reddit, Discord, and GitHub can provide platforms for discussion and knowledge exchange. These communities often feature forums where users share insights, ask questions, and collaborate on projects (Giungato et al., 2021). Active participation in such forums can enhance understanding and provide exposure to diverse perspectives.
3. **Social Media and Professional Networks**: Following thought leaders and organizations on platforms like Twitter and LinkedIn can keep individuals informed about the latest trends and developments in Web3 and blockchain. Engaging with content, participating in discussions, and sharing knowledge can enhance one's visibility in the field and help establish professional connections (Karafillidis & Korkontzelos, 2021).

10.3. Hands-On Experience: Working on Projects and Contributing to Open-Source Initiatives

Practical experience is essential for deepening knowledge and understanding of Web3 and blockchain technologies.

1. **Project-Based Learning**: Actively working on projects, whether personal, academic, or professional, allows individuals to apply theoretical concepts in practical scenarios. Developing dApps, creating smart contracts, or participating in hackathons can provide valuable experience and enhance technical skills (Bürgel et al., 2021).

2. **Open-Source Contributions**: Contributing to open-source blockchain projects on platforms like GitHub not only helps individuals gain hands-on experience but also fosters collaboration and community engagement. Many successful projects welcome contributions from developers of all skill levels, offering opportunities to learn from others while enhancing the project (Lerner & Tirole, 2020). Engaging with open-source communities can also lead to networking opportunities and exposure to industry practices.
3. **Internships and Co-op Programs**: Securing internships or co-op positions with organizations that focus on Web3 and blockchain can provide invaluable real-world experience. These positions often allow individuals to work on significant projects and collaborate with experienced professionals, enhancing their skill sets and understanding of industry dynamics (Suresh Babu, C. V. & Sanjai Das, 2023).

11.0. SCOPE OF THE PROJECT

The scope of this project, titled "Designing and Developing a Web3 Mobile Platform: Integrating Blockchain and AI for Enhanced Functionality, Security, and User Experience," outlines the boundaries and focus areas of the development process. This section details the inclusions and exclusions of the project, as well as the assumptions and constraints that will guide the implementation.

11.1. Inclusions: Blockchain and AI Integration, User Interface Design, Security Enhancements, Scalability Solutions

1. **Blockchain and AI Integration**: This project emphasizes the seamless integration of blockchain technology and artificial intelligence (AI) to enhance the functionality of the mobile platform. The blockchain component will ensure decentralized data storage, transparency, and immutability, while AI algorithms will facilitate data analysis, user behavior prediction, and personalized recommendations (Duan et al., 2021). The integration aims to create a platform that leverages the strengths of both technologies, providing users with a secure and intelligent experience.
2. **User Interface Design**: A key focus of the project is the design of an intuitive and user-friendly interface that enhances user experience (UX). This involves employing user-centered design principles, conducting user research, and iterating on design prototypes based on user feedback (Nielsen & Molich, 2021). The goal is to create a visually appealing and accessible interface that caters to diverse user needs and abilities, ensuring ease of navigation and interaction.

3. **Security Enhancements**: Given the importance of security in Web3 applications, the project will implement robust security measures to protect user data and transactions. This includes encryption protocols, secure key management practices, and regular security audits to identify vulnerabilities (Kumar et al., 2020). The objective is to build a platform that prioritizes user trust and safeguards sensitive information against potential threats.
4. **Scalability Solutions**: To ensure that the platform can handle increased user activity and data volume, scalable solutions will be incorporated. Techniques such as layer-2 scaling solutions and sharding will be explored to enhance transaction throughput without compromising performance (Suresh Babu, C. V. & Abhinaba Pal. 2023).. This aspect of the project aims to provide a responsive and efficient user experience, even as the user base grows.

11.2. Exclusions: Traditional Web Application Development, Non-Web3 Technologies

1. **Traditional Web Application Development**: The project will not include traditional web application development practices that do not leverage the decentralized capabilities of blockchain technology. While conventional methods may provide certain functionalities, they do not align with the core objectives of creating a Web3 platform that emphasizes user control and ownership of data.
2. **Non-Web3 Technologies**: Technologies that do not support the principles of decentralization, such as centralized cloud services or traditional database management systems, will be excluded from the project's scope. The focus will remain on utilizing blockchain, AI, and related decentralized technologies that contribute to the overall vision of the project (Buterin, 2018).

11.3. Assumptions and Constraints: Tools, Technologies, User Testing, Time, Budget, Technical Limitations

1. **Assumptions**: The project operates under several key assumptions:
   - Users have a basic understanding of blockchain technology and are willing to adapt to a new mobile platform.
   - The necessary tools and technologies for blockchain and AI integration are accessible and compatible with the intended platform design.
   - The development team possesses the required expertise to implement complex functionalities related to blockchain and AI.
2. **Constraints**: The project will face various constraints that may impact its execution:

- **Tools and Technologies**: The availability of specific tools and frameworks for blockchain and AI development may limit certain functionalities (Wang et al., 2021). The choice of blockchain platform (e.g., Ethereum, Polkadot) will also influence development decisions.
- **User Testing**: Limited access to representative user testing groups may constrain the ability to gather comprehensive feedback, potentially impacting design iterations and overall usability.
- **Time and Budget**: The project timeline and budget will impose limitations on the extent of features that can be developed and tested (Kuo et al., 2020). Balancing scope with available resources will be crucial for successful project completion.
- **Technical Limitations**: The inherent challenges of blockchain technology, such as latency and energy consumption, may impose constraints on the performance of the mobile platform. Addressing these limitations will require careful planning and innovative solutions.

12.0. LITERATURE REVIEW

The integration of artificial intelligence (AI) and blockchain technology has garnered significant interest in both academic and industrial circles. This literature review discusses existing research on the intersection of these two transformative technologies and identifies gaps in practical implementations and scalability solutions.

12.1. Existing Research on AI and Blockchain Integration

Research on the integration of AI and blockchain has primarily focused on their complementary strengths, enhancing security, transparency, and efficiency in various domains. Several studies highlight the potential of this integration in optimizing data management, automating processes, and improving decision-making (Wang et al., 2020).

1. **Data Management and Security**: Blockchain's decentralized nature ensures data integrity, while AI can analyze vast amounts of data in real-time. For instance, Xu et al. (2020) emphasize that AI can enhance the security of blockchain networks by identifying anomalous behavior patterns, which is crucial for detecting and mitigating security threats. The combination of AI and blockchain has been proposed as a solution to strengthen cybersecurity protocols by providing a transparent audit trail of data transactions (Zhang et al., 2021).

2. **Automation and Smart Contracts**: The automation capabilities of AI can streamline processes within blockchain ecosystems. Smart contracts—self-executing contracts with the terms of the agreement directly written into code—can benefit from AI algorithms that enable them to execute complex conditions and optimize performance (Suresh Babu, C. V. & Sanjai Das 2023). By integrating machine learning with smart contracts, it becomes feasible to create adaptive contracts that can adjust based on changing data inputs.
3. **Decision-Making Processes**: The synthesis of AI and blockchain can facilitate enhanced decision-making capabilities. For instance, Chen et al. (2021) discuss how AI-driven predictive analytics can leverage blockchain data to forecast trends and inform business strategies. This integration allows organizations to make more informed, data-driven decisions while ensuring data authenticity through blockchain.

12.2. Gaps in Practical Implementations and Scalability Solutions

Despite the promising potential of AI and blockchain integration, several gaps exist in the literature concerning practical implementations and scalability solutions.

1. **Practical Implementations**: While theoretical frameworks and prototypes exist, there is a lack of comprehensive case studies that document real-world applications of AI-blockchain integration (Nguyen et al., 2022). Most research tends to focus on conceptual models rather than empirical evidence from live deployments. This gap highlights the need for more extensive pilot projects and documentation to showcase successful integrations across various industries, such as healthcare, supply chain management, and finance.
2. **Scalability Solutions**: Scalability remains a critical challenge for both blockchain and AI technologies. Blockchain networks often struggle with transaction throughput and latency issues, while AI models may require extensive computational resources, which can hinder their deployment at scale (Voshmgir, 2020). Although some studies suggest solutions such as sharding and layer-2 scaling techniques for blockchain, few research efforts have explored how these methods can be synergistically applied with AI-driven solutions to create scalable architectures (Dai et al., 2021). There is a pressing need for research that focuses on developing integrated frameworks that address both the scalability of blockchain networks and the resource efficiency of AI algorithms.
3. **Interoperability Challenges**: Interoperability among different blockchain systems and AI models is another gap in the existing research. Many studies highlight the potential benefits of integrating AI with blockchain; however, they

often overlook the complexities associated with different protocols, standards, and data formats used across various platforms (Mansoori et al., 2021). Developing a standardized approach to ensure seamless interaction between diverse systems is essential for realizing the full potential of AI-blockchain integrations.

13.0. METHODOLOGY

This chapter employs a comprehensive methodology to design and develop a Web3 mobile platform integrating blockchain and artificial intelligence (AI). The methodology is structured to encompass an exploratory and developmental approach, focusing on user feedback and experimental data collection, employing qualitative and quantitative analysis methods, and utilizing various tools and technologies relevant to Web3 development and AI.

13.1. Research Design: Exploratory and Developmental Approach

The research design for this chapter is characterized by an exploratory and developmental approach, allowing for a thorough investigation of existing technologies and their integration into a cohesive mobile platform. The exploratory phase involves a literature review and analysis of current trends in Web3, AI, and blockchain to identify best practices and potential gaps in the existing platforms (Creswell & Creswell, 2017).

This initial exploration is followed by a developmental phase, wherein a prototype of the Web3 mobile platform is constructed. This prototype aims to incorporate user-centered design principles to create an intuitive user experience while integrating advanced functionalities provided by blockchain and AI technologies. The development is iterative, with cycles of testing and refinement based on user feedback and system performance (Suresh Babu, C. V. & Sanjai Das 2023)..

13.2. Data Collection: User Feedback and Experimental Data

Data collection methods in this research are twofold: user feedback and experimental data.

1. **User Feedback**: User feedback is collected through surveys and usability testing sessions. Surveys will gather insights on user expectations, preferences, and pain points related to current Web3 applications. Usability testing sessions involve real users interacting with the prototype to assess the platform's intuitiveness and

functionality. This feedback will be analyzed to identify areas for improvement and validate design choices (Brooke, 2013).

2. **Experimental Data**: Experimental data will be collected during the development of the mobile platform. This includes performance metrics such as transaction speeds, resource consumption, and responsiveness of AI-driven features. Automated testing frameworks will be employed to measure system performance under different conditions and loads, ensuring the platform meets scalability and efficiency requirements (Lerner et al., 2021).

13.3. Analysis Methods: Qualitative and Quantitative Analysis

The analysis methods utilized in this chapter encompass both qualitative and quantitative approaches.

1. **Qualitative Analysis**: Qualitative data collected from user feedback will be analyzed using thematic analysis. This method allows for the identification of recurring themes and patterns within user responses, providing deeper insights into user experiences and preferences (Braun & Clarke, 2006). The analysis will focus on understanding user motivations, satisfaction levels, and suggestions for enhancements.
2. **Quantitative Analysis**: Quantitative data from experimental measurements will be subjected to statistical analysis to evaluate the platform's performance objectively. Metrics such as response times, transaction success rates, and resource usage will be analyzed using descriptive statistics and inferential tests, enabling the assessment of the system's efficiency and scalability (Field, 2013).

13.4. Tools and Technologies: Web3.js, Ethers.js, Solidity, AI Frameworks

The development of the Web3 mobile platform will leverage various tools and technologies that facilitate blockchain integration and AI capabilities.

1. **Web3.js**: This JavaScript library allows interaction with the Ethereum blockchain and other decentralized networks. It provides a convenient API for building dApps and interacting with smart contracts, making it essential for the platform's front-end development (Buterin, 2014).
2. **Ethers.js**: Ethers.js is another powerful library for interacting with the Ethereum blockchain. It offers a simple interface for developers to create and manage wallets, sign transactions, and communicate with smart contracts, ensuring a seamless user experience (Rosenfeld, 2021).

3. **Solidity**: Solidity is the primary programming language for writing smart contracts on Ethereum. It will be used to develop the smart contracts that facilitate the platform's functionality, ensuring security and efficiency (Huang et al., 2018).
4. **AI Frameworks**: To integrate AI capabilities into the platform, various AI frameworks such as TensorFlow and PyTorch will be utilized. These frameworks support the development and deployment of machine learning models that can enhance user experience through features like predictive analytics and personalized recommendations (Abadi et al., 2016).

14.0. SOLUTION DESIGN AND IMPLEMENTATION

Integration of AI and Blockchain

The Web3 mobile platform leverages **blockchain for decentralization and security** while **AI enhances decision-making and automation**. The architecture comprises:

1. **Blockchain Layer** – Ensures secure transactions with smart contracts and consensus mechanisms.
2. **AI Layer** – Processes blockchain data to enhance security, user personalization, and automation.
3. **User Interface Layer** – Provides an intuitive experience for seamless blockchain-AI interaction.

System Architecture

- **Decentralized Blockchain Network** (e.g., Ethereum, Polkadot) enables peer-to-peer transactions with integrity (Suresh Babu, C. V. & Sanjai Das 2023).
- **AI Engine** analyzes transaction data for trend predictions, security enhancements, and fraud detection.
- **User Interface (UI)** delivers personalized content, transaction histories, and AI-driven recommendations.

Machine Learning Models for Smart Contracts & User Personalization

- **Decision Trees & Random Forests** – Predict smart contract outcomes based on historical data.
- **Neural Networks** – Identify complex user behavior patterns for recommendations and automation.

- **Clustering Algorithms (K-means)** – Segment users for targeted experiences and marketing.
- **Natural Language Processing (NLP)** – Enables chatbots and virtual assistants for user support.

Data Preprocessing for Blockchain Data

1. **Data Cleaning** – Eliminates noise, duplicates, and inconsistencies for accurate AI processing.
2. **Feature Engineering** – Extracts key variables (e.g., transaction frequency, user interactions).
3. **Normalization & Scaling** – Standardizes data for improved machine learning performance.
4. **Data Splitting & Cross-Validation** – Ensures model accuracy and generalization.

This structured approach enhances **security, automation, and user experience**, making the platform **adaptable to evolving Web3 trends**.

15.0. RESOURCE REQUIREMENTS

1. Human Resources:

Developing a Web3 mobile platform integrating blockchain and AI requires a multidisciplinary team:

- **Project Manager** – Oversees development, manages risks, and ensures project alignment.
- **Blockchain Developer** – Implements smart contracts, blockchain protocols, and decentralized components.
- **AI Specialist** – Develops machine learning models, predictive analytics, and NLP features.
- **UX Designer** – Designs intuitive, user-friendly interfaces based on usability principles.
- **QA Tester** – Conducts functional, performance, and security testing.

2. Technical Resources:

Key technologies and tools include:

- **Development Environment** – IDEs like Visual Studio Code, IntelliJ IDEA.
- **Blockchain Tools** – Web3.js, Ethers.js, Truffle Suite for smart contract and dApp development.
- **AI Frameworks** – TensorFlow, PyTorch, scikit-learn for machine learning integration.
- **Cloud Infrastructure** – AWS, Azure, or Google Cloud for hosting and processing.

3. Budget Considerations:

- **Personnel Costs:** $60,000–$130,000 per role annually.
- **Software Licenses:** Costs for proprietary tools.
- **Hardware Costs:** $5,000–$15,000 for testing infrastructure.
- **Cloud Services:** $1,000–$5,000 monthly for hosting and AI processing.
- **Contingency Funds:** 10-20% of the total budget for unexpected expenses.

Efficient resource allocation is essential for ensuring functionality, security, and user experience in the Web3 mobile platform.

16.0. RISK MANAGEMENT

Effective risk management is critical in the development of a Web3 mobile platform integrating blockchain and AI. This section highlights key risks and corresponding mitigation strategies to ensure security, scalability, and user adoption.

Key Risks

1. **Security Vulnerabilities** – Smart contract flaws and AI-related data integrity issues may lead to breaches and financial losses.
2. **Scalability Issues** – Increased transaction volume can cause bottlenecks, leading to delays and higher operational costs.
3. **User Adoption Challenges** – Complexity, security concerns, and lack of Web3 awareness may hinder widespread adoption.

Mitigation Strategies

- **Regular Security Audits** – Conducting audits with third-party experts and automated security tools to identify vulnerabilities.
- **Iterative Testing & Refinement** – Using Agile/DevOps methodologies and beta testing for continuous improvement.
- **User Feedback Integration** – Implementing usability testing and educational resources to enhance user experience and adoption.

- **Scalability Planning** – Leveraging layer-2 solutions, sharding, and AI-driven predictive analytics for system optimization.
- **Regulatory Compliance** – Ensuring adherence to data protection laws (e.g., GDPR, CCPA) and staying updated on evolving regulations.

By proactively managing these risks, the Web3 platform can achieve greater security, efficiency, and user engagement, driving its long-term success.

17.0. EVALUATION AND METRICS

To ensure the success of a Web3 mobile platform integrating blockchain and AI, clear evaluation criteria and performance metrics are essential. These help assess functionality, security, and user experience.

Criteria for Success

1. **User Satisfaction** – Measured through surveys, user feedback, and Net Promoter Scores (NPS) to gauge user experience and loyalty.
2. **Transaction Efficiency** – Evaluated by transaction confirmation times and network throughput to ensure speed and reliability.
3. **Security Robustness** – Assessed through the frequency and severity of security incidents, phishing attempts, and the effectiveness of security measures like multi-factor authentication and encryption.

Performance Metrics

1. **Response Time** – Tracks how quickly transactions are processed and confirmed, enhancing user experience.
2. **Security Incident Frequency** – Monitors occurrences of data breaches, unauthorized access, and vulnerabilities to evaluate security effectiveness.
3. **User Engagement** – Measured through daily active users (DAU), session duration, and interaction rates to assess platform usability.
4. **Scalability Metrics** – Examines transaction throughput and system performance under increasing loads to ensure future growth readiness (Suresh Babu, C. V. & Abhinaba Pal. 2023).

By leveraging these success criteria and performance metrics, developers can continuously refine the Web3 mobile platform, optimizing security, efficiency, and user engagement.

18.0. EXPECTED OUTCOMES AND IMPACT

The development of a Web3 mobile platform integrating blockchain and AI aims to deliver a user-friendly, secure, and scalable application while driving broader adoption and setting new standards for decentralized applications (Suresh Babu C.V, Naveen Akash V., et. al. 2024).

Expected Results

1. **User-Friendly Interface** – Designed for seamless navigation and accessibility, making blockchain interactions intuitive for users of all technical backgrounds.
2. **Robust Security Features** – Implements encryption, secure key management, and security audits to protect user data and transactions.
3. **Scalability Solutions** – Utilizes sharding and layer-2 solutions to maintain performance and efficiency under increasing user and transaction loads.

Impact

1. **Enhanced User Trust** – Strengthened through security measures and an intuitive user experience, addressing concerns about blockchain usability.
2. **Greater Adoption of Web3 Technologies** – Encourages users to transition from traditional web applications to decentralized alternatives, driving mainstream adoption.
3. **Improved dApp Standards** – Establishes benchmarks for security, usability, and scalability, setting a foundation for higher-quality Web3 applications.

By achieving these outcomes, the platform contributes to a more secure, efficient, and widely accepted Web3 ecosystem, fostering innovation and trust in decentralized technologies.

19.0. CONCLUSION

This chapter explored the key aspects of designing and developing a Web3 mobile platform that integrates blockchain and AI to enhance functionality, security, and user experience. It established the transformative potential of Web3 technologies by outlining goals, methodologies, and expected outcomes.

Key Takeaways

- **Current Challenges in Web3 Apps** – Issues like poor usability, security risks, and scalability limitations hinder adoption.

- **Integrating Blockchain and AI** – AI-driven security, predictive analytics, and personalized user experiences improve efficiency and trust.
- **User-Centric and Secure Design** – Implementing intuitive interfaces, encryption, and secure key management fosters greater user engagement and confidence.
- **Scalability Solutions** – AI-powered automation and decentralized architecture ensure seamless expansion as user demand grows.

Call to Action

- **Developers** – Prioritize accessibility, security, and usability in application design.
- **Investors** – Support projects aligned with decentralization and user empowerment.
- **Regulators** – Establish balanced guidelines to promote innovation while protecting user rights.
- **Users** – Engage with and provide feedback to enhance Web3 applications.

By addressing these challenges and fostering collaboration among stakeholders, this Web3 platform can drive a secure, scalable, and user-friendly digital ecosystem, accelerating mainstream adoption of decentralized applications.

REFERENCES

Babu, C. V. S., & Manoharan, S. (2024). AI and Blockchain Revolution in Communication Education: Future of Work in the Age of Industrial Robotics. In Eduard Babulak, I. G. I. (Ed.), *Applied AI and Humanoid Robotics for the Ultra-Smart Cyberspace* (pp. 63–84). Global., DOI: 10.4018/979-8-3693-2399-1.ch003

Braun, V., & Clarke, V. (2006). Using thematic analysis in psychology. *Qualitative Research in Psychology*, *3*(2), 77–101. DOI: 10.1191/1478088706qp063oa

Brooke, J. (2013). SUS: A quick and dirty usability scale. In *Usability Evaluation in Industry* (pp. 189-194). CRC Press.

Buterin, V. (2014). *A next-generation smart contract and decentralized application platform*. Ethereum Foundation. https://ethereum.org/en/whitepaper/

Chong, W. K.. (2021). Predictive analytics in blockchain technology: Trends and applications. *Journal of Management Analytics*, *8*(2), 127–144. DOI: 10.1080/23294885.2020.1799357

Cohen, A., McCauley, M., & Robison, A. (2020). Blockchain-based voting: A revolutionary step towards secure democracy. *Journal of Digital Governance*, *1*(1), 23–35. DOI: 10.1007/s42455-019-00006-7

Creswell, J. W., & Creswell, J. D. (2017). *Research Design: Qualitative, Quantitative, and Mixed Methods Approaches* (5th ed.). Sage Publications.

Dai, H. N.. (2021). Blockchain and AI-based solutions for sustainable agriculture: A review. *Computers and Electronics in Agriculture*, *181*, 105951. DOI: 10.1016/j.compag.2020.105951

Dinh, T. N., Liu, R., Zhang, L., & Chen, G. (2018). Untangling blockchain: A data processing view of blockchain systems. *IEEE Access : Practical Innovations, Open Solutions*, *6*, 19056–19067. DOI: 10.1109/ACCESS.2018.2821901

Duan, Y.. (2021). Integrating blockchain and artificial intelligence: The role of data in digital transformation. *Business Horizons*, *64*(3), 339–348. DOI: 10.1016/j.bushor.2021.01.004

Dufour, S., Benaissa, A., & Cheikhrouhou, N. (2023). A Decentralized Approach to AI: Addressing Data Privacy and Bias in AI Algorithms. *Journal of Information Technology & Politics*, *20*(1), 35–51.

Ethereum Foundation. (2024). Web3.js. Retrieved from https://web3js.readthedocs.io/en/v1.7.0/

European Commission. (2020). Data protection in the European Union. https://ec.europa.eu/info/law/law-topic/data-protection_en

Field, A. (2013). *Discovering Statistics Using IBM SPSS Statistics* (4th ed.). Sage Publications.

Frolov, A., Gubarev, M., & Ponomareva, N. (2023). Trends in Web3 Application Development: Opportunities and Challenges. *International Journal of Information Management*, *65*, 102453.

Gao, H., Zhao, J., & Zhang, W. (2023). Enhancing User Experience in Web3 Applications Through AI-Powered Personalization. *Journal of Systems and Software*, *205*, 110767.

Garrett, J. J. (2011). *The elements of user experience: User-centered design for the web and beyond*. New Riders.

Giungato, P.. (2021). The role of online communities in promoting blockchain knowledge: A systematic review. *Journal of Knowledge Management*, *25*(6), 1397–1416. DOI: 10.1108/JKM-01-2021-0120

Gupta, V., & Rathore, H. (2024). Leveraging AI for enhanced blockchain scalability: Challenges and solutions. *International Journal of Information Management*, *66*, 102459.

Hassan, S., Babar, M. I., & Khan, A. N. (2021). Decentralized Autonomous Organizations (DAOs): A governance perspective. *IEEE Access : Practical Innovations, Open Solutions*, *9*, 157220–157230. DOI: 10.1109/ACCESS.2021.3128918

Helo, P., & Shamsuzzoha, A. (2021). AI and blockchain in supply chain management: A systematic literature review. *Advanced Intelligent Systems*, *3*(6), 2000204. DOI: 10.1002/aisy.202000204

Huang, J., ... (2018). Solidity: A programming language for writing smart contracts. *arXiv preprint arXiv:1808.05233*.

Huang, R., Liu, X., & Xu, Z. (2023). Usability Challenges in Web3: Bridging the Gap Between Blockchain and Users. *Computers in Human Behavior*, *145*, 107560.

Huang, Y.. (2019). Trust, risk and the acceptance of blockchain technology: A survey. *Journal of Information Technology*, *34*(3), 197–214. DOI: 10.1177/0268396218792025

Kahneman, D. (2011). *Thinking, fast and slow*. Farrar, Straus and Giroux.

Karafillidis, A., & Korkontzelos, A. (2021). The role of social media in knowledge sharing in blockchain communities: A case study. *International Journal of Information Management, 59*, 102359. DOI: 10.1016/j.ijinfomgt.2021.102359

Khan, A.. (2021). Leveraging AI for enhancing scalability in blockchain. *Computers & Security, 105*, 102240. DOI: 10.1016/j.cose.2021.102240

Khan, M., Ahmad, N., & Saleem, A. (2024). Decentralized Finance: A New Paradigm in Financial Services. *Finance Research Letters, 49*, 103348.

Kim, H. K., Park, Y. J., & Lee, S. (2021). Improving usability in cryptocurrency wallet applications through user feedback. *Computers in Human Behavior, 116*, 106642. DOI: 10.1016/j.chb.2020.106642

Kostiainen, K.. (2019). Secure key management for blockchain applications. *IEEE Security and Privacy, 17*(3), 28–37. DOI: 10.1109/MSP.2019.2915746

Kouhizadeh, M., & Sarkis, J. (2021). Blockchain and supply chain management: A systematic review and future directions. *International Journal of Production Economics, 231*, 107851. DOI: 10.1016/j.ijpe.2020.107851

Krause, A.. (2020). Networking and collaboration in the blockchain community: An analysis of industry conferences. *Journal of Business Research, 116*, 418–426. DOI: 10.1016/j.jbusres.2019.10.025

Kuo, T. T.. (2020). The role of blockchain technology in the management of supply chain risks: A review and future research agenda. *International Journal of Production Economics, 219*, 109–121. DOI: 10.1016/j.ijpe.2019.04.014

Lerner, J., & Tirole, J. (2020). The governance of blockchain initiatives. *The Journal of Economic Perspectives, 34*(2), 107–130. DOI: 10.1257/jep.20191203

Lidwell, W., Holden, K., & Butler, J. (2010). *Universal Principles of Design*. Rockport Publishers.

Mackey, T. K.. (2021). The role of blockchain technology in advancing global health: A systematic review. *Health Policy and Technology, 10*(2), 100–111. DOI: 10.1016/j.hlpt.2021.03.001

Makhdoom, I.. (2021). Blockchain technology in healthcare: A systematic review. *Journal of Biomedical Informatics, 113*, 103634. DOI: 10.1016/j.jbi.2020.103634

Mansoori, Y.. (2021). Interoperability in blockchain technology: A review. *Journal of Network and Computer Applications, 188*, 103115. DOI: 10.1016/j.jnca.2021.103115

Miers, I.. (2013). ZK-proof-based protocols for anonymous transactions. *ACM Transactions on Information and System Security*, *16*(4), 1–24. DOI: 10.1145/2482768.2482770

Narayanan, A., Bonneau, J., Felten, E., Miller, A., & Goldfeder, S. (2016). *Bitcoin and Cryptocurrency Technologies*. Princeton University Press.

Nguyen, T. N.. (2022). Blockchain and AI in health care: A systematic review. *Health Informatics Journal*, *28*(2), 14604582221084341. DOI: 10.1177/14604582221084341

Nielsen, J., & Molich, R. (2021). Heuristic evaluation of user interfaces. *Proceedings of the SIGCHI Conference on Human Factors in Computing Systems*, 249-256. https://doi.org/DOI: 10.1145/674044.674096

Oluoch, M.. (2020). Real-time anomaly detection in blockchain transactions using deep learning. *Journal of Cybersecurity and Privacy*, *1*(1), 61–79. DOI: 10.3390/jcp1010005

Paszke, A., ... (2019). PyTorch: An imperative style, high-performance deep learning library. In *Advances in Neural Information Processing Systems* (pp. 8024-8035).

Peters, G.. (2021). Blockchain education: Trends and approaches for the future. *Computers in Human Behavior Reports*, *4*, 100124. DOI: 10.1016/j.chbr.2021.100124

Peters, G. W., Panayi, E., & Chapelle, A. (2023). Scalability Solutions for Blockchain: Layer-2 and Beyond. *Journal of Financial Technology*, *1*(1), 5–20.

Reid, F., Subramanian, A., & Ali, S. (2022). Security Vulnerabilities in Decentralized Applications: A Comprehensive Review. *IEEE Access : Practical Innovations, Open Solutions*, *10*, 10345–10363.

Rosa, A. M., da Silva, R. F., & Freire, L. (2021). Accessibility in web applications: A systematic review of studies. *Journal of Web Engineering*, *20*(1), 1–26. DOI: 10.13052/jwe1540-9589.2010

Rosenfeld, M. (2021). *Ethers.js: A Complete Guide*. https://docs.ethers.io/v5/

Singh, A., & Sandhu, R. (2021). *Blockchain and Decentralized Applications*. Academic Press.

Singh, R.. (2020). Integrating blockchain and AI: Opportunities and challenges. *Proceedings of the IEEE International Conference on Data Science and Advanced Analytics (DSAA)*, 375-386. https://doi.org/DOI: 10.1109/DSAA.2020.00053

Soni, P., Verma, S., & Sharma, S. (2022). AI in Blockchain: A Comprehensive Survey. *Artificial Intelligence Review*, *55*(4), 2541–2576.

Stallings, W., & Brown, L. (2019). *Computer Security: Principles and Practice*. Pearson.

Suite, T. (2024). Truffle Suite. Retrieved from https://www.trufflesuite.com/truffle

Suresh Babu, C. V. & Abhinaba Pal. (2023). Securing Decentralized Finance Through Blockchain Technologies. In R. Thanigaivelan, S. Kaliappan, & C. Jegadheesan (Eds.), Cyber-Physical Systems and Supporting Technologies for Industrial Automation (pp. 351-372). IGI Global. https://doi.org/DOI: 10.4018/978-1-6684-9267-3.ch020

Suresh Babu, C. V. & Sanjai Das (2023). Impact of Blockchain Technology on the Stock Market. In K. Mehta, R. Sharma, & P. Yu (Eds.), Revolutionizing Financial Services and Markets Through FinTech and Blockchain (pp. 44-59). IGI Global. DOI: 10.4018/978-1-6684-8624-5.ch004

Suresh Babu, C. V., Dharma Sastha, B., Naveen Akash, V., Praveen, S., & Santhosh Kumar, D. (2024). Enhancing Sustainability in Smart Energy Systems Through Anomaly Detection Algorithms. In Naoui, M., Ben Khalifa, R., & Sbita, L. (Eds.), *Modeling, Analysis, and Control of Smart Energy Systems* (pp. 119–136). IGI Global., DOI: 10.4018/979-8-3693-2999-3.ch007

Swan, M. (2015). *Blockchain: Blueprint for a new economy*. O'Reilly Media.

Tapscott, D., & Tapscott, A. (2016). *Blockchain Revolution: How the Technology Behind Bitcoin is Changing Money, Business, and the World*. Penguin.

Tiwari, S., Kumar, V., & Kumari, R. (2023). Understanding User Frustrations in Web3 Applications: A Survey Study. *International Journal of Information Technology : an Official Journal of Bharati Vidyapeeth's Institute of Computer Applications and Management*, *15*(1), 101–115.

Tönnies, B., Naegele, M., & Lutz, M. (2022). Usability in Blockchain Applications: A Review and Future Directions. *ACM Transactions on Internet Technology*, *22*(4), 56.

Vaswani, A., ... (2017). Attention is all you need. In *Advances in Neural Information Processing Systems* (pp. 5998-6008).

Voshmgir, S. (2020). *Token Economy: How Blockchains and Smart Contracts Revolutionize the Financial Industry*. BlockchainHub.

Wang, J.. (2020). Blockchain and artificial intelligence in financial services: A systematic literature review. *Technological Forecasting and Social Change*, *146*, 854–861. DOI: 10.1016/j.techfore.2018.10.010

Wang, X.. (2021). An overview of blockchain technology in smart cities. *Journal of Network and Computer Applications*, *177*, 102920. DOI: 10.1016/j.jnca.2020.102920

Wood, G. (2016). Polkadot: Vision for a scalable decentralized network. *Web3 Foundation*. Retrieved from https://polkadot.network/Polkadot-Whitepaper-v0.9.8.pdf

Xu, J.. (2020). A survey on blockchain-based intelligent security systems: Challenges and opportunities. *Journal of Network and Computer Applications*, *170*, 102766. DOI: 10.1016/j.jnca.2020.102766

Zhang, C., Liang, H., & Zhang, Y. (2023). Smart Contracts: Security Challenges and Solutions. *Computer Standards & Interfaces*, *85*, 103595.

Zhang, P., Schmidt, D., & Hinton, J. (2020). Decentralized identity: The foundation for self-sovereign identity. *IEEE Software*, *37*(1), 32–38.

Zhang, Q., Schmidt, D., & White, J. (2022). *AI in Blockchain Applications for the Next Generation of Decentralized Services*.

Zhang, Y.. (2021). A blockchain-based approach for secure and efficient data management in smart cities. *Future Generation Computer Systems*, *116*, 105–115. DOI: 10.1016/j.future.2020.10.024

Compilation of References

Abdulsaeed, A., Burhanuddina, M., Ismaelb, M., Abd Ghania, M. K., Elzamly, A., & Doheir, M. (2019). Adoption of cloud based solutions for E-learning technologies and their relative perspectives for higher education. *Revista Aus*, *26*(10), 105–114.

Ablin, J. L. (2008). Learning as problem design versus problem solving: Making the connection between cognitive neuroscience research and educational practice. *Mind, Brain, and Education/Mind. Mind, Brain and Education : the Official Journal of the International Mind, Brain, and Education Society*, *2*(2), 52–54. DOI: 10.1111/j.1751-228X.2008.00030.x

Ablyazov, T., & Rapgof, V. (2019). Digital platforms as the basis of a new ecological system of socio-economic development. *IOP Conference Series. Materials Science and Engineering*, *497*, 012002. DOI: 10.1088/1757-899X/497/1/012002

Aborujilah, A., Al-othmani, A. Z., Hussien, N. S., Mokhtar, S. A., Long, Z. A., & Nizam, M. (2024). Cybersecurity Risk Assessment Approach for Malaysian Organizations : Malaysian Universities as Case Study. *2022 9th International Conference on Electrical and Electronics Engineering (ICEEE)*, 440–450. DOI: 10.1109/ICEEE55327.2022.9772546

Abu-Al-Aish, A., and Love, S. (2013). Factors influencing students' acceptance of m-learning: an investigation in higher education. Int. Rev. Res. Open Distributed Learn. 14, 83–107. acceptance model: four longitudinal field studies. Manage. Sci. 46, 186–204.doi: .DOI: 10.19173/irrodl.v14i5.1631

Adamopoulou, E., & Moussiades, L. (2020). An Overview of Chatbot Technology. In *IFIP Advances in Information and Communication Technology* (Vol. 584). IFIP., DOI: 10.1007/978-3-030-49186-4_31

Adorni, G., & Koceva, F. (2016). Educational Concept Maps for Personalized Learning Path Generation. In Lecture notes in computer science (pp. 135–148). DOI: 10.1007/978-3-319-49130-1_11

Advan, A. (2015). Taksim Gezi Park protest in the framework of social movements and the use of social media (Doctoral thesis). Retrieved from: https://tez.yok.gov.tr/UlusalTezMerkezi/tezDetay.jsp?id=ebVax1OsckbMgNOJfdQ3Mg&no=kBZOEKmrfhGGibOKiM4rig

Agarwal, R., Gupta, A. K., & Kraut, R. (2008). The interplay between digital and social networks. *Information Systems Research, 19*(3), 243–252. DOI: 10.1287/isre.1080.0200

Aguilar, S. J. (2015). Web 3.0 technologies and enhanced learning environments: An analysis of students' perceptions. *International Journal of Educational Technology, 2*(1), 1–8.

Ahmad, A. (2023). Optimizing Educational Delivery: Cloud-Based Solutions for Effective Distance Learning. *Jurnal Sistem Informasi dan Teknik Informatika (JAFOTIK) [Journal of Information Systems and Informatics Engineering], 1*(2), 41-46.

Ahmad, M., Muhammad, K. H. N., Mobo, F. D., Tahir, M. W., & Akram, M. (2024). Navigating the Journey: How Chatbots Are Transforming Tourism and Hospitality. In Darwish, D. (Ed.), *Design and Development of Emerging Chatbot Technology* (pp. 236–255). IGI Global., DOI: 10.4018/979-8-3693-1830-0.ch014

Ahmad, S. F., Alam, M. M., Rahmat, M. K., Mubarik, M. S., & Hyder, S. I. (2022, January). Academic and administrative role of artificial intelligence in education. *Sustainability (Basel), 14*(3), 1101. DOI: 10.3390/su14031101

Ahmad, S. F., Rahmat, M. K., Mubarik, M. S., Alam, M. M., & Hyder, S. I. (2021, November). Artificial intelligence and its role in education. *Sustainability (Basel), 13*(22), 12902. DOI: 10.3390/su132212902

Ahmed, A. A., Elmi, A. H., Abdullahi, A., & Ahmed, A. Y. (2023). *Cybersecurity awareness among university students in Mogadishu : a comparative study. 32*(3), 1580–1588. DOI: 10.11591/ijeecs.v32.i3.pp1580-1588

Akbar, H., Zubair, M., & Malik, M. S. (2023). The Security Issues and challenges in Cloud Computing. *International Journal for Electronic Crime Investigation, 7*(1), 13–32. DOI: 10.54692/ijeci.2023.0701125

Akgun, S., & Greenhow, C. 2022. "Artificial Intelligence (AI) in Education: Addressing Societal and Ethical Challenges in K-12 Settings." In *Proceedings of International Conference of the Learning Sciences, ICLS.*

Akil, H., Martone, M., & Van Essen, D. C. (2011). Challenges and Opportunities in mining Neuroscience data. *Science, 331*(6018), 708–712. DOI: 10.1126/science.1199305 PMID: 21311009

Al-Abdullatif, A. M. (2023). Modeling Students' Perceptions of Chatbots in Learning: Integrating Technology Acceptance with the Value-Based Adoption Model. *Education Sciences, 13*(11), 1151. Advance online publication. DOI: 10.3390/educsci13111151

Al-Abdullatif, A. M., Al-Dokhny, A. A., & Drwish, A. M. (2023). Implementing the Bashayer Chatbot in Saudi Higher Education: Measuring the Influence on Students' Motivation and Learning Strategies. *Frontiers in Psychology, 14*, 1129070. Advance online publication. DOI: 10.3389/fpsyg.2023.1129070 PMID: 37255522

Alalwan, A. A., Rana, N. P., Dwivedi, Y. K., & Algharabat, R. (2017). Social media in marketing: A review and analysis of the existing literature. *Telematics and Informatics, 34*(7), 1177–1190. DOI: 10.1016/j.tele.2017.05.008

Al-Azawei, A., Parslow, P., & Lundqvist, K. (2016). Investigating the effect of learning styles in a blended e-learning system: An extension of the technology acceptance model (TAM). *Australasian Journal of Educational Technology, 32*(5), 17–32. DOI: 10.14742/ajet.2741

Albreem, M. A., Sheikh, A. M., Alsharif, M. H., Jusoh, M., & Mohd, N. M. Y. (2021). Green Internet of Things (GIoT): Applications, Practices, Awareness, and Challenges. *IEEE Access : Practical Innovations, Open Solutions, 9*, 38833–38858. Advance online publication. DOI: 10.1109/ACCESS.2021.3061697

Aldosari, S. A. M. (2020). The future of higher education in the light of artificial intelligence transformations. *International Journal of Higher Education, 9*(3), 145–151. DOI: 10.5430/ijhe.v9n3p145

Alexei, A., & Alexei, A. (2021). Cyber security threat analysis in higher education institutions as a result of distance learning. *International Journal of Scientific & Technology Research, 10*(3), 128–133. www.ijstr.org

Alexiou, M. (2018). Modeling guided tour participants' experiences. *International Journal of Culture, Tourism and Hospitality Research, 12*(3), 257–276. DOI: 10.1108/IJCTHR-10-2017-0104

Almarashdeh, I. A., Sahari, N., Zin, N. A. M., & Alsmadi, M. (2010). The success of learning management system among distance learners in Malasian universities. *Journal of Theoretical and Applied Information Technology, 21*(2).

Al-Mushasha, N. F., & Nassuora, A. B. (2012). Factors determining e-learning service quality in Jordanian higher education environment. *Journal of Applied Sciences (Faisalabad), 12*(14), 1474–1480. DOI: 10.3923/jas.2012.1474.1480

Al-Nuaimi, M. N., Al Sawafi, O. S., Malik, S. I., Al-Emran, M., & Selim, Y. F. (2022, April). Evaluating the actual use of learning management systems during the covid-19 pandemic: An integrated theoretical model. *Interactive Learning Environments*, •••, 1–26. DOI: 10.1080/10494820.2022.2127777

Alomari, I., Al-Samarraie, H., & Yousef, R. (2019). The Role of Gamification Techniques in *Promoting Student Learning*: A Review and Synthesis. *Journal of Information Technology Education, 18*, 395–417. DOI: 10.28945/4417

Aloqayli, A., & Abdelhafez, H. (2023). Intelligent Chatbot for Admission in Higher Education. *International Journal of Information and Education Technology (IJIET), 13*(9), 1348–1357. Advance online publication. DOI: 10.18178/ijiet.2023.13.9.1937

Alotaibi, M. B. (2020). A comprehensive cybersecurity framework for e-learning systems. *Computers & Security, 97*, 101963. DOI: 10.1016/j.cose.2020.101963

Alrawashdeh, T. A. (2012). Factors affecting acceptance of web-based training system: Using extended Utaut and structural equation modeling. *Int. J. Comput.Sci. Eng. Inf. Technol., 2*(2), 45–54. DOI: 10.5121/ijcseit.2012.2205

Alshamrani, A., Myneni, S., Chowdhary, A., & Huang, D. (2019). A survey on advanced persistent threats: Techniques, solutions, challenges, and research opportunities. *IEEE Communications Surveys and Tutorials, 21*(2), 1851–1877. DOI: 10.1109/COMST.2019.2891891

Alshar'e, M. (2023). *Cyber Security Framework Selection: Comparison of Nist and ISO27001. 3*(1), 245–255.

AlSheikh Theeb, T., Chuang, R., & Pandit, S. (2022). *Key considerations when developing an ICT in Education strategy (Helpdesk Response No. 43)*. EdTech Hub., DOI: 10.53832/edtechhub.0100

Alsulami, M. H., Alharbi, F. D., Almutairi, H. M., & Almutairi, B. S. (2021). *Measuring Awareness of Social Engineering in the Educational Sector in the Kingdom of Saudi Arabia*. 1–13.

Alzighaibi, A. R. (2021). Cybersecurity Attacks on Academic Data and Personal Information and the Mediating Role of Education and Employment. *Journal of Computer and Communications, 09*(11), 77–90. DOI: 10.4236/jcc.2021.911006

AlZu'bi, S., Mughaid, A., Quiam, F., & Hendawi, S. (2024). Exploring the Capabilities and Limitations of Chatgpt and Alternative Big Language Models. *Artificial Intelligence and Applications (Commerce, Calif.), 2*(1), 28–37. DOI: 10.47852/bonviewAIA3202820

Amornkitpinyo, T., Yoosomboon, S., Sopapradit, S., & Amornkitpinyo, P. (2021). The structural equation model of actual use of cloud learning for higher education students in the 21st century. *Journal of E-Learning and Knowledge Society*, *17*(1), 72–80. DOI: 10.20368/1971-8829/1135300

Anand, A., & Bhambri, P. (2018). Rotation, Scale and Translation Invariant Character Recognition System using Neural Network. I.K.Gujral Punjab Technical University, Jalandhar (M.Tech. thesis).

Anand, A., & Bhambri, P. (2018). *Rotation, Scale and Translation Invariant Character Recognition System using Neural Network. I.K.Gujral Punjab Technical University*. Jalandhar.

Anderson, C. A. (2018). Educational Technology and Web 3.0: Transforming Learning Experiences. *Educational Technology Research and Development*, *66*(6), 1323–1336.

Ankara Metropolitan Municipality. (2019). The capital walls are colorful… Retrieved from: https://www.ankara.bel.tr/haberler/baskent-duvarlari-rengarenk

Anna, L. (2018). Value creation by engaging customers in the process of product and business design in a virtual environment. Handel Wewnetrzny, (375), 160-168. Retrieved from https://search-proquest-com.proxy.uwasa.fi/docview/2129933661?accountid=14797

Apampa, K. M., Wills, G., & Argles, D. (2020). Cybersecurity and in-course assessment practices in distance learning: Perspectives from international institutions. *Computers & Security*, *96*, 101924. DOI: 10.1016/j.cose.2020.101924

Appleton, J. J., Christenson, S. L., Kim, D., & Reschly, A. L. (2006). Measuring cognitive and psychological engagement: Validation of the Student Engagement Instrument. *Journal of School Psychology*, *44*(5), 427–445. DOI: 10.1016/j.jsp.2006.04.002

Archambault, L., Leary, H., & Rice, K. (2022). Pillars of online pedagogy: A framework for teaching in online learning environments. *Educational Psychologist*, *57*(3), 178–191. DOI: 10.1080/00461520.2022.2051513

Arrighi, P.-A., & Mougenot, C. (2019). Towards user empowerment in product design: A mixed reality tool for interactive virtual prototyping. *Journal of Intelligent Manufacturing*, *30*(2), 743–754. DOI: 10.1007/s10845-016-1276-0

Arufe Giráldez, V., Sanmiguel-Rodríguez, A., Ramos Álvarez, O., & Navarro-Patón, R. (2022). Can gamification influence the academic performance of students? *Sustainability (Basel)*, *14*(9), 5115. DOI: 10.3390/su14095115

Attali, Y., & Arieli-Attali, M. (2015). Gamification in assessment: Do points affect test performance? *Computers & Education, 83*, 57–63. DOI: 10.1016/j.compedu.2014.12.012

Attri, R., & Bairagi, R. (2022). Guthali – challenges in marketing Indian handicrafts and handloom. *Emerald Emerging Markets Case Studies, 12*(1), 1–23. DOI: 10.1108/EEMCS-09-2021-0298

Audet, É. C., Levine, S. L., Metin, E., Koestner, S., & Barcan, S. (2021). Zooming their way through university: Which Big 5 traits facilitated students' adjustment to online courses during the COVID-19 pandemic. *Personality and Individual Differences, 180*, 110969. DOI: 10.1016/j.paid.2021.110969 PMID: 36540325

Au, Y. A., Carpenter, D., Chen, X., & Clark, J. G. (2009). Virtual organizational learning in open source software development projects. *Information & Management, 46*(1), 9–15. DOI: 10.1016/j.im.2008.09.004

Avgousti, A., Papaioannou, G., & Hermon, S. (2024). Enhancing Online Accessibility of Digitized Artifacts from Small Museum Collections in Cyprus: An Empirical Evaluation of the CyprusArk Solution. *Journal on Computing and Cultural Heritage, 17*(3), 1–24. Advance online publication. DOI: 10.1145/3648229

Ayhan, A. (2021). Kent mekânında bir çeviri biçimi olarak sokak sanatı. *Çeviribilim ve Uygulamaları Dergisi*, [Street art as a form of translation in urban space. Journal of Translation Studies and Applications] 31, 91-107. Retrieved from: chrome-extension://efaidnbmnnnibpcajpcglclefindmkaj/https://dergipark.org.tr/en/download/article-file/2059888

Babu, C. V. S., & Manoharan, S. (2024). AI and Blockchain Revolution in Communication Education: Future of Work in the Age of Industrial Robotics. In Eduard Babulak, I. G. I. (Ed.), *Applied AI and Humanoid Robotics for the Ultra-Smart Cyberspace* (pp. 63–84). Global., DOI: 10.4018/979-8-3693-2399-1.ch003

Badamasi, B., & Utulu, S. C. A. (2021). Framework for Managing Cybercrime Risks in Nigerian. *Proceedings of the 1st Virtual Conference on Implications of Information and Digital Technologies for Development,* 2021, 853–866.

Baggett, M., & Gibbs, R. (2014). Historypin and Pinterest for Digital Collections: Measuring the Impact of Image-Based Social Tools on Discovery and Access. *Journal of Library Administration, 54*(1), 11–22. Advance online publication. DOI: 10.1080/01930826.2014.893111

Bahrudin, F. I., Rahim, A. A., & Alias, N. U. (2022). Online Learning Experiences for Integrated Multidisciplinary Course During the Covid-19 Pandemic. *Design Ideals Journal*, *4*(2), 38–44.

Bakri, M. Q., ... (2019). A review on service robots: mechanical design and localization system. IOP Conf. Ser.: Mater. Sci. Eng. 705 012003. Retrieved from: chrome-extension://efaidnbmnnnibpcajpcglclefindmkaj/https://iopscience.iop.org/article/10.1088/1757-899X/705/1/012003/pdf

Bakshi, P., Bhambri, P., & Thapar, V. (2021). A review paper on wireless sensor network techniques in Internet of Things (IoT). Wesleyan Journal of Research, 14(7), 147-160. Retrieved from https://www.wesleyanjournal.in/

Bamakan, Seyed Mojtaba Hosseini, and Saeed Banaeian Far. 2024. "Distributed and Trustworthy Digital Twin Platform Based on Blockchain and Web3 Technologies." *Cyber Security and Applications*, 100064.

Bandura, A. (1986). *Social foundations of thought and action*. Prentice-Hall.

Banksy (2005). *Banksy wall and piece*. Wemding: Apply Druck.

Baptista, G., & Oliveira, T. (2019). Gamification and serious games : A literature metaanalysis and integrative model. *Computers in Human Behavior*, *92*, 306–315. DOI: 10.1016/j.chb.2018.11.030

Barken, T. L., Bonacina, S., Bostad, R., Gabarron, E., Garcia, B., Haddeland, K., Hanssen, Ø., Hartvigsen, E., Hartvigsen, G., Hejlesen, O., Henriksen, A., Horsch, A., Iversen, A., Jaccheri, L., Johannessen, E., Johnsen, H. M., Martinez, S. G., Martinez Millana, A., Pelagatti, S., & Årsand, E. (2023). University campus as a smart technology-supported active learning arena. *Septentrio Reports*, (1). Advance online publication. DOI: 10.7557/7.7222

Barocas, S., Hardt, M., & Narayanan, A. (2020). *Fairness in Machine Learning Limitations and Opportunities*. Book.

Bates, L. (2014). *Bombing, Tagging, Writing: An Analysis of the Significance of Graffiti and Street Art.* (Master thesis). University of Pennsylvania, Philadelphia, PA. Retrieved from: https://repository.upenn.edu/hp_theses/570/

Bates, T., Cobo, C., Mariño, O., & Wheeler, S. (2020). Can artificial intelligence transform higher education? *International Journal of Educational Technology in Higher Education*, *17*(1), 42. Advance online publication. DOI: 10.1186/s41239-020-00218-x

Bazoukis, G., Hall, J., Loscalzo, J., Antman, E. M., Fuster, V., & Armoundas, A. A. (2022). The inclusion of augmented intelligence in medicine: A framework for successful implementation. *Cell Reports Medicine*, *3*(1), 1–8. DOI: 10.1016/j.xcrm.2021.100485 PMID: 35106506

Becker, S. A., Cummins, M., Davis, A., & Freeman, A. (2017). *NMC/CoSN Horizon Report: 2017 K-* (12th ed.). The New Media Consortium.

Beerkens, M. (2022). An evolution of performance data in higher education governance: A path towards a "big data" era? *Quality in Higher Education*, *28*(1), 29–49. DOI: 10.1080/13538322.2021.1951451

Bell, J., & Loane, S. (2010). New-wave' global firms: Web 2.0 and SME internationalisation. *Journal of Marketing Management*, *26*(3/4), 213–229. DOI: 10.1080/02672571003594648

Benotti, L., Martínez, M. C., & Schapachnik, F. 2014. "Engaging High School Students Using Chatbots." In *ITICSE 2014 - Proceedings of the 2014 Innovation and Technology in Computer Science Education Conference*. DOI: 10.1145/2591708.2591728

Benotti, L., Martínez, M. C., & Schapachnik, F. (2018). A Tool for Introducing Computer Science with Automatic Formative Assessment. *IEEE Transactions on Learning Technologies*, *11*(2), 179–192. Advance online publication. DOI: 10.1109/TLT.2017.2682084

Berners-Lee, T. (2006). Linked data. Retrieved from: https://www.w3.org/DesignIssues/LinkedData.html

Bertacchini, E., Revelli, F., & Zotti, R. (2024). The economic impact of UNESCO World Heritage: Evidence from Italy. *Regional Science and Urban Economics*, *105*, 103996. Advance online publication. DOI: 10.1016/j.regsciurbeco.2024.103996

Bhambri, P., & Gupta, O. P. (2018). Implementing Machine Learning Algorithms for Distance based Phylogenetic Trees. I.K.Gujral Punjab Technical University, Jalandhar (Ph.D. thesis).

Bhambri, P., Singh, S., Jain, S., & Dhanoa, S. I. (2023). Plants recognition using leaf image pattern analysis with focus on advanced smart computing technologies. In AIP Conference Proceedings 2916, 020003 (2023). https://doi.org/DOI: 10.1063/5.0179534

Bhambri, P. (2024a). NFTs: Transforming Digital Ownership in the Web 3 Era. In Darwish, D. (Ed.), *Decentralizing the Online Experience With Web3 Technologies* (pp. 151–167). IGI Global., DOI: 10.4018/979-8-3693-1532-3.ch007

Bhambri, P., & Khang, A. (2024). Basics of greener living. In Khang, A., Abdullayev, H. V., Litvinova, E., Musrat, G. E., & Avramovic, Z. Ž. (Eds.), *Revolutionizing automated waste treatment systems: IoT and bioelectronics* (pp. 396–412). IGI Global., DOI: 10.4018/979-8-3693-6016-3.ch024

Bhambri, P., & Khang, A. (2024a). Managing and Monitoring Patient's Healthcare Using AI and IoT Technologies. In Khang, A. (Ed.), *Driving Smart Medical Diagnosis Through AI-Powered Technologies and Applications* (pp. 1–23). IGI Global., DOI: 10.4018/979-8-3693-3679-3.ch001

Bhambri, P., & Khang, A. (2024b). AI-Integrated Biosensors and Bioelectronics for Healthcare. In Khang, A. (Ed.), *AI-Driven Innovations in Digital Healthcare: Emerging Trends, Challenges, and Applications* (pp. 82–96). IGI Global., DOI: 10.4018/979-8-3693-3218-4.ch004

Bhambri, P., & Khang, A. (2024c). Machine Learning Advancements in E-Health: Transforming Digital Healthcare. In Khang, A. (Ed.), *Medical Robotics and AI-Assisted Diagnostics for a High-Tech Healthcare Industry* (pp. 174–194). IGI Global., DOI: 10.4018/979-8-3693-2105-8.ch012

Bhambri, P., & Khang, A. (2024d). Biosensor Applications and Principles of Agricultural and Aquacultural Sectors. In Khang, A. (Ed.), *Agriculture and Aquaculture Applications of Biosensors and Bioelectronics* (pp. 1–17). IGI Global., DOI: 10.4018/979-8-3693-2069-3.ch001

Bhambri, P., & Khang, A. (2024e). Challenges and future directions on business intelligence. In Özsungur, F. (Ed.), *Generating entrepreneurial ideas with AI* (pp. 117–146). IGI Global., DOI: 10.4018/979-8-3693-3498-0.ch006

Bhambri, P., & Rani, S. (2024a). Ethical Issues for Climate Change and Mental Health. In Samanta, D., & Garg, M. (Eds.), *Impact of Climate Change on Mental Health and Well-Being* (pp. 178–198). IGI Global., DOI: 10.4018/979-8-3693-2177-5.ch012

Bhambri, P., & Rani, S. (2024b). *Challenges, Opportunities, and the Future of Industrial Engineering with IoT and AI. Integration of AI-Based Manufacturing and Industrial Engineering Systems with the Internet of Things*. CRC Press.

Bhambri, P., Sinha, V. K., & Jaiswal, M. (2019). Change in iris dimensions as a potential human consciousness level indicator. *International Journal of Innovative Technology and Exploring Engineering*, *8*(9S), 517–525. DOI: 10.35940/ijitee.I1082.0789S19

Bhattacherjee, A., and Hikmet. (2008). Reconceptualizing organizational support and its effect on information technology usage: Evidence from the health care sector. *Journal of Computer Information Systems*, *48*, 69–76. DOI: 10.1080/08874417.2008.11646036

Bianet (2017). More than 20 thousand gas cartridges were used in ıstanbul during the gezi resistance. Retrieved from: https://bianet.org/bianet/insan-haklari/187962-gezi-direnisinde-istanbul-da-20-binden-fazla-gaz-fisegi-kullanildi?utm_content=buffer620bd&utm_medium=social&utm_source=twitter.com&utm_campaign=buffer

Bikakis, N., Giannopoulos, G., Sidiropoulos, N., Flouda, C., Doupas, A., Giouli, V., Karioris, P., Botini, P., Vacalopoulou, A., & Stainhaouer, G. (2023). Exposing Geospatial Cultural Heritage Content in Map-based Applications. *CEUR Workshop Proceedings*, ●●●, 3379.

Bilquise, G., Ibrahim, S., & Sa'Ed, E. M. S. (2023). Investigating Student Acceptance of an Academic Advising Chatbot in Higher Education Institutions. *Education and Information Technologies*. Advance online publication. DOI: 10.1007/s10639-023-12076-x

Bisen, I. E., Arslan, E. A., Yildirim, K., & Yildirim, Y. (2021). *Artificial intelligence and machine learning in higher education. In machine learning approaches for improvising modern learning systems*. IGI Global., DOI: 10.4018/978-1-7998-5009-0.ch001

Blaschitz, E., Mayr, E., & Oppl, S. (2022). Too Low Motivation, Too High Authority? Digital Media Support for Co-Curation in Local Cultural Heritage Communities. *Multimodal Technologies and Interaction*, *6*(5), 33. Advance online publication. DOI: 10.3390/mti6050033

Bloom, B. S. (Ed.). (1956). Taxonomy of educational objectives: Vol. 1. *Cognitive domain*. David McKay.

Bogdanova, G., Todorov, T., & Noev, N. (2020). Accessibility testing of digital cultural heritage. *Digital Presentation and Preservation of Cultural and Scientific Heritage, 10 2020-September*. DOI: 10.55630/dipp.2020.10.16

Boldt, R., & Carvalho, M. (2018). Virtual prototyping as an evaluation method for functional clothing. *IOP Conference Series. Materials Science and Engineering*, *460*(1), 012040. Advance online publication. DOI: 10.1088/1757-899X/460/1/012040

Bonadio, E. (2017). Copyright protection of street art and graffiti under UK law. *Intellectual Property Quarterly,* 2, 1-39. Retrieved from: https://papers.ssrn.com/sol3/papers.cfm?abstract_id=2946360

Bonadio, E. (2018a). Graffiti gets vara protection: The 5Pointz case (March 6, 2018). *European Intellectual Property Review, 2018,* Forthcoming, Retrieved from: *SSRN*: https://ssrn.com/abstract=3135118

Bonadio, E. (2018b). Street art, graffiti and copyright. In Bonadio, E., & Lucchi, N. (Eds.), *Non-conventional copyright – do new and atypical works deserve protection?* (pp. 83–110). Edward Elgar. DOI: 10.4337/9781786434074.00012

Bongiovanni, I. (2019). *The least secure places in the universe? A systematic literature review on information security management in higher education.*

Boonchutima, S., Chongkolrattanaporn, T., & Kongchan, W. (2023, October). Cognitive Load Theory in Online Education: Leveraging Interactive Media, Testing, Interaction and to Enhance Engagement and Active Learning. *Region 10 Conference (TENCON)* (pp. 2-9). IEEE.

Boontarig, W., Chutimaskul, W., Chongsuphajaisiddhi, V., & Papasratorn, B. (2012). "Factors influencing the Thai elderly intention to use smartphone for e-Health services," in *2012 IEEE Symposium on Humanities, Science and Engineering Research,* 479–483. DOI: 10.1109/SHUSER.2012.6268881

Borah, B., Pathak, D., Sarmah, P., Som, B., & Nandi, S. 2019. "Survey of Textbased Chatbot in Perspective of Recent Technologies." In *Communications in Computer and Information Science.* Vol. 1031. DOI: 10.1007/978-981-13-8581-0_7

Borin, E., & Donato, F. (2023). Financial Sustainability of Digitizing Cultural Heritage: The International Platform Europeana. *Journal of Risk and Financial Management, 16*(10), 421. Advance online publication. DOI: 10.3390/jrfm16100421

Bose, M. M., Yadav, D., Bhambri, P., & Shankar, R. (2021). Electronic customer relationship management: Benefits and pre-implementation considerations. *Journal of Maharaja Sayajirao University of Baroda, 55*(01(VI)), 1343–1350.

Boudreau, C. A., & Kromrey, J. D. (1994). A longitudinal study of the retention and academic performance of participants in freshmen orientation course. *Journal of College Student Development, 35,* 444–449.

Bouncken, R. B., & Reuschl, A. J. (2018). Coworking-spaces: How a phenomenon of the sharing economy builds a novel trend for the workplace and for entrepreneurship. *Review of Managerial Science, 12*(1), 317–334. DOI: 10.1007/s11846-016-0215-y

Bower, M., Howe, C., McCredie, N., Robinson, A., Grover, D., & Tyack, A. (2017). A design-based research approach to enhancing inquiry-based learning in geography using geospatial technologies. *Learning Environments Research, 20*(2), 191–210.

Braganza, A., Chen, W., Canhoto, A., & Sap, S. (2021). Productive employment and decent work: The impact of AI adoption on psychological contracts, job engagement and employee trust. *Journal of Business Research, 131*, 485–494. DOI: 10.1016/j.jbusres.2020.08.018 PMID: 32836565

Braun, V., & Clarke, V. (2006). Using thematic analysis in psychology. *Qualitative Research in Psychology*, *3*(2), 77–101. DOI: 10.1191/1478088706qp063oa

Brooke, J. (2013). SUS: A quick and dirty usability scale. In *Usability Evaluation in Industry* (pp. 189-194). CRC Press.

Brown, M., & Green, T. (2016). *The essentials of instructional design: Connecting fundamental principles with process and practice*. Routledge.

Brynskov, M., Heijnen, A., Balestrini, M., & Raetzsch, C. (2018). Experimentation at scale: Challenges for making urban informatics work. *Smart and Sustainable Built Environment*, *7*(1), 150–163. DOI: 10.1108/SASBE-10-2017-0054

Buchanan, C., Howitt, M. L., Wilson, R., Booth, R. G., Risling, T., & Bamford, M. (2021). *"Predicted Influences of Artificial Intelligence on Nursing Education: Scoping Review." JMIR Nursing*. JMIR Publications Inc., DOI: 10.2196/23933

Bughin, J., Byers, A. H. and Chui, M. (2011). How social technologies are extending the organization. *McKinsey Quarterly Report.*

Bu, Q. (2022). Ethical Risks in Integrating Artificial Intelligence into Education and Potential Countermeasures. *Science Insights*, *41*(1), 561–566. Advance online publication. DOI: 10.15354/si.22.re067

Buterin, V. (2014). *A next-generation smart contract and decentralized application platform*. Ethereum Foundation. https://ethereum.org/en/whitepaper/

Caccavale, F., Gargalo, C. L., Gernaey, K. V., & Krühne, U. 2022. "To Be Fair: Ethical and Fair Application of Artificial Intelligence in Virtual Laboratories." In *SEFI 2022 - 50th Annual Conference of the European Society for Engineering Education, Proceedings*. DOI: 10.5821/conference-9788412322262.1398

Cachat-Rosset, G., & Klarsfeld, A. (2023). Diversity, Equity, and Inclusion in Artificial Intelligence: An Evaluation of Guidelines. *Applied Artificial Intelligence, 37*(1), 2176618. Advance online publication. DOI: 10.1080/08839514.2023.2176618

Cacioppo, J. T., & Decety, J. (2011). Social neuroscience: Challenges and opportunities in the study of complex behavior. *Annals of the New York Academy of Sciences, 1224*(1), 162–173. DOI: 10.1111/j.1749-6632.2010.05858.x PMID: 21251011

Çakır, M. S. (2015). Graffiti and street art in Türkiye (Master thesis). Retrieved from: https://tez.yok.gov.tr/UlusalTezMerkezi/tezDetay.jsp?id=z1h8wuUu352yX48C4QpBMw&no=dTdcSQotHaQ44PhQzSb5xg

Calvaresi, D., Eggenschwiler, S., Mualla, Y., Schumacher, M., & Calbimonte, J. P. (2023). Exploring Agent-Based Chatbots: A Systematic Literature Review. *Journal of Ambient Intelligence and Humanized Computing, 14*(8), 11207–11226. Advance online publication. DOI: 10.1007/s12652-023-04626-5

Capurro, C., Plets, G., & Verheul, J. (2023). Digital heritage infrastructures as cultural policy instruments: Europeana and the enactment of European citizenship. *International Journal of Cultural Policy*. Advance online publication. DOI: 10.1080/10286632.2023.2193401

Capurro, C., & Severo, M. (2023). Mapping European Digital Heritage Politics: An Empirical Study of Europeana as a Web-based Network. *Heritage & Society*, 1–21. Advance online publication. DOI: 10.1080/2159032X.2023.2266801

Carletti, L. (2016). Participatory heritage: Scaffolding citizen scholarship. *The International Information & Library Review, 48*(3), 196–203. DOI: 10.1080/10572317.2016.1205367

Carvalho, L., Martinez-Maldonado, R., Tsai, Y.-S., Markauskaite, L., & De Laat, M. (2022). How can we design for learning in an AI world? *Computers and Education: Artificial Intelligence, 3*, 100053. DOI: 10.1016/j.caeai.2022.100053

Catteeuw, F. E. F., & Vonderhorst, J. (2007). Employee engagement: Boosting productivity in turbulent times. *Organization Development Journal, 25*(2), 151–157.

Challco, G. C., Bittencourt, I. I., & Isotani, S. (2020). Can Ontologies Support the Gamification of Scripted Collaborative Learning Sessions? In: Bittencourt, I., Cukurova, M., Muldner, K., Luckin, R., Millán, E. (eds) Artificial Intelligence in Education. AIED 2020. Lecture Notes in Computer Science(), vol 12163. Springer, Cham. https://doi.org/DOI: 10.1007/978-3-030-52237-7_7

Chamorro-Atalaya, O., Olivares-Zegarra, S., Sobrino-Chunga, L., Guerrero-Carranza, R., Vargas-Diaz, A., Huarcaya-Godoy, M., Rasilla-Rovegno, J., Suarez-Bazalar, R., Poma-Garcia, J., & Cruz-Telada, Y. (2023). Application of the Chatbot in University Education: A Bibliometric Analysis of Indexed Scientific Production in SCOPUS, 2013-2023. *International Journal of Learning, Teaching and Educational Research, 22*(7), 281–304. Advance online publication. DOI: 10.26803/ijlter.22.7.15

Chang, C. C., Yan, C. F., & Tseng, J. S. (2012). Perceived convenience in an extended technology acceptance model: Mobile technology and English learning for college students. *Australasian Journal of Educational Technology, 28*(5), 809–826. DOI: 10.14742/ajet.818

Chang, C.-C. (2013). Library mobile applications in university libraries. *Library Hi Tech, 31*(3), 478–492. DOI: 10.1108/LHT-03-2013-0024

Chang, Y.-H., Yan, Y.-C., & Lu, Y.-T. (2022). Effects of Combining Different Collaborative Learning Strategies with Problem-Based Learning in a Flipped Classroom on Program Language Learning. *Sustainability (Basel), 14*(9), 9. Advance online publication. DOI: 10.3390/su14095282

Chao, T. C., & Lo, H. C. (2018). An exploratory study on applying Web 3.0 tools to conduct e-learning in virtual communities. *Turkish Online Journal of Distance Education, 19*(1), 124–136.

Chatterjee, S., & Bhattacharjee, K. K. (2020). (2020)Adoption of artificial intelligence in higher education: A quantitative analysis using structural equation modelling. *Education and Information Technologies, 25*(5), 3443–3463. Advance online publication. DOI: 10.1007/s10639-020-10159-7

Chatterjee, S., Rana, N. P., Khorana, S., Mikalef, P., & Sharma, A. (2021). Assessing organizational users' intentions and behavior to AI integrated CRM systems: A meta-UTAUT approach. *Information Systems Frontiers, 25*(4), 1299–1313. DOI: 10.1007/s10796-021-10181-1

Chaudhry, I. S., Sarwary, S. A. M., El Refae, G. A., & Chabchoub, H. (2023). Time to revisit existing student's performance evaluation approach in higher education sector in a new era of ChatGPT — A case study. *Cogent Education, 10*(1), 2210461. DOI: 10.1080/2331186X.2023.2210461

Chedrawi, C., & Howayeck, P. (2019). Artificial intelligence a disruptive innovation in higher education accreditation programs: Expert systems and AACSB. *Lecture Notes in Information Systems and Organisation, 30*, 115–129. DOI: 10.1007/978-3-030-10737-6_8

Chen, C., Landa, S., Padilla, A., & Yur-Austin, J. (2021). Learners' experience and needs in online environments: Adopting agility in teaching. *J. Res. Innov. Teach. Learn., 14*(1), 18–31. DOI: 10.1108/JRIT-11-2020-0073

Cheng, E. C. K., & Wang, T. (2022). Institutional Strategies for Cybersecurity in Higher Education Institutions. *Information (Basel), 13*(4), 192. Advance online publication. DOI: 10.3390/info13040192

Cheng, S. (2024). Applications of Web 3.0. In *Web 3.0: Concept, Content and Context* (pp. 109–145). Springer. DOI: 10.1007/978-981-99-6319-5_5

Cheng, X., Bao, Y., Yang, B., Chen, S., Zuo, Y., & Siponen, M. (2023). Investigating Students' Satisfaction with Online Collaborative Learning During the COVID-19 Period: An Expectation-Confirmation Model. *Group Decision and Negotiation, 32*(4), 749–778. DOI: 10.1007/s10726-023-09829-x PMID: 37304175

Cheng, X., Bao, Y., Zarifis, A., Gong, W., & Mou, J. (2022, March). Exploring consumers' response to text-based chatbots in e-commerce: The moderating role of task complexity and chatbot disclosure. *Internet Research, 32*(2), 496–517. DOI: 10.1108/INTR-08-2020-0460

Cheng, Y. M. (2012). Effects of quality antecedents on e-learning acceptance. *Internet Research, 22*(3), 361–390. DOI: 10.1108/10662241211235699

Chen, J., Liu, L., & Zhu, L. (2022). An intelligent training system based on virtual reality technology. *Computers in Human Behavior, 130*, 107086. DOI: 10.1016/j.chb.2022.107086

Chen, P. H., & Chen, Y. L. (2018). Integrating Web 3.0 Technologies in Higher Education: A Constructivist Framework. *Journal of Educational Technology & Society, 21*(2), 222–236.

Chen, X., Li, S., Liu, S., Fowler, R., & Wang, X. (2023, October). MeetScript: Designing Transcript-based Interactions to Support Active Participation in Group Video Meetings. *Proceedings of the ACM on Human-Computer Interaction, 7*(CSCW2), 1-32. DOI: 10.1145/3610196

Chen, Y., Jensen, S., Albert, L. J., Gupta, S., & Lee, T. (2023). Artificial Intelligence (AI) Student Assistants in the Classroom: Designing Chatbots to Support Student Success. *Information Systems Frontiers, 25*(1), 161–182. Advance online publication. DOI: 10.1007/s10796-022-10291-4

Cheong, C., Filippou, J., & Cheong, F. (2014). Toward the gamification of learning: Investigating student perceptions of game elements. *Journal of Information Systems Education, 25*(3), 233.

Chevet, S. (2018). Blockchain technology and non-fungible tokens: reshaping value chains in creative industries. Retrieved from https://papers.ssrn.com/sol3/papers.cfm?abstract_id=3212662

Chocarro, R., Cortiñas, M., & Marcos-Matás, G. (2023). Teachers' Attitudes towards Chatbots in Education: A Technology Acceptance Model Approach Considering the Effect of Social Language, Bot Proactiveness, and Users' Characteristics. *Educational Studies*, *49*(2), 295–313. Advance online publication. DOI: 10.1080/03055698.2020.1850426

Choi, B. Y., Song, S., & Zaman, R. (2020, September). Smart Education: Opportunities and challenges induced by COVID-19 pandemic:[A survey-based study]. *International Smart Cities Conference (ISC2)* (pp. 1-8). IEEE. DOI: 10.1109/ISC251055.2020.9239063

Choi, K.-S. (2020). Opportunities for higher education of artificial intelligence in korea. *International Journal of Engineering Research & Technology (Ahmedabad)*, *13*(11), 3428–3430. https://www.scopus.com/inward/record.uri?eid=2-s2. DOI: 10.37624/IJERT/13.11.2020.3428-3430

Chong, W. K.. (2021). Predictive analytics in blockchain technology: Trends and applications. *Journal of Management Analytics*, *8*(2), 127–144. DOI: 10.1080/23294885.2020.1799357

Christensen, R., & Knezek, G. (2015, October). The technology proficiency self-assessment questionnaire (TPSA): Evolution of a self-efficacy measure for technology integration. In Proceedings of the KEYCIT2014: Key Competencies in Informatics and ICT Conference, KEYCIT, Potsdam (pp. 311–318).

Chuan-Chuan Lin, J., & Lu, H. (2000). Towards an understanding of the behavioural intention to use a web site. *International Journal of Information Management*, *20*(3), 197–208. DOI: 10.1016/S0268-4012(00)00005-0

Clarizia, F., Colace, F., Lombardi, M., Pascale, F., & Santaniello, D. (2018). Chatbot: An Education Support System for Student. In. Lecture Notes in Computer Science: Vol. 11161. *Including Subseries Lecture Notes in Artificial Intelligence and Lecture Notes in Bioinformatics)*. LNCS., DOI: 10.1007/978-3-030-01689-0_23

Clark, D., & Mayer, R. E. (2016). *E-learning and the science of instruction: Proven guidelines for consumers and designers of multimedia learning*. John Wiley & Sons. DOI: 10.1002/9781119239086

Coates, H., Xie, Z., & Hong, X. (2021). Engaging transformed fundamentals to design global hybrid higher education. *Studies in Higher Education, 46*(1), 166–176. DOI: 10.1080/03075079.2020.1859683

Cohen, A., McCauley, M., & Robison, A. (2020). Blockchain-based voting: A revolutionary step towards secure democracy. *Journal of Digital Governance, 1*(1), 23–35. DOI: 10.1007/s42455-019-00006-7

Colliander, J., & Dahlén, M. (2011). Following the Fashionable Friend: The Power of Social Media - Weighing the Publicity Effectiveness of Blogs versus Online Magazines. *Journal of Advertising Research, 51*(1), 313–320. DOI: 10.2501/jar-51-1-313-320

Collins, G. J. (2021, September). Redesigning a Postgraduate Software Engineering Module to Increase Engagement. *44th International Convention on Information, Communication and Electronic Technology (MIPRO)* (pp. 1524-1529). IEEE. DOI: 10.23919/MIPRO52101.2021.9597084

Conklin, T. R. (2012). *Street Art, Ideology, and Public Space* (Master thesis). Doi: DOI: 10.15760/etd.761

Corns, A., Davidson, L., Namberi, S., O Reilly, R., & Shaw, R. (2024). Developing enhanced and enriched 3d models of cultural heritage assets as part of the eu co-funded 5dculture project. *International Archives of the Photogrammetry, Remote Sensing and Spatial Information Sciences - ISPRS Archives, 48*(2). DOI: 10.5194/isprs-archives-XLVIII-2-W4-2024-157-2024

Corrêa, J. S., Pereira de Araújo Neto, A., Rebouças Pinto, G., Daniel Batista Lima, L., & Soares Teles, A. (2023). Lhia: A Smart Chatbot for Breastfeeding Education and Recruitment of Human Milk Donors. *Applied Sciences (Basel, Switzerland), 13*(12), 6923. Advance online publication. DOI: 10.3390/app13126923

Cowick, C. (2015). Preserving street art: uncovering the challenges and obstacles. *Art Documentation: Journal of the Art Libraries Society of North America, 34,* 29-44. Retrieved from: https://www.jstor.org/stable/10.1086/680563

Cox, W., Alexander, A., West, H., Abzhaparova, A., & Hill, J. (2023). How to thrive when studying online. *Journal of Geography in Higher Education, 47*(3), 502–511. DOI: 10.1080/03098265.2022.2087214

Crawford, K., & Calo, R. (2016). There Is a Blind Spot in AI Research. *Nature, 538*(7625), 311–313. Advance online publication. DOI: 10.1038/538311a PMID: 27762391

Creative Commons. (2023) Attribution-sharealike 4.0 international (CC BY-SA 4.0). Retrieved from: https://creativecommons.org/licenses/by-sa/4.0/

Cremene, M., Suciuc, M., Dumitrescu, D., and Pallezc D. (2019). "Comparison of multi-objective evolutionary algorithms for QoS:aware web service composition", published July 14, 2019 in the Springer Nature LNICST Series.

Creswell, J. W., & Creswell, J. D. (2017). *Research Design: Qualitative, Quantitative, and Mixed Methods Approaches* (5th ed.). Sage Publications.

Crosby, M., Pattanayak, P., Verma, S., & Kalyanaraman, V. (2016). Blockchain technology: Beyond bitcoin. Applied Innovation, 2, 6-10. https://j2-reed.com/papers/npb16.pdf

Cui, W., & Xue, Z., & Thai, K.-P. (2019). Performance comparison of an AI-Based adaptive learning system in China. In 2018 Chinese Automation Congress, CAC 2018, pp. 3170–3175. Institute of Electrical and Electronics Engineers Inc. https://doi.org/DOI: 10.1109/CAC.2018.8623327

Daalhuizen, J., & Timmer, R. Martijn van, d. W., & Gardien, P. (2019). An architecture of design doing: A framework for capturing the ever-evolving practice of design to drive organizational learning. *International Journal of Design*, 13(1), 37-52. Retrieved from https://search-proquest-com.proxy.uwasa.fi/docview/2226896677?accountid=14797

Dabouis, B., Boccara, V., & Yannou, B. (2023). Retrospective coding of the ux design process for ux design enhancement in design agencies. *Proceedings of the Design Society*, *3*, 3105–3114. DOI: 10.1017/pds.2023.311

Dai, H. N.. (2021). Blockchain and AI-based solutions for sustainable agriculture: A review. *Computers and Electronics in Agriculture*, *181*, 105951. DOI: 10.1016/j.compag.2020.105951

Dale, S. (2014). Gamification: Making work fun, or making fun of work? *Business Information Review*, *31*(2), 82–90. DOI: 10.1177/0266382114538350

Daud, M., & Hawa, S. (2020). E-JAVA Chatbot for Learning Programming Language: A Post-Pandemic Alternative Virtual Tutor. *International Journal of Emerging Trends in Engineering Research*, *8*(7), 3290–3298. DOI: 10.30534/ijeter/2020/67872020

Davies, J. (2012). Art crimes?: Theoretical perspectives on copyright protection for illegally-created graffiti art. *Maine Law Review*, *65*, 27–35. https://digitalcommons.mainelaw.maine.edu/mlr/vol65/iss1/3/

Davis, M. H., & McPartland, J. M. (2012). High School Reform and Student Engagement. In Christenson, S. L., Reschly, A. L., & Wylie, C. (Eds.), *Handbook of Research on Student Engagement* (pp. 515–539). Springer US., DOI: 10.1007/978-1-4614-2018-7_25

de la Torre, M. (2013). Values and Heritage Conservation. *Heritage & Society*, *6*(2), 155–166. Advance online publication. DOI: 10.1179/2159032X13Z.00000000011

De Reu, J., Plets, G., Verhoeven, G., De Smedt, P., Bats, M., Cherretté, B., De Maeyer, W., Deconynck, J., Herremans, D., Laloo, P., Van Meirvenne, M., & De Clercq, W. (2013). Towards a three-dimensional cost-effective registration of the archaeological heritage. *Journal of Archaeological Science*, *40*(2), 1108–1121. Advance online publication. DOI: 10.1016/j.jas.2012.08.040

De Roover, K., Vermunt, J. K., & Ceulemans, E. (2022). Mixture multigroup factor analysis for unraveling factor loading noninvariance across many groups. *Psychological Methods*, *27*(3), 281–306. DOI: 10.1037/met0000355 PMID: 33271027

Dede, C. (2017). Immersive interfaces for engagement and learning. *Science*, *317*(5839), 66–69. PMID: 19119219

Dede, C. (2022). The future of immersive technologies in education. In Khine, M. S. (Ed.), *Immersive Learning and Virtual Reality in Education* (pp. 1–17). Springer., DOI: 10.1007/978-981-16-9164-6_1

Deebak, B. D., & Al-Turjman, F. (2021). Digital-twin assisted: Fault diagnosis using deep transfer learning for machining tool condition. *International Journal of Intelligent Systems*, *37*(12), 10289–10316.

Del Moral, P., Nowaczyk, S., & Pashami, S. (2022). Why is multiclass classification hard? *IEEE Access : Practical Innovations, Open Solutions*, *10*, 80448–80462. DOI: 10.1109/ACCESS.2022.3192514

Dell'Era, C., & Verganti, R. (2009). Design-driven laboratories: Organization and strategy of laboratories specialized in the development of radical design-driven innovations. *R & D Management*, *39*, 1–1.

DeLone, W. H., & McLean, E. R. (1992). Information systems success: The quest for the dependent variable. *Information Systems Research*, *3*(1), 60–95. DOI: 10.1287/isre.3.1.60

Delone, W. H., & McLean, E. R. (2003). The DeLone and McLean model of information systems success: A ten-year update. *Journal of Management Information Systems*, *19*(4), 9–30. DOI: 10.1080/07421222.2003.11045748

Deng, X., & Yu, Z. (2023). *A Meta-Analysis and Systematic Review of the Effect of Chatbot Technology Use in Sustainable Education.* Sustainability., DOI: 10.3390/su15042940

Deterding, S. (2011, September 15). Gamification Research Network. Retrieved from A Quick Buck by Copy and Paste: http://gamification-research.org/2011/09/a-quick-buck-bycopy-and-paste/

Dhiman, S. andSharma, P. (2009). "Performance Testing: Comparative and Statistical Analysis of Web Services and Tests", International Journal of Computer Science and Network Security (IJCSNS), Vol. 9. No. 4, p. 84-90.

Dieguez, T., Loureiro, P., & Ferreira, I. (2021). *Entrepreneurship and leadership in higher education to develop the needed 21st Century skills. In 17th European Conference on Management, Leadership and Governance, ECMLG 2021.* Academic Conferences International Limited., https://www.scopus.com/inward/record.uri?eid=2-s2

Digital, N. Z. (n.d.). *Getting started with digitisation.* Retrieved from: https://digitalnz.org/make-it-digital/getting-started-with-digitisation

Dinh, T. N., Liu, R., Zhang, L., & Chen, G. (2018). Untangling blockchain: A data processing view of blockchain systems. *IEEE Access : Practical Innovations, Open Solutions, 6,* 19056–19067. DOI: 10.1109/ACCESS.2018.2821901

Donato, E., & Giuffrida, D. (2019). Combined methodologies for the survey and documentation of historical buildings: The castle of scalea (cs, italy). *Heritage, 2*(3), 2384–2397. Advance online publication. DOI: 10.3390/heritage2030146

Downer, J. T., Rimm-Kaufman, S. E., & Pianta, R. C. (2007). How do classroom conditions and children's risk for school problems contribute to children's behavioral engagement in learning? *School Psychology Review, 36*(3), 413–432. DOI: 10.1080/02796015.2007.12087938

Downes, S. (2018). Learning networks and connective knowledge. Instructional Technology Forum, 2006(3), 14-27.

Duan, Y.. (2021). Integrating blockchain and artificial intelligence: The role of data in digital transformation. *Business Horizons, 64*(3), 339–348. DOI: 10.1016/j.bushor.2021.01.004

Duarte, A., & Riedl, K. (2021). "Virtually" the same learning outcomes. A case study of a virtual client briefed communication project across borders. *ICONO 14, Revista de comunicación y tecnologías emergentes [Journal of Communication and Emerging Technologies], 19*(2), 189-211.

Dudley, N. M., & Kachka, M. P. (2019). The role of user experience in educational technology: A literature review. *Educational Technology Research and Development, 67*(1), 97–125.

Dufour, S., Benaissa, A., & Cheikhrouhou, N. (2023). A Decentralized Approach to AI: Addressing Data Privacy and Bias in AI Algorithms. *Journal of Information Technology & Politics, 20*(1), 35–51.

Dulle, F. W., & Minishi-Majanja, M. K. (2011). The suitability of the unified theory of acceptance and use of technology (utaut) model in open access adoption studies. *Information Development, 27*(1), 32–45. DOI: 10.1177/0266666910385375

Dumaska, I.. (2021). E-commerce and M-commerce as global trends of international trade caused by the Covid-19 pandemic. *WSEAS Transactions on Environment and Development, 17*, 386–397. DOI: 10.37394/232015.2021.17.38

Durak, H. Y. (2018). Flipped learning readiness in teaching programming in middle schools: Modelling its relation to various variables. *Journal of Computer Assisted Learning, 34*(6), 939–959. DOI: 10.1111/jcal.12302

Du, X., Jiao, J., & Tseng, M. (2006). Understanding customer satisfaction in product customization. *International Journal of Advanced Manufacturing Technology, 31*(3–4), 396–406. DOI: 10.1007/s00170-005-0177-8

Dyson, M. C., & Moran, K. (2000). Informing the design of web ınterfaces to museum collections. *Museum Management and Curatorship, 18*(4), 391–406. DOI: 10.1080/09647770000501804

Eaton, M. (2017). The flipped classroom. *The Clinical Teacher, 14*(4), 301–302. DOI: 10.1111/tct.12685 PMID: 28703501

Erdoğan, G. (2009). Street Art in Public Space: Graffiti Istanbul, Beyoğlu, Yüksek Kaldırım Street Analysis (Master thesis). Retrieved from: https://tez.yok.gov.tr/UlusalTezMerkezi/tezDetay.jsp?id=eSyrdfAApPq4gJghJX9Txw&no=Ljcw59xkWxqAsNt4-QQreg

Essel, H. B., Vlachopoulos, D., Tachie-Menson, A., Johnson, E. E., & Baah, P. K. (2022). The Impact of a Virtual Teaching Assistant (Chatbot) on Students' Learning in Ghanaian Higher Education. *International Journal of Educational Technology in Higher Education, 19*(1), 57. Advance online publication. DOI: 10.1186/s41239-022-00362-6

Essien, A., Chukwukelu, G., & Essien, V. (2020).

Ethereum Foundation. (2024). Web3.js. Retrieved from https://web3js.readthedocs.io/en/v1.7.0/

European Commission. (2014). Communication from the commission to the European Parliament, the council, the European Economic and Social Committee and the Committee of the Regions, towards an integrated approach to cultural heritage for Europe. Retrieved from: https://eur-lex.europa.eu/legal-content/en/ALL/?uri=CELEX:52014DC0477

European Commission. (2015). Getting cultural heritage to work for Europe, report of the Horizon 2020 expert group on cultural heritage. Retrieved from: https://op.europa.eu/en/publication-detail/-/publication/b01a0d0a-2a4f-4de0-88f7-85bf2dc6e004

European Commission. (2020). Data protection in the European Union. https://ec.europa.eu/info/law/law-topic/data-protection_en

Evans, C. (2019). The effectiveness of m-learning in the form of podcast revision lectures in higher education. *Computers & Education*, *50*(2), 491–498. DOI: 10.1016/j.compedu.2007.09.016

Faiella, F., & Ricciardi, M. (2023). Virtual reality in education: A tool for learning in the experience age. Journal of e-Learning and Knowledge Society, 19(1), 167-178. https://doi.org/DOI: 10.20368/1971-8829/1866

Fair, D. A., Dosenbach, N. U., Moore, A. H., Satterthwaite, T. D., & Milham, M. P. (2021). Developmental cognitive neuroscience in the era of networks and big data: Strengths, weaknesses, opportunities, and threats. *Annual Review of Developmental Psychology*, *3*(1), 249–275. DOI: 10.1146/annurev-devpsych-121318-085124

Fajar, A. N., & Legowo, N. (2018). Services modeling based on soa and bpm for information system flexibility improvement. [IJECE]. *International Journal of Electrical and Computer Engineering*, *8*(4), 2451. DOI: 10.11591/ijece.v8i4.pp2451-2455

Falk, M. T., & Hagsten, E. (2024). Factors with ambiguous qualities for Cultural World Heritage Sites. *Journal of Cultural Heritage*, *66*, 384–391. Advance online publication. DOI: 10.1016/j.culher.2023.12.009

Fanni, R., Steinkogler, V. E., Zampedri, G., & Pierson, J. (2023). Enhancing Human Agency through Redress in Artificial Intelligence Systems. *AI & Society*, *38*(2), 537–547. Advance online publication. DOI: 10.1007/s00146-022-01454-7 PMID: 35692234

Farah, J. C., Spaenlehauer, B., Sharma, V., Rodriguez-Triana, M. J., Ingram, S., & Gillet, D. 2022. “Impersonating Chatbots in a Code Review Exercise to Teach Software Engineering Best Practices.” In *IEEE Global Engineering Education Conference, EDUCON*, 2022-March:1634–42. IEEE Computer Society. DOI: 10.1109/EDUCON52537.2022.9766793

Farheen Ansari, M. (2022). An Effective Cybersecurity Awareness Training Model: First Defense of an Organizational Security Strategy. *International Research Journal of Engineering and Technology (IRJET), 9*(4), 1–6. www.irjet.net

Fayomi, J. O., & Sani, Z. A. (2023). Application and challenges of web 3.0 in smart cities. *JO. Fayomi and ZA. Sani. Application and Challenges of Web*, *3*, 31–42.

Featherman, M. S., & Pavlou, P. A. (2003). Predicting E-Services Adoption: A Perceived Risk Facets Perspective. *International Journal of Human-Computer Studies*, *59*(4), 451–474. DOI: 10.1016/S1071-5819(03)00111-3

Field, A. (2013). *Discovering Statistics Using IBM SPSS Statistics* (4th ed.). Sage Publications.

Figueira, C. (2017). A Joint Communication to the European Parliament and the Council: Towards an EU Strategy for International Cultural Relations, by the European Commission, 2016. *Cultural Trends*, *26*(1), 81–85. DOI: 10.1080/09548963.2017.1274371

Fishbein, M., & Ajzen, I. (1977). Belief, attitude, intention, and behavior: An introduction to theory and research. *Philosophy & Rhetoric*, •••, 10.

Floridi, L, J Cowls, M Beltrametti, and others. 2022. “AI 4People’s Ethical Framework for a Good AI Society: Opportunities, Risks, Principles, and Recommendations (2020).”

Foia i, T., Pantazi-Băjenaru, M., & Gurău, D. (2023). Personal Design, the New Fashion Trend with Applications of Innovative Technologies. Leather & Footwear Journal. *Revista de Pielarie - Încaltaminte*, *23*(3), 199–208. DOI: 10.24264/lfj.23.3.5

Folmar, D. (2015). *Game it up: Using gamification to incentivize your library*. Rowman & Littlefield.

Følstad, A., Araujo, T., Effie, L. C. L., Brandtzaeg, P. B., Papadopoulos, S., Reis, L., & Baez, M.. (2021). Future Directions for Chatbot Research: An Interdisciplinary Research Agenda. *Computing*, *103*(12), 2915–2942. Advance online publication. DOI: 10.1007/s00607-021-01016-7

Fornell, C., & Larcker, D. F. (1981). Evaluating Structural Equation Models with Unobservable Variables and Measurement Error. *JMR, Journal of Marketing Research, 18*(1), 39. DOI: 10.2307/3151312

Fornell, C., & Larcker, D. F. (1981). Evaluating structural equation models with unobservable variables and measurement error. *JMR, Journal of Marketing Research, 18*(1), 39–50. DOI: 10.1177/002224378101800104

Forstmann, B. U., & Wagenmakers, E. (2015). An Introduction to Model-Based Cognitive Neuroscience. In *Springer eBooks*. https://doi.org/DOI: 10.1007/978-1-4939-2236-9

Fouad, N. S. (2021). *Securing higher education against cyberthreats : from an institutional risk to a national policy challenge*. DOI: 10.1080/23738871.2021.1973526

Franzoni, V., Milani, A., Mengoni, P., & Piccinato, F. (2020). Artificial intelligence visual metaphors in e-learning interfaces for learning analytics. *Applied Sciences (Basel, Switzerland), 10*(20), 1–25. DOI: 10.3390/app10207195

Freitag, A. M., & Camargo-Borges, C. (2024). The Digital Bow: Exploring the Potential of Digital Presence for Indigenous Community-Based Tourism in Brazil. *Tourism Planning & Development, 21*(6), 755–772. Advance online publication. DOI: 10.1080/21568316.2024.2307974

Frey, K., Lüthje, C., & Haag, S. (2011). Whom Should Firms Attract to Open Innovation Platforms? The Role of Knowledge Diversity and Motivation. *Long Range Planning, 44*(5–6), 397–420. DOI: 10.1016/j.lrp.2011.09.006

Frivold, G., Krokstie, R., & Hassini, E. (2023). Exploring the Role of Web 3.0 in Higher Education: A Systematic Literature Review. *Education Sciences, 13*(2), 112.

Frolov, A., Gubarev, M., & Ponomareva, N. (2023). Trends in Web3 Application Development: Opportunities and Challenges. *International Journal of Information Management, 65*, 102453.

Füller, J., & Matzler, K. (2007). Virtual product experience and customer participation—A chance for customer-centred, really new products. *Technovation, 27*(6–7), 378–387. DOI: 10.1016/j.technovation.2006.09.005

Gadelha, M. R., & Silva, A. P. D. (2023). Design and evaluation of an augmented reality-based educational game for teaching mathematics to children. *Computers & Education, 178*, 104343. DOI: 10.1016/j.compedu.2022.104343

Gan, W., Ye, Z., Wan, S., & Yu, P. S. (2023). Web 3.0: The Future of Internet. *arXiv preprint arXiv:2304.06032*. DOI: 10.1145/3543873.3587583

Gao, H., Zhao, J., & Zhang, W. (2023). Enhancing User Experience in Web3 Applications Through AI-Powered Personalization. *Journal of Systems and Software*, *205*, 110767.

Garba, S. andMohmad, R. (2021). "Web Services for Dynamic Mobile Environments": A Case Study - International Journal of Electronic Services and Mobile Applications Volume 13 - Issue 4 - October-December.

Gardner, H. (2017). *Multiple intelligences: New horizons in theory and practice*. Basic Books.

Garrett, J. J. (2011). *The elements of user experience: User-centered design for the web and beyond*. New Riders.

Garrison, D. R., Anderson, T., & Archer, W. (2016). Critical thinking, cognitive presence, and computer conferencing in distance education. *American Journal of Distance Education*, *15*(1), 7–23. DOI: 10.1080/08923640109527071

Geake, J., & Cooper, P. (2003). Cognitive Neuroscience: Implications for education? *Westminster Studies in Education*, *26*(1), 7–20. DOI: 10.1080/0140672030260102

Gee, J. P. (2019). What video games have to teach us about learning and literacy. [CIE]. *Computers in Entertainment*, *1*(1), 20–20. DOI: 10.1145/950566.950595

Ge, Z., & Hu, Y. (2020) Innovative application of artificial intelligence (AI) in the Management of higher education and teaching. In *2020 International Conference on Artificial Intelligence and Information Technology, ICAIIT 2020*. Institute of Physics Publishing. https://doi.org/DOI: 10.1088/1742-6596/1533/3/032089

Gibson, A., & Martínez-Maldonado, R. (2017). That dashboard looks nice, but what does it mean? *Proceedings of the 29th Australian Conference on Computer-Human Interaction*. DOI: 10.1145/3152771.3156171

Gillespie, B., Doyle, P., Jiang, Z., & Humble, D. (2022). Sustainable international engagement using a partner co-hosted teaching model. *Irish Journal of Academic Practice*, *10*(1), 1–13. DOI: 10.21427/as8x-eq43

Gill, S. S., Xu, M., Patros, P., Wu, H., Kaur, R., Kaur, K., Fuller, S., Singh, M., Arora, P., Parlikad, A. K., Stankovski, V., Abraham, A., Ghosh, S. K., Lutfiyya, H., Kanhere, S. S., Bahsoon, R., Rana, O., Dustdar, S., Sakellariou, R., & Buyya, R. (2024). Transformative Effects of ChatGPT on Modern Education: Emerging Era of AI Chatbots. *Internet of Things and Cyber-Physical Systems*, *4*, 19–23. Advance online publication. DOI: 10.1016/j.iotcps.2023.06.002

Giungato, P.. (2021). The role of online communities in promoting blockchain knowledge: A systematic review. *Journal of Knowledge Management, 25*(6), 1397–1416. DOI: 10.1108/JKM-01-2021-0120

Gnaur, D., Hindhede, A. L., & Andersen, V. H. (2020, October). Towards hybrid learning in higher education in the wake of the COVID-19 crisis. *European Conference on e-Learning* (pp. 205-211). Academic Conferences International Limited.

Goel, A. K., Bakshi, R., & Agrawal, K. K. (2022). Web 3.0 and decentralized applications. *Materials Proceedings, 10*(1), 8.

Gonda, D. E., & Chu, B. 2019. "Chatbot as a Learning Resource? Creating Conversational Bots as a Supplement for Teaching Assistant Training Course." In *TALE 2019 - 2019 IEEE International Conference on Engineering, Technology and Education*. DOI: 10.1109/TALE48000.2019.9225974

Gonda, D. E., Luo, J., Wong, Y. L., & Lei, C. U. 2018. "Evaluation of Developing Educational Chatbots Based on the Seven Principles for Good Teaching." In *Proceedings of 2018 IEEE International Conference on Teaching, Assessment, and Learning for Engineering, TALE 2018*. DOI: 10.1109/TALE.2018.8615175

González, C. S., Gómez, N., Navarro, V., Cairós, M., Quirce, C., Toledo, P., & Marrero-Gordillo, N. (2016). Learning healthy lifestyles through active videogames, motor games and the gamification of educational activities. *Computers in Human Behavior, 55*, 529–551. DOI: 10.1016/j.chb.2015.08.052

Goosen, L., & Van Heerden, D. (2013a). Project-Based Assessment Influencing Pass Rates of an ICT Module at an ODL Institution. In E. Ivala (Ed.), *Proceedings of the 8th International Conference on e-Learning*. 1, pp. 157-164. Cape Town: Academic Conferences and Publishing.

Goosen, L., & Van Heerden, D. (2015). e-Learning Management System Technologies for Teaching Programming at a Distance. In C. Watson (Ed.), *Proceedings of the 10th International Conference on e-Learning (ICEL)* (pp. 116 - 126). Nassua: Academic Conferences and Publishing International. Retrieved from https://scholar.google.co.za/scholar?oi=bibs&cluster=16255326938393691479&btnI=1&hl=en

Goosen, L., & Van Heerden, D. (2016). e-Learning Environment Tools to Address Online and Open Distance Education Context Challenges. In R. M. Idrus, & N. Zainuddin (Ed.), *Proceedings of the 11th International Conference on e-Learning (ICEL)* (pp. 275 - 284). Kuala Lumpur, Malaysia: Academic Conferences and Publishing International.

Goosen, L., & Van Heerden, D. (2017). Beyond the Horizon of Learning Programming with Educational Technologies. In U. I. Ogbonnaya, & S. Simelane-Mnisi (Ed.), *Proceedings of the South Africa International Conference on Educational Technologies* (pp. 78 - 90). Pretoria: African Academic Research Forum.

Goosen, L., & Van Heerden, D. (2018). Assessment of Students in Higher Education – Information and Communication Technology Tools and Tips. *Progressio, 40*(1), #4704 23 pages. DOI: 10.25159/0256-8853/4706

Goosen, L. (2018). Ethical Data Management and Research Integrity in the Context of e-Schools and Community Engagement. In Sibinga, C. (Ed.), *Ensuring Research Integrity and the Ethical Management of Data* (pp. 14–45). IGI Global., DOI: 10.4018/978-1-5225-2730-5.ch002

Goosen, L., & Van Heerden, D. (2013b). Project-based learning and assessment of an IT module in an ODL context. [SAJHE]. *South African Journal of Higher Education, 27*(6), 1430–1443.

Goosen, L., & Van Heerden, D. (2019a). Promoting Research-Based Opportunities for First Year Programming Learners: Relevant and Quality Information Technology Education. In Govender, N., Mudaly, R., Mthethwa, T., & Singh-Pillay, A. (Ed.), *Proceedings of the 27th Conference of the Southern African Association for Research in Mathematics, Science and Technology Education (SAARMSTE)* (pp. 215 - 228). Durban: University of KwaZulu-Natal.

Goosen, L., & Van Heerden, D. (2019b). Student Support for Information and Communication Technology Modules in Open Distance Environments: Towards Self-Directed Learning. In Van Wyk, M. M. (Ed.), *Student Support Toward Self-Directed Learning in Open and Distributed Environments* (pp. 26–58). IGI Global., DOI: 10.4018/978-1-5225-9316-4.ch002

Gopalan, B. (2019). 'A Study on Variables, Technology Facilitators and Measures of Value Co-creation for Management', Acta Wasaensia 417, Doctoral dissertation, University of Vaasa. Vaasan yliopisto.

Gopalan, B., & Kohtamäki, M. (2017). Customer-The Value Co-Creator. *International Journal of Scientific & Technology Research*, Volume 6 – Issue 4, April 2017 Edition. ISSN 2277-8616.

Gordon, K. (2021). Using color to enhance your design. Retrieved from: https://www.nngroup.com/articles/color-enhance-design/

Gordon, E., & Silva, A. (2011). *Net Locality: Why Location Matters in a Networked World*. Wiley-Blackwell. DOI: 10.1002/9781444340679

Goswami, U. (2008). Principles of Learning, Implications for Teaching: A Cognitive Neuroscience perspective. *Journal of Philosophy of Education*, *42*(3–4), 381–399. DOI: 10.1111/j.1467-9752.2008.00639.x

Gottlieb, L. (2008). *Graffiti art styles a classification system and theoretical analysis*. McFarland & Company, Inc., Publishers.

Gowda, M. P. C., Srivastava, A., Chakraborty, S., Ghosh, A., & Raj, H. 2021. "Development of Information Technology Telecom Chatbot: An Artificial Intelligence and Machine Learning Approach." In *Proceedings of 2021 2nd International Conference on Intelligent Engineering and Management, ICIEM 2021*. DOI: 10.1109/ICIEM51511.2021.9445354

Graf, A. M. (2018). *Facets of graffiti art and street art documentation online: A domain and content analysis* (Doctoral thesis). Retrieved from ProQuest Dissertations and Theses. (UMI No. 10810618).

Gray, P. H., Parise, S., & Iyer, B. (2011). Innovation Impacts of using Social Bookmarking Systems. *Management Information Systems Quarterly*, *35*(3), 629–643. DOI: 10.2307/23042800

Green, B. P. (2018). Ethical Reflections on Artificial Intelligence. *Scientia et Fides*, *6*(2), 9. Advance online publication. DOI: 10.12775/SetF.2018.015

Groh, F. (2012). Gamification: state of the art definition and utilization. In Proceedings of the 4th seminar on Research trends in media information, (pp. 39-46). February 14. Ulm

Grover, V. and Kohli, R. (2012). Cocreating IT Value: New Capabilities and Metrics for Multifirm Environments. *MIS Quarterly (36, 1), pp. 225-232.*

Gummesson, E. (2008). Extending the service-dominant logic: From customer centricity to balanced Centricity. *Journal of the Academy of Marketing Science*, *36*(1), 15–17. DOI: 10.1007/s11747-007-0065-x

Gummesson, E., & Mele, C. (2010). Marketing as value co-creation through network interaction and resource integration. *Journal of Business Market Management*, *4*(4), 181–198. DOI: 10.1007/s12087-010-0044-2

Guo, Y. (2023). A review of Machine Learning-based zero-day attack detection: Challenges and future directions. *Computer Communications*, *198*, 175–185. DOI: 10.1016/j.comcom.2022.11.001 PMID: 36741076

Gupta, S., Modgil, S., Choi, T. M., Kumar, A., & Antony, J. (2023). Influences of artificial intelligence and blockchain technology on financial resilience of supply chains. *International Journal of Production Economics*, *261*, 108868. DOI: 10.1016/j.ijpe.2023.108868

Gupta, V., & Rathore, H. (2024). Leveraging AI for enhanced blockchain scalability: Challenges and solutions. *International Journal of Information Management*, *66*, 102459.

Halili, S. H., & Sulaiman, H. (2018). Factors influencing the rural students' acceptance of using ICT for educational purposes. *Kasetsart Journal of Social Sciences*, *40*, 574–579. DOI: 10.1016/j.kjss.2017.12.022

Hamari, J., & Koivisto, J. (2014). Measuring flow in gamification: Dispositional flow scale-2. *Computers in Human Behavior*, *40*, 133–143. DOI: 10.1016/j.chb.2014.07.048

Hamzah, W., Wan, M. A. F., Ismail, I., Yusof, M. K., Syarilla, I. M. S., & Yacob, A. (2021). Using Learning Analytics to Explore Responses from Student Conversations with Chatbot for Education. *International Journal of Engineering Pedagogy*, *11*(6), 70–84. Advance online publication. DOI: 10.3991/ijep.v11i6.23475

Hanafizadeh, P., Behboudi, M., Koshksaray, A. A., & Tabar, M. J. S. (2014). Mobile-Banking Adoption by Iranian Bank Clients. *Telematics and Informatics*, *31*(1), 62–78. DOI: 10.1016/j.tele.2012.11.001

Hasal, M., Nowaková, J., Saghair, K. A., Abdulla, H., Snášel, V., & Ogiela, L. 2021. "Chatbots: Security, Privacy, Data Protection, and Social Aspects." In *Concurrency and Computation: Practice and Experience*. Vol. 33. DOI: 10.1002/cpe.6426

Hassan, S., Babar, M. I., & Khan, A. N. (2021). Decentralized Autonomous Organizations (DAOs): A governance perspective. *IEEE Access : Practical Innovations, Open Solutions*, *9*, 157220–157230. DOI: 10.1109/ACCESS.2021.3128918

Heidemann, W., & Elgert, L. (2023). Virtual and augmented reality in education: Recent developments and future trends. *Educational Technology Research and Development*, *71*(1), 1–14. DOI: 10.1007/s11423-022-10040-w PMID: 37016716

Heilporn, G., Lakhal, S., & Bélisle, M. (2021). An examination of teachers' strategies to foster student engagement in blended learning in higher education. *International Journal of Educational Technology in Higher Education*, *18*(1), 1–25. DOI: 10.1186/s41239-021-00260-3 PMID: 34805484

Helo, P., & Shamsuzzoha, A. (2021). AI and blockchain in supply chain management: A systematic literature review. *Advanced Intelligent Systems*, *3*(6), 2000204. DOI: 10.1002/aisy.202000204

Hernández-Fernández, A., Olmedo-Torre, N., & Peña, M. (2020). Is classroom gamification opposed to performance? *Sustainability (Basel)*, *12*(23), 9958. DOI: 10.3390/su12239958

Hine, C. (2005). Internet Research and the Sociology of Cyber-Social-Scientific Knowledge. *The Information Society*, *21*(4), 239–248. DOI: 10.1080/01972240591007553

Hofacker, C. F., de Ruyter, K., Lurie, N. H., Manchanda, P., & Donaldson, J. (2016). Gamification and Mobile Marketing Effectiveness. *Journal of Interactive Marketing*, *34*(1), 25–36. DOI: 10.1016/j.intmar.2016.03.001

Hoffmann, A. L., Roberts, S. T., Wolf, C. T., & Wood, S. (2018). Beyond Fairness, Accountability, and Transparency in the Ethics of Algorithms: Contributions and Perspectives from LIS. *Proceedings of the Association for Information Science and Technology*, *55*(1), 694–696. Advance online publication. DOI: 10.1002/pra2.2018.14505501084

Höflich, J. R., Kircher, G. F., and Linke, C. (2010). Mobile Media and the Change of Everyday Life. *Frankfurt, DEU: Peter Lang AG, 2010. ProQuest ebrary. Web. 10 November 2014.* Copyright © 2010. Peter Lang AG. All rights reserved.

Holmes, E., Nicholson, J. K., Lodge, S., Nitschke, P., Kimhofer, T., & Wist, J.. (2021a). Diffusion and relaxation edited proton NMR spectroscopy of plasma reveals a high-fidelity supramolecular biomarker signature of SARS-CoV-2 infection. *Analytical Chemistry*, *93*(8), 3976–3986. DOI: 10.1021/acs.analchem.0c04952 PMID: 33577736

Holmes, W., Porayska-Pomsta, K., Holstein, K., Sutherland, E., Baker, T., Shum, S. B., Santos, O. C., Rodrigo, M. T., Cukurova, M., Bittencourt, I. I., & Koedinger, K. R. (2022). Ethics of AI in Education: Towards a Community-Wide Framework. *International Journal of Artificial Intelligence in Education*, *32*(3), 504–526. Advance online publication. DOI: 10.1007/s40593-021-00239-1

Hong, J. C., Hwang, M. Y., Tai, K. H., & Lin, P. H. (2019). Improving cognitive certitude with calibration mediated by cognitive anxiety, online learning self-efficacy and interest in learning chinese pronunciation. *Educational Technology Research and Development*, *67*(3), 597–615. DOI: 10.1007/s11423-018-9628-4

Hooda, M., Rana, C., Dahiya, O., Rizwan, A., & Hossain, M. S. (2022). Artificial intelligence for assessment and feedback to enhance student success in higher education. *Mathematical Problems in Engineering*, *2022*, 1–19. DOI: 10.1155/2022/5215722

Hopcan, S., Polat, E., Ozturk, M. E., & Ozturk, L. (2022). Artificial Intelligence in Special Education: A Systematic Review. *Interactive Learning Environments*. Advance online publication. DOI: 10.1080/10494820.2022.2067186

Hou, M., Zhu, H., Zhou, M., & Arrabito, G. G. (2011). Optimizing operator&#x-2013;agent interaction in intelligent adaptive interface design: A conceptual framework. *IEEE Transactions on Systems, Man, and Cybernetics. Part C, Applications and Reviews*, *41*(2), 161–178. DOI: 10.1109/TSMCC.2010.2052041

Hrastinski, S. (2017). Asynchronous and synchronous e-learning. *EDUCAUSE Quarterly*, *31*(4), 51–55.

Huang, J., ... (2018). Solidity: A programming language for writing smart contracts. *arXiv preprint arXiv:1808.05233*.

Huang, C., Samek, T., & Shiri, A. (2021). AI and Ethics: Ethical and Educational Perspectives for LIS. *Journal of Education for Library and Information Science*, *62*(4), 351–365. Advance online publication. DOI: 10.3138/jelis-62-4-2020-0106

Huang, R., Liu, X., & Xu, Z. (2023). Usability Challenges in Web3: Bridging the Gap Between Blockchain and Users. *Computers in Human Behavior*, *145*, 107560.

Huang, Y.. (2019). Trust, risk and the acceptance of blockchain technology: A survey. *Journal of Information Technology*, *34*(3), 197–214. DOI: 10.1177/0268396218792025

Hunt, S. D., Sparkman, R. D.Jr, & Wilcox, J. B. (1982). The pre-test in survey research: Issues and preliminary findings. [intrinsic motivation, and emotion into the technology acceptance model. Inf.]. *JMR, Journal of Marketing Research*, *19*(2), 269–273. DOI: 10.1177/002224378201900211

Huotari, K., & Hamari, J. (2017). A definition for gamification: Anchoring gamification in the service marketing literature. Electronic Markets, (27/1), p. 21-31.

Huttunen, M. (2024). Heritage for sustainable peace: The politics of contested histories and the Nanjing controversy at UNESCO. *Frontiers in Political Science*, *6*, 1249745. Advance online publication. DOI: 10.3389/fpos.2024.1249745

Ifelebuegu, A. O., Kulume, P., & Cherukut, P. (2023). Chatbots and AI in Education (AIEd) Tools: The Good, the Bad, and the Ugly. *Journal of Applied Learning and Teaching*, *6*(2).

Ijaz, K., & Ahmad, S. (2022). Augmented reality: An innovative approach in education and learning. *Journal of Educational Computing Research, 60*(5), 1081–1106. DOI: 10.1177/07356331211058791

IKEA HOME PLANNER. Ikea.com, n.d. Web. 19 Dec. 2014. <https://www.ikea.com/ms/en_JP/rooms_ideas/splashplanners.html>

Illescas, C., Ortega, T., & Jadán-Guerrero, J. 2023. "Gender Bias in Chatbots and Its Programming." In *Smart Innovation, Systems and Technologies.* Vol. 337 SIST. DOI: 10.1007/978-981-19-9099-1_33

Innovation Management / Crowdsourcing / Challenges / Competitions. Innocentive.com, n.d. Web. 19 Dec. 2014. <https://www.innocentive.com/>

Intriligator, S. S. (2015). *Local heritage as a participatory digital culture: the rise and fall of "Anglesey: a bridge through time" website* [PhD Dissertation]. ProQuest Dissertations and Theses (UMI No. 27609710)

IPFS. (2024). Persistence, permanence, and pinning. Retrieved from https://docs.ipfs.tech/concepts/persistence/#long-term-storage

Isa, S. S., & Liem, A. (2021). Exploring the role of physical prototypes during co-creation activities at LEGO company using case study validation. *CoDesign, 17*(3), 330–354. DOI: 10.1080/15710882.2020.1715443

Ishii, H., Ratti, C., Piper, B., Wang, Y., Biderman, A., & Ben-Joseph, E. (2004). Bringing clay and sand into digital design — Continuous tangible user interfaces. *BT Technology Journal, 22*(4), 287–299. https://www.proquest.com/scholarly-journals/bringing-clay-sand-into-digital-design-continuous/docview/215203715/se-2?accountid=177896. DOI: 10.1023/B:BTTJ.0000047607.16164.16

Izaguirre, J. I., Ferrari, A. A., & Acuto, F. A. (2024). Exploring cultural heritage and archaeological research from a VR-based approach. *Digital Applications in Archaeology and Cultural Heritage, 32*, e00318. Advance online publication. DOI: 10.1016/j.daach.2024.e00318

Jadresin Milic, R., McPherson, P., McConchie, G., Reutlinger, T., & Singh, S. (2022). Architectural History and Sustainable Architectural Heritage Education: Digitalisation of Heritage in New Zealand. *Sustainability (Basel), 14*(24), 16432. Advance online publication. DOI: 10.3390/su142416432

Jain, A. and Solanki, S. (2019). "An Efficient Approach for Multiclass Student Performance Prediction based upon Machine Learning," 2019 International Conference on Communication and Electronics Systems (ICCES), Coimbatore, India, pp. 1457-1462, doi: 10.1109/ICCES45898.2019.9002038.

Jarrahi, M. H. (2018). Artificial Intelligence and the Future of Work: Human-AI Symbiosis in Organizational Decision Making. *Business Horizons*, *61*(4), 577–586. DOI: 10.1016/j.bushor.2018.03.007

Jasin, J., Ng, H. T., Atmosukarto, I., Iyer, P., Osman, F., Peng, Y. K. W., Pua, C. Y., & Cheow, W. S. (2023). The Implementation of Chatbot-Mediated Immediacy for Synchronous Communication in an Online Chemistry Course. *Education and Information Technologies*, *28*(8), 10665–10690. DOI: 10.1007/s10639-023-11602-1 PMID: 36779194

Javornik, A., & Verhagen, H. (Eds.). (2022). *Augmented Reality and Virtual Reality in Education: Innovative Instructional Approaches* (1st ed.). Routledge., DOI: 10.4324/9781003189983

Jobin, A., Ienca, M., & Vayena, E. (2019). The Global Landscape of AI Ethics Guidelines. *Nature Machine Intelligence*, *1*(9), 389–399. Advance online publication. DOI: 10.1038/s42256-019-0088-2

Johnson, L., Adams Becker, S., Estrada, V., & Freeman, A. (2015). *NMC/CoSN Horizon Report: 2015 K-* (12th ed.). The New Media Consortium.

Jokilehto, J. (1999). A century of heritage conservation. *Journal of Architectural Conservation*, *5*(3), 14–33. Advance online publication. DOI: 10.1080/13556207.1999.10785249

Jony, A. I., & Hamim, S. A. (2024). Navigating the Cyber Threat Landscape: A Comprehensive Analysis of Attacks and Security in the Digital Age. *Journal of Information Technology and Cyber Security*, *1*(2), 53–67. DOI: 10.30996/jitcs.9715

Joo, Y. J., Bong, M., & Choi, H. J. (2000). Self-efficacy for self-regulated learning, academic self-efficacy, and internet self-efficacy in web-based instruction. *Educational Technology Research and Development*, *48*(2), 5–17. DOI: 10.1007/BF02313398

Jumani, A. K., Siddique, W. A., & Laghari, A. A. (2023). *Cloud and Machine Learning Based Solutions for Healthcare and Prevention. Image Based Computing for Food and Health Analytics: Requirements, Challenges, Solutions and Practices (IBCFHA)*. Springer International Publishing.

Jun, Z., & Shaokang, G. (2018). Exploration of product design based on behavioral interaction and emotional guidance. *2018 1st International Conference on Education, Art, Management and Social Sciences (EAMSS)*. Retrieved from chrome-extension://efaidnbmnnnibpcajpcglclefindmkaj/https://www.clausiuspress.com/conferences/LNEMSS/EAMSS%202018/E0431.pdf

JUUL J. (2005). *Half-Real: Video Games Between Real Rules and Fictional Worlds.* MIT Press.

K, A. and T, R. (2024), "Beyond the loom: understanding handloom product purchase motivations using the extended theory of planned behavior", Research Journal of Textile and Apparel, Vol. ahead-of-print No. ahead-of-print. DOI: 10.1108/RJTA-01-2024-0019

Kaçmaz, O. (2019). *Contemporary street art in Kadıköy special* (Master thesis). Retrieved from: https://www.proquest.com/openview/d4528d067e0e4c24ec0b59d773ff2aa3/1?pq-origsite=gscholar&cbl=2026366&diss=y

Kahneman, D. (2011). *Thinking, fast and slow.* Farrar, Straus and Giroux.

Kalavani, A., Kazerani, M., & Shekofteh, M. (2018). Acceptance of evidence based medicine (EBM) databases by Iranian medical residents using unified theory of acceptance and use of technology (UTAUT). *Health Policy and Technology, 7*(3), 287–292. DOI: 10.1016/j.hlpt.2018.06.005

Kang, H. S., Noh, S. D., Son, J. Y., Kim, H., Park, J. H., & Lee, J. Y. (2018). The FaaS system using additive manufacturing for personalized production. *Rapid Prototyping Journal, 24*(9), 1486–1499. DOI: 10.1108/RPJ-11-2016-0195

Kapp, K. M. (2012). The Gamification of Learning and Instruction: Game-based Methods and Strategies for Training and Education.

Karaca, A., & Kılcan, B. (2023). The Adventure of Artificial Intelligence Technology in Education: Comprehensive Scientific Mapping Analysis. *Participatory Educational Research, 10*(4), 144–165. Advance online publication. DOI: 10.17275/per.23.64.10.4

Karafillidis, A., & Korkontzelos, A. (2021). The role of social media in knowledge sharing in blockchain communities: A case study. *International Journal of Information Management, 59*, 102359. DOI: 10.1016/j.ijinfomgt.2021.102359

Kari, R., & Steinert, M. (2021). Human factor issues in remote ship operations: Lesson learned by studying different domains. *Journal of Marine Science and Engineering, 9*(4), 385. DOI: 10.3390/jmse9040385

Kaur, J., & Bhambri, P. (2019). Design of Paddy Crop Prediction Technique based on K-Mean, Naïve Bayes, KNN and SVM Classifiers. I.K. Gujral Punjab Technical University, Jalandhar (M.Tech. thesis).

Kaur, R. (2023). *Artificial intelligence for cybersecurity : Literature review and future research directions. 97*(January). DOI: 10.1016/j.inffus.2023.101804

Kaur, A., Singh, S., Chandan, J. S., Robbins, T., & Patel, V. (2021). Qualitative Exploration of Digital Chatbot Use in Medical Education: A Pilot Study. *Digital Health, 7*, 20552076211038151. Advance online publication. DOI: 10.1177/20552076211038151 PMID: 34513002

Kay, R. H. (2016). Exploring the use of video podcasts in education: A comprehensive review of the literature. *Computers in Human Behavior, 28*(3), 820–831. DOI: 10.1016/j.chb.2012.01.011

Kelling, G. L., & Wilson, J. Q. (1982). Broken windows: The police and neighborhood safety. Retrieved from: https://www.theatlantic.com/magazine/archive/1982/03/broken-windows/304465/

Kelly, A., Sullivan, M., & Strampel, K. (2023). Generative artifiicial intelligence: University student awareness, experience, and confiidence in use across disciplines. *Journal of University Teaching & Learning Practice, 20*(6). Advance online publication. DOI: 10.53761/1.20.6.12

Kelly, D., Conway, C., Harney, S., & McKeague, H. (2022). Temporary Transitions to Online Problem-Based Learning: Advice for Tutors and Learners. *Journal of Problem Based Learning in Higher Education, 10*(1), 1–19. DOI: 10.54337/ojs.jpblhe.v10i1.6362

Ketonen-Oksi, S., & Valkokari, K. (2019). Innovation ecosystems as structures for value co-creation. *Technology Innovation Management Review, 9*(2), 25–35. https://search-proquest-com.proxy.uwasa.fi/docview/2197276312?accountid=14797. DOI: 10.22215/timreview/1216

Khalaf, R. W. (2024). Adopting a Holistic Approach to Cultural and Natural Heritage Protection Under the UNESCO World Heritage Convention. In *Law and Visual Jurisprudence* (Vol. 12). DOI: 10.1007/978-3-031-47347-0_7

Khamparia, A., & Pandey, B. (2020). Association of learning styles with different e-learning problems: A systematic review and classification. *Education and Information Technologies, 25*(2), 1303–1331. DOI: 10.1007/s10639-019-10028-y

Khan, A.. (2021). Leveraging AI for enhancing scalability in blockchain. *Computers & Security, 105*, 102240. DOI: 10.1016/j.cose.2021.102240

Khan, M., Ahmad, N., & Saleem, A. (2024). Decentralized Finance: A New Paradigm in Financial Services. *Finance Research Letters, 49*, 103348.

Khan, N., Sarwar, A., Chen, T. B., & Khan, S. (2022). Connecting digital literacy in higher education to the 21st century workforce. *Knowledge Management and E-Learning, 14*(1), 46–61. DOI: 10.34105/j.kmel.2022.14.004

Khoshelham, K., & Elberink, S. O. (2022). Augmented reality in education: A review. *Journal of Computer Assisted Learning*, *38*(1), 3–13. DOI: 10.1111/jcal.12663

Khoza, S. B., & Mpungose, C. B. (2022). Digitalised curriculum to the rescue of a higher education institution. *African Identities*, *20*(4), 310–330. DOI: 10.1080/14725843.2020.1815517

Kim, B., Lim, H., Chung, J., Kim, J., Lim, K., Sohn, D., Cho, J.-Y., Yu, K.-S., Shin, S.-G., Paick, J.-S., & Jang, I.-J. (2008). Safety, tolerability and pharmacokinetics of udenafil, a novel PDE-5 inhibitor, in healthy young Korean subjects. *British Journal of Clinical Pharmacology*, *65*(6), 848–854. DOI: 10.1111/j.1365-2125.2008.03107.x PMID: 18318773

Kim, H. K., Park, Y. J., & Lee, S. (2021). Improving usability in cryptocurrency wallet applications through user feedback. *Computers in Human Behavior*, *116*, 106642. DOI: 10.1016/j.chb.2020.106642

Kim, J. W., Choi, J., Qualls, W., & Han, K. (2008). It takes a marketplace community to raise brand commitment: The role of online communities. *Journal of Marketing Management*, *24*(3/4), 409–431. DOI: 10.1362/026725708X306167

Kireyev, I. V., & Zhabotynska, N. V. (2020). Modern tools for the implementation of distance learning. In *Pedagogy in modern conditions: collective monograph* (pp. 222-225). Boston: Primedia eLaunch. DOI: 10.46299/ISG.2020.MONO.PED.III

Kirschner, P. A., & van Merriënboer, J. J. (2013). Do learners really know best? Urban legends in education. *Educational Psychologist*, *48*(3), 169–183. DOI: 10.1080/00461520.2013.804395

Kistyanto, A., Rahman, M. F. W., Adhar Wisandiko, F., & Setyawati, E. E. P. (2022). Cultural intelligence increase student's innovative behavior in higher education: The mediating role of interpersonal trust. *International Journal of Educational Management*, *36*(4), 419–440. DOI: 10.1108/IJEM-11-2020-0510

Klimova, B., Pikhart, M., & Kacetl, J. (2023). Ethical Issues of the Use of AI-Driven Mobile Apps for Education. *Frontiers in Public Health*, *10*, 1118116. Advance online publication. DOI: 10.3389/fpubh.2022.1118116 PMID: 36711343

Kline, B., & Best, S. (2023). Virtual reality in higher education: A comparative case study. *Interactive Learning Environments*, *31*(1), 80–95. DOI: 10.1080/10494820.2021.1977123

Klinke, H., Surkemper, L., & Underhill, J. (2018). In Conversation with CyArk: Digital Heritage in the 21st Century. *International Journal for Digital Art History*, *0*(3). https://journals.ub.uni-heidelberg.de/index.php/dah/article/view/49914

Koenig, N., Anzelmi, G., Naso, D., Nienhaus, M., & Grasso, E. "An Improved IDIM Technique for Sensorless Control of Single-Phase Electromagnetic Drives," 2019 IEEE 10th International Symposium on Sensorless Control for Electrical Drives (SLED), Turin, Italy, 2019, pp. 1-6, DOI: 10.1109/SLED.2019.8896303

Kolotylo-Kulkarni, M., Xia, W., & Dhillon, G. (2021). Information disclosure in e-commerce: A systematic review and agenda for future research, March 2020. *Journal of Business Research*, *126*, 221–238. DOI: 10.1016/j.jbusres.2020.12.006

KONDA. (2014). Trip report. Society's perception of the 'Gezi Park Events'. Who were the people in Gezi Park? Retrieved from: https://konda.com.tr/uploads/konda-geziraporu2014-be80cf101d80fe3a74322f7690203132abd2f22b1c69b31a6bbad80d1a227cf1.pdf

Koohang, A., Riley, L., Smith, T., & Schreurs, J. (2009). E-learning and constructivism: From theory to application. *Interdisciplinary Journal of E-Learning and Learning Objects*, *5*(1), 91–109. DOI: 10.28945/3321

Kooli, C. (2023). Chatbots in Education and Research: A Critical Examination of Ethical Implications and Solutions. *Sustainability (Basel)*, *15*(7), 5614. Advance online publication. DOI: 10.3390/su15075614

Kostiainen, K.. (2019). Secure key management for blockchain applications. *IEEE Security and Privacy*, *17*(3), 28–37. DOI: 10.1109/MSP.2019.2915746

Kouhizadeh, M., & Sarkis, J. (2021). Blockchain and supply chain management: A systematic review and future directions. *International Journal of Production Economics*, *231*, 107851. DOI: 10.1016/j.ijpe.2020.107851

Kour, R., & Karim, R. (2020). Cybersecurity workforce in railway: Its maturity and awareness. *Journal of Quality in Maintenance Engineering*, *27*(3), 453–464. DOI: 10.1108/JQME-07-2020-0059

Kraft Customer Co-creation Case Study / Communispace. Communispace.com, n.d. Web. 19 Dec. 2014. <http://www.communispace.com/Kraft-South-Beach-Diet-case-study/>

Krause, A.. (2020). Networking and collaboration in the blockchain community: An analysis of industry conferences. *Journal of Business Research*, *116*, 418–426. DOI: 10.1016/j.jbusres.2019.10.025

Kritika (2024). A comprehensive literature review on phishing URL detection using deep learning techniques. Journal of Cyber Security Technology, 1–29. DOI: 10.1080/23742917.2024.2378552

Kshetri, N. (2018). Blockchain's roles in strengthening cybersecurity and protecting privacy. *Telecommunications Policy*, *41*(10), 1027–1038. DOI: 10.1016/j.telpol.2017.09.003

Kuhail, M. A., Alturki, N., Alramlawi, S., & Alhejori, K. (2023). Interacting with Educational Chatbots: A Systematic Review. *Education and Information Technologies*, *28*(1), 973–1018. Advance online publication. DOI: 10.1007/s10639-022-11177-3

Kuh, G. D. (2009). The national survey of student engagement: Conceptual and empirical foundations. *New Directions for Institutional Research*, *2009*(141), 5–20. DOI: 10.1002/ir.283

Kuo, T. T.. (2020). The role of blockchain technology in the management of supply chain risks: A review and future research agenda. *International Journal of Production Economics*, *219*, 109–121. DOI: 10.1016/j.ijpe.2019.04.014

Kuzhaloli, S., Devaneyan, P., Sitaraman, N., Periyathanbi, P., Gurusamy, M., & Bhambri, P. (2020). Invention titled "IoT based Smart Kitchen Application for Gas Leakage Monitoring" (Application No. 202041049866A). Published on 27th November 2020 (Issue No. 48/2020, Page No. 59674). Retrieved from http://ipindia.nic.in/writereaddata/Portal/IPOJournal/1_4929_1/Part-1.pdf

Labadi, S., Giliberto, F., Rosetti, I., Shetabi, L., & Yildirim, E. (2021). Heritage and the sustainable development goals: Policy guidance for heritage and development actors. In *International Council on Monuments and Sites - ICOMOS*.

Labadze, L., Grigolia, M., & Machaidze, L. (2023). Role of AI Chatbots in Education: Systematic Literature Review. *International Journal of Educational Technology in Higher Education*, *20*(1), 56. DOI: 10.1186/s41239-023-00426-1

Lacity, M. C., & Lupien, S. C. (2022). *Blockchain Fundamentals for Web 3.0*. University of Arkansas Press.

Lahcen, R. A., Mohapatra, R., & Chen, B. (2020, November 16). Prioritizing strategies for a better transition to remote instruction. *EDUCAUSE Review*. Retrieved from https://er.educause.edu/articles/2020/11/prioritizing-strategies-for-a-better-transition-to-remote-instruction

Lai, K. W. (2024). Augmented reality in education: A meta-analysis. *Educational Technology Research and Development*, *72*(2), 331–349. DOI: 10.1007/s11423-023-10051-1

Lallie, H. S., & Titis, E. (2023). *Understanding Cyber Threats Against the Universities, Colleges, and Schools*. Elsevier.

Lameras, P., & Arnab, S. (2022). Power to the Teachers: An Exploratory Review on Artificial Intelligence in Education. *Information (Basel)*, *13*(1), 14. Advance online publication. DOI: 10.3390/info13010014

Laurillard, D. (2017). *Rethinking university teaching: A conversational framework for the effective use of learning technologies*. Routledge.

Lave, J., & Wenger, E. (2019). *Situated learning: Legitimate peripheral participation*. Cambridge University Press.

Lechner, U., & Hummel, J. (2002). Business models and system architectures of virtual communities: From a sociological phenomenon to peer-to-peer architectures. *International Journal of Electronic Commerce*, *6*(3), 41–53. DOI: 10.1080/10864415.2002.11044242

Leclercq, T., Poncin, I., & Hammedi, W. (2017). The engagement process during value co-creation: Gamification in new product development platforms. *International Journal of Electronic Commerce*, *21*(4), 454–488.

Lee, B. C., Yoon, J. O., & Lee, I. (2009). Learners' acceptance of e-learning in South Korea: Theories and results. *Computers & Education*, *53*(4), 1320–1329. DOI: 10.1016/j.compedu.2009.06.014

Lee, E. A. L., & Wong, K. W. (2022). Enhancing student engagement through augmented reality in education. *Interactive Learning Environments*, *30*(8), 1121–1134. DOI: 10.1080/10494820.2021.1923496

Lego Digital Designer. Lego.com, n.d. Web. 19 Dec. 2014. http://ldd.lego.com/en-us/

Lehoux, P. (2004). Patients' perspectives on high-tech home care: A qualitative inquiry into the user-friendliness of four technologies. *BMC Health Services Research*, *4*(1), 28. Advance online publication. DOI: 10.1186/1472-6963-4-28 PMID: 15462682

Lerner, J., & Tirole, J. (2020). The governance of blockchain initiatives. *The Journal of Economic Perspectives*, *34*(2), 107–130. DOI: 10.1257/jep.20191203

Le, T. D., Le-Dinh, T., & Uwizeyemungu, S. (2024). Search engine optimization poisoning: A cybersecurity threat analysis and mitigation strategies for small and medium-sized enterprises. *Technology in Society*, *76*, 102470. DOI: 10.1016/j.techsoc.2024.102470

Li, S. and Yan, C. (2024). "Governing Decentralized Autonomous Organizations as Digital Commons." *Journal of Business Venturing Insights* 21. .DOI: 10.1016/j.jbvi.2024.e00450

Liang, X., Lu, Y., & Martin, J. (2021). A review of the role of social media for the cultural heritage sustainability. *Sustainability (Basel)*, *13*(3), 1055. Advance online publication. DOI: 10.3390/su13031055

Lidwell, W., Holden, K., & Butler, J. (2010). *Universal Principles of Design*. Rockport Publishers.

Li, G., Lin, S., & Tian, Y. (2024). Immersive Museums in the Digital Age: Exploring the Impact of Virtual Reality on Visitor Satisfaction and Loyalty. *Journal of the Knowledge Economy*. Advance online publication. DOI: 10.1007/s13132-024-01782-7

Li, H., Edwards, S. M., & Lee, J.-H. (2002). Measuring the intrusiveness of advertisements: Scale development and validation. *Journal of Advertising*, *31*(2), 37–47. DOI: 10.1080/00913367.2002.10673665

Lihra, T., Buehlmann, U., & Graf, R. (2012). Customer preferences for customized household furniture. *Journal of Forest Economics*, *18*(2), 94–112. DOI: 10.1016/j.jfe.2011.11.001

Li, J., Li, J., Yang, Y., & Ren, Z. (2021). Design of higher education system based on artificial intelligence technology. *Discrete Dynamics in Nature and Society*, *2021*, 1–11. DOI: 10.1155/2021/3303160

Li, L., & Hsiao, K. F. (2023). Exploring the affordances of virtual reality in education: A systematic review. *British Journal of Educational Technology*, *54*(2), 308–327. DOI: 10.1111/bjet.13183

Li, L., Wang, Y., & Wang, H. (2018). The impact of instructional design in an online collaborative learning environment. *Computers & Education*, *55*(2), 681–690.

Lin, F. R., Liu, Y. L., & Yuan, S. M. (2019). The impact of user satisfaction with online learning management system on learner performance. *Behaviour & Information Technology*, *38*(2), 125–134.

Lin, H. (2007). The Ethics of Instructional Technology: Issues and Coping Strategies Experienced by Professional Technologists in Design and Training Situations in Higher Education. *Educational Technology Research and Development*, *55*(5), 411–437. Advance online publication. DOI: 10.1007/s11423-006-9029-y

Lin, H. Y., & Hsu, Y. C. (2023). The effects of virtual reality and augmented reality on learning outcomes in K-12 education: A meta-analysis. *Computers & Education*, *181*, 104450. DOI: 10.1016/j.compedu.2022.104450

Lin, Y. T., & Jian, H. Y. (2023). Development of an Educational Chatbot System for Enhancing Students' Biology Learning Performance. *Wangji Wanglu Jishu Xuekan*, *24*(2), 275–281. DOI: 10.53106/160792642023032402006

Li, P., & Chen, J.-H. (2018). A model of an e-customized co-design system on garment design. *International Journal of Clothing Science and Technology*, *30*(5), 628–640. DOI: 10.1108/IJCST-01-2018-0011

Liu, L., Subbareddy, R., & Raghavendra, C. G. (2022). AI Intelligence Chatbot to Improve Students Learning in the Higher Education Platform. *Journal of Interconnection Networks*, *22*(Supp02), 2143032. Advance online publication. DOI: 10.1142/S0219265921430325

Liu, Z., & Kang, J. (2022). Virtual reality in education: A comprehensive review. *Education and Information Technologies*, *27*(5), 5189–5211. DOI: 10.1007/s10639-022-11063-4 PMID: 35013667

Li, Y., Duan, Y., Fu, Z., & Alford, P. (2012). An empirical study on behavioural intention to reuse e-learning systems in rural China. *British Journal of Educational Technology*, *43*(6), 933–948. DOI: 10.1111/j.1467-8535.2011.01261.x

Li, Y., Zhao, L., Chen, Y., Zhang, N., Fan, H., & Zhang, Z. (2023). 3D LiDAR and multi-technology collaboration for preservation of built heritage in China: A review. *International Journal of Applied Earth Observation and Geoinformation*, *116*, 103156. Advance online publication. DOI: 10.1016/j.jag.2022.103156

Luekveerawattana, R. (2024). Enhancing innovation in cultural heritage tourism: Navigating external factors. *Cogent Social Sciences*, *10*(1), 2301813. Advance online publication. DOI: 10.1080/23311886.2024.2301813

Lund, B. D., & Wang, T. (2023). Chatting about ChatGPT: How May AI and GPT Impact Academia and Libraries? *Library Hi Tech News*, *40*(3), 26–29. Advance online publication. DOI: 10.1108/LHTN-01-2023-0009

Luo, Y., & Du, H. (2022). Learning with desktop virtual reality: Changes and interrelationship of self-efficacy, goal orientation, technology acceptance and learning behavior. *Smart Learning Environments*, *9*(1), 1–22. DOI: 10.1186/s40561-022-00203-z

Macharia Njoroge, M. P. (2021). An Examination of Threats facing Assets in Use in Kenyan Public Universities. [IJSRP]. *International Journal of Scientific and Research Publications*, *11*(5), 687–695. DOI: 10.29322/IJSRP.11.05.2021.p11372

Mackey, T. K.. (2021). The role of blockchain technology in advancing global health: A systematic review. *Health Policy and Technology, 10*(2), 100–111. DOI: 10.1016/j.hlpt.2021.03.001

Madhavan, G., Mythily, M., Sharon, R., & Isaac Ritharson, P. 2023. "Chatbots Embracing Artificial Intelligence Solutions to Assist Institutions in Improving Student Interactions." In *Proceedings of the International Conference on Circuit Power and Computing Technologies, ICCPCT 2023*. DOI: 10.1109/ICCPCT58313.2023.10245835

Maecenas (2018). Andy Warhol's 14 small electric chairs to be sold in blockchain art auction. Retrieved from: https://blog.maecenas.co/andy-warhols-14-small-electric-chairs-to-be-sold-in-blockchain-art-auction/

Magazines, F. Flipboard.com, n.d. Web. 19 Dec. 2014. <https://about.flipboard.com/magazines/>

Maietti, F. (2022). Digital Documentation for Enhancement and Conservation of Minor or Inaccessible Heritage Sites. In *Contributions to Management Science*. DOI: 10.1007/978-3-031-14121-8_8

Mailizar, M., Burg, D., & Maulina, S. (2021). Examining university students' behavioural intention to use e-learning during the COVID-19 pandemic: An extended TAM model. *Education and Information Technologies, 26*(6), 7057–7077. DOI: 10.1007/s10639-021-10557-5 PMID: 33935579

Mainardes, E. W., Teixeira, A., & Romano, P. C. S. (2017). Determinants of co-creation in banking services. *International Journal of Bank Marketing, 35*(2), 187–204. https://search-proquest-com.proxy.uwasa.fi/docview/1868279930?accountid=14797. DOI: 10.1108/IJBM-10-2015-0165

Makhdoom, I.. (2021). Blockchain technology in healthcare: A systematic review. *Journal of Biomedical Informatics, 113*, 103634. DOI: 10.1016/j.jbi.2020.103634

Malhi, M. S., Iqbal, U., Nabi, M. M., & Malhi, M. A. (2020). E-learning based on cloud computing for educational institution: Security issues and solutions. *International Journal of Electronics and Information Engineering, 12*(4), 162–169.

Malone, T. W. (1980). What makes things fun to learn? Heuristics for designing instructional computer games. In *Proceedings of the 3rd ACM SIGSMALL symposium and the first SIGPC symposium on Small systems* (pp. 162–169). ACM. DOI: 10.1145/800088.802839

Mansoori, Y.. (2021). Interoperability in blockchain technology: A review. *Journal of Network and Computer Applications, 188*, 103115. DOI: 10.1016/j.jnca.2021.103115

Mantra, I. Abd. Rahman, A., & Saragih, H. (2020). Maturity Framework Analysis ISO 27001: 2013 on Indonesian Higher Education. In *International Journal of Engineering & Technology* (Vol. 9, Issue 2, p. 429). DOI: 10.14419/ijet.v9i2.30581

Maranga, J. (2019). *Emerging Issues in Cyber Security for Institutions of Higher Education. August.*

Marchese, F. T., & Shergill, M. P. K. (2012). 500 year documentation. In *Proceedings of the 2012 ACM symposium on Document engineering (DocEng '12).* Association for Computing Machinery, New York, NY, USA, 157–160. https://doi.org/DOI: 10.1145/2361354.2361391

Marcinkowski, F. (2020). Implications of AI (un-)fairness in higher education admissions: The effects of perceived AI (un-)fairness on exit, voice and organizational reputation. In 3rd ACM Conference on Fairness, Accountability, and Transparency, FAT* 2020. Association for Computing Machinery, Inc, pp. 122–130. https://doi.org/DOI: 10.1145/3351095.3372867

Markellou, M. (2023). Cultural Heritage Accessibility in the Digital Era and the Greek Legal Framework. *International Journal for the Semiotics of Law*, *36*(5), 1945–1969. Advance online publication. DOI: 10.1007/s11196-023-10027-w

Marks, B., & Thomas, J. (2022). Adoption of virtual reality technology in higher education: An evaluation of five teaching semesters in a purpose-designed laboratory. *Education and Information Technologies*, *27*(1), 1287–1305. DOI: 10.1007/s10639-021-10653-6 PMID: 34257511

Martinez-Garcia, A., Horrach-Rosselló, P., & Mulet-Forteza, C. (2023). Evolution and current state of research into E-learning. *Heliyon*, *9*(10), e21016. DOI: 10.1016/j.heliyon.2023.e21016 PMID: 37867823

Masciotta, M. G., Morais, M. J., Ramos, L. F., Oliveira, D. V., Sánchez-Aparicio, L. J., & González-Aguilera, D. (2021). A Digital-based Integrated Methodology for the Preventive Conservation of Cultural Heritage: The Experience of HeritageCare Project. *International Journal of Architectural Heritage*, *15*(6), 844–863. Advance online publication. DOI: 10.1080/15583058.2019.1668985

Maulana, R., Anita, F., & Putra, M. I. (2022, June). EFL Students' Critical Thinking in Speaking Activities. *Jurnal Pendidikan Bahasa*, *11*(1), 139–152. DOI: 10.31571/bahasa.v11i1.3528

McAlister, A. R., Alhabash, S., & Yang, J. (2024). Artificial Intelligence and ChatGPT: Exploring Current and Potential Future Roles in Marketing Education. *Journal of Marketing Communications*, *30*(2), 166–187. Advance online publication. DOI: 10.1080/13527266.2023.2289034

McNealy, J. E. (2023). "Who's Liable?: Agency and Accountability in Human–Machine Communication." In *The Sage Handbook of Human–Machine Communication*. DOI: 10.4135/9781529782783.n52

Md, M. H. O., & Miraz, M. H. (2016). Comparative Performance Analysis of Blockchain as a Service (BaaS) Platforms. *Applied Soft Computing*, *39*, 124–139.

Means, B., & Neisler, J. (2019). Using technology to support at-risk students' learning. *Journal of Educational Computing Research*, *35*(4), 381–399.

Medaglia, J. D., Lynall, M., & Bassett, D. S. (2015). Cognitive Network Neuroscience. *Journal of Cognitive Neuroscience*, *27*(8), 1471–1491. DOI: 10.1162/jocn_a_00810 PMID: 25803596

Mekler, E. D., Brühlmann, F., Tuch, A. N., & Opwis, K. (2017). Towards understanding the effects of individual gamific. elements on intrinsic motivation and performance. *Computers in Human Behavior*, *71*, 525–534. DOI: 10.1016/j.chb.2015.08.048

Melaku, H. M. (2023). Context-Based and Adaptive Cybersecurity Risk Management Framework. *Risks*, *11*(6), 101. Advance online publication. DOI: 10.3390/risks11060101

Mendelson-Shwartz, E., Shwartz, O., & Mualam, N. (2023). Protecting street art rights using an NFT-based system. *Journal of Urban Technology*, *30*(3), 81–100. DOI: 10.1080/10630732.2023.2180983

Mendoza, S., Sánchez-Adame, L. M., Urquiza-Yllescas, J. F., González-Beltrán, B. A., & Decouchant, D. (2022). A Model to Develop Chatbots for Assisting the Teaching and Learning Process. *Sensors (Basel)*, *22*(15), 5532. Advance online publication. DOI: 10.3390/s22155532 PMID: 35898035

Men, L. R., Zhou, A., & Wan, H. S. T. (2022). Harnessing the Power of Chatbot Social Conversation for Organizational Listening: The Impact on Perceived Transparency and Organization-Public Relationships. *Journal of Public Relations Research*, *34*(1–2), 20–44. Advance online publication. DOI: 10.1080/1062726X.2022.2068553

Messinger, P. R., Stroulia, E., Lyons, K., Bone, M., Niu, R. H., Smirnov, K., & Perelgut, S. (2009). Virtual worlds - past, present, and future: New directions in social computing. *Decision Support Systems*, *47*(3), 204–228. DOI: 10.1016/j.dss.2009.02.014

Miers, I.. (2013). ZK-proof-based protocols for anonymous transactions. *ACM Transactions on Information and System Security*, *16*(4), 1–24. DOI: 10.1145/2482768.2482770

Mikusa, M. E. (2015). The effect of technology self-efficacy and personal engagement on students' and teachers' attitudes toward technology use in education(Doctoral dissertation). Appalachian State University

Miles, J. (2014). Tolerance and Variance inflation factor. Wiley StatsRef: Statistics Reference Online, https://doi.org/.DOI: 10.1002/9781118445112.stat06593

Milgram, P., & Kishino, F. (2023). Taxonomy of mixed reality visual displays. *IEICE Transactions on Information and Systems*, *E77-D*(12), 1321–1329. DOI: 10.1587/transinf.77.d.1321

Minkevics, V., & Kampars, J. (2021). Artificial intelligence and big data driven is security management solution with applications in higher education organizations. In Chemouil, P.. (Ed.) *17th International Conference on Network and Service Management, CNSM 2021*. Institute of Electrical and Electronics Engineers Inc. pp. 340–344. https://doi.org/DOI: 10.23919/CNSM52442.2021.9615575

Miroshnyk, R., Matviy, I., Halaz, L., & Bahlai, I. (2022, November). Trends in the Development of Online Platforms for Distance Learning. *17th International Conference on Computer Sciences and Information Technologies (CSIT)* (pp. 260-264). IEEE. DOI: 10.1109/CSIT56902.2022.10000065

Mishra, N., & Mukherjee, S. (2019). Effect of artificial intelligence on customer relationship management of Amazon in Bangalore. *International Journal of Management (Kolkata)*, *10*(4), 168–172. DOI: 10.34218/IJM.10.4.2019.016

Mishra, P., & Koehler, M. J. (2006). Technological pedagogical content knowledge: A framework for teacher knowledge. *Teachers College Record*, *108*(6), 1017–1054. DOI: 10.1111/j.1467-9620.2006.00684.x

Mishra, R. (2019). Usage of data analytics and artificial intelligence in ensuring quality assurance at higher education institutions. In *2019 Amity International Conference on Artificial Intelligence, AICAI 2019*. Institute of Electrical and Electronics Engineers Inc. pp. 1022–1025. https://doi.org/DOI: 10.1109/AICAI.2019.8701392

Mitic, V. (2019) Benefits of Artificial Intelligence and Machine Learning in Marketing. In Sinteza 2019-International Scientific Conference on Information Technology and Data Related Research (pp. 472-477). Singidunum University.

Mohamed Zabri, S., Mohammad Abakar, Y., & Ahmad, K. (2023). Exploring the acceptance of online learning among students in technical and non-technical programmes at a higher education institution. *Cogent Education*, *10*(2), 2284552. DOI: 10.1080/2331186X.2023.2284552

Mohammadi, H. (2015). A Study of Mobile Banking Usage in Iran. *International Journal of Bank Marketing*, *33*(6), 733–759. DOI: 10.1108/IJBM-08-2014-0114

Mohammadi, M., Zahedi, M., & Baraani, A. (2020). Cybersecurity in e-learning systems: A systematic review. *Journal of Computer Assisted Learning*, *36*(5), 648–662. DOI: 10.1111/jcal.12440

Mohammed, CM. and Subhi R. M. (2021). Zeebaree Cloud Comparison: IaaS, PaaS and SaaS: A Review. Journal of Web Semantics Volume 1, Issue 3, April 2004, No. Page 309 - 320 page

Mokmin, N. A. M., & Ibrahim, N. A. (2021). The Evaluation of Chatbot as a Tool for Health Literacy Education among Undergraduate Students. *Education and Information Technologies*, *26*(5), 6033–6049. Advance online publication. DOI: 10.1007/s10639-021-10542-y PMID: 34054328

Mónica Faria, B., Vasconcelos, S., Paulo Reis, L. and Lau, N. (2012). A Methodology for Creating Intelligent Wheelchair Users' Profiles. In Proceedings of the 4th International Conference on Agents and Artificial Intelligence - Volume 2: ICAART; ISBN 978-989-8425-95-9; ISSN 2184-433X, SciTePress, pages 171-179. DOI: 10.5220/0003749701710179. DOI: 10.3390/s22155830 PMID: 35957387

Moosa, J., & Bahaaudeen, A. (2023, March). Programming courses Teaching methods Before, During, and After COVID-19 Pandemic. *International Conference on IT Innovation and Knowledge Discovery (ITIKD)* (pp. 1-5). IEEE. DOI: 10.1109/ITIKD56332.2023.10099736

Moura, A. M. C., & Borges, M. R. S. (2022). Virtual reality in the education of health professionals: A systematic review. *Revista Brasileira de Enfermagem*, *75*(1), e20200401. DOI: 10.1590/0034-7167-2020-0401

Murtarelli, G., Gregory, A., & Romenti, S. (2021). A Conversation-Based Perspective for Shaping Ethical Human–Machine Interactions: The Particular Challenge of Chatbots. *Journal of Business Research*, *129*, 927–935. Advance online publication. DOI: 10.1016/j.jbusres.2020.09.018

Mutibwa, D. H., Hess, A., & Jackson, T. (2020). Strokes of serendipity: Community co-curation and engagement with digital heritage. *Convergence (London)*, *26*(1), 157–177. Advance online publication. DOI: 10.1177/1354856518772030

Nachtigall, T., Mironcika, S., Tomico, O., & Feijs, L. (2020). Designing ultra-personalized product service systems. *CoDesign*, *16*(4), 274–292. DOI: 10.1080/15710882.2020.1842454

Nagamachi, M. (2010). *Kansei/affective engineering*. CRC Press.

Naidu, V. R., Najah, S., Saqib, M., Swathi, R., & Pandey, N. (2023). Transforming E-Learning through Cloud-Based Interactive Multimedia Authoring Solutions. *SHS Web of Conferences. 156.* EDP Sciences. DOI: 10.1051/shsconf/202315609001

Namkoong, M., Park, Y., Lee, S., & Park, G. (2024). Effect of AI counsellor's nonverbal immediacy behaviour on user satisfaction: Serial mediation of positive expectancy violation and rapport. *Behaviour & Information Technology*, •••, 1–17. DOI: 10.1080/0144929X.2024.2367691

Narayanan, A., Bonneau, J., Felten, E., Miller, A., & Goldfeder, S. (2016). *Bitcoin and Cryptocurrency Technologies*. Princeton University Press.

Nardi, A., & Ranieri, M. (2019). Comparing paper-based and electronic multiple-choice examinations with personal devices: Impact on students' performance, self-efficacy and satisfaction. *British Journal of Educational Technology*, *50*(3), 1495–1506. DOI: 10.1111/bjet.12644

Nardo, D., & Carminati, L. (2023). Using virtual reality to enhance soft skills: A systematic review. *Interactive Learning Environments*, *31*(2), 228–244. DOI: 10.1080/10494820.2021.1978540

Ndeda, L. A., Odoyo, C. O., Systems, I., Town, B., & Town, K. (2019). Cyber Threats and Cyber Security in the Kenyan Business Context. *Global Scientific Journal*, *7*(9), 576–582.

Nepali, S. (2017). *Evaluation of GPU based Cloud Solutions (Scalability of Deep Learning in the Cloud).* (Master thesis). University of Oslo.

Nesprava, M., Zarishniak, I., Koropetska, O., Kurinna, A., Syvash, S., & Sushchenko, L. (2023). Formation of Communicative Competencies of Applicants for Higher Education in the Context of Distance Learning. *Revista Romaneasca pentru Educatie Multidimensionala [Romanian Journal for Multidimensional Education]*, *15*(1), 247-260.

Neuendorf, H. (2018). Street artist revok and H&M settle dispute over an ad that featured his work without permission. Retrieved from: https://news.artnet.com/art-world/revok-hm-ad-campaign-1345127

Neumann, C., Stroud, K. M., Bailey, S., Allison, K., & Everts, S. S. (2021). 21st-century competencies in higher education: A practitioner's guide. In *Handbook of research on barriers for teaching 21st-Century competencies and the impact of digitalization* (pp. 293–315). IGI Globalpp., DOI: 10.4018/978-1-7998-6967-2.ch016

Ngugi, J. K., & Goosen, L. (2021). Innovation, Entrepreneurship, and Sustainability for ICT Students Towards the Post-COVID-19 Era. In Carvalho, L. C., Reis, L., & Silveira, C. (Eds.), *Handbook of Research on Entrepreneurship, Innovation, Sustainability, and ICTs in the Post-COVID-19 Era* (pp. 110–131). IGI Global., DOI: 10.4018/978-1-7998-6776-0.ch006

Nguyen, Q. N., Sidorova, A., & Torres, R. (2022). User Interactions with Chatbot Interfaces vs. Menu-Based Interfaces: An Empirical Study. *Computers in Human Behavior, 128*, 107093. Advance online publication. DOI: 10.1016/j.chb.2021.107093

Nguyen, T. N.. (2022). Blockchain and AI in health care: A systematic review. *Health Informatics Journal, 28*(2), 14604582221084341. DOI: 10.1177/14604582221084341

Nielsen, J. (2001). 13 design guidelines for homepage usability. Retrieved from: https://www.nngroup.com/articles/113-design-guidelines-homepage-usability/

Nielsen, J. (2020). 10 usability heuristics for user interface design. Retrieved from: https://www.nngroup.com/articles/ten-usability-heuristics/

Nielsen, J., & Molich, R. (2021). Heuristic evaluation of user interfaces. *Proceedings of the SIGCHI Conference on Human Factors in Computing Systems*, 249-256. https://doi.org/DOI: 10.1145/674044.674096

NikeID Customize Shoes and Accessories. Nike.com, n.d. Web. 19 Dec. 2014. https://www.nike.com/us/en_us/c/nikeid

Nogel, C. N. (2015). Decolonial arts pedagogy and the visual metaphor: the great wall of los angeles mural project. (Master thesis). Retrieved from: https://escholarship .org/uc/item/99m0v13q

Nomeikaite, L. (2017). Street art, heritage, embodiment. *Street Art and Creativity, 3*, 43-53. Doi: https://doi.org/DOI: 10.25765/sauc.v3i1.62

Novak, D. (2014). Methodology for the measurement of graffiti art works: Focus on the piece. *World Applied Sciences Journal, 32*, 40–46. DOI: 10.5829/idosi.wasj.2014.32.01.301

Novak, D. (2015). Photography and classification of information. *SAUC - Street Art & Urban Creativity Scientific Journal,* 1, 13-25. Doi: DOI: 10.25765/sauc.v1i1.22

Nunnally, J. C. (1978). *Psychometric theory* (2nd ed.). McGraw-Hill.

Nussli, N., Oh, K., & Davis, J. P. (2024). Capturing the successes and failures during pandemic teaching: An investigation of university students' perceptions of their faculty's emergency remote teaching approaches. *E-Learning and Digital Media, 21*(1), 42–69. DOI: 10.1177/20427530221147112

Odhiambo, G. (2016). Higher education in Kenya: An assessment of current responses to the imperative of widening access. *Journal of Higher Education Policy and Management, 38*(2), 196–211. DOI: 10.1080/1360080X.2016.1150551

Oh, L. and Teo, H. (2010). Consumer value co-creation in a hybrid commerce service-delivery system. *International Journal of Electronic Commerce (14:3), pp. 35-62.*

Okanovic, V., Ivkovic-Kihic, I., Boskovic, D., Mijatovic, B., Prazina, I., Skaljo, E., & Rizvic, S. (2022). Interaction in eXtended Reality Applications for Cultural Heritage. *Applied Sciences (Basel, Switzerland), 12*(3), 1241. Advance online publication. DOI: 10.3390/app12031241

Okonkwo, Chinedu Wilfred, and Abejide Ade-Ibijola. (2021). "Chatbots Applications in Education: A Systematic Review." *Computers and Education: Artificial Intelligence*. .DOI: 10.1016/j.caeai.2021.100033

Olapade, D. T., Aluko, T. B., Adisa, A. L., & Abobarin, A. A. (2023). A framework for assessment of customary land delivery institutions: Instrument development, content validity and reliability testing. *Property Management, 41*(5), 729–752. DOI: 10.1108/PM-06-2022-0041

Oliveira, J. D. S., Espindola, D. B., Barwaldt, R., Luciano, M. I. R., & Pias, M. (2019). "IBM Watson Application as FAQ Assistant about Moodle." In *Proceedings - Frontiers in Education Conference, FIE*. Vol. 2019-October. DOI: 10.1109/FIE43999.2019.9028667

Oliveira, N., & Cunha, J. (2019). Co-design and Footwear: Breaking Boundaries with Online Customization Interfaces. *The International Journal of Visual Design, 13*(1), 1–26. DOI: 10.18848/2325-1581/CGP/v13i01/1-26

Oluoch, M.. (2020). Real-time anomaly detection in blockchain transactions using deep learning. *Journal of Cybersecurity and Privacy, 1*(1), 61–79. DOI: 10.3390/jcp1010005

Omachonu, V. K., & Einspruch, N. G. (2010). Innovation in healthcare delivery systems: A conceptual Framework. *The Innovation Journal, 15*(1), 1–20.

Oomen, J., & Aroyo, L. (2011). Crowdsourcing in the cultural heritage domain: opportunities and challenges. Proceedings of the 5th International Conference on Communities and Technologies (C&T '11) In Association for Computing Machinery (p. 138–149). New York, USA. Doi: https://doi.org/DOI: 10.1145/2103354.2103373

Opportunities and challenges of adopting artificial intelligence for learning and teaching in higher education. In Fostering communication and learning with underutilized technologies in higher education, pp.67–78. IGI Global. https://doi.org/.DOI: 10.4018/978-1-7998-4846-2.ch00

Orphanidou, Y., Efthymiou, L., & Panayiotou, G. (2024). Cultural Heritage for Sustainable Education Amidst Digitalisation. *Sustainability (Basel)*, *16*(4), 1540. Advance online publication. DOI: 10.3390/su16041540

Ozuem, W., Howell, K. E., & Lancaster, G. (2008). Communicating in the new interactive marketspace. *European Journal of Marketing*, *42*(9/10), 1059–1083. DOI: 10.1108/03090560810891145

Panagiotis, F., Theodoros, M., Leinfellner, R., & Yasmine, R. (2016). Climbing Up the Leaderboard : An Empirical Study of Applying Gamification Techniques to a Computer Programming Class. *Electronic Journal of e-Learning*, *14*, 94–110.

Papa, R., & Jackson, K. M. (2021). "Enduring Questions, Innovative Technologies: Educational Theories Interface with AI." In *Intelligent Computing - Proceedings of the 2021 Computing Conference*. DOI: 10.1007/978-3-030-80126-7_51

Papagiannis, H. (2022). *Augmented Human: How Technology Is Shaping the New Reality*. O'Reilly Media.

Pardamean, E., Roan, W., Iskandar, K. T. A., Prayangga, R., & Hariyanto, T. I. (2022). Mortality from coronavirus disease 2019 (Covid-19) in patients with schizophrenia: A systematic review, meta-analysis and meta-regression. *General Hospital Psychiatry*, *75*, 61–67. DOI: 10.1016/j.genhosppsych.2022.01.010 PMID: 35182908

Parsons, S., & Cobb, S. (2023). Augmented reality and education: A review of the literature. *Journal of Interactive Learning Research*, *34*(3), 293–316.

Paszke, A., ... (2019). PyTorch: An imperative style, high-performance deep learning library. In *Advances in Neural Information Processing Systems* (pp. 8024-8035).

Payton, S., & Hague, C. (2010). *Digital Literacy in Practice: Case Studies of Primary and Secondary Classrooms*. Futurelab.

Pediredla, V. K., Chandrasekaran, K., Annamraju, S., & Thondiyath, A. (2021). Design, analysis, and control of a 3-dof novel haptic device displaying stiffness, texture, shape, and shear. *IEEE Access : Practical Innovations, Open Solutions*, *9*, 72055–72065. DOI: 10.1109/ACCESS.2021.3079175

Pehlivan, S. (2021). Sanatın ve hareketin mekânı sokaklar. Retrieved from: https://narmanlisanat.com/sokak-sanati/

Pelet, J.-É. (2021b). Introduction to the Book: User Experience in Web 2.0 Technologies and Its Impact on Universities and Businesses. In *Handbook of Research on User Experience in Web 2.0 Technologies and Its Impact on Universities and Businesses* (pp. 1-18). IGI Global.

Pelet, J. É., Belda, S., & Arezki, D. (2023). Use of AI in Predicting Trends in Vegetation Dynamics in Africa. In *Encyclopedia of Data Science and Machine Learning* (pp. 31–56). IGI Global.

Pelet, J. É., & Ettis, S. A. (2022). Social media advertising effectiveness: The role of perceived originality, liking, credibility, irritation, intrusiveness, and Ad destination. [IJTHI]. *International Journal of Technology and Human Interaction*, *18*(1), 1–20. Advance online publication. DOI: 10.4018/IJTHI.2022010106

Pelet, J.-E. (Ed.). (2021a). *Handbook of Research on User Experience in Web 2.0 Technologies and Its Impact on Universities and Businesses*. IGI Global., Retrieved from https://www.igi-global.com/book/handbook-research-user-experience-web/244230 DOI: 10.4018/978-1-7998-3756-5

Pereira, J., Fernández-Raga, M., Osuna-Acedo, S., Roura-Redondo, M., Almazán-López, O., & Buldón-Olalla, A. (2019). Promoting Learners' Voice Productions Using Chatbots as a Tool for Improving the Learning Process in a MOOC. *Technology, Knowledge and Learning*, *24*(4), 545–565. Advance online publication. DOI: 10.1007/s10758-019-09414-9

Pérez, J. Q., Daradoumis, T., & Joan, M. M. P. (2020). Rediscovering the Use of Chatbots in Education: A Systematic Literature Review. *Computer Applications in Engineering Education*, *28*(6), 1549–1565. Advance online publication. DOI: 10.1002/cae.22326

Perić, B. Š., Šimundić, B., Muštra, V., & Vugdelija, M. (2021). The role of unesco cultural heritage and cultural sector in tourism development: The case of EU countries. *Sustainability (Basel)*, *13*(10), 5473. Advance online publication. DOI: 10.3390/su13105473

Perrenoud, P. (2015). Travail réel des enseignants et formation. *Recherches & Educations, 14*, 205–208.

Peters, G. W., Panayi, E., & Chapelle, A. (2023). Scalability Solutions for Blockchain: Layer-2 and Beyond. *Journal of Financial Technology, 1*(1), 5–20.

Peters, G.. (2021). Blockchain education: Trends and approaches for the future. *Computers in Human Behavior Reports, 4*, 100124. DOI: 10.1016/j.chbr.2021.100124

Peters, M., & Edler, J. (2024). The potential of augmented reality in education: A systematic review. *Educational Research Review, 43*, 100518. DOI: 10.1016/j.edurev.2021.100518

Pikkarainen, M., Huhtala, T., Kemppainen, L., & Häikiö, J. (2019). Success factors for data–driven service delivery networks. *Journal of Innovation Management, 7*(4), 14–46. DOI: 10.24840/2183-0606_007.004_0003

Pillay, A. K., & Sharma, N. A. (2022). Applicable Cyber Security Recommendations to Prevent Cyber Attacks in Universities. *2022 IEEE Asia-Pacific Conference on Computer Science and Data Engineering (CSDE)*, 1–5. DOI: 10.1109/CSDE56538.2022.10089360

Pinheiro, A. J., & Martins, H. (2024). The World Heritage Classification in Urban Tourism Destinations: Perspectives for the City of Porto, Portugal. *Advances in Science. Technology and Innovation*. Advance online publication. DOI: 10.1007/978-3-031-49536-6_16

Pituch, K. A., & Lee, Y. (2006). The influence of system characteristics on e-learning use. *Computers & Education, 47*(2), 222–244. DOI: 10.1016/j.compedu.2004.10.007

Polyportis, A., & Pahos, N. (2024). Understanding Students' Adoption of the ChatGPT Chatbot in Higher Education: The Role of Anthropomorphism, Trust, Design Novelty and Institutional Policy. *Behaviour & Information Technology*. Advance online publication. DOI: 10.1080/0144929X.2024.2317364

Pomerantz, N. K. (2006). Student engagement: A new paradigm for student affairs. *The College Student Affairs Journal, 25*(2), 176–185.

Poncin, I., Garnier, M., Slim Ben Mimoun, M., & Leclercq, T. (2017). Smart technologies and shopping experience: Are gamification interfaces effective? The case of the Smartstore. *Technological Forecasting and Social Change, 124*, 1–12. DOI: 10.1016/j.techfore.2017.01.025

Poole, K. (2020). Arts organizations engaging audiences through street art. Unpublished master thesis. ProQuest Dissertations and Theses veri tabanından erişildi. (UMI No. 27999258)

Popenici, S. A. D., & Kerr, S. (2017). Exploring the impact of artificial intelligence on teaching and learning in higher education. *Research and Practice in Technology Enhanced Learning*, *12*(1), 22. Advance online publication. DOI: 10.1186/s41039-017-0062-8 PMID: 30595727

Pradana, M., Elisa, H. P., & Syarifuddin, S. (2023). Discussing ChatGPT in education: A literature review and bibliometric analysis. *Cogent Education*, *10*(2), 2243134. DOI: 10.1080/2331186X.2023.2243134

Prahalad, C. and Ramaswamy, V., (2003). The New Frontier of Experience Innovation. MIT Sloan Management Review (44:4), pp. 12-18.

Prensky, M. (2001). *Digital game-based learning*. McGraw Hill.

Prensky, M. (2018). *Don't bother me mom—I'm learning!: How computer and video games are preparing your kids for 21st century success and how you can help!* Paragon House.

Prieto-Andreu, J. M., Gómez-Escalonilla-Torrijos, J. D., & Said-Hung, E. (2022). Gamification, motivation, and performance in education: A systematic review. Rev. Electrón. *Educare (San José)*, *26*, 251–273.

Prinsloo, P., & Kaliisa, R. (2022). Data privacy on the African continent : Opportunities, challenges and implications for learning analytics. *British Journal of Educational Technology Published by John Wiley & Sons Ltd on Behalf of British Educational Research Association. 894, December 2021*, 894–913. DOI: 10.1111/bjet.13226

Prokopyev, N., Ustin, P., Gafarov, F., & Popov, L. (2024). Methods of social network texts analysis for a psychometric model of personal behavior. *BIO Web of Conferences. 116*. EDP Sciences. DOI: 10.1051/bioconf/202411606010

Qafzezi, E. (2023). Online Collaborative Learning in Higher Education in Albania: Some Necessary Innovations. *International Journal of Management. Knowledge and Learning*, *12*. Advance online publication. DOI: 10.53615/2232-5697.12.S1-11

Rafaeli, S. & Noy, A. (2002). Online auctions, messaging, communication and social facilitation: A simulation and experimental evidence. *European Journal of Information Systems*, 11(3), 196-196-207.

Raghav, S., & Joshi, S. (2023). Virtual reality in education: A systematic review of empirical studies. *Education and Information Technologies, 28*(2), 1597–1626. DOI: 10.1007/s10639-022-11097-8

Rahimi, A. R., & Tafazoli, D. (2022). The role of university teachers' 21st-century digital competence in their attitudes toward ICT integration in higher education: Extending the theory of planned behavior. *The JALT CALL Journal, 18*(2), 238–263. DOI: 10.29140/jaltcall.v18n2.632

Rahman, A. M., Abdullah, A. M., and Alma, I. (2018). "Programming Challenges of Chatbot: Current and Future Prospective." In *5th IEEE Region 10 Humanitarian Technology Conference 2017, R10-HTC 2017*. Vol. 2018-January. DOI: 10.1109/R10-HTC.2017.8288910

Rai, A., Pavlou, P., Im, G., and Du, S. (2012). Interfirm IT capability profiles and communications for cocreating relational value: Evidence from the logistics industry. *MIS Quarterly (36:1), pp. 233-262.*

Ramandanis, D., & Xinogalos, S. (2023). *Designing a Chatbot for Contemporary Education: A Systematic Literature Review*. Information., DOI: 10.3390/info14090503

Ramayah, T., Ahmad, N. H., & Lo, M. C. (2010). The role of quality factors in intention to continue using an e-learning system in Malaysia. *Procedia: Social and Behavioral Sciences, 2*(2), 5422–5426. DOI: 10.1016/j.sbspro.2010.03.885

Rana, R., & Bhambri, P. (2024). Digital Twin for Sustainable Industrial Development. In Rani, S., Bhambri, P., Kumar, S., Pareek, P. K., & Elngar, A. A. (Eds.), *AI-Driven Digital Twin and Industry 4.0: A Conceptual Framework with Applications* (1st ed., pp. 241–253). CRC Press., DOI: 10.1201/9781003395416-15

Rana, R., Bhambri, P., & Chhabra, Y. (2024). Evolution and the Future of Industrial Engineering with the IoT and AI. In *Integration of AI-Based Manufacturing and Industrial Engineering Systems with the Internet of Things* (pp. 19–37). CRC Press.

Rani, S., Bhambri, P., Kaur, J., & Sangwan, Y. S. (2024). Exploring the application domains of ML-based facial emotion recognition systems: Framework, techniques and challenges. In *Second International Conference on Computing and Communication Networks (ICCCN 2022)* (pp. 090008-1–090008-9). AIP Conf. Proc. 2919. https://doi.org/DOI: 10.1063/5.0184852

Rathor, S., Zhang, M., & Im, T. (2023). Web 3.0 and Sustainability: Challenges and Research Opportunities. *Sustainability (Basel), 15*(20), 15126. DOI: 10.3390/su152015126

Raza, S. A., Qazi, W., Khan, K. A., & Salam, J. (2021). Social isolation and acceptance of the Learning Management System (LMS) in the time of COVID-19 pandemic: An expansion of the UTAUT Model. *Journal of Educational Computing Research*, *59*(2), 183–208. DOI: 10.1177/0735633120960421

Razzaq, A. (2024). A Web3 Secure Platform for Assessments and Educational Resources Based on Blockchain. *Computer Applications in Engineering Education*, *32*(1), e22677. Advance online publication. DOI: 10.1002/cae.22677

Rees, G., Hunt, A., Vitale, V., Horgan, J., & Strachan, P. (2023). Discovering the local in national cultural heritage collections. How web maps can help the UK public engage with their 'own places.'. *Information Communication and Society*, *26*(15), 2885–2903. Advance online publication. DOI: 10.1080/1369118X.2022.2113819

Reeves, T. C., Herrington, J., & Oliver, R. (2017). *A guide to authentic e-learning*. Routledge.

Reid, F., Subramanian, A., & Ali, S. (2022). Security Vulnerabilities in Decentralized Applications: A Comprehensive Review. *IEEE Access : Practical Innovations, Open Solutions*, *10*, 10345–10363.

Reinoso, M. S., & Monzonis, J. L. (2023). Augmented reality and mathematics education: A systematic review. *Journal of Educational Computing Research*, *60*(4), 871–896. DOI: 10.1177/07356331211019019

Reiss, M. J. (2021). The Use of AI in Education: Practicalities and Ethical Considerations. *London Review of Education*, *19*(1). Advance online publication. DOI: 10.14324/LRE.19.1.05

Rezaei, N., Nofre, J., & Ghaderi, Z. (2024). World heritage classification and tourism: Divergent trajectories in Marrakech Medina (Morocco) and M'Zab Valley (Algeria). *Journal of Heritage Tourism*, *19*(1), 111–128. Advance online publication. DOI: 10.1080/1743873X.2023.2259509

Riegner, C. (2007). Word of mouth on the web: The impact of Web 2.0 on consumer purchase decisions. *Journal of Advertising Research*, *47*(4), 436–447. DOI: 10.2501/S0021849907070456

Riel, J. 2020. "Essential Features and Critical Issues with Educational Chatbots: Toward Personalized Learning via Digital Agents." In *Handbook of Research on Modern Educational Technologies, Applications, and Management (2 Vol.)*. DOI: 10.4018/978-1-7998-3476-2.ch015

Rienties, B., & Kinchin, I. M. (2014). Understanding (in) formal learning in an academic development programme: A social network perspective. *Teaching and Teacher Education*, *39*, 123–135. DOI: 10.1016/j.tate.2014.01.004

Rindfleisch, A., & Im, S. (2019). Enhancing customer centricity via 3D printing. Handbook on Customer Centricity. Robert Palmatier, Christine Moorman, and Ju-Yeon Lee, (Eds), Edward Elgar, New York.

Robson, K., Plangger, K., Kietzmann, J. H., McCarthy, I., & Pitt, L. (2015). Is it all a game? Understanding the principles of gamification. *Business Horizons*, *58*(4), 411–420. DOI: 10.1016/j.bushor.2015.03.006

Roca, J. C., Chiu, C.-M., & Martínez, F. J. (2006). Understanding elearning continuance intention: An extension of the Technology Acceptance Model. *International Journal of Human-Computer Studies*, *64*(8), 683–696. DOI: 10.1016/j.ijhcs.2006.01.003

Roemer, E., Schuberth, F., & Henseler, J. (2021). HTMT2–an improved criterion for assessing discriminant validity in structural equation modeling. *Industrial Management & Data Systems*, *121*(12), 2637–2650. DOI: 10.1108/IMDS-02-2021-0082

Romero, D., & Molina, A. (2011). Collaborative networked organizations and customer communities: Value co-creation and co-innovation in the networking era. *Production Planning and Control*, *22*(5-6), 447–472. DOI: 10.1080/09537287.2010.536619

Rosa, A. M., da Silva, R. F., & Freire, L. (2021). Accessibility in web applications: A systematic review of studies. *Journal of Web Engineering*, *20*(1), 1–26. DOI: 10.13052/jwe1540-9589.2010

Rosenfeld, M. (2021). *Ethers.js: A Complete Guide*. https://docs.ethers.io/v5/

Roued-Cunliffe, H. (2019). *Open heritage data: an introduction to research, publishing and programming with open data in the heritage sector*. Facet., DOI: 10.29085/9781783303618

Roued-Cunliffe, H., & Copeland, A. (Eds.). (2017). *Participatory heritage*. Facet., DOI: 10.29085/9781783301256

Rudolph, J., Tan, S., & Tan, S. (2023). ChatGPT: Bullshit spewer or the end of traditional assessments in higher education? *Journal of Applied Learning & Teaching*, *6*(1). Advance online publication. DOI: 10.37074/jalt.2023.6.1.9

Rueda Márquez de la Plata, A., Cruz Franco, P. A., & Ramos Sánchez, J. A. (2023). Applications of Virtual and Augmented Reality Technology to Teaching and Research in Construction and Its Graphic Expression. *Sustainability (Basel), 15*(12), 9628. Advance online publication. DOI: 10.3390/su15129628

Rukhiran, M., Phaokla, N., & Netinant, P. (2022). Adoption of Environmental Information Chatbot Services Based on the Internet of Educational Things in Smart Schools: Structural Equation Modeling Approach. *Sustainability (Basel), 14*(23), 15621. Advance online publication. DOI: 10.3390/su142315621

Rusli, M. (2020). The effects of various modes of online learning on learning results. *International Journal of Advanced Computer Science and Applications, 11*(4), 100–105. DOI: 10.14569/IJACSA.2020.0110414

Russell, D. L. (2021). Design, Development, Implementation, and Support (DDIS): Supporting Online Nontraditional Doctoral Candidates. *Higher Learning Research Communications, 11*(1), 14–26. DOI: 10.18870/hlrc.v11i1.1186

Ryan, R. M., & Deci, E. L. (2000). Self-Determination Theory and the Facilitation of Intrinsic Motivation, Social Development, and Well-Being. *The American Psychologist, 55*(1), 11. DOI: 10.1037/0003-066X.55.1.68 PMID: 11392867

S. D. A. Bujang et al., "Multiclass Prediction Model for Student Grade Prediction Using Machine Learning," in IEEE Access, vol. 9, pp. 95608-95621, 2021, doi: 10.1109/ACCESS.2021.3093563.

Salahdine, F., Mrabet, Z. El, & Kaabouch, N. (2021). Phishing Attacks Detection A Machine Learning-Based Approach. *2021 IEEE 12th Annual Ubiquitous Computing, Electronics & Mobile Communication Conference (UEMCON)*, 250–255. DOI: 10.1109/UEMCON53757.2021.9666627

Salomon, G. (1988). AI in Reverse: Computer Tools That Turn Cognitive. *Journal of Educational Computing Research, 4*(2), 123–139. Advance online publication. DOI: 10.2190/4LU7-VW23-EGB1-AW5G

Salt Araştırma. (2023). 13th news about Antalya international film and art festival painting and sculpture symposium. (1976). Pure research archive. Inventory Number: DRKDOC010. URI: https://archives.saltresearch.org/handle/123456789/11637

Salt Beyoğlu. (2013). They are afraid of the mural. Retrieved from: https://saltonline .org/tr/471/duvar-resminden-korkuyorlar

Sánchez, D. O., & Trigueros, I. M. G. (2019). Gamification, social problems, and gender in the teaching of social sciences : Representations and discourse of trainee teachers. *PLoS One*, *14*(6), e0218869. DOI: 10.1371/journal.pone.0218869 PMID: 31242248

Sánchez, D. R., Langer, M., & Kaur, R. (2019). Gamification in the classroom : Examining the impact of gamified quizzes on student learning. *Computers & Education*, *103666*. Advance online publication. DOI: 10.1016/j.compedu.2019.10366

Sanders, E. B. N., & Stappers, P. J. (2008). Co-creation and the new landscapes of design. *CoDesign*, *4*(1), 1, 5–18. DOI: 10.1080/15710880701875068

Sanusi, M. S. (2022). Action research to reassess the acceptance and use of technology in a blended learning approach amongst postgraduate business students. *Cogent Education*, *9*(1), 2145813. DOI: 10.1080/2331186X.2022.2145813

Sarkar, I.H., Kayes, A.S.M., Badsha S., Alqahtani, H., Watters, P. and Ng, A., (2020). Cybersecurity data science: an overview.

Särmäkari, N. (2023). Digital 3D Fashion Designers: Cases of Atacac and The Fabricant. *Fashion Theory*, *27*(1), 85–114. DOI: 10.1080/1362704X.2021.1981657

Savin-Baden, M., Tombs, G., & Bhakta, R. (2015). Beyond Robotic Wastelands of Time: Abandoned Pedagogical Agents and New Pedalled Pedagogies. *E-Learning and Digital Media*, *12*(3–4), 295–314. Advance online publication. DOI: 10.1177/2042753015571835

Sayed Al Mnhrawi, D. N. T. A., & Alreshidi, H. A. (2022). A systemic approach for implementing AI methods in education during COVID-19 pandemic: Higher education in Saudi Arabia. *World Journal of Engineering*, *20*(5), 808–814. DOI: 10.1108/WJE-11-2021-0623

Sayedi, M., & Santhanam, R. (2022). The impact of virtual reality on learning and student engagement: A meta-analysis. *Computers & Education*, *174*, 104332. DOI: 10.1016/j.compedu.2021.104332

Schallmo, D., Williams, C. A., & Boardman, L. (2017). Digital transformation of business models best practice, enablers, and roadmap. International Journal of Innovation Management, 21, 08, 1740014. Retrieved from https://www.worldscientific.com/doi/abs/10.1142/S136391961740014X?srsltid=AfmBOooPZRAZ8Kwl83b9pqgDCfgNQTZsGO5ZqDCpxse21h_mkd2fHINl

Schiavone, F., Leone, D., Sorrentino, A., & Scaletti, A. (2020). Re-designing the service experience in the value co-creation process: An exploratory study of a healthcare network. *Business Process Management Journal*, *26*(4), 889–908. DOI: 10.1108/BPMJ-11-2019-0475

Schlosser, A. E., White, T. B. and Lloyd, S. M. (2006). Converting Web Site Visitors into Buyers: How Web Site Investment Increases Consumer Trusting Beliefs and Online Purchase Intentions. *Journal of Marketing* (70:2), pp.133-148.

Setiawan, E. B., & Setiyadi, A. (2015). A compares the performance of different web hosting servers. *International Journal of Database Theory and Application*, *8*(3), 297–312.

Sharkey, A. J. C. (2016). Should We Welcome Robot Teachers? *Ethics and Information Technology*, *18*(4), 283–297. Advance online publication. DOI: 10.1007/s10676-016-9387-z

Sharma, D., Sharma, A.K. (2010). "Comparative Analysis of Web Page Ranking Algorithms". International Journal of Computer Science thiab. *Engineering (London)*, *2*(08), 2670–2676.

Sharma, A. (2022). Review on Major Cyber security Issues in Educational Sector International Journal of Computer Sciences and Engineering Open Access Review on Major Cyber security Issues in Educational Sector. *International Journal on Computer Science and Engineering*, (January). Advance online publication. DOI: 10.26438/ijcse/v9i12.2629

Sharma, S. K., Srivastava, P. R., Kumar, A., Jindal, A., & Gupta, S. (2023). Supply chain vulnerability assessment for manufacturing industry. *Annals of Operations Research*, *326*(2), 653–683. DOI: 10.1007/s10479-021-04155-4 PMID: 34149141

Shue, E., Liu, L., Li, B., Feng, Z., Li, X., & Hu, G. (2023). Empowering Beginners in Bioinformatics with ChatGPT. *Quantitative Biology*, *11*(2), 105–108. Advance online publication. DOI: 10.15302/J-QB-023-0327 PMID: 37378043

Shukla, A. K., Chowdury, M. A. M., Nath, R. and Muhuri, P. K. (2021). "Fuzzy Reliability Redundancy Allocation Problem Using Multi-factorial Evolutionary Algorithm," 2021 IEEE International Conference on Systems, Man, and Cybernetics (SMC), Melbourne, Australia, 2021, pp. 2512-2517, doi: 10.1109/SMC52423.2021.9658908.

Siemens, G. (2018). Connectivism: A learning theory for the digital age. *International Journal of Instructional Technology and Distance Learning*, *2*(1), 3–10.

Siemens, G., & Tittenberger, P. (2009). *Handbook of emerging technologies for learning*. University of Manitoba.

Siemons, J., & Markopoulos, P. (2023). Augmented reality in primary schools: Designing and evaluating a learning tool. *Journal of Educational Computing Research, 59*(5), 829–856. DOI: 10.1177/0735633119863108

Signorelli, C. M. (2018). "Can computers overcome humans? consciousness interaction and its implications," in *2018 IEEE 17th International Conference on Cognitive Informatics & Cognitive Computing* (Berkeley, CA). DOI: 10.1109/ICCI-CC.2018.8482038

Silic, M., & Back, A. (2017). Impact of gamification on user's knowledge-sharing practices: Relationships between work motivation, performance expectancy and work engagement. In T. X. Bui. and R. Sprague (Eds.), 50th annual Hawaii international conference on System Sciences, HICSS 2017 (pp. 1308–1317). IEEE Computer Society. https://www.scopus.com/inward/record.uri?eid=2-s2. 0-85086568517&partnerID=40&md5=

Silva, A. L., & Terra, A. L. (2024). Cultural heritage on the Semantic Web: The Europeana Data Model. *IFLA Journal, 50*(1), 93–107. Advance online publication. DOI: 10.1177/03400352231202506

Sims, L. (2022). Teaching critical thinking and cultural intelligence via virtual exchange: A practice report on the utilization of research-based principles to support and assess learning outcomes. *Journal of Virtual Exchange, 5*, 133–143. DOI: 10.21827/jve.5.38804

Singh, G., & Bhambri, P. (2023). Simulation Analysis of AODV and DSDV Routing Protocols for Secure and Reliable Service in Mobile Adhoc Networks (MANETs). In Integration of AI-Based Manufacturing and Industrial Engineering Systems with the Internet of Things (pp. 205-216). CRC Press.

Singh, A., & Sandhu, R. (2021). *Blockchain and Decentralized Applications*. Academic Press.

Singh, R.. (2020). Integrating blockchain and AI: Opportunities and challenges. *Proceedings of the IEEE International Conference on Data Science and Advanced Analytics (DSAA)*, 375-386. https://doi.org/DOI: 10.1109/DSAA.2020.00053

Singh, S., Lal, Y., Bhambri, P., Kumar, A., & Dhanoa, I. S. (2021). Advancements in social data security and encryption: A review. *Natural Volatiles and Essential Oils, 8*(4), 15353–15362.

Sohn, K., & Kwon, O. (2020a). Technology acceptance theories and factors influencing artificial intelligence-based intelligent products. *Telematics and Informatics*, *47*, 101324. DOI: 10.1016/j.tele.2019.101324

Soma Disaster. (2014, May 14). In Wikipedia. Retrieved from (26 March 2023): https://tr.wikipedia.org/wiki/Soma_Facias%C4%B1

Songkram, N., Songkram, N., Chootongchai, S., & Samanakupt, T. (2021). Developing students' learning and innovation skills using the virtual smart classroom. [iJET]. *International Journal of Emerging Technologies in Learning*, *16*(4), 34–51. DOI: 10.3991/ijet.v16i04.15221

Soni, P., Verma, S., & Sharma, S. (2022). AI in Blockchain: A Comprehensive Survey. *Artificial Intelligence Review*, *55*(4), 2541–2576.

Spector, J. M., Merrill, M. D., Van Merriënboer, J. J., & Driscoll, M. P. (2013). *Handbook of research on educational communications and technology*. Springer.

Srivastava K., Kumar M, Verma R, Maurya P., (2024). Assessment of Quality Attributes of Mobile Learning Applications on Students' Satisfaction Source Title: Architecture and Technological Advancements of Education 4.0. DOI:.DOI: 10.4018/978-1-6684-9285-7.ch007

Srivastava. K, Kumar. Manoj (2017). An Empirical Examination of Perceived Risk in Mobile-Banking Business, Economics, Computer Science Adhyayan: A Journal of Management Sciences DOI: Corpus ID: 169118936DOI: 10.21567/adhyayan.v7i02.10762

Stallings, W., & Brown, L. (2019). *Computer Security: Principles and Practice*. Pearson.

Statham, N. (2019). Scientific rigour of online platforms for 3D visualisation of heritage. *Virtual Archaeology Review*, *10*(20), 1–16. DOI: 10.4995/var.2019.9715

Steinkuehler, C., & Duncan, S. (2008). Scientific habits of mind in virtual worlds. *Journal of Science Education and Technology*, *17*(6), 530–543. DOI: 10.1007/s10956-008-9120-8

Stephen, A. T., & Toubia, O. (2010). Deriving Value from Social Commerce Networks. *JMR, Journal of Marketing Research*, *47*(2), 215–228. DOI: 10.1509/jmkr.47.2.215

Suite, T. (2024). Truffle Suite. Retrieved from https://www.trufflesuite.com/truffle

Su, J., & Yang, W. (2022). *"Artificial Intelligence in Early Childhood Education: A Scoping Review." Computers and Education: Artificial Intelligence*. Elsevier B.V., DOI: 10.1016/j.caeai.2022.100049

Suki, N. M., & Suki, N. M. (2017). Determining students' behavioural intention to use animation and storytelling applying the UTAUT model: The moderating roles of gender and experience level. *International Journal of Management Education, 15*(3), 528–538. DOI: 10.1016/j.ijme.2017.10.002

Sulistyarini, W. (2022). Analysis of Cognitive Aspects of Test Techniques in Islamic education Learning. *EDUKASI: Jurnal Pendidikan Islam (e-Journal), 10*(2), 166-190.

Šumak, B., & Šorgo, A. (2016). The acceptance and use of interactive whiteboards among teachers: Differences in UTAUT determinants between pre- and post-adopters. *Computers in Human Behavior, 64*, 602–620. DOI: 10.1016/j.chb.2016.07.037

Sun, H., Ni, W., & Farouk, A. (2022). Design and application of an AI-Based text content moderation system. *Scientific Programming, 2022*, 1–9. DOI: 10.1155/2022/2062791

Suresh Babu, C. V. & Abhinaba Pal. (2023). Securing Decentralized Finance Through Blockchain Technologies. In R. Thanigaivelan, S. Kaliappan, & C. Jegadheesan (Eds.), Cyber-Physical Systems and Supporting Technologies for Industrial Automation (pp. 351-372). IGI Global. https://doi.org/DOI: 10.4018/978-1-6684-9267-3.ch020

Suresh Babu, C. V. & Sanjai Das (2023). Impact of Blockchain Technology on the Stock Market. In K. Mehta, R. Sharma, & P. Yu (Eds.), Revolutionizing Financial Services and Markets Through FinTech and Blockchain (pp. 44-59). IGI Global. DOI: 10.4018/978-1-6684-8624-5.ch004

Suresh Babu, C. V., Suruthi, G., Indhumathi, C., & Sushruth, S. (2024b). Integrated approach for network intrusion detection: Combining KNN algorithm, Karhunen-Loève transform, and genetic algorithm optimization. In Metaheuristic and machine learning optimization strategies for complex systems (p. 21). DOI: 10.4018/979-8-3693-7842-7.ch002

Suresh Babu, C. V. (2023). *Artificial Intelligence and Expert Systems*. Anniyappa Publications.

Suresh Babu, C. V., Dharma Sastha, B., Naveen Akash, V., Praveen, S., & Santhosh Kumar, D. (2024). Enhancing Sustainability in Smart Energy Systems Through Anomaly Detection Algorithms. In Naoui, M., Ben Khalifa, R., & Sbita, L. (Eds.), *Modeling, Analysis, and Control of Smart Energy Systems* (pp. 119–136). IGI Global., DOI: 10.4018/979-8-3693-2999-3.ch007

Suresh Babu, C. V., & Praveen, S. (2023). Swarm Intelligence and Evolutionary Machine Learning Algorithms for COVID-19: Pandemic and Epidemic Review. In Suresh Kumar, A., Kose, U., Sharma, S., & Jerald Nirmal Kumar, S. (Eds.), *Dynamics of Swarm Intelligence Health Analysis for the Next Generation* (pp. 83–103). IGI Global., DOI: 10.4018/978-1-6684-6894-4.ch005

SureshBabu. C. V., Sudhir Manoharan., L., G. K., & V., S. K. (2024). Application of Support Vector Machine Algorithm in Automated Lending Protocols for Decentralized Finance Platforms. In L. Vardari & I. Qabrati (Eds.), Decentralized Finance and Tokenization in FinTech (pp. 1-20). IGI Global. DOI: 10.4018/979-8-3693-3346-4.ch001

Sutherland, A., & Goodchild, A. (2022). Virtual reality for learning: A critical review of the use of VR in primary and secondary education. *Education and Information Technologies*, *27*(3), 2139–2172. DOI: 10.1007/s10639-022-10859-2

Sutton, R. S., & Barto, A. G. (2018). *Reinforcement learning: An introduction* (2nd ed.). The MIT Press. Syst. Res. 11, 342–365. DOI: 10.1287/isre.11.4.342.11872

Swan, M. (2015). *Blockchain: Blueprint for a new economy*. O'Reilly Media.

Tabachnick, B. G., & Fidell, L. S. (2013). Using multivariate statistics: International edition. Pearson 2012.

Taber, K. S. (2018). The use of Cronbach's alpha when developing and reporting research instruments in science education. *Research in Science Education*, *48*(6), 1273–1296. DOI: 10.1007/s11165-016-9602-2

Tadejko, P. (2020). Cloud cognitive services based on machine learning methods in architecture of modern knowledge management solutions. In *Data-Centric Business and Applications: Towards Software Development* (Vol. 4, pp. 169-190). Springer. Retrieved from https://link.springer.com/chapter/10.1007/978-3-030-34706-2_9

Taecharungroj, V. (2023). 'What Can ChatGPT Do?' Analyzing Early Reactions to the Innovative AI Chatbot on Twitter. *Big Data and Cognitive Computing*, *7*(1), 35. Advance online publication. DOI: 10.3390/bdcc7010035

Tajuddin, R. A., Baharudin, M., & Hoon, T. S. (2013). System quality and its influence on students' learning satisfaction in UiTM Shah Alam. *Procedia: Social and Behavioral Sciences*, *90*, 677–685. DOI: 10.1016/j.sbspro.2013.07.140

Tam, N. T., Hoang, V., Bình, H. T. T., & Vĩnh, L. T. (2022). Multi-objective teaching–learning evolutionary algorithm for enhancing sensor network coverage and lifetime. *Engineering Applications of Artificial Intelligence*, *108*, 104554. DOI: 10.1016/j.engappai.2021.104554

Tam, W., Huynh, T., Tang, A., Luong, S., Khatri, Y., & Zhou, W. (2023). Nursing Education in the Age of Artificial Intelligence Powered Chatbots (AI-Chatbots): Are We Ready Yet? *Nurse Education Today*, *129*, 105917. Advance online publication. DOI: 10.1016/j.nedt.2023.105917 PMID: 37506622

Tapscott, D., & Tapscott, A. (2016). *Blockchain Revolution: How the Technology Behind Bitcoin is Changing Money, Business, and the World.* Penguin.

Taş, O., & Taş, T. (2015). Street art in Ankara: right to the city, protest and resistance. Mulkiye Journal, 39, 85-114. Retrieved from: https://dergipark.org.tr/en/download/article-file/1093

Tellis, G. J., & Gaeth, G. J. (1990). Best value, price-seeking, and price aversion: The impact of information and learning on consumer choices. *Journal of Marketing*, *54*(2), 34–45. DOI: 10.1177/002224299005400203

Teng, Y., Zhang, J., & Sun, T. (2022). Data-driven decision-making model based on artificial intelligence in higher education system of colleges and universities. *Expert Systems: International Journal of Knowledge Engineering and Neural Networks*, *40*(4), e12820. Advance online publication. DOI: 10.1111/exsy.12820

Thorat, V. A., Rao, P., Joshi, N., Talreja, P., & Shetty, A. (2024). The Role of Chatbot GPT Technology in Undergraduate Dental Education. *Cureus*. Advance online publication. DOI: 10.7759/cureus.54193 PMID: 38496058

Tihomiroves, J., & Grab, J. (2016). "Comparison of SOAP and REST-based web services using software benchmarks." ISSN 2255-9086 (Print) December, Vol. 19 Ib., p. 92-97 DOI: 10.1515/itms-2016-0017

Tihomirovs and Grabis. (2004). Comparison of SOAP and REST-based web roles. *Management*, *17*(2), 275–297.

Tiwari, S., Kumar, V., & Kumari, R. (2023). Understanding User Frustrations in Web3 Applications: A Survey Study. *International Journal of Information Technology : an Official Journal of Bharati Vidyapeeth's Institute of Computer Applications and Management*, *15*(1), 101–115.

Tobar-Munoz, H., & Ruiz-Blanco, J. A. (2023). Impact of augmented reality on creativity in primary education. *Computers & Education*, *182*, 104505. DOI: 10.1016/j.compedu.2022.104505

Todorova, L., Fattinger, E., Url, E., Vandemaele, S., Pott, U., Strebel, H., Merklein de Freitas, C., Christopher, A., Hendriks, S., & Prellwitz, M. (2022). COPILOT – Development and Implementation of International Cooperative Online Intercultural Learning. *Journal of Occupational Therapy Education*, *6*(2). Advance online publication. DOI: 10.26681/jote.2022.060219

Tönnies, B., Naegele, M., & Lutz, M. (2022). Usability in Blockchain Applications: A Review and Future Directions. *ACM Transactions on Internet Technology*, *22*(4), 56.

Traymbak, S., Sharma, M., Anand, A., & Shukla, A. (2024). Chatbot Technology in the Education Sector: A Bibliometrics Analysis Using VOS Viewer. *International Journal of System Assurance Engineering and Management*. Advance online publication. DOI: 10.1007/s13198-023-02230-6

Trentin, A., Perin, E., & Forza, C. (2012). Product configurator impact on product quality. *International Journal of Production Economics*, *135*(2), 850–859. DOI: 10.1016/j.ijpe.2011.10.023

Trujillo-Torres, J. M., & Trujillo-Pisanty, D. (2024). Virtual reality and augmented reality in education: A review and systematic meta-analysis. *Computers & Education*, *174*, 104385. DOI: 10.1016/j.compedu.2022.104385

Tsiodra, M., Panda, S., Chronopoulos, M., & Panaousis, E. (2023). Cyber Risk Assessment and Optimization: A Small Business Case Study. *IEEE Access : Practical Innovations, Open Solutions*, *11*(May), 44467–44481. DOI: 10.1109/ACCESS.2023.3272670

Tulke, J. (2020). Archiving dissent: (ım)material trajectories of political street art in Istanbul and Athens. A. McGarry, I. Erhart, H. Eslen-Ziya. In Jenzen, O., & Korkut, U. (Eds.), *The Aesthetics of Global Protest* (pp. 121–140). Visual Culture and Communication., DOI: 10.2307/j.ctvswx8bm.11

Tuncel, R. (2021, May 29). We commemorate those who died in Gezi with a demand for justice. Bianet. Retrieved from: https://m.bianet.org/bianet/insan-haklari/244857-gezi-de-olenleri-adalet-talebiyle-aniyoruz

Uddin, M., & Preston, D. (2015). Systematic Review of Identity Access Management in Information Security. *Journal of Advances in Computer Networks*, *3*(2), 150–156. DOI: 10.7763/JACN.2015.V3.158

Udeaja, C., Trillo, C., Awuah, K. G. B., Makore, B. C. N., Patel, D. A., Mansuri, L. E., & Jha, K. N. (2020). Urban heritage conservation and rapid urbanization: Insights from Surat, India. *Sustainability (Basel)*, *12*(6), 2172. Advance online publication. DOI: 10.3390/su12062172

Uğur, O. (2023). *Sokak sanatına erişim: Türkiye için bir web sayfası önerisi* [Access to street art: A webpage proposal for Türkiye]. Unpublished master thesis. Hacettepe University, Ankara.

Uğur, O., & Öztemiz, S. (2024). Usability evaluation of street art websites. *Bilgi Yönetimi*, 7(2), 305-324. https://dergipark.org.tr/tr/pub/by/issue/89621/1578190

Uludag, K. (2024). Exploring the Association Between Textual Parameters and Psychological and Cognitive Factors. *Psychology Research and Behavior Management*, *17*, 1139–1150. DOI: 10.2147/PRBM.S460503 PMID: 38505355

Ulven, J. B., & Wangen, G. (2021). A systematic review of cybersecurity risks in higher education. *Future Internet*, *13*(2), 1–40. DOI: 10.3390/fi13020039

UNESCO World Heritage Centre. (2024). *World Heritage Site*. https://whc.unesco.org/en/list

Uzunboylu, H., & Ozdamli, F. (2023). A meta-analysis on the effects of augmented reality applications in education. *Computers in Human Behavior*, *126*, 107018. DOI: 10.1016/j.chb.2021.107018

van der Hoeven, A. (2020). Valuing urban heritage through participatory heritage websites: Citizen perceptions of historic urban landscapes. *Space and Culture*, *23*(2), 129–148. DOI: 10.1177/1206331218797038

van Dijk, J. A. G. M., Peters, O., & Ebbers, W. (2008). Explaining the acceptance and use of government Internet services: A multivariate analysis of 2006 survey data in the Netherlands. *Government Information Quarterly*, *25*(3), 379–399. DOI: 10.1016/j.giq.2007.09.006

Van Doorn, J., Lemon, K. E., Mittal, V., Nab, S., Pick, D., Pirner, P., & Verhoef, P. C. (2010). Customer engagement behavior: Theoretical foundations and research directions. *Journal of Service Research*, *13*(3), 253–266. DOI: 10.1177/1094670510375599

Van Heerden, D., & Goosen, L. (2019, November 7 - 8). Assessments Used in an Open Distance e-Learning Environment to Promote Self-Directed Learning. In R. Ørngreen, M. Buhl, & B. Meyer (Ed.), *Proceedings of the 18th European Conference on e-Learning (ECEL 2019)* (pp. 593 - 602). Copenhagen: Academic Conferences and Publishing International Limited. DOI: 10.34190/EEL.19.003

Van Heerden, D., & Goosen, L. (2020b, December). Information and Communication Technologies to Change Education. In M. Motseke, M. Chitiyo, U. I. Ogbonnaya, O. C. Dada, & G. Charles-Ogan (Ed.), *Proceedings of the South Africa International Conference on Education* (pp. 241-250). Pretoria: African Academic Research Forum.

Van Heerden, D., & Goosen, L. (2021a). Students' Perceptions of e-Assessment in the Context of Covid-19: The Case of UNISA. In M. Qhobela, M. M. Ntsohi, & L. G. Mohafa (Ed.), *Proceedings of the 29th Conference of the Southern African Association for Research in Mathematics, Science and Technology Education (SAARMSTE)* (pp. 291-305). Maseru, Lesotho: SAARMSTE.

Van Heerden, D., & Goosen, L. (2021b). The Future of Information and Communication Technology Courses? (K. Arai, Ed.) *Lecture Notes in Networks and Systems, 285*, 507-526. DOI: 10.1007/978-3-030-80129-8_36

van Heerden, D., & Goosen, L. (2023b). Investigating the Assessment Submission Rates of a First Year Programming Module at an African Open and Distance e-Learning University. (K. Arai, Ed.) *Lecture Notes in Networks and Systems, 739*, 827–847. DOI: 10.1007/978-3-031-37963-5_57

Van Heerden, D., & Goosen, L. (2012). Using Vodcasts to Teach Programming in an ODL Environment. *Progressio, 34*(3), 144–160.

Van Heerden, D., & Goosen, L. (2020a, July). Promoting the Growth of Fourth Industrial Revolution Information Communication Technology Students: The Implications of Open and Distance e-Learning. In Buckley, S. B. (Ed.), *Promoting Inclusive Growth in the Fourth Industrial Revolution* (pp. 118–147). IGI Global., DOI: 10.4018/978-1-7998-4882-0.ch005

Van Heerden, D., & Goosen, L. (2023a). The Implications of COVID-19 for Fostering Diversity and Inclusion Through Curriculum Transformation: Teaching Open and Distance E-Learning Students. In Tabane, C., Diale, B., Mawela, A., & Zengele, T. (Eds.), *Fostering Diversity and Inclusion Through Curriculum Transformation* (pp. 73–100). IGI Global. DOI: 10.4018/978-1-6684-6995-8.ch005

Vanderveen, G., & van Eijk, G. (2016). Criminal but beautiful: A study on graffiti and the role of value judgments and context in perceiving disorder. *European Journal on Criminal Policy and Research, 22*(1), 107–125. DOI: 10.1007/s10610-015-9288-4

Vaquero-Gonzalez, L. M., & Alcover, C. M. (2022). Virtual reality and mathematics learning: A systematic review of empirical studies. *Journal of Educational Computing Research, 60*(4), 897–924. DOI: 10.1177/07356331211019020

Vaswani, A., ... (2017). Attention is all you need. In *Advances in Neural Information Processing Systems* (pp. 5998-6008).

Velaj, Y., Dolezal, D., Ambros, R., Plant, C., & Motschnig, R. (2022, October). Designing a Data Science Course for Non-Computer Science Students: Practical Considerations and Findings. *Frontiers in Education (FIE) Conference* (pp. 1-9). IEEE.

Venhuizen, N. J., Basile, V., Evang, K., & Bos, J. 2013. Gamification for Word Sense Labeling. In *Proceedings of the 10th International Conference on Computational Semantics (IWCS 2013) – Short Papers*, pages 397–403, Potsdam, Germany. Association for Computational Linguistics.

Venkatesh, V., & Davis, F. D. (1996). A model of the antecedents of perceived ease of use: Development and test. *Decision Sciences*, *27*(3), 451–481. DOI: 10.1111/j.1540-5915.1996.tb01822.x

Venkatesh, V., & Davis, F. D. (2000). A theoretical extension of the technology acceptance model: Four longitudinal field studies. *Management Science*, *46*(2), 186–204. DOI: 10.1287/mnsc.46.2.186.11926

Venkatesh, V., Morris, , Davis, , & Davis, . (2003). User acceptance of Information technology: Toward a unified view. *Management Information Systems Quarterly*, *27*(3), 425–478. DOI: 10.2307/30036540

Verma, R., Teixeira, J., Patrıcio, L., Nunes, N. J., Nobrega, L., Fisk, R. P., & Constantine, L. (2012). Customer experience modeling: From customer experience to service design. *Journal of Service Management*, *23*(3), 362–376. DOI: 10.1108/09564231211248453

Vivek, S. D., Beatty, S. E., Dalela, V., & Morgan, R. M. (2014). A generalized multidimensional scale for measuring customer engagement. *Journal of Marketing Theory and Practice*, *22*(4), 401–420. DOI: 10.2753/MTP1069-6679220404

Voshmgir, S. (2020). *Token Economy: How Blockchains and Smart Contracts Revolutionize the Financial Industry*. BlockchainHub.

Wagh, K. and Thool, R. (2008). "A Comparative Study of SOAP and REST Web Services Configuration Techniques for Mobile Hosting," Proceedings of the 17th International World Wide Web Conference, p. 287-296.

Wagner, C., & Majchrzak, A. (2006). Enabling Customer-Centricity Using Wikis and the Wiki Way. *Journal of Management Information Systems*, *23*(3), 17–43. DOI: 10.2753/MIS0742-1222230302

Wang, J.. (2020). Blockchain and artificial intelligence in financial services: A systematic literature review. *Technological Forecasting and Social Change*, *146*, 854–861. DOI: 10.1016/j.techfore.2018.10.010

Wang, S. K., Hsu, H. Y., & Campbell, T. (2015). Using the cloud-based mobile learning environment to support collaborative learning in higher education. *Computers & Education*, *78*, 78–88.

Wang, S., & Li, Q. (2023). Remote collaborative process optimization in research and design of industrial manufacturing. *Autonomous Intelligent Systems*, *3*(10), 10. Advance online publication. DOI: 10.1007/s43684-023-00056-4

Wang, T., & Yang, M. (2023). Using augmented reality to support learning: A systematic review and meta-analysis. *Journal of Educational Computing Research*, *60*(3), 587–613. DOI: 10.1177/07356331211019023

Wang, W. T., & Wang, C. C. (2009). An empirical study of instructor adoption of web-based learning systems. *Computers & Education*, *53*(3), 761–774. DOI: 10.1016/j.compedu.2009.02.021

Wang, X.. (2021). An overview of blockchain technology in smart cities. *Journal of Network and Computer Applications*, *177*, 102920. DOI: 10.1016/j.jnca.2020.102920

Wang, Y. (2021). Artificial Intelligence in Educational Leadership: A Symbiotic Role of Human-Artificial Intelligence Decision-Making. *Journal of Educational Administration*, *59*(3), 256–270. Advance online publication. DOI: 10.1108/JEA-10-2020-0216

Wareham-Morris, K., & McGowan, J. (2018). Gamified Learning : A Rationale for Ludopedagogy and Gamified Classrooms. *Worcester Journal of Learning and Teaching*, *12*, 23–31.

Warshaw, P. R., & Davis, F. D. (1985). Disentangling behavioral intention and behavioral expectation. *Journal of Experimental Social Psychology*, *21*(3), 213–228. DOI: 10.1016/0022-1031(85)90017-4

Waycott, J., Sheard, J., Thompson, C., & Clerehan, R. (2017). Making students partners and producers of technology for learning. In *Proceedings of the 22nd annual conference of the Australasian Society for Computers in Learning in Tertiary Education (ASCILITE)* (pp. 839-843).

Wen, T., Dobson, E., & Hvaara, R. (2020, October). Mesh Learning: A Cloud and Edge–based Computing Network Providing Data–Driven Solutions to the Oil and Gas Industry. *Offshore Technology Conference Asia.* OnePetro. Retrieved from DOI: 10.4043/30365-MS

Wenge, M. (2021). Artificial intelligence-based real-time

West, R. E. (2019). Transformative Learning in the Design Studio: A Case Study of Web 3.0 in Architectural Education. *Journal of Educational Technology & Society*, *22*(2), 172–184.

Whitenton, K. (2015). Menu Design: Checklist of 15 UX Guidelines to Help Users. Retrieved from: https://www.nngroup.com/articles/menu-design/

Widiartha, I. B., Hwang, J. S., Yoon, H. Y., & Pratiwi, O. N. (2023). Analysis of Resilience of Education System in Higher Education Due to Covid-19 Pandemic in Indonesia: A Systematic Literature Review. [JOIV]. *JOIV: International Journal on Informatics Visualization*, *7*(2), 439–445. DOI: 10.30630/joiv.7.2.1814

Wiggins, G., & McTighe, J. (2005). *Understanding by design*. ASCD.

Williams, M. D., Dwivedi, Y. K., Lal, B., & Schwarz, A. (2009). Contemporary trends and issues in IT adoption and diffusion research. *Journal of Information Technology*, *24*(1), 1–10. DOI: 10.1057/jit.2008.30

Wilson, A. S., & McDonagh, J. E. (2014). A Gamification Model to Encourage Positive Healthcare Behaviours in Young People with Long Term Conditions. *EAI Endorsed Transactions on Game-Based Learning*, *1*(2), e3. Advance online publication. DOI: 10.4108/sg.1.2.e3

Wolff, K., Herholz, P., Ziegler, V., Link, F., Brügel, N., & Sorkine, H. O. (2023). Designing Personalized Garments with Body Movement. *Computer Graphics Forum*, *42*(1), 180–194. DOI: 10.1111/cgf.14728

Wood, G. (2016). Polkadot: Vision for a scalable decentralized network. *Web3 Foundation*. Retrieved from https://polkadot.network/Polkadot-Whitepaper-v0.9.8.pdf

Woodbridge, J. (2024). Digital Innovations In Computer-Aided Design Software For Weaving: CAD developers are able to react to client's needs and also anticipate future needs to offer the textile industry the tools it requires for modern production. *Textile World*, *174*(1), 32–35.

Woodward, S. C., & Cooke, L. (2022). World Heritage and the Sustainable Development Goals. In *World Heritage*. DOI: 10.4324/9781003044857-12

Wu, E. H. K., Chun, H. L., Ou, Y. Y., Chen, Z. L., Wei, K. W., & Chi, Y. C. (2020). Advantages and Constraints of a Hybrid Model K-12 E-Learning Assistant Chatbot. *IEEE Access : Practical Innovations, Open Solutions*, *8*, 77788–77801. Advance online publication. DOI: 10.1109/ACCESS.2020.2988252

Xue, J., Wang, Y.-C., Wei, C., Liu, X., Woo, J., & Jay Kuo, C.-C. (2024). Bias and Fairness in Chatbots: An Overview. *APSIPA Transactions on Signal and Information Processing*, *13*(2). Advance online publication. DOI: 10.1561/116.00000064

Xu, J.. (2020). A survey on blockchain-based intelligent security systems: Challenges and opportunities. *Journal of Network and Computer Applications, 170*, 102766. DOI: 10.1016/j.jnca.2020.102766

Xu, M., Ren, X., Niyato, D., Kang, J., Qiu, C., Xiong, Z., & Leung, V. C. (2023). When quantum information technologies meet blockchain in web 3.0. *IEEE Network*.

Yadav, U.S. and Tripathi, R. (2024), "Impact of innovation, entrepreneurial orientation and entrepreneurial leadership on supply chain resilience in handicraft industry: moderating role of supply chain orientation", Benchmarking: An International Journal, Vol. ahead-of-print No. ahead-of-print. DOI: 10.1108/BIJ-09-2023-0615

Yaga, D., Mell, P., Roby, N., & Scarfone, K. (2018). *Blockchain technology overview*. National Institute of Standards and Technology., DOI: 10.6028/NIST.IR.8202

Yanes, N., Mostafa, A. M., Ezz, M. and Almuayqil, S. N. (2020). "A Machine Learning-Based Recommender System for Improving Students Learning Experiences," in IEEE Access, vol. 8, pp. 201218-201235, doi: 10.1109/ACCESS.2020.3036336.

Yang, Y., Asaad, Y., and Dwivedi, Y. (2017). Examining the impact of gamification on intention of engagement and brand attitude in the marketing context, Computers in Human Behavior, Volume 73, Pages 459-469, ISSN 0747-5632, DOI: 10.1016/j.chb.2017.03.066

Yang, J., Chen, Y. L., Por, L. Y., & Ku, C. S. (2023). *A Systematic Literature Review of Information Security in Chatbots*. Applied Sciences., DOI: 10.3390/app13116355

Yang, S., Song, Y., Chen, S., & Xia, X. (2017). Why are customers loyal in sharing-economy services? a relational benefits perspective. *Journal of Services Marketing, 31*(1), 48–62. DOI: 10.1108/JSM-01-2016-0042

Yaokumah, W., & Dawson, A. A. (2019). Network and Data Transfer Security Management in Higher Educational Institutions. *Advances in Information Security, Privacy, and Ethics*, (February), 1–19. DOI: 10.4018/978-1-5225-8455-1.ch001

Yilmaz, R. (2018). The effects of Web 3.0 technology on learning and teaching: A case study in teacher education. *Journal of Educational Technology & Society, 21*(2), 222–236.

Yoo, E., & Yu, J. (2024). Evaluating the Impact of Presentation on Learning and Narrative in AR of Cultural Heritage. *IEEE Access : Practical Innovations, Open Solutions, 12*, 25876–25887. Advance online publication. DOI: 10.1109/ACCESS.2024.3365696

Yousif Yaseen, K. A. (2022). Importance of Cybersecurity in The Higher Education Sector 2022. *Asian Journal of Computer Science and Technology*, *11*(2), 20–24. DOI: 10.51983/ajcst-2022.11.2.3448

Yuen, Y. L. E., & Leslie, C. A. (2024). Enriching Museum Student Users' Curriculum Interpretation, Learning, and Worldview through Digital Archive Approach with HistoryPin. *The International Journal of the Inclusive Museum*, *17*(1), 23–48. Advance online publication. DOI: 10.18848/1835-2014/CGP/v17i01/23-48

Yu, L., & Yu, Z. (2023). Qualitative and Quantitative Analyses of Artificial Intelligence Ethics in Education Using VOSviewer and CitNetExplorer. *Frontiers in Psychology*, *14*, 1061778. Advance online publication. DOI: 10.3389/fpsyg.2023.1061778 PMID: 36968737

Yusif, S., & Hafeez-baig, A. (2023). Cybersecurity Policy Compliance in Higher Education : A Theoretical Framework Cybersecurity Policy Compliance in Higher Education : A. *Journal of Applied Security Research*, *0*(0), 1–22. DOI: 10.1080/19361610.2021.1989271

Zabalo, E. A., Erle, G. L., & Gerrikagoitia, J. K. (2018). *Evaluating the human machine interface experience in industrial workplaces*. Electronic Workshops in Computing., DOI: 10.14236/ewic/HCI2018.93

Zahidi, Z., Lim, Y. P., & Woods, P. C. (2013). User experience for digitization and preservation of cultural heritage. In *2013 International Conference on Informatics and Creative Multimedia,* 2013, (p. 13-16). Kuala Lumpur, Malaysia Doi: DOI: 10.1109/ICICM.2013.11

Zawacki-Richter, O., & Naidu, S. (2016). Mapping research trends from 35 years of publications in Distance Education. *Distance Education*, *37*(3), 245–269. DOI: 10.1080/01587919.2016.1185079

Zeithaml, V. A. (1988). Consumer perceptions of price, quality, and value: A means-end model and synthesis of evidence. *Journal of Marketing*, *52*(3), 2–22. DOI: 10.1177/002224298805200302

Zhang, C., Li, G., Hashimoto, H., & Zhang, Z. 2022. "Digital Transformation (DX) for Skill Learners: The Design Methodology and Implementation of Educational Chatbot Using Knowledge Connection and Emotional Expression." In *IEEE Global Engineering Education Conference, EDUCON*. Vol. 2022-March. DOI: 10.1109/EDUCON52537.2022.9766384

Zhang, Q., Schmidt, D., & White, J. (2022). *AI in Blockchain Applications for the Next Generation of Decentralized Services*.

Zhang, C., Liang, H., & Zhang, Y. (2023). Smart Contracts: Security Challenges and Solutions. *Computer Standards & Interfaces*, *85*, 103595.

Zhang, K., González del Valle-Brena, A., Ramos Riera, I., & Zhao, J. (2024). Ancient routes, new gateways: A systematic literature review of China's cultural route heritage. *Journal of Cultural Heritage Management and Sustainable Development*, *14*(2), 266–281. Advance online publication. DOI: 10.1108/JCHMSD-06-2021-0114

Zhang, P., Schmidt, D., & Hinton, J. (2020). Decentralized identity: The foundation for self-sovereign identity. *IEEE Software*, *37*(1), 32–38.

Zhang, Y.. (2021). A blockchain-based approach for secure and efficient data management in smart cities. *Future Generation Computer Systems*, *116*, 105–115. DOI: 10.1016/j.future.2020.10.024

Zheng, Z., Xie, S., Dai, H., Chen, X., & Wang, H. (2018). Blockchain challenges and opportunities: A survey. *International Journal of Web and Grid Services*, *14*(4), 352–375. DOI: 10.1504/IJWGS.2018.095647

Zhou, J., Chen, F., Berry, A., Reed, M., Zhang, S., & Savage, S. 2020. "A Survey on Ethical Principles of AI and Implementations." In *2020 IEEE Symposium Series on Computational Intelligence, SSCI 2020*. DOI: 10.1109/SSCI47803.2020.9308437

Zhou, Z. H., & Feng, J. (2017) Deep Forest: Towards an Alternative to Deep Neural Networks. arXiv *preprintarXiv*:1702.08835. https://arxiv.org/pdf/1702.08835.pdf DOI: 10.24963/ijcai.2017/497

Zichemann, G. & Cunningham, C. (2011). Gamification by design: Implementing game mechanics in web and mobile apps. CA: O'Reilly Media Inc.

Zomerdijk, L. G., & Voss, C. A. (2010). Service design for experience-centric services. *Journal of Service Research*, *13*(1), 67–82. DOI: 10.1177/1094670509351960

About the Contributors

Jean-Eric Pelet is an Associate Professor at IAE Amiens (France). He holds an MBA in Information Systems, a PhD in Management Science, and a Habilitation to Supervise Researches in Management. His current research focuses on Web3, e-commerce platform interfaces, connected objects, gamification in the wine industry and consumer behavior. His work has been published in international journals such as the European Journal of Information Systems, Systèmes d'Information et Management, Information and Management, Review of Managerial Science, Journal of Consumer Behaviour, International Journal of Wine and Business Research and others. He is the author of several academic and professional books focusing on digital technologies, consumer behavior, user experience, and e-commerce. His recent works include User Experience in Web 2.0 Technologies and its Impact on Universities and Businesses (2020, IGI Global) and Advanced Web Applications and Progressing E-Learning 2.0 Technologies in Higher Education (2019, IGI Global), exploring the impact of Web 2.0 and e-learning in higher education. His book E-Commerce: How to Design, Build, and Manage Your Website (2018, Dunod) provides a practical guide to e-commerce, while Mobile Platforms, Design, and Apps for Social Commerce (2017, IGI Global) delves into mobile technologies for social commerce. He also co-authored Handbook of Research on User Behavior in Ubiquitous Online Environments (2013, IGI Global) and authored M-Commerce (2014, Pearson), focusing on mobile commerce.

***

Munir Ahmad is a seasoned professional in the realm of Spatial Data Infrastructure (SDI), Geo-Information Productions, Information Systems, and Information Governance, boasting over 25 years of dedicated experience in the field. With a PhD in Computer Science, Dr. Ahmad's expertise spans Spatial Data Production, Management, Processing, Analysis, Visualization, and Quality Control.

Throughout his career, Dr. Ahmad has been deeply involved in the development and deployment of SDI systems specially in the context of Pakistan, leveraging his proficiency in Spatial Database Design, Web, Mobile & Desktop GIS, and Geo Web Services Architecture. His contributions to Volunteered Geographic Information (VGI) and Open Source Geoportal & Metadata Portal have significantly enriched the geospatial community. As a trainer and researcher, Dr. Ahmad has authored over 50 publications, advancing the industry's knowledge base and fostering innovation in Geo-Tech, Data Governance, and Information Infrastructure, and Emerging Technologies. His commitment to Research and Development (R&D) is evident in his role as a dedicated educator and mentor in the field.

Pankaj Bhambri is affiliated with the Department of Information Technology at Guru Nanak Dev Engineering College in Ludhiana. Additionally, he fulfills the role of the Convener for his Departmental Board of Studies. He possesses nearly two decades of teaching experience. His research work has been published in esteemed worldwide and national journals, as well as conference proceedings. Dr. Bhambri has garnered extensive experience in the realm of academic publishing, having served as an editor for a multitude of books in collaboration with esteemed publishing houses such as CRC Press, Elsevier, Scrivener, and Bentham Science. In addition to his editorial roles, he has demonstrated his scholarly prowess by authoring numerous books and contributing chapters to distinguished publishers within the academic community. Dr. Bhambri has been honored with several prestigious accolades, including the ISTE Best Teacher Award in 2023 and 2022, the I2OR National Award in 2020, the Green ThinkerZ Top 100 International Distinguished Educators award in 2020, the I2OR Outstanding Educator Award in 2019, the SAA Distinguished Alumni Award in 2012, the CIPS Rashtriya Rattan Award in 2008, the LCHC Best Teacher Award in 2007, and numerous other commendations from various government and non-profit organizations. He has provided guidance and oversight for numerous research projects and dissertations at the postgraduate and Ph.D. levels. He successfully organized a diverse range of educational programmes, securing financial backing from esteemed institutions such as the AICTE, the TEQIP, among others. Dr. Bhambri's areas of interest encompass machine learning, bioinformatics, wireless sensor networks, and network security.

Gerald W. Chege is an Assistant Professor of Information Systems and Technology in USIU. He was the coordinator of Information Systems and Technology in USIU from 2002 to September 2006. He has over 15 years as a university lecturer and consulting experience. He taught at the Institute of Computer Science, University of Nairobi 1987-1994 before joining USIU. He graduated with a BSc in Physics, 1st class honours from the University of Nairobi, an MSc in Electrical Engineering, at

University of York, UK. He also has a Ph.D. in Parallel Computing from University of York. Dr. Chege has consulted for both private and public sectors in providing Information Systems and Technology solutions including Central Bank of Kenya, Sameer Africa Ltd, Athi Water Services Board, KTDA, Kenya Pipeline, Kenya Tourist Board, Kenya Agricultural Research Institute and Tourist Trust Fund (TTF) amongst others. He teaches both undergraduate and graduate courses. Dr. Chege has published several papers in his field and presented some in seminars, both locally and internationally. His areas of specialization include database management systems, computer networks, programming languages, systems analysis and design, internet architectures and protocols and web applications development. He has been an external examiner in computer science for Egerton University, University of Nairobi and African Nazarene University

Caleb Chidozie Chinedu is a senior lecturer at the Faculty of Technical and Vocational Education, Universiti Tun Hussein Onn Malaysia. He holds a PhD, M. Ed and a bachelor's degree in Technical and Vocational Education with over seven years of teaching, research and administrative experience in TVET and teacher education research. His research interest centres on Education for Sustainable Development, higher-order thinking skills (HOTS), curriculum development and pedagogy, Leadership, and Management in TVE, the evolving impact of Generative AI on education.

Leila Goosen is a full professor in the Department of Science and Technology Education of the University of South Africa. She holds a C2 rating via the South African National Research Foundation. Prof. Goosen was an Associate Professor in the School of Computing, and the module leader and head designer of the fully online signature module for the College for Science, Engineering and Technology, rolled out to over 92,000 registered students since the first semester of 2013. She usually supervises around ten Masters and Doctoral students, and has successfully completed supervision of 43 students at postgraduate level. Previously, she was a Deputy Director at the South African national Department of Education. In this capacity, she was required to develop ICT strategies for implementation. Before that, she had been a lecturer of Information Technology (IT) in the Department for Science, Mathematics and Technology Education in the Faculty of Education of the University of Pretoria. Her research interests have included cooperative work in IT, effective teaching and learning of programming and teacher professional development.

Balaji Gopalan is an Assistant Professor in the Department of Decision Sciences at the CMS Business School (Bangalore). His area of specialization is Production and Operations Management, Logistics and Supply Chain Management and Value Co-creation. He has 20 years of experience in academics, research and consulting and has worked at institutes in India, Finland and the USA. He holds a Doctorate in Industrial Management from the University of Vaasa, Finland. He has a M.Sc. in Information Studies from Florida State University, USA, M.E. in Manufacturing Systems from BITS-Pilani, Rajasthan and B.E. in Industrial Production from SJCE (University of Mysore).

Hafsa Hamid Butt is an accomplished scholar who has recently completed her M.Phil in Linguistics from Minhaj University, Lahore. She has been a consistent achiever throughout her academic journey, with a remarkable track record of success in literature, education, and linguistics. Her Master's research project reflects her unwavering commitment and passion for the field of linguistics. With her exceptional academic credentials. Hafsa is undoubtedly a valuable asset to any institution that is fortunate enough to have her as a part of their team.

Er. Kritika is an accomplished researcher and dynamic keynote speaker specializing in the intersection of cybersecurity and neuroscience. She has made significant contributions to the field through a diverse array of publications, including peer-reviewed articles, book chapters and books. Her expertise lies in uncovering new insights and best practices in cybersecurity, particularly, through the lens of Generative AI, neuroeconomics, good governance, neuroethics and neuro-driven technologies. She has solely authored 2 books, 15+ research papers and 10+ book chapters. With a distinguished body of Scopus-indexed publications, book chapters, and authored books, she has consistently pushed the frontiers of knowledge across multiple disciplines. Her exceptional contributions to both academia and industry have been recognized with numerous prestigious awards, including the Trailblazer Award for Security/ Safety in Education (2025), Best Researcher Award (2024), Young Engineer Award (2024), and Young Researcher Award (2023). The author is serving as Member(ISC2), Lifetime Member of International Association of Engineers(IAENG), Member of Women In Cybersecurity(WiCys) India Affiliate, professional member of Institute of Scholars(InSc) and book and journal reviewer for various reputed publications like IEEE, Elsevier, IGI Global, etc. Her visionary research continues to shape the future of technology, making a lasting impact on the global scientific community.

Manoj Kumar currently working as Associate Professor in the Institute of Management, Commerce and Economics at Shri Ramswaroop Memorial University, having an experience of more than 15 years in the field of accounting and finance. He holds a doctorate degree in Commerce, from the Department of Commerce,

University of Lucknow. His area of research includes Mobile Banking, Artificial Intelligence, Insolvency Resolution, Management Accounting. He is having many publications in various Scopus Indexed and national and international journal, presented many papers in national and international conferences and attended large number FDPs and QIP's to update his knowledge.

Maida Maqsood did MS in English from Government College Women University, Sialkot. Throughout her academic journey, she has achieved notable successes that have strengthened her foundation in literature, education and linguistics. Her Master's research reflects her dedication to exploring critical themes in literature with the use of linguistics style. Additionally, her active participation in different conferences and seminars, such as The International Conference on Modern Trends in Applied Linguistics, and 7th ASNeT International Multidisciplinary Academic Conference 2024 (AIMAC 2024) highlight her commitment to staying updated with current trends in her field.

Pratibha Maurya presently working as Assistant Professor Grade -III in Amity Institute of Information Technology, Amity University, Lucknow Campus, have teaching experience of more than 15 years in the area of IT and CS. She holds M.Sc. (CS), M.Tech. (IT) and PhD degrees in Computer Science. Her research interest includes Artificial Intelligence and Machine Learning, Big Data and Information Retrieval. She is having a long list of publications in various Scopus and national & international journal, presented many papers in national and international conferences of repute and attended many FDPs and QIP's. She has been member of Technical program committees for conferences and reviewer for indexed journals

Collins Oduor is an Assistant Professor, Information Systems. Dr. Oduor holds a PhD in Information Systems – University of Nairobi with specialty areas: Information systems, distributed systems and parallel systems. Dr Oduor has good teaching and research experience at university level and a vast experience in the fields of ICT Consultancies and Teaching, lifelong learning, and ICT 4 development programs. Collins has vast experience in ICT integration in education through training for teacher trainees in Primary Teacher Training Colleges in Kenya. He has also participated in the Accelerated 21st Century Education (ACE) ICT integration in Education Pilot Project for Ministry of Education, Teacher Education Professional Development Program 2009-2012 as a consultant and as a master trainer. Collins has also participated in the Inter University Council of East Africa (IUCEA) Staff mobility program as external examiner 2015 & 2018 in addition Dr. Oduor is also an External examiner for Namibia University of Science and Technology (Namibia) and University of Venda (South Africa). Collins has been a Panel Presenter/Speaker in

Academia roundtable "New teaching approaches for higher learning institutions in the digital era" presentation at the World Summit on Information Systems (WSIS) organized by the International Telecommunication Union (ITU) Geneva Switzerland. Dr Oduor has supervised over twenty masters students thesis/projects, participated in various curricula development for so many universities in the region. In addition to the membership in professional bodies, Dr Oduor has also published scholarly books, books chapters and over ten papers in referred journals publications plus additional international conference paper presentations on ICT. Collins has been a reviewer and editor of papers for some International Journals. On community service, participated in the Hultz Prize Nairobi Regional Summits as a judge and also currently a mentor in the Presidential Digital Talent Program (PDTP) and that Collins is now keen on research areas covering more on ICT integration in Education, ICT4Development, Design and behavioral design in ICT systems, Citizen Science, Community

Beatrice Akoth Owino is from Nairobi, Kenya, and is currently affiliated with the United States International University in Africa. She holds a Master of Science Degree in Information Systems Technology (Cyber Security) and is currently pursuing her Ph.D. in Information Systems Technology, in the Computing Department, in the School of Science and Technology, USIU-Africa. Her research interests include cyber security and forensics, AI & ethics, information systems management, and security. She holds various certifications, including Certified Ethical Hacker (CEH), MCITP, ITIL, and Microsoft Azure.

Semanur Öztemiz is an associate professor at Department of Information Management, Hacettepe University, Ankara, Türkiye. Her main research interests include user studies, cultural heritage literacy, digital humanities and social informatics. She has numerous works about bibliotherapy, cultural heritage, digitization process in cultural memory institutions, copyright, and digitisations issues, semantic web and cultural heritage, usability in digital libraries and social informatics.

Mahona Joseph Paschal is an interdisciplinary scholar, experienced educator, and author with a Master's in Education Management and Planning from St Augustine University of Tanzania. He is currently furthering his education at the University of Duisburg-Essen in Germany. He recently completed another professional development course with the Arizona State University, USA. Paschal's life mission is to empower and inspire young people & educational leaders reach their full potentials. He has been involved in educational leadership, research & innovation, and continously strives to make changes in his local and global communities. Using theory, practice, and humor, he challenges teams to become collaborative, data-driven, and digitally connected. Paschal is the author of Responsive Classroom: Student's Relationship and Academic Performance in Tanzania (2020), several Peer Reviewed Articles, Book Chapters in Edited Volumes and Learning Models. He is always seeking to learn new skills, techniques and approaches himself and he is dedicated to getting the most out of everything he does.

Sita Rani is a Faculty of Computer Science and Engineering at Guru Nanak Dev Engineering College, Ludhiana. She earned her Ph.D. in Computer Science and Engineering from I.K. Gujral Punjab Technical University, Kapurthala, Punjab in 2018. She has also completed Post Graduate Certificate Program in Data Science and Machine Learning from Indian Institute of Technology, Roorkee in 2023. She has completed her Postdoc from Big Data Mining and Machine Learning Lab, South Ural State University, Russia in August, 2023. She has more than 20 years of teaching experience. She is an active member of ISTE, IEEE and IAEngg. She is the receiver of ISTE Section Best Teacher Award- 2020, and International Young Scientist Award-2021. She has contributed to the various research activities while publishing articles in the renowned SCI and Scopus journals and conference proceedings. She has published seven international patents and authored, edited and coedited 7 books. Dr. Rani has delivered many expert talks in A.I.C.T.E. sponsored Faculty Development Programs and key note talks in many National and International Conferences. She has also organized many International Conferences during her 20 years of teaching experience. She is the member of Editorial Board and reviewer of many international journals of repute. She is also the vice-president of SME and MSME (UT Council), Women Indian Chamber of Commerce and Industry (WICCI) from last 3 years. Her research interest includes Parallel and Distributed Computing, Data Science, Machine Learning, Internet of Things (IoT), and Smart Healthcare.

S. Yogananthan is a Senior Professor with the Department of Decision Sciences at the Faculty of Management Studies, CMS Business School (Bangalore), Jain-deemed-to-be University. He teaches Production and Operations Management and Logistics and Supply Chain Management.

Ravishankar S. Ulle is an Assistant Professor with the Department of Decision Sciences at the CMS B School, Bangalore, Karnataka (India). He area of specialization is Production and Operations Management and Logistics and Supply Chain Management.

C.V. Suresh Babu is a pioneer in content development. A true entrepreneur, he founded Anniyappa Publications, a company that is highly active in publishing books related to Computer Science and Management. Dr. C.V. Suresh Babu has also ventured into SB Institute, a center for knowledge transfer. He holds a Ph.D. in

Engineering Education from the National Institute of Technical Teachers Training & Research in Chennai, along with seven master's degrees in various disciplines such as Engineering, Computer Applications, Management, Commerce, Economics, Psychology, Law, and Education. Additionally, he has UGC-NET/SET qualifications in the fields of Computer Science, Management, Commerce, and Education. Currently, Dr. C.V. Suresh Babu is a Professor in the Department of Information Technology at the School of Computing Science, Hindustan Institute of Technology and Science (Hindustan University) in Padur, Chennai, Tamil Nadu, India. For more information, you can visit his personal blog at https://sites.google.com/view/cvsureshbabu/.

Sanjay Taneja is currently a Professor in Research at Graphic Era University, Dehradun, India. His significant thrust areas are Banking Regulations, Banking and Finance (Fin Tech, Green Finance), Risks, Insurance Management, Green Economics and Management of Innovation in Insurance. He holds a double master's degree (MBA &M.Com.) in management with a specialization in Finance and Marketing. He received his PG degrees in Management (Gold Medalist) from Chaudhary Devi University, Sirsa, India in 2012. He earned his Doctor of Philosophy (Sponsored By ICSSR) in Banking and Finance entitled "An Appraisal of financial performance of Indian Banking Sector: A Comparative study of Public, Private and Foreign banks in 2016 from Chaudhary Devi University, Sirsa, India. He received his Post Doctoral Degree from faculty of Social Sciences, Department of Banking and Insurance, Usak University, Turkey entitled on "Impact of the European Green Deal on Carbon (CO2) Emission in Turkey" in 2023. He has published research papers in reputed SCOPUS/Web of Science/SCI/ABDC/UGC Care Journals. Prof. Taneja has more than fifty publications in total (Scopus/ABDC/Web of Science- 27)

Orhun Uğur is an archaeologist who has completed a master's degree in the field of information management. He aims to contribute to the sustainable management of heritage data through his acquired education. Besides participating in archaeological excavations, he previously worked as a digital archivist at BIAA (British Institute at Ankara) and Imagining Futures project, gaining experience in digitisation processes and information management. Additionally, he has a particular interest in street art as cultural heritage, participatory heritage approaches, crowdsource methods, and usability domains.

Dalize van Heerden is a lecturer in the School of Computing at the University of South Africa. She started working for UNISA in 1999 and has been teaching programming modules ever since. Her main research interests include e-learning, m-learning and technology-enhanced learning. She has received numerous institutional awards for her innovative teaching and learning practices.

Rinki Verma currently working as Associate Professor in the School of Management at Babu Banarsi Das University, Lucknow, having an experience of more than 13 years in the area of Marketing and General Management. She holds doctorate degree from MNNIT, Allahabad. Her research area includes Public Private Partnership, Internet Advertising, E- Service Quality, Artificial Intelligence. She is having publications in various Scopus indexed, and reputed national & international journal and presented research papers in national and international conferences organized by reputed institutions and attended many MDPs, QIP's etc. She has been a trainer in the training programs on Conflict Management, Behavioral Change, Change Management, etc for Primary Medical Staff (PMS-DOCTORS) and senior officers (Non-Defense Academy).

Index

A

B

C

D

E

G

H

I

K

L

M

N

O

P

R

S

T

U

V

W